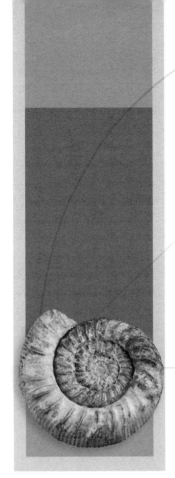

ROCK SOLID ANSWERS

The Biblical Truth Behind 14 Geologic Questions

Michael J. Oard and John K. Reed, Editors

With contributions also from:
Aaron Hutchinson, Emil Silvestru, Peter Klevberg, Rick Bandy,
John H. Whitmore, Andrew A. Snelling, and Ian Juby

First printing: October 2009
Second printing: October 2011

ISBN: 978-0-89051-567-9
Library of Congress Number: 2009938719

Please consider requesting that a copy of this volume be purchased by your local library system.

Printed in the United States of America

For other great titles please visit the Master Books® website at www.masterbooks.net
or the Creation Research Society website at www.creationresearch.org

For information regarding author interviews,
please contact the publicity department at (870) 438-5288.

Creation Research Society Books
6801 North Hwy. 89
Chino Valley, AZ 86323

Master
Books®
A Division of New Leaf Publishing Group
www.masterbooks.net

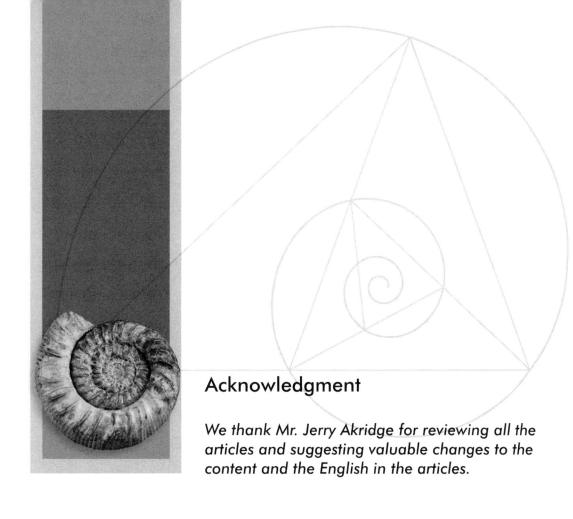

Acknowledgment

We thank Mr. Jerry Akridge for reviewing all the articles and suggesting valuable changes to the content and the English in the articles.

Contents

Preface

The Fall and Rise of Flood Geology

During the 18th and early 19th centuries, new ideas swept the West. The forces of the Enlightenment were not content with "ivory tower" philosophy but pushed their new worldview aggressively into every area of life. Early on, they set their sights on the new science of geology, recognizing its strategic importance as a springboard to a more vital target — the repudiation of biblical history and the subsequent overthrow of biblical authority. Although most intellectuals had rejected Genesis during the latter half of the 18th century (Rudwick 2005), there was strong public support into the early 19th century. But this quickly waned. A growing antipathy by opponents of Christianity and a growing apathy among Christians ushered in the desired "geological revolution." Scientists gave lip service to the Bible, providing an excuse for the professional clergy. But by 1850, Flood geology was a minority position, well outside the scientific mainstream. By 1900, it had been reduced to an object of ridicule. Enlightenment philosophy had carried the day.

So we find ourselves at the beginning of the 21st century with natural (earth) history firmly lodged within the domain of secular geology. As with any monopoly, those who enjoy its privileges are also jealous to guard against competition — a reality ironically at odds with the spirit of scientific inquiry loudly proclaimed by the monopolists long ago. But competition is always present in the marketplace of ideas. During the latter decades of the 20th century, the ghost of Georges Cuvier (1769–1832) returned to haunt mainstream geology. Lyell's uniformitarianism fell beneath the onslaught of a revived secular catastrophism, often known as "neocatastrophism." Evidence from the channeled scablands of the Pacific Northwest and the features formed by the eruption of Mount St. Helens proved inexplicable to the reigning uniformitarianism, which leaned heavily on low-energy analogs of modern depositional environments to interpret the rock record.

Ironically, the neocatastrophists were several decades behind the times. A new Flood geology had appeared in the early 1960s, challenging the same uniformitarian monopoly. Rather than open the door to the ancient taboo of Noah's Flood, modern geologists have shown an amazing flexibility by converting en masse to neocatastrophism, desperate to maintain their vast geologic past, but with no real underlying principle to guide interpretation. Even the word "uniformitarianism" has come under fire, with a retreat to the older and more restricted methodological term, "actualism." One might say that geologists have proven that they can accept a variety of historical models as long as they exclude the Bible. At a minimum, recent decades have shown that trends in geological history are driven by philosophical — not scientific — commitments.

Why are geologists so resistant to the alternative framework of Flood geology? Is not science advanced by the interplay between multiple working hypotheses? Some argue that Flood geology, because of its ties to the Bible, has no place at the table. Of course this ignores the *equally* religious commitments of those who reject the Bible. It also illustrates how the outmoded philosophy of positivism (science is the key to truth) lurks in the minds of scientists. Neither history nor science can proceed purely on the strength of self-authenticating data. Both require assumptions about reality and time derived from philosophy or theology. Most creationists understand that, but many secular scientists do not. In other words, they are forced to rely on "antediluvian" philosophy.

No philosopher still believes that science is pure, objective, and untainted by philosophical presuppositions or psychological prejudice. That "modern" myth has become a post-modern farce — even more so when geologists are faced with the burden of using science to do history — the investigation of unique past events. It is as if the failure of Marxism, which signaled the collapse of a "scientific history," has no relevance to geology. If geology does not become more flexible, it will validate the accusations of some that "open-minded" scientists are often the most dogmatic of people.

But whether they like it or not, Flood geology is here to stay because the Christian Church is waking up to its necessity in their faith. Many Christians have had a fling with compromise, but now understand that the circle cannot be squared. They see the intellectual schizophrenia of denying biblical history while clinging to biblical authority, and have found that contrary position equally unsatisfying to both heart and head. They see theological compromises as threadworn and the aura of omniscient science as tarnished. They have also ceased to buy the outmoded "religion versus science" argument that kept them at arm's length for so long. That mindset has been superseded by an understanding of the role of integrated worldviews in this debate.

Christians are not the only people to react to the new understanding of the uncertainties of science. The scientist no longer stands on his mid-20th century pedestal. Some, like postmodernists, have simply thrown up their hands at the possibility of truth; denigrating religious truth and scientific truth with equal relish. They are opposed by die-hard scientists who still believe that truth is possible, but cling to the outmoded idea that science is the path to enlightenment. These academics have hunkered down inside their campus fortresses to fight off the barbarian hordes — only to find that the barbarians are the philosophy department in the adjacent building.

Neither option — denying truth or claiming all truth comes from science — is tenable today. A third way is possible. A new generation of Christians has come to appreciate that truth comes from God and cannot be ceded to secular science. They are striving to rebuild the ruins of the biblical worldview, the only one that has historically been able to integrate knowledge and insure truth. Secular natural history, whether uniformitarian or neocatastrophist, resists the new Flood geology precisely because it forces this clash of worldviews out in the open. As the myths of the Enlightenment fall by the wayside, the secular position becomes increasingly tenuous. Theological, metaphysical, and epistemological commitments exist on all sides. Christians are willing to admit theirs and show how they integrate well with real science and real history. Sadly, many secularists resist that step, knowing that their assumptions rest on sand.

Though Flood geology is hampered by a paucity of practitioners, few publishing outlets, and no public or industry funding, it has one crucial asset that secular geologists lack — a healthy consistency between axioms, methods, and conclusions. Furthermore, it offers the possibility of breaking out of a hidebound dogmatism that forces geologists to squeeze 21st-century discoveries into a 19th-century framework. Flood geology offers an opportunity to explore ideas and evaluate data within a new and more intellectually satisfying paradigm. Needless to say, that paradigm has been attacked.

Rock Solid Answers seeks to defend against those attacks. We recognize that truth involves *defending* propositions as well as advancing them. The truth of the Genesis Flood, reasserted during the last half of the 20th century, has been challenged on a variety of fronts. Many of those arguments have been ably answered, especially in the arenas of theology and the life sciences. However, geological challenges appear to be in the forefront for most secular apologists, and diluvial geology has convinced a smaller cross-section of people than creationist positions in other disciplines. Therefore, the Creation Research Society has assembled a team of scholars to answer some of the most persistent arguments leveled by the geological establishment.

Contributions to this book are interesting in their own right, and demonstrate that advocates of Flood geology are careful, well-informed scientists. The chapters also reveal a common flaw in attacks on Flood geology — the old logical bugaboo of "begging the question," or circular reasoning. Those opposed to Flood geology use conclusions driven by their presupposition of the truth of their own position, even arguing for uniformitarian processes in a neocatastrophist world. Evidently they fail to recognize that all they are really doing is finding new and complicated ways of saying, "my presuppositions are different from yours."

We can only conclude that they fail to see this logical error, clinging to faith commitments outside of science. For years they have believed that science is the synonym of truth, and they have shoved metaphysics, theology, and history under that umbrella. It is no surprise that they are less capable when faced anew with arguments of this sort. For Christians are not simply content to disagree with David Hume's famous burn-everything-that's-not-science-or-math tirade, but have even had the audacity to point out that science is not even *possible* absent Christianity (e.g., Lisle 2009; Pearcy and Johnson 2004; Reed 2001; Stark 2003).

Thus, as you read through this book, it is vital to recognize that deeper disagreements color the positions of secular and Flood geologists. Otherwise the following chapters will devolve into a simplistic back and forth of disparate "facts," and truth is likely to be lost as the quantity of information becomes the basis for belief. However, if the reader will discern the more fundamental differences of opinion reflected in these chapters, the debate will assume a new clarity that we hope will lead to the discovery that diluvial geology is not simply a legitimate alternative to uniformitarianism and secular catastrophism, but is a door to a worldview that offers the more satisfying prospect of a unity of truth across the spectrum of knowledge.

References

Lisle, J. 2009. *The Ultimate Proof of Creation: Resolving the Origins Debate.* Green Forest, AR: Master Books.

Pearcey, N.R., and Johnson, P.E. 2004. *Total Truth: Liberating Christianity from Its Cultural Captivity.* Wheaton, IL: Crossway Books.

Reed, J.K. 2001. *Natural History in the Christian Worldview: Foundation and Framework.* St. Joseph, MO: Creation Research Society Books.

Rudwick, M.J.S. 2005. *Bursting the Limits of Time: The Reconstruction of Geohistory in the Age of Revolution.* Chicago, IL: University of Chicago Press.

Stark, R. 2003. *For the Glory of God.* Princeton, NJ: Princeton University Press.

Chapter 1

A Context for the Flood Geology Debate

John K. Reed • *PhD — Geology*
Michael J. Oard • *MS — Atmospheric Science*

A major challenge, perhaps even the greatest challenge, for Flood geologists is to simply get started — to reach the point where debate is taking place. Too many times, the only "debate" on the part of secular geologists is to simply dismiss with ridicule the diluvial position as one held only by ignorant Christians, clinging to an outmoded faith. This in part is driven by the old secular myths about the origin of geology, where brave empiricists (Hutton, Playfair, and Lyell) overcame the repressive persecution of an anti-intellectual church to lead humanity into a more enlightened and scientific view of the past. Only recently has historical research put the lie to that nonsense (Gould 1987; Rudwick 2005, 2008). This "victimized by Christianity" appeal was nothing more than the first line of defense by equally religious atheists, and was applied across the spectrum of knowledge. As the sociologist Rodney Stark (2003, p. 123) noted:

> The reason that we didn't know the truth concerning these matters is that the claim of an inevitable and bitter warfare between religion and science has, for more than three centuries, been the primary polemical device used in the atheist attack on faith. From Thomas Hobbes through Carl Sagan and Richard Dawkins, false claims about religion and science have been used as weapons in the battle to "free" the human mind from the "fetters of faith."

If the historians and Stark are correct, then another way of looking at the issue is the first step required. One that makes the most sense is that geology is one of many areas where a much greater debate is underway between *opposing worldviews* (figure 1). No other explanation explains the historical data, which show a causal link between Christianity and science, and between Christianity and history. How can Christianity be "anti-intellectual" if its scholars were responsible for the origin of both disciplines, as well as numerous others? Western culture was built on the Christian religion . . . overtly until the Enlightenment, and implicitly even after. And that historical tipping point provides a clear clue as to Christianity's opposite number, Enlightenment naturalism. This is confirmed by a simple piece of logic.

That logic goes like this: if the *affirmation* of biblical truth and authority is a religious position, then the *denial* of biblical truth and authority must also be a religious position. Thus, we must look for a religious point of view behind the anti-Christian "science" of the past two centuries. Is there a relationship between uniformitarian geology and naturalism, and is there evidence that a conscious effort was made to remove Christianity from natural history in the late 18th and early 19th centuries? Clearly, the answer to both questions is "yes." For example, the Comte de Buffon (1707–1788) and James Hutton (1726–1797) were two Enlightenment authors advocating theories of earth's past. Both overtly rejected biblical history. After

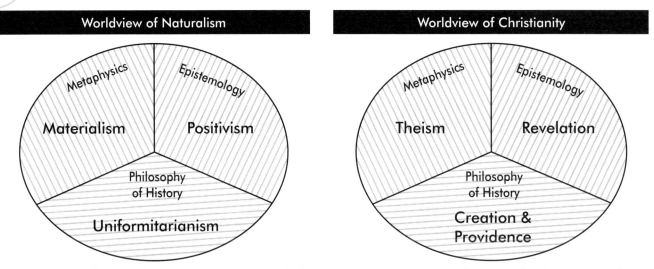

Figure 1. The differences between the worldviews of Christianity and naturalism at their most fundamental levels are stark in all three areas: metaphysics, epistemology, and their philosophy of history.

the excesses of the French Revolution, anti-Christian activity became more circumspect, but Lyell's obvious later animosity toward biblical Christianity (Mortenson 2006) was undeniable, as was that of Darwin, and their descendents down to our day.

If the context of the debate is a clash of worldviews, then clearly empirical evidence must be evaluated carefully, because commitments outside science might be driving the selection and interpretation of these "facts." Another conclusion would be that the two sides are separated not by a disagreement over particular data, but by distinct faith commitments. Modern examples of these can be seen in any of the books by the "New Atheists." Their arguments, while cloaked in science, are ultimately philosophical, and although they might be suspect, the authors' passion is quite real. Thus, all of the following chapters must be read while keeping in mind this fundamental religious opposition between Christianity and naturalism (e.g., Reed et al. 2004).

Other points worth considering as we begin the debate arise from the worldview battle. First, it is important to clarify differences between conclusions drawn from the faith commitments of naturalism, and those derived from the *science* of geology. Often the two are intermixed; a careful account is given of strata in a particular location, and then we are told that their characteristics "prove" an old earth with low-energy continuous processes shaping its surface. Second, we must recognize that debates over the meaning of empirical data will not ultimately resolve the issue. Since worldviews are involved, only the demonstrable formal invalidity of one or the other

can settle the argument. Finally, the disparity in the opposing positions must be taken into account. Secular geology controls academia, government agencies, almost all journals, almost all museums, public education, and the media. Thus the quantity of information is to be expected to reside in their corner. Fortunately, truth is not determined by the amount of data presented.

Given this framework, what consideration should a fair-minded person give to the following chapters? If there is a conflict between worldviews, then we must examine the consequences. Three significant ones come to mind. The first is the emphasis on formal errors in the discussion of empirical data. These may be difficult to detect, but provide the most direct means of evaluating the truth claims of the opposing positions. Second, we must assess the possibility of common ground; after all, if there is a religious conflict, are we just talking past each other? Finally, given the monopoly of naturalism, what reasons can we advance to convince them of the importance of holding an open debate?

Formal Errors in Arguments against Flood Geology

If secular geologists have propagated their worldview in their interpretations of the past, then we must beware of formal as well as empirical errors. For example, early interpretations of history demonstrated their antipathy toward Christianity by proposing ahistorical, steady-state visions of the past. Hutton's system was clearly timeless in the chronological sense understood in the West, being driven by his faith commitment to deism. Buffon's first system and even Lyell's initial proposal of uniformity were both ahistorical, denying not only the content of biblical history, but even its framework of linear, chronological time (Gould 1987; Rudwick 2005). That was a step too far at the time and implicitly destroyed the possibility of a real history for the prehuman past. So a consensus developed for a linear, progressive geohistory that could be measured by chronological events.

But when we examine this closely, the philosophy becomes clear. The nature of time is a question to be resolved by philosophy or theology, not by science. Furthermore, this *framework* of history was *Christian* (Rudwick 1999). More importantly, it could only be justified theologically, by Christianity (Lisle 2009; Reed 2001). Thus, when we see a Christian concept of time used to debunk Christianity, logical alarms begin to sound. And if naturalism does not possess an equally-valid justification for this concept of time, then the alarms should be heeded.

Likewise, the geologic time scale asserts that the path of history can be traced by a sequence of rocks. But this requires the assumption that during each of the proposed geological eras, rocks were being deposited at the same time all over the world that could be later correlated *by their chronology* (Reed 2008). This assumption is also outside of science and could certainly not be demonstrated in the early 19th century when the time scale was being fashioned . . . if for no other reason than that vast reaches of the world's geology were completely unknown.

Arguments involving conflicting worldviews proceed on multiple levels. The following chapters will primarily address the empirical level. But while they do not dwell on formal arguments, logical flaws in secular arguments become apparent as you read — errors that reside in the accepted wisdom that is being countered. First, most of those secular positions are based on uniformitarianism. Even though many geologists have become "neocatastrophists," many of the standard arguments are rooted in their uniformitarian past. And most, surreptitiously yet systematically, *assume* the conclusion they are trying to prove — that uniformitarianism is true! If one assumes present causes have operated over deep time, then one looks for low-energy processes.

Evidence that this framework was a conclusion reached apart from science is seen in the fact that it took 150 years for the interpretations of secular neocatastrophism to gain traction, despite their having been proposed by scientists like Cuvier prior to Lyell's uniformitarian theory. Clear and compelling evidence was ignored or suppressed because it

did not fit the model. That is why it took J Harlen Bretz decades to convince geologists of the catastrophic nature of the Glacial Lake Missoula flood that formed the channeled scablands of the Pacific Northwest (Oard 2004).

Another common error in logic appears in arguments against the Flood. It can be boiled down to the simplest form of proposition: "Datum X requires interpretation Y. Interpretation Y is contrary to my perception (time/ energy/extent) of the biblical Flood. *Ergo*, Flood geology is invalid and secular geology is vindicated."

The logical shortcoming is evident in the very beginning of that proposition. Does X *require* Y, or is there a hidden assumption beneath X that surreptitiously directs one toward Y? In other words, does interpretation flow from self-authenticating data, or does it arise from an interaction between data philosophical assumptions, faith commitments, and social or psychological factors? We affirm the latter and consider the former a relict of a naïve and antiquated view of science. The position that science is the door to truth is called positivism. It was popular in the 19th century and in the 20th century in a modified form. But that view has become increasingly untenable in the face of recent developments in both philosophy and science. Unfortunately, scientists tend to lag behind developments in philosophy and so the error crops out repeatedly in the challenges presented in the following chapters.

Thus, in addition to convincing empirical arguments, Flood geologists present secular counterparts with the more important challenge of correcting the formal flaws that flow from Naturalism (Reed et al. 2004). It is strange that many opponents of the Flood are so blind to this particular problem. Perhaps the dominance of their paradigm for two centuries has left them overconfident. The habit of secular scientists to dismiss the diluvial position with ridicule rather than with reason certainly suggests that.

Creationists have long argued that the interplay between belief structures or worldviews and forensic data found in earth's crustal features are significant and must be factored into any interpretation. The issue is not "religion versus science" but the history of one worldview versus the history of the other worldview. Working with this blend of science, history, and philosophy is inescapable because natural history is a mixed question (Adler 1965); one that requires the cooperation of multiple disciplines to reach the most comprehensive conclusions. Flood geology is a subset of a framework that is theistic, rather than atheistic; sets revelation as the arbiter of truth instead of science; and accepts biblical narrative as an outline of history, rather than an extrapolation from present processes.

So in one sense, the two positions are far enough apart that a simple empirical back and forth cannot produce resolution. If that is true, can there be a meeting of the minds — a common ground?

Finding Common Ground

Before common ground can be defined, the differences between the two positions must be understood by both sides. Secular geologists have long dismissed Flood geology as theistic superstition; a statement no more meaningful than its opposite: that they are indulging in *atheistic* superstition! The conversation has nowhere to go from there. So if common ground for discussion is to be achieved, the first step is seeing beyond the "facts" to the conflicting visions of history inherent to naturalism and Christianity. These two perspectives have widely varying positions about the nature of reality, the nature of knowledge, and the nature of history. Each side must understand the worldview of the other.

Advocates of naturalism see natural history as simply a matter of scientific inquiry. Since it deals with a time long before the advent of any scientific observer, there can be no valid human record of "prehistoric" times. This was the logic of the Enlightenment thinkers, who divorced a part of earth's past from its biblical moorings and handed the study of it over to science. Their reasoning, influenced by the emerging science of archeology (Rudwick 2005), was that since a forensic approach was needed, science was the logical choice to investigate the ancient past. Their error was in forgetting that the definition of history is the empirical study of unique past events. And they compounded that error in their atheistic assumption that if God either does not exist or is not a legitimate subject for science, then the Bible has no relevance to the discussion.

The Flood geologist, on the other hand, recognizes that the investigation of unique past events is distinct from science per se. Furthermore, he sees science resting on axioms that are only justified by philosophy or theology. Since he affirms a God who reveals Himself, then the biblical record is not lightly dismissed or reinterpreted. Instead, it acts as a boundary for his forensic investigation. So finding common ground is a real challenge.

Despite these differences, there is common ground, and both sides should strive to meet there. Even if they do not agree about the origin and proper extent of science, both sides do agree that science is a valid tool in natural history, if used properly. Both agree that the addition of empirical data to the debate is a positive step. Flood geologists may be skeptical of uniformitarian or neocatastrophist

conclusions, but not because they dispute the empirical data. *Rather, they question the part of the interpretation that rests on non-empirical assumptions and non-empirical bias.* Therefore, a key to common ground is the clear statement by both sides of their own assumptions and bias. Once this is done, they can be factored into the debate. Any refusal by either side to perform that simple step should be seen as diagnostic of dogmatism.

But what about all the Christians who advocate the deep time or evolution of secular natural history and who deny the Flood in its global extent? We respond by noting that an individual does not have to be consistent with their worldview; many people are not. We do admit that atheists over the past two centuries have been more consistent in their opposition to Christianity, and we regret that Christians have not been equally consistent by holding to a biblical earth history. However, the debate is not about the opinions of individuals, but about the truth of propositions by competing worldviews.

Therefore, we affirm the common respect for the scientific method, the belief in a real chronological history, and the desire to find truth. If nothing else, we recognize that common ground is found in naturalism being the philosophical child of Christianity (e.g., Glover 1984). The meeting place is found in a common set of ground rules which both sides recognize as comprising science. Though there is disagreement about the extent of the *domain* of science, there is sufficient agreement about the *method* for the debate to proceed in a meaningful way much further than it has at present.

Finally (though perhaps most importantly), the question should be raised as to why such a debate should occur. Ironically, advocates of naturalism seem to have lost their historical position of being the heralds of a skeptical openness in matters of science that would seem to demand a serious hearing for Flood geology — at least in its empirical aspects. Flood geologists are now the skeptics, calling for a new open-minded examination of multiple hypotheses in investigating earth's past.

Reasons for Open Debate

So despite empirical and formal differences between the opposing worldviews, common ground does exist. Given that, can Flood geology exist as a respectable minority report in the earth sciences? Most secular geologists refuse to admit the possibility, and that is surprising, given their empirical methodology and the inherent uncertainties that follow empiricism. For example, as you read in the following chapters, you might weigh the evidence and conclude that there is a 70 percent probability that the argument against the Flood is valid. Then you might read the next chapter and conclude that the same probability is only 20 percent. This uncertainty demonstrates that while Flood geology might not be a *winner* in each topic of debate, that it is certainly a *competitor*. If nothing else, the possibility of new evidence being found in the future makes such competition real. Furthermore, the history of science, littered as it is with myriads of rejected ideas, should instill an inherent caution in any scientist to reject out of hand something that might be powerfully supported by the next discovery.

For that very reason, final victory for *either* side cannot come from any amount of empirical data. Both sides can exist as competing concepts, but only the *formal* invalidity of one can result in a firm conclusion of truth or falsehood. The ongoing dismissal of Flood geology in the absence of a compelling demonstration of its formal invalidity is symptomatic of a rigid dogmatism. Furthermore, since Christians have made cases for the formal invalidity of naturalism (e.g., Lisle 2009; Reed 2001), secular geologists are faced with the necessity of both answering those cases as well as countering the empirical information in the following chapters.

If secular geologists assert that Flood geology is no competitor at all, they are in essence arguing a universal negative, and thus face a heavy burden of proof. There is a fault line running through geology that reflects anti-Christian psychology, not logic and science. On one hand, it poses as a bastion of skepticism; advocating an empirical, probabilistic view of truth. This is a holdover from attacks on the dogmatism of some Christians in earlier centuries. But they need to be consistent. Now that the naturalists are the dogmatists, can they recover that tradition, set aside their prejudice, and examine the evidence with an open mind? If not, they have created another logical inconsistency in their worldview. If, as we believe, this book readily answers common objections to Flood geology in a coherent and compelling fashion, then the continued refusal to admit creationists to the table of natural history reveals a dogmatism at odds with their own traditions.

Why are secular geologists so unwilling to consider theistic alternatives? Their refusal is evident: any geologist or student of geology who articulates such a view will find the road to a rewarding professional career blocked. Secular universities discriminate against both students and professors on this basis (Bergman 2008). No secular journal will publish diluvial ideas. The petroleum and mining industries follow academia and refuse to consider exploration within a diluvial framework. This is diagnostic not of a confident empirical position, but of an entrenched monopoly.

These monopolists may claim they discriminate because Flood geology is so clearly wrong, but the presence of a worldview conflict in natural history and the arguments presented in the following chapters refute that claim. During the late 18th century, there was a call to do away with hoary traditions and unsupported dogma and embrace an open-minded methodology. Modern geology was in the middle of that movement, calling for tolerance when they were the minority. Seemingly, the children of the Enlightenment have become what their fathers fought against, recalling the old adage: "We have met the enemy and he is us."

Another reason for open debate is that the object of our investigations is history, not science. There is a residue of positivism that pervades most scientific thinking. Even if science was the doorway to truth, a little common sense reflection tells us that repeated controlled experiments are quite different from speculation about unique unobserved past events. One only has to watch a special on the History Channel to see now nebulous theories of history can be. It seems as if every episode is reinterpreting a previously popular theory. Logic tells us that the self-congratulations of the hosts are premature; they seem blissfully unaware of the implication that their "new" version of "truth" can (and probably will) be debunked just as easily when another new piece of evidence is unearthed.

Finally, open debate would bring an economic advantage. Geology, as a science, has been stimulated and funded because of its important and direct economic applications. Oil and gas, all forms of mining, and groundwater occurrence and protection all affect the lives of nearly every human and depend on geologic thinking. Yet our imperfect understanding of the earth's crust injects uncertainty into all these ventures. Anything that would provide greater insight into investigation and understanding would have significant economic advantage in reducing the expense of resource discovery.

The Biblical Case for a Global Flood

Flood geology is opposed within Christianity as well as by secular geology. For many years, many Christians sought compromise positions with an ascendant uniformitarian geology and evolutionary biology. Their ploys are well known. Days became ages. Billion-year gaps appeared in Genesis 1. The first part of Genesis was poetry. It was not intended for modern, sophisticated

Europeans. The Flood was an inundation of the Euphrates, the Tigris, the Black Sea, the Persian Gulf, or any other convenient body of water. But none of these ideas make sense, geologically or theologically. Secular advocates of naturalism and many Christians recognize that, and are reconciled to holding divergent views.

But there are Christians who still wish to have uniformitarian (or neocatastrophist) geology and the Bible too. It is to that group we address this section. Despite all of the attempts to twist words and phrases, the biblical case for a global Flood of a year's duration is overwhelming. The reasons for accepting what was the consensus view of the Church up until the Enlightenment are no less textually and theologically compelling than they were two thousand years ago. First, the context and language of the relevant texts strongly indicates a global Flood — there are dozens of phrases in Genesis 6–9 alone that are universal. Second, if the Flood were local, why bother with an ark? Third, if such a craft floated on the waters of a local flood, it would travel downstream and out into the ocean, not end up atop a mountain. The biblical story of the ark's landfall is perfectly consistent with a global Flood, as is the account of mountaintops being the first land seen as the waters fell. Fourth, Genesis 8:5 states that these mountaintops appeared 70 days after the ark landed, suggesting that its resting place was at a high elevation. Fifth, the duration of 371 days makes any local flood incredible at best, especially given the wording that suggests violent inundation. Sixth, men and animals were commanded to *repopulate* the earth, something not needed unless life had been extinguished. Finally, and probably most importantly, the local flood theory impugns the honor of God. He promised to Noah to never bring another similar flood on the earth again. If the Flood were not the global cataclysm described in Genesis, then God's promise was false — a position no Christian can afford to take.

Ironically, creationists and atheists find common ground here. They both agree that the Bible teaches the historical occurrence of a global Flood, both disagreeing with the fence-sitting Christians who want to have the best of both worlds. But as Elijah warned Israel, limping around between two contrary opinions is neither safe nor sane, and God calls them to choose fidelity to Him and to His revelation of His works.

The Road Ahead

This book addresses only a fraction of the challenges that face Flood geology — many of which have not yet been discovered or elucidated. Of course, that is no different

than uniformitarian geology or any other human investigative enterprise of such large scope — all face many intellectual challenges, which is why we enjoy them so much.

Furthermore, there are many challenges for which there are, at present, no satisfactory answers. Again, this is true for both sides. The lack of answers can be attributed to several causes. We may not understand the phenomena to be explained as well as we should. We may have too few people working the problem or insufficient funding. Finally, some things may never be explicable by human knowledge. But both sides will continue to strive toward answers like those provided in the chapters to come.

The topics discussed in this book were selected by several criteria. First, they are perceived as popular objections to Flood geology based on the frequency with which they are used by its opponents. Second, we had to find authors who had knowledge of the subject area and were willing to contribute to this project. Finally, we believe that these discussions help illustrate the role that non-scientific bias often plays in interpretation. All the authors agree that this book is not the final word on these topics; it is merely a step forward. Our uniformitarian counterparts may find new arguments that will require new answers. But we will continue our work too, perhaps publishing more books of this type. We are confident that as time, effort, and thought have provided answers to these challenges, additional progress will continue to enable us to answer new challenges as they are presented.

A significant advantage held by uniformitarian geologists is their entrenched position in academia and industry. Unable to access those resources, diluvialists must look elsewhere for support. Private institutions are beginning to provide some (e.g., the recent RATE project),[1] but that is still a drop in the bucket compared to funding and manpower available to uniformitarian scientists. Who knows what progress could be made in Flood geology were there even a small percentage of the same resources available!

It is the nature of any investigative effort to take on new challenges. If it weren't, the profession of geology would be boring and dry. Everyone starting his or her career yearns for some great discovery. Yet sometimes the adversarial view

---

1. RATE stands for **R**adioisotopes and the **A**ge of **t**he **E**arth. It was a joint research project by the Institute for Creation Research and the Creation Research Society to explore the many problems with radioactive dating methods that support an old age for the earth. Among the groundbreaking results, RATE showed that there may have been a period of accelerated radioactive decay within the past 6,000 years (see chapter 11).

of Flood geology prevents that same mindset from being applied to its challenges. Instead of being seen as opportunities, they are thought to invalidate the whole paradigm. That is both unfortunate and unfair, and we hope that one effect of the following chapters will be to change that perception. Flood geologists enjoy new challenges as much as anyone and appreciate the opportunity for exciting new discoveries in an underexplored paradigm. Once the nature of the conflict between uniformitarianism and diluvialism is seen in its proper context — that of competing worldviews — we are confident that a level playing field will become more acceptable to reasonable people. After all, geologists advocating different theories *within* uniformitarianism are at least able to work together with a professional attitude. Disagreement is kept to the level of objective discussion and debate. We ask for nothing more than the same professional courtesy.

Challenges for All

The debate between secular geology and Flood geology presents distinct challenges for all parties. Secular geologists are challenged to practice the scientific tolerance that they preach. Flood geologists are challenged to engage the data and build their models. If secular universities and government will not fund these activities, then Christian institutions should do so. Finally, readers of this book are also challenged. As you move through the chapters, you should carefully evaluate the arguments on both sides, on their merit as demonstrated by logic and evidence. You should also look beneath the empirical arguments and identify unstated assumptions springing from the different worldviews, and be prepared to see formal errors springing from those frameworks. You should evaluate the role of presuppositions — by both sides — that direct the interpretation of the data, noting especially how both sides can agree on the empirical content and come to dramatically varying conclusions.

Then, and only then, will you be participating in a genuinely open debate between the two positions.

References

Adler, M.J. 1965. *The Conditions of Philosophy*. NY: Atheneum Press.

Glover, W. 1984. *Biblical Origins of Modern Secular History*. Macon, GA: Mercer University Press.

Gould, S.J. 1987. *Time's Arrow, Time's Cycle: Myth and Metaphor Is the Discovery of Geological Time*. Cambridge, MA: Harvard University Press.

Kuhn, T.S. 1962. *The Structure of Scientific Revolutions*. Chicago, IL: University of Chicago Press.

Lisle, J. 2009. *The Ultimate Proof of Creation: Resolving the Origins Debate*. Green Forest, AR: Master Books.

Mortenson, T. 2006. The historical development of the old-earth geological time-scale. In J.K. Reed and M.J. Oard (editors). *The Geologic Column: Perspectives within Diluvial Geology*. Chino Valley, AZ: Creation Research Society Books.

Oard, M.J., 2004. *The Lake Missoula Flood Controversy and the Genesis Flood*. Chino Valley, AZ: Creation Research Society Books.

Reed, J.K. 2001. *Natural History in the Christian Worldview*. Chino Valley, AZ: Creation Research Society Books.

Reed, J.K. 2008. "Toppling the Timescale, Part II: Unearthing the Cornerstone." *Creation Research Society Quarterly* 44(4):256–263.

Reed, J.K., P. Klevberg, C.R. Froede Jr., C.B. Bennett, and T. Lott. 2004. "Beyond Scientific Creationism." *Creation Research Society Quarterly* 41(3):216–230.

Rudwick, M.J.S. 1999. {Geologists' time: a brief history." In K. Lippincott (editor). *The Story of Time*. London: Merrell Holbertin, p. 250–253.

Rudwick, M.J.S. 2005. *Bursting the Limits of Time: The Reconstruction of Geohistory in the Age of Revolution*. Chicago, IL: University of Chicago Press.

Rudwick, M.J.S. 2008. *Worlds Before Adam: The Reconstruction of Geohistory in the Age of Reform*. Chicago, IL: University of Chicago Press.

Stark, R. 2003. *For the Glory of God*. Princeton, NJ: Princeton University Press.

Chapter 2

Mt. Everest and the Flood

Michael J. Oard • MS — Atmospheric Science

Abstract

This chapter provides an answer to the common criticism that the Flood could not have covered Mt. Everest. This challenge is voiced by skeptics and echoed by supposedly conservative Christians. It is easily answered: Psalm 104:8 states that God caused the mountains to rise and the valleys to subside during the Flood. These differential vertical tectonic movements are demonstrated in Wyoming and documented worldwide. Evidence suggests that tectonic motions also occurred on a large scale: continents rose and the ocean basins sank.

Introduction

Skeptics and liberal scholars object to the Genesis Flood by avowing that the Flood water could never have covered Mt. Everest. The same argument applies to practically all the high mountain ranges of the world, but Mt. Everest is the showcase. If earth's surface were leveled, the ocean would average about 1.7 miles (2.7 km) deep — not nearly enough to cover Everest. The argument may or may not apply to volcanic mountains, since these mountains could have formed either late in or after the Flood. Furthermore, the rocks that form most of the mountains of the world were once below the surface of the ocean. Marine fossils are often found at the tops of these mountains. For instance, there are marine crinoid fossils in limestone at the top of Mount Everest (Gansser 1964, p. 164).

Many theologians and other scholars have tripped over this "problem" for centuries (Young 1995). For instance, Old Testament scholar Bernard Ramm (1954, p. 165–166) typifies the objection of many critics:

> There is a problem of the amount of water required by a universal flood. All the waters of the heavens, poured all over the earth, would amount to a sheath seven inches thick. If the earth were a perfect sphere so that all the waters of the ocean covered it, the depth of the ocean would be two and one-half to three miles. To cover the highest mountains would require eight times more water than we now have. It would have involved a great creation of water to have covered the entire globe, but no such creative act is hinted at in the Scriptures.

Mathematical errors are ubiquitous in Ramm's statement. First, there is only an average of about two inches of liquid water in the present atmosphere, not seven. Second, the amount of water in his hypothetical ocean would only be 1.7 miles (2.7 km) deep, not 2.5–3 miles (4–5 km). Third, Mt. Everest is 29,035 feet (8,850 m) or 5.5 miles high. So, given Ramm's water depth of 2.5–3 miles (4–5 km), there would need to be only about two or three times, not eight times, the amount of ocean water. Otherwise, the volume of seawater would need to be around four times greater than its current average to cover Mt. Everest. So Ramm has a point, although his poor math casts doubt on the rest of his scholarship.

Ramm seems to typify a number of modern-day writers. Take for instance the popular *NIV Application Commentary: Genesis*, in which John Walton (2001, p. 322) considers a global Flood an extreme belief because the water cannot cover the high mountains:

> According to the conventional interpretation of the Genesis version of Noah's story, the sea level rose for 150 days until it covered the tops of the mountains and then subsided for another 150 days. It is easy to prove that this is physically impossible.

However, there are logical and biblical problems with Ramm's and Walton's arguments. They presume to know how the Flood worked and to understand its hydrodynamic, tectonic, and destructive ability. But, like so many other critics, they believed too much of what secular scientists have said about the unscientific past. In other words, they believed the *speculations of sinful men who did not observe what happened* (observations and repeatability are keys to science) over the clear word of God. Ramm (1954, p. 8) admits his basic naïve trust in what he believes are scientific facts (really speculations of the past) in his preface: "With reference to technical details of the sciences I must depend on what other men say, and I am thereby at their mercy."

Instead, Ramm, Walton, and other Christian critics of the creation and the Flood should apply 1 Thessalonians 5:21 from the New American Standard Bible (NASB): "But examine everything *carefully*; hold fast to that which is good" (emphasis added). They need to hold fast to the whole Bible from Genesis to Revelation. Then they should carefully examine the statements made by evolutionary/uniformitarian scientists. With some persistence a different picture usually emerges.

Answer Found in Psalm 104:6–9

Actually, the Bible provides an easy solution in Psalm 104:6–9 (NASB, brackets added for clarity):

> *You [God] covered it [Earth] with the deep as with a garment;*
> *The waters were standing above the mountains.*
> *At Your rebuke they fled,*
> *At the sound of Your thunder they hurried away.*
> *The mountains rose; the valleys sank down*
> *To the place which You established for them.*

> *You set a boundary that they may not pass over,*
> *So that they may not return to cover the earth.*

Many consider Psalm 104 to speak of creation, and maybe that is the reason few scholars view verses 6–9 as referring to the Flood. That is one reason local-Flood advocate Davis Young (1995, p. 4) believes these verses refer to day 3 of creation. The psalm is really a praise of God's greatness. These verses refer to a time when earth was completely flooded, since verse 6 states that the mountains were covered with water. There were only two times in biblical history when earth was so covered. The first was during the second and early on the third days of creation (Gen. 1), and the second was during the Genesis Flood (Gen. 6–9). On day 2 of creation week, God separated the waters by an "expanse" and then made the dry land appear on day 3 (Gen. 1:6–10). However, Psalm 104:6–9 must refer to the Flood because verse 9 states that God set a boundary that the waters may not pass over to cover earth. These verses likely refer to the *last* time earth was totally inundated. Furthermore, in verse 6 God *covered* earth, while on day 3 the dry land *appears*, so that the land was *uncovered*. Therefore, Psalm 104:6–9 must refer to the Genesis Flood and not to the earlier creation week. Regardless, the only possible way to go from a totally flooded earth to the topography observed today is for part of earth's crust to rise and part to subside.

These verses fit this praise psalm because the Flood *re*-created earth's surface; the Flood formed the surface features we see today. The early verses praise God for His creation. Starting with verse 10, this passage talks about Flood-formed features and other things that we can observe today, like springs, valleys, mountains, and the beasts of the field. Of course, many scholars who think Genesis 6–9 refers to a local flood continue to believe that Psalm 104:6–9 refers to day-3 events, but this belief is likely incorrect.

Notice in verse 8 that when God caused the water to recede, *the mountains rose and the valleys sank down*. Some versions of the Bible, such as the NIV, translate verse 8: ". . . they [the waters] flowed over the mountains, they went down into the valleys." However, this version is not the proper translation (Taylor, 1998; 1999), while the NASB quoted above is more accurate to the Hebrew text. Verse 8 implies that to drain the Flood water, mountains rapidly rose and valleys (basins) rapidly sank down. So, the mountains with their sedimentary rocks and fossils *rose up out of the Flood water*, not the reverse, in which Flood water had to cover their *current* heights (figure 1). Given

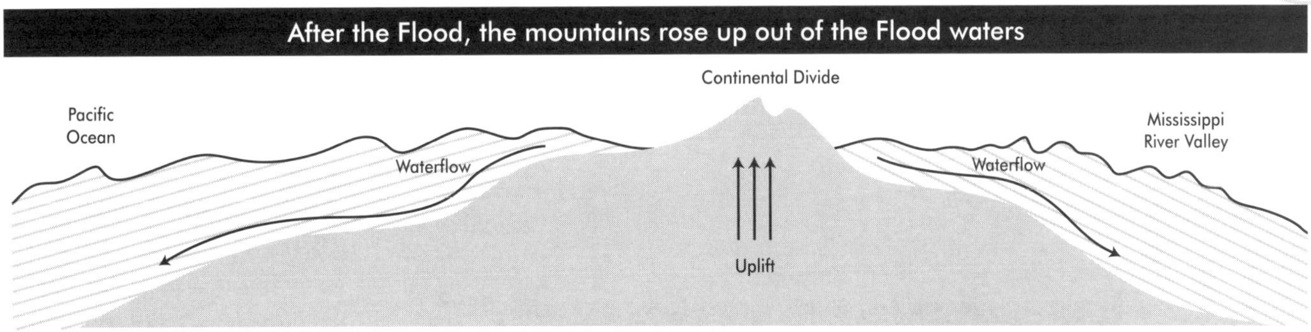

After the Flood, the mountains rose up out of the Flood waters

Figure 1. Schematic showing the Flood waters moving off the uplifting western United States and the water rushing toward the Pacific Ocean and down the east slopes of the Rockies (drawn by Daniel Lewis of AIG).

the clarity of the text, one wonders how theologians could possibly have tripped over this "problem." And even if Psalm 104:6–9 did refer to day 3, the high mountains of the earth could still have risen up out of the Flood water.

Evidence for Differential Vertical Crustal Movements

Is there geological evidence for such differential crustal movement? Actually, rising mountains and sinking basins are tectonic themes *all over earth*. Many mountain ranges are adjacent to deep valleys, for instance, the Himalaya Mountains and the Ganges Plain of India. Other examples, including the mountains and basins in Wyoming, record differential vertical tectonics in the crust.

Differential Crustal Tectonics in Wyoming

Good examples of upward and downward crustal motions are shown by the mountain ranges in Wyoming. These ranges are separated by generally flat-bottomed valleys (figure 2). Granite cores many of these mountains, indicating that they were uplifted. The Beartooth Mountains of south-central Montana and north-central Wyoming average about 10,000 feet (3,000 m) above mean sea level (msl), with the highest peaks reaching about 13,000 feet (4,000 m) msl. These mountains are mostly composed of granitic rocks capped by at least one large sedimentary erosional remnant containing marine fossils (figure 3). These remnants indicate that great thicknesses of sedimentary rock were eroded from the Beartooth Mountains. The adjacent Bighorn Basin to the east

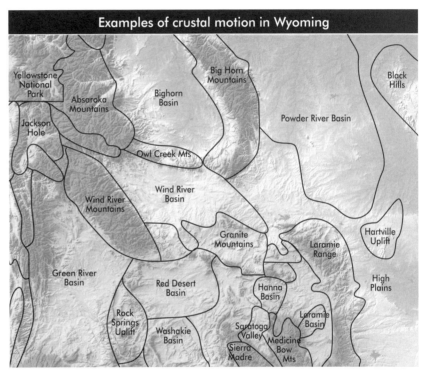

Figure 2. Map of major basins and mountain uplifts in Wyoming (from Love 1960, p. 204).

Figure 3. Beartooth Butte within a low spot on top of the Beartooth Mountains.

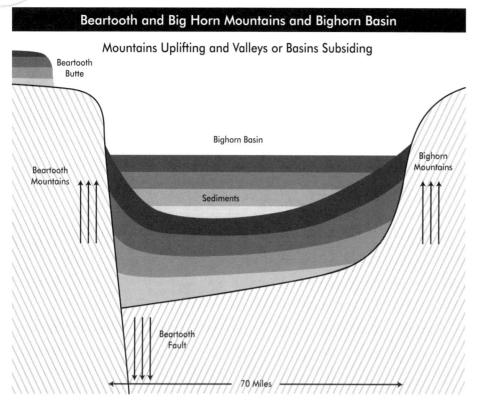

Beartooth and Big Horn Mountains and Bighorn Basin

Mountains Uplifting and Valleys or Basins Subsiding

Figure 4. Schematic of Beartooth fault showing about 23,000 feet (7,000 m) of vertical displacement (taken from Coffin 1983, and redrawn by Mark Wolfe).

likely started before uplift, since sedimentary rocks at the edge of the basin are draped over the uplifts and lie at high angles (figure 5). These sedimentary rocks often form "flatirons," triangular features exposing bedding planes with a pointed apex and broad base resembling a flatiron for ironing clothes. The history of the basins included large-scale erosion of the Beartooth Mountains and adjacent mountain ranges, with some of the resulting sediments deposited in the Bighorn Basin. Flood currents flowing through the basin would also have deposited sediment from more distant areas undergoing erosion.

Similar vertical motions are seen by the relative elevation of granite in other mountain ranges and basins of Wyoming (table 1). Note that the granite in the relatively small Hanna Basin is as deep as 31,000 feet (9,450 m) below sea level (Otteman and Snoke 2005). Based on the height of granite

is about 4,500 feet (1,370 m) msl. The Bighorn Mountains rise to the east of the basin. The Bighorn Basin is filled with generally horizontally bedded sandstone, shale, and coal; the top layers have been eroded. The granite basement of the northern Bighorn Basin is over 10,000 feet (3,000 m) below sea level (deeper in the southern Bighorn Basin) with the greatest depth in the western Bighorn Basin adjacent to the Beartooth Mountains (Wise 2000, p. 362). The basin is offset from the uplifted Beartooth Mountains by the Beartooth fault (figure 4). It seems clear that the Beartooth Mountains rose and/or the Bighorn Basin (valley) sank.

The northern Bighorn Basin is filled with over 14,000 feet (4,250 m) of sedimentary rocks (which were once thicker), indicating that the vertical movement started in deep water during the Flood. Sedimentation in the Bighorn Basin

Sedimentary rocks in the Big Horn Basin

Figure 5. Tilted Paleozoic and Mesozoic strata at the northwest edge of the Bighorn Basin at Clark Canyon adjacent to southeast Beartooth Mountains.

in the Wind River Mountains (near 14,000 ft.; 4,270 m) and its depth in the Hanna Basin, Love (1960) estimated a total vertical change of 45,000 feet (13,715 m) in Wyoming! Given these uplifts, the 30,000-foot (9,150 m) uplift of Mt. Everest and the Himalayas is not a problem and could easily have occurred during the retreating stage of the Flood.

Differential Crustal Tectonics Worldwide

The juxtaposition of uplifted mountains and downwarped basins is a *fundamental* property of continents and ocean basins all over the earth. Evolutionary geomorphologist Lester King (1983, p. 16, 71, emphasis his) summarized:

> So the fundamental tectonic mechanisms of global geology are *vertical, up or down*: and the normal and most general tectonic structures in the crust are also vertically disposed. . . . But one must bear in mind that every part of the globe — on the continents or in the ocean basins — provides direct geological evidence that formerly it stood at different levels, up or down, and that it is subject *in situ* to vertical displacements.

Cliff Ollier and Colin Pain (2000) stated in their book *The Origin of Mountains* that the greatest uplift of practically all the major mountains of the world occurred in the last several million years — only recently in geological time. In the biblical timeframe, this tectonic activity would have been one of the last major geological events in the Flood. However, these authors also concluded that they do not know why the mountains rose, and they provided over 20 possible mechanisms. Scientists need

Mountains		Basins	
Wind River Mountains	14,000 ft	Wind River Basin	-23,000 ft
Beartooth Mountains	13,000 ft	Bighorn Basin	-21,000 ft
Bighorn Mountains	13,000 ft	Powder River Basin	-14,000 ft
Medicine Bow Mountains	12,000 ft	Hanna Basins	-31,000 ft
Owl Creek Mountains	9,000 ft	Washakie Basin	-21,000 ft
Laramie Range	10,000 ft	Red Desert Basin	-23,000 ft
		Green River Basin	-14,000 ft

Table 1. Estimates of altitudes of granitic rocks in some mountains and below the sedimentary fill in adjacent basins in Wyoming (Love 1960, p. 205).

to know more about the crust and mantle to better understand these vertical motions.

Continents Uplifted and Ocean Basins Sank

As mountains rose out of the Flood water, tremendous erosion would have occurred, filling subsiding basins with eroded sediments. The western United States shows uplift that occurred at a variety of scales: local, regional, and subcontinental. Figure 6 shows a schematic of this

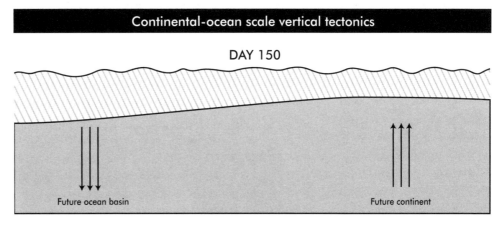

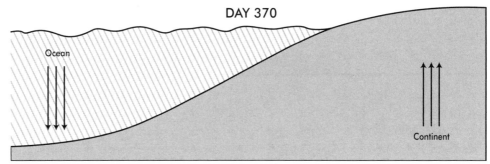

Figure 6. Schematic of vertical uplift of the future continents and subsidence of the ocean crust during the Retreating Stage of the Flood (drawn by Mark Wolfe).

differential uplift of the continents and subsidence of the oceans' basins during the Flood.

Evidence of Continental Uplift

Evidence for rising continents and the concomitant rapid draining of the Flood water is provided by a host of geomorphic observations (Klevberg and Oard 1998; Oard 2001a, 2001b, 2004a, 2004b, 2008; Oard and Klevberg 1998, 2005). This evidence includes tall igneous and sedimentary erosional remnants that should have been destroyed by millions of years of erosion, planation surfaces, pediments, water and wind gaps, and rocks transported long distances by water.

Evidence of Oceanic Subsidence along the Continental Margin

At the same time the continents rose, the ocean basins sank. Sinking continental margins accumulated up to 12 miles (20 km) of sediment (Deptuck et al. 2003; Pickering et al. 1989) eroded from rising continents (Pazzaglia and Gardner 1994; Uchupi and Emory 1967). King (1983, p. 200, emphasis and brackets added) also stated in regard to coastal areas and their offshore basins:

The formations and unconformities [of the continental margin] have been tilted seaward (monoclinally) at intervals during the later Cenozoic. There have been repeated tectonic episodes: *always in the same sense — the lands go up and the sea floor down. . . .*

This statement by a uniformitarian geomorphologist is remarkably similar to Psalm 104:8.

Evidence of Subsidence Far from Land

Guyots, flat-topped seamounts (figure 7), provide further evidence for the subsidence of the ocean basins. Many seamounts are flat-topped guyots (Clague et al. 2000a; Searle 1983; Simkin 1972; Wessel 2001). For instance, most of the numerous seamounts in the western Pacific are guyots (Shipboard Scientific Party 1993a). Guyots also are found elsewhere on the ocean bottom but are less abundant; for instance, in the northeast Pacific (Carsola and Dietz 1952; Turner et al. 1980) and the eastern Atlantic (Verhoef and Collette 1987). Just like seamounts, guyots commonly occur in linear chains (Smoot and King 1997). Harry Hess (1946) was the first geologist to describe guyots. Their origin remains a difficult uniformitarian problem (Winterer and Metzler 1984, p. 9,969): "Since Hess first recognized them in 1946, the origin of flat-topped seamounts, or guyots, has remained one of the most persistent problems in marine geology."

Not all guyots are sheared volcanic cones. Recent investigators have concluded that some guyots, especially in the western Pacific, are *drowned carbonate platforms that have broken up* (Wilson et al. 1998). Some of these guyots cover large areas and are capped by thick carbonate, once thought to be drowned reefs or atolls. But the carbonate is now considered to be a *carbonate bank with fossils*, similar to the Bahamas (Jenkyns and Wilson 1999). In the western Pacific, many guyot

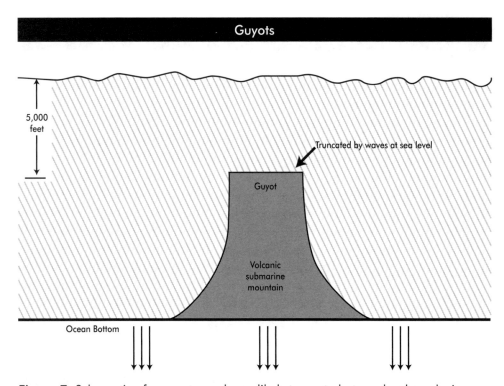

Figure 7. Schematic of a guyot, a volcano likely truncated at sea level producing a flat top. Guyots are currently at an average depth of 5,000 feet (1,525 m) below sea level. There are thousands of guyots on the ocean bottom, especially in the western Pacific, indicating that the ocean basins have sunk (drawn by Mark Wolfe).

tops have an area larger than 195 mi^2 (500 km^2). On Dutton Ridge, a series of guyots just east of the junction of the Mariana and Izu-Bonin Trenches have tops larger than 195 mi^2 (500 km^2). The largest is Lamont Guyot with an area of 615 mi^2 (1,590 km^2) (Smoot 1989). Dutton Ridge is thought to be a broken-up carbonate platform, not only because of the large size of the guyot tops, but also because the guyots are found at variable depths, ranging from 4,265 to 7,800 feet (1,300–2,375 m) below msl. It appears that pronounced vertical tectonic displacements have been involved in the destruction of these ancient carbonate platforms. The Mid-Pacific Mountains are also thought to be a carbonate platform that was broken up and drowned (Shipboard Scientific Party 1993b). Mai Tai Guyot and Sio Guyot in the eastern Mariana Basin have summit top areas of 585 mi^2 (1,515 km^2) and 1,100 mi^2 (2,850 km^2), respectively (Kellogg et al. 1987).

Furthermore, researchers are coming to the conclusion that some volcanic seamounts can apparently form generally flat tops deep underwater (Lonsdale and Spiess 1979; Simkin 1972). A number of guyots near the East Pacific Rise are attributed to calderas being infilled by small lava flows (Clague et al. 2000a; Clague et al. 2000b; Fornari et al. 1984; Mitchell 2001). However, they are small compared to the classical guyots in the western Pacific (Batiza and Vanko 1983/1984; Lonsdale 1983; Searle 1983; Wessel 2001).

Therefore, there are several ways to produce a guyot: volcanic infilling of a caldera, erosion at sea level, and deposition (Winterer and Metzler 1984). None of these mechanisms are mutually exclusive, and most guyot tops are likely a combination of mechanisms.

The flat tops of the larger seamounts and the carbonate platforms are still considered to have formed near sea level and subsequently sunk. Investigators have concluded that the carbonate was laid down in shallow water, based on shallow-water fossils (Sager et al. 1993; Shipboard Scientific Party 1993c). Thus, the depth of these guyots is still considered an ancient sea level indicator within the uniformitarian model (Caplan-Auerbach et al. 2000; Smoot and King 1997).

The most important point is that guyots have subsided an average of 5,000 feet (1,525 m) below msl, implying that the ocean basins have sunk to the same extent (Sager et al. 1993). Guyot depths vary significantly, indicating that some areas have sunk much more (Oard 2001a). Maximum subsidence seems to be around trenches, such as a guyot near the Japan Trench at 12,135 feet (3,700 m) below msl (Menard 1984). Capricorn Guyot is located at the edge of the Tonga Trench and has been tilted slightly down toward the trench, indicating the trench has sunk more than surrounding areas (Crawford et al. 2003). Hoernle et al. (2004) discovered new guyot-like seamounts on the volcanic Hikurangi Oceanic Plateau, indicating that this plateau sank about 5,250 feet (1,600 m) in the southwest and about 10,825 feet (3,300 m) in the northeast. Furthermore, these sinking guyots occurred *recently*, (King 1983, p. 168, 71, emphasis and brackets mine, parentheses his):

> Marine volcanic islands which have been truncated by the waves and since subsided below sea level are called guyots. Most of them seem to have sunk by 600 to 2000 m [1,970 to 6,560 feet] and it is evident that they afford a measure of the amount by which the ocean floor has sunk in *late geologic time.* The Pacific floor especially has subsided. . . . All the ocean basins afford evidence of subsidence (amounting to hundreds and even thousands of meters) in areas far from land.

In a Flood model, all sea level indicators are equivocal. Uniformitarian scientists assume that guyots were truncated at sea level or even above sea level. However, in the Flood model, the truncation likely occurred rapidly by Flood currents. Since currents in deep water are generally expected to be strongest near the surface and decrease with depth, the erosion of a guyot need not occur right at sea level. The currents, say at 300 feet (90 m) deep, may be sufficient to flatten a seamount top. Although guyots in the Flood model likely are not necessarily ancient sea level indicators, guyots still indicate substantial subsidence of the ocean bottom.

Conclusions

The problem of the Flood water covering Mt. Everest has an easy solution from Scripture in Psalm 104:6–9. In addition, geology provides overwhelming support for differential vertical tectonic movement of earth's crust at a variety of scales. The mountains rose out of the Flood water as the valleys and basins sank, often being filled with sediments that later formed sedimentary rocks. Such differential crustal motions (and likely parts of the mantle) not only explain how the Flood water drained, but also account for all the high mountains once being covered by water. The mountains were elevated late in the Flood, therefore the Flood water did not need to reach the elevations of present-day mountains.

References

AAPG: American Association of Petroleum Geologists Bulletin
CRSQ: Creation Research Society Quarterly
CENTJ: Creation Ex Nihilo Technical Journal (now Journal of Creation)

Batiza, R., and D. Vanko. 1983/1984. Volcanic development of small oceanic central volcanoes on the flanks of the East Pacific Rise inferred from narrow-beam echo-sounder surveys. *Marine Geology* 54:53–90.

Caplan-Auerbach, J., F. Duennebier, and G. Ito. 2000. Origin of intraplate volcanoes from guyot heights and oceanic paleodepth. *Journal of Geophysical Research* 105 (B2):2,679–2,697.

Carsola, A.J., and R.S. Dietz. 1952. Submarine geology of two flat-topped northeast Pacific seamounts. *American Journal of Science* 250:481–497.

Clague, D.A., J.G. Moore, and J.R. Reynolds. 2000. Formation of submarine flat-topped volcanic cones in Hawaii. *Bulletin of Volcanology* 62:214–233.

Clague, D.A., J.R. Reynolds, and A.S. Davis. 2000. Near-ridge seamount chains in the northeastern Pacific Ocean. *Journal of Geophysical Research* 105 (B7):16,541–16,561.

Crawford, W.C., J.A. Hildebrand, R.M. Dorman, S.C. Webb, and D.A. Wiens. 2003. Tonga Ridge and Lau Basins crustal structure from seismic refraction data. *Journal of Geophysical Research* 108 (B4):EPM6:1–17.

Deptuck, M.E., R.A. MacRae, J.W. Shimeld, G.L. Williams, and R.A. Fensome. 2003. Revised upper Cretaceous and lower Paleogene lithostratigraphy and depositional history of the Jeanne d'Arc Basin, offshore Newfoundland, Canada. *AAPG* 87:1,459–1,483.

Fornari, D.J., W.B.F. Ryan, and P.J. Fox. 1984. The evolution of craters and calderas on young seamounts: insights from Sea Mark I and sea beam sonar surveys of a small seamount group near the axis of the East Pacific Rise at ~10°N. *Journal of Geophysical Research* 89 (B13):11,069–11,083.

Gansser, A. 1964. *Geology of the Himalayas*. New York: Interscience Publishers.

Hess, H.H., 1946. Drowned ancient islands of the Pacific Basin. *American Journal of Science* 244:772–791.

Hoernle, K., F. Hauff, R. Werner, and N. Mortimer. 2004. New insights into the origin and evolution of the Hikurangi Oceanic Plateau. *EOS* 85(41):401, 408.

Jenkyns, H.C., and P.A. Wilson. 1999. Stratigraphy, paleoceanography, and evolution of Cretaceous Pacific guyots: relics from a greenhouse earth. *American Journal of Science* 299:341–392.

Kellogg, J.N., B.S. Wedgeworth, and J. Freymueller. 1987. Isostatic compensation and conduit structures of western Pacific seamounts: results of three-dimensional gravity modeling. In Keating, B.H., P. Fryer, R. Batiza, and G.W. Boehlert (editors). *Seamounts, Islands, and Atolls*. Geophysical Monograph 43, American Geophysical Union, p. 85–96.

Klevberg, P., and M.J. Oard. 1998. Paleohydrology of the Cypress Hills Formation and Flaxville gravel. In Walsh, R.E. (editor). *Proceedings of the Fourth International Conference on Creationism*. Pittsburgh, PA: Creation Science Fellowship, p. 361–378.

King, L.C. 1983. *Wandering Continents and Spreading Sea Floors on an Expanding Earth*. New York: John Wiley and Sons.

Lonsdale, P. 1983. Laccoliths(?) and small volcanoes on the flank of the East Pacific Rise. *Geology* 11:706–709.

Lonsdale, P., and F.N. Spiess. 1979. A pair of young cratered volcanoes on the East Pacific Rise. *Journal of Geology* 87:157–173.

Love, J.D. 1960. Cenozoic sedimentation and crustal movement in Wyoming. *American Journal of Science* 258-A:204–214.

Menard, H.W. 1984. Origin of guyots: the *Beagle* to *Seabeam*. *Journal of Geophysical Research* 89 (B13):11,117–11,123.

Mitchell, N.C. 2001. Transition from circular to stellate forms of submarine volcanoes. *Journal of Geophysical Research* 106 (B2):1,987–2,003.

Oard, M.J. 2001a. Vertical tectonics and the drainage of floodwater: a model for the middle and late diluvian period — Part I. *CRSQ* 38 (1):3–17.

———. 2001b. Vertical tectonics and the drainage of floodwater: a model for the middle and late diluvian period — Part II. *CRSQ* 38 (2):79–95.

———. 2004a. *The Missoula Flood Controversy and the Genesis Flood*. Creation Research Society Monograph No. 13, Chino Valley, AZ.

———. 2004b. Pediments formed by the Flood: evidence for the Flood/post-Flood boundary in the Late Cenozoic. *TJ* 18(2):15–27 (now *Journal of Creation*).

___. 2008. *Flood by Design: Receding Water Shapes the Earth's Surface*. Green Forest, AR: Master Books.

Oard, M.J., and P. Klevberg. 1998. A diluvial interpretation of the Cypress Hills Formation, Flaxville gravels, and related deposits. In R.E. Walsh (editor). *Proceedings of the Fourth International Conference on Creationism*. Pittsburgh, PA: Creation Science Fellowship, p. 421–436.

————. 2005. Deposits remaining from the Genesis Flood: rim gravels in Arizona. *CRSQ* 42(1):1–17.

Ollier C., and C. Pain. 2000. *The Origin of Mountains*. Routledge, London.

Otteman, A.S., and S.W. Snoke. 2005. Structural analysis of a Laramide, basement-involved, foreland fault zone, Rawlins uplift, south-central Wyoming. *Rocky Mountain Geology* 40(1):65–89.

Pazzaglia, F.J., and T.W. Gardner. 1994. Late Cenozoic flexural deformation of the middle U.S. Atlantic passive margin. *Journal of Geophysical Research* 99(B6):12,143–12,157.

Pickering, K.T., R.N. Hiscott, and F.J. Hein. 1989. *Deep-Marine Environments*. London: Unwin Hyman.

Ramm, B. 1954. *The Christian View of Science and Scripture*. Grand Rapids, MI: William B. Eerdmans Publishing Co.

Sager, W. et al. 1993. Examining guyots in the Mid-Pacific Mountains. *EOS* 74(17):201, 205–207.

Searle, R.C. 1983. Submarine central volcanoes on the Nazca Plate — high-resolution sonar observations. *Marine Geology* 53:77–102.

Shipboard Scientific Party, 1993a. Introduction. In Premoli Silva, I., J. Haggerty, F. Rack, et al. (editors). *Proceedings of the Ocean Drilling Program*, Initial Reports 144:3–4.

————. 1993b. Synthesis of results, Leg 143. In W.S. Sager, E.L. Winterer, J.V. Firth, et al. (editors). *Proceedings of the Ocean Drilling Program*, Initial Reports 143:13–29.

————. 1993c. Introduction and scientific objectives. In W.S. Sager, E.L. Winterer, J.V. Firth, et al. (editors). *Proceedings of the Ocean Drilling Program, Initial Reports* 143:7–12.

Simkin, T. 1972. *Origin of some flat-topped volcanoes and guyots*. Geological Society of America Memoir 132, Boulder, CO, p. 183–193.

Smoot, N.C. 1989. The Marcus-Wake seamounts and guyots as paleofracture indicators and their relation to the Dutton Ridge. *Marine Geology* 88:117–131.

Smoot, N.C., and R.E. King. 1997. The Darwin Rise demise: the western Pacific guyot heights trace the trans-Pacific Mendocino fracture zone. *Geomorphology* 18:223–235.

Taylor, C. 1998. Did mountains really rise according to Psalm 104:8? *CENTJ* 12(3):312–313.

————. 1999. More on mountains — Charles Taylor replies. *CENTJ* 13(1):70–71.

Turner, D.L., R.D. Jarrard, and R.B. Forbes. 1980. Geochronology and origin of the Pratt-Welker seamount chain, Gulf of Alaska: a new pole of rotation for the Pacific plate. *Journal of Geophysical Research* 85(B11):6,547–6,556.

Uchupi, E., and K.O. Emery. 1967. Structure of continental margin off Atlantic coast of United States. *AAPG* 51 (2):223–234.

Verhoef, J., and B.J. Collette. 1987. Lithospheric thinning under the Atlantis Meteor seamount complex (North Atlantic). In: B.H. Keating, P. Fryer, R. Batiza, and G.W. Boehlert (editors). *Seamounts, islands, and atolls*. Geophysical Monograph 43. Washington, DC: American Geophysical Union, p. 391–405.

Walton, J.H. 2001. *The NIV Application Commentary: Genesis*. Grand Rapids, MI: Zondervan.

Wessel, P. 2001. Global distribution of seamounts inferred from gridded Geosat/ERS-1 altimetry. *Journal of Geophysical Research* 106(B9):19,431–19,441.

Wilson, P.A., H.C. Jenkyns, H. Elderfield, and R.L. Larson. 1998. The paradox of drowned carbonate platforms and the origin of Cretaceous Pacific guyots. *Nature* 392:889–894.

Winterer, E.L., and C.V. Metzler. 1984. Origin and subsidence of guyots in Mid-Pacific Mountains. *Journal of Geophysical Research* 89(B12):9,969–9,979.

Wise, D.U. 2000. Laramide structures in basement and cover of the Beartooth uplift near Red Lodge, Montana. *AAPG* 84 (3):360–375.

Young, D.A. 1995. *The Biblical Flood: A Case Study of the Church's Response to Extrabiblical Evidence*. Grand Rapids, MI: William B. Eerdmans Publishing Company.

Chapter 3

Mercury Toxicity and the Genesis Flood

Aaron R. Hutchinson • PhD — Chemistry

Abstract

Geophysicist Glenn R. Morton has argued that a dangerous concentration of the toxic metal mercury would have been released by the Genesis Flood. This belief is based on the assumptions that the pre-Flood crust contained a concentration of mercury similar to that of the modern crust, that 90 percent of this mercury would be released as dissolved mercury ions by the Flood, and that the resulting mercury concentration of 100 parts per billion (ppb) would have been devastating to life on earth. However, a careful study of the relevant literature shows that none of these assumptions are warranted. There is good reason to believe that the pre-Flood crust contained less mercury than Morton estimated, because many mercury deposits were most likely formed by hydrothermal activity during or after the Flood. Furthermore, it is unlikely that the Flood would have fully dissolved what mercury was present, because most of it would have been in the form of highly insoluble mercury sulfide. Of the mercury that was dissolved, only 2–20 percent would be expected to be methyl mercury, which is by far the most dangerous form of the metal. It is primarily methyl mercury that accumulates in food chains and poses the greatest threat to higher life forms. There are also numerous instances documented in the literature of plant life surviving in waters with a mercury concentration higher than 100 ppb. Therefore, Morton's challenge to the Genesis Flood does not stand; there is no reason to question the Genesis account based on mercury chemistry.

Introduction

The account of the great Flood found in Genesis 6–8 is one of the most fascinating passages in the Scriptures. In one mighty act of righteous judgment, God destroyed the world that was and created the world we see today. Many important lessons concerning God's character and our lives can be drawn from the Genesis account of this event.

The Genesis Flood, however, is more than just a moral lesson; it was also a real historical event — one of the greatest in earth's geological history. Today, however, many geologists dispute that such an episode could have occurred, and their concerns should be answered directly and forthrightly. If the Bible is God's Word and therefore true, and if truth about nature can also be found via the proper application of the scientific method, then when the findings of science appear to be at odds with Scripture, there are only two possible reasons. Either my understanding of Scripture must be in error or there is a problem with the scientific evidence (Brand 1997).

With that in mind, let us examine one challenge to the veracity of the Genesis Flood — that the Flood would have released sufficient mercury to have made the survival of Noah and his family unlikely (Morton 1998). If true, it poses a serious challenge to a literal interpretation of Genesis. Conversely, if Genesis is true, that argument cannot be. Since numerous Bible scholars have demonstrated that Genesis is presented as an historical account (Morris, 1985), then it is likely that there is a problem with the scientific basis for this argument. To evaluate that fairly, let's start by defining the challenge.

The Challenge

This argument was published by geophysicist Glenn R. Morton (1998). He claims that dangerous concentrations of toxic heavy metals, particularly mercury, would have been released during the Flood. However, Genesis infers that some aquatic animals and plant life survived the Flood itself, and that the post-Flood world was habitable by Noah, his family, and the animals aboard the ark, contradicting Morton's claim of a toxic post-Flood world. If you wish to read Morton's argument in his own words, please see appendix 1.

Essentially, Morton argues that all of the current sedimentary rock was formed from igneous rock eroded by the Flood. During this process of erosion, he believes that 90 percent of the mercury contained in these rocks would be released. Assuming that the mercury concentration in these igneous rocks was the same as that of the modern crust, which Morton estimates at 0.1 parts per million (ppm), and that the volume of water in the Flood was essentially the same as the volume of water in modern oceans, this gives a concentration of 100 micrograms of mercury per liter of water or 100 parts per billion (ppb) for the Flood water. Morton goes on to argue that this concentration would pose a grave threat to the reestablishment of life on earth.

The basic questions we must answer are these: (1) would a global Flood really release enough mercury to create an average concentration of 100 ppb throughout the world's oceans, and (2) would such a concentration threaten the continued existence of life afterward? To answer these questions, we must first review the basic properties and behavior of mercury in the environment.

Mercury Chemistry

Mercury (Hg) is a very interesting and unique chemical element. It is a liquid and releases an appreciable amount of vapor at room temperature, which is highly unusual for a metal. It will also dissolve many other metals, forming amalgams (solutions of one metal dissolved in another metal) (Greenwood and Earnshaw 1984). Due to this ability, mercury has been used to remove precious metals, such as gold and silver, from ore since as early as perhaps 2700 B.C. (Malm 1998). In fact, much of the mercury

pollution that exists today in the Western United States (Pirrone et al. 1998) or South America (Malm 1998) stems from gold mining by amalgamation. Mercury amalgams have also been traditionally used as tooth fillings, although this practice has become somewhat controversial in recent years (Aposhian et al. 1995; Bjorkman et al. 1997; Jones 2004; Lorscheider et al. 1995).

Mercury pollution is a concern due to the metal's high toxicity. This toxicity partly stems from one of mercury's most significant properties, its ability to form especially strong chemical bonds with sulfur. Mercury tends to bind to sulfur whenever possible. Since a number of key chemical compounds within the body contain sulfur, mercury can bind to these sulfurs, preventing the compounds from performing their intended function (Silbergeld and Devine 2000; Winker et al. 2002). Within the human body, mercury can also create reactive oxygen species (Gasso et al. 2001), affect the immune system (Silva et al. 2005; Tchounwou et al. 2003; Yokoo et al. 2003), and cause birth defects (Domingo 1995; Tchounwou et al. 2003). In adults, symptoms of mercury poisoning include damage to the central nervous system (manifested as diminished fine motor skills, tremors, and memory loss), stomach pains, pain or loss of feeling in the hands and feet, vision and hearing loss, and eventually death (Auger et al. 2005; Clarkson 1998; Harada et al. 2001; Stern 2005; Tchounwou et al. 2003; Yokoo et al. 2003). In fact, the mental effects of mercury exposure were recognized long ago, although their cause was not fully understood; the phrase "mad as a hatter" refers to the tendency of haberdashers to go insane due to handling mercury, which they used to remove lint from their hats.

Mercury appears in a number of different chemical forms, including the metallic liquid Hg^0 (this is the form many readers are most likely familiar with, since it is found in older thermometers), the water-soluble ionic (an ion is a charged atom) species Hg^{2+}, the rare Hg_2^{2+} ion (technically an ion in which each atom has a positive one charge), and the carbon-containing molecule methyl mercury (technically CH_3Hg^+ or $(CH_3)_2Hg$, although for simplicity's sake in this paper I will refer to all organic mercury compounds as methyl mercury). While all of these forms are toxic, methyl mercury is by far the most toxic; only a few drops on the skin can kill an adult human (Holden 1997). This is because methyl mercury in many ways behaves like an organic molecule of the type living things routinely interact with. Therefore, it is usually absorbed rather than excreted by the body (Boening 2000). Most of the major cases of mercury poisoning in recent history have involved methyl mercury. It was methyl mercury stemming from waste dumped by a local chemical plant that contaminated fish in Minamata Bay, Japan, leading to a massive outbreak of human mercury poisoning that affected 2,262 people between 1956 and 1998, and gave mercury poisoning its clinical name of Minamata disease (Futatsuka et al. 2000). Methyl mercury, used as a fungicide to treat seed wheat sent to Iraq to stave off famine in 1971, was also responsible for the hospitalization of 6,530 people and death of 459 when hungry farmers turned the wheat into bread rather than planting it (Bakir et al. 1973). When mercury toxicity is discussed, methyl mercury is the form of most interest.

Clearly, it is not enough to simply say mercury is highly toxic, as does Morton. No matter how toxic, if mercury is not available to living things in the environment, then it does not pose a real threat.

Figure 1

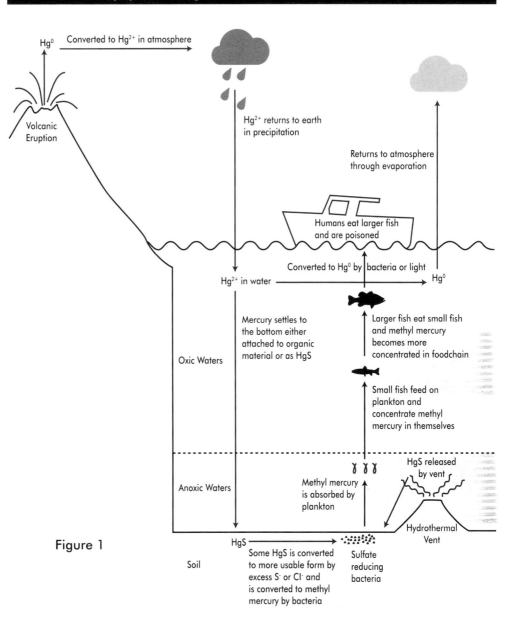

How mercury cycles through the environment and enters the food chain

Hg⁰ Converted to Hg²⁺ in atmosphere

Volcanic Eruption

Hg²⁺ returns to earth in precipitation

Returns to atmosphere through evaporation

Humans eat larger fish and are poisoned

Converted to Hg⁰ by bacteria or light

Hg²⁺ in water → Hg⁰

Mercury settles to the bottom either attached to organic material or as HgS

Oxic Waters

Larger fish eat small fish and methyl mercury becomes more concentrated in foodchain

Small fish feed on plankton and concentrate methyl mercury in themselves

Anoxic Waters

Methyl mercury is absorbed by plankton

HgS released by vent

Hydrothermal Vent

HgS

Soil

Some HgS is converted to more usable form by excess S⁻ or Cl⁻ and is converted to methyl mercury by bacteria

Sulfate reducing bacteria

The real issue is whether a global Flood would actually release enough mercury in a sufficiently dangerous form (i.e., methyl mercury) to poison the post-Flood world. To be able to intelligently answer that question, we need to know how mercury actually behaves in natural waters.

Mercury's behavior in an aquatic environment differs greatly between oxygen-rich (oxic) and oxygen-poor (anoxic) waters. Because the chemical reactions are different in these two environments, different chemical compounds are generated that mercury will react with. The amount of oxygen in water is, in turn, often dependent upon depth (figure 1). In general, there is more oxygen near the surface than in deeper water. Regardless of depth, mercury atoms are rarely found alone. Rather, they tend to

be chemically bonded to other elements, creating a variety of compounds that will undergo different reactions.

In oxic surface waters, mercury tends to bind to the hydroxide ion (OH^-) or the chloride ion (Cl^-), although it will bind to sulfur if a sufficient amount is present (Morel et al. 1998). If a great deal of organic material (decaying plants and animals) is present and a significant amount of that material contains sulfur atoms, then as much as 95 percent of the mercury may be attached to that (Morel et al. 1998; Ravichandran 2004). In these waters, mercury is usually in the Hg^{2+} form, although it can be converted to Hg^0 by bacteria or sunlight. Some bacteria possess, as a defense against mercury poisoning, a group of genes called the *mer* operon, which will convert Hg^{2+} and/or methyl mercury to Hg⁰ (Kiyono et al. 2003; Wagner-Dobler et al. 2000). Thus, these bacteria convert the mercury from a more toxic form to a less toxic form, a fact that could have a significant impact on mercury's behavior during the Flood. It is also possible for Hg^{2+} to be converted to Hg^0 by light. In general, the reaction with light is most important if the mercury concentration is too low to activate the *mer* operon; otherwise, the bacterial route dominates (Morel et al. 1998). Once it has become Hg^0, the mercury will evaporate into the atmosphere, be converted back to Hg^{2+} there, and return to earth elsewhere in rain. It is also possible for Hg^{2+} to be converted to methyl mercury in oxic water, but only if the concentration of Cl^- is in the right range and the correct bacteria are present (Najera et al. 2005). Oxic surface waters are not considered a major area for methyl mercury production.

Higher concentrations of mercury are often found in anoxic waters (Mason et al. 1999; Morel et al. 1998). These include deeper waters and swamps or peat bogs, where bacterial decomposition of dead plant material uses up a great deal of oxygen and poor circulation fails to replenish it. The excess organic material helps make swamps natural mercury traps (United States Geological Survey [USGS] 2004), since this organic material will bind the mercury and the sulfate-reducing bacteria common in these environments will convert sulfate to sulfide, the form of sulfur most reactive with mercury. The sediments below deeper anoxic waters also contain these bacteria, accounting for their higher concentrations of sulfide (and therefore mercury) than the oxic waters above. In fact, mercury chemistry in anoxic environments is dominated by its reaction with sulfide (Morel et al., 1998). The primary compound formed by the reaction of mercury with sulfide is mercury sulfide or cinnabar (HgS). Most of the mercury in sediments is, in fact, found as cinnabar (Greenwood and Earnshaw 1984). Cinnabar itself is highly insoluble, so formation of cinnabar would have the net effect of removing mercury from water. Cinnabar can form more soluble compounds in the presence of other sulfides (Morel et al. 1998), elemental sulfur (Morel et al. 1998), acidic waters containing Cl^- (Mikac et al. 2003), or excess organic material (Ravichandran 2004).

Not only are sulfate-reducing bacteria partly to blame for increased mercury concentrations in anoxic waters, they are also the source of deadly methyl mercury (Morel et al. 1998). An enzyme in these bacteria will convert Hg^{2+} to methyl mercury (Choi et al. 1994). The methyl mercury is then absorbed by one-celled organisms, which are in turn eaten by larger organisms. In this way, the mercury moves up the food chain. For example, if 10 percent of the total mercury in an aquatic ecosystem is methyl mercury, approximately 15 percent of the mercury in tiny phytoplankton would normally be methyl mercury, increasing to 30 percent in the zooplankton that feed on the phytoplankton, and 95 percent in the fish near the top of the food chain (Morel et al. 1998) (figure 1). This can result in significant amounts of methyl mercury accumulating in the top predators, which can be toxic if eaten by humans.

Therefore, Morton greatly oversimplifies the problem. Fish have a very low uptake rate for Hg^{2+} and will not accumulate significant amounts of it (Morel et al. 1998). High levels of Hg^{2+} are of concern primarily because of its ability to be converted to methyl mercury. In fact, the U.S. Environmental Protection Agency (EPA) is considering setting new groundwater mercury standards based not on the total concentration of mercury in the water, but on the concentration of methyl mercury in fish living in a body of water (Southworth et al. 2004). Even in the Everglades, an almost ideal environment for methyl mercury production, only 20 percent of the total mercury is methyl mercury (Cai et al. 1999). By comparison, only 3 percent of the total mercury dissolved in rivers and 2 percent in coastal ocean waters is methyl mercury (Mason et al. 1999). One more recent study found that between 1.2 and 17.2 percent of the total mercury in peaty stream banks was methyl mercury, while less than 1 percent was methyl mercury in the soil 65 feet (20 m) from the stream (Skyllberg et al. 2003), while another found that 0.3 percent and 8 percent of the total mercury in a number of Virginia and Tennessee streams was methyl mercury (Southworth et al. 2004). Therefore, of the mercury released by the Flood, less than 20 percent (probably closer to 1 percent) would have been methyl mercury. Furthermore, we must keep in mind that methyl mercury poisoning is not an instantaneous process. We learn from the great mercury poisoning incident in Minamata Bay, Japan, that mercury began to be dumped into the bay in the 1930s, yet symptoms of poisoning were not reported in humans until approximately 20 years later, and at least a year after new procedures at the plant significantly increased the amount of mercury released (Eto 2000; McCurry 2006).

Historically, mercury has had a number of industrial uses and has therefore been mined as a mineral. Approximately three-quarters of the world's mercury production comes from just five major mercury belts (Rytuba 2003). Since these represent a major reservoir of mercury in today's environment, they are of great importance for our discussion of mercury and the Flood.

Geologic mercury is usually found in one of three types of deposits: Almaden-type deposits, silica-carbonate deposits, and hot spring deposits (Rytuba 2002). More than one-third of all mercury mined worldwide comes from the world's largest cinnabar deposit near Almaden, Spain (Jebrak et al. 2002), the type of locale for Almaden-type deposits. These ores formed from large submarine hydrothermal vents or submarine volcanoes. Although there is still some debate as to exactly how and when the Almaden deposit was created, the consensus seems to be that the main deposits were deposited from hydrothermal fluids as, or shortly after, the sedimentary rock layers containing them formed, while secondary deposits were formed by the remobilization of that mercury, perhaps in conjunction with the introduction of new hydrothermal mercury during later hydrothermal events (Hernandez et al. 1999; Hugueras et al. 1999; Jebrak et al. 2002). The layer of rock (primarily the rock quartzite) containing the mercury has been assigned to the Silurian age (Hernandez et al. 1999; Rytuba 1986a). This is a geological period that young-Earth geologists believe corresponds to a time early in the Flood (Whitmore 2007), consistent with the Almaden volcanic/hydrothermal activity being part of the erupting "fountains of the deep."

Silica-carbonate mercury deposits are found along fault zones associated with the mineral serpentinite (Rytuba 2002, 2003), which has been transformed by an influx of carbonate and silica from low-temperature hydrothermal fluids (Rytuba 2002; Sherlock and Logan 1995). These fluids also contained mercury, which was deposited as cinnabar along fractures in the altered serpentinite (Rytuba 1986b; Sherlock and Logan 1995). These are believed to have formed during the Tertiary, well after the Almaden deposit (Ash 1996; Rytuba 1986b), and are often associated with "prehistoric" mineral springs (Sherlock and Logan 1995).

Hot spring mercury deposits form in similar fashion, but with hotter hydrothermal fluids (Sherlock and Logan 1995). They are not associated with serpentinite (Panteleyev 1996; Rytuba 2002) and often occur in environments nearer to the surface than silica-carbonate deposits (Rytuba 2002). Some are still forming today in places like Sulphur Bank, California (Sherlock and Logan 1995). Although not usually classified as one of the three major deposit types, the world's second largest mercury deposit occurs at Idrija, Slovenia. It is believed to have formed in a manner similar to hot springs and silica-carbonate

deposits with hydrothermal fluids infiltrating through already-established sedimentary rock layers and depositing mercury. However, a significant amount of mercury also may have been in the black shale present prior to hydrothermal enrichment (Lavric and Spangenberg 2003). The association between mercury and black shale will be discussed later.

With this brief overview in mind, let's examine the first key question relating to Morton's challenge: would the Flood release sufficient mercury to create an average concentration of 100 ppb worldwide?

How Much Mercury Would the Flood Release?

Morton assumes that there was little to no sedimentary rock present before the Flood and that the current volume of sedimentary rock corresponds to the amount of igneous rock crushed and redeposited by the Flood. While this is probably an overstatement, we can use it as a maximum for Flood erosion. Morton then assumes that Earth's crust contains 0.1 ppm mercury and that erosion would release 90 percent of that mercury, leading to a 100 ppb average mercury concentration in the world's waters. Morton considers 0.1 ppm a "very conservative" estimate, basing this number on a USGS report (Parker 1967). This report actually listed three values for mercury in Earth's crust and two for igneous rock. In both cases, the oldest value was 0.5 ppm, while newer estimates were approximately 0.08 ppm. More recent papers estimate 0.05 ppm (Lavergren 2005; United Nations Environment Progamme 2003).

Therefore, 0.1 ppm is not conservative; if anything, it seems a little high. Furthermore, these estimates are for the mercury concentration of the *modern* crust. If the major mercury deposits observed today (such as Almaden) were formed during or after the Flood, pre-Flood crustal mercury might have been much lower, especially since it appears that they formed by mercury migrating in hydrothermal fluids from Earth's interior. Perhaps a better estimate would come from looking at the mercury concentration in the bulk silicate earth, which includes the crust and mantle. This might better approximate the primitive mantle prior to the formation of a true crust (Baumgardner 2000; Kargel and Lewis 1993; McDonough and Sun 1995). This number would be 10 ppb, or 0.01 ppm, an order of magnitude less than Morton's "conservative" estimate (Baumgardner 2000; McDonough and Sun 1995). However, that is only his first error.

Morton's 90 percent estimate of mercury mobilization comes from a USGS paper (Siegel and Siegel 1987) discussing mercury being released by volcanoes in Hawaii. Volcanoes are a major source of mercury; significant spikes in total atmospheric mercury correspond to volcanic eruptions (Schuster et al. 2002). Morton refers to a section of this paper that discusses mercury lost by erosion of a cooled lava flow. However, the context is the slow release of mercury from the lava flow over a century. Morton apparently assumes that the same amount would be released by rapid weathering (over the course of perhaps days) during the Flood. However, this assumption appears flawed. To understand why, let's take a closer look at the paper Morton is referencing, one paragraph of which is quoted by Morton. Here is the paragraph directly preceding the one he quotes:

> Lava flows constitute another source of mercury. Weathering brings about the slow release of soluble or solubilized constituents as the igneous materials degrade into soil minerals. Lava samples were analyzed by digestion of 100-mesh powder with 0.1 N HCl to remove soluble and loosely bound mercury. This was followed by hot 2N HNO$_3$ digestion to remove any mercury complex with organic ligands, and then concentrated HF to destroy the silicate matrix (Siegel and others, 1975). Samples from flows of 1840, 1923, and 1955 were obtained with the assistance of the late Gordon Macdonald; fresh Pauahi samples were collected in 1979. The results . . . suggest a 50 percent release in about 50 years and a gradual infiltration of oxidizable, presumably humic, complexing substrates (Siegel and Siegel 1987, p. 832–833).

This paragraph is followed by a table (see table 1) listing how much mercury was removed from rock samples of different ages by each of the three methods described above. The estimate of 90 percent mercury loss over the course of 100 years comes from comparing the total amounts of mercury (from all three measurement methods) for samples of different age. However, this is not the only significant thing we can learn from this data. For all the samples, the 0.1N HCl (HCl is a strong acid and normality [N] is a unit of concentration, a 0.1N solution of HCl would have a pH of 1) removed only a small amount of the total mercury. For every sample but the oldest, the 2N HNO$_3$ removed far less mercury than the concentrated HF.

Morton states that sedimentary rocks in the Flood were formed from mechanically crushed and chemically weathered igneous rocks, releasing mercury in the process. The igneous rocks in the study he cites were crushed, then treated with various acids to remove the mercury for analysis. This laboratory procedure was probably more chemically destructive and therefore more likely to release mercury than anything occurring during the Flood. Furthermore, it is clear that only the most extreme laboratory conditions actually removed the majority of mercury from these samples. Digestion in 0.1N HCl is a very chemically destructive process, and 2N HNO$_3$ is slightly more than an order of magnitude more acidic (plus more chemically reactive in other ways) than 0.1N HCl. Yet only in the sample from 1840 was more than 21 percent of the total measured mercury removed by the HCl and HNO$_3$ combined. In that sample, roughly 66 percent of the total mercury was removed by both procedures. The HF was successful at removing the mercury not because it is a stronger acid than the others (it's actually weaker), but because a specific chemical reaction between the HF and silicon in the igneous rock literally breaks up the chemical structure of the rocks (this is what the authors meant by "destroy the silicate matrix"). The authors concluded that the mercury released by HCl was only loosely attached to the rock. Mercury released by HNO$_3$, on the other hand, was interpreted as being attached to organic compounds that had gradually entered the lava flow; HNO$_3$ will destroy organic material through an oxidation reaction. However, organic material presumably was not destroyed by the Flood water, nor would the Flood water have resembled

Year lava flow formed	Hg extracted by HCl (ppb)	% of total Hg extracted by HCl	Hg extracted by HNO$_3$ (ppb)	% of total Hg extracted by HNO$_3$	Hg extracted by HF (ppb)	% of total Hg extracted by HF
1840	5	3.82%	81	61.8%	45	34.4%
1923	16	4.08%	66	16.8%	310	79.1%
1955	10	0.962%	59	5.68%	970	93.4%
1979	0	0.00%	15	1.15%	1,290	98.8%

Table 1. The extraction of mercury from cooled lava flows (Siegel and Siegel 1987)

concentrated HF. Therefore, the digestion in HCl is probably the only process analogous to those of the Flood, and the Flood water would have been less acidic than the HCl. For the two oldest lava samples, approximately 4 percent of the mercury was removed by the HCl; in other words, only 4 percent of the mercury was readily soluble in very acidic water even after the rocks were physically pulverized, and not the 90 percent suggested by Morton!

This would not be surprising to any chemist; most of the mercury would be in the form of mercury sulfide, which is extremely insoluble. Mercury does not become a pollution problem because large amounts of mercury sulfide will dissolve in water; rather, the mercury either enters the water in a more soluble form or very tiny amounts of mercury sulfide dissolve and are then (over time) magnified up the food chain. Many studies have documented the insolubility of HgS, even in strong acids (Fernandez-Martinez and Rucandio 2003, 2005; Martin-Doimeadios et al. 2000; Mikac et al. 2003). Excess Cl^- is required to make mercury sulfide soluble. How much Cl^- would have been available during the Flood? At present, it is estimated that the crust only contains 185 ppm chlorine (Parker 1967), while that in the silicate earth is estimated at 17 ppm (McDonough and Sun 1995). Even the higher figure (assuming all of it converted to soluble Cl^- and using the same figures Morton used to estimate the concentration of mercury in Flood water) only corresponds to 0.00586 N Cl^-. This is approximately 17 times less Cl^- than is present in 0.1N HCl, which was ineffective in extracting mercury. Mikac et al. (2003) noted that in the presence of 0.01N Cl^-, greater than 1N HNO_3 was required to extract significant amounts of mercury. The Flood water simply would not have been that acidic.

Although this fact is not mentioned by Morton, it has also been reported in the literature (Revis et al. 1989; Han et al. 2008) that a saturated solution of sodium sulfide will extract significant amounts of mercury from HgS-contaminated soils. The reality is that moderate or low concentrations of sulfide will remove mercury from water as HgS and prevent its redissolving (Piao and Bishop, 2006), while high concentrations will render it soluble again. However, using calculations such as those used for chlorine in the preceding paragraph, it is clear that even if all the sulfur in the earth's crust was dissolved and converted to sulfide, the resulting Flood waters would contain a much lower concentration of sulfur than a saturated Na_2S solution would; sodium sulfide is very soluble! Therefore, this would not significantly help Morton to get the HgS in the earth's crust dissolved. In fact, the sul-

fide in the Flood waters would most likely have been at a low enough level (once the interaction of sulfur with other elements in the water is considered) to significantly decrease the solubility of the mercury. Han et al. (2008) also showed that mercury can be somewhat more easily extracted from HgS residing in soil that has been planted with crops for several seasons. However, only a small fraction of the crust destroyed by the Flood would have been topsoil involved in agriculture and much stronger acids than we would expect in the Flood waters were required to extract the mercury in that study. These findings do not make Morton's thesis any more believable.

For the last word on this subject, Professor Donard, an environmental chemist from France who studied the extractability of mercury sulfide from the mines at Almaden, Spain, noted (Martin-Doimeadios et al. 2000, p. 365):

> The total extraction results and the sequential extraction procedure have shown that mercury in the Almaden's sediments is quite stable and presents low chemical availability. This lack of availability renders inorganic mercury methylation difficult. The results are consistent with mineralogy of mercury deposits, since cinnabar has an extremely low solubility in water, is resistant to physical and chemical weathering, and is hardly leached under acid drainage.

Although Morton's basic thesis is clearly in error, let's examine other ways that mercury could get into the Flood environment. First, the 40 days and nights of rain would have moved essentially all of the mercury from the atmosphere. However, this would have been insignificant: even after more than a century of industrial activity, which has dramatically increased the amount of mercury in the atmosphere (Schuster et al. 2002), there are only 6,000–10,000 tons of mercury there today (Lin and Pehkonen 1999). In the pre-Flood world, atmospheric mercury would have presumably been much less. Second, volcanoes would have released mercury, and we assume a tremendous amount of volcanic activity during the Flood. Likewise, undersea hydrothermal vents would have released mercury (Ruelas-Inzunza et al. 2003). If the "fountains of the deep" mentioned in Genesis 7:11 indicate hydrothermal activity, these might have been a significant source of mercury pollution (although for reasons I will explain later, I somewhat doubt it). Overall, these processes probably elevated the amount of mercury in the Flood environment. Still, given Morton's miscalculation of both the total available mercury and the percentage released into the environment, the total concentration would have been considerably less than Morton's 100 ppb.

So what is a more reasonable estimate for the amount of mercury released by the Flood? From the outset, I want to acknowledge that this is not a simple question; as has already been shown, there would have been a number of factors affecting mercury concentration (many of which simply cannot be determined millennia later), and therefore the best that can be provided is a rough estimate. However, I believe I can at least give an estimate that is closer to reality than Morton's. To start with, in place of Morton's too high estimate of 0.1 ppm, let's use Lavergren's 0.05 ppm value (Lavergren 2005; United Nations Environment Programme 2003), which immediately cuts Morton's number in half and equates to 50 ppb mercury in the Flood waters. Also, since Morton's assumption that 90 percent of the mercury in the crust would be dissolved is far too high, let's reduce that to a more reasonable value of 5 percent. (In light of the extreme insolubility of mercury sulfide, I think this is a generous estimate.) That would reduce the concentration to 2.78 ppb in the Flood waters. If we started with the bulk silicate earth mercury value of 0.01 ppm for the crust's concentration (Baumgardner 2000; McDonough and Sun 1995), that would reduce the final value by a factor of five, giving a final concentration of 0.56 ppb mercury. Admittedly, my assumption that 5 percent of the mercury would dissolve, while in line with the published data, might be downplaying the unique properties of the Flood. If we assume that my estimate of mercury solubility is too low and arbitrarily triple it to 15 percent, that still results in mercury concentrations of less than 10 ppb, a tenth of Morton's estimate. So I would conclude that there was between 0.5 and 10 ppb mercury in the Flood waters, with the real value probably lying closer to the smaller number. Furthermore, no more than 20 percent, and probably closer to 2 percent, of this would be the deadly methyl mercury. As we will see in the next section, while such a concentration is far from desirable, it is not catastrophic.

So Morton's estimate of mercury released by the Flood is massively too high. However, for the sake of argument, let us assume that Morton is right and the Flood water contained 100 ppb mercury for our evaluation of the second big question: the threat such a release would actually pose to the environment.

Was Mercury a Threat to the Post-Flood World?

It is not enough for sufficient mercury to be released to yield a 100-ppb concentration in the Flood water. The mercury must have remained dissolved for enough time to have worked its way into the food chain. As noted above, the Flood water would represent a very complex chemical system. A mercury concentration near 100 ppb would have presumably activated the bacterial *mer* operon, so bacteria would have been converting Hg^{2+} to Hg^0, which would evaporate into the atmosphere. Morton argues in his paper that Hg^0 evaporation would not be an issue because the continual rainfall during the Flood would have removed it from the atmosphere. Although that would be true for the 40 days and 40 nights of rainfall, it was during this period that the Flood water was still rising, and presumably the mercury had not then reached its maximum concentration. Once the rain ended, mercury could begin to accumulate in the atmosphere, lowering the concentration in the water. However, the interplay between evaporation and precipitation would probably prevent this from being a major form of mercury removal.

There would have been a great deal of organic matter (decomposing plant and animal life) in the Flood water. This organic matter would have trapped a major amount (current studies suggest as much as 95 percent) of the mercury. If this organic bound mercury was in an oxic environment, it is unlikely that it would have been converted to methyl mercury. Thus it would pose a smaller threat because aquatic animals would not have retained Hg^{2+} to the same degree as methyl mercury. Morton does not make this distinction, simply noting that the U.S. EPA's permissible concentration for mercury in drinking water is 2 ppb and assuming anything above this concentration would be problematic. Obviously, any significant concentration of mercury in drinking water is not good; however, it is naïve to simply assume that the EPA limit represents the absolute maximum mercury concentration above which great harm occurs. The truth is that many humans routinely drink a liquid with greater that 2 ppb mercury, namely our saliva. The amalgams used for dental fillings contain a significant concentration of mercury, and that mercury tends to find its way into saliva. One study found that people with amalgam fillings have saliva mercury concentrations anywhere from 0 ppb to 500 ppb, with an average of ~3.5 ppb before chewing and ~31.5 ppb after chewing (Ganss et al. 2000). These values were reported to be in good accord with previously published values. A slightly more recent study of Hg^{2+} leaching from amalgams into simulated saliva reported a concentration of 15 ppb after 6 hours of contact with the amalgam and 101 ppb after 90 hours contact (Sanna et al. 2002). While it is outside the scope of this paper to discuss the controversy over the health effects of mercury dental amalgams, it is worth noting that human life is not being imperiled by ingesting concentrations of Hg^{2+} greater than the EPA drinking water limit and approaching Morton's too-high estimate for the Flood water. The primary health threat from mercury does not come from ingesting water containing Hg^{2+}.

In an anoxic environment, on the other hand, a significant amount of methyl mercury could begin to form. This would have been the real threat: the formation and availability of sufficient methyl mercury to infiltrate the food chain and poison life. However, only a relatively small amount of the total mercury in a system is normally methyl mercury. Under ideal anoxic conditions, it would reach no more than 20 percent of the total; in less ideal conditions, it would have been only 2–3 percent of the total. So, even if the total concentration of mercury reached 100 ppb, we would only expect ~2–20 ppb to exist in that dangerous form. In reality, it was probably less than that.

In a previous section, I mentioned that hydrothermal vents could have been a source of mercury contamination for the Flood. However, it is also possible they removed mercury from the system. Not only do these vents release mercury, they also release hydrogen sulfide, and sulfides react with mercury to form insoluble mercury sulfide. Therefore, excess sulfide would have removed mercury the vent released, forming cinnabar deposits. Mercury in the Flood water near the vent would also have been captured.

The Almaden mercury belt described earlier could be an example of this process. The source of mercury at Almaden was hydrothermal fluids and magma released during elevated hydrothermal activity, probably during the Flood. The mercury is believed to have been deposited at the same time that the surrounding sedimentary rock was forming or after it had formed. Since sedimentary rocks would have formed rapidly during the Flood, and since the vents were at the interface of the Flood water and the seafloor (including former continental surfaces), the vents and associated mercury were buried by Flood sediment. This is not only consistent with the geology of the Almaden deposit, but would have resulted in limiting the deposit's contribution to contamination of the Flood water. Modern hydrothermal systems tend to be sources of mercury pollution, but during the Flood they were more likely sinks, chemically binding free mercury that was then rapidly covered by thick sediments.

Since deepwater vents would also coincide with anoxic environments, this entrapment of mercury would preferentially lock up the more dangerous methyl mercury, in my opinion. Mercury methylation in the Flood would have been occurring in deeper waters, where organic material would have been sinking down and decaying, helping to deplete the water of oxygen. With most of the mercury being bound to organic material or occurring as mercury sulfide, it would have been settling to the bottom anoxic zone as well. Normally this would generate excess mercury methylation, but in the Flood, it would have only trapped mercury in the new sedimentary rocks.

There is still debate as to the average concentration of mercury in sedimentary rock (Parker 1967; Yudovich and Ketris 2005). However, black shales are enriched with mercury, with concentrations perhaps as much as an order of magnitude above the average of other sedimentary rock (Lavergren 2005; Parker 1967; Yudovich and Ketris 2005). Also, there is still a significant debate in the geological literature as to how black shales form (Kenig et al. 2004; Lavergren 2005; Lyons and Kashgarian 2005; Schultz 2004). The consensus seems to be that they represent at least intermittently anoxic environments rich in organic material and sulfides. Such an environment would trap mercury, both in its organic material and by hydrogen sulfide generated by the sulfate-reducing bacteria expected to flourish there during anoxic periods, and promote its methylation. We know these sediments were converted into rock. And we know that these rocks contain a great deal of mercury, probably averaging between 0.4 and 0.22 ppm (Lavergren 2005; Parker 1967; Yudovich and Ketris 2005). While all the black shale seen today likely did not form during the Flood (some of it appears rather late in the geologic column for that), it is reasonable to assume that much of it did. The mercury in these shales represents a tremendous quantity that was effectively removed from the system by sedimentation. Furthermore, since the environment that most likely formed the black shales would have been conducive to mercury methylation, this would have removed the mercury most likely to be transformed into methyl mercury. Similarly, coal is often enriched in mercury (Yudovich and Ketris 2005). Rapid coal formation during the Flood would likewise bind great amounts of mercury from the environment. Please recall that the process of converting Hg^{2+} to methyl mercury and then infiltrating it into the food chain in hazardous quantities is not fast. The rapid sedimentation of the Flood would have prevented this from occurring to any great extent.

A recent study (Orihel et al. 2008) supports this view. The authors added mercury spiked with various radioactive elements (so they could track the specific mercury they had added) to an experimental lake once a year for two years. They found that most of the mercury they added the first year had found its way into the sediment by the second year. A similar study (Tessier et al. 2007) using aquariums as simulated bodies of water found that most (87.9–96.2 percent) of the mercury added had found its way into the sediment within a month. Orihel and coworkers also found that most of the mercury was not converted to methyl mercury, and much of the methyl mercury that was produced remained in the sediment and was not available to be consumed by many of the organisms. This was occurring in an environment with much slower sedimentation than the flooded earth. The best evidence suggests that natural processes would have buried much of the mercury released by the Flood before it entered the foodchain (figure 2).

Even in areas where mercury methylation could occur without being removed by sedimentation, there is reason

to believe that net methylation of mercury would have been less than predicted. This is because the Flood would have been an "equal opportunity" polluter; the waters would have contained more than just mercury. Using Morton's methods, we see that the same rocks contain approximately 5 percent iron (Parker 1967). The silicate earth concentration is estimated at between 18 and 19 percent (McDonough and Sun 1995). In either case, there would have been a great deal of iron in the Flood water. Studies have shown that high concentrations of iron will decrease the rate of mercury methylation (Mehrotra and Sedlak 2005). In fact, those authors suggest adding iron to wetland sediments as a way to decrease methyl mercury pollution. Between the rapid sedimentation and the high concentration of iron in the *Flood water*, it seems unlikely that methyl mercury formation posed a great problem during the Flood.

Morton suggests that the high concentration of Hg^{2+} in the Flood water would have harmed plant life, even if it was not methyl mercury. Of course, we have already established that total mercury in the Flood water was much less than Morton's 100 ppb, but for the sake of argument, let's grant him that figure. To support his contention that this would have been devastating to

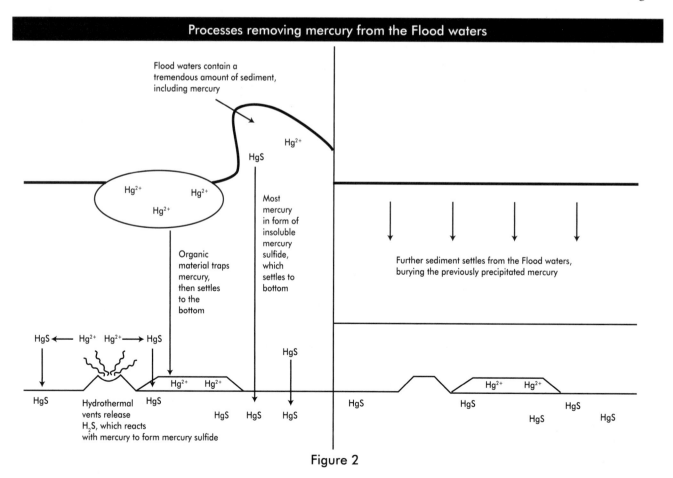

Figure 2

plant life, Morton references some data suggesting that "typically, plant-cell damage takes place with aqueous solutions containing as little as 10 [micro]g/L of Hg ion" (Morton 1998). This comes from the same paper (Siegel and Siegel 1987) on mercury and volcanoes that Morton used to get his estimate of 90 percent mercury loss during weathering. We have already seen that his presentation of that data required further scrutiny. Thus, it comes as no surprise that this one does, too.

Siegel and Siegel (1987) only mentioned this figure in passing to set up a contrast with the relatively low toxicity of Hg^0 to plant life. They cite a paper (Siegel 1977) as the original source of the data. If we look at this original paper, we see that Morton's figure for plant damage, while presumably made in good faith, is misleading. That is because the ten micrograms per liter value in the original paper was not referring to "plants growing in mercury-rich ground water [sic]" as Morton states, but to tobacco protoplasts. A protoplast is a cell without its protective cell wall. In this case, the author wanted to see how toxic some metals were to plant cells if they got through all the plant's defenses and actually reached the cell. Although this is an important topic for study, it is not a very realistic analogy of how the whole organism would respond to mercury, nor was it intended by the author to be taken in that way. Still, even accepting that this study is showing the tobacco cells at their most vulnerable state, it should be noted that, while cell damage may have occurred at a 10 ppb concentration, 100.3 ppb was required to kill 50 percent of the protoplasts. In the Flood, plants did not exist as lone protoplasts, but rather as seeds or shoots that later grew into mature organisms. Therefore, a far more realistic appraisal of mercury toxicity to plants would be the concentration required to inhibit seed germination. The seed, of course, contains multiple cells with cell walls and, therefore, as Siegel stressed in this paper, is more resistant to poisoning. In fact, he reported that a concentration of approximately 802 ppb was required to inhibit the germination of 10 percent of the tobacco seeds, and that slightly over 2,200 ppb were necessary to prevent 50 percent from germinating.

This is not an isolated example. To the contrary, as Morton should have realized, the ability of plants to survive in waters containing very high mercury concentrations has been reported many times in the literature. For example, a more recent paper concerning mercury toxicity to tobacco states, "Tobacco has been shown to be highly resistant to environmental mercury, accumulating up to 5,000 μg/g under chronic low-level exposure with no symptoms of toxicity" (Suszcynsky and Shann 1995). This means the tobacco can accumulate within it 5,000 ppm mercury without seeing any ill effect. Now, one might argue that this is only referring to chronic low-level exposure, not a sudden high-level exposure such as the Flood could cause. The paper addresses this as well. The author submerged the roots of tobacco plants in solutions with varying concentrations of mercury and observed the effects on the plants. Keep in mind that Morton's estimate for mercury in the Flood water (far too high to begin with) is only 100 ppb or 0.1 μg/ml. Suszcynsky and Shann (1995, p. 65) noted:

> An inhibition of whole plant growth was demonstrated in plants whose roots were exposed to $HgCl_2$ with the severity of inhibition corresponding to increasing treatment levels. Plants at higher treatment levels (>10.0 μg Hg^{2+}/ml) displayed minor visible symptoms of toxicity (chlorosis) but no tissue death. . . . Although growth in plants exposed to lower treatment levels (≤ 1.0 μg Hg^{2+}/ml) was slightly inhibited, there was no apparent threat to their viability as that which occurred in plants exposed to higher treatment levels.

In other words, the survival of the tobacco plants was not threatened by a mercury concentration ten times higher than Morton's estimate, and there was no actual tissue death in plants to a concentration ten times higher than that! Tobacco is not the only plant resistant to mercury. Another study reported that 47 percent of alfalfa seedlings exposed to an approximately 600 ppb Hg^{2+} solution for 24 hours showed no ill effect, and 11 percent showed no effect after 24 hours' exposure to 6,000 ppb mercury (Ortega-Villasante et al. 2005). Seedlings from two types of rice were shown to undergo slightly over 50 percent germination in a solution of more than 20,000 ppb mercury, while the germination rate was between 70 and 80 percent in a solution a tenth as concentrated (Mishra and Choudhuri 1999). While these may have been far from healthy rice plants, they were surviving in waters that contained orders of magnitude more mercury than even Morton suggests the Flood would have contained. A study of the aquatic plant *Vallisneria Spiralis* did not note ill effects on plants from exposure to any concentration less than approximately 200 ppb mercury (Gupta and Chandra 1998). Water lettuce is reported as surviving, albeit with complete inhibition of new root formation, for three weeks (the plants did not all die at the end of three weeks, the study just ended) in solutions of over 100,000 ppb mercury (Odjegba and Fasidi 2004). In fact, the author of that study suggested that these plants could be used to remove mercury from polluted waters, a process known as *phytoremediation*. The water hyacinth has also been suggested for phytoremediation due to its ability to survive in mercury-contaminated waters and accumulate the mercury within itself (Riddle et al. 2002). To summarize all of this, many plants can survive exposure to concentrations of mercury many times higher than Morton claimed would be lethally toxic during the Flood. Clearly, his estimates of mercury toxicity are just as confused as his calculations of mercury concentration in the Flood water.

Conclusions

Based upon an honest look at the available evidence, Morton's challenge to the Genesis Flood does not stand. First, earth's crust at the time of Noah likely did not contain the 0.1 ppm mercury he estimated. Even if it had, it is unlikely that the Flood would have released more than a small percent of that mercury, much less 90 percent. And even if that much mercury *were* released, it would have been removed from the water by: (1) binding to organic matter, (2) precipitation as a sulfide, and (3) rapid burial by sedimentation (figure 2). Furthermore, to enter the food chain, the mercury would need to be converted to methyl mercury, and both sedimentation and the iron released by the Flood would have inhibited that. Finally, even if the concentration of mercury did reach 100 ppb, plant life still would have survived. There is no reason to question the Genesis account based on mercury chemistry.

While this paper has been focused on that one specific contaminant, I am confident that careful study will show that the release of other environmental toxins also fails to threaten the Flood model.

Appendix 1: Morton in His Own Words

It [Morton's paper] will consider the amount of mercury (element symbol Hg) that must have been released by the erosion of the pre-Flood igneous type of rock which was then made into sedimentary rock containing fossils. The YEC [Young Earth Creationist] paradigm requires that there be very little sedimentary rock prior to the flood. This is because none would have been made at creation (it would be a deception to make rocks appear sedimentary which were in fact not sedimentary). Thus we can calculate how much igneous rock must have been eroded to form the presently observed volcanic rocks. The total of sedimentary rocks can be calculated as 630×10^6 km^3. (See

R. Morton [this is me] "Prolegomena to the Study of the Sediments," *CRSQ*, Dec. 1980, p. 162–167). All of this material must have come from igneous rock.

Given that igneous rocks are around 3.3 g/cc (3300 kg/m^3) and sedimentary rocks are around 2.5 g/cc, we can correct for this and we find a .75 reduction factor to put the sedimentary rocks back to igneous. Thus, 477×10^6 km^3 or 4.77×10^{17} cubic meters of igneous rocks must have been eroded.

An earlier version of this note was criticized for not making explicit an assumption. The assumption is this. Within the YEC model, the prediluvial rock, which mostly would have been granite and basalt, must have been mechanically crushed, and then rapidly altered chemically to separate the feldspar and quartz fractions. Only in this way can the vast quantities of sand and shale seen in the sedimentary rocks be explained. For God to have created the vast quantities of sand and shale on the primeval earth would be a case of God deceptively creating the appearance of age when no such appearance would be needed. On the primeval earth, only a thin layer of soil would be required, not 40 to 60,000 feet of it. By the process of mechanical crushing and rapid chemical weathering, much of the mercury contained in the rock would have been released. This is consistent with what is known to occur in the weathering of basalts in which 90 percent of the mercury in the basalts is released to the environment in about a century.

"If Kilauea lava typically cools with about 1,000 [micro] g/kg of mercury and proceeds to release 90 percent, then this still constitutes only a minor source of the element. The 1840 eruption produced about 400×10^6 m^3 of lava weighing perhaps 16×10^9 kg. Thus this lava contained a total of 16×10^6 g (16 tons) of mercury, of which about 14 tons was released in about a century. In contrast, Halemaumau yields 260 tons annually when it is not erupting" (Siegel and Siegel 1987, p. 833).

What is the mercury content of the crust of the earth? Using the very conservative value of .1 parts per million (ppm) we find that the flood would have ground up and released $.0000001 * 4.77 \times 10^{17}$ cubic meters x 3300 kg/m^3 x .9= 1.4×10^{14} kg or 1.4×10^{17} g or 1.4×10^{23} micrograms. I place this in all three units because of the need below.

All of this would have been released into the oceans for the fish to ingest. The volume of the ocean is 1.4×10^{21} liters. So the amount of mercury in a liter is 1.41×10^{23} micrograms/1.4×10^{21} liters = 100 micrograms per liter of water.

How bad is it? Consider this: "Typically, plant-cell damage takes place with aqueous solutions containing as little as 10 [micro]g/L of Hg ion" (Siegel and Siegel 1987, p. 830).

An expert might question the relevance of this fact to the Flood since the above refers to plants growing in mercury-rich ground water [sic]. Since plants were not taken on the ark, they must have survived by floating on the surface of the flood waters. And many young-earth creationists have suggested that such vegetable mats were responsible for the coal bed formation. Thus, the damage which mercury laden waters would cause to these floating plants is something that must be addressed by global flood advocates.

The EPA does not allow more than 2.4 micrograms/liter, which is the EPA's Critical Maximum Concentration for fresh water discharge from an industrial site. This was set up to protect aquatic life from deleterious effects from mercury (Gray and Sanzolone 1996, p. 5).

How about for animal ingestion? This was found on the Internet: "The EPA has set a limit of 2 parts of mercury per billion parts of drinking water (2 ppb = 2 micrograms/liter). The EPA requires that discharges or spills of 1 pound or more of mercury be reported" (http://atsdr1.atsdr.cdc.gov:8080/tfacts46.html).

For those who don't know, 100 micrograms per liter is 50 times more than the EPA would allow for an anthropogenic release. I guess the EPA would initiate regulatory action against Noah's Flood for polluting the oceans.

Acknowledgments

I would like to thank Dr. John Whitmore for elucidating many of the finer points of Flood geology to a simple chemist such as myself and for providing numerous editorial suggestions on this work. I would also like to thank Dr. John Reed for his significant editorial input. Finally, I would like to thank Dr. Heather Kuruvilla for useful guidance on the subject of protoplasts versus whole organisms.

References

Aposhian, H.V., R.M. Maiorino, D. Gonzalez-Ramirez, M. Zuniga-Charles, Z. Xu, K.M. Hurlbut, P. Junco-Munoz, R.C. Dart, and M.M. Aposhian. 1995. Mobilization of heavy metals by newer, therapeutically useful chelating agents. *Toxicology* 97:23–38.

Ash, C. 1996. Silica-carbonate mercury. In *Selected British Columbia Mineral Deposit Profiles*, Volume 2, Metallic Deposits. British Columbia, Canada: British Columbia Ministry of Employment and Investment., p. 75–76.

Auger, N., O. Kofman, T. Kosatsky, and B. Armstron. 2005. Low-level methylmercury exposure as a risk factor for neurologic abnormalities in adults. *Neurotoxicology* 26:149–157.

Bakir, F., S.F. Damluji, L. Amin-Zaki, M. Murtadha, A. Khalidi, Y. Al-Rawi, S. Tikriti, H.I. Dhahir, T.W. Clarkson, J.C. Smith, and R.A. Doherty. 1973. Methylmercury poisoning in Iraq. *Science* 181:230–241.

Baumgardner, J.R. 2000. Distribution of radioactive isotopes in the earth. In Vardiman, L., A.A. Snelling, and E.F. Chaffin (editors), *Radioisotopes and the Age of the Earth*. El Cajon, CA: Institute for Creation Research, p. 49–94.

Bjorkman, L., G. Sandborgh-Englund, and J. Ekstrand. 1997. Mercury in saliva and feces after removal of amalgam fillings. *Toxicology and Applied Pharmacology* 144:156–162.

Boening, D.W. 2000. Ecological effects, transport, and fate of mercury: a general review. *Chemosphere* 40:1335–1351.

Brand, L. 1997. *Faith, Reason, and Earth History: A Paradigm of Earth and Biological Origins by Intelligent Design*. Berrien Springs, MI: Andrews University Press, p. 90–96.

Cai, Y., R. Jaffe, and R.D. Jones. 1999. Interactions between dissolved organic carbon and mercury species in surface waters of the Florida Everglades. Applied. *Geochemistry*. 14:395–407.

Choi, S.C., T. Chase Jr., and R. Bartha. 1994. Enzymatic catalysis of mercury methylation by Desulfovibrio desulfuricans LS. *Applied and Environmental Microbiology* 60:1342–1346.

Clarkson, T.W. 1998. Human toxicology of mercury. *The Journal of Trace Elements in Experimental Medicine* 11:303–317.

Domingo, J.L. 1995. Prevention by chelating agents of metal-induced developmental toxicity. *Reproductive Toxicology* 9:105–113.

Eto, K. 2000. Minamata Disease. *Neuropathology* 20:S14–S19.

Fernandez-Martinez, R., and M.I. Rucandio. 2003. Study of extraction conditions for the quantitative determination of Hg bound to sulfide in soils from Almaden (Spain). *Analytical and Bioanalytical Chemistry* 375:1089–1096.

———. 2005. Study of the suitability of HNO_3 and HCL as extracting agents of mercury species in soils from cinnabar mines. *Analytical and Bioanalytical Chemistry* 381:1499–1506.

Futatsuka, M., T. Kitano, M. Shono, Y. Fukuda, K. Ushijima, T. Inaoka, M. Nagano, J. Wakamiya, and K. Miyamoto. 2000. Health surveillance in the population living in a methyl mercury-polluted area over a long period. *Environmental Research* 83:83–92.

Ganss, C., B. Cottwald, I. Traenckner, J. Kupfer, D. Eis, J. Monch, U. Gieler, J. Klimek. 2000. Relation between mercury concentrations in saliva, blood, and urine in subjects with amalgam restorations. *Clinical Oral Investigations* 4:206–211.

Gasso, S., R.M. Cristofol, G. Selema, R. Rosa, E. Rodriguez-Farre, and C. Sanfeliu. 2001. Antioxidant compounds and Ca^{2+} pathway blockers differentially protect against methylmercury and mercuric chloride neurotoxicity. *Journal of Neuroscience Research* 66:135–145.

Gray, John E., and Richard F. Sanzolone. 1996. "Environmental Studies of Mineral Deposits in Alaska," U.S. Geological Survey Bulletin 2156. Washington, DC: U.S. Gov. Printing Office.

Greenwood, N.N., and A. Earnshaw. 1984. *Chemistry of the Elements*. Tarrytown, NY: Pergammon Press.

Gupta, M., and P. Chandra. 1998. Bioaccumulation and toxicity of mercury in root-submerged macrophyte Vallisneria Spiralis. *Environmental Pollution* 103:327–332.

Han, F.X., S. Shiyab, J. Chen, Y. Su, D.L. Monts, C.A. Waggoner, and F.B. Matta, 2008. Extractability and bioavailability of mercury from a mercury sulfide contaminated soil in Oak Ridge, Tennessee, USA. *Water, Air, and Soil Pollution* 194:67–75.

Harada, M., J. Nakanishi, E. Yasoda, M.C.N. Pinheiro, T. Oikawa, G.A. Guimaraes, B. Cardoso, T. Kizaki, and H. Ohno. 2001. Mercury pollution in the Tapajos River basin, Amazon: mercury level of head hair and health effects. *Environment International* 27:285–290.

Hernandez, A., M. Jebrak, P. Higueras, R. Oyarzun, D. Morata, and J. Munha. 1999. The Almaden mercury mining district, Spain. *Mineralium Deposita* 34:539–548.

Holden, C. 1997. Death from lab poisoning. *Science* 276:1797.

Hugueras, P., R. Oyarzun, R. Lunar, J. Sierra, and J. Parras. 1999. The Las Cuevas Deposit, Almadden District (Spain): an unusual case of deep-seated advanced argillic alteration related to mercury mineralization. *Mineralium Deposita* 34:211–214.

Jebrak, M., P.L. Higueras, E. Marcoux, and S. Lorenzo. 2002. Geology and geochemistry of high-grade, volcanic rock-hosted, mercury mineralization in the Nuevo Entredicho deposit, Almaden district, Spain. *Mineralium Deposita* 37:421–432.

Jones, L.M. 2004. Focus on fillings: a qualitative health study of people medically diagnosed with mercury poisoning, linked to dental amalgam. *Acta Neuropsychiatrica* 16:142–148.

Kargel, J.S., and J.S. Lewis. 1993. The composition and early evolution of Earth. *Icarus* 105:1–25.

Kenig, F., J.D. Hudson, J.S.S. Damste, and B.N. Popp. 2004. Intermittent euxinia: reconciliation of a jurassic black shale with its biofaces. *Geology* 32:421–424.

Kiyono, M., H. Omura, T. Omura, S. Murata, and H. Pan-Hou. 2003. Removal of inorganic and organic mercurials by immobilized bacteria having mer-ppk fusion plasmids. *Applied Microbiology & Biotechnology* 62:274–278.

Lavergren, U. 2005. Black shale as a metal contamination source. *The EES Bulletin* 3:18–31.

Lavric, J.V., and J.E. Spangenberg. 2003. Stable isotope (C, O, S) systematics of the mercury mineralization at Idrija, Slovenia: constraints on fluid source and alteration process. *Mineralium Deposita* 38:886–899.

Lin, C.J., and S.O. Pehkonen. 1999. The chemistry of atmospheric mercury: a review. *Atmospheric Environment* 33:2067–2079.

Lorscheider, F.L., M.J. Vimy, A.O. Summers, and H. Zwiers. 1995. The dental amalgam mercury controversy — inorganic mercury and the CNS; genetic linkage of mercury and antibiotic resistances in intestinal bacteria. *Toxicology* 97:19–22.

Lyons, T.W., and M. Kashgarian. 2005. Paradigm lost, paradigm found: the Black Sea-black shale connection as viewed from the anoxic basin margin. *Oceanography* 18:87–99.

Malm, O. 1998. Gold mining as a source of mercury exposure in the Brazilian Amazon. *Environmental Research* 77:73–78.

Martin-Doimeadios, R.C.R., J.C. Wasserman, L.F.G. Bermejo, D. Amouroux, J.J.B. Nevado, and O.F.X. Donard. 2000. Chemical availability of mercury in stream sediments from Almaden area, Spain. *Journal of Environmental Monitoring* 2:360–366.

Mason, R.P., N.M. Lawson, A.L. Lawrence, J.J. Leaner, J.G. Lee, and G. Sheu. 1999. Mercury in the Chesapeake Bay. *Marine Chemistry* 65:77–96.

McCurry, J. 2006. Japan remembers Minamata. *The Lancet* 367:99–100.

McDonough, W.F., and S.S. Sun. 1995. The composition of the earth. *Chemical Geology* 120:223–253.

Mehrotra, A.S., and D.L. Sedlak. 2005. Decrease in net mercury methylation rates following iron amendment to anoxic wetland sediment slurries. *Environmental Science and Technology* 39:2564–2570.

Mikac, N., D. Foucher, S. Niessen, S. Lojen, and J. Fischer. 2003. Influence of chloride and sediment matrix on the extractability of HgS (cinnabar and metacinnabar) by nitric acid. *Analytical and Bioanalytical Chemistry* 377:1196–1201.

Mishra, A., and M.A. Choudhuri. 1999. Monitoring of phytotoxicity of lead and mercury from germination and early seedling growth indices in two rice cultivars. *Water, Air, and Soil Pollution* 114:339–346.

Morel, F.M.M., A.M.L. Kraepiel, and M. Amyot. 1998. The chemical cycle and bioaccumulation of mercury. *Annual Review of Ecology & Systematics* 29:543–566.

Morris, H.M. 1985. *Scientific Creationism*, second edition. Green Forest, AR: Master Books.

Morton, G.R. *The fish is being served with a delicate creamy mercury sauce.* 1998. <http://home.entouch.net/dmd/mercury.htm> (March, 2005).

Najera, I., C.C. Lin, G.A. Kohbodi, and J.A. Jay. 2005. Effect of chemical speciation on toxicity of mercury to *Escherichia coli* biofilms and planktonic cells. *Environmental Science and Technology* 39:3116–3120.

Odjegba, V.J., and I.O. Fasidi. 2004. Accumulation of trace elements by *Pistia Straiotes:* Implications for phytoremediation. *Ecotoxicology* 13:637–646.

Orihel, D.M., M.J. Paterson, P.J. Blanchfield, R.A. Bodaly, C.C. Gilmour, and H. Hintelmann. 2008. Temporal change in the distribution, methylation, and bioaccumulation of newly deposited mercury in an aquatic ecosystem. *Environmental Pollution* 154:77–88.

Ortega-Villasante, C., R. Rellan-Alvarez, F.F. Del Campo, R.O. Carpena-Ruiz, and L.E. Hernandez. 2005. Cellular damage induced by cadmium and mercury in *Medicago Sativa*. *Journal of Experimental Botany* 56:2239–2251.

Panteleyev, A. 1996. Hot Spring Hg. In D.V. Lefebure, and T. Hoy (editors). *Selected British Columbia Mineral Deposit Profiles Volume 2: Metallic Deposits*. British Columbia, Canada: British Columbia Ministry of Employment and Investment, p. 31–32.

Parker, R.L. 1967. Composition of the earth's crust. In Michael Fleischer, editor, *Data of Geochemistry*, Sixth Edition, Professional Paper 440-D. Reston, VA: US, p. D14–D15.

Piao, H., and P.L. Bishop. 2006. Stabilization of mercury-containing wastes using sulfide. *Environmental Pollution* 139:498–506.

Pirrone, N., I. Allegrini, G.J. Keeler, J.O. Nriagu, R. Rossmann, and J.A. Robbins. 1998. Historical atmospheric mercury emissions and depositions in North America compared to mercury accumulations in sedimentary records. *Atmospheric Environment.* 32:929–940.

Ravichandran, M. 2004. Interactions between mercury and dissolved organic matter — a review. *Chemosphere* 55:319–331.

Revis, N.W., T.R. Osbourne, D. Sedgley, and A. King. 1989. Quantitative method for determining the concentration of mercury (II) sulphide in soils and sediments. *Analyst* 114:823–825.

Riddle, S.G., H.H. Tran, J.G. Dewitt, and J.C. Andrews. 2002. Field, laboratory, and x-ray absorption spectroscopic studies of mercury accumulation by water hyacinths. *Environmental Science and Technology* 36:1965–1970.

Ruelas-Inzunza, J., L.A. Soto, and F. Páez-Osuna. 2003. Heavy-metal accumulation in the hydrothermal vent clam *Vesicomya gigas* from Guaymas Basin, Gulf of California. *Deep-Sea Research I* 50:757–761.

Rytuba, J.J. 1986a. Descriptive model of Almaden Hg. In D.P. Cox and D.A. Singer (editors). *Mineral Deposit Models*. Bulletin 1693. Reston, VA: USGS, p. 180.

———. 1986b. Descriptive model of silica-carbonate Hg. In D.P. Cox and D.A. Singer (editors). *Mineral Deposit Models*. Bulletin 1693. Reston, VA: USGS, p. 181–182.

———. 2002. Mercury geoenvironmental models. In R.R. Seal II and N.K. Foley (editors). *US Geological Survey Open File Report 2002-195: Progress on Geoenvironmental Models for Selected Mineral Deposit Types*. Reston, VA: USGS, p. 161–175.

———. 2003. Mercury from mineral deposits and potential environmental impact. *Environmental Geology* 43:326–338.

Sanna, G., M.I. Pilo, P.C. Piu, N. Spano, A. Tapparo, G.G. Campus, and R. Seeber. 2002. Study of the short-term release of ionic fraction of heavy metals from dental amalgam into synthetic saliva, using anodic stripping voltammetry with microelectrodes. *Talanta* 58:979–985.

Schultz, R.B. 2004. Geochemical relationships of a late Paleozoic carbon-rich shale of the midcontinent, USA: a compendium of results advocating changeable geochemical conditions. *Chemical Geology* 206:347–372.

Schuster, P.F., D.P. Krabbenhoft, D.L. Naftz, L.D. Cecil, M.L. Olson, J.F. Dewild, D.D. Susong, J.R. Green, and M.L. Aboot. 2002. Atmospheric mercury deposition during the last 270 years: a glacial ice core record of natural and anthropogenic sources. *Environmental Science and Technology* 36:2303–2310.

Sherlock, R.L., and M.A.V. Logan. 1995. Silica-carbonate alteration of serpentinite: implications for the association of mercury and gold mineralization in Northern California. *Exploration and Mining Geology* 4:395–409.

Siegel, B.Z., and S.M. Siegel. 1987. Hawaiian volcanoes and the biogeology of mercury. In Decker, R.W., T.L. Wright, and P.H. Stauffer (editors). *Volcanism in Hawaii*. Professional Paper 1350. Reston, VA: USGS, p. 827–839.

Siegel, S.M. 1977. The cytotoxic response of 'Nicotiana' Protplasts to metal ions: a survey of the chemical elements. *Water, Air, and Soil Pollution* 8:294–304.

Silbergeld, E.K., and P.J. Devine. 2000. Mercury — are we studying the right endpoints and mechanisms. *Fuel Processing Technology* 65-66:35–42.

Silva, I.A., J. Graber, J.F. Nyland, and E.K. Silbergeld. 2005. In vitro $HgCl_2$ exposure of immune cells at different stages of maturation: effects on phenotype and function. *Environmental Research* 98:341–348.

Skyllberg, U., J. Qian, W. Frech, K. Xia, and W.F. Bleam. 2003. Distribution of mercury, methyl mercury, and organic sulphur species in soil, soil solution, and stream of a boreal forest catchment. *Biogeochemistry* 64:53–76.

Southworth, G.R., M.J. Peterson, and M.A. Bogle. 2004. Bioaccumulation factors for mercury in stream fish. *Environmental Practice* 6:135–143.

Stern, A.H. 2005. A review of the studies of the cardiovascular health effects of methylmercury with consideration of their suitability for risk assessment. *Environmental Research* 98:133–142.

Suszcynsky, E.M., and J.R. Shann. 1995. Phytotoxicity and accumulation of mercury in tobacco subjected to different exposure routes. *Environmental Toxicology and Chemistry* 14:61–67.

Tchounwou, P.B., W.K. Ayensu, N. Ninashvili, and D. Sutton. 2003. Review: environmental exposure to mercury and its toxicopathologic implications for public health. *Environmental Toxicology* 18:149–175.

Tessier, E., R.C.R. Martin-Doimeadios, D. Amouroux, A. Morin, C. Lehnoff, E. Thybaud, E. Vindimian, and O.F.X. Donard. 2007. Time course transformations and fate of mercury in aquatic model ecosystems. *Water, Air, and Soil Pollution* 183:265–281.

United Nations Environment Progamme. 2003. *Global Mercury Assessment*. Geneva, Switzerland: UNEP Chemicals.

United States Geological Survey. *Mercury studies in the Florida Everglades*. November 9, 2004. <sofia.usgs.gov/publications/fs/166-96/printfood.html> (January, 2006).

Wagner-Dobler, I., H. Von Canstein, Y. Li, K.N. Timmis, and W.D. Deckwer. 2000. Removal of mercury from chemical wastewater by microoganisms in technical scale. *Environmental Science and Technology* 34:4628–4634.

Whitmore, J. 2007. Personal communication.

Winker, R., A.W. Schaffer, C. Konnaris, A. Barth, P. Giovanoli, W. Osterode, H.W. Rudiger, and C. Wolf. 2002. Health consequences of an intravenous injection of metallic mercury. *International Archives of Occupational and Environmental Health* 75:581–586.

Yokoo, E.M., J.G. Valente, L. Grattan, S.L. Schmidt, I. Platt, and E.K. Silbergeld. 2003. Low level methylmercury exposure affects neuropsychological function in adults. *Environmental Health* 2:8.

Yudovich, Y.E., and M.P. Ketris. 2005. Mercury in coal: a review part 1 geochemistry. *International Journal of Coal Geology* 62:107–134.

Chapter 4

Karst and the Age of the World

Emil Silvestru • PhD — *Sedimentology/Stratigraphy of Karst Terrain*

Abstract

Karst is seen by many as a major, virtually definitive challenge to diluvial geology. Not only are features visible today (caves, speleothems, etc.) believed to take tens of thousands of years to form, but alleged ancient karst features (paleokarst) have been reported in rocks as old as the Precambrian. This seems to render a short geological time frame of around 6,000 years utterly preposterous. Like many other areas of geology, if one is to search for an alternative explanation of field data, the issue of karst has to be reanalyzed from its initial assumptions.

Several Necessary Definitions

Karst is a term introduced by Austrian geographers in the 19th century, referring to the limestone terrains east of Trieste, in what is now Slovenia. They actually germanicized the Slovenian name "Kras" used to define that particular area. The most specific features of this type of relief are caves, potholes, swallow holes, karst springs, sinkholes, and karren.[1] There are many definitions of karst but few true karstological ones, that is, approaching the issue from a systems perspective, and from solid field and laboratory experience. Karst is essentially a set of features that ensure the flow of water through, rather than on top of, a rock sequence. Karst-like features can

form on virtually any rocks even if there is no subterranean flow of water. One definition that I have found useful is as follows: karst is an aquifer presenting a set of surface and subsurface forms organized in order to evacuate subterranean waters through an outlet (Bakalowicz 1993).

Though it may sound a bit reductionist, this is in fact one of the most comprehensive definitions because it emphasizes the main characteristic of karst, namely its hydrologic function. Without water moving through karst (at least at some point in its history), the term itself is not proper, since similar surface morphologies can form on virtually any rock without a subterranean drain being involved.

Paleokarst is defined not just as an "ancient karst" but rather as a karst that has been covered by consolidated sediments (and therefore has undergone at least one geologic process — diagenesis in this case) in contrast with *buried karst,* which was covered by unconsolidated sediments (Silvestru 2003). By definition, paleokarst is completely disconnected from present karsting processes (Ford and Williams 1992), while buried karst can still be active under the sediment cover (Silvestru 1997).

Karstogenesis
General Remarks

The complex processes that are involved in the formation of karst features in present times are fairly well understood. As a perfect example of uniformitarianism, they are

---

1. Also called "grikes," "pavements," "runnels," and many other names.

extrapolated into the more or less distant past, thus providing a substantially long geologic time frame. Karstogenesis has been dealt with in standard textbooks[2] and will therefore not be covered in detail in the present text.

There is a clear distinction between endogenous and exogenous karsts (Silvestru 1990). The former is generated by *ascending* solutions originating in earth's crust (driven by thermal convection), while the latter is the result of *descending* solutions originating at earth's surface (driven by gravity). Only the latter has been directly investigated and its dynamics subjected to measurement. The former has not been seen forming today and is therefore referred to as "paleokarst," being found in geological settings always connected to hot solutions circulating around igneous bodies that also provide the solutions that dissolve the limestone. Endogenous karst is always considered "paleokarst" and is sometimes responsible for significant ore accumulations within the hydrothermal and hydrothermal-metasomatic domains (Mârza and Silvestru 1988). As a general rule, exogenous karst is believed to be controlled by hydrodynamic factors, since it is essentially a drainage system (see Bakalowicz's definition on previous page). As a consequence, the vast majority of karst features (surficial or subsurface) are connected to a karst aquifer. In very rare cases, karren and small-scale hollows on the surface are the result of surficial processes and do not play a role in the transfer of water to the karst aquifer. It is worth mentioning that karst-like features also occur on non-carbonate rocks and are thus labeled pseudokarst — features forming on any type of rock mainly by processes other than chemical erosion — or parakarst — features forming on non-carbonate rocks mainly by chemical erosion (Silvestru 1990). The use of only such features in assessing paleokarst is thus questionable.

Karst features are interpreted as morphological expressions of a dynamic process — the transit (with or without a temporary storage) of water *through* lithostructural units. This process consists of several stages. *Input* can be areal or concentrated. This will send most of the runoff and a part of the hydrographic network (watercourses) into the lithostructural units. Water then will circulate

through the rock toward the output, and part will be temporarily stored in the karst aquifer. The lithostructural unit where the circulation and storage occur is considered a *throughput*. These stages are also present in the vertical classification of karst aquifers: *infiltration zone, vertical flow zone, amphibious passage zone,* and *flooded (saturated) zone* (Bleahu 1974).

The stages above are classical elements of a system; hence karst is usually viewed as a system (figure 1). Unlike some systems where the throughput is considered a "black box," the karst "box" is "gray" because some

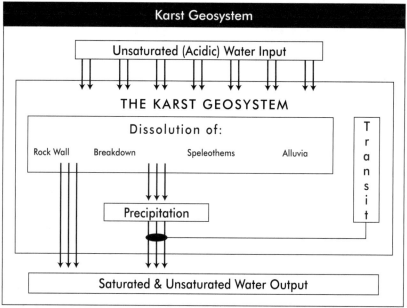

Figure 1. The karst geosystem is represented in fact by the throughput in this diagram. Once penetrated into the rock, water can either simply transit or — and this is where karsting takes place — interact with the rock. The interaction can be mechanical (erosion), chemical (corrosion usually called dissolution), and combined (erosion and corrosion and/or erosion/corrosion followed by collapse/breakdown). These processes create in essence excavations (i.e., the karst cavities). There are, however, antagonistic processes (i.e., building of new rock) because of the precipitation of calcite and other minerals from the karst waters.

caves can be accessed. However, much is still unknown, and those uncertainties create controversy over fluid flow in the karst aquifer. Though there are many theories and models, the only one that is truly backed by systematic field research and substantial experiments (including extensive pumping/recharging) is the *drain and annexes* model (figure 2) proposed by Mangin (1975). The drain is the main conduit that discharges the aquifer, while the annexes — a vast network of partly or completely flooded chambers interconnected by various size passages — have a double function. At normal to high flows they store excess water. At low flows (drought), the

---

2. Ford and Williams (1992) is one of the most comprehensive.

The drain and annexes model

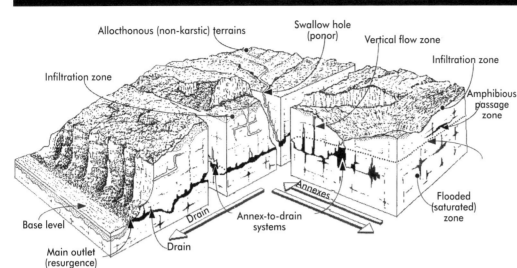

Figure 2. Mangin's (1975) "drain and annexes" model of the karst geosystem. Based on extended field work and interdisciplinary approaches complemented by repeated pumping experiments, this model was not only confirmed but found to make accurate predictions regarding the behavior of the karst aquifer.

annexes supply the drain so that the karst spring maintains a remarkably constant flow, longer than any other type of aquifer.

In limestone (and rock salt or rock gypsum), all surface input features are connected to more or less vertical channels through which water circulates toward the storage section. If there is no output for the stored water, the entire lithostructural unit becomes waterlogged, long before karren, sinkholes, and blind valleys can form. In such cases, there are no distinctive karst landforms (except karren in some cases). Therefore a twofold distinction emerges: (1) not all small-scale surface karst and parakarst features can be associated with proper karstification (karsting) processes, and (2) whenever medium- to large-scale surface (and subsurface) karst and parakarst features are present, they indicate the existence of all four stages of the karstification process. Consequently, any correct assessment of a paleokarst should start with the identification of at least parts of the drain and/or annexes.

Depth in cm	15	70
Air in the atmosphere	0.03	
Pine forest	1.13	9.39
Beech forest	0.62	1.19
Moss cover	1.93	7.98
Grass cover	0.60	4.13
Bare soil	1.19	7.02

Table 1. CO_2 contents (percent of air volume) in various soils and at various depths (from Schoeller, 1962)

Karstification Today

The uniformitarian principle demands that whatever karst processes are recorded today should also be responsible for karstification in the geologic past. There is a vast array of both experimental and field data that shows several factors essential to karsting.

Chemical Factors

Precipitation (rain and meltwater) that infiltrates through soil increases its content of carbon dioxide (CO_2) (see table 1). Most of the CO_2 dissolves in water as mild carbonic acid (H_2CO_3), which dissolves limestones, dolostones, rock gypsum, and chalk (usually referred to as *karstic rocks*). In certain cases, humic acids from the soil further increase the acidity. The amount of rock put into solution has been measured fairly accurately (see table 2), and it is referred to as rate of *karst denudation*, that is, the amount of rock dissolved in 1,000 years (measured as millimeters of lowering of the surface per millennium). Climate (as the table shows) plays an important role in the rate of karst denudation. This rate does not include mechanically eroded rock — impossible to quantify but sometimes significant.

Reliable data are not available for dissolution inside caves and throughout the fissure network inside the limestone. In some cases, saturated waters can mix inside the karst aquifer; the resulting mixture becomes acidic again (*mixing corrosion*, Bögli 1964). Some authors have estimated the overall dissolution rate by the mineral contents of karst springs, but that represents the sum of all rocks put into solution within the karst system

Area	Rate of karst denudation mm/millenium
Dry arctic climate	
Blomstrand (Spitzbergen)	40
Port Radium (Northwest Territories, Canada)	24
Very wet arctic climate	
Gold Creek (Northeast Alaska)	530
Capilano (British Columbia, Canada)	420
Cold oceanic climate	
Saint Casimir (Quebec, Canada)	160
Lismore Island (Scotland)	150
Temperate oceanic climate	
Cuilcagh (Ireland)	50
Vuerne (Belgium)	50
Quercy (France)	12
Alpine oceanic climate	
Vercors Massif (France)	240
Silbern (Switzerland)	112
Continental climate	
Fort Simpson (Northwest Territories, Canada)	40
Jasper (Alberta, Canada)	40
Bothnian Bay (Finland)	30
Wet Mediterranean climate	
Timavo (Italy)	64
Temperate climate with dry, warm summers	
Bow River (Canadian Rockies, Alberta)	40
Dry Mediterranean climate	
Calanques (near Marseille, France)	10
Algeria	6
Wet tropical climate	
Rio Champoton (Yucatan Pen., Mexico)	16
Key West (Florida, USA)	10
Dry tropical climate	
Grand Canyon (Arizona, USA)	6.6

Table 2. Rate of karst denudation in various areas of the world (from Bleahu 1974, p.133)

(including sediments, breakdown blocks, and even speleothems), and gives little indication of the amount of limestone removed from the bedrock.

Lithological Factors

Observed true karst (*orthokarst*, Silvestru 1990) forms on carbonate rock only, mainly by dissolution. There is no report (to my knowledge) of observed ongoing karsting on any other rock type. Therefore, we shall only deal with carbonate rocks. All the elements that define the lithological factor (structure, texture, grain size, grain contour, the matrix, porosity, etc.) influence karsting rates. Table 3 shows the average solubility of various types of carbonate (karst) rocks at temperatures similar to field conditions.

Bedding planes play a major role in the initial penetration of water into the limestone, especially when they are associated with discontinuities. The thinner the layers, the more bedding planes there are, with consequently higher infiltration rates.

Tectonic Factors

Tectonics, or crustal motions, play by far the most important role in karsting by providing numerous ways of access for infiltrating acidic water. Many passages follow a fault line (usually called *master joint*), and large subterranean rooms are often located at the intersection of two or more fault lines.

Hydrological Factors

Various amounts of precipitation rapidly sink into limestone terrains by areal (diffuse) infiltration and through local sinks in streams, creeks, and rivers known as *swallets* or *swallow holes* (*ponors* in Europe). After various durations of *residence time*,[3] infiltrated water resurfaces through *karst*

---

3. The total time water spends under the ground inside the karst aquifers.

Karst aquifers, Fontaine de Vaucluse

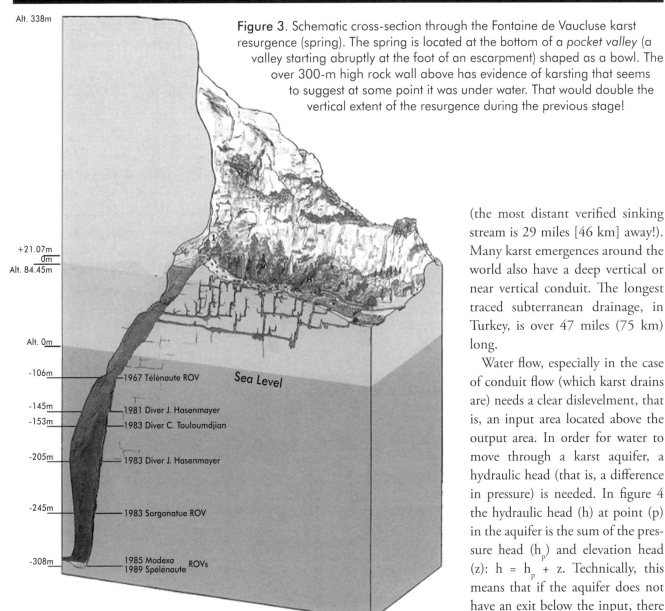

Figure 3. Schematic cross-section through the Fontaine de Vaucluse karst resurgence (spring). The spring is located at the bottom of a *pocket valley* (a valley starting abruptly at the foot of an escarpment) shaped as a bowl. The over 300-m high rock wall above has evidence of karsting that seems to suggest at some point it was under water. That would double the vertical extent of the resurgence during the previous stage!

Alt. 338m

+21.07m
0m
Alt. 84.45m

Alt. 0m

-106m — 1967 Télénaute ROV   Sea Level

-145m — 1981 Diver J. Hasenmayer
-153m — 1983 Diver C. Touloumdjian

-205m — 1983 Diver J. Hasenmayer

-245m — 1983 Sorgonatue ROV

-308m — 1985 Modexa   ROVs
          1989 Spélénaute

(the most distant verified sinking stream is 29 miles [46 km] away!). Many karst emergences around the world also have a deep vertical or near vertical conduit. The longest traced subterranean drainage, in Turkey, is over 47 miles (75 km) long.

Water flow, especially in the case of conduit flow (which karst drains are) needs a clear dislevelment, that is, an input area located above the output area. In order for water to move through a karst aquifer, a hydraulic head (that is, a difference in pressure) is needed. In figure 4 the hydraulic head (h) at point (p) in the aquifer is the sum of the pressure head (h_p) and elevation head (z): $h = h_p + z$. Technically, this means that if the aquifer does not have an exit below the input, there will be no flow.

springs.[4] Obviously, the movement of water is generally controlled by gravity, but karst aquifers also have massive upwelling flows like the famous resurgence Fontaine de Vaucluse, in Southern France, which discharges an average 19 tons/second! The hydrographic basin supplying this karst aquifer covers an area of about 1,200 km² (470 mi²). This resurgence's morphology is quite spectacular, consisting of a nearly vertical shaft 1,011 feet (308 m) deep, through which the water ascends (figure 3). The emerging water is essentially neutral and thus could not have created the shaft and the deep, flooded cave passages

Type of rock	$CaCO_3$ (mg/l)	$MgCO_3$ (mg/l)
Limestone	16.1	1.1
Dolomitic limestone	10.6	3.65
Calcareous dolomite	18.6	10.8
Dolomite	10.8	10.5

Table 3. Average $CaCO_3$ and $MgCO_3$ concentration in solutions resulting from the dissolution of various karst rocks (Bleahu 1974, p.187)

4. *Resurgences* or *emergences*, depending on whether the source of the water is known or not.

Karst aquifer elements

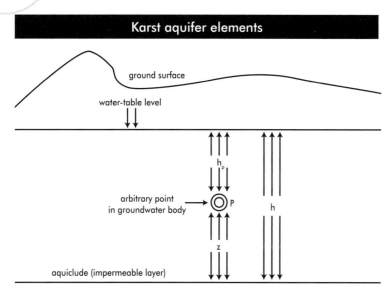

ground surface

water-table level

h_p

arbitrary point in groundwater body → P

h

z

aquiclude (impermeable layer)

Figure 4. The elements that define the hydraulics of an unconfined karst aquifer (from Ford & Williams 1992). See details in the text.

A general outline of the karsification process

Precipitation

CO_2 ····▶ H_2O ◀···· Carbonate

UNSATURATED ZONE

Infiltaration zone

Vertical circulation zone

Amphibious passage zone

$H_2O + CO_2, H_2O + (HCO_3 + Ca^{2+})$

$H_2O + HCO_3 + Ca^{2+} + (CO_3^{2-})$

WATER TABLE

$H_2O + CO_2, nH_2O$ ◀···· Carbonate

SATURATED ZONE

$H_2O + HCO_3^- + Ca^{2+} + (CO_3^{2-})$

SPEED	
Of Reaction	Of Flow
····▶ Slow	──▶ Slow
····▶ Fast	──▶ Fast

PHASE	
○	Gas
▭	Liquid
◇	Solid

Figure 5. Bakalowicz's (1977) outline of the main chemical reactions and processes involved in karsting.

All of these factors show that a true karst geo-system would leave a clear, deep signature in the relief. Even after burial and other geological processes, that signature should still be visible today.

The First Challenge — Present-day Karst

There are a huge number of caves today — karstlands cover about 12 percent of the ice-free landmasses (Ford and Williams 1992). The vast majority is interpreted as recent, mostly Quaternary age within the uniformitarian time scale. Standard karstification models postulate periods of hundreds of thousands or even millions of years for the formation of mature caves, cave systems, and karstlands. These figures are calculated by extrapolating values of today's karst denudation rate and the rate of limestone dissolution by dilute carbonic acid according to the well-known set of reactions. Bakalowicz (1977) presented a general outline of the karsification process (figure 5) in which the simplified chemical reactions point toward a sort of continuum in which soluted calcite ($H_2O + HCO_3 + Ca^{2+} + CO_3^{2-}$) and precipitating calcite ("carbonate" in the diagram) often coexist.

Radiometric dating of speleothems has also been used to calculate the rates of cave formation, but there are many problems in this dating (appendix 1). Since stalagmites[5] accumulate only once, there is no more flooding of the respective passage (i.e., the passage is "fossil"), the distribution of dated speleothems at various levels is believed to represent stages of development of the cave systems as they adjusted to downcutting base level. Calculated rates of cave downcutting range between 20 and 500 mm/ka (Ford and Williams 1992). Quite obviously, such estimates are a function of the accuracy of speleothem dating.

All these ages clearly challenge the biblical timeframe, especially since Lot and his daughters are said to have dwelt in caves (Gen. 19:30) merely 400 years after the Flood (Silvestru 2008).

---

5. Stalactites cannot be used for radiometric dating.

Problems with Long-Ages Model

Let us first take a look at some of the problems with the standard, long-age karstogenetic and speleogenetic models.

I will concentrate on a marked discrepancy in karstology. Many speleothems have been recorded growing very fast while others, which have formed inside mines[6], are indirect but irrefutable proof that speleothem growth occurs rapidly. Completely disregarding this data or considering such cases the exception, the dating of speleothems—in a classical case of the reinforcement syndrome—concentrates on speleothems believed to have grown for tens or even hundreds of thousands of years (Lauritzen and Mylroie 2000; Maire and Quinif 1989; Soriaux 1982).

This means that the drip point for all those stalagmites must have remained virtually unchanged for tens or hundreds of thousands of years. The point where the dripping water reaches the ceiling of a cave is a function of the geometric feedwater conduit, which is significantly influenced by surface conditions of the limestone (the input area). Minor changes on the surface drastically influence the functioning of feedwater conduits. In fact, many environmental battles over karst terrains were based on the preservation of the natural conditions on the surface, especially the forests that provide protection from excessive erosion, the soil cover, and through it the vital supply of CO_2, crucial for the formation of speleothems (Silvestru 1994). Erosion, especially after forests are gone, drastically modifies the surface features that are responsible for transferring the runoff. Once the vegetation is gone, soil is rapidly washed into limestones, clogging many infiltration pathways.

In the Siebenhengste massif north of Lake Thun in the Swiss Alps (Jeanin 1991; Silvestru 2000), the Cretaceous Schrattenkalk limestone was exposed by essentially glacial erosion from under the Hohghant Sandstone of Late Eocene age at the end of the Ice Age. The glacial erosion was completely erased by karsting processes so that today only typical karst features (extensive karren) are visible on most of this high alpine ridge. The effects of the glacial erosion are only visible on the adjacent sandstone and in the many erratic blocks of limestone that also show intense karsting. Such significant erosion of the limestone would have undoubtedly affected the infiltration pathways. Finally, as acidic water travels along the infiltration pathways, it dissolves limestone, actively modifying the size and geometry of feedwater conduits.

On the other hand, remarkable drip point stability is demonstrated by "candles" or "broomsticks" — tall, thin[7] stalagmites that grew several meters high and maintained a minimal diameter. On rare occasions, the position of the drip point on the ceiling slightly shifted, resulting in "stepped stalagmites," that is, with the growth axis repeatedly shifted a few centimeters in one or several directions.

However, the observed sensitivity of the karst system to environmental changes makes it quite difficult to accept that the dripping will stay constant for hundreds of thousands of years, through several stadial and interstadial events during the Quaternary! Yet this is what old speleothems demand. Strangely enough, *observed processes* are considered unimportant for one and only one reason: that the long-established, fiercely defended reigning paradigm of long ages is preserved and confirmed.

Elementary logic requires a simpler, testable interpretation: that speleothems are younger than the tens or hundreds of thousands of years many of them have been dated.

The Problem with Water Saturation

Apart from the chemical processes, the most important condition in the karst system is the continued circulation of water. If the water is stagnant, its ability to dissolve limestone is limited. Once saturation is reached, dissolution basically stops, and caves will not form or grow. The vast majority of infiltration paths in karstic rocks are narrow, mostly capillary discontinuities like cracks, joints, and bedding planes, which often become too narrow for any flow. However, an ongoing source of acidic water will help enlarge the conduit and allow the flow to resume. The problem is evident: as it dissolves the rock, the water in the capillary conduits becomes saturated and cannot be refreshed because capillary flow does not allow any form of secondary circulation. Thus, unsaturated water from the surface cannot flow through the saturated water in the capillary conduit to refresh it, and eventually the saturated water will reach the surface.

A vast array of field and laboratory data has revealed that sufficient acidity is lost within the first 13 to 33 feet (4 to 10 m) from the surface,[8] which puts karstogenetic theory in a delicate position: *existing models cannot explain*

---

6. See for example http://www.answersingenesis.org/creation/v23/i3/kathleen.asp.

7. The minimum diameter of a stalagmite is of the order of three cm (Ford and Cullingford, 1976).

8. For a list of references see Silvestru (2003).

how the extensive cave systems of today grew from simple infiltration of acidic runoff through a discontinuous network of fissures.

The only solution offered thus far is to postulate that all large cave systems formed in areas where a consistent and extended network of joints and fissures already existed. In this case, "consistent" essentially means that the network has to have a lower opening to allow a pressure head for flow to occur. This convenient explanation is contradicted by concrete field situations of which one is most striking — the Floridan karst.

Florida has two superimposed aquifers: the Upper Floridan Aquifer (UFA) with Tertiary limestones reaching the surface, and a deep confined aquifer in limestones that do not reach the surface and descend to 7,875 feet (2,400 m) below surface or 7,545 feet (2,300 m) below mean sea level (Jordan 1950).

The UFA limestones are literally filled with fresh water, clearly visible in the countless ponds that dot the landscape, all of them entrances to vast mazes of flooded cave passages. There are also countless karst springs on the periphery of the limestones, with discharges ranging up to 990 feet^3/sec (28 m^3/sec)! A large number of the many boreholes drilled in the Florida Peninsula have reached this confined aquifer and often encountered flooded cave passages — up to 20 feet (6 m) across, some of them very deep, down to 5,900 feet (1,800 m) (Jordan, 1950). ^{14}C dating of the karst waters has yielded alleged ages up to 28,000 years, which corresponds to a speed of subterranean water circulation of 6 to 40 feet (2–12 m) per year (Henshaw et al. 1965). These data raise several serious questions.

1. What creates karstic voids so deep below a significant regional base level without any known or even imaginable outlet? According to Back et al. (1966), at the deepest points ever reached by drilling, the water is saturated in calcite and dolomite (never in aragonite) so it cannot possibly further dissolve limestone and create karst voids. Hippenmeier (1964) tried to solve this problem by invoking paleogeography, that is, at a time when the rocks were close enough to the surface to be karsted. Yet this explanation cannot be accepted except for the coastal area and at shallow depth. There is absolutely no geological marker that would even hint to such an explanation, and the geology of the area does not support it, unless the Atlantic Ocean level has dropped over 4,920 feet (1,500 m)!

2. Geochemical studies (Back et al. 1966) have also revealed that at great depth there are karst waters allegedly 8,000 years old that are still unsaturated. Given the very slow speed of karst water circulation (see previous page), such a long time of residence without saturation defies all known mechanisms.

Known Alternative Karsting Processes

The discovery of sulfuric acid karsting came as a surprise to the karstological community, and not because karst is formed by sulfuric acid — that has been known for quite some time — but because of the extent and speed of this process. The best known example is from the Guadalupe Mountains of New Mexico and Texas, generated by *ascending* solutions. The resulting caves are called "endogenous" (Silvestru 1990) or "hypogene" (Ford and Williams 1992). They include the famous Carlsbad Caverns, its neighbor Lechuguilla Cave (probably the most beautiful cave in the world), and 30 other major caves (Hill 1987). This karst system is outstanding for its large rooms and passages, blind pits, and abundant, splendidly crystallized, evaporite speleothems (Hill 1987). Apparently there is no significant connection with the surface except for entrances opened by erosion.

Karstologists are split about how the Guadalupe karst formed, because the caves contain huge calcite and evaporite speleothems. Some support *per ascensum* genesis by hydrogen sulfide (H$_2$S) that originated from the underlying Permian oil and gas fields. They interpret the calcite speleothems as secondary features (Hill, 1987). Others, such as Ford and Williams (1992), invoke a classical karstification process of which the calcite speleothems are by-products. Nevertheless, these authors propose a polygenetic origin, suggesting that there was some H$_2$S involvement, especially in a late phase, when H$_2$S-rich backwater ponding generated the enormous evaporite speleothems. Yet the massive maze of passages of Lechuguilla Cave, for example (in excess of 118 miles [190 km]), bears no resemblance to any known cave system formed by infiltrating carbonic acid, but strikingly resembles hydrothermal karst from locations around the world (Bakalowicz et al. 1987; Dubliyanski 1980; Kovacs and Muller 1980; Muller and Sarvary 1977).

Similar karst has been identified in Italy at Grotte di Frasassi (Ford and Williams 1992) and the Republic of Georgia at Akhali Atoni Cave (Titilozov 1983). Interestingly, some consider the latter to be of hydrothermal origin (Dubliyanski 1980).

The discovery of an alternative mechanism opens a new approach to karsting as a whole, especially within the conditions one would assume occurred during and immediately after the Flood. I have previously approached the possibility of caves being formed by hydrothermal activity (Silvestru 2003). The vast amount of hydrothermal solutions[9] (HTS) through the karstic rocks was responsible for the formation of vast cave systems in the final stages of the Flood and immediately after. This flow was not restricted to existing conduits like those found in carbonic acid karsting (e.g., bedding planes); it rather proceeded en masse through the rocks. Wilson et al. (2001) presented a simulation of the dolomitization process inside carbonate platforms. They pointed out that geothermal convection of seawater moving in reaction fronts (i.e., mass flow of fluids not in equilibrium with the host rock) can explain the complex process of dolomitization. The authors have also pointed out that high temperatures played an important role in this process. Those conditions sound very similar to those expected during the Flood.

In the case of the Guadalupe karst, I believe the supporters of the *per ascensum*, hypogene formation of this karst are correct; the karst was carved mainly by sulfuric acid (H_2SO_4). They propose that H_2S originated from the subjacent Permian oil and gas fields, rose to the water table, and oxidized to H_2SO_4. Since corrosion by H_2SO_4 is much faster than that by HCO_3, the amount of H_2S required to generate Carlsbad Caverns' Big Room (in excess of 35 million feet[3] [10^6 m^3]) is small — less than 10 percent of one year's commercial production from the nearby gas fields in New Mexico (Hill 1987). Bakalowicz (1986) pointed out that the aggressiveness of sulfuric acid solutions can be further increased by CO_2 inside the limestone. Under such circumstances, I believe the Guadalupe karst could have formed in several centuries.

A Young-Earth Model and Answer to the Challenge

In an integrated young-earth approach, the starting point should be the early stages of the formation of the karstic rocks followed by the diagenetic and post-diagenetic processes. This view can be described in a series of stages.

Stage 1. Hydrothermal circulation through the thick sediments deposited during the Flood leads to accelerated diagenesis. The majority of sedimentary rocks are terrigenous, and their porosity today typically ranges from 5 to 25 percent (Selley 2000). The original (primary) porosity of the unbound sediment must have been higher, around 35 to 40 percent. The cement that binds the clasts together filled a part of that primary porosity, and this means that 10–35 percent of all terrigenous rocks is cement (i.e., a chemical precipitate). I believe this represents just a part of the HTS that moved in reaction fronts through the lithosphere during the Flood and immediately after (for more details, see Silvestru 2003). Karstic rocks therefore could rapidly form and their diagenesis contribute to increased local acidity.

Tectonic uplift would have resulted in a dense fissural network, further increasing penetration by the acidic HTS. Thus, hydrothermal karst (HTK) could have started to form in the first (deeper) karstic rocks even before the end of the Flood. Very large chambers connected through narrow conduits could have formed, and oftentimes the conduits and even chambers could have followed tectonic pathways ("master joints") that formed during diagenesis and quite possibly under the pressure of the ascending fluids and gasses. The larger the chambers, the slower the karsting, so that the largest chambers could have acted eventually as reservoirs for HTS, and further upward circulation was more strictly controlled by petrographic and structural factors. I would compare these chambers and the way they supplied karsting above and around them to batholiths and their associated dikes and sills.

I would like to reemphasize that karsting is a process that increases porosity; hence the flow paths become more efficient and, as long as the HTS supply is abundant, the rate of hydrothermal karsting increases. The replacement of large volumes of rock with fluids could have resulted in some positive isostatic movements. This corroborates the fact that the most developed type of karst — the tower karst — has been proven not to be the result of only tropical climate conditions as previously believed (Balazs 1962; Lehman 1954) but also and mainly of very rapid regional (isostatic) uplift and erosion (Mangin and Bakalowicz 1990).

Stage 2. As deep hydrothermal activity decreases and the karstic rocks approach the surface, the *per ascensum*, convectional movement of solutions is gradually replaced by gravitational *per descensum* movement of solutions from the newly formed karst reservoirs. By this time, due to isostatic and orogenic movements, new tectonic pathways have become accessible, and dissolution shifts from chambers to conduits. Incipient cave systems begin to

_____

9. "Hydrothermal" is used here in its proper geologic sense (i.e., a postmagmatic stage prior to the formation of thermal waters), the same process being responsible for the formation of countless hydrothermal ore deposits around the world.

develop, and subaqueous speleothems may also begin to form. Most present-day cave systems include large chambers alternating with rather narrow conduits.

Stage 3. Hydrothermal activity now restricted to deeper levels, the reservoirs begin emptying, supplying hypogene karsting below them. This would create a significant hydraulic head for any liquids present above. The drawdown would drain all voids above, and consequently conduit karsting would intensify. In a very short time (due to high potential energy from accelerated uplift), surface solutions of the type Austin (1980) suggested (i.e., highly acidic because of organic decomposition) would reach hydrothermal karst and consequently a mixing of solutions and processes would occur. This also causes a vertical staging of chambers and conduits, a setting known today as "multiphase cave systems" (Ford and Williams 1992).

Stage 4. Based on local/regional conditions, some of the chambers/reservoirs rise above local base level and drain whatever fluids left in them toward the base level collector. While they may have played a role in stage 3, the flow-induced primary porosity pathways are probably decisive during this stage, controlling the onset of drain conduits. By this time, hypogene karsting has completely given way to exogene karsting, followed by an ample and rapid reshaping of the old HTK (breakdown and collapse being the major agencies). Surface karsting — starting as soon as karstic rocks are subjected to subaerial conditions — dramatically increases as surface and hypogene karst become connected.

As the water receded from the newly formed continents in massive sheet flows, wherever the rocks were riddled with karst voids and therefore weakened, landscapes like the tower karst rapidly formed. It was during this stage that most of the hydrographic networks that control karst drains today were created.

Massive post-Flood precipitation (rain in the lower latitudes, snow in the higher ones) would have also contributed to accelerated karsting. The huge amounts of dissolved limestone were rapidly precipitating in intense speleothem growth episodes. The onset of the Ice Age slowed both karsting and speleothem growth (in temperate and arctic areas) to values probably less than the ones measured today. This should be — and actually is — recorded by many speleothems. The Holocene witnessed an increase in karsting processes, and lately the increase in atmospheric CO_2 has further accelerated them, but far less than during stages 1–3 (Silvestru 2003).

The Second Challenge — Paleokarst
What Is Paleokarst after All?

The existence of paleokarst, that is, karst preserved in rocks that are claimed to have been deposited during the Flood, represents a major challenge to a diluvialist geological model (DGM). I would like to emphasize that a diluvialist model implies an extremely catastrophic geology, which by definition rules out deep time. Because the first alleged paleokarst has been described from the Lower Proterozoic (Silvestru 2000) throughout the entire stratigraphic column, none of the proposed Flood boundaries in it can avoid this challenge.

A rather broad array of meanings is assigned to paleokarst. Geographers tend to emphasize landforms; geologists stress a particular mineral paragenesis; karstologists (like Bakalowicz) place emphasis on hydrodynamics and morphologies. In the most comprehensive treatise on paleokarst published so far, Bosak et al. (1989) wrote about a "terminological jungle." This can be proven by several examples from some of the classical treatises. There are two terms — *paleokarst* and *fossil karst* — closely mingled from the early times of karst studies, as de Martonne (1910) pointed out. These two terms have been used as everything from synonyms to two different categories. Appendix 2 presents what are considered "standard" definitions of terms.

These definitions, however, do not cover all reality. Buried karst is ambiguous, since there are karsts with features that form before the present morphogenic set of conditions, are then covered by other rocks, and yet function as elements of the present karst system. Such an example is the Padis karst plateau in the Apuseni Mountains of Romania (Silvestru 2000), where sediments as thick as 280 feet (85 m) cover sinkholes that still act as concentrated inlets for the runoff. The sinkholes feed a limestone aquifer (which includes caves) discharged through one outlet. No "paleo" features in this! In fact, it is practically impossible for any ancient karst feature to be completely decoupled from some type of solution. Even when located deep under the surface, infiltrated water reaches them and reshapes them (Silvestru 1985). At greater depth, hydrothermal solutions invade and even enlarge pre-existing karst features, depositing a wide array of minerals, including ores (Silvestru 1985). Karst has also been identified within pneumatolithic conditions (with temperatures and pressures superior to hydrothermal conditions), with garnets depositing on top of calcite speleothems (Mârza and Silvestru 1988). Development of such features will always occur since they are usually within the range of some type of aqueous solution. There is strong evidence that thermo-mineral solutions are also active in creating karst features deep inside limestones, deposition — if it occurred — taking place after the acidity of solutions has been dampened by the limestones (Silvestru 2000).

Relict karst (Bosak et al. 1989) is also a misleading term since it is based on the undefined concept of "survival." What survives of "karst landforms that were created at earth's surface under one set of morphogenic conditions"? Morphologies? The presumed paleokarst maintains its hydrogeological functions, and one cannot truly separate old morphologies from more recent ones. In most cases, hydrographic and geomorphic criteria depend on how the researcher believes the hydrogeologic setting was functioning in the past. Ford and Williams (1992) emphasize this problem and leave the issue open by introducing the category of true paleokarst or buried karst. These authors also use the term "fossilized" for this category. Obviously, they mean to equate the concept with "extinct." However, while an extinct and buried creature is literally "decoupled" from the present system, no lithostructure, let alone a buried landform (which represents an important anisotropy inside a lithostructure), can be truly decoupled from the present hydrogeochemical system.

Exhumed karst, as defined by all authors, cannot be differentiated — when "stripped of its cover beds" — from *relict karst*. Again, the researcher's preconceived view of the whole system decides which landform is what, *if any, of the terms in appendix 2 are used.*

In my view, paleokarst cannot be interpreted purely as a landform (or a geographic feature). It is a lithostructural (or geological) feature, and hence, must have undergone at least one geologic event, that is, a chemical, physical and/or tectonic change due to geological processes (Silvestru and Ghergari 1994). True paleokarst may range from voids (acting as secondary porosity) to intrastratal breccias and complex petrographic structures, including some ore deposits. Any other karst or fossil karst feature that is still a landform, that is, is exposed to surface processes, no matter its actual age or geomorphic setting, is just a stage in the history of a given karst geosystem. The use of the term *fossil karst* is essential in such a case, because it implies that no diagenesis had affected the karst geosystem.

In the case of true paleokarst, diagenesis does not normally wipe away the difference — essential to karstification — between soluble and insoluble (or rather highly soluble and less soluble) rocks. Moving water was discovered at extreme depth in the ultra-deep Kola borehole

outside any karst aquifer and not far from the calculated upper boundary for burial metamorphism (which would obviously eliminate karst features).[10] This suggests that recognizable paleokarst can be affected by infiltrating water, which would then accentuate karst features, at almost any depth. It may be argued that deeper water will be saturated and therefore noncorrosive, but erosion and uplift should eventually bring the paleokarst to "corrosive water depth." By the time erosion and uplift brought the paleokarst to the surface again, clear neokarst features should be superimposed on the original paleokarst. The literature makes no clear reference to such features. Bosak (1995, p. 117) actually admits this problem:

> To distinguish what is ancient from what could have been remodelled in recent times is very difficult. The rejuvenation of karst making the conserved fossil record degraded and unreadable is caused by numerous factors generally leading to the renewal of the hydrological function of the karst and of karst water circulation.

Can Paleokarst Survive Unchanged during Deep Time?

My 30-plus years of experience have confirmed that most paleokarst features, when exhumed or brought closer to the surface, amplify the subsequent processes of karstification and cryptokarstification (hidden karstification) irrespective of their position with respect to the water table. If close enough to the surface, such cryptokarst can influence or even generate surface karst features (Silvestru 2000). Take for example the formation of modern sinkholes associated with bauxite ore bodies inside limestones (which mark an alleged paleokarst of Berriasian-Valanginian age) in the Padurea Craiului Mountains in Romania. Sinkholes are present whenever a bauxite ore body is close enough to the surface (Cociuba and Silvestru 1989). They never occur right above the bauxite but always downstream with respect to the local underground drainage, which points to a direct and dynamic link between surface and subsurface karst. It is believed that enhanced chemical activity associated with the bauxite bodies accelerates karsting.

The "Paleokarstic" Fills from Iglesiente, Sardinia, Italy

Located in the southwestern part of Sardinia, the Iglesiente lead, zinc, barite, and fluorite mining area is composed of rocks ranging from Cambrian to Quaternary. The paleokarst features are located in the Cambrian Gonessa Formation — dolomites and fossil-rich limestones about

---

10. http://www.nkj.ru/archive/articles/4172.

2,297 feet (700 m) thick, overlain by nodular limestones and slates (Bini et al. 1988). The underlying Nebida Formation (Lower-Middle Cambrian) is rich in fossils (stromatolites, echinids, brachiopods, trilobites, oncolites, stenotecoids, and algae). The top of the Gonessa Formation appears to have been karsted in a period of emergence during the Caledonian orogeny. During the Hercynian orogeny, granites were emplaced in the adjacent area, and volcanism was active during the Late Oligocene and Miocene.

The paleokarst features range from karren, pinnacles, pockets, and sinkholes filled with terra rossa, to sediment-filled cracks and larger voids up to cave-sized. A sinkhole-like feature in the fossiliferous limestone of the Gonessa Formation was cut through in a local mine. It was filled with transgressive Triassic sandstones that also appear to be carved by a perfectly overlapping "sinkhole" of unknown age, filled with terra rossa. The top of the Triassic sandstones appears to be weathered and covered by a thin layer of sparry calcite, carved by karren and pinnacles. Inside the terra rossa fill, sparry calcite is also present as conical structures resembling speleothems. According to the authors, this setting is recurrent in the area (figure 6). They claim that the paleokarst was generated during the Lower Ordovician, survived unfilled (or filled and then mysteriously unfilled) for 200 million years until the Triassic, was filled during that period, karsted again, and refilled with terra rossa of unknown age. The same explanation is given for a number of cave-like cavities that are now completely filled with sediment. The authors conclude:

> While these caves developed mostly during the Paleozoic and Mesozoic . . . the sediments have been deposited after the Cenozoic volcanic activities . . . (Bini et al. 1988, p. 151).

This uniformitarian explanation has many problems. If the Triassic fill of the "sinkhole" in figure 5 is transgressive, then why isn't the layering more or less parallel? The underlying limestones are horizontal and the claimed unconformity is, too. It is not plausible to invoke suffosion[11] as there is no trace of subjacent voids into which

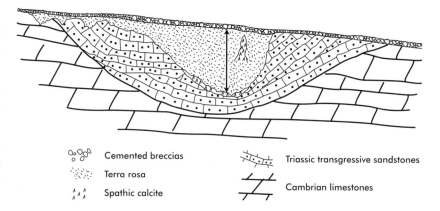

Cross section of alleged doline sinkhole

Cemented breccias

Terra rosa

Spathic calcite

Triassic transgressive sandstones

Cambrian limestones

Figure 6

fines could be washed. The feature is easily explained if the sandstones were initially deposited horizontally over a seep area. After degassing, the still-plastic sediments slumped into the newly created void, to be rapidly cemented by seep precipitates. The same precipitates generated the irregular sparry calcite layer and, quite possibly, the conical speleothem-like formation in the terra rossa fill.

The carbonate sequence of the Gonessa Formation covers the middle and upper part of the Lower Cambrian — supposedly some 12 million years. Yet, as shown by the stratigraphic column in figure 6, the alleged sinkholes formed throughout this entire period. This implies repeated emergence and karsting, but there are no unconformities inside the limestones or dolomites. A syngenetic origin for the "sinkholes" is more reasonable, and the most likely mechanism is paleoseep activity. This rules out a long period of karstogenesis.

If the intense, recurrent, and chemically variable magmatism occurred after the caves had formed, then why is there no sign of hydrothermal fill? All the cave fills described by the authors are of the classical karst type. Yet all the economically significant mineralization is located inside the limestones. Furthermore, there is no mention of secondary migration of cations (Pb, Zn, Ba) toward the paleokarstic voids. This is most unusual. It all makes sense, however, if the "paleokarst" is younger than the igneous rocks, so young that leaching and migration of the cations toward the voids has not occurred.

Several other field examples of paleokarst are examined in appendix 3.

---

11. A category of piping through the evacuation of fines by a combination of solution and downwashing.

A Creationist Interpretation of Iglesiente and an Answer to the Challenge

The Gonessa Formation was deposited during the Flood and subject to recurrent paleoseep activity originating from the ascent of HTS discussed earlier. This also left its signature on the organic-rich Nebida Formation. Fluids formed pockmarks, sometimes overlapping, and seep precipitates. Subsequent diagenesis preserved the pockmarks, which are strikingly similar to paleosinkholes.

Toward the end of the Ice Age, a classical karst began developing on the island, and as the climate became warmer and more humid, sediments began filling the karstic voids. Rapidly rising sea level restricted the formation of large cave systems to the higher elevations. However, the small cavities at lower levels might have been subjected to marine invasion and erosion.

Paleokarst Summary

In conclusion, I believe that the case of paleokarst remains doubtful: there appear to be no known features that cannot be explained within a DGM framework. While the standard, old-age interpretation of paleokarst can be applied as part of the larger, naturalistic paradigm, it remains riddled with problems: some unanswered, some inadequately answered, and some completely ignored.

In my view, and accepting definitions by Ford and Williams (1992), the vast majority of the karst visible today are reactivated *paleokarst* that formed during the final stages of the Flood, and function today as *relict karst* with some instances of *new karst* (neokarst) formed since the end of the Ice Age, all of which fits the time frame required by the DGM.

Appendix 1

The Problem with Speleothem Dating

The dating of speleothems has become a standard for karstology, paleoclimatology, and many other areas of "historical sciences." The ^{230}Th/^{234}U method is the most frequently used and most versatile method. There are two parent uranium isotopes in the limestones: ^{238}U ($\lambda = 4.47 \times 10^9$ a^{-1}) and ^{235}U ($\lambda = 7.13 \times 10^8$ a^{-1}), where λ is the half life of the isotope. Among their intermediate daughters are ^{234}U ($\lambda = 2.48 \times 10^5$ a^{-1}) and ^{230}Th ($\lambda = 7.52 \times 10^4$ a^{-1}). The uranium isotopes decay by α decay, while thorium undergoes β decay. All three uranium isotopes are more or less soluble, but ^{234}U is more soluble than the others. This leads to "daughter excess." ^{230}Th is insoluble and believed to be completely absorbed by clays and other insoluble components of the limestone. In order for speleothems to be dated, they need to have a crystalline structure that has recorded growth with as few gaps as possible and without contaminants (usually clay minerals). Recrystallization has to be completely absent. In reality, many speleothems are partly or completely recrystallized and many are porous. As a result, ^{234}U will be preferentially leached. This is why stalactites are not recommended for dating since they have a central feeding canal. The principle is rather simple: ^{234}U is leached out from the limestone, transported by the solution that dissolved the limestone, and eventually incorporated in the calcite precipitating in stalagmites. A necessary assumption is that the system is closed after precipitation of the calcite. Yet recrystallization is common; on a microscopic scale, the vast majority of speleothems reveal many imperfections of the crystalline lattice (i.e., openings of the system). Furthermore, one must assume that no ^{230}Th is deposited in the precipitating calcite; that all ^{230}Th is the daughter of the ^{234}U. However, most calcite contains contaminants; ^{230}Th, ^{232}Th ($\lambda = 1.39 \times 10^{10}$ a^{-1}), and ^{231}Pa ($\lambda = 3.43 \times 10^4$ a^{-1}) (Ford and Williams 1992) and speleothems can incorporate the contaminants. Recent discoveries may present serious challenges to speleothem dating. Foraminifer shells[12] that under normal optical microscopy seemed free of recrystallization showed intense recrystallization under electron microscopy. Since the standard diagnosis only involves binocular microscope investigation, a large number of shells probably have been recrystallized, rendering them useless for dating purpose (Pearson et al. 2001; Schrag 1999). To my knowledge, dated speleothems are not first checked for recrystallization by electron microscopy; a thorough visual examination, sometimes with a loupe, is all that is normally done to assess recrystallization. I believe that many dated speleothems would reveal widespread recrystallization at an ultramicroscopic level of investigation. For more information on the many problems in radiometric dating, see Humphreys et al. (2003), Vardiman et al. (2000, 2005), and chapter 11 in this book.

Appendix 2

"Standard" Definitions of Paleokarst and Other Terms

Paleokarst: "karst developed largely or entirely during past geological periods." It is divided into *buried karst:* "karst phenomena formed at the surface of the earth and then covered by later rocks"; *intrastratal karst:* "karst formed within rocks already buried by younger strata";

---

12. Regularly used for oxygen isotope ratios in paleotemperature reconstructions.

and *relict karst*: "karst landforms that were created at the earth's surface under one set of morphogenic conditions and which survive at the surface under a present, different set of conditions" (Bosak et al. 1989, p. 32–35). *Relict karsts* are "karsts removed from the situation in which they were developed, although they remain exposed to and are modified by processes operating in the present system." *Paleokarst* or *buried karst* "are completely decoupled from the present hydrogeochemical system; they are fossilized. When stripped of their cover beds they reveal an *exhumed karst*" (Ford and Williams 1992, p. 507). *Fossil karst landforms* are of two main kinds. First, those formed in earlier geological periods and never covered by later rocks; these may be called *relict landforms*. And secondly, those formed in earlier geological periods, subsequently covered by non-limestone rocks and later re-exhumed; these are *exhumed* or *resurrected landforms* (Sweeting 1973, p. 153–154). *Fossil* or *paleokarst* "occurs beneath unconformities where solutional features of land surface have been covered by later deposits" (Ford and Cullingford 1976, p. 109–110).

Appendix 3

Some Field Examples

Alleged paleokarst buried by thick sediments can still accommodate active drainages like in the territory between the Danube and the Black Sea in Romania, called Dobrogea (the lowest land in Romania). In its southern third, this territory consists of a thick pile of various types of sedimentary carbonates resting on Paleozoic crystalline formations and covered by Quaternary deposits (mainly loess). There are two karst aquifers in these sediments: a lower one in Jurassic-Barremian (Mesozoic) limestones that is 1,300–3,300 feet (400–1,000 m) thick, which lies directly on the Paleozoic formations, and an artesian aquifer in Sarmatian (Upper Neogene) limestones (Davidescu et al. 1991). They are separated by an aquiclude of Aptian (Mid-Cretaceous) clays. The lower aquifer demonstrates unexpected characteristics. Boreholes drilled through the entire hydrogeologic sequence encountered voids at a depth of 1,476 feet (450 m) (400 m below sea level) with intense fresh water circulation and even quartz sand eruptions (Bleahu 1974). Extremely strong water circulation mixed with sand broke a drill bit and more than one meter of piping. The karst aquifer is fed by aerial infiltration some 124 miles (200 km) away in the pre-Balkan region in Bulgaria (Davidescu et al. 1991). Isotope dating of the water in this aquifer next to the Black Sea yielded "ages" up to 25,000 years (Tenu and Davidescu 1995),

which corresponds to a dismal groundwater flow of 0.25 feet/year (0.08 m/year)! Obviously, such tranquil velocities could not destroy drilling equipment.

On the other hand, such a rapid, massive local flow of water would normally occur above the water table in the vadose zone, implying an extensive cave system. According to Bleahu (1974, p. 474), the existence of karst drainages inside this aquifer cannot be attributed to a paleokarst that was buried under thick Miocene and Quaternary sediments because pre-Miocene voids could not survive under the lithostatic pressure (there are no syngenetic fillings of the voids that could have been later corroded). Even if Bleahu is wrong (and I don't think he is), if these voids were really generated during an ancient karstification phase, they were clearly reused by the recent karst aquifer. Whatever traces of paleokarst might have existed would then have been wiped away by recent karstification.

As with the Floridan "paleokarst," the attempt to solve the mystery by interpreting the actual karst as paleokarst failed. Furthermore, the characteristics of the confined aquifer show that even such a deep and buried karst is active and in connection with the surface. Similar cases are encountered even in metamorphic lithostructures. In Northern Romania, the Rodnei Mountains are mostly comprised of crystalline formations. One is an important carbonate sequence (marble) over 4,920 feet (1,500 m) thick. Inside the sequence, mining activities have encountered various karst aquifers. One of these is located in a crystalline limestone sequence lying on and overlain by moderately metamorphosed garnet schists. The limestones have no lateral connection with the surface — over 492 feet (150 m) above. Yet they are far from being sealed from surface infiltrations. A multitude of faults, fractures, and associated joints were encountered that were (and still are) draining fresh water, sometimes under high pressure. Flows of up to 2 feet³/sec (60 liters/sec) were recorded (Silvestru 1985). It is obvious that if paleokarst features had somehow survived metamorphism, they would be highly active in organizing karst drains, and even more so since the pneumatolithic karsting (Mârza and Silvestru 1988) also occurred in this same lithostructure. The hot and hyperactive solutions would have exploited any existing paleokarst. Considering these facts (as opposed to theoretical models), I find it difficult to accept the idea that paleokarst features have been preserved *unchanged* for millions or hundreds of millions of years. It seems more probable that any primary morphology initially preserved inside soluble rocks would be subsequently reshaped beyond recognition by karstification or cryptokarstification or, if buried at greater depth, by diagenesis.

Karst features are morphological expressions of a dynamic process — the movement of water through lithostructural units — and consequently only features preserved inside rocks that can positively be linked to this circulation (or/and storage in karst aquifers) can be called paleokarst. On the other hand, if karst-like features are found in the geological record without being associated with proper karstification processes, what other genetic mechanisms could be involved? A possible solution is provided by *oil and gas seeps* (Silvestru 2001). Such sites extend far beyond hydrocarbon provinces. Seeps are located on practically all continental margins, where they constitute a general feature of the hydrogeologic system and where the vast majority of karsted limestones were deposited.

Seeps are also present on the continents and, in some cases, *submarine seeps are connected hydrologically to terrestrial groundwater systems*. Their output includes natural gas, carbon dioxide, nitrogen, hydrogen sulfide, other gases, and oil. Many seeps support chemosynthetic biotopes and produce a variety of ocean bottom morphologies such as *seep precipitates (carbonates and hydrates), pockmarks, piping, and rills*, ranging in scale from meters to kilometers. From a sedimentary point of view, some of the most significant seep signatures are carbonate bodies such as irregular mounds, dikes, and flat hardground-type surfaces. Many of these features follow fault lines. Sometimes small-scale parallel, ring, and columnar structures, resembling speleothems, are present inside these carbonate bodies (Moore 1999). Cylindrical to conical structures were identified recently at some seep locations on the ocean bottom. The structure of many paleoseep carbonate bodies is practically identical with modern ones, potentially permitting paleoclimate, hydrological, chemical, and biological reconstructions. Paleoseeps seem to have a definite life span, being buried by newer sediments after "death."

As we consider alternative mechanisms for karst-like features, seep morphologies such as pockmarks, piping and rills, and seep precipitates are most relevant. Another significant seep feature is the endogenous cave — a cave generated by corrosive fluids ascending through the sedimentary deposits.

Pockmarks are crater-like depressions ranging from less than 3 to 2,300 feet (1 to 700 m) across, and from 3 to 100 feet (1 to 30 m) in depth (Silvestru 2001). Their density may be as high as 93/mi² (240/km²) (Hovland and Judd 1988). Similar densities of sinkholes are also present in modern karst areas (Silvestru 1997). My investigations in the Padis Plateau area (Romania), based on extrapolating measurements from areas smaller than one square kilometer, have revealed densities up to 108 per square mile (280/km²). At such densities, subsequent evolution of the ocean bottom could easily shape the pocked surface into what would appear to be an incipient cockpit, mogote, or tower karst (Ford and Williams 1992). Once seep activity ceased, these features would be buried and preserved. If at some later stage they emerged, karstification processes would certainly exploit such "inherited" conditioning, and true tower karst would form very quickly. Sometimes such features have survived on steep submarine slopes without being buried. For example, grooves and pitting have been identified at depths ranging from 3,280 to 9,840 feet (1,000 to 3,000 m) off the Iberian Peninsula (Maire 1986). This is far too deep to be explained by Quaternary eustatic sea level fluctuations.

There is a secondary feature of tower karst that has not been satisfactorily explained by normal karstification processes. This is the *case-hardening of residual hills and limestone surfaces* (Ford and Williams 1992). However, it is easily explained by seep activity. Case-hardening is an induration of highly porous, weak limestone on the slopes of tower karst. It is currently interpreted as a secondary feature, although ^{230}Th/^{234}U dating has failed to yield interpretable ages (Ford and Williams 1992). Explaining case-hardening as a syngenetic seep-generated carbonate deposit on the slopes of pockmarks is logical and elegant. Obviously, radiometric dating of such features would be of little use, even if possible.

Standard karst interpretations try to relate "buried karsts" to plate tectonics, since most large carbonate deposits were laid down on passive continental margins. Interpreting "buried karsts" as seep-induced pseudokarst — given that seeps are also present on continental margins — makes a lot of sense, and this syngenetic seep scenario dramatically reduces the time scale for the karstification processes. Most signature-relevant seeps are hydrocarbon-generated. Gold (1999) has convincingly shown that this overlap has to do with ascending primordial hydrocarbons that gradually lose hydrogen and combine with calcium oxides to form calcite. Thus, potentially huge volumes of neo-carbonates could be available not only for such pseudokarst features but also for limestone diagenesis! Thus, features usually defined as "paleokarst" are questionable and can be interpreted as pseudokarst instead.

References

Aubert, D. 1967. Éstimation de la solution superficielle dans le Jura. *Buletin de la Societé Spéléologique Vaudoise*, 324, 69(8):365–376.

Austin, S.A. 1980. Origin of limestone caves. *Impact* 79:vii–viiii.

Back, W., N. Cherry, and B.B. Henshaw. 1966. Chemical equilibrium between the water and minerals of a carbonate aquifer. *Bulletin of the National Speleological Society* 28(3):119–126.

Bakalowicz, M. 1977. Relations entre la dynamique des eaux du karst et les processus de karstification. *Proceedings of the 7th International Speleological Congress*: 10–12 (Sheffield).

———. 1986. La karstification: processus, modèles et examples. *Proceedings of the 9th International Speleological Congress*. III:59–63 (Barcelona).

Bakalowicz, M., D.C. Ford, T.E. Miller, A.N. Palmer, and M.V. Palmer. 1987. Thermal genesis of solution caves in the Black Hills, South Dakota. *Geological Society of America Bulletin* 99:729–738.

Balázs, D. 1962. Beiträge zur Speläologi des Süchinesichen Karstgebeites. *Karst es Barlangkutatás*. 2:3–82 (Budapest).

Bini, A., M. Cremaschi, P. Forti, and G. Perna. 1988. Paleokarstic fills in Iglesiente (Sardinia, Italy): sedimentary processes and age. *Annales de la Societé Géologiqué du. Belgique* 111:149–161 (Liège).

Bleahu. M.D. 1974. *Morfologia Carstica*. Ed. Stiintifica, Bucuresti.

Bögli, A. 1964. Corrosion par mélange des eaux. *Intern. Journ. Speleol.* 1, part 1+2:61–70.

Bosák, P., D.C. Ford, J. Glazek, and I. Horaček (editors). 1989. *Paleokarst — A Systematic and Regional View*. Prague: Academia.

Bosák, P. 1995. Paleokarst of the Bohemian Massif in the Czech Republic: short review, *Acta Carsologica* XXIV:109–121 (Ljubliana).

Cociuba, I., and E. Silvestru. 1989. Hypothesis on a genetical relation between the actual karst and the bauxite-bearing paleokarst at the Jurassic/Creatceous boundary in the Piatra Craiului Mountains (Romania), *Travaux de l'Institut de Spéologie 'Emil Racovitza'* XXVIII:87–90 (Bucharest).

Davidescu, F.D., A. Tenu, and A. Slavescu. 1991. Environmental isotopes in karst hydrology: a layout of problems with exemplifications in Romania. *Theoretical and Applied Karstology* 4:77–86 (Bucharest).

Dubliyamski, V.N. 1980. Hydrothermal Karst in Alpine Folded Belt of Southern Part of U.S.S.R.. *Kras I speleologia*. 3(12):18–36.

Ford, D.C., and P.W. Williams. 1992. *Karst Geomorphology and Hydrology*. London: Chapman & Hall.

Ford, T.D., and C.H.D. Cullingford. 1976. *The Science of Speleology*. London-New York-San Francisco: Academic Press.

Gold, T. 1999. *The Deep Hot Biosphere*. New York: Copernicus.

Hanshaw, B.B., W. Back, and M. Rubin. 1965. Carbonate equilibria and radiocarbon distribution related to groundwater flow in the Floridan limestone aquifer, U.S.A, Hydr.des roches fissure. *Actes des Géologié de Dubrovnik*, AIHS-UNESCO, vol. II: 601–614.

Hill, C.A. 1987. Geology of Carlsbad Caverns and other caves of the Guadalupe Mountains, New Mexico and Texas. *New Mexico Bureau of Mines and Mineral Resources Bulletin* 117.

Hovland, M., and A.G. Judd. 1988. *Seabed Pockmarks and Seepages — Impact on Geology, Biology and the Marine Environment*. London: Graham and Trottman.

Humphreys, R., J.R. Baumgradner, S.A. Austin, and A. Snelling. 2003. Helium diffusion rates support accelerated nuclear decay. In R.E. Walsh (editor). *Proceedings of the Fifth International Conference on Creationism*, technical symposium sessions. Pittsburgh, PA: Creation Science Fellowship, p. 175–195.

Jeanin, P.Y. 1991. La région karstique du Nord du lac de Thoune (Suisse). *Actes de 9ͤ Congrès National de Spéléologie*, Charmey:123–126.

Jordan, R.H. 1950. An interpretation of Floridan karst. *Journal of Geology* 58(4):291–268.

Kovacs, J., and P. Muller. 1980. A Budai hegyek hévizes tevékanségyenek kialakulása és nyomai. *Karszt es Barlang* (ii):93–98.

Lauritzen, S.E., and J.E. Mylroie. 2000. Results of speleothem U/Th dating reconnaissance from the Hedelberg Plateau, New York. *Journal of Cave & Karst Studies*. April:20–26.

Lehmann, H. (editor). 1954. Das Karstphænomen in den Verschieden Klimazonen. *Erdkunde* 8:112–139.

Maire, R. 1986. Apropos des karsts sous-marins. *Karstologia* 7:55.

Maire, R., and Y. Quinif. 1989. Les dépôts de la galerie Aranzadi. *ARSIP* 16:6995.

Mangin, A. 1975. Contribution a l'étude hydrodinamique des aquiferes karstiques. Thèse Doct.Sci.Nat. in *Annales de Spéléologie* 29(3):283–332; (4):495–601; 30(1):21–124.

Mangin, A., and M. Bakalowicz. 1990. Le karst conique: sa genèse à partir de l'example du karst du sud de la Chine. *Comptes Rendues de l'Académie des Sciences de Paris*. 310(II):301–307.

Martonne, E., de. 1910. *Traité de Géographie Physique*. Paris.

Mârza, I., and E. Silvestru. 1988. First mention of the hydrothermal karst phenomenon associated to Neogene metasomatic suplhide ore deposits from Rodna Veche. Studia Universitatis "Babes-Bolyai." *Geologica-Geographica,Cluj-Napoca*, XXXIII: 77–81.

Moore, C.J. 1999. Fluid seeps at continental margins; a report of a workshop defining critical research issues affecting geology, biology, the oceans, and the atmosphere. www.soest.hawaii.edu/margins/seeps_workshop.html (as posted in 2004).

Muller, P., and I. Sarvary. 1977. Some aspects of developments in Hungarian speleology theories during the last ten years. *Karszt es Barlang* 53–59 (Budapest).

Pearson, P.N., P.W. Ditchfield, J. Singano, K.G. Harcourt-Brown, C.J. Nicholas, R.K. Olsson, N.J. Shackelton, and M.A. Hall. 2001. Warm tropical sea surface temperatures in the Late Cretaceous and Eocene epochs. *Nature* 413:482.

Schoeller, H. 1962. *Les Eaux Souterraines*. Paris: Masson.

Schrag, D.P. 1999. Effects of diagenesis on the isotopic record of Late Paleogene tropical sea surface temperatures. *Chemical Geology* 161:215–224.

Selley, R.C. 2000. *Applied Sedimentology*. London: Academic Press.

Silvestru, E. 1985. Aspects of karstification in the crystalline limestones on the southern slope of Rodnei Mountains. *Theoretical and Applied Karstology* 2:87–95 (Bucharest).

———. 1990. Propositions pour une classification litho-génétiquedes formes karstiques et apparentées. *Karstologia* 15:55–57 (France).

———. 1994. Karst and environment: a Romanian approach. In D. O'Halloran, C. Green, M. Harley, M. Stanley, and J. Knill (editors). *Geological and Landscape Conservation*. London: Geological Society, p. 221–225.

———. 1997. *Stratigrafia si sedimentologia depozitelor carstice din exo- si endocarstul zonei Padis-Cetatile Ponorului, Muntii Bihor*. PhD thesis, Universitatea «Babes-Bolyai» Cluj-Napoca, Romania.

———. 2000. Paleokarst — a riddle inside confusion. *Creation Ex Nihilo Technical Journal* 14 (3):100–108.

———. 2001. Bubbles of surprise. *TJ* 15(2):89–93.

———. 2003. A hydrothermal model of rapid post-Flood karsting. In Walsh, R.E. (editor). *Proceedings of the Fifth International Conference on Creationism*, technical symposium sessions. Pittsburgh, PA: Creation Science Fellowship, p. 233–239.

———. 2008. *The Cave Book*. Green Forest, AR: Master Books.

Silvestru, E., and L. Ghergari. 1994. On the paleokarst in the cave Ghetarul de la Scarisoara (Bihor Mountains, Romania). *Theoretical and Applied Karstology* 7:155–161 (Bucharest).

Soriaux, P. 1982. Contribution à l'étude de la sédimentation en milieu karstique. Le système Niaux-Lombrives-Sabart (Pyrénées ariégeoises). PhD thesis, «Paul Sabatier» University, Toulouse, Geol.régionale, structurale et appliquée, Laboratoire souterrain CNRS.

Sweeting, M. 1973. *Karst Landforms*. New York: Columbia University Press.

Tenu, A., and F. Davidescu. 1995. Environmental isotopic studies in karstic calcareous areas of Romania, *Theor. Appl. Karst.* 8:9–24 (Bucharest).

Titilozov, Z.K. 1983. *Akhali Atoni cave system*. Tbilisi: Metsniereba.

Vardiman, L., A. Snelling, and E. Chaffin (editors). 2000. *Radioisotopes and the Age of the Earth*. El Cajon, CA: Institute for Creation Research and Chino Valley, AZ: Creation Research Society.

———. 2005. *Radioisotopes and the Age of the Earth: Results of a Young-Earth Creationist Research Initiative*, El Cajon, CA: Institute for Creation Research and Chino Valley, AZ: Creation Research Society.

Wilson, A.M., W. Sanford, F. Whitaker, and P. Smart. 2001. Spatial patterns of diagenesis during geothermal circulation in carbonate platforms. *American Journal of Science* 301:727–752.

Chapter 5

Do Soils Indicate Long Ages?

Peter Klevberg • BS — Engineering Science, P.E.
Rick Bandy • BS — Forestry, minor in Soil Science

Abstract

Many believe that most soils require long periods of time to form. This argument has been used in an attempt to refute the Bible's claims for a global Flood only 5,000 years ago. In addition to arguments based on formation of existing soils, many geologists or paleopedologists see evidence of multiple fossil soil horizons or *paleosols* in the geologic record. Few, if any, of these researchers have examined carefully the assumptions behind their arguments. In this chapter, we define soil, examine the commonly recognized soil-forming factors, analyze the limitations of the soil-forming factor approach, and describe the complex interactions of environmental factors and soil-forming mechanisms. Arguments for the necessity of time in pedogenesis are summarized. Predictions by uniformitarian and diluvial approaches to natural history are compared to a rigorous analysis of soil-forming mechanisms. Data from soil science are more easily accommodated by a diluvial view of earth history.

Introduction

Uniformitarians claim that modern soil profiles may take millions of years to form — a challenge to the short time frame of the Bible. This chapter will examine those claims and demonstrate that observed soil formation rates, even for very heavily weathered soils, fit the diluvial time frame.

We will be contrasting the Establishment Geologic Paradigm (EGP) with the Diluvial Geological Paradigm (DGP). The EGP is the view of earth history that holds to gradualism, philosophic naturalism, an ancient earth, and evolutionism. Its counterpart, DGP, proffers catastrophism, supernaturalism, biblical history (in particular the Deluge), and creation.

What Is Soil?

Most think that soil is just "dirt." However, the definition is not that simple; there is considerable confusion and controversy over the definition by engineers, agriculturalists, and geologists (Hunt 1972). This controversy is described in appendix 1. We define *soil* in a nongenetic way as *an unconsolidated mixture of natural materials that serves or may serve as a rooting medium.*

Basic Characteristics of Soils

To understand how to predict and interpret soils in the real world, one must understand what influences a soil to appear and function as it does. Klevberg and Bandy (2003) describe five environmental factors that influence the type of soil formed. These include climate, parent material, geomorphology/topography, biology, and groundwater. The EGP substitutes time for groundwater, but there is a problem with including time as an environmental factor. The environmental factors and the time problem are described in appendix 2.

				Horizons: a sequence of layers found when soil is examined
O_i				Horizon of undecomposed organic matter
O_e				Organic horizon of partially decomposed organic matter (O_i & O_e usually absent on prairie soils)
A_p	A			Surface mineral horizon that has an accumulation of well-decomposed organic matter that coats the mineral particles and darkens the soil. A_p is used when surface layer is plowed. Granular structure common
	E			Subsurface horizon that has lost organic matter, clay, iron, or aluminum through eluviation (or other processes) with concentration of resistant sand and silt-sized particles. Platy structure common. Not common in prairie soils. More often found in forested soils
B_w	B_t		B_w	- Nontransitional mineral horizon characterized by: 1. Development of color contrast, blocky or prismatic structure, or both 2. No apparent illuviation
			B_t	- Mineral horizon characterized by: 3. Relatively greater concentration of silicate clay; may be entirely illuvial or partly epimorphic 4. Clay films, lamellae, bridges, or other evidence of illuviation
				B_w and B_t horizons are mutually exclusive.
B_k				Mineral horizon characterized by accumulations of calcium carbonate ($CaCO_3$). Not always present in soil profile
B_y				Mineral horizon characterized by accumulations of gypsum ($CaSO_4$). Not always present in soil profile
B_z				Mineral horizon characterized by accumulations of soluble salts. Not always present in soil profile
C				Mineral horizon that has been little affected by soil-forming processes but may be otherwise weathered.
C_r				Weakly consolidated bedrock or saprolite. It can be dug through with some difficulty. Roots do not penetrate except along fracture planes
R				Relatively unweathered bedrock. Generally penetrable only by drilling or specialized equipment

Figure 1. Generalized soil profile. Note: Other horizons are possible.

When all five factors are exactly the same, then the soil — no matter where — will be *exactly* the same, too. Change one of the factors and the soil will be different in one way or another. If one has a good understanding of each of these factors in a local area, one can predict with great accuracy what type of soil will be found at a given site.

Each soil type has its own set of characteristics. When one examines a soil pit closely, one will find a sequence of layers that soil scientists call *horizons*. The type and depth of each horizon are influenced by the five environmental factors. There are three major horizons that may be found in many soils: a major surface horizon, a major horizon in the subsoil, and a major horizon in the substratum (figure 1). The surface and subsurface may have an O, A, and/or an E horizon. All three of these may be present, or only one may be present. The B horizon is considered the subsoil, and a C horizon is considered the substratum. The R horizon signifies hard bedrock. Each of these horizons can be subdivided based on how the environmental factors have influenced a particular soil, as shown in figure 1.

Long Age Claims for Common Soils

The formation of distinctive horizons, contrasting in texture, fabric, mineralogy, color, and organic content, has been used as an argument for long periods of time for soil formation far in excess of biblical history (Birkeland 1974, 1984; Chadwick et al. 1994; Natural Resources Conservation Service 1997; Weaver 1989). Although uniformitarian soil scientists acknowledge that some soils form quickly (Birkeland 1984; Bown and Kraus 1981), several soil orders are widely believed to require long periods of time to generate (see appendix 3). The geographic ranges where the various soil orders dominate is shown in figure 2.

Others argue more directly against the Deluge — that soil conditions at the end of the Deluge would have been

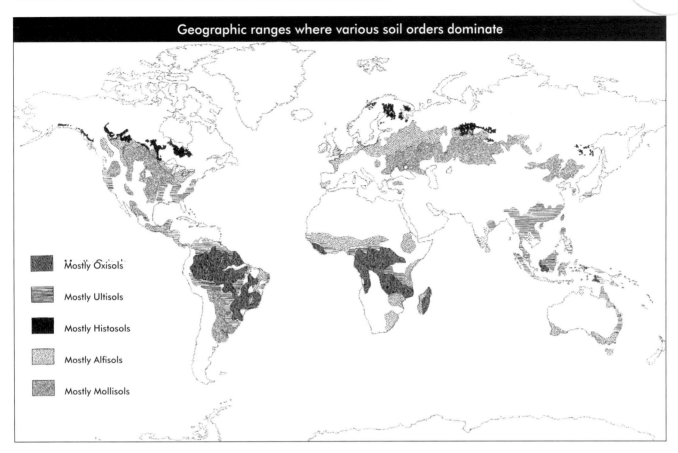

Figure 2. Dominant soil orders of the world. Modified from USDA sources and Brady (1974).

inimical to plant life (Harding 2001; Yake 1995). However: (1) seed survival during the Genesis Flood appears reasonable (Howe 1971); (2) the initial salt content of parent materials at the end of the Deluge is not known; and (3) NaCl (salt) is relatively mobile and easily leached.

How Soil Forms

Clearly, time estimates require a good understanding of the processes involved in soil formation (pedogenesis) and how they act over time. These processes are really influenced by: (1) the environment in which the soil forms (the environmental factors), and (2) within the environment certain mechanisms *physically* acting within the soil to alter the parent material. These processes are illustrated in figures 3 and 4. Traditionally, uniformitarian geologists have approached pedogenesis just in terms of *soil-forming* (environmental) *factors*, described in appendix 2.

The Four Soil-Forming Mechanisms

Soil-forming mechanisms (table 1) are those processes that actually turn the parent material into soil (figure 4). The rates at which soil-forming mechanisms operate and the pathways they follow are determined by environmental

factors (figure 3). The four mechanisms include (1) epigenesis, (2) physical weathering, (3) leaching, and (4) presence of organic matter.

Epigenesis

Epigenesis describes mineral transformations due to chemical weathering. As one of the most important mechanisms in soil development, it has received much attention. In general, silicate minerals are transformed into silicate clays (physils), hydrous aluminum, and iron oxides. Carbonate minerals are typically dissolved, leaving a silicate residuum. In general, weathering rates are greatest for minerals at the top of Bowen's Reaction Series[1] (figure 5) and least for quartz, at the bottom.

Physical Weathering

Physical weathering includes the breakdown of individual rock and mineral grains and translocation of soil particles

---

1. Bowen's Reaction Series is a hierarchy of igneous minerals illustrating an upward-increasing elevation of temperature and pressure for mineral stability, with quartz formed at the lowest temperature and pressure and olivine and anorthite at the highest.

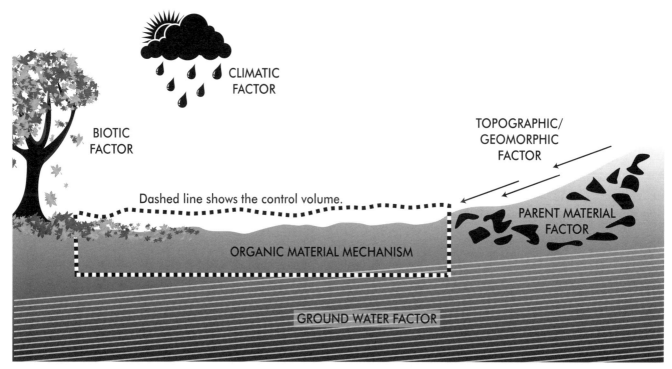

Figure 3. The five soil-forming environments. The dashed area is blown up in figure 4.

(i.e., particle movement within the control volume). The former produces an increasingly finer-grained texture. The latter enhances soil development by the formation of argillic or cambic horizons, color contrasts, and stratification. Physical processes, including surface winnowing by wind or water and translocation in the subsurface (eluviation/illuviation), tend to segregate particles by size and may result in a texture-contrast soil with visually identifiable horizons. Bioturbation also mixes different-sized particles and blends organic matter, producing thicker and better-developed topsoils.

Leaching

Leaching of ions from the upper soil horizons (the solum) by meteoric water is a function of vadose zone hydrology and geochemistry. Free water must be available to transport soluble bases and cations from the upper portion of the solum, and it must remain in contact with mineral grains or hygroscopic water long enough for ions to enter solution. Soluble substances in soil organic matter may also be leached, sometimes resulting in complex reactions with minerals and ions released from the minerals. Iron and aluminum oxides are most resistant to leaching

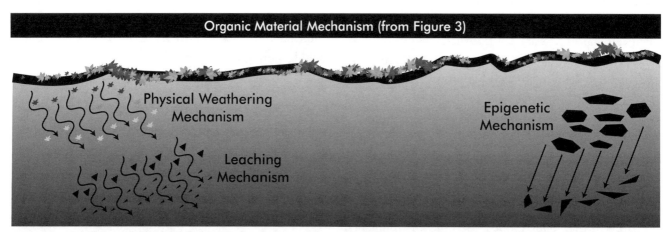

Figure 4. The four physical mechanisms for the formation of a soil

Table 1. The Four Soil-Forming Mechanisms

MECHANISM	DESCRIPTION	DESCRIPTION
E	Epigenetic soil-forming mechanism	Change in soil state due to effects of epigenesis
P	Physical weathering soil-forming mechanism	Change in soil state due to effects of physical weathering
L	Leaching soil-forming mechanism	Change in soil state due to effects of leaching of ions from the solum
O	Organic matter soil-forming mechanism	Change in soil state due to effects of organic matter

and tend to persist in highly leached soils. Ions leached from the upper A soil horizon may be redeposited in the subjacent B horizon, often forming a calcic (B_k), gypsic (B_y), natric (B_n), salic (B_z), or spodic (usually B_s, B_h, or B_{hs}) horizon.

Organic Matter

Organic matter in the soil is contributed by plants, animals, and microbes. It is essential to soil productivity and affects other soil-forming mechanisms.

> As a result of the near-surface breakdown of dead organic matter, the carbon dioxide concentration at the biosphere/lithosphere interface can be up to ten times greater than the normal atmospheric level. Around living plant roots the hydrogen-ion concentration is even greater (Paton et al. 1995, p. 17).

Organic matter may accumulate above mineral matter (an O horizon) or mix with mineral matter to form topsoil (A horizon).

Pedogenesis and Paradigms

Now that the mechanisms that result in pedogenesis are understood, we can address the argument against the DGP. The basic argument is that the Bible allows insufficient time for observed soil profiles. Since five soil orders (oxisols, ultisols, histosols, alfisols, and mollisols) discussed in appendix 3 are especially thought to require too long to form, we will evaluate rates of change in soil state due to soil-forming mechanisms for these soils and the influence of environmental factors on these rates within both paradigms of earth history. Parts of the world where these soils are most common are shown in figure 2. The variables governing soil formation are myriad and complex in their interaction (figure 6), and include chemical reactions

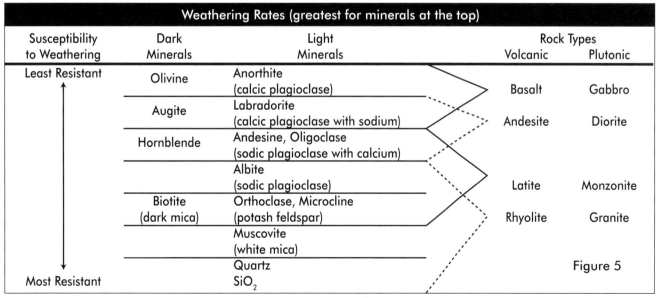

Figure 5. Bowen's Reaction Series. Susceptibility to weathering of various minerals is greatest for those that crystallize first. Not illustrated are the effects of crystal size (larger crystals are more susceptible to weathering) and fractures or defects.

and physical processes governed by thermodynamic rate laws (Lavkulich 1969). None of these environmental variables — climate, parent material, topography, biology, groundwater — or soil-forming mechanisms — epigenesis, translocation, leaching, or organic decay — are independent of time. Even parent material is a function of time when mineral transport is acknowledged. Therefore, time is often *assumed,* and *presuppositions* about natural history profoundly affect inferences about pedogenesis. EGP claims must be shown to be independent of those axioms if its criticisms are to be meaningful.

Because time is implicit in the traditional EGP soil-forming factor variables, complexities abound in analyzing rates of soil formation. Because most soil formation occurred in the past, pedogenesis is properly *history*; science, while valuable, is subordinate. Predictions of physical and chemical changes in soil formation are influenced by observers' paradigms of earth history — the EGP or DGP.

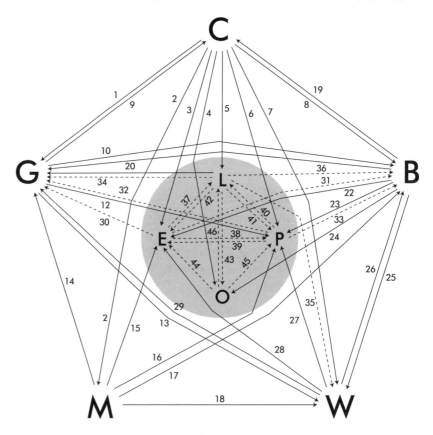

The Variables Involved in Soil Formation

Figure 6. Interrelationships of environmental factors and soil-forming mechanisms

Soil History Based on View of Earth History

EGP soil scientists (pedologists) tend to assume that soil formation has been a slow, gradual process (Brady 1974; Natural Resource Conservation Service 1997; Weaver 1989). By contrast, diluvialists (recognizing the influence of environmental factors on soil-forming mechanisms) emphasize *individual* factors and assume that rates have varied in the past — perhaps greatly. They also assume that types of soil formation might have varied in the past, perhaps significantly. Finally, diluvialists would predict that many soils have complex histories. Specific differences between the two paradigms of earth history are summarized as follows:

EGP Expectations

- Climate influences pedogenesis over long ages, and climate change has been gradual, allowing soils to reach or approach equilibrium with their environment.
- Parent material exerts the principal influence at the onset of pedogenesis but becomes less

important over time. Thus, it is unimportant for mature soils.

- Geography is constantly changing and exerts, therefore, a constantly changing influence on pedogenesis.
- Biology is strongly influenced by climate. Its influence, though sometimes slight, may result in a great cumulative effect over time.
- Groundwater is secondary, largely determined by climate and topography.
- Epigenesis is largely determined by climate and topography. Over time, many soils reach maturity, and specific physils are assumed to be products of epigenesis.
- Greater time favors translocation of physils and ions, resulting in formation of soil horizons, including argillic and cambic horizons.
- Greater time leads to highly leached soils.

While organic matter rapidly reaches equilibrium in soil, it can have a great effect on both leaching and the formation of horizons over time.

DGP Expectations

- Climate has exerted its influence on pedogenesis over a relatively short period of postdiluvian time. Climate change has been significant — possibly exponential, damped sinusoidal, or stochastic — and was likely warmer and wetter in early post-diluvian time.

- Parent material exerted the principal influence at the onset of pedogenesis; it is likely to be more important than perceived by EGP adherents. Parent material may exhibit stratification, oxidation, well-developed weathering profiles, and an initial physil content that might falsely be considered pedogenic.

- Geography has probably changed little since the Deluge, and topography may have remained constant in many places. Their effect, therefore, has been a relatively constant modifying influence on the other factors.

- Biology is strongly influenced by climate. Organic matter could be expected on much of the ground surface or incorporated into sediments at the onset of the postdiluvian period (Scheven 1996). A warmer, wetter climate would have encouraged rapid growth of plants and both microscopic and macroscopic animals, expediting soil formation.

- Groundwater would begin at its maximum, with saturated ground and a moist climate, approaching modern levels in response to climatic changes, topography, and hydrogeologic properties of the parent material.

- Epigenesis may have been profoundly affected by significant climate change, atmospheric aerosols, and high carbon dioxide levels due to decaying organic matter.

- Given limited time, translocation of physils would be slight in some soils, and a nonlinear (possibly exponentially decreasing) function with time.

- Highly leached soils, in both extent and magnitude, would result from parent material that was already leached by geologic processes, accelerated weathering in the postdiluvial climate, or more

rapid leaching rates than expected for the modern environment.

- Time for organic leaching and bioturbation would be small. Thus, pedogenesis attributed to these processes would be expected to be less or modern rates may be understated or past rates may have been significantly higher, if climate was different.

Comparisons between the Two Paradigms

Based on the above expectations from the two paradigms, the differences of how each views the traditional five soil-forming environmental factors are expanded in appendix 4.

In regard to the actual soil-forming mechanisms, which are influenced by the soil-forming environment, the differences between the two paradigms are analyzed in appendix 5.

Traditional Views in Light of Modern Data

A century of pedologic research has not validated the old-earth natural history. Instead, the complexity of pedogenesis has stymied attempts to infer times of formation from soil "maturity." Newer dating methods suffer from circular reasoning and the interdependence of so-called independent methods (Klevberg 2000). In fact, estimates based on the EGP actually produce soil-forming rates lower than those observed operating today (table 2)!

The DGP envisions an initial maximum of soil-formation rates immediately after the Deluge, declining to the present rate for many soils. These expectations are more compatible with observed rates than EGP predictions. Non-zero initial values, the result of organic and inorganic diluvial detritus, would further reduce the requisite time to reach the current state of soil development. Finally, soils are not static: *some profiles probably could not have been preserved as long as envisioned by the EGP.*

Pedogenesis and the Question of Time

In spite of uniformitarian claims that pedogenesis requires much greater time than available in the DGP, observed processes and their rates do not support those claims. However, since they are pressed particularly on five types of soils (appendix 3), we will examine each of those types (appendix 6).

Evaluating Rates of Pedogenesis

Evaluating rates of pedogenesis and the history of particular soils is difficult:

Table 2. Comparison of Expected Rates of Soil Formation

DGP/EGP[1]	Environmental Factors[2]				
Soil-Forming Mechanism[3]	C	M	G	B	W
E	►	►	NA	►	►
P	►	►	0	◎	►
L	►	NA	0	►	►*
O	►	►*	NA	►/◎	NA

[1]Qualitative comparison of DGP to EGP: ► soil formation due to indicated relationship more rapid in DGP scenario than EGP scenario; ◎ soil formation expected to be more extensive in EGP than DGP; 0 degree of expected soil formation similar in DGP and EGP; NA relationship between indicated factors not apparent or deemed minor.
[2]Environmental factors: C - climatic factor, M - parent material factor, G - geomorphic factor, B - biotic factor, W - groundwater factor.
[3]Soil-forming mechanisms: E - epigenesis (mineral transformation), P - physical weathering, L - leaching, O - soil organic matter.
*Evaluation based on inferred initial conditions.

As more pedological research is carried out and more soils are observed and studied, the pedologist is recognizing that many of the soils occurring on the present landscape are polygenetic soils which have formed in part under environments different from those of the present (Lavkulich 1969, p. 26).

Age estimates of soils based on assumptions of linear weathering or leaching rates are grossly simplistic (Ruhe 1975). Vreeken (1984) reviewed methods of dating soils by dating surfaces, average pedogenic index, variable pedogenic index, paleopedogenic index, and soil-landscape analysis. He exposed faulty assumptions and circular reasoning that render these methods untenable. He is not alone.

Evidence has been presented that pedogenic processes have either been discontinuous through time, or there has been considerable variation in intensity of process. This work shows that soils scientists should be cautious about conjectures regarding soil genesis based largely upon soil-profile characteristics (Daniels et al. 1971, p. 76).

Because soil formation is so complex and site-specific, obtaining a quantitative mathematical description of pedogenesis is virtually impossible:

In order to compare soil data on even a semiquantitative basis, *a time scale must be adopted* (Birkeland 1974, p. 153, emphasis added).

In other words, *one's view of natural history determines his bias in evaluating soil data.* Thus, soil formation is no less compatible with the DGP than the EGP. Furthermore, as new research is indicating, the DGP appears to be a superior framework for soil research.

Conclusions

As is true of many other phenomena documented in this book, anticreationist arguments usually boil down to uniformitarians repackaging their assumptions (implicit or explicit) as *conclusions*, forcing them on particular phenomena with little regard to the scientific details, and then claiming that their "scientific" conclusions disprove the DGP. The flaws in that approach are too numerous to mention.

Soil formation is ultimately an historic question dependent in part on the presuppositions of existing paradigms of natural history. We have shown that the long ages required for soil formation rely less on empirical data than on the old-earth assumptions of the EGP — especially its uniformitarian bias toward linear rates of soil formation through history. A number of faulty assumptions drive equally faulty conclusions:

- Parent material is assumed to be unweathered, unstratified, and barren of "mature" physils or organic matter.

- Rates of soil-forming mechanisms are assumed to be linear and similar to modern rates, despite evidence of significant past climate change and evidence that soil profile development would affect the rates of soil-forming mechanisms.

- Faulty "dating" and other methods that *assume* the EGP are used to assign soil formation rates independent of the pedologic data.

- Physical weathering over long periods is invoked where rapid chemical weathering may have caused the same features.

- Pedologic explanations are sought where geologic explanations are more likely (e.g., bauxite bone beds).

Current knowledge of pedogenesis demonstrates that even "problem soils" are congruent with the DGP. Oxisols may form more rapidly than commonly believed, and probably reflect the influence of parent material more strongly than climate. Evidence for a purely pedological formation of oxisols is equivocal, while evidence for a geologic origin of some oxisols is clear. Many may be polygenetic. Ultisols and alfisols would have formed more quickly in the warmer, wetter postdiluvial climate (a nonlinear, decreasing function). Histosol and mollisol formation is readily accommodated within the DGP, even using rates of organic matter accumulation assumed by EGP adherents.

The natural history scenario of the DGP predicts more rapid soil formation than the EGP, and accumulating data support it. Even oxisols and ultisols can form within the 4,000–5,000 years since the Deluge. The biblical record is not contradicted by pedologic data and is in many cases superior to the EGP in interpreting observed soil characteristics and rates of pedogenesis.

Appendix 1. The Soil Definition Controversy

Soil scientists generally define *soil* as the natural rooting medium of plants (Brady 1974). Typically, this means that soil extends to a depth of less than two meters from the surface, even though the sedimentary deposit may extend much deeper. To geologists and engineers, *soil* is any surficial, unconsolidated sediment or collection of mineral grains and other solid particles (McCarthy 1988, p. 1). Thus, from a geologic perspective, soil may extend down tens or even hundreds of meters. The geologic/engineering definition treats soil as a category of sedimentary deposit or a result of in situ weathering. It does not necessarily recognize development of features distinctive to *soil-forming processes* that affect the suitability of the material as a rooting medium.

Blatt et al. (1972) defined soil as unconsolidated earth material marked by the presence of soil horizons and the direct influence of organic matter. According to Selley (1976, p. 54), it is "that part of the weathering profile which is the domain of biological processes. Soil consists of rock debris and humus." Soil is distinguished from underlying regolith by (1) characteristic layering, (2) an organic-rich and biochemically weathered upper layer, (3) abundance of organisms, and (4) more intense weathering (Brady 1974). Olson (1981, p. 1) defined soils as "discrete bodies produced by interactions of climate, vegetation, and surficial geologic materials." Some of these definitions exclude unconsolidated, surficial earth materials where biologic processes are minimal (e.g., in Antarctica).

Pedology (the study of soils) considers the soil as a natural body and places minor emphasis on its immediate practical utilization (Brady 1974, p. 6).

While pedological definitions such as these may be incomplete or tautological (use the proposed definition to define themselves), they emphasize what distinguishes *soil* from other earth materials. Soils definitions and taxonomy continue to be areas of debate. Early definitions were largely theory driven and genetic (based on assumed origin):

> . . . whereas in 1938 the emphasis was explicitly on zonal pedogenesis, with classification being derived from it, by 1975 the emphasis was almost entirely classificatory, with zonal pedogenesis being implicit at best (Paton et al. 1995, p. 9).

Pedogenesis is the formation of a soil from mineral and organic matter.

Lavkulich (1969) did somewhat better. In a ponderous but comprehensive definition, he included the requirement that soil-forming factors must have acted over time to differentiate *soil* from its parent material. But the definition still remained rooted to history, while Paton et al. (1995) emphasized the shift toward scientific (i.e., objective, descriptive) soil classification criteria and away from an unscientific (i.e., subjective, genetic) approach to soil science. As they noted (p. 9):

> The continuing belief by a considerable number of pedologists that, by using this approach of more precise definition in soil classification, a better pedogenic model would eventually emerge reflects a belief in induction. This means that objective and unbiased conclusions can only be reached by measuring and describing what is encountered without having any prior hypotheses, or preconceived expectations. This viewpoint had been decisively repudiated as long ago as the middle of the nineteenth century, when it was shown to lead to an intellectual impasse and one moreover that no scientist had followed.

They are right insofar as rationalism or positivism is implied. They are wrong insofar as they address induction as an *element* in the scientific method, Popper and others notwithstanding (Klevberg 1999; Malcolm 1997; Reed 1998, 2000a). Contrary to Paton et al. (1995), this attempt to correct the inherently unscientific emphasis on zonal pedogenesis, with its "degree of maturity," has been helpful. Generally, changes in soil taxonomy over the past

Table 3. Comparison of Parameters — Soil-Forming Factors

FACTOR	DESCRIPTION	NOTATION	DESCRIPTION
C	Climatic soil-forming factor	$\partial S/\partial C$	Change in soil state as a result of climatic influences
M	Parent material soil-forming factor	$\partial S/\partial M$	Change in soil state as a result of mineralogical influences
G	Geomorphic (topographic) soil-forming factor	$\partial S/\partial G$	Change in soil state as a result of influences of topography or geomorphology
B	Biotic soil-forming factor	$\partial S/\partial B$	Change in soil state as a result of influences of vegetation, animals, and microbes
t	Time soil-forming factor	$\partial S/\partial t$	Change in soil state due to time

century show that soil science (in contrast to many disciplines) has become more scientific and less subjective. Following that trend, we define soil in a non-genetic way as *an unconsolidated mixture of natural materials that serves or may serve as a rooting medium.*

Appendix 2. Soil-Forming versus Environmental Factors

Soil formation is a complex process with many variables (Brady 1974). Isolation of independent variables is difficult; there is no comprehensive equation of state for soil. More general soil-forming factors are therefore applied: complex variables that can act in independent, dependent, or interdependent ways. These include the following: (1) climate, (2) parent material, (3) topography (or geography), (4) biology, and (5) time (table 3). This approach relies on the assumption that the variables, plus accessory factors, suffice to define any soil. These factors are purely observational, and their validity depends on the skill and experience of the investigators. Though not strictly quantitative, it represents a distinct advantage over earlier, speculative approaches (Jenny 1941). The fact that these variables are often not independent in the field often precludes a rigorous quantitative assessment (Birkeland 1974).

Climate

Climate is likely the most important factor (Brady 1974), though some disagree (Paton et al. 1995). Weaver (1989, p. 106) stated, "The rate of chemical weathering and soil formation is largely controlled by climate." Because climate includes both temperature and moisture variables, it determines the rate of soil formation as well as many secondary minerals resulting from epigenesis. It is worth noting that the assumption that soil formation requires extended time tends to exaggerate the role of climate (Brady 1974; Selley 1976). Both EGP and DGP

researchers acknowledge significant climate change in the past, though they differ on the extent of the past itself.

Parent Material

Parent material is an important variable; distinct soils have been documented under similar conditions of climate, topography, and vegetation (figure 7). Parent material can change over time as regolith is added by deposition or removed by erosion. But what constitutes parent material? Some define it as the subjacent, unweathered bedrock (Paton et al. 1995; Tarbuck and Lutgens, 1984); some as all the regolith beneath recognizable soil horizons (Brady 1974); and some as the soil state at an arbitrarily selected initial time (Jenny 1941, p. 52–53):

> In view of these logical and practical difficulties, we prefer to define parent material as *the initial state of the soil system* and thus avoid special reference to the strata below the soil, which may or may not be parent material.
>
> Mathematically speaking, we should say that parent material becomes soil after an infinitely small time interval (Jenny 1941, p. 45).

Some believe that parent material is initially the most important soil-forming factor, with climate becoming dominant later (Weaver 1989). If so, the disparate soil types illustrated in figure 7 should become increasingly similar over time.

Topography (Geomorphology)

The importance of the topographic factor is illustrated by figure 8. Geomorphology (topography and geography) influences geohydrology, which is very important to soil genesis (Daniels et al. 1971). On a smaller scale, changes in slope can profoundly affect pedogenesis. Topographic position also influences microclimate, altering the temperature regime by slope position and the soil moisture regime by slope angle. It therefore modifies climate —

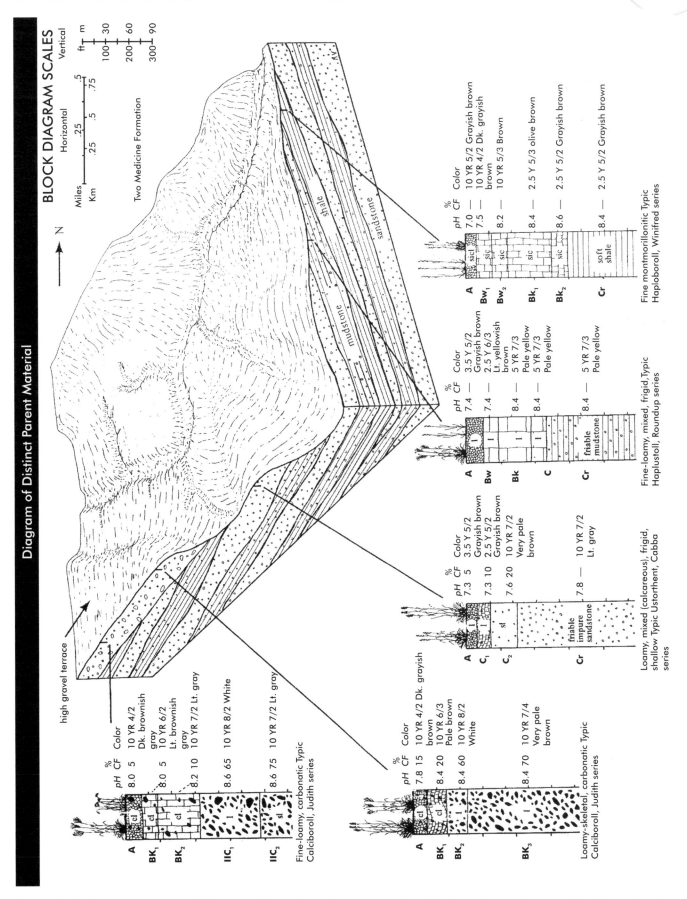

Figure 7. Role of parent material illustrated by soil development on Two Medicine Formation. Modified from Veseth and Montagne (1980).

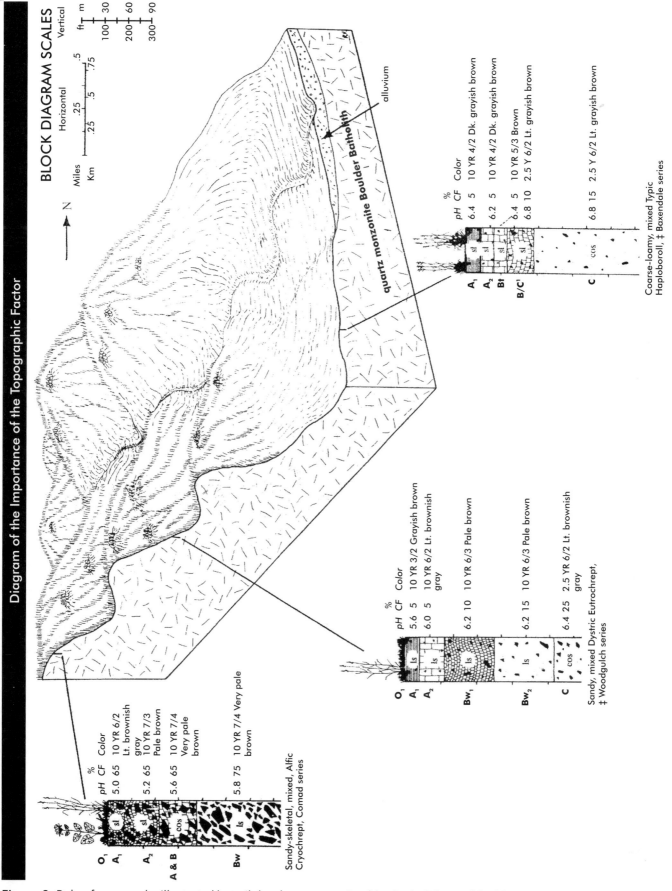

Figure 8. Role of geography illustrated by soil development on Boulder Batholith. Modified from Veseth and Montagne (1980).

probably its most important effect (Brady 1974). Geomorphologists emphasize the larger scale (i.e., geography), including inferred differences in parent material and the more general (and speculative) geologic history.

Biology

The biotic/biologic factor is important to epigenesis (Birkeland 1984), leaching, and fertility. According to some (Paton et al. 1995), biology is mainly responsible for the development of texture-contrast soil horizons. Microbes, vegetation, and animals all influence pedogenesis through both physical and chemical effects on parent material. Lichens can produce a measurable weathering effect on exposed rock surfaces (Birkeland 1984; Chadwick et al. 1994).

> As soon as plants gain a foothold in a weathering rock or in recently deposited soil material, the development of a soil profile has begun (Brady 1974, p. 310).

Decaying vegetation produces greatly elevated levels of carbonic acid, produces organic sesquioxide complexes, and binds, mixes, and moves soil particles (Paton et al. 1995; Brady 1974). The development of "laterites" (acroperox) is thought to depend on vegetation, based on its near absence prior to the "Devonian" (Blatt et al. 1972). Both plants and animals produce bioturbation; creatures as diminutive as ants and earthworms are capable of significant soil mixing (Paton et al. 1995).

Time

Time (t) is the factor that reveals the conflicts between the EGP and DGP. Weaver (1989, p. 106, emphasis added) revealed the EGP bias toward low rates and deep time when he stated:

> The rate of chemical weathering and soil formation is largely controlled by climate. Regardless of the climate, *the rate is relatively slow.*

Long periods of time are *assumed* and sometimes inferred, from: (1) differences in soils in glaciated versus unglaciated areas (Brady 1974), (2) argillic horizons or horizons of carbonate accumulation (Gile and Grossman 1968), or (3) rates of leaching or epigenesis (Chadwick et al. 1994).

> We see from this brief review of soils that long periods of time are required for physils to form in soils; superimposed soil profiles are common and

may represent as much as 100 m.y. [million years] of weathering (Weaver 1989, p. 107).

Most systems of soil classification contain, in some form or another, the idea of soil-forming factors. Among these, the factor time or degree of maturity occupies the most prominent role (Jenny 1941, p. 48).

In general, uniformitarianism distorts time in two ways: (1) as of primary importance to pedogenesis, and (2) as being in vast supply. Jenny's advice (1941, p. 31, emphasis added) should be heeded:

> The estimation of relative age or degree of maturity of soils is universally based on horizon differentiation. In practice, it is generally maintained that the larger the number of horizons and the greater their thickness and intensity the more mature is the soil. However, it should be kept in mind that *no one has ever witnessed the formation of a mature soil.* In other words, our ideas about soil genesis as revealed by profile criteria are inferences. They are theories, not facts.

The list of controversial soil types is quite long. Whatever the correct interpretation may be, it is evident that the issues center around the factor of time in soil formation.

Groundwater

Although not traditionally one of the major soil-forming factors considered by the EGP, we include groundwater as a significant agent of pedogenesis. The presence or absence of an elevated water table is important, and not implicit in any of the other factors. Jenny (1941, p. 92) noted that groundwater, sometimes included in topography/geography, is often on par with other factors, at least locally, though it may be neglected when more than about three millimeters below the ground surface. We consider the presence or absence of groundwater to be of greater significance than acknowledged by many establishment pedologists, though some have recognized its importance (Birkeland 1974; Daniels et al. 1971; Hunt 1972; Twidale 1990). Groundwater occurrence is affected by topography but may also affect topography.

> Many familiar landforms, major and minor, originate at the weathering front through the interplay of groundwater and bedrock (Twidale 1990, p. 36).

Proximity of groundwater also strongly influences vadose zone moisture through capillarity and vapor phase diffusion. The presence and movement of water in and through the soil is clearly one of the most important variables in the formation of soil from parent material (Brady 1974; Jenny 1941; Twidale 1990).

Problems with Time

DGP adherents note that expanded time is *assumed* by soil scientists. This is illustrated by a mathematical definition of the five variables (table 3). If climate is a function of time, how can it be considered a soil-forming factor distinct from time? Time is related to climate, not distinct from it. The same is true of the other factors. It is like defining white as "the color white" — one cannot use the same term to define itself! Instead, these factors are interdependent. As Jenny observed (1941, p. 267): "It is improbable that a function between two s properties that possesses general validity will ever be found." Others have also admitted this relationship (Birkeland 1974; Lavkulich 1969). If one could hold climate, parent material, geography, and biology constant while varying only time, *soil formation would not occur*, not in a year, not in a billion years, for it is the cumulative effect of these other processes that produces soil.

Time an Assumption in Pedogenesis

Some, though admitting this problem, have not seen its significance.

> Some workers have criticized Jenny for including time as one of the factors, because by itself time does nothing to a soil. Its importance, however, lies in the fact that most soil-forming processes are so slow that their effect on soil is markedly time-dependent (Birkeland 1974, p. 128).

Not only does this assertion fail to recognize the mathematical confusion introduced by simultaneously including time as a factor *and* an independent variable inherent to the other factors, but it displays a strong uniformitarian bias that cannot help resolve issues between the two paradigms. In practice, the only effective approach is an attempt to examine soils in similar and proximate locations where significant variation can be expected to be limited to only one factor (Birkeland 1974; Jenny 1941).

Time Ambiguities in Soil Boundary Conditions

Another cause of confusion is ambiguity in the initial conditions (the conditions a soil started with) of a given soil. It should be obvious that determination of the initial conditions of most soils is beyond the reach of science (Klevberg 1999). This may be alleviated in soil science studies by concentrating on observed changes in the soil state or simply assigning an arbitrary initial state (e.g., the state of the soil at the time observation began). A useful approach to this problem is that taken in physics and engineering: the use of a control volume — the space occupied by a specific soil, bounded vertically by the soil-atmosphere interface and arbitrarily assigned maximum rooting depth, and horizontally by common pedological demarcations between soils of a series. This enables us to distinguish between *environmental factors*, which principally influence soil formation from outside the control volume, and *soil-forming mechanisms*, operating within the control volume.

> A clear distinction should be made between factors and processes [soil-forming mechanisms] . . . processes form the soil. The factors, in contrast, define the state of the soil system (Birkeland 1974, p. 125).

Both environmental factors and soil-forming mechanisms are processes occurring within space-time; thus, expressions of changes in the soil state due to one of these processes must acknowledge its occurrence in time. We heed Birkeland's advice in distinguishing between environmental factors and soil-forming mechanisms and omitting time as a "soil-forming factor." The resulting environmental factors are shown in table 4.

Appendix 3. Soil Types That Are Believed to be Old

Some soil orders, including andisols, aridisols, gelisols, entisols, inceptisols, spodosols, and vertisols, can generally form quickly, usually within several centuries or less (Birkeland 1984; Fisher 1983; Hunt 1972; Jenny 1941; Lowe 1986). However, five soil types are especially considered indicative of long ages: (1) oxisols, (2) ultisols, (3) histosols, (4) alfisols, and (5) mollisols. Each of these will be described along with their old-age interpretations.

Oxisols

Oxisols, formerly known as *laterites* (1938 classification) are the most highly weathered soils (figure 9), typical of hot climates with nearly year-round moist conditions. They occupy land surfaces considered "geologically old" and occur mostly in the tropical and subtropical regions.

Table 4. The Five Environmental Factors of Pedogenesis

FACTOR	DESCRIPTION	DESCRIPTION
C	Climatic environmental factor	Change in soil state as a result of climatic influences
M	Parent material environmental factor	Change in soil state as a result of mineralogical influences
G	Geomorphic (topographic) environmental factor	Change in soil state as a result of influences of topography or geomorphology
B	Biotic environmental factor	Change in soil state as a result of influences of vegetation, animals, and microbes
W	Groundwater environmental factor	Change in soil state due to groundwater effects

The oxic subsurface horizon is generally very high in low-activity clay-size particles, predominantly hydrous iron and aluminum oxides. Weathering extends deeper than other soils. Combined with intense leaching, it removes much of the silica from the silicates in the oxic horizon (Brady and Weil 1999). Boundaries between subsurface horizons are indistinct, giving a uniform appearance with depth. Low-activity clays have a limited capacity to hold nutrients such as Ca^{++}, Mg^{++}, and K^+, resulting in low natural fertility and medium to strongly acidic soils. The lack of a unifying climatic similarity in their present distribution suggests climate change *after* soil formation or transport of a highly weathered parent material to arid areas (U.S.D.A. 1999). This intense weathering leads most pedologists to assign long ages:

> . . . residual deposits such as laterite require prolonged intensive chemical weathering for them to reach maturity (Selley 1976, p. 62).

Some believe oxisols require at least 100,000 years to form (Birkeland 1984), and some oxisols are thought to be more than one million years old based on amino acid dating and other criteria (Birkeland 1974; Boardman 1985). Nahon (1986) asserted that ferricretes (acrorthox or acroperox) require one to six million years to form. Retallack (1990, p. 112) went even further:

> The advanced weathering of these soils is due in part to their great age, often amounting to tens of millions of years.

Ultisols

Ultisols also exhibit a deeply leached weathering profile (figure 10) and are formed by clay mineral weathering, translocation of clays to an argillic or kandic horizon, and

leaching of base-forming cations from the profile (Brady and Weil 1999). They are more highly weathered and acidic than alfisols, but less acidic than oxisols (Brady and Weil 1999). They are commonly found on land surfaces considered "Pleistocene" or older according to the EGP.

Figure 9. Topical oxisol (m = meters, ft = feet). From USDA photograph.

Image of Utisol

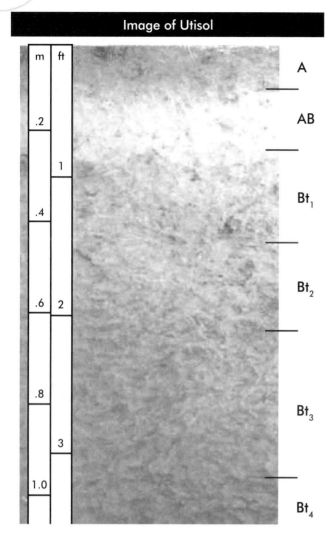

Figure 10. Typical ultisol (m = meters, ft = feet). From USDA photograph.

Histosols

Histosols are organic-rich soils, such as peat. They have undergone minimal profile development because of their anaerobic environment (figure 11), and consist of one or more thick layers of organic soil material. Generally, histosols have organic soil materials in more than half of the upper 80 centimeters (or upper two-thirds of a thin soil). These deposits accumulate in marshes, bogs, and swamps — habitats for water-loving plants such as pondweeds, cattails, sedges, reeds, mosses, shrubs, and even some trees. The residues of these plants sink into the water, generation after generation, creating anaerobic conditions that enhance their preservation (Brady and Weil 1999). Retallack (1990, p. 271) stated that 20 cm/year of peat accretion is a "maximum conceivable rate," while rates of less than 1 mm/year are typical (p. 272). On this basis, well-developed histosols in Finland, Siberia, North America, and elsewhere, sometimes several meters thick,

Image of Histosol

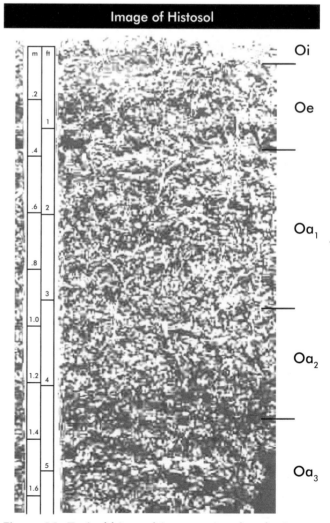

Figure 11. Typical histosol (m = meters, ft = feet). From USDA photograph.

They appear to form from a wide variety of parent materials, but few retain primary minerals that contain bases (with the exception of some micas). Most form under moist conditions in warm to tropical climates (Brady and Weil 1999), usually under forest vegetation. Ultisols commonly have both an epipedon and subsoil that are acidic and low in plant nutrients. When precipitation exceeds evapotranspiration (seasonally), water moves through the soils into a moist or wet substratum. The release of bases by weathering is equal to or less than removal by leaching, and most of the bases are commonly held in the vegetation and the upper few centimeters of the soils (USDA 1999). Some researchers believe ultisols in the United States required a million years or more to form (Birkeland 1984).

could require several thousand years to form. For example, at 0.5 mm/year, the Leteensuo Peat Bog in Finland, approximately 10 meters thick (Forsman et al. 1998), would be nearly 20,000 years old.

Alfisols

Alfisols form in cool-to-hot humid climates, semiarid tropics, and Mediterranean climates (figure 12). They are characterized by a diagnostic subsurface horizon in which silicate clay accumulates by illuviation (Brady and Weil 1999). This horizon is only moderately leached, and its cation exchange capacity is more than 35 percent saturated with base-forming cations (Brady and Weil 1999). Alfisols forming under a forest canopy have a leached, light-colored E horizon subjacent to the A horizon. In regions of mesic and frigid soil temperature regimes, alfisols are mostly found on deposits or surfaces classified "late Pleistocene." In warmer regions, they are also found

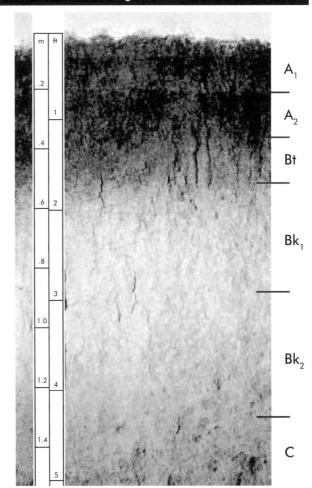

Figure 13. Typical mollisol (m = meters, ft = feet). From USDA photograph.

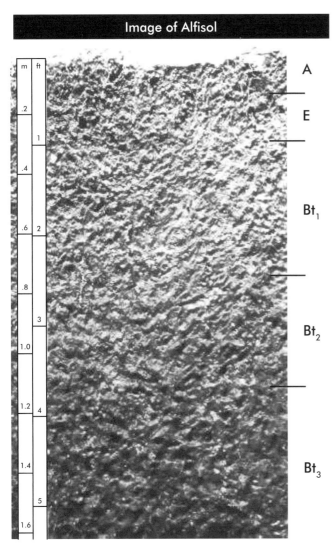

Figure 12. Typical alfisol (m = meters, ft = feet). From USDA photograph.

on "older" surfaces if the soils lose bases by leaching only infrequently or if there is an external source of bases, such as a calcareous dust from a desert (USDA 1999). Alfisols are thought to require at least 10,000 years to form (Birkeland 1984).

Mollisols

Mollisols exhibit strong surface horizon development (figure 13). The principal process in their formation is the accumulation of calcium-rich organic matter, largely from the dense root systems of prairie grasses, to form the thick, soft mollic epipedon that characterizes these soils (Brady and Weil 1999). Mollisols may have an argillic, albic, or cambic subsurface horizon. Most are found under grassland vegetation, and their high native fertility makes them among the world's most productive soils. Beyond the limits of glaciation, mollisols may exist on surfaces dating back

Table 5. Comparison of Parameters
Climatic Environmental Factor

Parameter	EGP	DGP
Climate	Very important to soil formation; largely dependent on G and various independent variables	Very important to soil formation; largely dependent on C_0, G and various independent variables
Initial Climate	On average, similar to current	May have been significantly warmer and wetter at end of Deluge
Climate Change	Gradual oscillations over long periods of time	Rapid change (probably exponential) following Deluge ($\partial C/\partial t \neq 0$)
Rate of Climate Change	Value small or zero	Value may have been large following Deluge ($\partial^2 C/\partial t^2 \neq 0$), decreasing with time
Climatic Factor	A roughly linear (gradual) change (soil formation) over vast periods of time	A generally exponential decrease in change (rate of soil formation) since Deluge

to the "mid-Pleistocene" or earlier (U.S.D.A. 1999). Mollisols are thought to require approximately 10,000 years to form when an argillic horizon is present, less when a cambic horizon exists (Birkeland 1984).

Appendix 4. DGP Versus EGP with the Five Environmental Factors

As summarized in table 5, expectations of the behavior of climate differ markedly between the EGP and DGP. In the biblical view of earth history, climate would probably describe a roughly exponential curve from initial conditions at the end of the Deluge to current "equilibrium" conditions (including normal fluctuations). Researchers in either paradigm recognize that historical climate change occurs, though unlike the EGP, the DGP suggests that climate change is nonlinear. Initial climatic conditions after the Genesis Flood would have been determined by long-term (equilibrium) factors in the antediluvian and diluvian periods, geomorphology after the global Flood, and postdiluvian ocean temperatures. Climatic equilibrium would have been dependent on atmospheric conditions (greenhouse gases, volcanic aerosols, variations in insolation) and changes in terrestrial conditions (land coverage by vegetation, water, or ice). The DGP envisions relatively warm, moist conditions in early postdiluvian time (Oard 1990), circumstances favorable to high rates of epigenesis, physical weathering, and leaching.

As summarized in table 6, expectations of the importance of parent material and nature of the "initial" materials differ significantly. According to the DGP, initial materials would result from the Deluge, and include unweathered rock, weathered rock, and unconsolidated sediment, depending on location. Very little fresh bedrock would

have been exposed by the waning currents; thus, the initial materials were not just homogeneous, unweathered rock. Retreating Flood water currents would have commonly deposited graded sequences of unconsolidated sediments. Thus, it may be difficult to differentiate between horizons resulting from diluvial sedimentation and buried soil horizons or profiles resulting from soil-forming processes. Eluviation and illuviation would suggest soil-forming processes (not unequivocally, cf. Birkeland 1974), though these rates were probably higher in the past. Fresh volcanic ash would have been initially abundant (Oard 1990; Whitcomb and Morris 1961) and may have been important in soil formation (including entisols and especially andisols).[2] Both paradigms note that parent material is not static, and both recognize that weathering occurs.

The point of disagreement is rate, especially if estimates are based on biased EGP "dating" methods. DGP researchers note that transport into and out of the control volume occurs (including clays), and EGP adherents are increasingly recognizing this, too (Chadwick et al. 1994; Daniels et al. 1971; Lavkulich 1969; Nettleton et al. 1990; Paton et al. 1995; Simonson 1959; Weaver 1989; Valentine and Dalrymple 1976), though they may not admit the variation in rate noted by the DGP.

As shown in table 7, there exists mixed agreement between the EGP and DGP on the likely role of geography. Substantial agreement between the two paradigms exists

___

2. Rapid formation of entisols (soils lacking distinct horizons) and andisols (derived from volcanic material) is often accepted in the EGP; however, volcanic ash may have been important in the formation of other soils (Froede 1995, 1996; Ping 2000; Selley 1976; Weaver 1989; Williams et al. 1998).

Table 6. Comparison of Parameters
Parent Material Environmental Factor

Parameter	EGP	DGP
Parent Material	Very important to soil formation; a complex result of C, G, and other variables	Very important to soil formation; primarily a result of M^0 modified by C, G, B, W, and other variables
Initial Parent Material	Often assumed homogeneous and unweathered	May have been heterogeneous and contained weathered materials already at end of Deluge
Weathering of Parent Material	Weathering occurs ($\partial M/\partial t \neq 0$) and is an important process; it has proceeded over vast ages.	Weathering occurs ($\partial M/\partial t \neq 0$) and is an important process; it may occur or have occurred more rapidly than commonly believed.
Rate of Weathering & Transport	Value of $\partial^2 M/\partial t^2$ small or zero	Value may have been large following Deluge ($\partial^2 M/\partial t^2 \neq 0$), decreasing with time
Parent Material Factor	A generally linear (gradual) change in soil state (i.e., soil formation) over vast periods of time	A generally exponential decrease in change (rate of soil formation) since Deluge (i.e., $\partial^3 S/\partial M \partial t^2 < 0$)

on the scale of local topography, despite substantial disagreement on larger scales. The EGP envisions vast changes in landscapes over deep time; the DGP envisions minor changes during the brief span of postdiluvian time because the abative and dispersive phases of the Deluge (Walker 1994) would have formed most of the present landscape. Later modification by wind, ice, and water would have been minor. Most soils thus formed in geomorphic environments similar to those today, even at large scales. Topographic changes are primarily a function of climate and parent material, since the presence of plants, important to slope stabilization, largely depends on these factors. As a result, erosion rates would have varied in the past, probably in a nonlinear fashion.

Erosion rates are roughly proportional to slope; other conditions being equal, doubling the angle of slope increases the loss of sediment by about two and a half times. Doubling the length of slopes increases the loss about one and a half times (Hunt 1972, p. 51).

Table 7. Comparison of Parameters
Geomorphic Environmental Factor

Parameter	EGP	DGP
Geomorphology and Topography	Important to soil formation; primarily a function of C and M, secondarily B and W	Important to soil formation; primarily a function of C, M, and G_0, secondarily B and W
Initial Geomorphology and Topography	May have been vastly different from present on both large and small scales	Geography at end of Deluge probably very similar to present; topography may differ
Change in Geomorphology and Topography	Erosion has produced great changes over vast periods of time ($\partial G >> G_0$)	Large-scale geomorphology probably has changed very little in postdiluvian time ($\partial G << G_0$ and $\partial G/\partial t$ is generally small), though significant local (small-scale) topographic changes may have occurred.
Change in Rates of Erosion	Value small and relatively constant, especially as long-term average	Value decreasing following Deluge ($\partial^2 G/\partial t^2 < 0$), especially with revegetation
Geomorphic Factor	A generally linear (gradual) change (soil formation) over vast periods of time	A generally static variable at large scale, episodic at small scale

Table 8. Comparison of Parameters
Biotic Environmental Factor

Parameter	EGP	DGP
Biotic Processes	Important to soil formation, but a secondary variable (i.e., B is highly dependent on C and M, also dependent on G, locally W)	Important to soil formation, but a secondary variable, i.e., B is highly dependent on C and M, also dependent on G, locally W
Initial Biologic Activity	On average, similar to present	May have been significant amounts of organic matter incorporated as O_0 at end of Deluge
Rate of Change of Biologic Activity	No significant global trend with time, but local changes over long periods could be great due to climate change, etc.	Rapid change (exponential) following Deluge ($\partial B/\partial t \neq 0$), especially revegetation; microbial activity probably optimized at end of Deluge
Change in Rate of Biologic Activity	Value small or zero	Value may have been large following Deluge ($\partial^2 B/\partial t^2 > 0$), decreasing with time ($\partial^2 B/\partial t^2 < 0$)
Biotic Factor	A generally linear (gradual) change in soil state (i.e., soil formation) over vast periods of time	Soil formation likely to be a complex, stochastic response to biologic mechanism due to number of variables

Thus, other variables assumed constant, erosion rates can be expected to slow as slope angles decrease.

The effects of biology also differ in the two paradigms (table 8). In general, DGP expectations include greater fluctuations in the magnitude of soil formation in the past than envisioned by the EGP. Immediately after the Flood, organic matter would have been present in many locations as residual debris (Genesis 8:11; Holroyd 1996; Oard 1995a; 1995b; Scheven 1996). Colonization of the denuded earth by plants would have been rapid (Genesis 8:11). Successions of flora would have been rapid early, especially with rapid climate change; this would have slowed in response to declining climate change. Since freshwater is less dense than saltwater, initial salt concentrations would not be expected to hinder plant growth in most surficial diluvial deposits. In addition, abundant moisture would have facilitated rapid leaching of the salts from soils. Meteoric water would also have diluted salts.

Table 9 summarizes the opposing views regarding the soil-forming effects of groundwater. Groundwater can affect pedogenesis more than typically acknowledged (Twidale 1990). First, weathering would be more rapid than anticipated from climate alone (Birkeland 1984).

> If appreciable water is available, not necessarily rainfall, and can move freely (relief, porosity, permeability) virtually any rock or aluminosilicate mineral will alter to kaolin-gibbsite-Fe oxides suite (Weaver 1989, p. 143).

The EGP envisions gradual change and little change in groundwater hydrology. The DGP envisions groundwater at a maximum at the end of the Deluge, declining (probably in a nonlinear fashion) to present conditions. The rate would be dependent on the hydrogeology of the site and climate, noting the influence of plants. Local topography would exert a strong influence in driving groundwater toward equilibrium. Insofar as pedogenesis was a function of groundwater, the rate of soil formation would follow this declining curve.

Appendix 5. DGP Versus EGP with the Four Soil-Forming Mechanisms

Soil-forming mechanisms, which operate within the control volume, seem to have received less attention than the well-known "soil-forming factors," but it is these mechanisms that transform parent material into soil.

Epigenesis

Table 10 summarizes the differences between the EGP and DGP views of epigenesis. The EGP can theoretically consider either rapid or slow mineral formation through alteration of parent materials, but in practice it defaults to "slow."

> Clay-mineral formation and transformation in the soil is a slow process (Birkeland 1974, p. 247).

It is often believed to require hundreds of thousands of years (Birkeland 1984). There is little incentive within the EGP to consider the possibility of rapid epigenetic

Table 9. Comparison of Parameters
Groundwater Environmental Factor

Parameter	EGP	DGP
Ground Water	Locally important to soil formation, but a secondary variable (i.e., W is highly dependent on C, M, and G, less so on B)	Locally very important to soil formation, but a secondary variable, i.e., W is highly dependent on C, M, and G, less so on B
Initial Water Level	May have been less or more than at present due to changes in C and G over vast periods of time.	Expected to be a maximum in most cases immediately following Deluge
Change in Ground Water Level with Time	Gradual changes expected locally over long periods due to changes in C and G	In most cases, expected to fall relatively rapidly (rate dependent on M) following Deluge ($\partial W/\partial t < 0$), driven toward equilibrium by C and G with lesser influence by B
Rate of Change in Water Level	Value small or zero	Value may have been large following Deluge ($\partial^2 W/\partial t^2 < 0$), decreasing with time (modern $\partial^2 W/\partial t^2 \neq 0$)
Groundwater Factor	Changes in water table likely to have been minor or gradual for most soils	Many soils may have experienced higher water table or soil moisture in past.

pathways, though some within the EGP are beginning to recognize the existence of specific physils or groups of physils in parent material, rather than just assuming these are products of epigenesis (Weaver 1989). Although much effort has been exerted to determine epigenetic pathways in response to climate, many physils in North American soils appear to be inherited from parent material unrelated to the present subjacent regolith (Hunt 1972). Weaver (1989) showed that EGP predictions do not match physil suites. Even where climate has been very important, parent material is not inconsequential:

> Again, the parent material helps determine the kind of clay that forms through availability and kind of bases (Birkeland 1974, p. 142).

Nettleton et al. (1990, p. 152, brackets added) found the following:

> The clays [in Redlands and Witt Aridisols] appear to be inherited from the parent material, or have accumulated from subsequent dust, because the primary sand and silt grains, except for biotite, are only slightly weathered.

Physil aggregates may have been deposited in high-energy environments where clay deposition would not normally be expected (Weaver 1989). Physils considered indicative of climate (e.g., montmorillonite) can form from a variety of parent materials (Weaver 1989) and can be found in various epimorphic combinations (Paton et al. 1995).

EGP rates of epigenesis are often biased by "absolute dates." While some may dispute this claim, evidence of bias is not difficult to find (Chadwick et al. 1994; Colman and Dethier 1986; Dahms et al. 1997; Hall and Shroba 1993; Leighton and MacClintock 1962; Locke 1986; Mahaney and Halvorson 1986; Nahon 1986; Taylor and Blum 1995).

Table 10. Comparison of Parameters
Epigenetic Soil-Forming Mechanism

Parameter	EGP	DGP
Epigenetic Mechanism	Generally assumed to occur gradually in response to climatic factor	May have occurred rapidly in response to varying climate and other environmental factors
Initial Epigenetic State	Often assumed to be zero (i.e., stable physils derived from parent material by epigenesis)	May be significant amount of inherited physils

Flawed assumptions in dating methods have resulted in disparate, inconclusive, or incorrect estimates for epigenetic rates, a fact even EGP adherents recognize (Foss and Segovia 1990; Grandstaff 1986; Hall and Martin 1986; Lowe 1986; Neall and Paintin 1986; Paton et al. 1995; White et al. 1986). This flawed dating, which tends to exaggerate age, has been debunked by observed instances of rapid soil formation: (1) at Kamenetz Fortress in Ukraine (Jenny 1941), (2) in volcanic soils, (3) on sand dunes, and (4) in the 19th-century work of Miss Shreck-enthall on moraines in the Alps. Epigenesis is particularly rapid in tropical entisols, and carbonates have been observed to form rapidly enough to clog drain pipes (Hunt 1972)! Although negligible desert varnish has formed at archaeological sites in the American Southwest since pueblos dated A.D. 1, it has been observed to form in railroad cuts and tunnels. The apparent necessary condition is the presence of water (Hunt 1972). Thus, rates of epigenesis may be easily underestimated and time for soil formation overestimated.

Evidence of significant epigenesis (physil development) has even been observed in Antarctica, on moraines believed to be between 17,000 and 21,000 years old (Ugolini 1986). Faster rates would be anticipated for temperate climates, especially where humid conditions exist. Lowe (1986) noted that the 10,000 to 15,000 years thought necessary for the transformation of volcanic glass and feldspar to halloysite via allophane was contradicted by the stratigraphy of New Zealand tephras.

> This implies that tephra composition and site weathering conditions frequently may have been underestimated in favor of the assumed tephra age-based weathering sequence (p. 270).

Halloysite (the end product) has been observed to form in 300 to 4,000 years in the humid tropics (Lowe 1986). Burial depth can affect the rate of epigenesis:

> The types and rates of formation and transformation of clay minerals derived from tephra deposits of acid to intermediate composition are determined chiefly by macro- and micro environmental factors together with the mineralogical and physicochemical composition of the parent deposits. *The length of time of weathering in clay mineral genesis is indirect and subordinate in its effect, in that weathering rates, and weathering products and their alteration, are largely dictated by other controls* (Lowe 1986, p. 281; emphasis ours).

Supposed intermediate species (allophane, imogolite) may persist, and supposed end products (halloysite, gibbsite) may form directly from tephra. These minerals can coexist and often do (Lowe 1986).

Similarly, King (1986) found little correlation between expected epigenetic products and a stratigraphic sequence of ash deposits in Canada. Surprisingly rapid epigenesis has also been observed in ash from the 1980 eruption of Mount St. Helens (White et al. 1986), with a rapidly declining rate of epigenesis attributed to a change from initial hydrochloric, nitric, and sulfuric acids to the much weaker carbonic acid, as chloride and sulfate were leached within three months of ash deposition (White et al. 1986). While many EGP pedologists agree that andisols can form rapidly, they seem to overlook the fact that many of their epigenetic pathways are similar to those of other soils. Thus:

> The rate of chemical weathering of geologic materials depends on the chemistry of weathering fluids and on the nature of reactions at mineral surfaces (Colman and Dethier 1986, p. 5).

Growth of new mineral phases as epigenesis progresses in mineral crystal defects may enlarge these conduits, accelerating weathering, or occlude these passages, depending on the secondary mineral species (Eggleton 1986). Weathering rinds with depth may result from variations in the rate of weathering, not the amount of time since deposition, since weathering in the shallow subsurface is generally greater than either surficial weathering or weathering at depth (Twidale 1990). Weathering rinds are probably more indicative of soil moisture than age (Twidale 1990). Oxisol formation appears to be greatly affected by lateral soil moisture movement, resulting in segregation of aluminum, magnesium, and iron, and possibly the formation of stone lines (Birkeland 1974). Organic matter and compounds can greatly accelerate chemical weathering in the solum (Birkeland 1984; Brady 1974; Paton et al. 1995; Ruhe 1975). The DGP envisions conditions generally more conducive to epigenesis during the early postdiluvian period than at present.

Physical Weathering

Table 11 summarizes differences regarding the role of physical weathering in soil formation. Although temperature fluctuations in themselves are probably a negligible factor (Birkeland 1974), ice lenses that form in soil attract water and grow, often inducing significant stresses (Hunt 1972), as do salts, clays, and plants (Birkeland 1974).

Table 11. Comparison of Parameters
Physical Weathering Soil-Forming Mechanism

Parameter	EGP	DGP
Physical Weathering Mechanism	Rates of mechanical breakdown of particles and translocation in solum typically slow — similar to modern rates — and often assumed to be linear	Rates of mechanical breakdown of particles and translocation may be relatively rapid, may have varied in the past, and may be more exponential than linear in response to buildup of resulting substances
Initial Physical Weathering	Often assumed to be virtually zero	May have been substantial at end of the Deluge

Table 12. Comparison of Parameters
Leaching Soil-Forming Mechanism

Parameter	EGP	DGP
Leaching Mechanism	Rate largely determined by climate, often assumed similar to present	Rate largely determined by climate, which may have been somewhat warmer and much moister than present
Initial Leaching	Often assumed to be zero	May have been quite high at end of Deluge

Evidence of physical weathering can be equivocal. Grus development to great depth has been observed in arid climates, indicating chemical rather than physical weathering, contrary to common belief (Birkeland 1974). Deep grus development may also indicate a wetter climate in these regions in the past — as predicted by the DGP. Patterned ground may be formed by processes other than freeze-thaw (Ruhe 1975). Stone lines may be formed pedogenically (Paton et al. 1995) or by creep, but often rounded or exotic clasts are present that neither process explains, indicating an unconformity (Ruhe 1975). Tephra accumulation over a'a lava, a rough-textured lava common in Hawaii, produces horizons free of rock fragments overlying the a'a (Chadwick et al. 1994), a profile that could be misinterpreted as evidence of physical weathering.

> Because cumulative soils have parent material continuously added to their surfaces, their features are partly sedimentologic and partly pedogenic. In a soil study, therefore, it is important that sedimentologic features are not ascribed to pedogenesis (Birkeland 1984, p. 185).

Formation of an argillic horizon by translocation of clay-size particles is one of the most important processes in soil profile development. It is impossible to distinguish clay translocated via suspension from that precipitated from solution, and even establishing whether that translocation has actually occurred can be difficult (Birkeland 1974). Argillic horizons are sometimes observed where they would not be expected, for example, in aridisols.

> Prominent argillic horizons occur only in soils [Redlands and Witt Aridisols] that formed primarily during the Pleistocene and hence are largely relict, yet many factors would tend to rapidly destroy these features, not preserve them (Gile and Grossman 1968, p. 14–15).

This suggests that they may be relatively young.

> Expression of the argillic horizon is related to soil age but not as closely as the horizon of carbonate accumulation (Gile and Grossman 1968, p. 15).[3]

Weaver (1989, p. 115) stated, "The time factor [re: clay translocation] has been difficult to quantify." Better defining the time factor will require more data on clay translocation rates and the effects of aeolian clay and silt on B horizon development in texture-contrast soils (Boardman 1985). Sesquioxide concentrations sometimes exceed what may be expected from parent material, indicating transport, but sesquioxides, carbonates, electrolytes, and positively charged colloids also inhibit clay migration, and above approximately 20–40 percent clay content (depending on physil species), clay translocation may virtually cease

---

3. Birkeland (1974) noted that the modern $CaCO_3$ influx to aridisols similar to those studied by Gile and Grossman is too low to explain observed concentrations, even with the ages ascribed to them by the EGP.

(Birkeland 1974; Blatt et al. 1972). Thus, modern rates may be substantially lower than in the past. Based on archaeological evidence, clay translocation in alfisols can readily occur in fewer than 3,000 years, and lateral groundwater movement may also be important in translocation (Fisher 1983).

Leaching

Table 12 summarizes paradigm differences over leaching as a soil-forming mechanism. The DGP predicts rapid initial leaching of already-weathered parent material, with the rate declining in response to drier climates and decreasing permeability of the solum. Leaching is largely a function of climate, needing excess moisture to provide free water for transport of ions from the solum (Locke 1986). "The most active agency in soil-profile formation is percolating water" (Jenny 1941, p. 47). White and Blum (1995) found that SiO_2 and Na weathering followed a linear function of precipitation and an Arrhenius temperature function (exponential), though no climatic correlation was observed for K, Ca, or Mg. Grandstaff (1986) found an Arrhenius relation to temperature and proportionality to free ligand concentration for olivine weathering in Hawaiian beach sand. The importance of excess soil water has been established in modern environments.

> Long term rates of desilication increase by nearly an order of magnitude as time-weighted median rainfall increases from 20 to 350 cm. Long-term rates of base action leaching increase by about a factor of about 4 over the same rainfall gradient (Chadwick et al. 1994, p. 102).

Common estimates for the rate of past soil formation are automatically uniformitarian.

> All regional and global estimates of chemical weathering are derived from dissolved load output from Earth's major river systems (Chadwick et al. 1994, p. 94).

Taylor and Blum's (1995) silicate weathering rates, derived from "known" ages, were 3.4 times faster than those based on stream flows. Yet observed rates are considerably in excess of those expected from the "known" ages of the moraines in their study, just as expected by diluvialists. Dahms et al. (1997) pointed out that Taylor and Blum erred by assuming a closed system and that their reported precision in estimating weathering rates is impossible. Similar efforts based on "known ages" have been made by Hall and Martin (1986), Locke (1986), Mahaney and Halvorson (1986), and others.

As has been demonstrated elsewhere (Oard, 1990), diluvialists would expect a higher temperature and precipitation regime over most of the earth immediately after the Deluge, with colder summers over mid-continental interiors. Initially high rates of leaching would be expected wherever wet conditions occurred, particularly when relatively warm, with rates later declining to present values. Since much of the heat would have resulted from extensive volcanism, the atmosphere may have contained considerable sulfuric acid, which would have greatly accelerated leaching. Thus, soil formation rates on the basis of leaching would have been very high at first in most parts of the postdiluvian world.

Permeability is not static, and rates of leaching would often be reduced by translocation. Just the formation of an argillic horizon would reduce soil permeability by about two orders of magnitude, suggesting that past leaching of the A horizon may have been less, and past leaching of the B horizon more for many ultisols and alfisols. For example, well-sorted sand may have a permeability of 10^{-2} cm/sec, but if silt or clay particles are introduced, permeability may decline to 10^{-4} cm/sec. Formation of laminae

Table 13. Comparison of Parameters
Organic Matter Soil-Forming Mechanism

Parameter	EGP	DGP
Organic Matter Mechanism	Rate largely determined by climate, often assumed similar to present or slightly more favorable for histosol formation during or after ice ages.	Rate largely determined by climate, which may have been somewhat warmer and much moister than present, possibly cooler at end of postdiluvial ice age
Initial Organic Matter	Normally assumed to be zero in parent material	May have been considerable at end of Deluge

in petrocalcic horizons may have been slow or rapid (Daniels et al. 1971).

Organic Matter

Table 13 summarizes EGP and DGP differences regarding the organic matter soil-forming mechanism.

> Organic matter probably reaches a steady state more rapidly than any other property of the soil. . . . Nevertheless, these and other data suggest that the time to achieve steady state may range from as little as 200 years to perhaps 10,000 years (Birkeland 1984, p. 203).

Organic matter as an argument for long time hinges on quantity of organic material and accumulation rates; for example, the amount of time required to form extensive peat bogs. Effects of organic matter on soil formation are also important, since organic matter can strongly influence the rate of formation of mineral soils. The question of organic matter accumulation may be illustrated by the Leteensuo Peat Bog (Klevberg and Bandy, 2003)[4]. Assuming no initial organic matter ($O_0 = 0$) and exponential decline in peat accretion from an initial maximum rate of 20 cm/year (Retallack, 1990) to 0.5 mm/year within four millennia, results in:

$$h = 200\,e^{-0.0015t} \qquad (1)$$

where h is net annual peat accumulation in millimeters and t is time in years since the Deluge. Total peat accretion, H, can therefore be calculated for any time period to the present:

$$H = \int 200\,e^{-0.0015t}\,dt \qquad (2)$$

This scenario results in total peat accretion of 436 feet (133 m) in 4,000 years — greatly in excess of observed histosol thicknesses, and at an average rate of accumulation *much less* than Retallack's "maximum conceivable rate." Using equation (2), the time required to form the Leteensuo Peat Bog would have been approximately 2,300 years with an *initial* (maximum) rate of 15.5 mm/year, roughly 8 percent of Retallack's "maximum conceivable rate." Even assuming a constant rate of formation of 2.5

---

4. While not the world's largest peat bog, it is certainly very large and representative of the vast accumulations of peat in Finland and other high latitude locations. It has also been explored more thoroughly than most bogs in preparation for building a road across it (Forsman, et al. 1998, p. 773); most peat bogs are not as well understood.

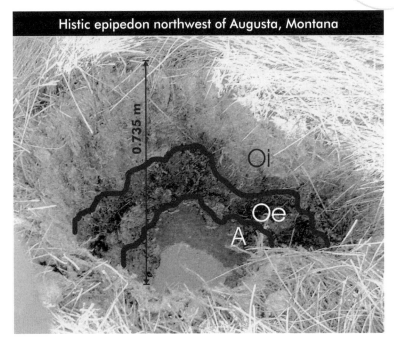

Histic epipedon northwest of Augusta, Montana

0.735 m

Oi

Oe

A

Figure 14. Test pit in Wetland near Augusta, Montana, showing nascent histosol.

mm/year and no initial organic matter, the Leteensuo Peat Bog could have easily formed in 4,000 years. In addition, in the DGP, O_0 was very likely *not* zero. Furthermore, rapid rates have been observed, even in less-than-optimal conditions: for example, a 7-inch (17.5 cm) thick histic epipedon constituting part of a mucky soil (a nascent histosol) 29 inches (73.5 cm) thick formed northwest of Augusta, Montana, in just 80 years (figures 14 and 15), following the commencement of irrigation.

Histosol formation is dependent on a narrow range of conditions that change over time, principally the position of the water table relative to the ground surface. It also assumes that average rates of net annual peat accumulation of much less than one mm/year are possible (Hunt 1972). In reality, site-specific environmental factors dominate, and therefore each example requires a site-specific hydrogeologic assessment. Finally, many peat deposits appear to be partially composed of *allocthonous* organic matter as indicated by the presence of calcite and dolomite nodules incompatible with modern swamps (Retallack 1990).

Old-age arguments made from radiocarbon dating of histosols are unreliable due to the mobility of carbon (Weaver 1989) and mixing with "old" carbon in soils containing carbonates (Ruhe 1975). Attempts to constrain weathering rates by radiocarbon dating tend to

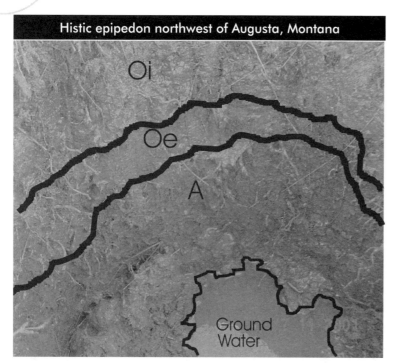

Figure 15. Closer view of figure 14, showing recently formed histic epipedon.

produce scattered data with no evident trend (Neall and Paintin 1986).

Perhaps recognizing the weakness of arguments from pedogenesis, Harding (2001) asserted that soils would have been sterile following the biblical Flood, but this is unlikely. Noting that humus increases the suitability of a soil to support plant life (Brady 1974), it could have been provided by some of the enormous antediluvian biomass.[5] Though much, no doubt, ended up as coal, oil, natural gas, and carbononiferous and kerygenous matter (Wood-morappe 1993), some would have been incorporated into surficial sediments, often on top (Holroyd 1996). Where present, it would have readily decayed in the warm, humid conditions expected at that time, resulting in rapid humus formation.

---

5. Humus is formed by microbial action on organic matter. It is difficult to say how long bacteria found in soils and organic matter might survive during the Genesis Flood, but they seem to be quite adaptable. When soils are periodically waterlogged due to rising water tables, aerobic bacteria go dormant and anaerobic bacteria become active. As these soils aerate, the reverse situation occurs. With large amounts of organic matter, as would be expected floating on the surface of the water during the Deluge and then being usually the last material deposited, it would seem quite reasonable to assume colonies of bacteria and fungi would be present and active.

Appendix 6. Analysis of the Five Supposed "Old" Soils

We apply what we have learned in this chapter to the five types of soils from appendix 3 that are claimed to always take long periods of time to form.

Oxisols

Oxisols, prominent for their lack of soil horizons and enrichment in aluminum and iron hydroxides, are claimed to be produced by prolonged, intense leaching in tropical climates. Oxisols, particularly acroperox, appear to provide strong evidence for an ancient earth. Estimates of acroperox formation from both granitic and ultramafic rocks are less than 50 mm/1000 yr (Nahon 1986). However, Boardman (1985) noted problems correlating soil redness with ambient temperatures. Also, Nahon's rate includes an unlikely linear rate over time, and many oxisols are relict (Nahon 1986). Because EGP adherents are biased toward long times, rates of oxisol formation are often based on radiometric dating of associated volcanics (Nahon 1986). Those methods are dubious (Austin 1992, 1994, 1996; Austin and Snelling 1998; Vardiman et al. 2005; Woodmorappe 1979, 1999a, 1999b), and therefore cannot substantiate the old ages for oxisols.

Retallack (1990, p. 343) recognized that "alumina enrichment can be caused both by hydrothermal alteration and by weathering, so that care must be taken in interpreting aluminous rocks [bauxite] in highly deformed and very ancient terranes." Yet he goes on to assert that kaolinite "has persisted in these profiles despite subsequent diagenetic alteration" (p. 344), an assertion clearly involving historic, nonscientific presuppositions! Selley (1976) noted three sources of clay origin: (1) hydrothermal alteration of feldspars, (2) intense weathering of diverse rocks, and (3) transport and deposition. Only the second is a pedogenic process, and even it can be diagenetic rather than pedogenic, which may be indicated by the variability of residual kaolins (Selley 1976). Traditional explanations for oxisols fall short: "There are many unsolved problems concerning this soil type" (Blatt et al. 1972, p. 257).

Evidence *against* a pedologic origin of some alleged oxisols is very clear. Ganisters and tonsteins in Europe are probably intensely weathered volcanic ash beds rather than leached soil horizons (Selley 1976). Extensive bauxite deposits in Romania contain bones of dinosaurs and other faunas that are virtually impossible to explain pedogenically, and many deposits in North America run afoul of paleoclimatologic inferences (Oard 1999). Some oxisols may be almost entirely geologic in origin, and others may be polygenetic. It is impossible to establish that any particular oxisol developed solely as the result of in situ weathering, and clearly some did not. We suggest pedologists consider *geologic* explanations for many oxisols.

Ultisols

Ultisols show a deeply leached weathering profile and translocation of clays. Both the EGP and DGP recognize that ultisol formation is a nonlinear function with time (Birkeland 1984), but diluvialists would expect rates of both leaching and translocation to have declined over time in response to soil profile development, as well as possible climate change. Present rates may represent *minima*, not averages. The response of leaching and translocation rates to soil profile development in ultisols can be evaluated by comparing them with alfisols, where formation within centuries or a few millennia has been observed. This suggests rapid formation of ultisols is likely. If leaching and translocation are nonlinear through time, then traditional ages for many ultisols are invalid. The importance of parent material in ultisol development may also have been unrecognized.

> Although the native fertility disadvantage of the Ultisols may be attributed in part to the higher rainfall and temperatures [assumed in their global warming scenario], this is not a totally valid relationship; parent material is undoubtedly a very significant soil forming factor contributing to differences in native fertility between Mollisols and Ultisols (Buol et al. 1990, p. 79, brackets added).

Histosols

Histosols no longer appear a convincing argument for long periods of formation. The rapid formation of histic epipedons in recent times appears to indicate that *observed histosols permit too little time for the EGP*, suggesting that continental glaciation (generally believed to have occurred where the majority of histosols are found today) may have occurred more recently than predicted by the EGP.

Alfisols

Alfisols, less intensively leached than ultisols, probably develop more rapidly. However, differences in climate and parent material may be more important than time. Consider the Thoeny and Creed soils of northern Montana (USDA 1986). The Thoeny series formed in "glacial till," a diamict with a fine-grained matrix, since the withdrawal of ice sheets from the area. The Creed series formed in the same region under the same climatic influences, but it formed in alluvium south of the ice limit. A typical pedon for both soils consists of A and E horizons to 6 inches (15 cm) with the base of the B_t horizon at 17 inches (43 cm) in the Thoeny and 16 inches (41 cm) in the Creed. According to the EGP, the Creed should be much older, and more highly developed with a much deeper B_k horizon. But climate, not time, most affected pedogenesis. Rapid pedogenesis also means that considerably less time was needed, as predicted by the DGP.

Mollisols

Mollisols are not as controversial. However, they provide good examples of "average" soils that call into question slow pedogenesis in other types. Consider the Telstad (USDA 1986) and Evanston soils of northern Montana (USDA 1988, and unpublished data). Both are fine-loamy, mixed, superactive, frigid, aridic argiustolls. The Telstad formed in "glacial till" north of the Missouri River. The Evanston formed in non-glacial alluvium south of the Missouri River.[6] Both exhibit a mollic epipedon 4–6 inches (10–15 cm) deep over an argillic horizon. The uniformity and degree of profile development of both is very similar, despite different supposed histories. They suggest equally rapid soil formation rather than slow development since glaciation.

References

CRSQ: Creation Research Society Quarterly
CENTJ: Creation Ex Nihilo Technical Journal (now Journal of Creation)

Austin, S.A. 1992. Excessively old "ages" for Grand Canyon lava flows. *Acts and Facts* 21(2):i–iv, Impact Article No. 224. Institute for Creation Research, El Cajon, CA.

———. 1994. *Grand Canyon: Monument to Catastrophe*. Santee, CA: Institute for Creation Research.

---

6. The Evanston series also occurs in alluvium that appears to be reworked till in various places north of the Missouri River; in these places, the Evanston is apparently *younger* than the Telstad, while south of the river it should be *older*.

————. 1996. Excess argon within mineral concentrates from the new dacite lava dome at Mount St. Helens volcano. *CENTJ* 10:335–343.

Austin, S.A., and A.A. Snelling. 1998. Discordant potassium-argon model and isochron "ages" for Cardenas Basalt (middle Proterozoic) and associated diabase of eastern Grand Canyon, Arizona. In Robert E. Walsh (editor). *Proceedings of the Fourth International Conference on Creationism.* Pittsburgh, PA: Creation Science Fellowship, p. 35–51.

Birkeland, P.W. 1974. *Pedology, Weathering, and Geomorphological Research.* New York: Oxford University Press.

————. 1984. *Soils and Geomorphology.* New York: Oxford University Press.

Blatt, H., G.V. Middleton, and R. Murray. 1972. *Origin of Sedimentary Rocks.* Englewood Cliffs, NJ: Prentice-Hall.

Boardman, J. 1985. Comparison of soils in Midwestern United States and Western Europe with the interglacial record. *Quaternary Research* 23:62–75.

Bown, T.M., and M.J. Kraus. 1981. Lower Eocene alluvial paleosols (Willwood Formation, northwest Wyoming, USA) and their significance for paleoecology, paleoclimatology, and basin analysis. *Palaeogeography, Palaeoclimatology, Palaeoecology* 34:1–30.

Brady, N.C. 1974. *The Nature and Properties of Soils*, eighth edition. New York: MacMillan Publishing Company.

Brady, N.C., and R.R. Weil. 1999. *The Nature and Properties of Soils*, twelfth edition. Upper Saddle River, NJ: Prentice-Hall Publishing Company.

Buol, S.W., P.A. Sanchez, S.B. Weed, and J.M. Kimble. 1990. Predicted impact of climatic warming on soil properties and use. In *Impact of Carbon Dioxide, Trace Gases, and Climate Change on Global Agriculture.* American Society of Agronomy Special Publication No. 53: 71–82.

Chadwick, O.A., C.G. Olson, D.M. Hendricks, E.F. Kelly, and R.T. Gavenda. 1994. Quantifying climatic effects on mineral weathering and neoformation in Hawaii. In *Transactions: 15th World Congress of Soil Science.* Acupulco, Mexico: International Society of Soil Science, p. 8a:94–105.

Colman, S.M., and D.P. Dethier (editors). 1986. *Rates of Chemical Weathering of Rocks and Minerals.* San Diego, CA: Academic Press.

Dahms, D.E., R.R. Shroba, J.C. Gosse, R.D. Hall, C.J. Sorenson, and M.C. Reheis. 1997. Relation between soil age and silicate weathering rates determined from the chemical evolution of a glacial chronosequence: comment and reply. *Geology* 25:381–382.

Daniels, R.B., E.E. Gamble, and L.A. Nelson. 1971. Relations between soil morphology and water-table levels on a dissected North Carolina Coastal Plain surface. *Soil Science Society of America Proceedings* 35:781–784.

Eggleton, R.A. 1986. The relation between crystal structure and silicate weathering rates. In S.M. Colman and D.P. Dethier (editors). *Rates of Chemical Weathering of Rocks and Minerals*, p. 21-40. San Diego, CA: Academic Press.

Fisher, P.F. 1983. Pedogenesis within the archaeological landscape at South Lodge Camp, Wiltshire, England. *Geoderma.* 29:93–105.

Forsman, J., E. Slunga, and P. Lahtinen. 1998. Geogrid and geocell reinforced secondary road over deep peat deposit. In R.K. Rowe (editor). *Sixth International Conference on Geosynthetics Conference Proceedings* 2:773–778. Industrial Fabrics Association International, Roseville, MN.

Foss, J.E., and A.V. Segovia. 1990. Rates of soil formation. In R.G. LaFleur (editor). *Groundwater as a Geomorphic Agent.* Boston, MA: Allen & Unwin.

Froede, C.R., Jr. 1995. A post-Flood (early Ice Age?) paleoenvironment in Mississippi. *CRSQ* 31:182–186.

————. 1996. A theory for the volcanic origin of radioactive shales and clays: Examples from the southeastern United States. *CRSQ* 33:160–168.

Gile and Grossman. 1968. Morphology of the argillic horizon in desert soils of southern New Mexico. *Soil Science* 106:6–15.

Grandstaff, D.E. 1986. The dissolution rate of forsteritic olivine from Hawaiian beach sand. In S.M. Colman and D.P. Dethier (editors). *Rates of Chemical Weathering of Rocks and Minerals.* San Diego, CA: Academic Press, p. 41–59.

Hall, R.D., and R.E. Martin. 1986. The etching of hornblende grains in the matrix of alpine tills and periglacial deposits. In S.M. Colman and D.P. Dethier (editors). *Rates of Chemical Weathering of Rocks and Minerals.* San Diego, CA: Academic Press, San Diego, p. 101–128.

Hall, R.D., R.E. Martin, and R.R. Shroba. 1993. Soils developed in the glacial deposits of the type areas of the Pinedale and Bull Lake glaciations, Wind River Range, Wyoming. *Arctic and Alpine Research* 25:368–373.

Harding, K. 2001. What would we expect to find if the world had flooded? http://www.geocities.com:0080/Tokyo/Temple/9917/flood.html.

Holroyd, E.W. III. 1996. Confirmation from debris flow at a forest fire site. *CRSQ* 33:141–151.

Hunt, C.B. 1972. *The Geology of Soils: Their Evolution, Classification, and Uses.* San Francisco, CA: W.H. Freeman and Company.

Jenny, H. 1941. *Factors of Soil Formation: A System of Quantitative Pedology.* New York: McGraw-Hill Book Company.

Klevberg, P. 1999. The philosophy of sequence stratigraphy — Part I: Philosophic background. *CRSQ* 36:72–80.

———. 2000. The philosophy of sequence stratigraphy — Part III: Application to sequence stratigraphy. *CRSQ* 37:94–104.

Klevberg, P., and R. Bandy. 2003. Postdiluvial soil formation and the question of time: Part I: Soil formation. *CRSQ* 39:252–68.

King, R.H. 1986. Weathering of holocene airfall tephras in the southern Canadian Rockies. In S.M. Colman and D.P. Dethier (editors). *Rates of Chemical Weathering of Rocks and Minerals.* San Diego, CA: Academic Press, p. 239–264.

Lavkulich, L.M. 1969. Soil dynamics in the interpretation of paleosols. In S. Pawluk (editor). *Pedology and Quaternary Research.* Edmonton, Canada: University of Alberta, p. 25–37.

Leighton, M.M., and P. MacClintock. 1962. The weathered mantle of glacial tills beneath original surfaces in north-central United States. *Journal of Geology* 70:267–293.

Locke, W.W. 1986. Rates of hornblende etching in soils on glacial deposits, Baffin Island, Canada. In S.M. Colman and D.P. Dethier (editors). *Rates of Chemical Weathering of Rocks and Minerals.* San Diego, CA: Academic Press, p. 129–145.

Lowe, D.J. 1986. Controls on the rates of weathering and clay mineral genesis in airfall tephras: A review and New Zealand case study. In S.M. Colman and D.P. Dethier (editors). *Rates of Chemical Weathering of Rocks and Minerals.* San Diego, CA: Academic Press, p. 265–330.

Mahaney, W.C., and D.L. Halvorson. 1986. Rates of mineral weathering in the Wind River Mountains, Western Wyoming. In S.M. Colman and D.P. Dethier (editors). *Rates of Chemical Weathering of Rocks and Minerals.* San Diego, CA: Academic Press, p. 147–167.

McCarthy, D.F. 1988. *Essentials of Soil Mechanics and Foundations: Basic Geotechnics,* third edition. Englewood Cliffs, NJ: Prentice Hall.

Nahon, D.B. 1986. Evolution of iron crusts in tropical landscapes. In S.M. Colman and D.P. Dethier (editors). *Rates of Chemical Weathering of Rocks and Minerals.* San Diego, CA: Academic Press, p. 169–191.

Natural Resources Conservation Service. 1997. In the time it took to form 1 inch of soil. United States Department of Agriculture poster.

Neall, V.E., and I.K. Paintin. 1986. Rates of weathering of ^{14}C-dated late quaternary volcaniclastic deposits in the western United States. In S.M. Colman and D.P. Dethier (editors). *Rates of Chemical Weathering of Rocks and Minerals.* San Diego, CA: Academic Press, p. 331–350.

Nettleton, W.D., A.B. Price, and G.A. Bowman. 1990. Argillic horizon formation in late Wisconsinan eolian materials in southwest Colorado, U.S.A. In L.A. Douglas (editor). *Soil Micromorphology.* Amsterdam: Elsevier, p. 149–154.

Oard, M.J. 1990. *An Ice Age Caused by the Genesis Flood.* San Diego, CA: Institute for Creation Research.

———. 1995a. Mid and high latitude flora deposited in the Genesis Flood — Part I: Uniformitarian paradox. *CRSQ* 32:107–115.

———. 1995b. Mid and high latitude flora deposited in the Genesis Flood — Part II: A creationist hypothesis. *CRSQ* 32:138–141.

———. 1999. What can 10,000 dinosaur bones in a bauxite lens tell us? *CENTJ* 13:8–9.

Olson, G.W. 1981. *Soils and the Environment.* New York: Chapman and Hall.

Paton, R.R., G.S. Humphreys, and P.B. Mitchell. 1995. *Soils: A New Global View.* New Haven, CT: Yale University Press.

Ping, C. 2000. Volcanic soils. In H. Sigurdsson (editor). *Encyclopedia of Volcanoes.* San Diego, CA: Academic Press, p. 1259–1270.

Retallack, G.J. 1990. *Soils of the Past — An Introduction to Paleopedology.* Boston, MA: Unwin Hyman.

Ruhe, R.V. 1975. *Geomorphology.* Boston, MA: Houghton Mifflin Company.

Scheven, J. 1996. The Carboniferous floating forest — an extinct pre-flood ecosystem. *CENTJ* 10:70–81.

Selley, R.C. 1976. *An Introduction to Sedimentology.* New York: Academic Press.

Simonson, R.W. 1959. Outline of generalized theory of soil genesis. *Soil Science of America Proceedings* 23:152–156.

Tarbuck, E.J., and F.K. Lutgens. 1984. *The Earth: An Introduction to Physical Geology.* Columbus, OH: Charles E. Merrill.

Taylor, A., and J.D. Blum. 1995. Relation between soil age and silicate weathering rates determined from the chemical evolution of a glacial chronosequence. *Geology* 23:979–982

Twidale, C.R. 1990. Weathering, soil development, and landforms. In R.G. LaFleur (editor). *Groundwater as a Geomorphic Agent*. Boston, MA: Allen & Unwin.

Ugolini, F.C. <AS> 1986. Processes and rates of weathering in cold and polar desert environments. In S.M. Colman and D.P. Dethier (editors). *Rates of Chemical Weathering of Rocks and Minerals*. San Diego, CA: Academic Press, p. 193–235.

USDA. 1986. *Soil Survey of Blaine County and Parts of Phillips County, Montana*. Soil Conservation Service [now Natural Resources Conservation Service], Washington, DC.

———. 1988. *Soil Survey of Fergus County, Montana*. Soil Conservation Service [now Natural Resources Conservation Service], Washington, DC.

———. Natural Resource Conservation Service. 1999. *Agriculture Handbook #436*. Washington, DC: Government Printing Office.

Valentine, K.W.G., and J.B. Dalrymple. 1976. Quaternary buried paleosols: A critical review. *Quaternary Research* 6:2:209–222.

Vardiman, L., A.A. Snelling, and E.F. Chaffin (editors). 2005. *Radioisotopes and the Age of the Earth: Results of a Young Earth Creationist Research Initiative*. El Cajon, CA: Institute for Creation Research, and Chino Valley, AZ: Creation Research Society.

Vreeken, W.J. 1984. Relative dating of soils and paleosols. In W.C. Mahaney (editor). *Quaternary Dating Methods*. New York: Elsevier, p. 269–281.

Walker, T.B. 1994. A biblical geologic model. In R.E. Walsh (editor). *Proceedings of the Third International Conference on Creationism* (technical symposium sessions). Pittsburgh, PA: Creation Science Fellowship, p. 581–592.

Weaver, C.E. 1989. *Clays, Muds, and Shales*. New York: Elsevier.

White, A.F., L.V. Benson, and A. Yee. 1986. Chemical weathering of the May 18, 1980, Mount St. Helens ash fall and the effect on the Iron Creek watershed, Washington. In S.M. Colman and D.P. Dethier (editors). *Rates of Chemical Weathering of Rocks and Minerals*. San Diego, CA: Academic Press,, p. 351–375.

Whitcomb, J.C., and H.M. Morris. 1961. *The Genesis Flood*. Philadelphia, PA: The Presbyterian and Reformed Publishing Company.

Williams, E.L., R.L. Goette, W.G. Stark, and G.T. Matzko. 1998. Fossil wood from Big Bend National Park, Texas (Dawson Creek Region), Part V — Origin and diagenesis of clays. *CRSQ* 35:31–38.

Woodmorappe, J. 1999a. Radiometric geochronology reappraised. In J. Woodmorappe. 1999. *Studies in Flood Geology*. San Diego, CA: Institute for Creation Research,, p. 145–175.

———. 1999b. *The Mythology of Modern Dating Methods*. San Diego, CA: Institute for Creation Research.

Yake, B. 1995. Objections from science to a global flood. *CRSQ* 32:12.

Chapter 6

Do Paleosols Indicate Long Ages?

Peter Klevberg • *BS — Engineering Science, P.E.*
Rick Bandy • *BS — Forestry, minor in Soil Science*
Michael J. Oard • *MS — Atmospheric Science*

Abstract

Paleosols, or "fossil soils," are being reported by uniformitarian geologists in increasing numbers. This is to be expected, since the deep time of their view of earth history would naturally result in the burial and preservation of many soils. However, not only do uniformitarian assumptions guide the investigation of paleosols, but the very definition of a paleosol is unscientific and called a "mixed question." This chapter addresses whether paleosols exist, how they may be identified, and how diluvialists should approach the investigation of alleged examples.

Introduction

Uniformitarian geologists have claimed that the existence of paleosols, especially as superposed multiple horizons, invalidates the short time scale of diluvial geology. A paleosol is defined as a fossil soil, that is, a soil that has been preserved in the geologic record or buried deeply enough that it is no longer subject to soil-forming processes. Strahler (1999, p. 286) noted:

> . . . the time constraints of Flood geology allow for only one major glaciation, and that leaves unexplained the nested alluvium fills and the ancient soil layers (paleosols) on buried terrace surfaces.

These claims rest in part on assertions that modern soil profiles take tens of thousands or even a million years or more to form — a proposition addressed in chapter 5. Like soils, the essential "problem" with paleosols is the challenge to the short time frame of diluvial geology. This chapter will examine those claims and demonstrate that although paleosols exist, they are often misidentified in the rock record because the identifying criteria are not credible. Most examples are shown to be inconclusive, and the diluvial prediction that true paleosols will be rare is concordant with the rock record.

The Apparent Problem of Paleosols

Paleosols, which are usually inferred to be buried soil horizons, pose two problems for diluvialists: (1) the improbability of a true soil horizon developing during the Noahic Flood — supposedly responsible for the bulk of the rock record — and (2) the time problems caused by superposed paleosol horizons (figure 1). This is because a true paleosol must develop normally as a soil, then be buried (sometimes being subjected to diagenesis), have another soil horizon develop, be buried, etc. Multiple paleosols are claimed by mainstream scientists (Retallack 1990; Selley 1976). Weaver (1989, p. 107) even asserted: ". . . superimposed soil profiles are the rule rather than the exception." Paleosols are used as an argument by anticreationists (Harding 2001), and even a few creationists see them as strong evidence for long periods of time (Robinson 1996).

Paleosols are assumed to form over long periods of time: "The time spans required to form soils are thousands to

Paleosols

Horizon Rich in Iron Oxide

Figure 1. Alleged paleosol, Cloudy Ridge, Alberta, Canada. The darker soil horizon contains more iron, and the profile is interpreted by some (Karlstrom 1988) as a paleosol. Brunton compass provides scale.

millions of years" (Retallack 1990, p. 13). They are also used to interpret ancient environments (Retallack 1990). By comparing "paleosol" properties to modern soils, EGP scientists infer properties of those environments:

> If a paleosol is very similar to a modern soil, then perhaps environments similar to those that formed the soil can be inferred for the paleosol (Retallack 1993, p. 1636).

Even if the Establishment Geologic Paradigm (EGP)[1] has distorted the age of many soils, would not sequences of multiple paleosols invalidate the Diluvial Geologic Paradigm (DGP)? Even soils forming as rapidly as a few centuries indicate the passage of great periods of time if sufficient numbers are stratigraphically superposed. The

---

1. The view of earth history that holds to gradualism, philosophic naturalism, an ancient earth, and evolutionism. Its counterpart, the "Diluvial Geologic Paradigm" or DGP, proffers catastrophism, supernaturalism, and a biblical history that highlights creation and the Deluge.

existence of such features would call into question biblical history. Some creationists accept the assertions of uniformitarians (Robinson 1996); others (including us) challenge them. Given the relative rapidity of soil formation observed in many modern environments, paleosols per se are not inimical to the DGP (Froede 1998). Rather, it is their stratigraphic location and abundance that is at issue.

Leighton and MacClintock (1962, p. 289) stated that "recognizing the proper distinctions between a profile of weathering and a soil profile is of the greatest importance to both geologists and pedologists." Yet this is seldom possible (Ruhe 1975), and even argillic horizons can form sedimentologically (Valentine and Dalrymple 1976). For example, identification of ancient B_k horizons (caliche or a soil cemented by calcium carbonate) is difficult at best:

> Correct recognition of ancient caliche is an art and, as with most art, the experts often disagree among themselves concerning the criteria to be used in an evaluation (Blatt et al. 1972, p. 259).

> It is the similarity of the processes and products of pedogenesis to those of diagenesis that is one of the major causes of confusion in the recognition of buried paleosols (Valentine and Dalrymple 1976, p. 210).

Various laboratory techniques, including mineral and ion ratios, although often useful, are rife with pitfalls and often equivocal (Brady 1974; Valentine and Dalrymple 1976). Alternative explanations *abound* for features some think diagnostic of paleosols, and the alternative explanations are often more likely (White 1998).

Paleosol Implications

Many define a paleosol simply as a buried soil or what they think is a buried soil (Bates and Jackson 1984), though disputes among paleopedologists are common (Froede 1998). We understand a paleosol to be a "fossil soil," or *a soil that has been preserved in the geologic record or buried deeply enough that it is no longer subject to soil-forming processes.* This implies recognizable soil horizons that are *in reality seldom seen.* Paleosols have been widely recognized in the "Quaternary" for over 100 years (Mahaney 1978). Retallack (1990) claimed that paleosols can even exist on the surface and be inactive — as if they would be distinct from normal soil horizons!

With the exception of underclays, a layer of clay lying directly below a coal bed, paleosols were long considered rare to nonexistent in pre-"Quaternary" sedimentary rocks. Then in the 1960s, a "renaissance" began (Retallack 1990). Ever since, claims of paleosols have multiplied: Retallack (1983) even claimed 87 paleosols in a 469-foot (143 m) stratigraphic section in Badlands National Park, South Dakota. From the EGP perspective, paleosols should be common in any terrestrial deposit:

> In view of the principle of uniformitarianism as applied to present-day alluvial sequences, we believe that fluvial rocks that do not contain pedogenic features are probably exceptional (Bown and Kraus 1981, p. 6).

Paleopedology — the study of ancient soils — is the basis for much modern research in "Quaternary" geology, and is certainly foundational to paleoclimatology and paleogeography. Although some researchers urge caution in using paleosols to infer paleoclimate, most still deduce the mean annual temperature and precipitation from "paleosol development" (Kraus 1999). Even some diluvialists have incorporated paleosol interpretations and paleoclimatic interpretations into their own research (Howe et al. 1995; Froede 1996; Robinson 1996). The best known application of paleoclimatological inferences is their use in distinguishing various glacial periods, for example, the traditional four "ice ages" in the Midwestern United States (Leighton and MacClintock 1962; Retallack 1990) and two or more "ice ages" in the Rocky Mountains (Hall et al. 1993, 1995). Interglacial weathering is assumed between glacial ages (Cioppa et al. 1995; Horberg 1956; Karlstrom 1982, 1987, 1988, 1990, 1991). However, these paleosols are often absent or dubious (Lemke et al. 1965). In recent years, some paleopedologic interpretations have run aground on physical evidences or the preference of many researchers for deep-sea cores or other paleoclimatological methods (Froede 1998). Nonetheless, paleopedology remains an important discipline in stratigraphy (Klevberg 2000a), and it probably will remain so for the foreseeable future.

While the DGP can accommodate the theoretical concept of paleosols, they are not expected to be common. On the other hand, the EGP virtually demands *ubiquitous* paleosols because of the assumptions of gradualism, localized catastrophes, and vast periods of time for earth history (Froede 1998). There is no doubt that the traditional understanding of paleosols conflicts with the biblical history of thousands of years and a global Flood. How can these "paleosols" represent so much time? Are they really buried soils? Can one really estimate paleoclimate from a paleosol? Are there alternative interpretations?

How to Study Paleosols

Because a paleosol represents particular events occurring in the past, its study is essentially *history*. Because soil studies are science, the issue is a mixed question — one in which information from different disciplines is applied to reach truth (Adler 1965). Paleopedology, as a subset of historical geology, is a subset of history, contrary to the modern positivist belief that it must be a field of science. A positivist is one who believes that science provides a superior path to truth. Extreme positivists believe that science provides the only path to truth. Although science plays an important role, it cannot act alone (Klevberg 1999; Morris 1984; Reed 2001). Conclusions about paleosols thus depend on presuppositions about the past. Since those of the EGP differ greatly from those of the DGP, EGP conclusions (driven primarily by EGP assumptions) cannot be valid arguments against the DGP.

Science functions as the forensic tool of natural history, and it can certainly help address the question of paleosols. However, tools like radiometric dating that are tainted by EGP assumptions will be less useful than more empirical methods. In theory, the EGP and DGP approach via science should be identical; unfortunately this is seldom the case, because historical bias is very strong.

But one scientific point is clear. Researchers from either paradigm must pay careful attention to properties that distinguish soil-forming processes from *other weathering processes* to determine whether or not specific layers in the rock record actually represent ancient soils.

Do Paleosols Exist?

Since soils have been buried by various natural phenomena in historic times, we can safely assert that if paleosols are defined as *buried soil horizons in which soil-forming processes are no longer operative,* paleosols *do* exist. Each part of this definition is important. For example, figure 2 shows a buried soil exposed in the bank of Cottonwood Creek, Fergus County, Montana. Note that while the A horizon has been disturbed, it is still distinct and well-preserved beneath nearly a meter of local flood deposits. A new soil is forming in the flood alluvium, complete with a new A horizon. Because the annual average depth of wetting at this site is deeper than the buried A horizon, the pre-Flood soil is merely a buried soil and *not* a paleosol.

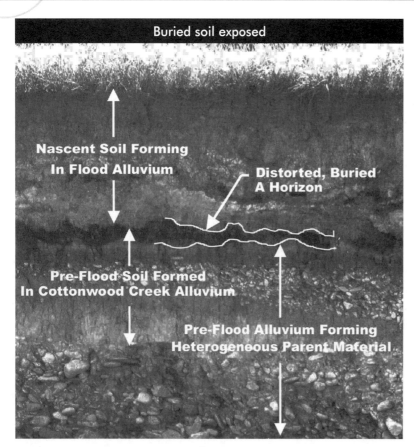

Figure 2. Buried soil in flood plain of Cottonwood Creek, Fergus County, Montana. Although slightly disturbed, the A horizon has been completely preserved. USDA photograph.

Figure 3. Goertzen Homestead, Near Hodgeville, Saskatchewan. Aeolian material during the Dust Bowl buried soil around the fence line to a depth of up to more than three feet (one meter).

Figure 3 shows a homestead in Saskatchewan. During the Dust Bowl, approximately a meter of aeolian deposits buried the pre-1930s soil (Lauber 1963) (figure 4). Today, soil-forming processes are active in the aeolian material in figure 3. Although the pre-1930s soil is buried, it cannot be conclusively identified as a paleosol because the average annual wetting depth is unknown. If a combination of permeability and microclimate (e.g., snow accumulation on a shaded lee slope or behind vegetation) enabled the wetting depth to extend deeper than one meter, this would be merely a buried soil. Another problem is preservation; if climate change resulted in increased depth of soil formation, a paleosol could be destroyed.

Figure 5 shows the lee mountainside covered by the Hebgen Lake earthquake slide in Montana. The pre-1959 soil is at least several meters beneath the present ground surface, too deep for most soil-forming mechanisms to be operative and too deep to act as a rooting medium for nearly all plants. It is thus a *true* paleosol. In similar cases, volcanic eruptions, debris flows, or other events have buried soils well beyond the reach of soil-forming processes. These, too, are now paleosols. However, all these paleosols are near the surface and were buried by typical post-diluvial geological processes.

Nonetheless, since the vast majority of alleged paleosols are stratigraphically *much deeper* in the rock record, the question is not so easily answered for these. The scientific method can disprove many individual cases, but that requires physical data and diagnostic properties. As Froede (1998, p. 25) noted:

> Uniformitarians state that soils have existed on earth for hundreds of millions of years, with some surviving into the present due to burial and preservation. This interpretation should be supported by the physical evidence (i.e., paleosols) if it is to be accepted.

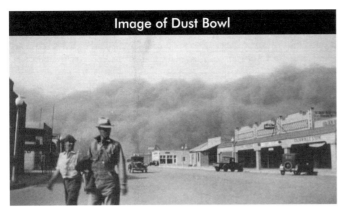

Image of Dust Bowl

Figure 4. Approaching dust storm, Springfield Colorado, in 1934. Photograph courtesy of Cecil and Lynn Walborn.

Image of mountainside covered by the Hebgen Lake earthquake slide

Source of debris

Earthquake Lake

Debris from 1959 landslide

Debris from 1959 landslide

Figure 5. A 1995 photograph of the Hebgen Lake earthquake slide in southwestern Montana which formed Earthquake Lake. Landslide debris from the other side of the valley moved up the slope to bury the pre-1959 soil, forming a paleosol.

Problems with Paleosol Criteria

Soil Profiles

Many earth materials form horizontal or subhorizontal layers, but not all of these represent soil profiles. Soil profiles show specific characteristics (Klevberg and Bandy 2003a) often specific to individual horizons and observable by close examination of undisturbed samples (see chapter 5). Paleosol horizons should assume a particular order if the strata actually represent a soil profile (table 1). Although some of the horizons could be missing, those present must appear in the correct order.

Some soils can appear structureless while really possessing structure; modern soils have definite soil horizons where the soil changes composition with depth due to soil-forming processes. Paleosols, in contrast with modern soils, have been buried and hence have undergone some degree of compaction and diagenesis. Although often

subject to significant alteration, supposedly they can still be distinguished from other sedimentary layers. Retallack (1990) recognized paleosols in the field by three main features: (1) root traces, (2) soil horizons, and (3) soil structures. These criteria, associated problems, and alternative explanations for each are summarized in table 2.

Trace Fossils

Retallack (1988) claimed that root traces alone are diagnostic of paleosols. However, he admitted that it is sometimes difficult to distinguish between a "root trace," a "burrow," and a gas escape structure (Retallack 1990). Trace fossils represent activities of certain organisms (burrowing, feeding, etc.), though interpretations are not always free from equivocation (Woodmorappe 2002). Root traces are considered diagnostic of plant growth in the particular stratum. The presence of other traces in a "paleosol" is problematic, because the EGP is biased

Table 1. Soil Horizon Descriptions

	Horizon	Description
Surface of Soil	O horizon	• An O horizon is considered a horizon dominated by organic material in various stages of decomposition. Little or no mineral material is present in this horizon.
	A horizon	• The A horizon is a mineral horizon that occurs either at the soil surface or directly below an O horizon (Soil Survey Manual 1993). This horizon typically is enriched with some organic material that causes a darkening of the horizon.
	E horizon	• The E horizon is a mineral horizon in which the main feature is loss of silicate clay, iron, aluminum, or some combination of these (cf. Soil Survey Manual, 1993). This horizon is highly leached and tends to be a very light gray to white color with little or no organic matter present.
Base of Solum	B horizon	• The B horizon is a subsurface horizon that, if present, is found below an A and/or E horizon. It shows one or more of the following features (cf. Soil Survey Manual, 1993): illuvial concentration of silicate clay, iron, aluminum, humus, carbonates, gypsum, or silica. • evidence of removal of carbonates • residual concentrations of sesquioxides • coatings of sesquioxides that make the horizon different in color from adjacent horizons • granular, blocky, or prismatic structure; or • brittleness
	C horizon	• The C horizon is little affected by pedogenic processes and lacks properties of O, A, E, B horizons (cf. Soil Survey Manual, 1993).
	R horizon	• The R horizon is hard bedrock.

Table 2. Distinguishing Criteria for Paleosol Identification

Criterion	EGP Interpretation	Alternative Processes
Trace fossils	Roots indicate growth position; burrows usually represent ordinary conditions.	"Trace fossils" may be evulsion structures; burrows may not indicate ordinary conditions (including escape burrows); root debris may have been simply buried, often upright.
Contrasting Horizons ("Profile")	Soil profile development has been preserved as a paleosol.	Mineralogic or sedimentologic stratification may produce horizons, as may nonpedogenic weathering processes.
Clay-Rich Horizons	Clay-rich horizons are indicative of illuviation and diagnostic of pedogenesis.	Clay-rich horizons may be syndepositional, hydrothermal, or due to diagenetic epigenesis.
Carbonate Horizons	Calcic or petrocalcic horizons are indicative of soil horizon formed in arid or semi-arid climate.	Carbonate may be syndepositional or deposited by groundwater.
Oxidation	Oxidation is indicative of surficial weathering in the zone of soil formation.	Oxidation may be syndepositional or diagenetic rather than pedogenic.
Underclays	Underclays represent soil in which forests grew or beneath swamps that were sources of organic material for coal formation.	Underclays result from typical hydrodynamic sedimentation effects (cyclothems, fining upward sequences); most coals are allochthonous, not autochthonous.
Glaebules	Glaebules are relict indicators of a previous soil where soil-forming conditions differed from extant ones.	Glaebules may be indicators of anisotropic parent material, the complexity of epigenesis, or a complex history for the formation of a given soil.
Physil ("Clay Mineral") Types	Physils (especially allophane and gibbsite) are evidence of epigenesis over long periods of pedogenic weathering.	Physils may be syndepositional or diagenetic and are often complex assemblages at the microscopic level

toward environments analogous to the present, excluding catastrophic or diluvial explanations a priori. For example, some traces may represent escape routes of organisms in danger of burial rather than dwelling or feeding burrows, or may consist of casts of root fragments buried in diluvial sediments rather than preserved in growth position. Furthermore, evulsion structures or other physical phenomena may easily be misinterpreted as trace fossils (Tucker 1990). Far from being diagnostic, the trace fossil criterion for paleosol identification is equivocal.

Soil Horizons

One of the diagnostic criteria of a paleosol is a sharply truncated upper horizon and a gradational lower horizon (Retallack 1990). The truncated upper horizon is interpreted to mean that the organic-enriched A horizon is missing (Birkeland 1984; Boardman, 1985), leaving behind a clay layer, a calcium carbonate layer, or a red layer, etc. These are *inferred* fossil soil horizons. That is convenient because it is the A horizon that *most readily* identifies a real paleosol. Since "paleosols" commonly lack an A horizon, they are often just a clay layer or a "weathered layer" (Retallack 1990). This is puzzling; preservation of an A horizon should not be unusual (figure 2). Diagenetic processes may result in formation of lignite, a low-grade coal, or some other carboniferous horizon, but *complete absence* of an A horizon makes a paleosol claim *suspect*. A true paleosol should correspond to the sequence illustrated in table 1.

Since the A horizon is usually missing, the literature focuses on the *inferred* B horizon. This "B horizon" supposedly validates the paleosol interpretation, as well as dating it, based on the "degree of development":

> The degree of development of a soil or paleosol is evaluated by the clayeyness of the B horizon and its type of clay, thickness of the B horizon, and the presence and strength of clayey structures, colors, and nodules . . . (Bestland 1997, p. 848).

As discussed in chapter 5, development of B_t or other B horizons is not just a time factor; parent material, topography, and climate (probably even biology) exert strong influences (Klevberg and Bandy 2003a). For example, potholes in glacial till contain soils that have thick, high-clay content B_t horizons. Soils outside the potholes have thinner B_t horizons with less clay, even though their soil-forming factors were identical in all other respects.

Soils with clay-enriched horizons are common. These horizons typically have formed from eluviation (clays leaching from surface horizons) and illuviation (clays being deposited in underlying horizons). Clay films on ped surfaces will usually distinguish between the two. Illuvial movement of clays into lower horizons should have clay films present on ped surfaces. Clay-rich horizons may also form from different parent materials being deposited on top of one another. Clay translocation can occur much more rapidly than is commonly assumed (Klevberg and Bandy 2003b).

Carbonate horizons (often called "caliche") can form pedogenically. Soil scientists call these calcic horizons, "petrocalcic horizons" or sometimes "calcrete" if cemented. Geologists utilize a variety of descriptive terms (e.g., lime-cemented conglomerate, carbonaceous sandstone, marl) to describe carbonate-dominated geologic units. Caliche is common in dry climates where leaching does not occur beyond the depth of the solum. Most soils in arid and semi-arid areas have a $CaCO_3$-enriched horizon that forms when $CaCO_3$ is leached into the solum past the average annual wetting depth.

These horizons are frequently cited as evidence for paleosols. Petrocalcic horizons in soils can easily be formed by *groundwater*. As the water evaporates or is used by plants, $CaCO_3$ is deposited, plugging the pores and cementing soil particles together. While it is true that $CaCO_3$-enriched horizons commonly occur in modern soils, pedogenesis is only one explanation. Carbonate may be syndepositional, emplaced at the same time as the sediment, or may be introduced later into geologic beds by groundwater. Many deposits have had complex histories with multiple sources of carbonate. Furthermore, B_k horizons in extant soils are not usually cemented.

Some paleosols are identified by oxidized horizons. However, oxidation occurs in most soils regardless of degree of weathering or depth of horizons. Reduction only occurs when anaerobic conditions are present along with the following:

- a food source
- temperatures above 5°C
- anaerobic bacteria present
- saturated soils

Where these conditions do not exist, oxidation will occur. Oxidized minerals are often found where hydrothermal alteration or other geologic processes have occurred. Palmer et al. (1989) recognized that many alleged paleosols are more readily explained by hydrothermal and metamorphic processes.

Underclays are probably the most commonly invoked "paleosols" of pre-"Quaternary" rocks (Froede 1998). These are often relatively structureless clays, subjacent to coal beds, and common in a cyclothem, a series of beds in which coal is one of the beds. In the EGP, these represent the C horizon of a histosol, an organically rich soil, in the classic coal swamp (Klevberg and Bandy 2003a). However, no soil profile is found in underclays (Scheven 1996), and the swamp theory for coal formation has been widely refuted (Coffin 1968, 1969; Rupke 1969; Snelling and Mackay 1984; Woodmorappe 1999). The presence of underclays in cyclothems suggests that their formation was part of a rapid depositional process (Berthault 1986; Woodmorappe 1999).

Soil Structures

Of special interest in the study of paleosols are peds (soil aggregates), cutans (the surfaces of peds), glaebules (aggregates of distinctive composition), and mineral crystals such as gypsum. Peds and cutans are hard to identify in paleosols because of compaction and diagenesis (Retallack 1990). Since glaebules and crystals can form in other types of sediments (Retallack 1990), they do not form solely in paleosols and *cannot*, therefore, be diagnostic of paleosols. Rather, the complexity of pedogenesis suggests that glaebules that are unrelated to paleosols should be common in many soils.

Physil species, sometimes considered diagnostic of soil-forming processes, have been observed in circumstances indicative of syngenetic or diagenetic processes (Klevberg and Bandy 2003b). Although they may be useful in testing various pedogenesis scenarios, they have multiple possible sources of origin and are thus *not* diagnostic of paleosols. They are actually diagnostic of parent material, not pedogenic history (Birkeland 1974).

Froede (1998, p. 25–26) noted the general difficulty facing paleopedologists in distinguishing paleosols in the geologic record:

> Presently, there is no standardized technique by which paleosols can be defined. Some investigators use modern soil science methods while others have developed their own schemes. . . . In many cases paleopedologists claim to be able to identify multiple buried soil horizons. . . . The identification of the purported paleosol horizons is based on a variety of soil classification techniques which allow for a highly interpretative framework. . . . This suggests an element of subjectivity involved in the "science."

We do well to heed the warning of James et al. (1993, p. 1,637):

> . . . many paleosols do not possess adequate characteristics to allow for proper classification at the order level following *Soil Taxonomy*. This is a fact.

Diagnostic criteria for paleosols are lacking, and perhaps because of this the methodology is scientifically weak (White 1998). As a consequence, claims that "paleosols" invalidate the DGP must be correspondingly weak.

The Argument from Rates of Soil Formation

As documented in chapter 5, modern soils, and by extension paleosols, are merely *assumed* to form over long periods of time. One reason for the extended rates of the EGP is the assumption that "Quaternary" soils are analogues for the time it would take a true paleosol to develop (Retallack, 1990, p. 13). Since the base of the "Quaternary" is nearly two million years in the past, it is little wonder that long ages are *automatically* built into "paleosols." Once again, the EGP *conclusion* is simply an outgrowth of the hugely inflated uniformitarian time scale (Klevberg and Bandy 2003a, 2003b).

In reality, modern soil-forming rates are *unknown* (Boardman 1985). Birkeland (1984, p. 118–119) admitted:

> It should be pointed out that it is very difficult to determine soil processes because few actual measurements can or have been made.

However, scientific observation has established one indisputable fact: soils can form quickly under the right conditions. For instance, a 9.4-inch (24-cm) thick andisol with distinct horizons formed within 74 years on Kodiak Island, Alaska (Ping 2000). A 14-inch (36-cm) thick andisol formed in just 45 years on volcanic ash deposited from the eruption of Krakatau (Leet and Judson 1965). Other soil orders, forming less quickly than andisols (those soils formed in volcanic material), may still take less time to form than commonly asserted, and some may even be partial relicts of geologic processes (Klevberg and Bandy 2003a, 2003b). Soil formation in the limestone of Kamenetz Fortress in Ukraine in a xeric moisture regime (a region dominated by mollisols, those with strong surface horizon development) amounted to 12 inches (30 cm) in 230 years, and comparable rates of soil formation have been observed in sand dunes and moraines in even relatively cool and dry climates

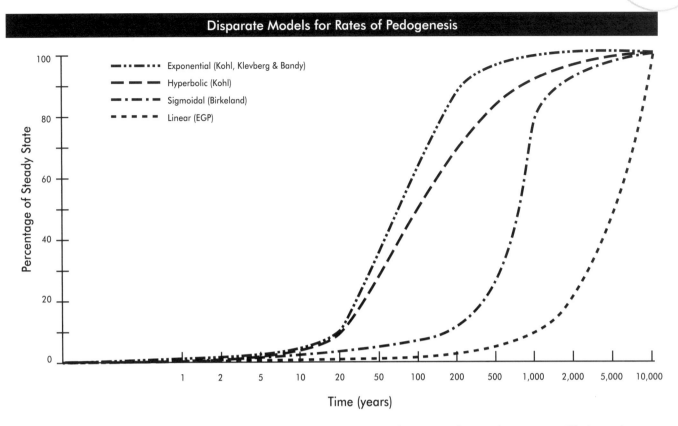

Figure 6. Disparate models for rates of pedogenesis. The term "steady state" refers to dynamic equilibrium of soil-forming processes with environmental factors (Klevberg and Bandy 2003a; Lavkulich 1969). The example used here is entirely arbitrary; ten thousand years might be accepted for a slow-forming mollisol, a typical alfisol, or a quick-forming ultisol.

(Jenny 1941). Caliche can form quickly enough to clog drain pipes (Hunt 1972). So, while rates are unknown, *observed* rates for many soils are much faster than traditionally thought (Burykin and Zasorinal 1989; Klevberg and Bandy 2003b).

For example, even if we granted the EGP assumption that a soil would take 10,000 years to reach "maturity," the actual rates of the various processes may differ greatly. As has been shown elsewhere (Klevberg and Bandy 2003a, 2003b), pedogenic processes are not generally linear, as recognized by Birkeland (1974), who proposed a sigmoidal rate function (a curve that increases upward more in the middle of the graph and slower at the upper and lower ends). Though more realistic than the linear assumption, Birkeland's EGP bias still caused him to overestimate the time required for pedogenesis. Note that if one selects an arbitrary percentage of steady state, say 50 percent, the inferred time of formation may differ by orders of magnitude. So, although many EGP adherents have come to recognize the rapidity with which some individual soils or soil series may form, the assumption

of great ages continues (Crocker 1960; Guggenberger et al. 1998; Klevberg and Bandy 2003b) because the conclusion of age is driven not by pedology, but by the EGP itself (figure 6).

We believe that early pedogenesis probably occurs more rapidly than even Birkeland proposed, and that an exponential or hyperbolic function (figure 6) is more realistic (Klevberg and Bandy 2003b; Kohl 2002). For example, rapid soil development occurred in many irrigated regions of the American West where land was leveled and then subjected to surface irrigation. Deep cuts on ridges exposed subsoil that was rapidly brought into production with good management (Kohl 2002). Development of natriustalfs (alfisols with natric horizons) took less than 60 years in South Dakota (Westin 1970, p. 17), and in cases of high-sodium irrigation water, as little as 2 years (Kohl 2003). In Alaskan soils, spodic and albic horizons have been observed to form in fewer than 150 years (Bormann et al. 1995). Water, particularly groundwater, has probably been more important in pedogenesis than recognized by many (Jenny 1941, p. 92; Klevberg and Bandy 2003a).

Also, plant succession can result in a highly nonlinear, decreasing-rate pedogenesis function (Bormann and Sidle 1990; Crocker 1960).

Alternative Explanations for Paleosols

What might a DGP explanation be if given a clay layer or a layer rich in calcium carbonate? Genetic interpretation should depend on the properties of these layers and not root traces or soil structures. There are at least three possible explanations, other than a paleosol, within the DGP:

1. A clay, calcium carbonate, or oxidized layer could simply be a result of aqueous deposition. Clay layers can be deposited rapidly by flocculation, while a red layer might indicate iron-rich water. While individual clay particles do not readily settle even in still water, aggregates of clay particles ("flocs") settle rapidly. Flocculation is commonly induced by the introduction of salts[2] (e.g., $CaCO_3$, $CaSO_4$, $Fe_2(SO_4)_3$, and especially $Al_2(SO_4)_3$, alum). Introducing approximately 25 mg alum for each liter of severely turbid water (or 300 mg of gypsum per liter) typically clears the water of suspended clay particles in a few hours (Hargreaves 1999). Physical means (typically limited to careful piping layout and discharge geometry) are used successfully to provide rapid deposition of clay-size tailings at many mines. Thus, contrary to the arguments of some (Bowden 2000, 2001; Froede 2001; Klevberg 2001), rapid deposition of clays — especially in the presence of iron and other salts — is not only possible, but likely to have occurred during the yearlong upheaval of the Deluge (Gen. 7:11), and subsequently on a smaller scale.

2. Sediment can be modified after deposition by meteoric water. Hydrothermal alteration can alter mineralogy. If rapid deposition occurred during the Genesis Flood — perhaps hundreds of meters in less than a day — accumulating lithostatic pressure would force excess water out. Chemically saturated waters moving under high pressure would quickly alter the sediment through which they flowed. Even practitioners of the EGP admit this. For instance, gray loams in the rocks of the Rhenish Massif have been interpreted as *both* the product of surficial weathering and the result of rock decomposition by ascending hydrothermal solutions (Meyer et al. 1983). Deeply kaolinized granite in southwest England (the Cornubian Batholith) is believed to be a reaction product of hydrothermal origin by some (Thomas 1994). Other batholiths exhibit weathering that is probably diagenetic rather than epigenetic (Snelling and Woodmorappe 1998). "Precambrian paleosols" in South Africa may be the products of hydrothermal alteration along lithological contacts (Palmer et al., 1989). This appears to be true of similar deposits (Williams 1969). Ollier and Pain (1996, p. 62) admitted:

   > Rising water, steam, and other emanations from deep in the earth move upwards through enclosing country rock and bring about some alteration. This may include the formation of tourmaline or fluorite in hard rocks, but it may also include the formation of clays. This is not [surficial] weathering, but hydrothermally altered rocks may come to look very much like weathered rocks. . . .

3. Third, a paleosol can be formed by less dramatic diagenetic processes. Diagenesis includes any alteration of sediment between the categories of weathering and metamorphism. It includes compaction, cementation, oxidation, reduction, hydrolysis, bacterial action, and replacement. Froede (1998) noted that diagenetic changes can be misidentified as paleosol horizons, as do some EGP researchers (Valentine and Dalrymple 1976; Bowen 1978). During the Deluge, one would expect a large variety of diagenetic changes due to various combinations of heat, pressure, chemistry, etc., that those adhering to the EGP would exclude from their thinking. Some investigators have found that early diagenetic groundwater alteration can mimic hydromorphic soil features, such as pseudogley mottling and calcic horizons (Kraus 1999).

At a minimum, identifying soil profiles and structures in the geologic record can be fraught with difficulties,

---

2. An exception is NaCl, since Na^+ is effective as a dispersing agent.

especially if the horizon in question has been clearly subjected to diagenesis (Retallack 1990). If altered enough, the layer may be indistinguishable from a zone of hydrothermal alteration (Retallack 1990). We have seen that alleged paleosols seldom exhibit a recognizable soil profile (table 1). Furthermore, the existence of roots or "root traces" cannot automatically define a paleosol. One should especially be suspicious when the supposed soil-forming process did not erase bedding planes or ripple marks, as admitted by Retallack (1990). Alternative explanations not only exist; they often appear more reasonable (White 1998).

The Equivocal Nature of Prominent Paleosols

EGP adherents usually cite a few prominent paleosols to support their arguments against the DGP. How well do they stand up to detailed examination based on the criteria discussed above?

The most well-known paleosols are those used to distinguish North American "interglacials." However, these are difficult to identify, patchy, and lack an A horizon, among other problems (Valentine and Dalrymple 1976; Oard 1990). Furthermore, the traditional glacial/interglacial scheme is now considered wrong; there are supposedly many more glaciations over a longer period than earlier indicated by the paleosol evidence (Boellstorff 1978; Woida and Thompson 1993). These glaciations are based on oxygen isotope ratios in deep-sea cores (Oard 1984a, 1984b, 1985).

Another group of well-known paleosols are underclays, often associated with coal seams. However, these are often structureless, with no evidence of soil profile development. Also, many overlying coal seams exhibit evidence of allocthonous depositional processes, invalidating the EGP "coal swamp" scenario. These deposits are often stacked in cyclothems; recent work by Berthault (1986, 2002a, 2002b) indicates rapid, energetic deposition, not soil formation.

Another EGP staple is the example of stacked sequences of paleosols. Unlike cyclothems, these generally do not occur as repeated combinations of particular sedimentary rocks. Instead, the number of paleosols and their vertical extent are often matters of debate (Froede 1998). However, those distinctions are essential if a pedostratigraphic column is to be formulated. And any interpretation about age, paleogeography, and paleoclimatology requires an accurate stratigraphic column.

A Diluvial Approach

In light of the information presented above, let us again consider the question, "Can paleosols exist?" Both paradigms affirm the existence of paleosols (Froede 1998), as long as *paleosol* is defined as *a buried soil horizon in which soil-forming processes are no longer operative*. However, the DGP does not admit the same genesis of paleosols. Indeed, it is this point of history that produces conflict between the EGP and DGP. If soil formation requires the length of time widely credited to it by the EGP, then formation of a single soil horizon, let alone multiple paleosols, is impossible within the diluvial time scale. However, observations of both rapid pedogenesis and catastrophic burial of soils is more congruent with the DGP than the EGP. The DGP predicts that paleosols will be less common, less laterally extensive, and more rapidly formed (Froede 1998; Klevberg and Bandy 2003b).

Implications for Paleopedology and Pedostratigraphy

In scientific research, error ranges or degrees of precision are very important and regularly reported. It is often critical to know the confidence interval of a result, and no measurement is complete without an implicit or explicit statement of precision. In historical research, a similar situation exists. One of the most important tasks of the historian is to weigh the relative reliability of conflicting witnesses. In neither case can we be assured of reaching "absolute truth." Both disciplines are human endeavors subject to human limitations. Yet geologists and paleopedologists can display incredible dogmatism. It is vital that we remember that any paleopedologic interpretation is just that — an *interpretation* — and the answers we give to these mixed questions are always tentative, and only as good as our historical and scientific data and inferences. We are limited by both our ability to concoct historical scenarios and to scientifically disprove them.

Pedostratigraphy naturally derives from paleopedology. Stratigraphy is the correlation of discrete bodies of earth materials to deduce their geometric orientation and relation to each other. One goal of investigating outcrops or boring logs is to construct a local stratigraphic column (figure 7). As with any stratigraphic method, great care must be taken to distinguish between scientific observation and historical inference (Reed et al. 2006).

Stratigraphers often refer to "independent lines of evidence" that have established a certain age-dating or stratigraphic scheme. The unwillingness to admit that

How a stratigraphic column is developed

Rock or soil properties, fossil content, or other properties are used to distinguish individual rock or soil units. An attempt is made to match these laterally and to develop a stratigraphic column that illustrates the way the units relate spatially in nature. Many also attempt to relate the units temporally (which is an effort in historical speculation, not science).

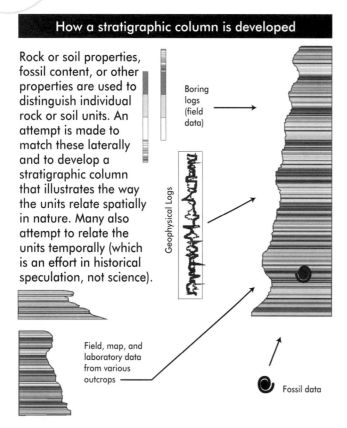

Boring logs (field data)

Geophysical Logs

Field, map, and laboratory data from various outcrops

Fossil data

Figure 7. How a stratigraphic column is assembled.

Correspondence

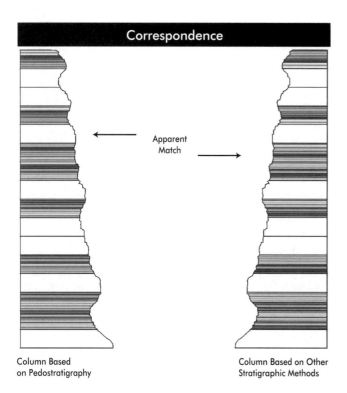

Apparent Match

Column Based on Pedostratigraphy

Column Based on Other Stratigraphic Methods

Figure 8. Apparent stratigraphic match which is not unique. In this illustration, pedostratigraphy appears to provide a perfect fit with other stratigraphic methods. However, because the correspondence is not unique, this may be coincidental or contrived.

historical inquiries are mixed questions challenges these because it reveals a remarkable ignorance of the parameters of investigation. Often such evidence is simply an example of the reinforcement syndrome (Klevberg 2000b; Oard 1997; Thompson and Berglund 1976), a psychological phenomenon wherein researchers increasingly attempt — and possibly succeed — in finding data to support a popular new hypothesis. They "jump on the bandwagon" until the hypothesis becomes "common knowledge" among the scientific mainstream. Although science is supposed to inhibit such behavior, a passing acquaintance with the current state of scientific thought reveals otherwise. Furthermore, pedostratigraphy is not a strictly *scientific* approach, whatever other merits it may have (Klevberg 2000a). So what of the "agreement" between various methods? There are several possibilities:

1. Assuming that the paleopedologic interpretation is right, and it is in agreement with magnetostratigraphy, biostratigraphy, etc., then it would tend to support the EGP interpretation. However, this support is weak if the correspondence is not *unique*, as has been demonstrated elsewhere relative to cyclothems (Zeller 1964) and eustatic, or sea level, curves (Miall 1992). Although the apparent correspondence between the stratigraphic sequence determined by different methods is impressive, it also may indicate a cyclic pattern in the rock record or researcher bias. Correspondence may be fortuitous or contrived (figure 8). If, for example, data from many sources all show alternating, meter-thick beds of sandstone and claystone that are virtually indistinguishable from similar beds above and below, any shift of two meters up or down will make any two boring logs match. A pattern such as that in figure 8 could fool a geologist into a false correlation. Pedostratigraphy may produce a sequence that appears identical to one determined using geophysical methods (e.g., resistivity or remanent magnetization), yet this sequence still may be correlated incorrectly, as illustrated by figure 9.

2. Assuming that the paleopedologic sequence is right, and it is in agreement with other stratigraphic methods, but the time required to form the sequence differs from other "dating" methods, then (although rarely admitted) the time scales of the other methods may be in error (figure 10). Radiometric "dates" are often used

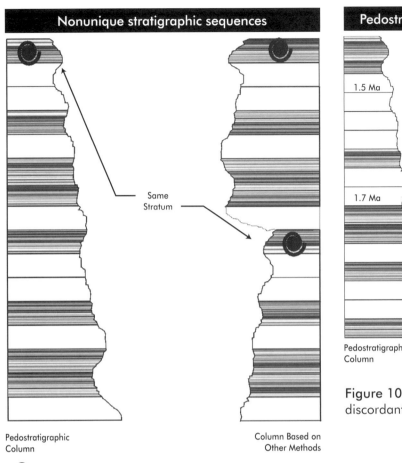

Nonunique stratigraphic sequences

Same Stratum

Pedostratigraphic Column

Column Based on Other Methods

◎ Fossil

Figure 9. Mistaken stratigraphic correlation of cyclic strata. Illustration of nonunique stratigraphic sequences with false apparent correspondence between stratigraphic methods.

Pedostratigraphic compared with other methods

1.5 Ma

1.7 Ma

2.5 Ma

5.3 Ma

If good agreement exists between stratigraphic columns, but the agreement does not extend to the "dates" assigned to the various units, then the "dating" methods are called into question. (Unfortunately, assumed evolutionary fossil succession usually governs the interpretation, often with rejection not only of radiometric "dates," but even of hard data when they conflict with EGP assumptions!)

Pedostratigraphic Column

Column Based on Other Methods

Figure 10. Matching stratigraphic columns with discordant "dates."

to *force* agreement from other data, and fossil assemblages are generally considered determinative. Either can add imaginary detail to the stratigraphic interpretation — hiatuses, overthrusts, paraconformities, etc. Conflicts between fossils, radiometric dates, and field stratigraphy are *seldom* used to force reevaluation of the method, and *never* to force reevaluation of the paradigm.

3. If a given sequence of strata is complicated or nearly random, agreement between a local stratigraphic column developed using paleopedology and a sequence developed using another stratigraphic method would tend to enhance confidence in the interpretation (figure 11). If the paleopedologic interpretation is wrong,

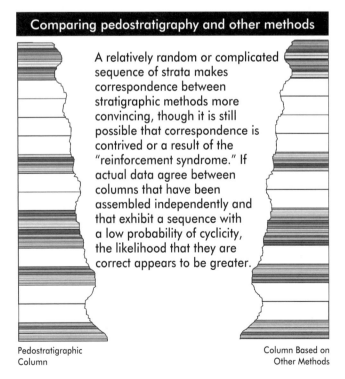

Comparing pedostratigraphy and other methods

A relatively random or complicated sequence of strata makes correspondence between stratigraphic methods more convincing, though it is still possible that correspondence is contrived or a result of the "reinforcement syndrome." If actual data agree between columns that have been assembled independently and that exhibit a sequence with a low probability of cyclicity, the likelihood that they are correct appears to be greater.

Pedostratigraphic Column

Column Based on Other Methods

Figure 11. Convincing correspondence between stratigraphic methods.

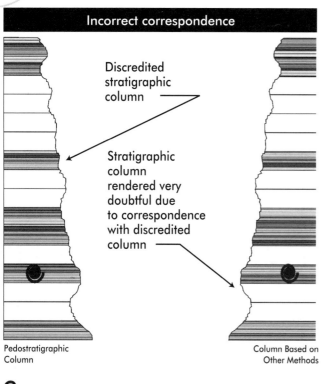

Incorrect correspondence

Discredited
stratigraphic
column

Stratigraphic
column
rendered very
doubtful due
to correspondence
with discredited
column

Pedostratigraphic
Column

Column Based on
Other Methods

 Fossil

Figure 12. Discredited column with good correspondence to other methods.

Doubtful interpretation

Discredited
stratigraphic
column

Stratigraphic
column rendered
somewhat doubtful
due to nonunique,
apparent
correspondence
with discredited
column

Column based
on Pedostratigraphy

Column Based on Other
Stratigraphic Methods

Figure 13. Doubtful correspondence with doubtful column.

and a sequence of strata represents a number of geologic events different from the paleopedologic scenario, then the alleged correspondence between pedostratigraphy and biostratigraphy or magnetostratigraphy is also wrong. This casts doubt on these other methods, especially if the correspondence between methods appears strong at the time one is discredited (figure 12).

4. If the paleopedologic interpretation is doubtful, and the correspondence with other methods is clearly not unique, then no mutual support between methods can be adduced, however convincing they may appear (figure 13).

5. If the paleopedologic interpretation conflicts with correlations based on other methods, at least one of the methods is invalid. This applies to any two stratigraphic (or "absolute dating") methods (figure 14).

6. To provide a truly meaningful comparison, the pedostratigraphic column must be developed *independently* of the other methods and then compared with the results from other methods. Unless this is done, bias can be expected and the results may be just another example of the

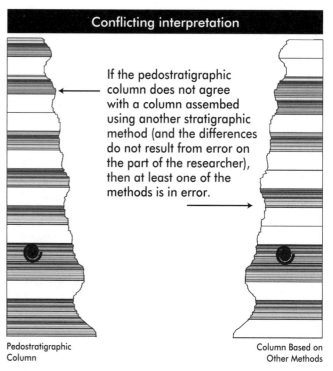

Conflicting interpretation

If the pedostratigraphic column does not agree with a column assembed using another stratigraphic method (and the differences do not result from error on the part of the researcher), then at least one of the methods is in error.

Pedostratigraphic
Column

Column Based on
Other Methods

Figure 14. Lack of correlation between stratigraphic methods.

reinforcement syndrome. In general, uniformitarians specifically *avoid* using pedostratigraphy independently of the other stratigraphic methods, though some warn of the need for quantitative data and care in avoiding this pitfall (Birkeland 1984).

When DGP assumptions are substituted for EGP assumptions, conclusions differ markedly. For example, suppose an EGP researcher believes 90 paleosols are represented in the wall of a canyon. His paradigm forces him to conclude that a low-energy, terrestrial environment was present for most of that time. If faced with sedimentological evidence suggesting energetic geologic processes, he must abandon one of his conclusions. One or both — his paleoenvironmental interpretation and his chronology — will be distorted. A DGP researcher might evaluate the same outcrop, note that the sedimentologic data demand deposition of the entire sequence in a very short time, and thus be directed toward diagenetic investigations (that he might not otherwise have pursued) that would explain the altered horizons. Which paradigm would be proven the most helpful? Yet the "open-minded" EGP adherent would never dream of exploring explanations outside his paradigm.

Conclusions

The field of paleopedology is primarily an historical enterprise that uses science as a forensic tool. Until advocates of the EGP admit this simple (and obvious) fact, their studies will be skewed toward a certainty that simply does not exist, all because they think they are doing "science." With regard to paleosols or any other natural history endeavor, that is the first advantage of the DGP.

Paleosols are not inimical to the DGP, but certainly lead to different interpretations. This is especially true in regard to the expected abundance and rate of formation of paleosols. EGP researchers are trapped by their long time frame just as much as DGP researchers are trapped by their short one. But *observation* supports rapid pedogenesis, contrary to EGP predictions. Furthermore, paleosols may be virtually impossible to identify in the field because the unique criteria that define soils are absent in ancient strata. Most uniformitarian examples are theory-driven and unconvincing. Common examples of paleosols are equally amenable to DGP interpretation. Given the depth of EGP bias, it may well be that most paleosols exist only in the mind of the beholder.

References

CRSQ: Creation Research Society Quarterly
CENTJ: Creation Ex Nihilo Technical Journal (now Journal of Creation)

Adler, Mortimer J. 1965. *The Conditions of Philosophy*. New York: Atheneum.

Bates, R.L., and J.A. Jackson (editors). 1984. *Dictionary of Geological Terms*, third edition. New York: Anchor Press/Doubleday.

Berthault, G. 1986. Experiments on lamination of sediments, resulting from a periodic graded-bedding subsequent to deposit. A contribution to the explanation of lamination of various sediments and sedimentary rocks. *Compte Rendus Academie des Sciences, Série II: Mecanique, Physique, Chimie, Sciences de la Terre et de l'Univers* 303:1569–1574.

———. 2002a. Analysis of main principles of stratigraphy on the basis of experimental data. *Lithology and Mineral Resources* 37:442–446.

———. 2002b. Geological dating principles questioned — paleohydraulics: A new approach. *Journal of Geodesy and Geodynamics* 22(3):19–26.

Bestland, E.A. 1997. Alluvial terraces and paleosols as indicators of early Oligocene climate change (John Day Formation, Oregon). *Journal of Sedimentary Research* 67(5):840–855.

Birkeland, P.W. 1974. *Pedology, Weathering, and Geomorphological Research*. New York: Oxford University Press.

———. 1984. *Soils and Geomorphology*. New York: Oxford University Press.

Blatt, H., G.V. Middleton, and R. Murray. 1972. *Origin of Sedimentary Rocks*. Englewood Cliffs, NJ: Prentice-Hall.

Boardman, J. 1985. Comparison of soils in Midwestern United States and Western Europe with the interglacial record. *Quaternary Research* 23:62–75.

Boellstorff, J. 1978. North American Pleistocene stages reconsidered in light of probable Pliocene-Pleistocene continental glaciations. *Science* 202:305–307.

Bormann, B.T., and R.C. Sidle. 1990. Changes in productivity and distribution of nutrients in a chronosequence at Glacier Bay National Park, Alaska. *Journal of Ecology* 78:561–578.

Bormann, B.T., H. Spaltenstein, M.H. McClellan, F.C. Ugolini, K. Cromack Jr., and S.M. Nay. 1995. Rapid soil development after windthrow disturbance in pristine forests. *Journal of Ecology* 83:747–757.

Bowden, M. 2000. Assessing creationist stratigraphy and the formation of clay. *CRSQ* 37:59.

———. 2001. Origin of clays — HTW (hydrothermal water) still the most viable. *CRSQ* 38:111–112.

Bowen, D.Q. 1978. *Quaternary Geology: A Stratigraphic Framework for Multidisciplinary Work*. New York: Pergamon Press.

Bown, T.M., and M.J. Kraus. 1981. Lower eocene alluvial paleosols (Willwood Formation, northwest Wyoming, USA) and their significance for paleoecology, paleoclimatology, and basin analysis. *Palaeogeography, Palaeoclimatology, Palaeoecology* 34:1–30.

Brady, N.C. 1974. *The Nature and Properties of Soils* (eighth edition). New York: MacMillan Publishing Company.

Brady, N.C., and R.R. Weil. 1999. *The Nature and Properties of Soils*, Twelfth Edition. Upper Saddle River, NJ: Prentice-Hall Publishing Company.

Burykin, A.M., and E.V. Zasorinal. 1989. Mineralization and humification of plant residues in young soils of technogenic ecosystems. *Soviet Soil Science* 21:90–98.

Cioppa, M.T., E.T. Karlstrom, E. Irving, and R.W. Barendregt. 1995. Paleomagnetism of tills and associated paleosols in southwestern Alberta and northern Montana: Evidence for late Pliocene–early Pleistocene glaciations. *Canadian Journal of Earth Sciences* 32:555–564.

Coffin, H.G. 1968. A paleoecological misinterpretation. *CRSQ* 5:85–87.

———. 1969. Research on the classic Joggins petrified trees. *CRSQ* 6:35–44, 70.

Crocker, R.L. 1960. The plant factor in soil formation. *Proceedings of the Ninth Pacific Science Congress, Bangkok, Thailand, 1957.*

Froede, C.R. Jr. 1996. A theory for the volcanic origin of radioactive shales and clays: Examples from the southeastern United States. *CRSQ* 33:160–168.

———. 1998. *Field Studies in Catastrophic Geology*. St. Joseph, MO: Creation Research Society Books.

———. 2001. Questions about clay-size particles formed during the Flood: A reply to Mr. Bowden. *CRSQ* 37:257–258.

Guggenberger, G., R. Bäumler, and W. Zech. 1998. Weathering of soils developed in eolian material overlying glacial deposits in eastern Nepal. *Soil Science* 163:325–337.

Hall, R.D., R.E. Martin, and R.R. Shroba. 1993. Soils developed in the glacial deposits of the type areas of the Pinedale and Bull Lake glaciations, Wind River Range, Wyoming. *Arctic and Alpine Research* 25:368–373.

———. 1995. Soil evidence for glaciation intermediated between the Bull Lake and Pinedale Glaciations at Fremont Lake, Wind River Range, Wyoming, USA. *Arctic and Alpine Research* 27(1):89–98.

Harding, K. 2001. What would we expect to find if the world had flooded? http://www.geocities.com:0080/Tokyo/Temple/9917/flood.html.

Hargreaves, J.A. 1999. *Control of Clay Turbidity in Ponds*. Southern Regional Aquaculture Center Publication No. 460.

Horberg, L. 1956. A deep profile of weathering on pre-Wisconsin drift in Glacier Park, Montana. *Journal of Geology* 64(1):201–218.

Howe, G.F., G.T. Matzko, R.R. White, W.G. Stark, and E.L. Williams. 1995. Fossil wood of Big Bend National Park, Brewster County, Texas: Part IV — wood structure, nodules, paleosols, and climate. *CRSQ* 31:225–232.

Hunt, C.B. 1972. *The Geology of Soils: Their Evolution, Classification, and Uses*. San Francisco, CA: W.H. Freeman and Company.

James, W.C., G.H. Mack, and H.C. Monger. 1993. Classification of paleosols: Discussion and reply. *Geological Society of America Bulletin* 105:1637.

Jenny, H. 1941. *Factors of Soil Formation: A System of Quantitative Pedology*. New York: McGraw-Hill Book Company.

Karlstrom, E.T. 1982. Stratigraphy and genesis of soils in "Kennedy Drift," Mokowan Butte, southwestern Alberta. *Geological Society of America Abstracts with Programs, Rocky Mountain Section*, 16(6):317.

———. 1987. Stratigraphy and genesis of five superposed paleosols in pre-Wisconsinan drift on Mokowan Butte, southwestern Alberta. *Canadian Journal of Earth Sciences* 24:2235–2253.

———. 1988. Multiple paleosols in pre-Wisconsinan drift, northwestern Montana and southwestern Alberta. *Catena* 15:147–178.

———. 1990. Relict periglacial features east of Waterton-Glacier parks, Alberta and Montana, and their palaeoclimatic significance. *Permafrost and Periglacial Processes* 1:221–234.

———. 1991. Paleoclimatic significance of Late Cenozoic paleosols east of Waterton-Glacier Parks, Alberta and Montana. *Palaeogeography, Palaeoclimatology, Palaeoecology* 85:71–100.

Klevberg, P. 1999. The philosophy of sequence stratigraphy — Part I: Philosophic background. *CRSQ* 36:72–80.

———. 2000a. The philosophy of sequence stratigraphy — Part II: Application to stratigraphy. *CRSQ* 37:36–46.

———. 2000b. The philosophy of sequence stratigraphy — Part III: Application to sequence stratigraphy. *CRSQ* 37:94–104.

———. 2001. Clays and basalt clarify stratigraphy. *CRSQ* 37:256–257.

Klevberg, P., and R. Bandy. 2003a. Postdiluvial soil formation and the question of time: Part I — soil formation. *CRSQ* 39:252–268.

———. 2003b. Postdiluvial soil formation and the question of time — Part II: Time. *CRSQ* 40:30–47.

Kohl, R. 2002. Personal communication.

———. 2003. Personal communication.

Kraus, M.J. 1999. Paleosols in clastic sedimentary rocks: Their geologic applications. *Earth-Science Reviews* 47:41–70.

Lauber, P. 1963. *Dust Bowl: The Story of Man on the Great Plains.* Eau Claire, WI: E.M. Hale & Company.

Lavkulich, L.M. 1969. Soil dynamics in the interpretation of paleosols. In S. Pawluk (editor). *Pedology and Quaternary Research.* Edmonton, Canada: University of Alberta, p. 25–37.

Leet, L.D., and S. Judson. 1965. *Physical Geology*, third edition. Englewood Cliffs, NJ: Prentice-Hall.

Leighton, M.M., and P. MacClintock. 1962. The weathered mantle of glacial tills beneath original surfaces in north-central United States. *Journal of Geology* 70:267–293.

Lemke, R.W., W.M. Laird, M.J. Tipton, and R.M. Lindvall. 1965. Quarternary geology of northern Great Plains. In H.E. Wright Jr. and D.G. Frey (editors). *The Quaternary of the United States.* Princeton, NJ: Princeton University Press, p. 15–26.

Mahaney, W.C. (editor) 1978. *Quaternary Soils.* Norwich, England: Geo Abstracts Ltd., University of East Anglia.

Meyer, W., H.H. Albers, H.P. Berners, K.V. Gehlen, D. Glatthaar, W. Löhnertz, K.H. Pfeffer, A. Schnütgen, K. Wienecke, and H. Zakosek. 1983. Pre-Quaternary uplift in the central part of the Rhenish Massif. In K.K. Fuchs, K. von Gehlen, H. Mälzer, H. Murawski, and A. Semmel. *Plateau Uplift: The Rhenish Shield — A Case History.* New York: Springer-Verlag, p. 39–46.

Miall, A.D. 1992. Exxon global cycle chart: An event for every occasion? *Geology* 20:787–790.

Morris, H.M. 1984. *The Biblical Basis for Modern Science.* Grand Rapids, MI: Baker Book House.

Oard, M.J. 1984a. Ice ages: The mystery solved? Part I: The inadequacy of a uniformitarian ice age. *CRSQ* 21:66–76.

———. 1984b. Ice ages: The mystery solved? Part II: The manipulation of deep-sea cores. *CRSQ* 21:125–37.

———. 1985. Ice ages: The mystery solved? Part III: Paleomagnetic stratigraphy and data manipulation. *CRSQ* 21:170–181.

———. 1990. *An Ice Age Caused by the Genesis Flood.* San Diego, CA: Institute for Creation Research.

———. 1997. *Ancient Ice Ages or Gigantic Submarine Landslides?* Creation Research Society Monograph No. 6. St. Joseph, MO.

Ollier, C., and C. Pain. 1996. *Regolith, Soils, and Landforms.* New York: John Wiley & Sons.

Palmer, J.A., G.N. Phillips, and T.S. McCarthy. 1989. Paleosols and their relevance to Precambrian atmospheric composition. *Journal of Geology* 97:77–92.

Ping, C. 2000. Volcanic soils. In H. Sigurdsson (editor). *Encyclopedia of Volcanoes.* San Diego, CA: Academic Press, p. 1,259–1,270.

Reed, J.K. 2001. *Natural History in the Christian Worldview.* Chino Valley, AZ: Creation Research Society Books.

Reed, J.K, P. Klevberg, and C.R. Froede Jr. 2006. Toward an empirical stratigraphy. In J.K. Reed and M.J. Oard (editors). *The Geologic Column: Perspectives within Diluvial Geology.* Chino Valley, AZ: Creation Research Society Books.

Retallack, G.J. 1983. *Late Eocene and Oligocene Paleosols from Badlands National Park, South Dakota.* Geological Society of America Special Paper 193, Boulder, Colorado.

———. 1988. Field recognition of paleosols. In J. Reinhardt and W.R. Sigleo (editors). *Paleosols and Weathering Through Geologic Time: Principles and Applications.* Special Paper 216. Boulder, CO: Geological Society of America, p. 1–20.

———. 1990. *Soils of the Past — An Introduction to Paleopedology.* Boston, MA: Unwin Hyman.

———. 1993. Classification of paleosols: Discussion and reply — discussion. *Geological Society of America Bulletin* 105:1635–1636.

Robinson, S.J. 1996. Can Flood geology explain the fossil record? *CENTJ* 10:32–69.

Ruhe, R.V. 1975. *Geomorphology.* Boston, MA: Houghton Mifflin Company.

Rupke, N.A. 1969. Sedimentary evidence for the allochthonous origin of stigmaria, carboniferous, Nova Scotia. *Geological Society of America Bulletin* 80:2019–2112.

Scheven, J. 1996. The Carboniferous floating forest — an extinct pre-Flood ecosystem. *CENTJ* 10:70–81.

Selley, R.C. 1976. *An Introduction to Sedimentology.* New York: Academic Press.

Snelling, A.A., and J. Mackay. 1984. Coal, volcanism, and Noah's flood. *CENTJ* 1:11–29.

Snelling, A.A., and J. Woodmorappe. 1998. The cooling of thick igneous bodies on a young earth. In R.E. Walsh (editor). *Proceedings of the Fourth International Conference on Creationism.* Pittsburgh, PA: Creation Science Fellowship, p. 527–545.

Strahler, A.N. 1999. *Science and Earth History: The Evolution/Creation Controversy.* New York: Prometheus Books.

Thomas, M.F. 1994. *Geomorphology in the Tropics: A Study of Weathering and Denudation in Low Latitudes.* New York: John Wiley & Sons.

Thompson, R., and B. Berglund. 1976. Late Weichselian geomagnetic "reversal" as a possible example of the reinforcement syndrome. *Nature* 263:490–491.

Tucker, M. 1990. *The Field Description of Sedimentary Rocks.* Buckingham, England: Open University Press.

Valentine, K.W.G., and J.B. Dalrymple. 1976. Quaternary buried paleosols: A critical review. *Quaternary Research* 6:2:209–222.

Weaver, C.E. 1989. *Clays, Muds, and Shales.* New York: Elsevier.

Westin, F.C. 1970. *Genesis of the Soils of Lake Dakota Plain in Spink County, South Dakota.* Agricultural Experiment Station Technical Bulletin 37. South Dakota State University, Brookings, SD.

White, E.M. 1998. South Dakota Badlands paleosols: Fact and fiction. *Soil Survey Horizons,* summer issue: 50–58.

Williams, G.E. 1969. Characteristics and origin of a pre-Cambrian pediment. *Journal of Geology* 77:183–207.

Woida, K., and M.L. Thompson. 1993. Polygenesis of a Pleistocene paleosol in southern Iowa. *Geological Society of America Bulletin* 105:1445–1461.

Woodmorappe, J. 1999. *Studies in Flood Geology.* San Diego, CA: Institute for Creation Research,.

———. 2002. Dinosaur footprints, fish traces and the Flood. *TJ* 16(2):10–12.

Zeller, E.J. 1964. *Cycles and Psychology.* Kansas Geological Survey Bulletin 169:631–636.

Chapter 7

Landslides Win in a Landslide over Ancient "Ice Ages"

Michael J. Oard • MS — Atmospheric Science

Abstract

In an attempt to rebut my book, *Ancient Ice Ages or Gigantic Submarine Landslides?*, Kevin Henke falls short by using an argument which reveals many weaknesses in a common uniformitarian position. His attempt falls short and at the same time reveals weaknesses in his uniformitarian position. Substantive empirical data show that the submarine landslide hypothesis — that practically all ancient "tillites" are really deposited by marine mass flows — is superior to the reigning ice age hypothesis. Features he insists are the result of an Ordovician "ice age" are now thought to be of non-glacial origin. The new Precambrian "snowball earth" concept is highly dubious. In addition to insufficient arguments, as well as making simplistic attacks on the Flood, Henke's bias and style all diminish the credibility of his points. His unusual definition of "actualism" reveals serious weaknesses in his paradigm.

Introduction

In *Ancient Ice Ages or Gigantic Submarine Landslides?* (Oard 1997), I presented the case that deposits commonly interpreted as those of ancient "ice ages" (hundreds of millions of years ago and sometimes lasting over one hundred million years) are more likely the result of gigantic submarine landslides during the Genesis Flood. Specifically, "tillites" (consolidated glacial till) and other diagnostic features are actually products of mass movement. Till is a mixture of materials from clay to boulders: eroded, transported, and deposited by glacial ice. Therefore, "tillite" refers to a glacial mode of origin. Diamictite and mixtite are descriptive terms for any consolidated rock containing stones of variable sizes within a fine-grained matrix, without regard to a mode of origin.

Table 1 shows the four proposed historic "ice ages" and their durations. It does not include the Pleistocene Ice Age, which diluvialists agree was real, occurring shortly after the Flood (Oard 1990, 2004). Other minor or local glaciations are not listed. During these proposed ice ages, uniformitarian scientists believe that sheets of ice would not have covered the whole area for the total duration but shifted with time and oscillated between "glacial" and "interglacial" pulses.

Geological Period	Secular Approximate Age Range (m.y. ago)
Late Paleozoic	256–338
Late Ordovician	429–445
Late Proterozoic	520–950
Early Proterozoic	2200–2400

Table 1. The four main "ancient ice ages" within the uniformitarian paradigm and their inferred age range in millions of years before the present. The age ranges for the Precambrian "ice ages" are admittedly rough estimates (from Crowell 1999, p. 3).

Evidence for these "ice ages" includes the following: (1) till-like textures in rock formations, (2) their large extent, (3) striated bedrock, (4) striated and faceted rocks in "tillites," and (5) dropstones (rocks released underwater by icebergs) in varvites (Figures 1–3). *Varvites* are consolidated varves, and varves are rhythmites deposited seasonally — a set of two layers per year. A *rhythmite* is a repeating sequence of two or more layers in a sedimentary succession. Figures 1–3 show the three main diagnostic criteria for the supposed ancient ice ages. Other (minor) diagnostic criteria are equivocal.

Henke (1999) challenged my submarine landslide interpretation of the "tillites" with an 89-page rebuttal from the website "No Answers in Genesis." He stated in his abstract:

> A review of Oard's book clearly shows that it is full of scientific errors, blatant misquotations of the literature, omissions of field and laboratory data that refute YECism, outdated references, and unjustified interpretations of scientific data (p. 1).

That is quite an indictment, but as this chapter will show, many of his criticisms are invalid or irrelevant, and this attempt failed to undermine the substantive arguments made in my book. Although Henke noted a few errors in my book, they were insignificant. While critical of the diluvial interpretation of varves and rhythmites, the answer to his ineffective points is found in Chapter 8. As we explore a number of scientific issues Henke addresses, we learn more about the structural flaws of his and similar arguments, as well as how bias plays a role in their conclusions.

Uniformitarian Bias

Uniformitarians like to present themselves as objective scholars, open-minded and fair. But like all adherents of a particular worldview (in this case, naturalism), they have their own dogma, and one has only to read a few paragraphs of Henke to see that he argues not as a scholar, but as an activist. This "rebuttal" of *Ancient Ice Ages or Gigantic Submarine Landslides?* is only one of a number of heated attacks on other creationists. Just as his efforts elsewhere fall short — a critique of Humphreys' RATE results (helium loss shows 6,000 years in zircons with 1.5 billion years' worth of uranium decay) was shown to be without merit in Humphreys' thorough reply[1] — his arguments for ancient glaciations do, too.

_____

1. See http://www.trueorigin.org/helium01.asp.

Figure 1. A striated, grooved, and polished pavement on dolomite from the late Paleozoic Dwyka Group, South Africa (photo by Gordon Davison).

Figure 2. Striated clast with more than one direction on a boulder in the assumed Kennedy drift of late "Pliocene" age, Saint Mary Ridge, east of Glacier Park, Montana.

Figure 3. Dropstone in rhythmites (arrow) from the early Proterozoic Gowganda Formation, Ontario, Canada. Some believe the rhythmites are varves while others believe they are distal turbidites.

Like other advocates of naturalism, Henke tries to tilt the playing field by claiming that "science" precludes the supernatural while explaining everything. He decries Christian "bias" but refuses to admit evidence of his own — claiming that the *interpretations* of uniformitarianism of rocks and fossils are solid forensic evidence: "In contrast, true peer review journals provide non-supernatural explanations for observations in nature . . ." (Henke 1999, p. 7). But many researchers recognize that being a scientist does not exclude bias:

> . . . even when they are looking, people usually see only what they expect to find and they do not see what they assume for whatever reason could not exist (Dement and Vaughan 1999, p. 34).

Better yet, Henke (1999, p. 64–65) should consider a point he himself has made:

> Dogma of any kind, whether religions, political, philosophical, or "scientific," will cause people to look for ways, reasonable or not, to undermine the reliability of data that they don't like and overlook the most blatant flaws in any data that they agree with.

At the same time he dismisses creation by intelligent design and the Genesis Flood, he advocates the principle of multiple working hypotheses — missing the fundamental truth that different assumptions of the past (the Bible is true versus the Bible is false) will drive different interpretations of the same observations (figure 4). Henke's criticisms of the Flood, the Bible, and God reveal a level of animosity at odds with objective observation.

Henke's bias is no different from that of many, including the founders of uniformitarianism, James Hutton and Charles Lyell, who were not objectively following the data of geology, but presenting a form of propaganda against the Flood (Gould 1987). Henke decries the dogma of creationism while ignoring his own.

The idea that creationists are biased and uniformitarians are not is clearly false. The real question is which side deals with their bias. Since creationists openly admit their dependence on their (supernatural) worldview and their opponents refuse to do the same with their (anti-supernatural) worldview, it is clear that creationists are one step ahead. It is not surprising then that creationists are open to different scientific models, discerning the

Figure 4. Two views or sets of presuppositions for looking at the same data from the world. One view is based on God's instruction book, the Bible, while the other is based on man's reason apart from God or the Bible (drawn by Dan Leitha of AiG).

difference between scientific open-mindedness (limited) and a metaphysical position (absolute). Henke should consider that since creationists are accustomed to being the "underdogs," they understand uniformitarian arguments quite well, while uniformitarians continue to display a remarkable ignorance of creationists' ideas. Unlike uniformitarians, creationists generally examine both sides of the issues.

Actualism, not Uniformitarianism?

Henke (1999) accuses creationists of attacking the "straw man" of outdated Lyellian uniformitarianism while neglecting the "actualism" of modern geologists. But the different terms carry a variety of confused meanings,[2] and Henke seems to understand them no better than anyone else. Ironically, much of that confusion comes from the work of secular neocatastrophists (those who believe in a few large catastrophes), who have popularized the empirical evidence for past geological catastrophes. His confusion is revealed in his definition of actualism:

> Oard (p. 55) is skeptical of this plausible argument because he chains himself to Lyell

---

2. For more information about the confusing multiple definitions of uniformitarianism, see Reed (1998).

uniformitarianism and claims that the process has never been observed in modern environments.

So what!! It's a plausible and natural explanation (Henke 1999, p. 40).

So the key to actualism is explanation that is "plausible" and "natural." The latter is merely a restatement of his anti-theistic bias. And "plausible" is a very elastic term. I find my thesis about submarine landslides "plausible" but Henke does not? That kind of subjectivism is decidedly contrary to science. Does he mean that it is only plausible if it is natural? Again, that is merely a restatement of his bias. If a professional geologist like Henke cannot supply a more precise definition for "actualism," then perhaps creationists are justifiably skeptical that geologists are using semantics to mask profound weaknesses in their uniformitarian dogma. It is not the creationists who are chained to Lyell, but the modern naturalists, who think that an explanation cannot be plausible unless it first passes the test of atheism.

This appeal to "actualism" leads him to improbable solutions to problems raised in my book. For example, he (p. 18) says that the absence of Pleistocene iceberg scour marks in pre-Pleistocene "tillites," means nothing because "past and present iceberg scour marks may vary in size and degree of preservation." That "actualism" is just special pleading. He (p. 69) uses the same excuse to avoid the absence of huge debris flow deposits in pre-Pleistocene strata, while large debris flows are common in Pleistocene and modern sediments.

As with other modern geologists, Henke admits that "natural" evidence demands catastrophism, such as meteorite impacts and the Lake Missoula flood, but he draws the line at the Bible.

Henke (p. 18) claims that I should have waited until scientists studied the rocks in more detail before presenting an interpretation — a standard that he does not apply to those advocating the glacial explanation. Geologists have been speculating on the subject of ancient ice ages for at least 80 years, both before and after the accumulation of an extensive body of literature.

Quoting Out of Context?

Anti-creationists frequently divert attention from substantive issues by focusing on minute ones. If they can show any error, no matter how insignificant, they think that they have won the argument. One of these ploys is the charge of "quoting out of context." While it is true in a few cases a more thorough job of setting the context in

my book could have been done, it was a sin of omission rather than of commission, and "in context" they have no bearing on the substance of the argument. I thank Henke for pointing out ways to clarify and strengthen my case for the second edition.

One of his examples was my failure to account for millions of years of erosion when questioning the glacial origin of older "tillites" based on their smaller sizes as compared to the recent Ice Age tills. However, the neo-catastrophist scientists, Oberbeck et al. (1993b, p. 680) also question the glacial origin of pre-Pleistocene diamictites based on their smaller area and much greater thicknesses.

In another place in my book discussing the non-glacial origin of "varvites" in Namibia, Henke (1999, p. 23–24) claims that I quoted Martin et al. (1985) out of context by not noting their theory of a metamorphic origin of the millimeter-scale banding in the "varvites." But he neglects the main point of Martin et al. (1985), who presented evidence *against* the dropstone varvite interpretation and reinterpreted the formation as of non-glacial origin. Martin et al. (1985) do say that the "pebbly schist" (their quotation marks) was originally of *mass flow origin and did have sedimentary bedding*. Second, some of the predominantly quartzite rocks are *not* pebbles but range from 60 centimeters to 1.5 meters in diameter and were considered dropstones. Third, *all workers* before them had interpreted the deposit as a glaciogenic dropstone varvite. I was simply pointing out that what had once been considered a "dropstone varvite" was reinterpreted as non-glacial — a context strangely not mentioned by Henke.

In another claim of quoting "out of context," Henke (1999, p. 34) stated:

> In the previous sentence, Oard (p. 98) claims that mass movements can form striations and grooves on HARD rocks. From the context, the reader might guess that the striated igneous rocks described by Harrington (1971) were hard and that these debris flows really did a fast and effective job of counterfeiting [sic] glacial striations on granites or other hard igneous rocks. However, Oard never tells his readers that the striated igneous rock in Harrington (1971, p. 1346) was on SOFT rhyolitic tuff.

This is what was actually said (Oard 1997, p. 98):

> Mass movement, however, can duplicate striations and grooves on hard rocks as well as on soft sediments (see chapter 7). For instance,

a debris flow from a flash flood striated a large igneous boulder held in place within basal debris (Harrington, 1971). The striations formed multiple sets which look like glacial striations.

First, by mentioning the extremes of hard rocks and soft sediments, it is implied that striations could form on soft igneous rocks, too. Second, Harrington (1971, p. 1,346–1,347) stated that the rhyolitic tuff, an igneous rock, was "rather soft" and "comparatively soft," which is quite different from a soft sediment. Third, Harrington (1971, p. 1,344) stated that the striations and grooves are oriented in several directions. This would be interpreted as glacial *without question* if found in a glaciated area. Fourth, Harrington was noting that "debris-laden torrential water flows" can cause striated glacial-like pavements — exactly my point!

After sifting through practically all of his claims of misquoting, misuse of references, sentences taken out of context, misinterpreted texts, etc., it is clear that it is Henke who does not understand or distorts the original references. When anti-creationists say "quoting out of context," they really mean that creationists do not agree with the *interpretations* of uniformitarians. For decades, creationists have used peer-reviewed scientific literature to make their points about the shortcomings of uniformitarianism and evolution. That is not "quoting out of context"; it is the essence of careful scholarship. With regard to my book, Henke misses two telling points: (1) the literature of those who advocate glaciations is the only place to find the data, since mainly those who advocate glaciations get published, and (2) the ability to make a creationist case from the literature of those who disagree with my interpretation is a sign of strength, not weakness.

Henke's note of other "distortions" occurred when I focused on particular aspects of papers without recounting their entirety, for example, focusing on striated pavements in a particular article without mentioning other supposed glaciogenic features. Was I not a creationist, it would be perfectly acceptable to limit discussion to the topic at hand — the whole point of citing literature! Anyone interested in the opinions or research pursuits of those authors is welcome to read their papers. Henke's standards would eliminate all scientific publication as we know it.

The "Context" Double Standard

Given Henke's bias against creationists, it is not surprising that he does not extend the sensitivity he shows to (uniformitarian) authors cited in my book to me or other creationist researchers. For instance, he (p. 18) stated that I argue that icebergs could not have produced the small scour marks in the late Paleozoic of Brazil described by Rocha-Campos et al. (1994). In the book I wrote:

> The above authors [Rocha-Campos et al. 1994] believe they found the first iceberg mark with associated iceberg debris in late Paleozoic rhythmites in the Paraná Basin, Brazil. . . . The furrows *seem much too small* to be iceberg scour marks (Oard 1997, p. 25).

Rather than admit that I said that the grooves "seem" too small to be iceberg scour marks, Henke (p. 18) emphatically states that I said "…that icebergs *could not have produced* these features" [emphasis mine]. My "context" was the contrast between the Pleistocene Ice Age and supposed pre-Pleistocene ice ages with regards to iceberg scour marks — they are *abundant* in Pleistocene glaciolacustrine and glaciomarine strata, while nearly absent in older sediments.

In another place, Henke (p. 37) states: "Oard (p. 53) claims that Petit (1987) found crescentic fractures and nailhead striae on fault surfaces." He then claims that Petit (1987, p. 599) does not say they are nailhead striations, implying that I misquoted Petit. In fact, what I said was "nailhead-*like* striae." So Henke is the one misquoting. Furthermore, had he read more thoroughly, he would have noted that while Petit (1987) does not use the term "nailhead striae," his description is the same: "During friction it forms deep striae (grooves) terminated at the final ploughing element position" (Petit 1987, p. 599). Petit even provides a picture (his figure 2a) showing the feature — quite similar to nailhead striae.

In another place, Henke (p. 9) states that I used an outdated quote from Crowell (1978) in noting that there were no glaciations between the Ordovician and late Paleozoic in the uniformitarian geological column (cf. table 1). I had actually stated that *major* ice ages are missing between the postulated Ordovician and late Paleozoic ice ages, being well aware of the minor "glaciations" between the major ones:

> Table 1.3 summarizes the four main pre-Pleistocene "ice ages" and their assumed dates. Other "ice ages" of short duration and small extent occurred in other geological periods . . . (Oard 1997, p. 5).

Henke (p. 59–60) also thinks I misrepresented several authors when I noted that they believe that *most and possibly all* pre-Pleistocene diamictites are debris from meteorite impacts:

> Furthermore, Oard (p. 17, 88) misrepresents Rampino (1992, 1994) and Oberbeck et al. (1993a, b; 1994) and claims that "most and possibly all" pre-Pleistocene glacial deposits could be debris from meteorite impacts. In reality, Rampino (1994, p. 439) and Oberbeck et al (1993a, p. 1; 1993b, p. 681; 1994, p. 488) only claim that SOME of the pre-Pleistocene glacial sediments could be impact deposits.

While these authors state (cautiously) that "some" diamictites interpreted to be glaciogenic are really of impact origin, a closer inspection of their manuscripts reveals that they are really challenging *most and possibly all* pre-Pleistocene "tillites." Rampino (1994, p. 441–443) goes through the main "ancient ice ages" and points out that many of their deposits are debris-flows, implying that they could be of impact origin. He notes that the best example of an ancient ice age deposit, the late Paleozoic Dwyka tillite of South Africa, has recently been reinterpreted as the product of glaciomarine sedimentation by debris flow and other mass flow processes. And if Rampino's position is in doubt, the following quote (1992, p. 99) makes his position quite clear (as does the title of his paper, "Ancient 'glacial' deposits are ejecta of large impacts: the ice age paradox explained"):

> Numerous studies have revealed that recognized tillite sequences were actually the products of massive debris flows, related density currents, and large-scale "rainout" of coarse sediment. As a result, tillites are now generally reinterpreted as glaciomarine debris-flow deposits — a problematic interpretation in terms of known depositional processes, rates, and scale. By contrast, the inferred glacial sequences have the essential characteristics of ballistic debris-flow ejecta created by large impacts. . . . The evidence suggests that episodic, widespread pre-Cenozoic tillites are actually the proximal ejecta of large impact events. . . .

Oberbeck et al. (1993a, p. 16, emphasis added) also challenged the Dwyka "tillite" interpretation:

> We suggest that prolonged impact cratering preceding breakup of Gondwanaland (*indicated by Permo-Carboniferous tillites in South Africa,*

South America, India, and Antarctica) could have extensively fractured the lithosphere and would have facilitated the final continental fragmentation.

Furthermore, Le Roux (1994) understood that Oberbeck et al. challenged this showcase for a pre-Pleistocene "ice age." He goes on to defend the glacial origin of the Dwyka "tillite" as opposed to the impact origin. Reimold et al. (1997, p. 517) also understood that a successful challenge of the Dwyka "tillite" would undermine the late Paleozoic "ice age":

> Diamictites, especially those deposited before the break-up of Gondwana in the Late Carboniferous and Permian, have recently been suggested to represent ejecta deposits from large comet or meteorite impact events. This is in contrast to the commonly held interpretation that these rocks represent glaciomarine sedimentary deposits.

Although the authors favoring impact origin of "tillites" claimed that they were challenging only *some* of the "ice age" deposits, in actuality upon reading all their material, they were challenging *most and possibly all* pre-Pleistocene "tillites."

Furthermore, Henke should have also clarified that Rampino (1994, p. 440, 445) wrote that the three major diagnostic features for glaciation are duplicated by impact ejecta deposits, which are essentially debris flows:

> The matter is compounded by the fact that known impact ejecta deposits can display features such as (1) clasts of various sizes showing multiple directions of striae and chattermarks; (2) dropstones (ballistic fallout); and (3) associated eroded and striated bedrock surfaces — features commonly inferred to be diagnostic of glacial origin. . . .

> Thus, debris-flow deposits produced by major impacts can apparently mimic many of the stratigraphic and sedimentological features considered diagnostic of diamictites of glacial origin.

In a response to the impact challenge by Young (1993), Oberbeck et al. (1993b, p. 681) pointed out: "We gave examples of all of the features that are commonly used to identify most of the ancient glacial deposits and we demonstrated that they occur in known impact deposits." This was precisely the case presented in my monograph.

Uniformitarians: Almost All "Tillites" Are Marine

Mass flows of various types can mimic most, if not all, features ascribed to pre-Pleistocene "ice ages," as noted above. The size of some of the "tillites" suggests large-scale mass flows — the types of mass flows *expected* during Noah's Flood and discussed in chapter 12 of *Ancient Ice Ages or Gigantic Submarine Landslides?*

Henke (p. 19) tries to avoid this by claiming another "misquote" of Deynoux and Trompette (1976, p. 1,313) about the marine origin of tillites. Although they admit that almost all ancient "glacial" deposits are really marine, Henke notes that they claimed to have found a widespread late Precambrian "continental glacial" deposit in West Africa:

> Nevertheless, it is obvious that Oard (p. 19) misrepresents Deynoux and Trompette (1976, p. 1313) by only quoting the section that is capitalized. Oard (p. 19) has refused to recognize that Deynoux and Trompette (1976, p. 1313) claim to have a real example of a continent-based glacial deposit and that not *all* pre-Pleistocene glacial deposits are marine (Henke 1999, p. 10–11, emphasis mine).

Again, Henke stretches too far. Deynoux and Trompette stated that *most or almost all* tillites are marine — which is exactly what I reported. Ironically, *Henke* admits in his conclusion that the vast majority of "tillites" are marine, despite his question mark appended to his title of that section.

Henke appears to be confused by the progression of logic used when citing other uniformitarian geologists who admitted that *most* pre-Pleistocene "tillites" are marine. First, by showing that even uniformitarians believe that most tillites are marine; then secondly, the case that even the ones they believe to be continental can be interpreted as marine because it is difficult to distinguish between marine and terrestrial glaciogenic deposits. Henke (1999, p. 12) virtually makes this case when he states:

> In conclusion, the vast majority of pre-Pleistocene glacial deposits are now recognized as marine, but many of them contain iceberg and other deposits that are incompatible with "Flood geology." Despite difficulties in distinguishing

pre-Pleistocene tillites from glaciomarine deposits, tillites have been identified and their existence is fatal to YECism.

However, Henke's case is weak. It is not clear that there are iceberg scour marks in pre-Pleistocene diamictites, and his insistence on the existence of ancient "tillites" rests on the same shaky criteria that have allowed most "tillites" to be reclassified by uniformitarians. That was the whole point of my book! For example, in a book-sized review of pre-Pleistocene "ice age" deposits, Eyles (1993, p. 1) stated that over 95 percent by volume of pre-Pleistocene "tillites" are actually marine. In essence, Henke is trying to show the remaining 5 percent makes me wrong, ignoring that it really makes uniformitarian dogma 95 percent wrong. And later in my book, I challenge the special features, such as iceberg plough marks, that supposedly make the remaining 5 percent glacial. All Henke can do is claim that I have "misquoted." Establishing the marine nature of practically all "tillites" goes a long way in making a case that the deposits in question are gigantic submarine landslides from the Flood.

Update on the Ordovician "Ice Age"

Henke (p. 50–59) strongly defends the Ordovician "ice age" in North Africa. He notes that it possesses many unique features rare or absent in other pre-Pleistocene "ice ages." These include drumlins, eskers, *roches moutonnées*, pingos, crescentic gouges, ice wedge casts, U-shaped paleovalleys, etc. However, these strata exhibit a number of anomalous features to "ice age" deposition (Oard 1997, p. 77–84). Also, data published since supports this interpretation.

Henke made several accusations in reference to these deposits that are easily disproven and explained. He stated:

> U-shaped valleys and other glacially eroded features are expected to be found underneath glacial deposits. Oard (p. 78–79) misuses the literature and tries to portray the contact between the glacial deposits of the Ordovician Tamadjert Formation and their underlying non-glacial rocks as "flat" and devoid of evidence of glacial erosion. . . . In reality, they all state that on a large or regional scale, the contact APPEARS flat, but locally the contact is uneven with up to several hundred meters of relief (p. 51–52)

Henke is confused by the scale of the features. I did err in including one reference (Biju-Duval et al. 1981) in the *seven* that mentioned that the surface below the diamictite is too flat for an "ice age" but more conducive toward a watery or mass flow origin. Biju-Duval et al. (1981) were referring to the surface on *top* of the diamictite (also exceptionally flat). Henke could have avoided the confusion by noting my statement:

> Although the lower boundary of the Tamadjert Formation is "dead flat" on a large scale, these U-shaped valleys are small-scale paleovalleys incised in the surface by a northward moving medium (Oard 1997, p. 83).

Thus, on the regional scale, the surface is "flat," while on the local scale, there are paleovalleys. Of course, U-shaped valleys are not necessarily indicative of glaciation, since they can also be formed by channelized mass flow: "Debris-flow valleys tend to be U-shaped" (Johnson 1970, p. 445).

Henke (p. 53) attempts to distract attention from the significance of the flat contact between the top of the "ice age" deposits and the overlying Silurian shale by saying that the contact has a lengthy history, as indicated by the top few centimeters of the sandstone below the contact being burrowed. In a rather lengthy digression, he stated that organisms could not dig burrows in the middle of rapidly depositing Flood sediments, and that burrows, paleosols, and animal trails both overlying and underlying the "glacial" sediments present numerous problems for the supposedly raging Flood (p. 24). But those smokescreens (addressed in Flood geology literature) cannot evade the main point: that the top of these "glacial" sediments is remarkably flat.

Henke (p. 54–55) attempts to downplay the comments by researchers that the Ordovician grooves and striations are remarkably parallel toward the north by stating that these features are also oriented to the northwest and north-northeast. Striations and grooves in one direction are more indicative of mass flow, while multiple directions are characteristic of glacial features. However, Biju-Duval et al. (1981) noted that there are *few exceptions* from the northward orientation. It is doubtful that even the huge ice sheet centered to the south, which Henke imagines, could produce such well-oriented, parallel markings. Furthermore, ice sheets melt and surge: one would expect that since the last events to scour the bedrock would be preserved, that scour would show multiple directions.

It has been common practice for uniformitarian geologists to define *multiple sets of striae* as evidence of glaciation (although mass flow can also duplicate this feature).

In fact, Le Roux (1994, p. 483), defending the Dwyka "tillite" from the challenge of the impact hypothesis, made the point that divergent striae (up to right angles on the same outcrop of polished pavements) provided evidence for glaciation. If that is the case, then why do the parallel grooves and striations associated with the Ordovician "ice age" not show the same variation?

In contrast to these "diagnostic" criteria for glaciation, Fairbridge (1971, p. 272) defended the "ice age" by stating:

> Schermerhorn proposes that the alleged glacial scour and grooving can be produced by slump

Figure 5. Striated pavement with more than one direction and with chattermarks from a debris flow on top of the Gravelly Mountains, southwest Montana. The pavement was broken up and tilted by faulting. The age is "Eocene" and was once assumed to be from an ancient ice age.

drag of pebbly mud flows. But could this occur over hundreds of miles and in parallel lines?

Although parallel grooves and striations normally imply mass flow (Schermerhorn 1971; Oard 1997), Fairbridge was arguing that the large scale of the parallelism required an ice sheet. But he fails to explain how an ice sheet might cause multiple sets of striae on a local scale, yet exhibit large-scale parallelism. A more reasonable explanation is a mass flow; the scale merely points to a *very large* mass flow, as would be expected in the Genesis Flood.

Henke (1999) claims that although glacial and nonglacial features can be confused, careful examination can rule out non-glacial counterfeits. But then he fails to specify diagnostic criteria; he simply cites *opinions* of various researchers. On the other hand, my book dealt with both primary and secondary diagnostic features of glaciation. Since uniformitarians now agree that the primary features are equivocal, let's examine the others.

Crossing sets of striae on rocks and pavements are thought to point to a glacial origin (Oard 1997, p. 51–52). I was able to provide several examples in which multiple sets of striae were caused by mass flows, including the striated pavement on top of the Gravelly Range in Montana (figure 5). Not only are there crossing sets, but there are also chattermarks — another secondary feature considered diagnostic of glaciation.

Recent research on grooves and striations in the Sahara Desert has concluded that they were not made by the direct scouring action of a glacier or by drifting icebergs (Deynoux and Ghienne 2004). Drifting icebergs (which Henke built his argument upon) do not even form parallel grooves over large areas (LeHeron et al. 2005). Deynoux and Ghienne (2004) proposed a new hypothesis — the stacked striated surfaces are *shear zones in unlithified water-laid sediments*, caused by a moving ice sheet. So the striations are not produced directly by glaciation, but indirectly. This new explanation is hypothetical and not observed in Pleistocene ice age deposits (Oard 2005). Also, the grooves and striations are vertically stacked and were formed in soft sediments, a problem noted by Schermerhorn (1971). Either way, they were not formed by ice — leaving no direct evidence of an ice age. The glacial hypothesis remains in fashion because researchers believe that other glaciogenic criteria support the Ordovician "ice age" in the Sahara Desert.

For example, Henke (p. 57–59) is convinced that eskers exist in the Sahara, and discussed at length my skepticism of them. An esker is a long sinuous ridge of stratified sand and gravel deposited below an ice sheet while it melts. Henke (p. 58) states that my criticisms are "invalid subjective biases." In that case, the same must be true of his fellow uniformitarian, Rampino (1994, p. 442), who is also skeptical of these "eskers." Furthermore, the most recent literature interprets these features as "large-scale channel-fill structures" (Ghienne and Deynoux 1998) or "tunnel valley fill" with the relief later inverted (Ghienne 2003; Ghienne et al. 2003; Moreau et al. 2005). Are all these authors hopelessly biased toward Flood geology?

Dome-like folds previously thought to be fossil pingos — large frost mounds in permafrost — are now believed to be caused by soft sediment deformation (Le Heron et al. 2005).

Furthermore, the features are found in *marine* strata. Many of the presumed lodgment tillites are not only difficult to recognize but have been reinterpreted as *sandy debris flows*:

> However, recent sedimentological work indicates that late Ordovician (lodgement [sic]-derived) diamictitic tills are difficult to recognize from upper Ordovician rocks with many previously described examples being reinterpreted as sandy debris flows (Le Heron et al. 2005, p. 76).

At the current rate, reinterpretation of supposed glaciogenic features as products of non-glacial processes will soon show that there is no "evidence" for the Ordovician "ice age." As I noted repeatedly, most "tillites" are being reinterpreted as (1) deposited in a marine environment, and (2) deposited by mass movement. Current research on the Ordovician "ice age" certainly continues that trend.

Snowball Earth

A recent hypothesis explores the idea of unique glaciation in the Precambrian — glaciation of the *whole* earth, and more than once. This is called the snowball earth hypothesis, and the idea has "snowballed" among uniformitarian geologists during the past ten years. Henke (p. 43) briefly discusses it, evidently believing the evidence for global glaciation is "overwhelming." I briefly mentioned the hypothesis in chapter 4 in my book.

Henke again misunderstands what I said when he claims that I believe there is widespread support for the Precambrian "glaciation." I actually said that there is widespread *acceptance* of the late Precambrian "ice age." Henke (p. 43) then claims: "The formation of continental glaciers at the Late Precambrian equator presents challenges for both YECs and scientists." Aside from his false dichotomy between creationists and other scientists, he errs again — most creationists do not believe in a late Precambrian glaciation.

But the challenge to uniformitarians is immense. Paleomagnetic evidence supposedly showing that the deposits are from *low* latitudes, combined with the *marine* nature of most of the "tillites," forces uniformitarians to postulate a *global* glaciation several times during the early and late Proterozoic (Hoffman and Schrag 2002; Evans 2003; Bodiselitsch et al. 2005; Kopp et al. 2005; Maruyama and Liou 2005). (The Proterozoic is the period dated 2.5 billion to about 0.5 billion years within the late Precambrian.) However, if the earth were ever totally covered by ice and snow, the resulting high albedo and cold temperatures would likely cause it to remain frozen. Also, thick limestones and dolomites in the Precambrian imply a warm ocean and atmosphere. There is even a dolomite cap on *top* of the "tillites," implying very warm temperature right after glaciation! The precipitation of dolomite requires warm to hot water. Although Henke (p. 44) admits that the vast majority of carbonates develop in warm climates, he needlessly belabors the point that some carbonates form in cold water, a point I already had noted in the book. He addresses the basic problem of huge volumes of carbonates associated with Precambrian "tillites" (making their warm water deposition likely) by appealing to the magic wand of actualism (p. 47):

> Contrary to YEC misconceptions, actualism does not demand modern analogs for dolomite formation, only that any explanation not violate the laws of chemistry and physics by invoking the supernatural.

It would be interesting to hear him explain how theism violates the laws of chemistry and physics to men like Boyle, Pasteur, Newton, Pascal, and Kelvin. But aside from an anti-theistic prejudice, if his scenario is accepted, the Precambrian climate must have rapidly oscillated between a global icebox and a global hothouse. "Actualism" takes Henke further and further away from scientific reality. Several speculative and far-fetched hypotheses have been suggested to account for such a unique climate. All face an additional obstacle; all of the climatic yo-yoing comes exactly prior to the Cambrian explosion: "The so-called Late Proterozoic snowball Earth disappeared at the beginning of Phanerozoic time" (Maruyama and Liou 2005, p. 775). The Phanerozoic is the time from 0.5 billion years to the recent time according to the uniformitarian time scale.

Given all of these problems with the "Precambrian ice age or ages" (Oard 2002), uniformitarian scientists, including Henke, should question their continued focus on it.

A Few Asides about the Flood

Like many others, Henke attacks his own straw man of the Flood to "disprove" it. The few legitimate problems that he raises are the subjects of current research and debate by creationists. Henke seems to lack a basic understanding of what a global Flood might accomplish.

He notes: "However, Oard never explains how all of this sediment could have formed on a young Earth and how it accumulated into huge mudflows during Noah's Flood" (p. 33). He ignores the many ways that copious sediment could be generated during the Flood. As noted by many creationists in the past, the real issue is one of energy and time: in the uniformitarian framework, time is virtually unlimited, while in the diluvial framework, energy is virtually unlimited. In addition to extrapolating the scale of observed events such as volcanoes, erosion, etc., the Flood probably included meteorite impacts, global tectonic disruption, etc. The migration of sediment as massive debris flows is not only congruent with the Flood model, but is expected, as was explained in several sections in chapter 12 of that book.

In another example, he says (p. 24), ". . . rhythmites indicate deposition under LOW ENERGY conditions, which is hardly consistent with a raging 'Biblical Flood.' " Though picturesque, he makes the typical mistake of assuming uniform conditions during the Flood. I know of no creationist who does. The Flood would accommodate a wide variety of depositional conditions in different places and different times. As to his specific objection, he is still wrong: rhythmites could easily have been deposited in distal turbidites, the common end products of fast-moving flows.

Pointing to strontium isotope ratios that indicate deposition of a late Paleozoic carbonate in fresh water, Henke

Image of Coconino Sandstone

Figure 6. Upper flat contact of the Toroweap Formation above the Coconino sandstone (arrow), west of Hermit's Rest, South Rim of the Grand Canyon. The lower contact is also flat but obscured by landslide debris.

Figure 7. Lower flat contact between the Coconino sandstone and the Hermit shale below (arrow). There is a supposed ten million-year gap in time at this contact. Upper contact is also flat but not as distinct at this location.

(p. 45) argues, "So, Oard will have to account for both fresh and salt waters into [sic] his 'Flood' scenario." Like hydraulic and tectonic energy, chemistry in the Flood would also have varied in both time and space. Given the events described, that would be the "actualistic" interpretation. So there really is not a problem accounting for fresh and salt water during the Flood, even assuming the uniformitarian interpretation of strontium isotope data is correct.

Henke (p. 49) then challenges the scale of debris flows during the Flood: "YECs want to believe that debris flows from Noah's Flood could have spread sediment over at least 250 km north to south and 400 km east to west across the Gowganda basin." This is 100,000 km². A debris flow of that magnitude is easily accommodated in a global Flood. Even modern, relatively low-energy flows cover large areas (Oard 1997). The Agulhas Slump off South Africa has an areal extent of 80,000 km² (Kid, 1982)!

Later, he (p. 70) dismisses the creationist interpretation of the Coconino Sandstone as a large Flood-deposited sand, claiming that it is a desert deposit. He ignores data that cast doubt on this interpretation (e.g., Austin 1994). If the Coconino Sandstone were a desert deposit, why was it spread over an area of 500,000 km² with a volume of 40,000 km³ (Austin 1994)? Why are its upper and lower contacts so flat in the Grand Canyon, if the Coconino is a wind-blown sand (figures 6 and 7)?

Summary

Henke's (1999) 89-page rebuttal of *Ancient Ice Ages or Gigantic Submarine Landslides?* is typical of anti-biblical bias. His appeals to actualism illustrate that. Yet, no amount of semantic manipulation can divert the many legitimate criticisms of the ancient ice age hypothesis for pre-Pleistocene "tillites." He accuses creationists of distortion, while doing the same. His few substantive issues, such as the "Ordovician ice age" and the "snowball earth" hypothesis, do not stand up to rigorous scrutiny — even by many uniformitarian researchers. Though presenting his work as a scientific critique, he ends up demonstrating the tenuous grasp of uniformitarian geologists on earth history.

My thesis that ancient "tillites" are in fact the products of gigantic submarine landslides during the Flood remains not only intact, but also reinforced by new research.

References

CRSQ: Creation Research Society Quarterly
TJ: Technical Journal (now Journal of Creation)

Austin, S.A., 1994. Interpreting strata of Grand Canyon. In S.A. Austin (editor). *Grand Canyon — Monument to Catastrophism*. Santee, CA: Institute for Creation Research, p. 21–56.

Biju-Duval, G., M. Deynoux, and P. Rognon. 1981. Late Ordovician tillites of the Central Sahara. In M.J. Hambrey and W.B. Harland (editors). *Earth's Pre-Pleistocene Glacial Record*. London: Cambridge University Press, p. 99–107.

Bodiselitsch, B., C. Koeberl, S. Master, and W.U. Reimold. 2005. Estimating duration and intensity of Neoproterozoic snowball glaciations form Ir anomalies. *Science* 308:239–242.

Crowell, J.C. 1978. Gondwanan glaciation, cyclothems, continental positioning, and climate change. *American Journal of Science* 278:1,345–1,372.

———. 1999. *Pre-Mesozoic Ice Ages: Their Bearing on Understanding the Climate System*. Geological Society of America Memoir 192, Boulder, CO.

Dement, W.C., and C. Vaughan. 1999. *The Promise of Sleep*. New York: Random House.

Deynoux, M., and J.F. Ghienne. 2004. Late Ordovician glacial pavements revisited: a reappraisal of the origin of striated surfaces. *Terra Nova* 16(3):95–101.

Deynoux, M., and R. Trompette. 1976. Discussion — Late Precambrian mixtites: glacial and/or nonglaical? Dealing especially with the mixtites of West Africa. *American Journal of Science* 276:1,302–1,315.

Evans, D.A.D. 2003. A fundamental Precambrian-Phanerozoic shift in earth's glacial style? *Tectonophysics* 375:353–385.

Eyles, N. 1993. Earth's glacial record and its tectonic setting. *Earth-Science Reviews* 35:1–248.

Fairbridge, R.W. 1971. Upper Ordovician glaciation in Northwest Africa? Reply. *GSA Bulletin* 82:269–274.

Ghienne, J.F. 2003. Late Ordovician sedimentary environments, glacial cycles, and post-glacial transgression in the Taoudeni Basins, West Africa. *Palaeogeography, Palaeoclimatology, Palaeoecology* 189:117–145.

Ghienne, J.F., and M. Deynoux. 1998. Large-scale channel fill structures in Late Ordovician glacial deposits in Mauritania, western Sahara. *Sedimentary Geology* 119:141–159.

Ghienne, J.F., M. Deynoux, G. Manatschal, and J.L. Rubino. 2003. Palaeovalleys and fault-controlled depocentres in the Late-Ordovician glacial record of the Murzuq Basin (central Libya). *Compes Rendus Geoscience* 335:1,091–1,100.

Gould, S.J. 1987. *Time's Arrow, Time's Cycle: Myth and Metaphor in the Discovery of Geological Time*. London: Cambridge University Press.

Harrington, H.J. 1971. Glacial-like "striated floor" originated by debris-laden torrential water flows. *AAPG Bulletin* 55:1,344–1,347.

Henke, K.R. 1999. *Ancient Ice Ages and Submarine Landslides, but not Noah's Flood: A Review of M. J. Oard's Assault on Multiple Glaciations*. http:home.austarnet.com.au/stear/henke_oard1.htm.

Hoffman, P.F., and D.P. Schrag. 2002. The snowball earth hypothesis: testing the limits of global change. *Terra Nova* 14(3):129–155.

Johnson, A.M. 1970. *Physical Processes in Geology*. San Francisco, CA: Freeman, Cooper and Company.

Kidd, R.B. 1982. Long-range sidescan sonar studies of sediment slides and the effects of slope mass sediment movement on abyssal plain sedimentation. In S. Saxov and J.K. Nieuwenhuis (editors). *Marine Slides and Other Mass Movements*. New York: Plenum Press, p. 289–303.

Koop, R.E., J.L. Kirschvink, I.A. Hilburn, and C.Z. Nash. 2005. The Paleoproterozoic snowball earth: a climate disaster triggered by the evolution of oxygenic photosynthesis. *Proceedings of the National Academy of Science* 102(32):11,131–11,136.

Le Heron, D.P., O.E. Sutcliffe, R.J. Whittington, and J. Craig. 2005. The origins of glacially related soft-sediment deformation structures in Upper Ordovician glaciogeneic rocks: implications for ice-sheet dynamics. *Palaeogeography, Palaeoclimatology, Palaeoecology* 218:75–103.

Le Roux, J.P. 1994. Impacts, tillites, and the breakup of Gondwanaland: a second discussion. *Journal of Geology* 102:483–485.

Martin, H., H. Porada, and O.H. Walliser. 1985. Mixtite deposits of the Damara sequence, Namibia, problems of interpretation. *Palaeogeography, Palaeoclimatology, Palaeoecology* 51:159–196.

Maruyama, S., and J.G. Liou. 2005. From snowball to Phaneorozic Earth. *International Geology Review* 47:775–791.

Moreau, J., J.F. Ghienne, D.P. Le Heron, J.L. Rubino, and M. Deynoux. 2005. 440 Ma ice stream in North Africa. *Geology* 33:753–756.

Oard, M.J. 1990. *An Ice Age Caused by the Genesis Flood*. El Cajon, CA: Institute for Creation Research.

———. 1997. *Ancient Ice Ages or Gigantic Submarine Landslides?* Creation Research Society Monograph 6, Chino Valley, AZ.

———. 2002. "Snowball Earth" — a problem for the supposed origin of multicellular animals. TJ 16 (1):6–9.

———. *Frozen in Time: Woolly Mammoths, the Ice Age, and the Bible*. Green Forest, AR: Master Books.

———. 2005. The Late Ordovician striated pavement in North Africa — not directly caused by glaciation. *TJ* 19(3):9–10.

Oberbeck, V.R., J.R. Marshall, and H. Aggarwal. 1993a. Impacts, tillites, and the breakup of Gondwanaland. *Journal of Geology* 101:1–19.

———. 1993b. Impacts, tillites, and the breakup of Gondwanaland: a reply. *Journal of Geology* 101:679–783.

Oberbeck, V.R., F. Hörz, and T Bunch. 1994. Impacts, tillites, and the breakup of Gondwanaland: a second reply. *Journal of Geology* 102:485–489.

Petit, J.P. 1987. Criteria for the sense of movement on fault surfaces in brittle rocks. *Journal of Structural Geology* 9:597–608.

Rampino, M.R. 1992. Ancient "glacial" deposits are ejecta of large impacts: the ice age paradox explained. *EOS*. American Geophysical Union Abstract Supplement, Washington, DC: American Geophysical Union, p. 99.

———. 1994. Tillites, diamictites, and ballistic ejecta of large impacts. *Journal of Geology* 102:439–456.

Reed, J.K. 1998. Demythologizing uniformitarian history. *CRSQ* 35(3):157–165.

Reimold, W.U., V. von Brunn, and C. Koeberl. 1997. Are diamictites impact ejecta? — no supporting evidence from South African Dwyka Group diamictite. *Journal of Geology* 105:517–530.

Rocha-Campos, A.C., P.R. Dos Santos, and J.R. Canuto. 1994. Ice scouring structure in late Paleozoic rhythmites, Paraná Basins, Brazil. In M. Deynoux, J.M.G. Miller, E.W. Domack, N. Eyles, I.J. Fairchild, and G.M. Young (editors). *Earth's Glacial Record*. London: Cambridge University Press, p. 234–240.

Schermerhorn, L.J.G. 1971. Upper Ordovician glaciation in Northwest Africa? Discussion. *GSA Bulletin* 82:265–268.

Young, G.M. 1993. Impacts, tillites, and the breakup of Gondwanaland: a discussion. *Journal of Geology* 101:675–679.

Chapter 8

Do Varves Contradict Biblical History?

Michael J. Oard • MS — Atmospheric Science

Abstract

Varves are thought to be a challenge to a young earth, although like others, the conflicts end up being mostly interpretive. While the rock record contains formations with thousands, even millions, of these rhythmites, it is not clear that they represent vast lengths of time. The first varves[1] to conflict with biblical history were those developed into the deglaciation and post-glacial time scales. Others came later from post–ice age lakes and marine basins, like Elk Lake, Minnesota, and the Santa Barbara Basin. Older varves have been identified in lithified rocks, like the Castile and Green River Formations. None of these are the problem once thought, for a variety of reasons. Primarily, new research has confirmed that many mechanisms can deposit varve-like rhythmites quite rapidly. Therefore, older long-age interpretations are suspect.

Introduction

A varve is narrowly defined as a thin sedimentary sequence laid down in water in one year. Rocks or sediments containing up to hundreds of thousands or millions of varves are relatively common. These varves imply far more time than the biblical chronology. Thus, they contradict its history, especially the Flood (Henke 1999; Morton 2003a; Strahler 1987; Wonderly 1987). Anti-creationist Strahler (1987, p. 231) summed up the problem:

> If large sequences of laminations are demonstrated beyond all reasonable doubt to be varves, Flood geology lies demolished and totally discredited.

Henke (1999, p. 19) piled on: "The consistency and diversity of varves and related geologic data are quickly driving the final nails in the YEC coffin."

But as with other "nails," this one deserves another look. The term "varve" is loaded, with only its definition demanding the time. A better word is the empirical term "rhythmite." A rhythmite is a repeating sequence of two or more laminae, a thin layer of sediment or sedimentary rock. Rhythmites differ from other laminations in that they show a repeating sequence, while other laminations show random alternations. The repeating sequence can be sand and silt, clay and diatom shells, or any number of different layers of particles, and is called a couplet. Fine sediment deposited slowly in water often exhibits laminations — thin layers that differ from each other by a change in color, texture, or composition. Sometimes the particles in a layer fine upward, forming graded bedding — commonly found in turbidites.[2]

---

1. Although "varve" is a genetic term implying annual deposition, its usage is so common in the literature that I will use it in this paper, even though many so-called varves might be rhythmites deposited by other mechanisms.

2. Turbidites are sediments deposited by a turbidity current, an underwater flow of sediment supported by fluid turbulence.

A true, classical varve is a couplet: a coarser layer of sand or silt laid down in summer and a finer layer of clay and organic matter laid down in winter. The term was originally applied in glacial lake environments but was extended to other rhythmite sequences deposited in either lakes or a marine environment (Anderson and Dean 1988). Consolidated varves are called "varvites." Occasional clasts larger than the thickness of the laminae are thought to be dropstones from icebergs or floating ice. The resulting rock is called "dropstone varvite" and is considered one of the three major proofs of past glaciation (see chapter 7).

This chapter will address the challenge varves present the creationist time scale. I will begin where varves were first used for chronology: Sweden. Then I will evaluate varves of lake and marine basins, specifically the Elk Lake varves in Minnesota and the marine varves in the Santa Barbara Basin off Southern California. Both of these units were deposited after the Flood (except possibly the lower sections of the Santa Barbara Basin). Other varves in the rock record probably formed during the Flood. I will analyze two classic examples, the Castile and Green River Formations. Finally, I will suggest a mechanism for the rapid formation of rhythmites and laminations.

The First Varve Time Scale

Rhythmites associated with the Ice Age look similar. Figure 1 shows varves in southern Ontario, Canada, associated with the deglaciation of eastern North America. The light layers are thought to be summer deposits, and the dark layers are considered winter sediments.

The first use of varves in a time scale was in Sweden, where Gerard De Geer counted thousands of couplets to reach the conclusion that the ice sheet took 13,500 years to move north across Sweden (Nelson 1948). The time from the end of the Ice Age to the present added about 9,000 more years (Cato 1987). The resulting time scale was considered the first "absolute" chronology (Oard 1992a, 1992b).

However, there was no single location that included all the varves. The chronology was set up by traveling north through Sweden and correlating sets of varves from one exposure to another (figure 2). The number of varves in each pit was usually less than 200 (Olsson 1970). The process is similar to tree ring chronologies — counting tree rings in many trees and matching partial sequences from one tree to another to establish a long chronology (e.g., the bristlecone pine chronology from the White Mountains in California).

Figure 1. A "varve" section taken from Twin Falls Dam, Ontario, Canada. Notice the abrupt change in couplet thickness near the bottom of the photograph. (Courtesy of the Geological Survey of Canada)

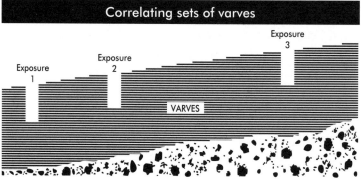

Figure 2. Schematic diagram illustrating "varve" correlations from three exposures. By measuring the couplet thickness pattern, the top portion of exposure 1 should match the bottom and middle portion of exposure 2. Modified from Nelson (1948, p. 47) by David Oard.

But De Geer simply *assumed* that the varves were annual layers: "The regular and continuous distribution of the varves convinced him [De Geer] that they, too, were annual" (Strömberg 1983, p. 97). Although De Geer's chronology was too long for biblical history, it was too short for previous estimates of post-glacial time of 500,000 to 1,000,000 years (Nelson 1948).

Later, a long "varve" chronology was set up in New England and southeast Canada by De Geer's student Ernst Antevs. Traveling up the Connecticut Valley in New England, Antevs was able to correlate sequences to reach a total of 4,400 years. Antevs also found a similar sequence in the Hudson Valley (Nelson 1948).

Up until the 1950s, the Swedish deglaciation varve chronology, which just happened to match the one in eastern North America by a "transcontinental" correlation (De Geer 1928), was considered the global standard (Schove and Fairbridge 1983). However, De Geer and Antevs had exaggerated the chronology. Even the anti-creationist Arthur Strahler (1987, p. 231) was critical of these early "varve" studies:

> De Geer's work was carried on in New England by Ernst Antevs in the 1920s and 1930s. Antevs, also assuming he was dealing with true varves, compiled a sequence for eastern North America spanning a north-south distance of over 100 km and yielding a chronology of 28,000 yr. There are three long gaps in this stretch, and much of the chronology rests on interpolation. Flint states that carbon-14 dates within the sequence "suggest a period of little more than 10,000 years."

Small wonder that creation scientists are highly critical of the varve studies of De Geer and Antevs. They need only to borrow and repeat the criticisms expressed by mainstream scientists. Something was wrong with the early varve chronologies, but a more interesting point is their *agreement*, another example of the pervasive *reinforcement* syndrome in the so-called historical sciences that reinforces beliefs and biases (Oard 1997).

Errors in "Varve" Correlations

Later I will show that varve-like rhythmites can form rapidly. But first we need to deal with the problems in varve correlation that led to problems in the early time scale — and likely continue today.

A typical varve sequence in Sweden has only about 200 couplets, so a complete sequence can only be built by correlating a large number of locations. Ideally, the bottom of a varve sequence in one location should correlate with the middle or top of the next sequence to the north, since the ice sheet retreated northward (figure 2). Continuing from

one location to another, the sequence is gradually built. How reliable are these correlations?

A close examination reveals many problems with the correlation procedure. One problem is that each "varve" section actually represents an *average* of many individual "varve" profiles from the same locality (Fromm 1970). Antevs (1925a, p. 120) explained the necessity for this averaging procedure:

> All individual curves [of varve thicknesses] were first matched and corrected for number of varves. If, for example, out of three measurements two agreed, but one had one varve less or more than the others, the exact location of the mistake was determined and the curve corrected by dividing one varve in two or uniting two varves in one, so that this curve agreed with the two others. Then the curves or such parts of them as included undisturbed varves of normal variation and thickness were selected for constructing the normal curve, and those curves were discarded that showed great difference in thickness from the majority or poor agreement in the shape of the curve.

But this procedure is subjective; the researcher can intentionally or unintentionally manipulate the data. One must remember that unconscious manipulation (or even conscious massaging) of data is probably a norm in science (Gould 1978).

Once each "type" section was constructed, all the sequences were *visually* matched in the direction of ice recession (there are computer methods available today for matching sequences). Distinctive varves or combinations aid in correlation. Although De Geer expressed considerable confidence in his chronology, difficulties have since surfaced (Lundqvist 1975; Ringberg 1979; Strömberg 1983). This is why the "Swedish Time Scale" giving the deglaciation chronology for Sweden was revised starting in the 1940s (Strömberg 1983). Strömberg (1985) summarized differences between the old correlations and the results of the revised Swedish Time Scale. North of Stockholm the revised chronology added about 10 percent more time. South of Stockholm, many hundreds of years were tacked onto the old chronology. These changes from De Geer's construct show that those early correlations were inaccurate. If correlation problems are inherent to the methodology, the new chronology may be just as inaccurate.

Many of the problems in correlating varves are illustrated by the Swedish rhythmites. They vary in sharpness, probably depending upon salinity variations in the Baltic Sea area, which has apparently ranged from freshwater to seawater. As a result, investigators have trouble even identifying a varve couplet (Strömberg 1983). This is especially true in the Stockholm-Uppsala area, De Geer's first study location (Strömberg 1985). In some areas, varves are missing, leaving the investigator the option of either interpolating or correlating to surrounding sections. Frequent sliding and slumping of the beds, difficult to detect in cores, also complicates correlation, and researchers today depend upon cores.

Accurate correlation is also difficult because few varves can be traced a significant distance (Ringberg 1979). Continuous horizontal exposures of lateral changes are rarely found in the field. Strömberg (1983) stated that past correlations have been poor, despite the enthusiasm of many investigators. De Geer's chronology was not as continuous as thought; he bridged a large gap in Sweden by using a varve series *outside* Europe (Schove and Fairbridge 1983). Although long distance correlation in Sweden is sometimes claimed (to the astonishment of some investigators), even very short distance correlations can be questionable. More recent correlations depend on varve sections that are much closer together, and even these correlations are sometimes difficult (Strömberg 1983). Stromberg showed a picture of varves in a two-foot-wide pit. The sublayers occasionally thicken and thin and two pinch out horizontally — just in that small pit. Knowing that, how could they expect to be credible correlating for any distance?

So, with these problems (and others), varve chronologies built on correlations are equivocal and must be "tuned" to other geological and climatic data, as admitted by Strömberg (1983, p. 100–101, emphasis mine):

> In reality only a few varve sequences contain the "correct" number of varves. . . . It is important to consider that correlations *agree with other geological criteria* in the area investigated.

Thus, "varve" chronologies, like most, if not all, geochronological methods, are subject to circular reasoning and the reinforcement syndrome (Oard 1997), which Henke (1999) minimizes as an effect of "historical science." Nowadays, all climatic data are made to fit the Milankovitch or astronomical theory for assumed multiple ice ages, which practically all uniformitarian scientists assume to be true (Oard 2005). This mechanism postulates cyclical glacial and interglacial phases caused by oscillations in the earth's orbital geometry around the sun. The Milankovitch mechanism has a very slow deglaciation

chronology that started about 18,000 years ago and ended around 6,000 to 10,000 years ago, depending upon the location. So the results of slow ice sheet melting from current "varve" chronologies "fits" with the Milankovitch paradigm.

The Questionable Glacial Lake Hitchcock "Varve" Chronology

The glacial Lake Hitchcock rhythmites also underscore many of the problems in deglaciation "varve" analysis. Lake Hitchcock was a lake south of the ice sheet in New England that occupied the Connecticut Valley (figure 3). The ice sheet melted northward up the valley, leaving behind a varve record more than 190 miles (300 km) long. Antevs (1922) correlated this section up the lake and claimed that it took 4,400 years for the ice sheet to recede. Although that rate fits quite well into uniformitarian deglaciation ideas, many difficulties exist with the Lake Hitchcock varves that also illustrate theoretical difficulties.

The varve couplets in Lake Hitchcock sediments vary considerably (Ashley 1972, 1975). For instance, the rhythmites range from 1 to 75 centimeters in thickness (Flint 1975). The coarse sublayer is sometimes not laminated, and when laminated, it may include as many as 40 laminae. The couplets vary significantly between outcrops,

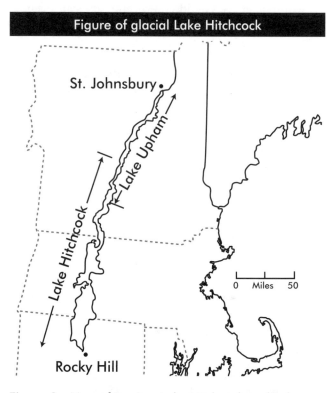

Figure 3. Map of Ice Age Lake Hitchcock and Lake Upham in New England. Modified from Ashley (1972) by Dale Niemeyer.

and they thin or disappear over basement irregularities — a sign that deposition was primarily by underflows or turbidity currents. And like those in Sweden, the number and thickness of each varve section must be interpolated from many measurements going northward.

Although admitting the couplets have not been proven to be annual, Ashley (1972, 1975) believes that they are, based partially on their similarity to the Swedish varves. But if the silt layers were deposited by underflows and turbidity currents, they are not annual. These flows can lay down multiple layers in one year, especially in a narrow lake with sediment entering from the sides.

Antevs (1922) misunderstood how lake rhythmites form, which distorted his correlations. He believed each couplet was formed by the settling from overflows of silt in summer and clay in winter. Thus, each couplet would extend a great distance southward down the lake and change thickness slowly (Gustavson 1975). This theory of varve formation, illustrated in figure 2, is only partially true. The coarse-grained sublayer is formed mainly by underflows that thin much more rapidly from their source than Antevs anticipated (Smith 1978; Smith et al. 1982; Smith and Ashley 1985). So correlating varve sections that are widely separated is questionable. Antevs' (1922) correlation points averaged about 3 miles (5 km) apart, but many were separated by more than 10 miles (16 km), too far for a reasonable coherence in the couplet pattern.

Lake rhythmites also vary across the width of a lake, further complicating correlation. Underflows and turbidity currents are often linear or lobe shaped, being thickest along the axis of flow and thinner on the flanks (Smith and Ashley 1985). Furthermore, the Coriolis force turns interflows and overflows to the right in the Northern Hemisphere. As a result, laminae formed by these flows, including the clay layers, thicken to the right in Northern Hemisphere lakes (i.e., Lake Hitchcock, Sweden), even in relatively small lakes (Sturm and Matter 1978; Smith et al. 1982; Smith and Ashley 1985).

Furthermore, deposition of the Lake Hitchcock rhythmites was predominantly nonglacial (excepting the basal rhythmite). The sediments were from deglaciated terrain to the west and east of the lake (Ashley 1975) (figure 4). Large deltas and cross-bedded silt layers show an easterly or westerly paleocurrent direction (Gustavson et al. 1975). The rhythmites connect to these deltas, and the coarse layer thins with distance from the deltas.

Based on rhythmites at only one location in the Connecticut Valley, Ridge and Larsen (1990) defended Antevs' correlations. But if the rhythmites were mostly deposited

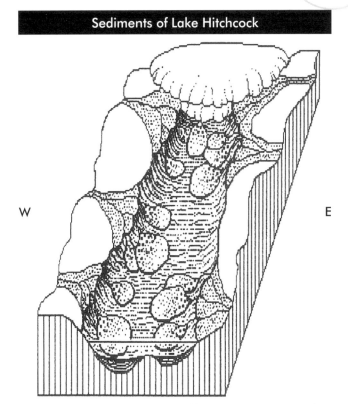

Sediments of Lake Hitchcock

W

E

Figure 4. Schematic diagram illustrating a portion of Ice Age Lake Hitchcock as the ice retreats northward up the valley. Note the sediment mostly enters the lake from the east and west, forming delta deposits and rhythmites. Modified from Ashley (1975) by Dale Niemeyer.

from the sides of the lake, how could the varves have been correlated up the *length* of the lake? It is hard to see how Antevs' (1922) correlations could be correct. In discussing them, Ashley (1972) agrees: "In my opinion, the method of visually matching curves drawn from varve tapes, which was so successful in Sweden, is unreliable for the Connecticut Valley." It is very likely unreliable in Sweden as well.

The Post-glacial Time Scale

Given the questionable correlations of deglaciation rhythmites in Sweden and the Connecticut River Valley, how are their ages related to the present? It was done by counting varves in the Ångermanälven River Valley in central Sweden, apparently the *only* one that provided a post-glacial chronology (Cato 1985). This valley was a shallow fjord at the end of the Ice Age, and the land was approximately 820 feet (250 m) lower than today, based on the highest Baltic Sea paleoshoreline. As the land rose by isostatic rebound after removal of the ice, the river delta prograded seaward and the bottom of the fjord became progressively exposed. During this time, sediments were

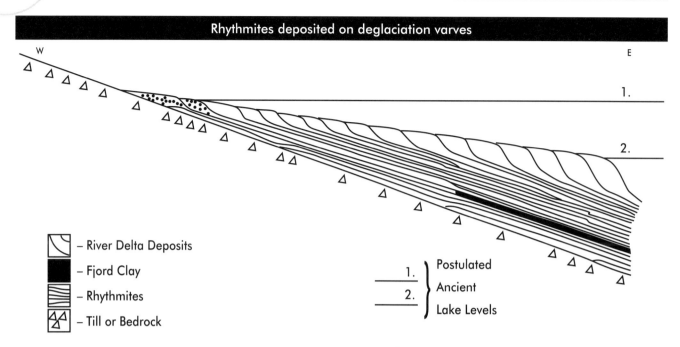

Figure 5. Typical section through the valley sediments along the Ångermanälven River Valley, central Sweden. The fjord clay (black) supposedly separates the deglaciation "varves" below from the post-glacial estuary "varves" above (redrawn from Cato 1987 by Dale Niemeyer).

transported down the river to the delta and then deposited in the brackish estuary. Because it was probably deep, rhythmites were deposited on top of the deglaciation varves (figure 5). A core through these sediments would reveal, starting from the top, delta deposits, followed by estuarine varves, then possibly a thin layer of fjord clay, and finally the deglaciation varves. By correlating short sequences of post-glacial rhythmites down valley from the point the ice last melted (the zero point), Lidén in 1915 developed a chronology to the present.

All the problems encountered in correlating lake rhythmites apply to these estuarine rhythmites. Other problems are inherent to estuaries. First, their rhythmites are very thin (Antevs 1925b), and thus notoriously difficult to correlate. Second, the two laminae in each couplet showed only slight differences in grain size and color (Antevs 1925a, 1925b), making it difficult to determine the annual layer sequence. Lidén even believed, at least in 1911, that the clay layer was deposited in the spring floods — the opposite of deglaciation varves. Moreover, rivers would deposit multiple pulses of sediment to the estuary from spring meltwater and rainstorms. At first, Lidén established the post-glacial period at 6,560 years, but later stretched it to 8,800 years (Antevs 1925b), probably because it was thought that post-glacial time in the area had been about 9,000 years. This illustrates

the subjectivity of his correlations and indicates that the results were altered to meet expectations.

It would help to have Lidén's original work, but he never published any varve diagrams or correlations during his lifetime. A brief summary of his conclusions came out in 1938 (Schove and Fairbridge 1983; Cato 1985, 1987). According to Cato (1987), Lidén's detailed work was ready in 1915 but was never published. I wonder why?

Besides the problems of determining the annual couplet and correlating these couplets downstream, two additional problems were encountered in developing the post-glacial varve time scale. First, the beginning of the sequence needed to be tied to the deglaciation sequence — called the "zero year." It was difficult — researchers had to distinguish the last "deglaciation varve" from the first "post-glacial varve." Second, Lidén could not connect the youngest rhythmite sequence to the present, since the youngest rhythmites were under water. The technology for taking underwater cores at the current 330 foot (100 m) depth had not been developed. His youngest core was taken about 40 feet (12 m) above sea level. So to connect that core to the present, he assumed a shoreline uplift rate of about 0.5 in/yr (1.25 cm/yr), and extrapolated its age to 980 years. Since then, geologists have cored the estuary. The current uplift rate is about 0.3 in/yr (0.76 cm/yr), so geologists have added another 365 years to Lidén's date.

Counting varves eastward down the Ångermanälven River Valley resulted in about 9,000 years added to the deglacial time scale to reach the present. However, this chronology is suspect, especially since Lidén never published his work, and there is difficulty in determining a varve and in correlating them.

Varves in Recent Non-glacial Lakes and Marine Basins

Varves have been identified in a variety of recent depositional environments, including many non-glacial lakes (Anderson and Dean 1988; Ludlam 1979; O'Sullivan 1983). Many of these rhythmites are very thin couplets of diatoms, calcium carbonate, mineral matter, or organic material. Rhythmites were once considered rare at the bottom of the ocean, but now are known to be common in isolated ocean basins and brackish estuaries of fjords (Dallimore et al. 2005; Pike and Kemp 1999; Smith et al. 1990).

They continue to be an argument against biblical history. Morton (2003a) claimed that varves cored in Lake Suigetsu, Japan, demonstrated the insufficiency of biblical history due to the 100,000 diatom/clay couplets, precise enough to tune the carbon-14 time scale to 45,000 years BP (Kitagawa and van der Plicht, 1998). Clay enters Lake Suigetsu from wind-blown dust derived from the Chinese Loess Plateau in central China (Fukusawa 1999). The dust adds nutrients to the lake that causes a diatom bloom. The two "independent time scales" were then presented as proof of an old earth. Unfortunately, there is very little literature on these varves in English, and so it is difficult to analyze them.

However the presence of rhythmites in other non-glacial lakes is well-known. Morton, along with other uniformitarians, interprets them using their bias. For example, they assume that the lake remained unchanged for thousands of years, ever since the first varve formed.

But couplets can be created rapidly, and this would have been especially true during the Ice Age. Diatom blooms can occur several times a year in a lake for example, during the spring and fall turnovers. So even a uniform rate can be faster than one year. Blowing dust was probably much greater during the Ice Age (Oard 2004). The Greenland ice sheet shows that Ice Age dust was 40 to 100 times greater than at present (Oard 2005). Dust originating from eastern Asia (Svensson et al. 2000) that would have crossed Japan likely occurred in pulses associated with strong, dry cold fronts. Each pulse of dust falling into the lake could have caused a diatom bloom. Consequently, dozens of diatom/clay couplets could have occurred each year as long as those atmospheric conditions persisted.

Also, the more scientific non-equilibrium model for carbon-14 dating and the change in the carbon-14/carbon-12 ratio before and after the Flood combine to produce much younger carbon-14 dates that fit well within the creationist time scale (Baumgardner 2005; Morris 1994). Thus, the carbon-14 "agreement" and the rate of rhythmite formation are both suspect at Lake Suigetsu. Other lacustrine varves can shed more light on these phenomena.

Elk Lake, Minnesota

Lake varves are not the same everywhere (O'Sullivan 1983). Clastic varves are those in which part of the couplet formed from material transported into the lake from its drainage basin or by wind. Non-clastic varves are those in which the rhythmites form from biological processes and mineral matter formed within the lake. Some sequences are a combination of both clastic and non-clastic layers. Some lakes show changes from clastic to non-clastic varves or vice versa. It is beyond the scope of this chapter to analyze the hundreds of lakes studied, so we will examine the well-known example of Elk Lake, Minnesota. A similar creationist explanation for varves in other lakes is probable.

Uniformitarian Interpretation

Elk Lake is a small lake in north-central Minnesota with an area of about one km^2 (figure 6). Minnesota was once glaciated, so these varves have accumulated only since the end of the Ice Age. Elk Lake is 50 miles (80 km) east of the present prairie-forest boundary (Dean 1997), and at the boundary between competing atmospheric air masses from the Arctic, the Gulf of Mexico, and the Pacific that would affect the deposition of varves. No permanent stream ever fed Elk Lake. In winter the lake freezes; in summer the bottom becomes anoxic (no oxygen). These conditions cause two vertical turnovers of the lake each year — in spring and autumn.

Deglaciation is assumed to have occurred about 10,000 years ago, which matches the approximate number of varves cored from the bottom of Elk Lake. Few other Holocene lakes in previously glaciated areas exhibit so many varves (Dean et al. 1984). One wonders if this "match" weights research toward Elk Lake. Its varves vary vertically in type, thickness, and sharpness of their contacts (Anderson 1992; Anderson et al. 1993; Dean 2002; Dean et al. 1984).

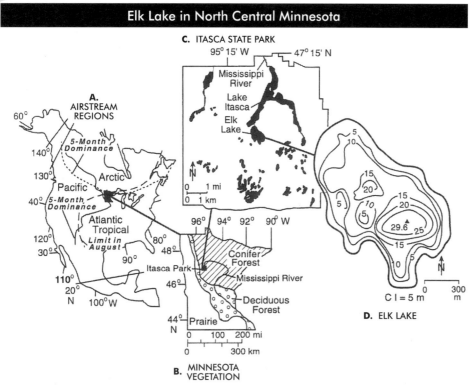

Figure 6. Maps showing (A) airstream regions in North America; (B) vegetation zones of Minnesota; (C) Itasca State Park with location of Elk Lake; (D) bathymetry of Elk Lake (Dean 1997, p. 331).

The Elk Lake cores are divided into three periods: the immediate post-glacial lake, the prairie lake, and the modern lake phases (figure 7). There are ten types of laminae in the cores that vary with time (Anderson 1993). The varves are said to be complex in parts, so the interpretation of the annual layer can also be complex and subjective (Anderson 1993). For example, two cores from the modern lake stage showed a 15 percent error in the varve counts (Anderson 1993).

The lowest portion of the cores, the immediate post-glacial phase (10,400 to ~8,000 years BP), has the most distinct, simple varves consisting of thin (<1 mm), sharply defined couplets of dark and light laminae. The light layer consists mainly of $CaCO_3$ and the other of organic matter, clay, and diatoms. It is thought that much of this sediment came from the dissolution of glacial till (Dean 1993). Shallow water deposits transported to the deep lake by turbidity currents are relatively common in this phase (Dean, 1993).

The middle portion of the cores, the prairie phase (8,000 to 4,000 years BP), is more clastic, with silt presumably carried into the lake as windblown dust. The prairie-forest boundary lay to the east, instead of to the west as at present. These varves consist of thick, light gray, clastic laminae separated by a very thin, dark gray, organic-rich layer. The appearance of the prairie phase varves is dramatically different from the immediate post-glacial phase. They are thicker, more variable, and less distinct, and the varved character of the sediment was nearly obliterated during peak influxes of dust (Dean et al. 1984). They are about three times thicker than those in the post-glacial phase and significantly thicker than those in the modern phase. An additional complication during the prairie phase was the erosion of sediments from shallow areas into the deeper part of the lake, adding to the amount of clastic material (Anderson 1993).

The modern lake phase varves (4,000 years to the present) contain very little clastic material, and are composed of complex alterations of diatoms, $CaCO_3$, $MnCO_3$, and amorphous flocs and gels of iron and manganese oxides and hydroxides. This phase likely corresponds to the modern forest environment around the lake.

Creationist Interpretation

The succession of varves at Elk Lake can be interpreted in the deglaciation and post–Ice Age chronology of a young earth (Oard 1990, 2004). Immediately following glacial retreat, there would have been significant meltwater inflow with associated turbidity currents. There are massive layers of turbidities in the immediate post-glacial rhythmites. There would have been significant clastic input during this period. After Mount St. Helens was denuded of forests, rapid deposition of many varve-like rhythmites occurred in Coldwater Lake (Anderson et al. 1985), so multiple rhythmites would be expected each year during this first phase.

After significant deglaciation, dry, strong winds would have deposited large amounts of dust into the lake (Oard 1990, 2004), resulting in multiple rhythmites per year, similar to the Ice Age varves in Lake Suigetsu, Japan.

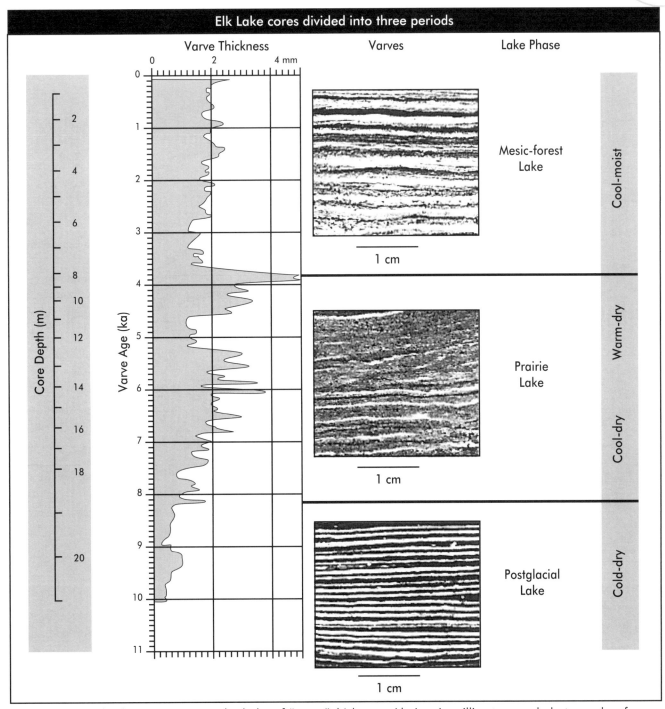

Figure 7. Core depth in meters, smoothed plot of "varve" thickness with time in millimeters, and photographs of typical "varve" sequences from the three post-glacial phases of Elk Lake (Anderson, Dean, and Bradbury 1993, p. 4).

The time involved could be as little as a hundred years or so.

The "annual" layer is difficult to determine for the modern annual lake phase. An analysis of the modern varves sometimes shows three or four laminae (Anderson 1993). There is a considerable variation in nutrients from year to year (Megard et al. 1993), which would affect biological productivity and thus varve thickness and composition:

Although only four of the ten types of laminations found in Elk Lake varved sediments occur in the modern lake stage . . . three and sometimes four of these types are found together in annual groupings that are difficult to interpret as annual accumulations (Anderson 1993, p. 57).

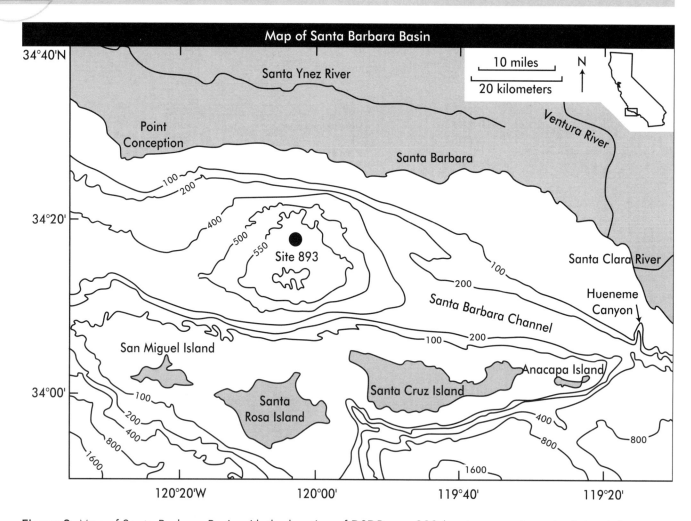

Figure 8. Map of Santa Barbara Basin with the location of DSDP core 893 (contours are in meters). Inset shows location of enlarged view of California coast (Kennet, Baldauf, et al. 1994, p. 17).

Furthermore, reworking of shallow water sediments during the modern phase is illustrated by charcoal layers from forest fires being redeposited in the deeper part of the lake (Bradbury 1996). During reworking, water circulation stirs up nutrients so that diatom blooms could add more layers (Bradbury 1996; Nuhfur et al. 1993). Thus, there is little reason to expect rhythmites in Elk Lake to represent annual deposits in any of the three periods.

Uniformitarians claim that their varve chronology is verified independently by carbon-14 dating, pollen stratigraphy, and paleomagnetism chronologies (Bradbury and Dean 1993). But none of these chronologies are independent; they are all built on many assumptions and are correlated to the Milankovitch hypothesis for ice ages (Oard 2005). Weaknesses in each method are downplayed simply because there are multiple (questionable) methods.

Santa Barbara Basin

Scientists have recently interpreted rhythmites as varves in many marine basins, bays, estuaries, and fjords, such as Saanich Inlet on Vancouver Island, southern British Columbia (Sancetta and Calvert 1988), and the Gulf of California (Pike and Kemp 1999). The marine varves in the Santa Barbara Basin (figure 8) off Southern California (Kennett et al. 1994) are the best studied. Because of a fairly large amount of literature available, an alternative creationist model can be suggested. It is possible that other marine rhythmites or laminations can be explained in a similar way.

Shallow Cores

Early (prior to the 1960s) shallow cores from the Santa Barbara Basin recovered rhythmites (Emery and Hülsemann 1962; Hülsemann and Emery 1961; Reimers et al. 1990). They were separated by homogeneous layers, turbidites, and disturbed rhythmites. It is estimated that about 5 percent of the top several meters consists of massive turbidites that vary in thickness from 0.04 to 5 inches (0.1–12 cm) (Schimmelmann and Kastner 1993). The Santa Barbara Basin is a productive environment for microorganisms (Schimmelmann and Kastner 1993), and diatoms are the dominant microorganisms deposited on the bottom. The rhythmites were claimed to be varves right from the beginning, based on carbon-14 dating, with a mean varve thickness of 0.06 to 0.08 inch/ yr (1.5 to 2.0 mm/yr) at 60–65 percent water content of the sediment (Emery and Hülsemann 1962; Hülsemann and Emery 1961; Soutar and Crill 1977). These varves consist of laminae of microorganisms containing pollen and silt alternating with clay or silt from coastal runoff. So the varves really represent alternating clastic and biogenic input.

Uniformitarians interpret the annual cycle to include microorganism blooms during the spring caused by strong upwelling, with clay and silt deposited during the winter. Upwelling brings nutrients to the surface, resulting in high surface biogenic productivity and silica sediments to the bottom. However, blooms of microorganisms can also occur in the fall (Black et al. 2001). Diatom blooms can be rapidly deposited by flocculation, coagulation of small particles into larger particles, and sometimes reach the bottom in 24 hours (Alldredge and Gotschalk 1989; Grimm et al. 1997). One diatom bloom put a shell layer 3.5 millimeters thick on the bottom (Grimm et al. 1996). Multiple blooms during the year can produce multiple layers. So the presumed annual cycle is much more complicated.

Clastic sedimentation is likewise more complex. Sedimentation into the deep basin does not correlate with the wet season because sediments from winter runoff are first deposited on the continental shelf (Soutar and Crill 1977). The input of silt and clay to the shelf is episodic, not regular. In 18 years of monitoring the Santa Clara River (the main input to the basin), half the total sediment was carried in just three floods, lasting a total of seven days (Milliman and Syvitski 1992)! Furthermore, shelf sediment is dispersed into the basin by a series of slumps and turbidity currents. So, silt and clay can be added to the bottom of the basin *at any time* during the year (Soutar and Crill 1977). The end result would be multiple annual couplets.

Rhythmites from El Niños during the past century and dating using short-lived radionuclides supposedly have proven the annual time scale of the varves (Krishnaswami

et al. 1973; Schimmelmann et al. 1990; Soutar and Crill 1977). The researchers did find that there were subannual rhythmites and that some supposed annual layers were weakly developed (Schimmelmann et al. 1990, p. 170):

> The seemingly obvious solution — to count varves downcore from the surface — presents some difficulties. . . . Moreover, water-rich seasonal layers with distinct coloration sometimes can be mistaken for annual layers. Also, varves may be weakly developed within certain intervals.

This suggests that defining annual layers is subjective. The uniformitarian scientists compensate by using marker horizons to date the rhythmites. However, this adds more complications and assumptions, mainly because researchers need to know the date of the marker horizon in advance. These dates may be scientifically defensible for recent events, but events older than about 200 years are hypothetical.

The first direct observations of sedimentation came from sediment traps suspended 165 feet (50 m) above the bottom (Thunell et al. 1995). The traps "verified" that the dark "winter" layers were caused by fine continental sediments from river and stream runoff while the light "summer" layers were caused by the spring onset of upwelling from increased northerly winds (Black et al. 2001). This is as expected from the varve interpretation.

However, in today's climate there are variables that can cause more than one couplet a year. First, a sediment trap 165 feet (50 m) above the surface would miss practically all mass flows and other movement of sediments along the bottom. A sediment trap only 7.5 feet (2.3 m) above the bottom of Coldwater Lake in the denuded area around Mount St. Helens missed most of the deposition there, which was by turbidity currents (Anderson et al. 1985).

Second, there is evidence that the supposed annual layer was punctuated by "event beds" comprising graded silt to clay, presumed to be reworking of basin deposits (Dean et al. 1999). Differentiation of these events from varves is difficult since event couplets resemble "varves." So it is likely that many rhythmites in the basin are formed by turbidity currents, undetected by suspended sediment traps. In fact, Emery et al. (1970, p. 99) believed that silt and clay in the Southern California borderland basins was deposited by turbidity currents:

> The fine-grained sediments are deposited first on the shelf, and later are placed in suspension by waves, tidal currents, and bottom currents to form

turbid bottom layers. These layers in turn form low-density, low-velocity turbidity currents that travel from the shelf into deeper water by way of submarine gullies and canyons.

Third, eddies are generated in the Santa Barbara Channel due to the convergence of two currents (Thunell 1998). These eddies possess distinct water properties that can potentially result in couplets on the basin bottom.

Deep Cores

In 1992, DSDP core 893 was drilled to 645 feet (196.5 m) (Kennett et al. 1994). Prior to this, piston and box cores had penetrated only a few meters into the sediments. The DSDP core found laminations separated by non-laminated intervals. However, below about 82 feet (25 m), there were large sections with few if any laminations. So most of the core below about 82 feet (25 m) was generally unlaminated, except for a 46-foot (14 m) interval at a depth of around 460 feet (140 m). These laminations were (of course) interpreted to be varves. Kennett and Ingram (1995) claimed that there are over 1.25 miles (2 km) of horizontal Quaternary sediments in the Santa Barbara Basin based on seismic profiles, implying a partial varve sequence extending back almost two million years.

However, DSDP core 893 was dated by the oxygen isotope ratio of benthic foraminifera (Berger et al. 1997). The Milankovitch hypothesis is assumed in dating deep-sea cores (Oard 2005). So an old age is automatically built into the core and climatic interpretations assume this age.

It is significant that the varves change down the core. At the surface, they were alternating layers of clay/silt with biogenic material (mainly diatoms), but at depth they become mainly variations in the amount of silt (Dean et al. 1999). A discontinuous to continuous thin diatom layer is superimposed on the silt variations. So the biogenic diatom component is sometimes barely present. Thus, these varves are likely due to variations in biogenic input superimposed on rapidly forming turbidites. Uniformitarians also arrive at an average sedimentation rate of around 0.02 in/yr (0.5 mm/yr) for the rhythmites (Dean et al. 1999), which is significantly less than that observed today, even discounting the water content. This suggests that their time scale is artificially expanded.

The time scale is even more questionable because the thickness of the biogenic laminae is much less in the glacial record than during the Holocene. This seems anomalous; one would expect glacial climates to cause more vigorous

ocean currents and greater upwelling of nutrients, which would generate more marine organisms. Even Berger et al. (1997, p. 622, brackets added) thought such a lack of marine organisms unusual:

> Given the usual pattern of high productivity during glacials in many regions of the ocean . . . it is surprising that opal deposition [from diatoms] was low within the basin during glacial time [references deleted].

Creationist Interpretation

In the creationist Ice Age model (Oard 1990, 2004) with its warm oceans and rapidly cooling surface temperatures, overturn would be strong, constantly bringing nutrients from depth to the surface. This would spur extremely large phytoplankton blooms (including diatoms), which would greatly increase the zooplankton, such as foraminifera. Therefore, the biological deposition rate during the Ice Age would be several orders of magnitude higher than expected by uniformitarians. Furthermore, precipitation in the southwest United States would have been up to four times the present rate early in the Ice Age, decreasing in the middle and late Ice Age (Oard 1993). This would increase runoff by much more than four times early in the Ice Age, since the relationship between precipitation and runoff is nonlinear. Sediment input into the ocean would have been much greater early in the Ice Age, tailing off during the remainder of the Ice Age. Thus, the combination of elevated sediment input and diatom blooms would have resulted in rapid formation of rhythmites in the Santa Barbara Basin, declining over time.

Much of the 1.25-mile (2 km) thick Quaternary sediments, mainly lower in the sequence, could be from the Flood, with only the top portion being the post-Flood period. The Santa Barbara Basin probably began as a deep basin more than 1.6 miles (2.5 km) deep with steep slopes. Turbidity currents and other mass flows would rapidly fill the basin, tapering off in the mid to late Ice Age to a minimal rate today. Thus, the late Flood, Ice Age, and post-Ice Age periods can easily account for the rhythmites and other sediments in the Santa Barbara Basin.

Varves in the Rock Record

There are many notable rhythmite sequences in the rock record that are claimed to be varves. Lithified varves are called varvites. If varvites contain rocks larger than the thickness of the couplet, the rocks are considered outsized clasts and the couplets are classified as "dropstone

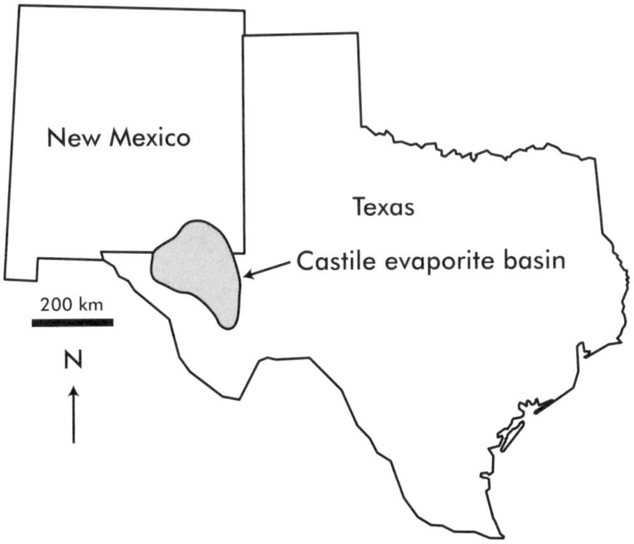

Figure 9. Location of the Castile "evaporite" basin (after Kirkland 2003, p. 900).

varvites," based on the assumption that these clasts were dropped from icebergs during glaciation. Dropstone varvites are one of the three main "proofs" of ancient ice ages (Oard 1997). However, there are other processes that can cause stones to be embedded in thin laminations, including mass movement.

I will delve into two of the classic examples of "varvites" that have a large literature base and have been used to challenge creationists. These are found in the Castile and the Green River Formations.

Castile Formation

A well-known sequence of rhythmites is found in the Upper Permian Castile Formation in the Delaware Basin of West Texas and adjacent southeast New Mexico (figure 9, Kirkland, 2000, p. 900). It is composed of evaporites and covers an area of about 9,800 mi² (25,400 km²) with an average thickness of about 1,650 feet (503 m). The formation is part of a giant deposit that covers 58,600 mi² (151,800 km²) and is up to 4,265 feet (1,300 m) thick (Lowenstein 1988). These rhythmites are interpreted as varvites. They are predominantly couplets of calcite and anhydrite (Anderson et al. 1972; Kirkland 2003), and are similar to many other evaporite sequences around the world (Kirkland 2003; Kushnir 1981).

The Castile Formation is said to contain 260,000 couplets representing 260,000 years of deposition. Some laminae can be correlated for distances of up to 71 miles (114

km) (Anderson et al. 1972). In fact, most can probably be correlated through almost the whole basin, despite being less than a millimeter thick (Kirkland et al., 2000)! Anderson et al. (1972) stated that the Castile Formation rhythmites have never been conclusively proven to be varves, but maintain that no other hypothesis has been seriously entertained. So, investigators have looked at the Castile varvites in only one way — as annual cycles. It is not surprising that they are thought to represent long periods of sedimentation.

Besides calcite/anhydrite laminations, there are also halite/anhydrite couplets; individual laminae of calcite; and triple laminae that are composed of anhydrite, calcite, and halite. Some layers are organic rich. The original Castile Formation is thought to have consisted of 5 percent calcite, 45 percent anhydrite, and 50 percent halite, but much of the halite and gypsum (the hydration product of anhydrite) dissolved from the western side of the basin by post-depositional processes (Kirkland et al. 2000; Kirkland 2003).

Wonderly (1987, p. 74–77) considered the Castile Formation a huge challenge to creationists. Morton (2003b) asserted that the Castile Formation varves cannot be explained by the Flood model, and that creationist leaders are covering up this fact:

It is pictures of varves which show amazing correlations over as much as 91 kilometers about 60 miles [sic]. The layers you see in the core are millimeters thick, which means that the same tranquil conditions had to prevail over that 60 miles. Such fine detail is difficult to explain during a turbulent global flood. The age of this is Permian, which places it in the middle of the geologic column. It is difficult to explain from a YE [young earth] vantage point. I submit this as more evidence that the YE leadership simply isn't telling their people what is actually in the geologic column.

This quote demonstrates many misconceptions about the Flood, one of which is that waters were turbulent everywhere at all times during the entire Flood. While there were certainly local areas of significant turbulence, one would also expect relatively calm areas away from such areas, especially in deep basins. It is such deep basins where "evaporites" can be deposited. In the Flood model, of course, evaporites (another loaded term) are probably "precipitites" deposited out of the water column due to supersaturation.

Castile Formation Challenges the Uniformitarian Paradigm

Many uniformitarians fail to see that the Castile evaporitic varvites are not a showcase for uniformitarianism, but present problems to their paradigm. First, it is difficult to verify that the Castile Formation rhythmites are varves (Kirkland et al. 2000). The various types supposedly formed as an elaborate response to a monsoonal climate (Kirkland 2003). This model is supposedly supported by the geochemistry of the deposits, the deposition of varves in modern salinas, the great regularity of rhythmites, and agreement with the amount of evaporation in a dry, hot environment (Kirkland et al. 2000).

One major problem for their model is that there is no modern analogue at that scale (Anderson et al. 1972). The modern environment presented is a pond 330–550 feet (100–168 m) in diameter and not more than 19 inches (48 cm) deep along the shore of the southern Sinai Peninsula (Kirkland 2003; Kushnir 1981), but it is much too small to explain the vast, pure evaporites of the Castile Formation.

When faced with the failure of the present to be the "key" to the past, uniformitarians attempt the semantic dodge of "actualism." Henke (1999) set the criteria for "actualism" as *naturalistic and plausible*. The former is a biased attempt to equate atheism with science, and the latter is subjective. The problem is that the meaning of

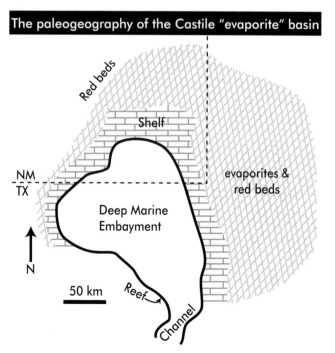

Figure 10. The paleogeography of the Castile "evaporite" basin showing the enclosed reef just before deposition (from Kirkland 2003, p. 901).

"uniformitarianism" has become equivocal. It originally had a very rigid definition, but the rock record cannot support that view. Since it originated as a replacement of the biblical Flood, geologists have been unwilling to reject it, resulting in the modern sloppy terminology. At present, they will accept catastrophism, as long as it isn't *biblical* catastrophism, and they can still call it "uniformitarianism."

These problems are illustrated by the Castile Formation varves: (1) there are no recognizable unconformities in the formation, (2) siliciclastics from the surrounding redbeds are *not* found in the chemical sediments, (3) origins proposed for apparent varves in other evaporite successions are likely invalid for the Castile varves, (4) it is difficult to explain the quantity of salt, (5) there is a lack of a mechanism for restricting seawater influx, (6) a pathway for brine discharge back to the sea is lacking, (7) there is a lack of a mechanism that would allow the basin to accumulate such a volume of "evaporites," and (8) there is no mechanism to explain the proportions of observed lithologies (Kirkland 2003). As a result, the latest proposed model by Kirkland (2003) may qualify as an "actualistic" mechanism, but it seems extremely far-fetched in explaining the above problems.

Kirkland (2003) proposed that the Delaware Basin was once quite deep and mostly surrounded by a dead or dying reef (now the Capitan Formation). But a channel connected the basin to the ocean (figure 10, Kirkland 2003, p. 901). Of course, the climate was arid part of the year because the paleolatitude was near the equator. So, evaporation was around 6.5 ft/yr (2.0 m/yr). Just before the first varves of the Castile Formation formed, the reef cut off the channel opening and formed a deep saline lake. This isolated the Delaware Basin from clastic material. Unfortunately, it also kept the seawater needed to produce the great volume of evaporites from flowing into the basin. The geochemistry of the Castile Formation reinforces the interpretation that the evaporites were derived from seawater (Kirkland et al. 2000). But how did the salts from the sea enter the enclosed lake basin? Kirkland (2003) proposed that seawater from the nearby ocean flowed through the *subsurface* part of the extinct, porous reef and its forereef rubble, surrounding the Delaware Basin, and into "Castile Salt Lake." The reef would have had to remain uncemented for many thousands of years to maintain its porosity and permeability.

But the amount of seawater needed to evaporatively create the varves would have been prodigious. The formation of just the 167-foot (51 m) thick Anhydrite I

Member of the Castile Formation would have required the evaporation of about 420,000 mi^3 (1,750,000 km^3) of seawater (Kirkland 2003), assuming the Permian Ocean had the same chemical composition as today's. This is 0.12 percent of the current volume of earth's present oceans. Total evaporation for the entire Castile "evaporites" is about 2.2 million mi^2 (9,170,000 km^3) of seawater, or about 0.65 percent of the volume of the modern ocean (Kirkland et al. 2000)! This vast volume of water would have to seep through a porous reef surrounding the evaporative lake.

There is also the problem with the ratios of the "evaporative" minerals; they are quite different from those found in modern seawater. Pure seawater will produce 30 times more halite than anhydrite, but the ratio in the Castile Formation is about one to one. Where does the extra anhydrite originate? Or is there a mechanism to selectively eliminate the salt? To solve this problem, Kirkland (2003) suggested a *return flow through the reef* of NaCl-rich brine from "Castile Salt Lake." So we have the situation where seawater can enter through the porous reef into the lake, but a halite brine must selectively be going the other way! To achieve this, he hypothesizes a special vertical stratification that supposedly occurred over part of the year. He goes on and on with other special conditions to account for the chemical deposition.

Others suggest that instead of the salt leaving the lake, gypsum (hydrated anhydrite) somehow entered from earlier evaporative deposits surrounding the Delaware Basin (Leslie et al. 1997). Uniformitarians do not lack creativity in solving their many problems, which could be one of the reasons why the uniformitarian paradigm looks so well supported to the public.

Final Questions

The models raise a number of questions. How did the NaCl actually become concentrated and leave through the reef, when seawater is moving in the opposite direction? Why would there be no siliciclastics, when the climate was supposed to be monsoonal (Kirkland 2003)? In an arid environment, it seems that even windblown silt would be significant over such a long time. How did the nearly dead reef protect the basin from river runoff during the monsoonal climate? Why was the bottom so undisturbed over the whole area for so long, especially when Kirkland (2003, p. 910) believes the lake overturned seasonally: "With equalization of brine densities, wind-induced overturn occurred." How could this be, when Kirkland (2003, p. 909) earlier stated:

Castile laminae accumulated "in an extremely protected 'zero energy' environment" (Holser, 1979). Their great lateral extent and complete lack of disruption are consistent with persistent brine stratification. Wind-induced currents apparently dissipated in the UBL [upper brine layer].

The persistent laminae (up to 113 km) are not evidence for the varve model but against it. True varves, even in large basins, change laterally. Ringberg (1979) stated in reference to the Swedish varves that an accurate correlation of sections is difficult because few varves can be traced any significant distance.

Green River Formation

Perhaps the most challenging claim for varves comes from the "Eocene" Green River Formation of southwest Wyoming, northeast Utah, and northwest Colorado (Henke 1999; Strahler 1987). Geologists estimate that there are about six million varves that were deposited over a few tens of millions of years (Bradley 1929). Henke (1999, p. 20) stated:

Some individual varves in the Green River Formation may extend for tens of kilometers (Fischer and Roberts 1991, p. 1148) and there are more than 5,000,000 individual couplets. . . .

Furthermore, Henke (1999, p. 21) pointed out that regular cycles are found in the varves, including the El Niño (ENSO) oscillation, the sunspot cycle, and the Milankovitch precession and eccentricity cycles. At first glance, this evidence seems difficult to explain within the creationist paradigm.

However, there are a number of indications that the Green River rhythmites are not varves. One of the most obvious is the presence of excellently preserved fossils, especially fossil fish. Such an observation indicates that these thin laminae are *not* varves since fish will rot in only a few weeks, even on the oxygen-less bottom of a deep, cold lake (Whitmore 2003).

After Bradley (1929) presented his varve hypothesis, other scientists expressed doubts and have continued to question the chronologies and cycles (Anderson and Dean 1988; Ripepe et al. 1991). Even Strahler (1987, p. 233) questions the number and regularity of the Green River varves, which is a good question given the proposed fluctuations in the lake level:

The Green River couplets are indeed a remarkable accumulation; their regularity and vast numbers are mind-boggling. How could such uniform deposition continue for 5 to 8 million years?

The varves average only about 0.04 to 0.08 inch (1 to 2 mm) thick with a minimum of 0.001 inch (0.03 mm) (Crowley et al. 1986), which is extremely thin for lake varves. Furthermore, it is claimed that there are subannual oscillations in the varve sequence (Ripepe et al. 1991), which may be hard to distinguish from "annual" oscillations.

Also, varves between two ash beds vary in thickness from 3.2 to 8.9 inches (8.1–22.6 cm) and in number between 1,160 to 1,568 couplets, between localities spaced up to 9.4 miles (15 km) apart (Buchheim and Biaggi 1988). In a later study, Church and Buchheim (2002) reinforced this conclusion with a slightly different rhythmite count. They counted the number of varves between the two ash beds over the 9.4-mile (15 km) distance as varying from 1,238 couplets at the edge of Fossil Basin to 1,661 couplets at the basin center.

The Green River Formation is famous for the immense number of excellently preserved fossils. This suggests that these thin laminae are not varves, since fish will rot in only a few weeks, even on the oxygen-starved bottom of a deep, cold lake (Whitmore 2003), contrary to Henke's (1999) assertion that the fish can lay on the bottom for years in an anaerobic environment while the very thin varves slowly cover them. Such well-preserved specimens are strong evidence for rapid burial, not the slow burial of annual varves.

The cycles found in the varves are presented as evidence that the laminations are true varves. However, the short period cycles, like the sunspot and ENSO cycles, are very weak. One would not expect these cycles to even be measurable. Furthermore, it is doubtful that the sunspot cycle would show a sedimentary effect (Crowley et al. 1986). In three short time series varying from 1,469 to 4,158 varve years, Crowley et al. (1986) did not discover any significant cycles, except for peaks of 10.8 and 5.4 years in a few parts of the series. Spectral analysis of up to 1,661 laminations in Fossil Basin did not show the 11-year sunspot cycle (Church and Buchheim 2002). This casts doubt on whether Ripepe et al. (1991) really found ENSO and sunspot cycles in their varve series, thus justifying a non-varve interpretation. In fact, since the 5.4-year peak is one-half the 10.8-year peak, it is quite possible that the former is just a harmonic of the latter (Crowley et al. 1986).

The longer period cycles are as questionable as the short period cycles. The 100,000-year Milankovitch eccentricity cycle hardly affects the solar radiation on earth (Oard 2005). The other Milankovitch cycles are also weak. One would not expect such cycles to be manifested in any set of rhythmites, especially the 100,000-year cycle.

There are also a number of other cycles that cannot be related to a possible natural cause, such as 30-year, 600-year, and 3,300-year cycles (Fischer and Roberts 1991; Maurizio et al. 1991). With so many cycles, it is not difficult to attribute natural causes to some of them. The finding of so many "cycles," including ones that should not show up, casts suspicion on the methodology for finding cycles in the Green River varves.

It is likely that the Green River Formation was deposited during the Flood (Oard and Klevberg 2008), though other creationists have suggested a post-Flood model (Oard and Whitmore 2006). The formation of the thin rhythmites during the rapid sedimentation in the Flood could account for many rhythmites, including those of the Castile and Green River formations (Berthault 1988, 1991, 1994).

Varve-like Rhythmites Can Form by Many Mechanisms

Real varves do occur today in a number of settings. These have been measured by sediment traps in the water column of lakes and in cores that can be calibrated with modern events. For instance, a retreating glacier in Norway left behind a lake in which the number of couplets in some cores matched the number of years since the glacier left the location (Ostrem 1975). But one core had twice as many couplets as years. It is not unusual for some yearly accumulations to have two couplets (O'Sullivan 1983).

However, it is quite a leap to suggest that most rhythmites associated with deglaciation, post-glacial time, and in the geological record are annual. Some may be, but there is evidence that many are not. Simply comparing De Geer and Antevs' chronologies to that accepted today indicates that these early works were either counting too many annual layers and/or the correlations were poor.

But even more devastating are recent discoveries of mechanisms to form rhythmites rapidly. In the early days, it was simply *assumed* that rhythmites were annual. Anderson and Dean (1988, p. 216) wrote:

> There was little questioning of the assumptions of annual deposition for proglacial lake sediments because seasonally regulated melting and freezing was so obvious, and early investigations . . . were convincing.

A proglacial lake is a lake that occurs at the edge of a glacier. Mackiewicz et al. (1984, p. 114) corroborate:

> Since its inception by De Geer (1912), the term varve has had a troubled history . . . the term "varve" has become a catch-all [sic] term to describe any interlaminated glacial sediment, and it is confusing and misleading.

Quigley (1983, p. 150) also states: "A single varve representing one year of deposition consists of a couplet of summer silt and winter clay; this time framework is difficult to demonstrate, however." Francis (1975, p. 63) maintains:

> Many glacial rhythmites are not varves and consist of laminated sediments in which the layers are alternately lighter-colored fine sand or coarse silt and darker fine silt or clay. . . .

As with most dating methods, its accuracy decreases with time. Varve sequences seem to change with time, and these changes are attributed to dry and wet cycles, change in vegetation cover, etc. It could be that these suggested climate changes are a result of the varves becoming more nonannual with depth.

Varves can be complex and variable. Those displayed in figure 1 are variable; they abruptly change thickness in the lower portion of the photograph. The character of lake varves depends upon many factors, including the quantity, grain size, and composition of the inflowing sediment; the size and bathymetry of the water body; the wind regime; the thermal and chemical stratification of the lake; the presence of burrowing organisms on the bottom, etc. (Ludlam 1979; O'Sullivan 1983; Smith et al. 1982).

Examples of Multiple Varve-Like Rhythmites Deposited within One Year

Measurements of clastic rhythmites, formed by input from the watershed in nonglacial lakes, indicate that more than one couplet can form each year.

Lake Walensee, Switzerland

Lambert and Hsü (1979) reported that 300–360 laminae formed in 160 years in Lake Walensee, Switzerland. The number and thickness of laminae varied with the location, which would make correlation by couplet thickness difficult. Generally, two couplets a year had formed, but at some locations five couplets were deposited in one year. The extra couplets were formed by turbidity currents caused by either melting snow or heavy rainstorms. Lambert and Hsü (1979, p. 454) note the implications of their research:

> Our investigation supports De Geer's first contention that sediment-laden flood-waters [sic] could generate turbidity underflows to deposit varves, but threw doubt on his second interpretation that varves or varve-like sediment are necessarily annual!

Henke (1999) claimed that I ignored (Oard 1997) crucial statements in Lambert and Hsü (1979) by creating the false impression that they denied the existence of any varve. However, I simply noted that they discovered that some rhythmites are non-annual. Furthermore, Henke claims that the false varves are easy to discern in Lake Walensee because the layering in their figure 4 is faint. Morton (1998) also claimed that the non-annual layers in Lake Walensee can easily be distinguished from the regular laminations in Lake Zurich. But since figure 4 in Lambert and Hsü (1979) shows many laminations for Lake Walensee, the *annual* varves must also be as faint as the non-annual varves. So, the faintness is likely due to peculiarities of Lake Walensee, such as the climate. Furthermore, the rhythmites shown for Lake Walensee are really not all that irregular, and those shown for Lake Zurich may simply represent a well-behaved interval.

Turbidity currents are technically defined as sporadic underflows supported by fluid turbulence. Turbidites are generally graded layers in the more proximal end, while they can be layered like varves in their distal ends. Crowell (1957, p. 1,005) stated: "Sandstone and mud sequences laid down by turbidity currents far removed from a glacial environment may be easily confused with varved sequences." I should add that clay, which usually settles slowly, can be rapidly brought to the bottom of a lake by turbidity currents and can form rhythmites quickly (Smith and Ashley 1985). Furthermore, clay can fall rapidly through the water column by flocculation.[3] It has been discovered that rhythmites not only form by underflows, but also can develop from interflows or overflows, or by all flows operating at different times. Interflows and overflows spread out from a river or stream at intermediate depths and at the surface, respectively, depending upon density contrasts.

Other Examples

Wood (1947) described three varve-like couplets deposited in a new reservoir in just two weeks. The couplets looked very much like varves and were formed by three peak river inflows caused by light showers.

---

3. The coagulation of clay particles due to chemical reactions, especially in salt or brackish water.

Pickrill and Irwin (1983) analyzed rhythmic sediments from a deep, glacial-fed lake in New Zealand and discovered an average of three couplets per year. They discovered that winter couplets form by the slumping of river delta deposits. A delta may become over steepened due to summer sedimentation and slump during winter. Their figure 9 showed non-annual couplets not much different than the annual couplets (except size), which were ascertained by ^{210}Pb dating. Henke (1999) claimed that annual and non-annual layers could be distinguished. But this distinction seems to be only by size after the radiometric dating. However, without radiometric dating it would have been easy to count many more annual layers.

Multiple, thin layers have been observed to form in fast flows today. For example, in 1965 a large flash flood on Bijou Creek, Colorado, formed thin couplets of sand and mud (McKee et al. 1967). A rapidly moving pyroclastic flow from the June 12, 1980, Mount St. Helens eruption deposited fine laminae with a total thickness of 26 feet (8 m) (Morris and Austin 2003). Others have noted fine laminations formed rapidly (Oard 1997).

Furthermore, "dropstones" can be emplaced laterally by mass flows and can be dropped from floating logs, kelp, etc. (Oard 1997). Multiple turbidites can form thick sequences of varve-like rhythmites. For example, Quigley (1983, p. 151) stated:

> It is very unfortunate from a sedimentological viewpoint that engineers describe any rhythmically laminated fine-grained sediment as "varved." There is increasing recognition that many sequences previously described as varves are multiple turbidite sequences of graded silt to clay units . . . without any obvious seasonal control on sedimentation.

Supposed Varve Diagnostic Criteria

Smith and Ashley (1985), realizing the confusion of multiple causes for the formation of varve-like couplets, attempted to define diagnostic criteria for determining the annual cycle. Three diagnostic criteria were presented: (1) a sharp break between the coarse sublayer and the overlying fine sublayer; (2) biogenic marks, usually in the fine-grained layer; and (3) the same thickness for the fine-grained layer throughout the lake basin. The first criterion is equivocal, since varves are now known to be quite complex (Antevs 1951; Eden 1955; Flint 1975). As far as the first criterion, Tauber (1970, p. 174) stated: "Many

transitional forms of gradation exist, and even well-graded varves (diatactic varves) may contain various patterns of microlamination."

Ashley (1972) showed that biogenic activity on clay layers, the second criterion, is rather uncommon in the rhythmites she studied in New England. It is difficult to demonstrate the third criterion for a lake or ancient lake basin. Ashley (1972, 1975) showed that the clay laminae, as well as couplet thickness, in her study area were laterally variable with a lack of clay on some topographic highs on the lake bottom. This observation nullifies the third criterion and suggests more of a turbidite or underflow mechanism.

A Suitable Modern Analogue for a Glacial Environment

Since the deglaciation rhythmites from the Ice Age occurred during the melting of the ice sheets and the temporary development of lakes along the edge, a proper analogue for the formation of rhythmites and true varves would be one adjacent to a rapidly receding glacier. This is especially true in view of the fact that in the creation-Flood model of the Ice Age, deglaciation would be rapid (Oard 1990, 2004). Such an analogue is provided by Muir Inlet, Alaska, in which Muir Glacier has been receding about 1,345 ft/yr (410 m/yr) up a fjord. Investigators have discovered that the debris from the base of Muir Glacier and other glaciers in Muir Inlet is continuously fed into the fjord. The debris often forms rhythmites similar to varves in glacial lakes (MacKiewicz et al. 1984). The rhythmites are formed mostly by interflows and overflows because of the higher density of the brackish water in the inlet. The sedimentation rate in the fjord varies from 43 ft/yr (13 m/yr) at the terminus of one glacier to about 3 ft/yr (1 m/yr) at ice-distal locations (MacKiewicz et al. 1984; Cowan et al. 1988). Most of this sediment is finely laminated silt and mud, and many couplets are deposited each year.

The rhythmites in Muir Inlet are formed by combinations of semidiurnal tides, diurnal meltwater discharges, internal waves resulting from water density contrasts in the estuary, heavy rainstorms, random debris flows, and (rarely) seiches[4] (Cowan et al. 1988; Ludlam 1979; MacKiewicz et al. 1984).

I made one mistake in my analysis of varves in Oard (1997) that Henke (1999) noted: I said there were two rhythmites a day, especially with the large spring tides,

---

4. Standing wave oscillations in an enclosed water body caused by earthquakes or strong winds.

formed in small bays of Muir Inlet, based on the work of Smith et al. (1990). Actually, it should have been one rhythmite per day, associated especially with the strong diurnal minus tide, but varve-like rhythmites also generally formed during the low amplitude neap tides (see Smith et al. 1990, p. 13, figure 6). Each couplet averages half a centimeter thick, and the sequence superficially looks like varves.

Henke (1999, p. 23) stated that I misinformed my readers on this situation:

> However, Oard (p. 60) does not tell his readers that the non-varves and varves described by Smith et al. (1990) were very different and distinguishable. In particular, Smith et al. (1990) described neap tidal deposits in Glacier Bay, Alaska, as being structureless or faintly laminated when compared with the more seasonal (spring) laminations.

Figure 11. Fine lamination resulting from flowing of dry sediment (photo courtesy of Guy Berthault).

Henke thinks that the "varves couplets," the annual cycle, in these bays of Muir Inlet are the spring and neap tidal rhythmites. But there are many more than one neap and spring tide per year. "Spring tides" occur during new moon and full moon, while the neap tides occur at quarter moon. So there will be at least 24 "spring tides" and 24 "neap tides" per year. The most significant tide in Muir Inlet bay is the minus tide. The "spring tide" shown in Smith et al. (1990, p. 13, figure 6) occurred *July 26 to August 1*. Regardless of whether one or two per day form, a large number of varve-like rhythmites can form in one year due to the melting of the glaciers. It is true that the neap tide is fainter than the spring tides with some structureless zones, but if this sequence were found in Swedish clays, they likely would be considered varves with some massive, non-varve zones.

Experimental Evidence for the Rapid Deposition of Varve-Like Rhythmites

Guy Berthault (1988, 1991, 1994) has shown that flowing sediment, like in a turbidity current or even in settling sediment, produces fine laminations (figure 11). The laminations are apparently caused when the sediments being deposited differ in grain size, shape, or density. Such laminations can form rapidly, and in a Flood model we would expect thousands of such laminations formed by sinking or current-transported sediments such as in a large basin. This might explain the rhythmites of the Castile and Green River Formations.

Henke (1999) simply dismissed Berthault's research by saying that his research could not explain laminations correlated over tens of kilometers and that clays would take too long to settle out. Henke is saying that experimental sedimentology has no relevance to the rock record — a position most sedimentologists would not accept. Certainly scientists must account for scale, but in a Flood model with rapid sedimentation in a basin and possible abrupt geochemical changes, one would indeed expect clay to flocculate and sink rapidly, or be transported rapidly to deep water in turbidity currents. Furthermore, the scale of the Flood is so large that it should not be difficult to deposit such correlated rhythmites over tens of kilometers, especially in deep, wide underwater basins. It is more of a problem for uniformitarians to explain fine laminations over long distances, such as in the Castile Formation. Can present processes of basin deposition form such even layers over such distances? No such large-scale rhythmites are being deposited today, nor would they be expected in the Ice Age.

Conclusions

Varves were assumed to be annual phenomena ever since the proposal of the concept, and it has been hard to break away from that error. It can be difficult determining an annual layer in a rhythmite sequence, mainly because there are several other mechanisms that can form varve-like rhythmites. There are many problems in correlating varve sequences from one locality to another. De Geer's "first absolute chronology" for deglaciation has long since been abandoned. The period from the end of deglaciation to the present in the Ångermanälven River Valley is fraught with even more problems, especially the thinness of the rhythmites, the little difference between the summer and the winter layers, and the connections to the beginning and the end.

In a creationist post-Flood model of the Ice Age (Oard 1990, 2004), varves would be laid down rapidly during catastrophic melting of the ice sheets. The rhythmites now forming in Muir Inlet in Alaska are a more suitable analogue for deglaciation. So most rhythmites associated with the Ice Age and the post-glacial period are not varves, but formed rapidly as subannual rhythmites.

So-called varves found in modern lakes and marine basins are tuned to the uniformitarian time scale. However, these varves present difficulties for the accepted annual model. They are more easily explained by rapid deposition during the Flood and/or the post-Flood period.

Rhythmites in the rock record were formed rapidly during the Flood by either turbidity currents or the rapid separation of particles of different sizes, shapes, densities, etc., during rapid settling in generally low current areas.

References

CRSQ: Creation Research Society Quarterly

Alldredge, A.L., and C.C. Gotschalk. 1989. Direct observations of the mass flocculation of diatom blows: characteristics, settling velocities, and formation of diatom aggregates. *Deep Sea Research* 36(2):159–171.

Anderson, R.Y. 1992. Possible connection between surface winds, solar activity, and the earth's magnetic field. *Nature* 358:51–53.

———. 1993. The varve chronometer in Elk Lake: record of climatic variability and evidence for solar-geomagnetic-^{14}C-climate connect. In J.P. Bradbury and W.E. Dean (editors). *Elk Lake, Minnesota: Evidence for Rapid Climate Change in the North-Central United States.* GSA Special Paper 226, Boulder, CO, p. 45–67.

Anderson, R.Y., and W.E. Dean. 1988. Lacustrine varve formation through time. *Palaeogeography, Palaeoclimatology, Palaeoecology* 62:215–235.

Anderson, R.Y., W.E. Dean, and J.P. Bradbury. 1993. Elk Lake in perspective. In J.P. Bradbury and W.E. Dean (editors). *Elk Lake, Minnesota: Evidence for Rapid Climate Change in the North-Central United States.* GSA Special Paper 226, Boulder, CO, p. 1–6.

Anderson, R.Y., W.E. Dean, D.W. Kirkland, and H.I. Snider. 1972. Permian Castile varved evaporite sequence, West Texas and New Mexico. *GSA Bulletin* 83:59–86.

Anderson, R.Y., E.B. Nuhfer, and W.E. Dean. 1985. Sedimentation in a blast-zone lake at Mount St. Helens, Washington — implications for varve formation. *Geology* 13:348–352.

Antevs, E. 1922. *The recession of the last ice sheet in New England.* Series No. 11. New York: American Geographical Society Research.

———. 1925a. *Retreat of the last ice-sheet in eastern Canada.* Memoir 146. Ottawa: Geological Survey of Canada.

———. 1925b. Swedish late-Quaternary geochronologies. *Geographical Review* 115:280–284.

———. 1951. Glacial clays in Steep Rock Lake, Ontario, Canada. *GSA Bulletin* 62:1,233–1,262.

Ashley, G.M. 1972. *Rhythmic sedimentation in glacial lake Hitchcock, Massachusetts-Connecticut.* Contribution No. 10. Amherst, MA: Department of Geology, University of Massachusetts.

———. 1975. Rhythmic sedimentation in glacial Lake Hitchcock, Massachusetts-Connecticut. In A.V. Jopling and B.C. McDonald (editors). *Glaciofluvial and Glaciolacustrine Sedimentation.* Society of Economic Paleontologists and Mineralogists Special Publication No. 23. Tulsa, OK, p. 304–320.

Baumgardner, J.R. 2005. [14]C evidence for a recent global Flood and a young Earth. In L. Vardiman, A.A. Snelling, and E.F. Chaffin (editors). *Radioisotopes and the Age of the Earth: Results of a Young-Earth Creationist Research Initiative.* El Cajon, CA: Institute for Creation Research and Chino Valley, AZ: Creation Research Society, p. 587–630.

Berger, W.H., C.B. Lange, and A. Weinheimer. 1997. Silica depletion of the thermocline in the eastern North Pacific during glacial conditions: clues from Ocean Drilling Program Site 893, Santa Barbara Basin, California. *Geology* 25:619–622.

Berthault, G. 1988. Experiments on laminations of sediments, resulting from a periodic graded-bedding subsequent to deposit — a contribution to the explanation of laminations of various sediments and sedimentary rocks. *TJ* 3:25–29.

———. 1991. "Perestroika" in stratigraphy. *TJ* 5:53–57.

————. 1994. Experiments on stratification. In R.E. Walsh (editor). *Proceedings of the Third International Conference on Creationism* (technical symposium sessions). Pittsburgh, PA: Creation Science Fellowship, p. 103–110.

Bradbury, J.P. 1996. Charcoal deposition and redeposition in Elk Lake, Minnesota, USA. *The Holocene* 6(2):339–344.

Bradbury, J.P., and W.E. Dean (editors). 1993. *Elk Lake, Minnesota: Evidence for Rapid Climate Change in the North-Central United States.* GSA Special Paper 226, Boulder, CO.

Bradley, W.H. 1929. *The Varves and Climate of the Green River Epoch.* U.S. Geological Survey Professional Paper 158. Washington, DC: U. S. Government Printing Office.

Buchheim, P.H., and R. Biaggi. 1988. Laminae counts within a synchronous oil shale unit: a challenge to the "varve" concept. *GSA Abstracts with Programs* 20(7):A317.

Cato, I. 1985. The definitive connection of the Swedish geochronological time scale with the present, and the new date of the zero year in Döviken, northern Sweden. *Boreas* 14:117–122.

————. 1987. On the definitive connection of the Swedish time scale with the present. *Sveriges Geologiska Undersökning Ser. Ca.* 68:1–55.

Church, M., and P.H. Buchheim. 2002. Varves and varve-derived climate cycles? Evidence from Eocene fossil lake, Green River Formation. *GSA Abstracts with Programs* 34(6):555.

Cowan, E.A., R.D. Powell, and N.D. Smith. 1988. Rainstorm-induced event sedimentation at the tidewater front of a temperate glacier. *Geology* 16:409–412.

Crowell, J.C. 1957. Origin of pebbly mudstone. *GSA Bulletin* 68:993–1,010.

Crowley, K.D., C.E. Duchon, and J. Rhi. 1986. Climate record in varved sediments of the Eocene Green River Formation. *Journal of Geophysical Research* 91(D8):8,637–8,647.

Dallimore, A., R.E. Thomson, and M.A. Bertram. 2005. Modern to Late Holocene deposition in an anoxic fjord on the west coast of Canada: implications for regional oceanography, climate and paleoseismic history. *Marine Geology* 219:47–69.

Dean, J.M., A.E.S. Kemp, D. Bull, J. Pike, G. Patterson, and B. Zolitschka. 1999. Taking varves to bits: scatting electron microscopy in the study of laminated sediments and varves. *Journal of Paleolimnology* 22:121–136.

Dean, W.E. 1993. Physical properties, mineralogy, and geochemistry of Holocene varved sediments from Elk Lake, Minnesota. In J.P. Bradbury and W.E. Dean (editors). *Elk Lake, Minnesota: Evidence for Rapid Climate Change in the North-Central United States.* GSA Special Paper 226, Boulder, CO, p. 135–157.

————. 1997. Rates, timing, and cyclicity of Holocene eolian activity in north-central United States: evidence from varved lake sediments. *Geology* 25:331–334.

————. 2002. A 1500-year record of climatic and environmental change in Elk Lake, Clearwater County, Minnesota II: geochemistry, mineralogy, and stable isotopes. *Journal of Paleolimnology* 27:301–319.

Dean, W.E., J.P. Bradbury, R.Y. Anderson, and C.W. Barnosky. 1984. The variability of Holocene climate change: evidence from varved lake sediments. *Science* 226:1191–1194.

De Geer, G. 1928. Geochronology as based on solar radiation, and its relation to archeology. *Smithsonian Report of 1928.* Washington, DC: U. S. Government Printing Office, p. 687–696.

Eden, W.J. 1955. A laboratory study of varved clay from Steep Rock Lake, Ontario. *American Journal of Science* 253:659–674.

Emery, K.O., and J. Hülsemann. 1962. The relationships of sediments, life, and water in a marine basin. *Deep-Sea Research* 8:165–180.

Emery, K.O, E. Uchup, J.D. Phillips, C.O. Bowin, E.T. Bunce, and S.T. Knott. 1970. Continental rise off eastern North America. *American Association of Petroleum Geologists Bulletin* 54:44–108.

Fischer, A.G., and L.T. Roberts. 1991. Cyclicity in the Green River Formation (lacustrine Eocene) of Wyoming. *Journal of Sedimentary Petrology* 61:1,146–1,154.

Flint, R.F. 1975. Features other than diamicts as evidence of ancient glaciations. In A.E. Wright and F. Moseley (editors). *Ice Ages: Ancient and Modern.* Liverpool: Seel House Press, p. 121–136.

Francis, E.A. 1975. Glacial sediments: a selective review. In A.E. Wright and F. Moseley (editors). *Ice Ages: Ancient and Modern.* Liverpool: Seel House Press, p. 43–68.

Fromm, E. 1970. Errors in the Swedish varve chronology. In I.U. Olsson (editor). *Radiocarbon Variations and Absolute Chronology.* New York: John Wiley and Sons, p. 163–172.

Fukusawa, H. 1999. Varved lacustrine sediments in Japan [sic]; recent progress. Daiyonki-Kenkyu (*Quaternary Research*) 38(3):237–243 (in Japanese with an English abstract).

Gould, S.J. 1978. Morton's ranking of races by cranial capacity. *Science* 200:503–509.

Grimm, K.A., C.B. Lange, and A.S. Gill. 1996. Biological forcing of hemipelagic sedimentary laminae: evidence from ODP

Site 893, Santa Barbara Basin, California. *Journal of Sedimentary Research* 66:613–624.

———. 1997. Self-sedimentation of phytoplankton blooms in the geologic record. *Sedimentary Geology* 110:151–161.

Gustavson, T.C. 1975. Sedimentation and physical limnology in proglacial Malaspina Lake, southeastern Alaska. In A.V. Jopling and B.C. McDonald (editors). *Glaciofluvial and Glaciolacustrine Sedimentation.* Special Publication No. 23. Tulsa, OK: Society of Economic Paleontologists and Mineralogists, p. 249–263.

Gustavson, T.C., G.M. Ashley, and J.C. Boothroyd. 1975. Depositional sequences in glaciolacustrine deltas. In A.V. Jopling and B.C. McDonald (editors). *Glaciofluvial and Glaciolacustrine Sedimentation.* Special Publication No. 23. Tulsa, OK: Society of Economic Paleontologists and Mineralogists, p. 264–280.

Henke, K.R. 1999. *Ancient ice ages and submarine landslides, but not Noah's Flood: a review of M.J. Oard's assault on multiple glaciations.* http:home.austarnet.com.au/stear/henke_oard1.htm.

Hülsemann, J., and K.O. Emery. 1961. Stratification in recent sediments of Santa Barbara Basin as controlled by organisms and water character. *Journal of Geology* 69:279–290.

Kennett, J.P., J.G. Baldauf, et al. 1994. Site 893. *Proceedings of the Ocean Drilling Program, scientific results, volume 146, part 2.* College Station, TX: Ocean Drilling Program.

Kennett, J.P., and B.L. Ingram. 1995. A 20,000-year record of ocean circulation and climate change from the Santa Barbara Basin. *Nature* 377:510–514.

Kirkland, D.W. 2003. An explanation for the varves of the Castile evaporites (Upper Permian), Texas and New Mexico, USA. *Sedimentology* 50:899–920.

Kirkland, D.W., R.E. Denison, and W.E. Dean. 2000. Parent brine of the Castile evaporites (Upper Permian), Texas and New Mexico. *Journal of Sedimentary Research* 70:749–761.

Kitagawa, H., and J. van der Plicht. 1998. Atmospheric radiocarbon calibration to 45,000 yr B.P.: late glacial fluctuations and cosmogenic isotope production. *Science* 279:1,187–1,190.

Krishnaswami, S., D. Lal, B.S. Amin, and A. Soutar. 1973. Geochronological studies in Santa Barbara Basin: ^{55}Fe as a unique tracer for particulate settling. *Limnology and Oceanography* 18:763–770.

Kushnir, J. 1981. Formation and early diagenesis of varved evaporite sediments in a coastal hypersaline pool. *Journal of Sedimentary Petrology* 51:1,193–1,203.

Lambert, A., and K.J. Hsü. 1979. Non-annual cycles of varve-like sedimentation in Walensee, Switzerland. *Sedimentology* 26:453–461.

Leslie, A.B., G.M. Harwood, and A.C. Kendall. 1997. Geochemical variations within a laminated evaporite deposit: evidence for brine composition during formation of the Permian Castile Formation, Texas and New Mexico, USA. *Sedimentary Geology* 110:223–235.

Lowenstein, T.K. 1988. Origin of depositional cycles in a Permian "saline giant": the Salado (McNutt zone) evaporites of New Mexico and Texas. *GSA Bulletin* 100:592–608.

Ludlam, S.D. 1979. Rhythmite deposition in lakes of the northeastern United States. In C. Schlüchter (editor). *Moraines and Varves — Origin/Genesis/Classification.* Rotterdam: A.A. Balkema, p. 295–302.

Lundqvist, J. 1975. Ice recession in central Sweden, and the Swedish time scale. *Boreas* 4:47–54.

MacKiewicz, N.E., R.D. Powell, P.R. Carlson, and B.F. Molnia. 1984. Interlaminated ice-proximal glaciomarine sediments in Muir Inlet, Alaska. *Marine Geology* 57:113–147.

McKee, E.D., E.J. Crosby, and H.L. Berryhill, Jr. 1967. Flood deposits, Bijou Creek, Colorado, June 1965. *Journal of Sedimentary Petrology* 37:829–851.

Megard, R.O., J.P. Bradbury, and W.E. Dean. 1993. Climatic and limnologic setting of Elk Lake. In J.P. Bradbury and W.E. Dean (editors). *Elk Lake, Minnesota: Evidence for Rapid Climate Change in the North-Central United States.* GSA Special Paper 226, Boulder, CO, p. 19–36.

Milliman, J.D., and J.P.M. Syvitski. 1992. Geomorphic/tectonic control of sediment discharge to the ocean: the importance of small mountainous rivers. *Journal of Geology* 100:525–544.

Morris, J.D. 1994. *The Young Earth.* Green Forest, AR: Master Books.

Morris, J., and S.A. Austin. 2003. *Footprints in the Ash: The Explosive Story of Mount St. Helens.* Green Forest, AR: Master Books.

Morton, G.R. 1998. Young-earth arguments: a second look, http://home.entouch.net/dmd/age.htm.

———. 2003a. Why radiocarbon dating works — Lake Suigetsu. http://home.entouch.net/dmd/suigetsu.htm.

———. 2003b. Varves and the global Flood. http://home.entouch.net/dmd/castile.htm.

Nelson, B.C. 1948. *Before Abraham: Prehistoric Man in Biblical Light.* Minneapolis, MN: Augsburg Publishing House.

Nuhfer, E.B., R.Y. Anderson, J.P. Bradbury, and W.E. Dean. 1993. Modern sedimentation in Elk Lake, Clearwater County, Minnesota. In J.P. Bradbury and W.E. Dean (editors). *Elk Lake,*

Minnesota: Evidence for Rapid Climate Change in the North-Central United States. GSA Special Paper 226, Boulder, CO, p. 75–96.

Oard, M.J. 1990. *An Ice Age Caused by the Genesis Flood.* El Cajon, CA: Institute for Creation Research.

———. 1992a. Varves — the first "absolute" chronology: part I — historical development and the question of annual deposition. *CRSQ* 29:72–80.

———. 1992b. Varves — the first "absolute" chronology: part II — varve correlation and the post-glacial time scale. *CRSQ* 29:120–125.

———. 1993. Comments on the breached dam theory for the formation of the Grand Canyon. *CRSQ* 30:39–46.

———. 1997. *Ancient Ice Ages or Gigantic Submarine Landslides?* Creation Research Society Monograph 6, Chino Valley, AZ.

———. 2004. *Frozen in Time: Woolly Mammoths, the Ice Age, and the Bible.* Green Forest, AR: Master Books.

———. 2005. *The Frozen Record: Examining the Ice Core History of the Greenland and Antarctic Ice Sheets.* El Cajon, CA: Institute for Creation Research.

Oard, M.J., and J.H. Whitmore. 2006. The Green River Formation of the west-central United States: Flood or post-Flood. *Journal of Creation* 10(1):45–85.

Oard, M.J., and P. Klevberg. 2008. Green River Formation very likely did not form in a post-diluvial lake. *Answers Research Journal* 1:99–107.

Olsson, I.U. (editor). 1970. *Radiocarbon Variations and Absolute Chronology.* New York: John Wiley and Sons.

Ostrem, G. 1975. Sediment transport in glacial stream. In A.V. Jopling and B.C. McDonald (editors). *Glaciofluvial and Glaciolacustrine Sedimentation.* Society of Economic Paleontologists and Mineralogists Special Publication No. 23. Tulsa, OK, p. 101–122.

O'Sullivan, P.E. 1983. Annually laminated lake sediments and the study of Quaternary environmental changes — a review. *Quaternary Science Reviews* 1:245–313.

Pickrill, R.A., and J. Irwin. 1983. Sedimentation in a deep glacier-fed lake — Lake Tekapo, New Zealand. *Sedimentology* 30:63–75.

Pike, J., and A.E.S. Kemp. 1999. Diatom mats in Gulf of California sediments: implications for the paleoenvironmental interpretation of laminated sediments and silica burial. *Geology* 27:311–314.

Quigley, R.M. 1983. Glaciolacustrine and glaciomarine clay deposition: a North American perspective. In N. Eyles (editor). *Glacial Geology — An Introduction for Engineers and Earth Scientists.* New York: Pergamon Press, p. 140–167.

Reimers, C.E., C.B. Lange, M. Tabak, and J.M. Bernhard. 1990. Seasonal spillover and varve formation in the Santa Barbara Basin, California. *Limnology and Oceanography* 35:1,577–1,585.

Ridge, J.C., and F.D. Larsen. 1990. Re-evaluations of Antevs' New England varve chronology and new radiocarbon dates of sediments from glacial Lake Hitchcock. *GSA Bulletin* 102:889–899.

Ringberg, B. 1979. Varve chronology of the glacial sediments in Blekinge and northeastern Skåne, southeastern Sweden. *Boreas* 8:209–215.

Ripepe, M., L.T. Roberts, and A.G. Fischer. 1991. ENSO and sunspot cycles in varved Eocene oil shales from image analysis. *Journal of Sedimentary Petrology* 61:1,155–1,163.

Sancetta, C., and S.E. Calvert. 1988. The annual cycle of sedimentation in Saanich Inlet, British Columbia: implications for the interpretation of diatom fossil assemblages. *Deep-Sea Research* 35(1):71–90.

Schimmelmann, A., and M. Kastner. 1993. Evolutionary changes over the last 1,000 years of reduced sulfur phases and organic carbon in varved sediments of the Santa Barbara Basin, California. *Geochimica et Cosmochimica Acta* 57:67–78.

Schimmelmann, A., C.B. Lange, and W.H. Berger. 1990. Climatically controlled marker layers in Santa Barbara Basin sediments and fine-scale core-to-core correlation. *Limnology and Oceanography* 35:165–173.

Schove, D.J., and R.W. Fairbridge. 1983. Swedish chronology revisited. *Nature* 304:583.

Smith, N.D. 1978. Sedimentation processes and patterns in a glacier-fed lake with low sediment input. *Canadian Journal of Earth Sciences* 15:741–756.

Smith, N.D., M.A. Venol, and S.K. Kennedy. 1982. Comparison of sedimentation regimes in four glacier-fed lakes of western Alberta. In R. Davison-Arnott, W. Nickling, and B.O. Fahey (editors). *Research in Glacial, Glaciofluvial, and Glaciolacustrine Systems.* Norwich, UK: Geobooks, p. 203–238.

Smith, N.D., A.C. Phillips, and R.D. Powell. 1990. Tidal drawdown: a mechanism for producing cyclic sediment laminations in glaciomarine deltas. *Geology* 18:10–13.

Smith, N.D., and G. Ashley. 1985. Proglacial lacustrine environments. In G. Ashley, J. Shaw, and N.D. Smith (editors). *Glacial Sedimentary Environments.* Tulsa, OK: Society of Economic Paleontologists and Mineralogists, p. 176–200.

Soutar, A., and P.A. Crill. 1977. Sedimentation and climatic patterns in the Santa Barbara Basin during the 19th and 20th centuries. *GSA Bulletin* 88:1,161–1,172.

Strahler, A.N. 1987. *Science and Earth History — The Evolution/ Creation Controversy*. Buffalo, NY: Prometheus Books.

Strömberg, B. 1983. The Swedish varve chronology. In J. Ehlers (editor). *Glacial Deposits in North-West Europe*. Rotterdam: A.A. Balkema, p. 97–105.

————. 1985. Revision of the late-glacial Swedish varve chronology. *Boreas* 14:101–105.

Sturm, M., and A. Matter. 1978. Turbidites and varves in Lake Brienz (Switzerland): deposition of clastic detritus by density. In A. Matter and M.E. Tucker (editors). *Modern and Ancient Lake Sediments*. London: Blackwell Scientific Publications, p. 147–168.

Svensson, A., P.E. Biscaye, and F.E. Grousset. 2000. Characterization of late glacial continental dust in the Greenland Ice Core Project ice core. *Journal of Geophysical Research* 105(D4):4,637–4,656.

Tauber, H. 1970. The Scandinavian varve chronology and C-14 dating. In I.U. Olsson (editor). *Radiocarbon Variations and Absolute Chronology*. New York: John Wiley and Sons, p. 173–196.

Thunell, R.C. 1998. Particle fluxes in a coastal upwelling zone: sediment trap results from Santa Barbara Basin, California. *Deep-Sea Research II* 45:1,863–1,884.

Thunell, R.C., E. Tappa, and D.M. Anderson. 1995. Sediment fluxes and varve formation in Santa Barbara Basin, offshore California. *Geology* 23:1,083–1,086.

Whitmore, J.H. 2003. *Experimental Fish Taphonomy with a Comparison to Fossil Fishes*. PhD Dissertation, Loma Linda University, Loma Linda, CA.

Wonderly, D.E. 1987. *Neglect of Geologic Data: Sedimentary Strata Compared with Young-Earth Creationists Writings*. Hatfield, PA: Interdisciplinary Biblical Research Institute.

Wood, A.E. 1947. Multiple banding of sediments deposited during a single season. *American Journal of Science* 245:304–312.

Chapter 9

Modern and Ancient Reefs

John H. Whitmore • *PhD — Geology*

Abstract

The existence of modern and ancient reefs has been one of the classic arguments used by uniformitarian geologists against Flood geology. They argue that modern reefs could not have grown to great size since the time of the Flood and that fossil reefs represent long periods of time. This chapter will discuss the difficulties in defining a "reef," review previous creationist work, briefly discuss the biology and growth rate of modern reefs, and discuss the important differences between modern and fossil reefs. These differences are important clues as to how fossil reefs may have formed during the Flood. A new hypothesis will be presented to explain the rapid, recent origin of large carbonate accumulations below Pacific atolls and guyots, and the underappreciated contributions of microbes to reefs will also be considered.

Introduction

When the term "reef" is used, one usually conjures up an underwater image of a beautiful and colorful array of corals, sponges, calcareous algae, fish, and other organisms. Indeed, coral reefs are some of the most wonderfully diverse and productive biological havens on earth, perhaps second only to rainforests. In today's tropical and subtropical oceans, reefs are typically formed by corals and algae. Corals, coralline algae, and other organisms can secrete hard exoskeletons of calcium carbonate ($CaCO_3$), which can accumulate and grow into a framework that forms the structure of the reef. Often living reef organisms grow on top of their dead predecessors, causing the reef to grow upward and outward over time. Some reefs have grown to immense sizes, both in thickness and in lateral extent. The largest and perhaps most famous is the Great Barrier Reef of Australia. It is actually a series of nearly 3,000 smaller reefs that follows the northeastern coastline of Australia for some 1,242 miles (2,000 km) (Spalding et al. 2001). Reefs can reach great thicknesses. One of the thickest known may be the Eniwetok Atoll in the Pacific. More than 4,035 feet (1,230 m) of supposed reefal limestone was penetrated by drilling before basalt was reached (Ladd 1961).

The Challenge: Too Much Time Represented by Modern and Ancient Reefs

The problem of reefs for Flood geology is twofold. First, is there enough time for modern reefs to have reached their current sizes since the end of the Flood? Second, there are many apparent fossil reefs in the geologic record that supposedly took eons to form. Weber (1980) discussed both of these difficulties, but they were recognized earlier by Whitcomb and Morris (1961). They suggested that coral reef growth rates were poorly known and that all modern living reefs probably had time to grow since the end of the Flood. They also suggested that accumulations of so-called in situ fossil reefs in the rock record may have been the result of pre-Flood growth and redeposition of reefal material during the Flood. Daniel Wonderly, an old-earth creationist, has suggested that fossil reefs, among other things, prove that immense amounts of geologic time have passed (1974, 1977). He argued that the growth rate of modern reefs is too slow to explain within a young-earth framework. He estimates the Eniwetok Atoll took at least 176,000 years to form at a growth rate of eight millimeters per year (1977). Another old-earth creationist, Davis Young, also claimed fossil reefs are irreconcilable within a young-earth framework (1982; Young and Stearly 2008). Besides problems of rapid growth during the Flood in turbid water and time for post-Flood reef growth, he explains that Whitcomb's and Morris's idea of transport and redeposition of huge reef blocks during the Flood is problematic, not only because of the immense sizes of many reefs, but also because no fossil reefs are known to be "upside-down." (Some transported, or allochthonous "reefs" have been documented and will be discussed later.) Admittedly, these are difficult problems, and we have yet to find solutions to all of them. This chapter will attempt to address some of these issues, offer some new hypotheses, and suggest further research.

What Is a "Reef"?

The definition of "reef" is problematic and has been misunderstood by laymen for decades. Modern reefs are typically thought of as wave-resistant frameworks of coral and algae. Young corals typically grow on their dead predecessors, and various types of coralline algae bind members of the reef together into a rigid framework. Loose debris from dead organisms (of all kinds) fills the empty spaces and crevices. Many void spaces remain unfilled below the reef, allowing for various "cryptic" organisms to thrive. Some have suggested that modern coral reefs should not be referred to as "coral" reefs but as "coralgal" or simply "algal" reefs because of the importance of coralline algae as the mortar that holds reefs together (Murphy 2002).

Unfortunately, paleontologists use a much wider definition for ancient reefs. This has led to confusion (on both sides of the debate) as to whether ancient reefs are present in the fossil record or not. One of the main problems is that reef-building organisms of today (primarily corals and algae) are not the same as reef-building organisms of the past. So "reefs" in the fossil record look completely different than coral reefs in the modern ocean. Many "reefs" in the fossil record were neither wave-resistant nor organically bound. They were simply small piles of unbound reef-building organisms — sometimes called bioherms. These

structures are often *interpreted* to be ancient reefs (or at least loosely referred to as reefs), implying all the problems of modern reefs that face creationists. Since the organisms of ancient reefs are different than those of today (primarily in Paleozoic and Mesozoic strata), comparisons between modern reefs and ancient ones need to be made carefully. Several excellent summary papers and books exist that discuss some of the differences between modern and ancient reefs (James 1983; James and Macintyre 1985; Longman 1981; Nevins 1972; Toomey 1981).

Modern reefs come in many shapes and sizes. Many (though not all) modern reefs have a rigid coral framework. James (1983) recognized several types of modern reefs, including Pacific atolls, marginal reefs, pinnacle reefs, patch reefs, reef mounds, algal reefs, stromatolites, and linear mud banks (his order, p. 431–434).

Atolls are circular reefs that surround a central lagoon. Drilling into atolls has appeared to confirm that many are located on ancient volcanic platforms (Ladd and Schlanger 1960), but this was far from certain for all atolls in the early 1960s (Ladd 1961). Apparently seafloor subsidence has long since caused the host volcano to become submerged, but vertical reef growth and/or carbonate accumulation has been able to match seafloor subsidence. This idea was originally proposed by Charles Darwin in 1842, in his book on coral reefs that went through several editions (Darwin, 1897).

A *marginal reef* (sometimes called a barrier reef or platform margin reef) often grows on the edge of the continental shelf and has a shallow lagoon between it and the continent. These types of reefs often have zones of characteristic sedimentary facies and organisms, according to water depth (figure 1). Atolls and marginal reefs represent the thickest buildups of modern-day reef organisms and have been the focus of most creationist challenges.

Pinnacle reefs are tall and column-like, 20–66 feet (6–20 m) tall and 16–164 feet (5–50 m) wide.

Patch reefs are not as tall at 10–20 feet (3–6 m) high.

Reef mounds occur in water 1,969–2,297 feet (600–700 m) deep and are elongate mounds up to 328 feet (100 m) long and 164 feet (50 m) high. The mounds are composed of concentric crusts of lithified mud and sand and are sometimes referred to as "lithoherms." They are covered with living crinoids, sea pens, corals, and sponges.

Algal reefs can take several forms. The algal cup reef can be up to 33 feet (10 m) high and a few tens of meters in diameter, consisting of several types of algae, including calcite-secreting coralline algae. Sometimes branching forms of algae make a reef, but they tend to fragment

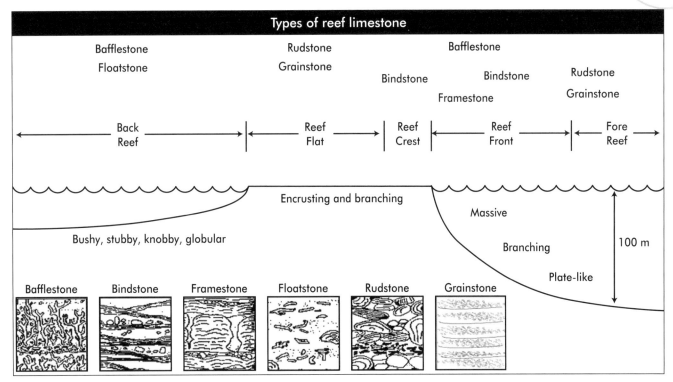

Figure 1. A generalized cross section through a modern marginal reef showing the most common organisms and limestone types that occur in each zone (modified from James 1983). The zones and limestone types are described in the text. Coralline algae are extremely important in binding corals together, especially in the reef crest and reef front. Note that this is only a generalized cross section and many variations can occur.

easily upon death, leaving only algal sand behind. No framework is preserved as a result of their growth.

Modern, living *stromatolites* occur in a variety of settings, including marine, lacustrine, and fluvial. They are composed of laminated microbial mats (cyanobacteria, diatoms, algae, etc.) that bind sediments. They assume a number of different morphologies, including the famous club-shaped stromatolites that have been found in Shark Bay, Australia (Logan 1961), Lake Tanganyika, Africa (Cohen et al. 1997), and at several other locations around the world (Decho et al. 2005). No large modern stromatolite "reefs" have been found that are comparable in size to those found in the fossil record. It is important to note that the term "reef" has been used in describing concentrations of modern and ancient stromatolites, especially when they are mound-shaped.

Linear mud banks are shallow mounds 10–13 feet (3–4 m) high of lime muds and molluscan skeletal debris that are occasionally exposed at low tide. They are often covered with sea grasses. James (1983) has nice color photographs, drawings, core samples, and descriptions of all these modern reef types. Note that some of these reef descriptions do not fit well within the typical definition of

"reef"; nonetheless, they are still considered reefs. Many fossil "reefs" fit within the categories of reef mounds, mud banks, and algal reefs. Paleontologists often use these wider definitions of "reefs," which are neither bound frameworks nor wave resistant.

The organisms and sediments of large modern reefs are often "zoned," or divided into sedimentary and biological facies (figure 1). The following descriptions of these zones are taken from James (1983), but others follow similar terminology (Longman, 1981). The *reef crest* is the highest part of the reef and absorbs tremendous amounts of energy from waves. In areas of extremely high and persistent energy, only encrusting or sheet-like organisms can grow. In other settings, short branching organisms can survive. The *reef front* is found seaward of the reef crest and can extend downward to about 328 feet (100 m), depending on water clarity. Near the surface, massive and branching corals are found. In deeper settings, more platelike corals are found. The fore reef extends into deeper water containing broken debris (sand to boulder size) from the reef. Behind the reef crest (shoreward) is the *reef flat*. The crest and the flat can be exposed during the lowest tides. Reef flats often occur as cemented pavements of skeletal debris covered with carbonate sands produced from deterioration of the reef. The *back reef* area often consists of quieter water in a shallow lagoon, shoreward of the reef flat. The water is generally quiet enough for mud to come out of suspension and be deposited. Large globular corals, various types of algae, and pinnacle and patch reefs can be found in this zone.

Because energy and processes vary in each of these zones, each zone has characteristic organisms and rock types. Sketches of these rock types (modified from James 1983) are also shown in figure 1. In the back reef area, *floatstones* (miscellaneous organismal fragments in a matrix of mud) will form in most areas because this zone is dominated by lower energy. Floatstones appear similar to a matrix-supported conglomerate. *Bafflestones* will form in some places when carbonate mud settles in between the branches of platy corals. The reef flat is typically a zone of high energy with well-washed sands and larger skeletal fragments. Resulting rock types are *rudstones* (similar to a clast supported conglomerate, but made of skeletal material from the reef) and *grainstones* (similar to a sandstone, but made of calcareous sand from the reef). The reef crest and reef front typically consist of *bindstones* (platelike organisms bound with coralline algae), *framestones* (frameworks made of platelike organisms and bound with coralline algae), and bafflestones.

As available sunlight and energy decrease with water depth, branching and platelike organisms become more common. The fore reef area usually consists of rubble produced from the active reef above, resulting in rudstones and grainstones. Estimates of the area that each facies covers varies from reef to reef, but Longman (1981) believes the following percentages from Pulau Putri (Indo-Pacific Basin) are representative: reef framework, 10 percent; reef-crest, 5 percent; reef flat, 12 percent; cor-algal sand, 73 percent. Note that the bulk of the "reef" is sand and not organically bound framework! These reef facies are well-known and easily identified in modern reefs, but are more difficult to recognize in the ancient rock record. Often ancient "reefs" are only known from an outcrop wall or drill cores. Rarely do we find good three-dimensional exposures where all of these facies can be studied together.

Let me offer this definition of a "reef" that can apply to both fossil and modern examples: *A reef is an in situ, aggregating community of organisms along with its associated facies and sediments, which are cemented together with both organic and inorganic carbonate cement, exhibiting topographic height* (inspired by Wood 1995). This is what most paleontologists have in mind when they talk about a reef. This definition is broad enough that it can apply not only to modern coral reefs, but also to various mollusks, sponges, and other organisms that have built reefs in the past. It also does not specify "a wave-resistant framework" to allow for deposits that have frequently been considered to be "reefs" in both modern and ancient settings. A reef should consist of in situ organisms. However, these organisms are often difficult to identify, even in modern reef limestones. In situ organisms are often smothered in mud and a large assortment of broken pieces of other organisms. Additionally, living reefs are active areas of boring and bioerosion that can reduce in situ organisms to piles of rubble. It has been difficult to identify in situ organisms in ancient "reefs," fueling the controversy as to what these deposits actually represent. Are ancient "reefs" actually reefs, or are they mass accumulations of carbonate debris from biological accumulations that used to be reefs? This is especially true of mud banks and reef mounds, which appear to be fairly common in the fossil record (Toomey 1981). This definition of reef not only applies to marine settings, but also to various lacustrine reefs, including stromatolites (Cohen et al. 1997; Roehler 1993) and caddis fly mounds (Leggitt and Cushman 2001).

Summary of Previous Creationist Work

There have been many articles about reefs published by creationists. I will summarize what I feel are some of the more important contributions, organized by publication date and author. Keep in mind that many of the following authors reject the existence of fossil "reefs" based on the description and dissimilarity to *modern platform margin reefs* (see figure 1). Most fossil "reefs" are small and do not consist of bindstones, bafflestones, and framestones; they consist of floatstones, grainstones, and rudstones.

Harold Clark (1968) recognized the presence of extensive "reefs" within the fossil record. He suggested two ideas to explain their origin: (1) pre-Flood growth and then in situ deposition during the Flood, or (2) pre-Flood growth and then transportation and burial of the entire reef structure during the Flood. He seemed to favor the latter based on stratigraphy.

Nevins (aka S.A. Austin) examined the Capitan Limestone and evaluated the literature to determine whether it was a reef or not. He defined a reef as (1972, p. 234): "a largely unbedded, wave-resistant structure composed of in situ, organically bound, frame-building organisms, cementing organisms, and sediment filling which modifies the surrounding sedimentation." His definition is based primarily upon the description of large barrier reefs observed today. He rejected the reef interpretation of the Capitan primarily based on its lack of clear "reef" facies relationships, organically bound fossils, and its lack of wave resistance. He proposed that the Capitan accumulated toward the end of the Flood year or shortly after. Wonderly (1974) critiqued Nevins' article, suggesting that there were numerous evidences of slow, depositional processes within the deposit and that Nevins had ignored most of the stratigraphy. Austin (Nevins 1974) replied, noting that Wonderly had failed to show sufficient evidences of long, depositional processes and that extensive fieldwork (by Austin) had failed to show that the Capitan Limestone met the definition of a reef. Therefore, he concluded that processes, other than in situ growth, should be considered.

D'Armond (1980) described supposed Silurian reef deposits from the Chicago area. He described and defined modern reefs and then dismissed the Thorton Quarry deposits as "reefs" because they failed to meet his criteria for modern reefs; that is, framework and wave resistance. His work showed a poor understanding of the differences conventional paleontologists recognize between modern reefs and ancient reefs. He proposed that these deposits were allochthonous, deposited catastrophically by large tsunamis during the Flood. Peczkis (1981) also did important work on the Thorton Reef and dolomites of the Chicago area. He also argued these deposits were catastrophic in origin.

Woodmorappe (1980, 1982) has contributed many articles about reefs. In his 1980 paper, he has brief sections with quotes from uniformitarian geologists and then comments on them. The sections are entitled: *Uniformitarian presuppositions and "ancient reefs"; Plasticity and accommodation of alleged reef characteristics; Difficulty of proving "ancient reefs"; Most "ancient reefs" admitted not to be reefs; Silurian "reefs" of U.S. Midwest are not reefs; and "Ancient reefs" are actually Flood deposits.* In these sections he shows that supposed ancient reefs are unlike modern reefs and concludes they may have been formed by the Flood. Woodmorappe followed a similar format in his 1982 paper. The sections are entitled: *Varying uniformitarian opinions concerning "ancient reefs"; Conjectural and imaginative character of uniformitarian reef models ascribed to ancient rock; Some "ancient reefs: merely artifacts of erosion; Capriciously dipping "reef flank" strata; Vague facies distinction between "reef core" and "reef flank"; Conspicuous absence of framework in "ancient reefs"; Evidence against reef origins from dearth of predation; Major differences in scale between modern and ancient "reefs"; Many claims of in situ reef organisms based upon conjecture; Reef organisms in growth position no proof for reef growth; Inorganic cementation of "ancient reef" deposits; "Reef" geometry no proof for a deposit being a reef; and "Ancient reefs" actually dune deposits.* The importance of these observations is that Woodmorappe documents that supposed ancient reef deposits are very different from framework-supported, wave-resistant structures of today, a fact not widely disputed by uniformitarians.

Read and Snelling (1985) tackled the problem of the age of Australia's Great Barrier Reef. They reported some results of a scientific study (Isdale 1984) that showed coral growth was positively correlated with high rainfall and runoff events. Coral growth rates were measured at 0.6 inches (15.3 mm) per year. They estimated that at this growth rate, the Great Barrier Reef could accumulate in about 3,700 years.

Hodges (1977, 1987; Hodges and Roth 1986) measured organism orientations in Paleozoic and Cenozoic reefs to determine if they were in situ or not. His results contradicted claims by D'Armond, Peczkis, and Woodmorappe that the Paleozoic "reef" deposits are unorganized mounds of debris. In many of Hodges' Silurian (and Pleistocene) localities, the organisms showed strong, preferred orientation to an upward or in situ "growth" position, especially in the reef cores. Only a few of his Silurian and his single Devonian locality did not show such orientation. His studies did not show any framework in the Silurian and Devonian reefs, and he thought they could better be described as "carbonate mud mounds." However, he noted (1987, p. 90):

> . . . coral bearing Paleozoic mounds, while relatively sparse in coral content, are not disordered piles of debris, especially in the central core region. Corals in the core are primarily upright in position, suggesting that either their cores are in their original position, with upright coral growth, or have been transported with no appreciable tilting. In conclusion, it is clear that the Paleozoic reefs of the Great Lakes region are markedly different in many respects from the modern-appearing Pleistocene reefs of Florida. Still, relatively little is known about the origin and ecology of the Paleozoic reefs of the Great Lakes region and their fascinating, important, and often-controversial role in deciphering Earth's history.

Ariel Roth has made a number of important contributions regarding reef growth. He recognized the problems with post-Flood growth of large reefs and the problems of fossil reefs. In his 1979 paper, there is an excellent summary of reef growth. He discussed factors required for rapid coral growth, including nutrient supply, sunlight, warm water, and low turbidity. Factors such as too much exposure to ultraviolet light slows coral growth, so modern reefs close to sea level may be poor places to conduct growth rate studies (if maximum potential growth rates are being sought). He discussed problems and potential solutions to the disparity between reported reef growth rates of between 0.03 and 3 inches (0.8 and 80 mm) per year. He noted that a distinction should be made between "reef growth" and "coral growth" rates, which are much higher. His graduate students "were able to double coral growth rates by increasing the water temperature 5°C or by increasing the carbonate ion concentration of the seawater" (p. 94).

Roth provided some potential solutions to fossil reefs in his 1995 paper. This is perhaps the best creationist paper to date on this subject. He remarks, "The term 'reef' has become too general a term for use in a discussion of fossil reefs. It can specify any rock unit that seems to have been elevated above its surroundings" (p. 88). He suggests that some fossil "reefs" are actually not reefs, but just mere accumulations of organic debris; that some fossil reefs may have formed prior to the Flood; and that some reefs are allochthonous (transported) blocks of pre-Flood material. He notes that "reefs" in the fossil record are smaller and are usually produced by different organisms and that some have what appear to be upright, in situ organisms. Specific examples are given of fossil reefs that have been reinterpreted, examples of "mud banks" that have been called "reefs," and examples of allochthonous reefs. Remarking about his joint publication with Hodges (1986) on oriented fossils within Silurian reefs, he stated (1995, p. 90):

> The orientation of the fossil in a reef is an important indicator of whether the reef formed by allochthonous or by autochthonous means. A position of growth suggests a slow autochthonous growth process, while unoriented fossils reflect an allochthonous transport process. Unfortunately, the identification of what is in growth orientation has too often turned out to be quite subjective. Also, allochthonous blocks of reef material can contain fossils in apparent growth position.

He concluded that ". . . fossil reefs do not present an undebatable time problem for the biblical scenario of a recent creation" (1995, p. 101).

The major contribution in Roth's 1998 text is a table summarizing various rates of coral growth and reef growth (see pages 235–241). He cited rates of coral growth between 0.027 and 16.3 inches (0.7 and 414 mm) per year and maximum rates of reef growth from 3.9 to 17 inches (99 to 432 mm) per year. At the most rapid currently observed growth rates, a 4,593-foot (1,400 m) reef could grow in as little as 3,240 years. He concluded that sufficient time has probably been available for even the thickest modern coral reef (Eniwetok Atoll) to grow since the time of the Flood.

Froede (1999) published an article on the Key Largo Limestone of south Florida, which was followed by Oard's letter to the editor (1999a), another short article by Froede (2000), and a final comment by Klevberg (2001). In his 1999 article, Froede proposed that the Key Largo Limestone (conventionally interpreted as a Pleistocene reef) developed during a 500- to 1,000-year time period when Flood water was retreating slowly and sea level was about 26 feet (8 m) higher than present. He argued that fast Flood water retreat would not have given the corals a chance to develop, but slow retreat would. Thus he argues that maximum glaciation did not occur until after the reef had formed, a minimum of 501 years following the Flood (p. 191). Oard (1999a) disagreed with Froede's model, mostly because he believes the Ice Age began almost immediately after the Flood (lowering sea level to make ice). Oard conceded the Key Largo Limestone may be a reef deposit, but may have been formed in a relatively short period following the Flood, caused by faster-than-normal coral growth, possibly due to warm water and other factors. Froede replied (2000) that it was highly unlikely that the limestone up to 171 feet (52 m) thick could grow in a short, 200-year time span following the Flood. He defended his original estimate by citing coral growth rate studies from living species that are found fossilized in the Key Largo Limestone. He also pointed out that most corals cannot withstand large fluctuations in temperature without adverse effects. Klevberg (2001) suggested the Key Largo Limestone might have been deposited during or after the Flood. He also pointed out that slight tectonic adjustments had not been considered by either author, and could cause significant local variations in sea level that could explain the formation of the thick limestone after the Flood.

Oard (1999b) tackled the problem of the apparent post-Flood growth and thickness of the Eniwetok Atoll based on some newly reported research, primarily from Wilson et al. (1998). He suggested several ideas for creationists

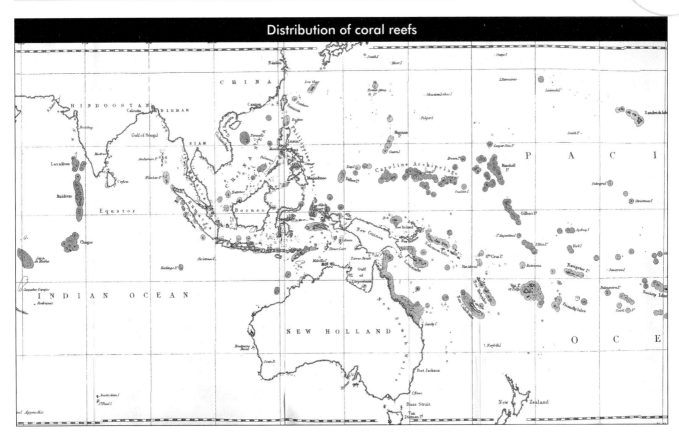

Figure 2. Part of Darwin's (1897) map (Plate III) showing the intense distribution of reefs in the warm, shallow waters of the Indo-Pacific region. Nearly all coral reefs grow in warm, tropical waters within 30° of the equator.

to consider when explaining guyots:[1] (1) some guyots are indeed eroded volcanic platforms that represent a large increase in relative sea level (usually explained by the Pacific floor subsiding), (2) the assumed reefal origin of some carbonate caps on guyots should be questioned because they have both organic and inorganic components (reefal organisms can be rare in guyot carbonates), and (3) it is possible that some guyots represent remnants of large, drowned carbonate platforms that broke up during the Flood (see Wilson et al. 1998). Oard proposed that if this third idea is correct, long periods of time might not be needed to explain the slow growth and accumulation of thick carbonates on islands like Eniwetok Atoll. The islands may simply be remnants of the large and thick carbonate platform that broke up during the Flood. If this is the case, rapid post-Flood growth of reefs is not needed to explain the thick accumulations of carbonate.

Wise (2003) and Wise and Snelling (2005) have identified what they think is an offshore pre-Flood reef made of stromatolites in the Precambrian rock of the Grand Canyon. They believe the in situ stromatolites grew in a hydrothermal environment, explaining why metazoans have not been found with the stromatolites.

Whitmore and Garner (2008) suggested, as part of their criteria model for Flood boundaries, that large in situ reef structures (like wave-resistant frameworks) would only be represented in certain parts of the sedimentary record. Since it takes large in situ structures more than one year to grow, they should only occur in rocks of pre-Flood or post-Flood times.

Reef Biology and Growth Rates

Many modern reef corals require warm, shallow water because of their calcium carbonate exoskeletons (calcium carbonate dissolves in cold water) and their symbiotic relationships with various kinds of algae and dinoflagellates (they need sunlight for photosynthesis). Hence, most modern reefs are found in shallow tropical or subtropical waters (figure 2). Reefs are areas of high production. They attract a wide variety of consumers and predators, making them some of the most diverse and complex ecosystems on earth.

---

1. Flat-topped, often deep, submarine volcanoes, often covered with a cap of carbonates and pelagic sediments.

Many reef organisms are sessile (attached) and feed by filtering nutrients. Most large reefs occur on the windward side of islands perhaps because wind-driven currents help flush the reef environment of sediment (James 1983). Many corals receive nutrients not only from filter feeding, but also from their endosymbionts[2] (Barnes and Chalker 1990; Murphy 2002). Other types of algae grow directly on corals and/or carbonate mud that surrounds the in situ organisms. Algae are the primary producers in the reef; photosynthesis occurring within various reef organisms converts solar energy into chemical energy for organisms.

Not all types of reefs require sunlight. In the broad definition of "reef" given above, deepwater carbonate mounds do not require sunlight. Many fossil "reefs" are made of filter feeders like brachiopods, sponges, echinoderms, or mollusks

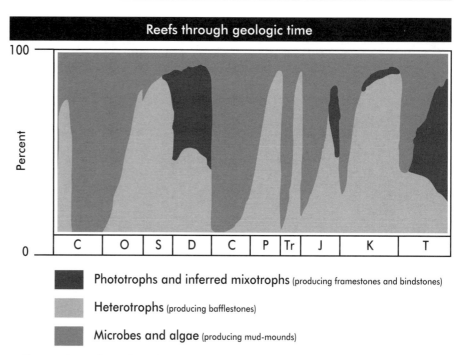

Figure 3. Reefs and reef types throughout conventional geological time. Note that most reefs have been formed by microbes and algae, until very recent times. Hetertrophic reefs are produced by organisms such as clams, which do not depend on symbiotic photosynthesis. Today, many coral reefs are photrophic or mixotrophic, greatly depending on photosynthetic organisms living symbiotically within them. (Modified from Wood 1993.)

that would not have required sunlight. Most fossil "reefs" have been considered to be predominantly *heterotrophic* instead of *phototrophic* (Wood et al. 1996). In fact, "most Phanerozoic reefs are revealed as having been built by microbes, various algae, and soft-substrate-dwelling heterotrophs" (Wood 1993, p. 536). This is illustrated in figure 3, which has been modified from Wood (1993, figure 3). In the examination of this figure, it should be noted that framework-type reefs (similar to many modern reefs of today) are a relative geological oddity and have only recently become a dominant reef type.

Reef growth is a balance between constructive and destructive processes and has proved particularly difficult to measure. Reefs are constructed by coral growth and sediment, which can settle and become cemented between the reef organisms. Modern reefs are destroyed by a number of processes, including active bio-eroders (parrotfish, sea urchins), chemical dissolution, boring organisms (sponges, clams, various worms), and storms. Boring organisms are so prevalent that they occur "in every piece of rock broken from the reef" (James 1983, p. 350). Waves from large

storms and tsunamis can break off large sections of the reef close to sea level and destroy it; sometimes these large reefal blocks are thrown *on top of* the reef, which can help produce an island above the submerged reef (Ladd 1961). Storms can cause considerable damage to reefs and wash broken pieces ashore (Bries et al. 2004), even when reefs occur on the leeward side of islands. Reef growth occurs by the addition of mass: ". . . corals add bulk, the algae function as cementing agents" (Ladd 1961, p. 704). It is important to realize coral growth rates are not equivalent to reef growth rates. Over time, corals grow, but they are also destroyed by the various processes mentioned above. Reef volume increases as living animals and their dead remains become cemented together with sediments to form the reef. Hence, the growth rate of a reef is slower than that of fast-growing corals.

With that in mind, a range of coral growth rates has been reported by many authors. Roth (1998) summarized many of these studies finding maximum reef growth rates between 3.9 and 17 inches (99 and 432 mm) per year. Some reefs have been observed to grow exceptionally fast. Ships hitting coral reefs in well-charted waters may indicate rapid growth (Ladd 1961; Roth 1998).

2. Unicellular algae and dinoflagellates that live symbiotically within their cells.

Rapid and large coral growth has been noted on sunken ships from World War II after only several decades (Earle 1976). *Acropora* colonies have reached 2.0–2.6 feet (60–80 cm) in diameter in just 4.5 years in some experimental rehabilitation studies (Fox 2005). Several studies have documented that although smaller corals have higher mortality rates, they are able to add mass exponentially faster than their larger counterparts (Lirman 2000; Yap et al. 1998). This is especially important for the reestablishment of a reef after it has been broken by a storm. Coral fragments can bud and produce a new colony. In some studies, temperature has a positive effect on coral growth rates. In a study of *Porites*, Lough and Barnes (2000) predicted calcification rates of coral reefs would increase due to global warming and an increase in sea surface temperatures, leading to increased worldwide reef mass.[3] Shinn (1966) found that coral growth rate was fastest between 28 and 30°C, and slowed considerably when water temperatures dropped. Some corals even died when temperatures approached 13°C. Higher than normal long-term temperature fluctuations can cause coral bleaching and death for many organisms of a colony (Riegl 2003). Corals have been noted to grow faster at the top of the colony than at the sides (Lough and Barnes, 2000), but upward coral and reef growth will certainly slow or stop when the low tide mark is reached.

Coral reef growth can be inhibited by ultraviolet light (Murphy 2002) exposure above sea level, nutrient-rich water laden with phytoplankton, and sediment that can suffocate the reef. Phytoplankton cloud the water, thereby reducing water clarity and blocking sunlight from reaching the imprisoned endosymbionts in the corals (Garrison 2006). Water that is frequently nutrient laden can cause frequent phytoplankton blooms, which *coral* reefs cannot endure. Coral reefs experiencing these kinds of conditions are often replaced with *algae*-dominated reefs (Tsai et al. 2005). According to Murphy (2002), modern "healthy" reefs have algae growing on them, but it is often microscopic because various vertebrate and invertebrate herbivores keep the algae so well trimmed that it is hardly visible. If the grazing capacity of herbivores is reduced or eliminated, the reef would soon become covered with algae and the corals below would die. At sites of high anthropogenic nutrient input and/or areas of overfishing, macroscopic algae is becoming more and more common on coral reefs (Stimson et al. 1996). Turbid water (from

sediment or phytoplankton) often inhibits coral reef growth, but some examples are known where corals can persist under these conditions (Smithers and Larcombe 2003).

Although the biochemistry is not completely understood, it is widely believed the symbiotic relationship that corals have with algae greatly enhances calcite deposition and reef building: "Photosynthesis by the algae results in increased rates of calcification by the host. This phenomenon is known as light-enhanced calcification" (Barnes and Chalker 1990, p. 109). Calcite, carbon dioxide, bicarbonate, carbonate, and carbonic acid are in equilibrium with each other in seawater, the concentrations of which are controlled by pH. The concentration of carbon dioxide in seawater is controlled by photosynthesis and the partial pressure of carbon dioxide in the atmosphere (see Faure 1998, p. 142–148, 433–437). In seawater, calcite reacts with carbonic acid and produces Ca and bicarbonate ions: $CaCO_3 + H_2CO_3 \circ Ca^{2+} + 2HCO_3^-$. Carbonic acid is in equilibrium with aqueous carbon dioxide: $H_2CO_3 \circ CO_2(aq) + H_2O$, which in turn is in equilibrium with gaseous carbon dioxide: $CO_2(aq) \circ CO_2(g)$. Hence, considering the reversal of these reactions, the partial pressure of gaseous carbon dioxide ultimately affects calcite precipitation. As CO_2 increases in the atmosphere, it ultimately causes an increase of carbonic acid in seawater, which lowers the pH, resulting in the *solution* of calcite. As CO_2 decreases in the atmosphere, the amount of CO_2 is decreased in the water, reducing the amount of carbonic acid (increasing pH), and leading to increased calcite *deposition*. However, aqueous photosynthesis can use up CO_2 in the water, resulting in higher pH and increased calcite deposition. Ca^{2+} and CO_3^{2-} are some of the most abundant ions in seawater (5th and 7th, respectively; Garrison 2006), making $CaCO_3$ (calcite, aragonite) deposition common when conditions of temperature and pH are favorable.

It has been found through experimental studies that increased atmospheric CO_2 levels (hence higher aqueous CO_2 levels) probably will have a negative effect on calcification levels in the ocean (Gattuso and Buddemeir 2000; Gattuso et al. 1998; Kleypas et al. 1999; Leclercq et al. 2000; Riebesell et al. 2000). Photosynthetic levels in carbonate-producing plankton will probably experience a slight increase, but this would not be offset by an equal increase in calcification levels (Riebesell et al. 2000). The current consensus in the literature appears to be that increased atmospheric CO_2 levels would probably have a negative impact on coral reef growth rates. This is causing

---

3. As will be seen later in the chapter, not all agree that global warming will lead to increased reef calcification rates.

great concern for the advocates of anthropogenic global warming. In addition, it appears that coral reefs are not carbon sinks. Coral reefs may actually add more CO_2 to the atmosphere than they ultimately remove due to respiration (Kawahata et al. 1997).

Experimental studies by Gattuso et al. (1998) have shown increased rates of calcification for corals living in water with greatly increased amounts of Ca^{2+}. Calcification increased nearly threefold when aragonite saturation was changed from 98 percent to 585 percent. These authors predict that if global levels of CO_2 continue to increase, it will ultimately affect seawater chemistry. Increased CO_2 levels will lower seawater pH, affecting the efficiency by which organisms could precipitate calcium carbonate. However, the authors also point out that increased atmospheric CO_2 levels probably would increase terrestrial weathering rates (via carbonic acid, H_2CO_3), releasing more Ca^{2+} into the oceans, and possibly counteracting the negative effects that higher CO_2 levels would have. Geochemical cycling is very complex with many variables and feedback mechanisms, often making these processes difficult to decipher. Flood and immediate post-Flood levels of these gases and ions are not specifically known, but it is likely the post-Flood atmosphere had higher amounts of CO_2, simply due to biological decay and volcanic activity.

It is well-known that many coral reefs exist in nutrient-poor ocean waters. How can these highly productive ecosystems exist in such conditions? Sorokin (1990, p. 401) stated: "The extremely high production of reef systems at a low level of nutrient supply has been and still remains one of the most exciting enigmas in marine biology." Part of the solution lies with the endosymbiotic dinoflagellates. They provide nutrients for the coral through photosynthesis, and they absorb waste products from the coral — such as nitrogen, carbon dioxide, and phosphorous (Murphy 2002). The dinoflagellates grow and divide with their coral hosts (Garrison 2006). Most of the modern "classic" coral reefs occur in "crystal clear" water. As discussed above, turbid water (often caused by phytoplankton blooms) often inhibits coral growth by blocking light needed for the symbiotic dinoflagellates. Coral reefs may exist in nutrient-poor waters because of the very fact that the waters are nutrient poor and that they will not be outcompeted by other organisms that would thrive in such conditions. Since corals are sessile and do not "move" once a settled polyp begins to grow, it will only thrive under conditions of sustained and sufficient light. These kinds of conditions frequently exist in shallow, nutrient-poor tropical waters.

Discussion

As documented above, considerable effort has been put forth by creationists to critique occurrences of "reefs" within the standard geologic column. Particular effort has been focused on Paleozoic "reefs" since most creationists believe these deposits must have been deposited catastrophically during the Flood, given reef organisms had little time to grow and cement themselves together during this time. Creationists still have much work to do in this area. With perhaps the exception of Nevins and Hodges, very few creationists have completed anything more than precursory fieldwork on ancient "reefs." More extensive, long-term fieldwork needs to be completed to discover how these deposits may have been formed during the Flood. Everything needs to be considered and wrapped into a comprehensive model (stratigraphy, sedimentology, and biology). We have been good at critiquing ancient "reefs"; now we need to look at the deposits more carefully and figure out how they might have formed within the context of the Flood.

One important and well-documented aspect of fossil reefs is that many of them are not comparable with the modern large coral frameworks. They vary greatly in size (the ancient ones are much smaller) and the types of organisms involved (figure 3). In discussing fossil reefs, Rosen (1990, p. 345) stated:

> Many modern coral reefs are extensive complex structures many kilometers across with a whole mosaic of carbonate facies. True framework is highly localized, not necessarily at the seaward rim of such complexes, and usually accounts for much less surface area and volume than bioclastic sediments, oolites (e.g., Bahamas), and evaporates. . . . Although some fossil build-ups are also seen as complexes (e.g., the Devonian of the Canning Basin), many are defined purely with respect to a local outcrop of a framework or relief feature, perhaps only meters across (e.g., the Silurian of British Wenlock). . . . The lagoonal patch reefs of Bermuda . . . are much more comparable in scale and structure to [the fossil] reefs of the British Wenlock.

In similar fashion, Longman (1981, p. 9–10) noted:

> Most modern coral reefs can be classified as "walled-reef complexes" because they contain a major rigid organic framework, a steep fore-reef wall, and a variety of associated high-energy facies,

Solitary Metazoans	Modular Metazoans
-clams, brachiopods, sponges, etc.	-corals
-aclonal reproduction	-clonal reproduction
-small buildups normal (m scale)	-large buildups possible (100s–1000s m scale)
-built on soft substrates	-require hard substrates
-low relief (m scale)	-high relief (10s–100s m scale)
-organisms more widely spaced	-tightly packed frameworks or colonies
-low diversity of organisms	-high diversity of organisms
-short-lived "reef"	-longer lived reef
-heterotrophic lifestyles	-phototrophic and mixotrophic lifestyles
-nutrient-rich environments	-nutrient-poor environments
-common in ancient rocks	-rare in ancient rocks
-form most of the "reefs" in the fossil record	-form most of the well-known reefs of today

Table 1. A generalized comparison between solitary and modular metazoan reefs (inspired by Wood 1995). Reefs of the first column are common in both ancient rocks and modern oceans. Reefs of the second column are only common in Cenozoic and are the conception that most people have of a reef.

whereas many ancient reefs would be classified as mud-mounds, knoll-reefs, patch-reefs, etc. . . . . Thus, study of modern reef complexes provides clues to interpreting ancient reefs, but modern reefs cannot and should not be viewed as direct analogs to ancient reefs, most of which were formed under different environmental conditions by organisms with different ecologic requirements.

This is only one of the many differences between modern and fossil reefs. Wood (1995) discussed many others, some of which are shown in table 1. Many ancient "reefs" are constructed of aclonal (individuals that are *not* "clones" of one another) and solitary metazoans (multi-cellular animals). Most modern (and Cenozoic) coral framework reefs are constructed of clonal (individuals that are "clones" of one another), modular metazoans. Wood proposed that these organismal and heterotrophic differences result in differences of reef morphology (size and framework structure) and in differences of the amount of carbonate build-up. This may answer in part why large framework-type structures are rare in the Paleozoic and Mesozoic from a Flood perspective. Modular types of metazoans (corals) would have had great difficulty building any kind of structure during the Flood. If one is willing to accept the broader definition of "reefs" as employed by most paleontologists, then yes, "reefs" do exist throughout much of the stratigraphic record. However,

most of these "reefs" have the characteristics of column one in table 1. Many of them are merely accumulations of various organisms *interpreted* to be in situ. The creationist literature cited above has argued that these small "reefs" could equally as well be interpreted as collections of transported debris, which is a distinct possibility. *Large* reefs that begin to have the characteristics of column 2 in table 2, do not begin to show up until the Cenozoic. In figure 3, note that framework-type reefs have four peaks (Silurian-Devonian, Jurassic, Cretaceous, and Tertiary). The pre-Tertiary (pre-Cenozoic) examples of framework-type reefs are generally very small and not comparable to the framework-type reefs of today (Toomey 1981).

Roth has suggested that some pre-Flood reefs may have been transported and reburied during the Flood (Roth 1995). These types of events may have occurred. Indeed, there are examples of large, allochthonous reef blocks that have been previously interpreted as in situ deposits, but are now known to have been transported (Conaghan et al. 1976; Polan and Stearn 1984). Based upon the severity of damage to modern reefs from hurricanes and tsunamis (Bries et al. 2004; Chavanich et al. 2005; Connell 1997), I would expect any pre-Flood framework reefs to have been nearly destroyed by early Flood processes. The cavernous nature of most coral reefs (marginal reefs) today is advantageous for water flow and nutrient circulation within the reef, and under most circumstances, the reef front and crest can withstand the wave energy normally dissipated against it. However, according to Murphy (2002), the bulk of the volume of most *modern* reefs is empty space, which is created by various reef "termites" that weaken the coral framework skeleton. This makes the reef highly susceptible to damage during larger than "normal" waves (Longman 1981). Even if some Paleozoic reef blocks were transported and redeposited, one difficult question that remains unresolved for Flood geologists is the apparent stratigraphic order (faunal succession) of the reef-producing organisms and whether transport and redeposition of pre-Flood reef blocks can explain that order. A transport and redeposition hypothesis probably will not work for all Paleozoic and Mesozoic "reefs."

Another scenario, but also with problems, might be that various reef-building organisms became dominant (or "bloomed") during various parts of the Flood and were able to build small reefs before they were buried or destroyed. There may not have been enough time, especially for larger metazoans. A possible hypothesis to account for Cenozoic and modern coral reef-building organisms is that they diversified from preexisting types of corals into the large framework builders of today, or that these organisms were small in number before the Flood and took advantage of new and more favorable post-Flood conditions to build their large frameworks. Like many marine animals, corals have embryonic planktonic life-forms that help distribute the species to new areas. It is likely that specially adapted, small colonies of pre-Flood corals were favored to adapt, diversify, and thrive under new conditions of temperature, depth, turbidity, nutrient levels, and ionic concentrations following the Flood. The "kinds" probably survived and diversified through their planktonic embryonic forms.

One criterion that I have not seen in the creationist literature is that modern reefs are extensively bored; that is, boring organisms drill into reefs for nutrients and domiciles. James (1983, p. 350) stated: "Boring organisms can be found in every piece of rock broken from the reef." Although clear examples of boring have been recognized by creationists in the rock record (Woodmorappe and Whitmore 2004), I am not sure that ancient "reef" deposits are as extensively bored as modern reefs. This might be a useful criterion to help us identify how long "aggregating communities" were together before burial. If pre-Flood boring was as common as it is today, surviving examples of pre-Flood reefs may be extensively bored, too. Roth (1995) suggested one example of a Devonian reef that is built on the Precambrian basement in Australia that may be a pre-Flood buried in situ reef. Clark (1968)

also suggested this as a possibility but did not provide any examples. Do examples exist? Further literature search and then consequent fieldwork needs to be completed to test this hypothesis.

The creationist literature has emphasized that many fossil reefs lack much in the way of an obvious framework, and instead are composed of copious amounts of carbonate mud; for example, the Capitan Reed of Texas (Nevins 1972). Wood et al. (1994) suggested that much of the sediment (micrite) in the Capitan might have been produced by microbes. They even speculated that the illusive framework of the Capitan might have been constructed, in part, by microbially bound sediment. Wood et al. (1996, p. 739) elaborated further:

> The metazoan reef community accounts for only a minor portion of the total reef fabric, occupying approximately 7–17 per cent of which 6–15 percent is occupied by the cryptic sponges. A substantial proportion of the reef fabric (25–50 percent) is now occupied by pale to mid-grey laminated micrite. This material has previously been interpreted as geopetal detrital sediment infill. Close inspection, however, reveals that micrite occurs not only as cavity fill but also as an encrustation around the open-surface community. The micrite has a layered, thrombolitic to peloidal texture in thin sections, and incorporates bioclastic debris. . . . We suggest this micrite to be of microbial origin which grew incrementally and became lithified synsedimentarily. . . . The micrite would have served to lend considerable rigidity to an otherwise relatively fragile reef framework, forming an open network of interconnected cavities and tunnels.

Recently the importance microbes play in the precipitation of calcite, dolomite, micrite, evaporates, and other substances has become widely known in both ancient and modern settings (Barton et al. 2001; Guo and Riding 1992; McKenzie and Vasconcelos 2001; Riding and Awramik 2000; Sánchez-Román et al. 2008; Shen and Xu 2005; Sprachta et al. 2001; Turner and Jones 2005; van Lith et al. 2003; Vasconcelos et al. 1995; Vasconcelos et al. 2000; Warnke 1997; Warren et al. 2001). Active microbes during the Flood may help solve several geological puzzles. The origin of thick deposits of dolomite ($CaMg(CO_3)_2$) has long been known as the "dolomite problem" because no thick accumulations of it can be found forming today, and therefore it is difficult to interpret within the uniformitarian paradigm. From the literature cited above, microbes may be an important part of the answer for both dolomite precipitation under "normal" temperatures and micrite formation during the Flood. The role of microbes in the rapid accumulation of the Capitan Reef during the Flood may be a fruitful avenue of research. Perhaps the Capitan has been a "reef" all along; all parties have simply failed to recognize the processes involved in its accumulation. Microbes may be a possible solution for loosely bound or "framework-less" reefs in other parts of the record as well. Bacteria have the ability to reproduce themselves within minutes, and modern seawater contains about 100 million bacteria per liter of seawater at all depths and latitudes (Duxbury and Duxbury 1997, p. 402)! Certainly Flood water had the potential to have even more bacteria due to increased nutrient supplies. Microbes may be the underappreciated "heroes" of dolomite and micrite in "reefs," and the solution to other geological problems.

Many anti-creationist criticisms have focused on the length of time that the Eniwetok Atoll may have taken to grow (Weber 1980; Wonderly 1977). Ladd and Schlanger (1960) report the drilling results of three deep holes and numerous shallow holes on the Atoll. Of special interest were the deep holes, one of which reached basalt at a depth of 4,157 feet (1,267 m) and the other presumed to have reached basalt at a depth of 4,610 feet (1,405 m). Many cavities and soft sediments were found throughout the deep holes. They remarked (p. 871):

> Perhaps the most conspicuous feature of the sedimentary sections found in the two deepest holes is the large proportion of soft or unconsolidated beds compared with layers that may be called firm or hard rock. In the first hole (F-1), on Elugelab, soft beds and cavities totaled 70 percent of the section. The cavities alone totaled 122 feet (pl. 265) and were found to depths of more than 2,700 feet. . . . The largest of the cavities in hole F-1 was 55 feet deep. In this and other intervals called cavities, the bit would drop with all the appearance of a free fall.

Describing the nature of the soft material in one of the deep holes, they said (p. 872):

> In hole F-1 a section of soft chalky limestone totaling approximately 1,000 feet was drilled starting at 2,900 feet (pl. 265). With nearly 1,000 feet of open hole, partly cavernous, above the

zone, and with no circulation, it was difficult to obtain samples. The material was much softer than anything drilled at higher levels, yet cuttings did not pack around the bit and drill collar as each succeeding joint of drill pipe was added. . . . This produced a small but recognizable sample consisting mainly of fine white chalky limestone, composed of grains of several sizes to a maximum of 1 millimeter — rods, spheres, discs, and arcuate and platy fragments. Most of these when pressed beneath the needle broke into a powder. A few grains contained clear, crystalline calcite that did not powder under the needle. When small lumps of the material were placed in fresh water they disintegrated, making the water milky.

The poorly lithified "chalky" limestone material appears difficult to understand within the context of modern reefs and may have been microbially produced. Additionally, modern reefs have caverns, but the percentage and size of some of the caverns encountered in the drilling of Eniwetok appear to be rather large. One solution, that may address both of these surprising findings, is that perhaps some of the carbonates in the atoll formed as a result of geothermal endo-upwelling (figure 4). This process has been described in modern reefs and is suggested for some of the ancient Pacific guyot reefs (Rougerie and Fagerstrom 1994) including the Eniwetok Atoll (Saller and Koepnick 1990). The process involves nutrient-rich deep ocean water entering the porous reef structure near its base on the volcanic guyot. The water entering the reef is driven upward through caverns in the reef structure by geothermal heat flow from the volcanic foundation. The convection of the nutrient-rich water delivers needed nutrients to the living reef above, including N, P, Si, CO_2, O_2, and Mg.

Considering these well-documented processes, I propose a new hypothesis for the post-Flood development of the Eniwetok Atoll. The reef began as a volcanic platform. Carbonates began to form on the platform as the result of the activity of bacteria and other organisms. Most of the carbonate was deposited at depth below sea level. Carbonate-producing organisms were brought to the platform as larval forms, transported by ocean currents. This explains the occasional occurrence of various corals and mollusks within the deeper parts of the drill core. Carbonate was able to form at depth because of the volcanic heat source warming the water. As the carbonate mound grew, spring activity from the volcanic

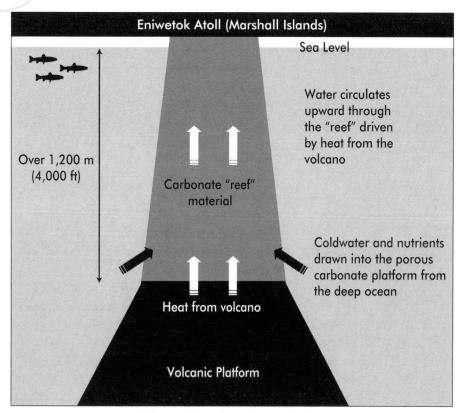

Figure 4. The process of geothermal endo-upwelling — a hypothesis which might explain rapid development of some of the world's thickest "reefs" in a short, post-Flood setting. The volcanic platform provides heat and leads to convection within the porous limestone reef material. Convection draws in cool, nutrient-rich, deep ocean water, which supplies nutrients to the reef organisms. Microbes help with carbonate precipitation, which is made possible by the volcanic heat source. Further details are explained in the text.

and guyots. It is possible that the bulk of many of these structures may have never been very close to sea level.

It is *unlikely* that high nutrient levels immediately following the Flood would have stimulated rapid coral reef growth in shallow water. As pointed out earlier, high amounts of CO_2 and nutrient levels hinder coral growth rates. Both may have been likely following the Flood. High nutrient levels in the open ocean lead to phytoplankton blooms, which increase water turbidity. Today's large reef builders require relatively clear water so the endosymbiotic dinoflagellates within the corals can perform photosynthesis. If geothermal endo-upwelling was a significant process in the formation of the Eniwetok Atoll, positive convection within the reef may have helped clear the waters immediately surrounding the reef of probable post-Flood turbidity.

Suggestions for Further Research

In this chapter, I have suggested several new hypotheses, which need further study and testing. As discussed, the importance of the microbial contribution to the formation of all types of carbonates is becoming widely recognized. Creationists need to further investigate this field as a potential, not only for the various Paleozoic reefal mud mounds, but also for larger and thicker micritic deposits in general. Many thick ancient limestones are micritic, like the Redwall Limestone of the Grand Canyon. It is time for another look at the Capitan Reef by creationists, especially in light of new hypotheses of micrite production and newer paleontological studies (Fagerstrom and Weidlich 1999; Saller et al. 1999; Senowbari-Daryan and Rigby 1996; Wood 1993; 1995; Wood et al. 1996; Wood et al. 1994). Further investigation should be completed on the Eniwetok Atoll to see if my hypothesis for its formation is feasible. A correct understanding of the formation of this atoll

platform supplied necessary acids to dissolve caverns in the limestone. The volcanic heat source allowed the process of geothermal endo-upwelling to begin and allowed the convection process to be efficient. The combination of nutrient supply and heat may have allowed the carbonate mound to grow much faster than observed coral reef growth rates today. As the carbonate mound approached sea level, phototrophic reef coral were permanently established and thrived as a result of the upwelling process.

Recent drilling has confirmed that many of the guyots in the western Pacific have thick carbonate caps.[4] It is possible these caps may have formed by processes described above. Combined with thermal subsidence of the seafloor (following the Flood), these combined processes might be sufficient to explain other thick carbonate-capped seamounts

---

4.   See http://www-odp.tamu.edu/index.html for summaries, especially of legs 143 and 144.

may have broader implications for guyots and other carbonate platforms scattered throughout the Pacific (Oard 1999b; Schlager 1981; Wilson et al. 1998). These projects and others mentioned in this chapter are going to require more than literature research; they will require original fieldwork!

Concluding Remarks

The study and interpretation of structures that are called "reefs" is a complex one. In understanding the differences between modern and ancient reefs, one first needs to dispense with the idea that a reef is a wave-resistant, framework-bound structure. Not all reefs, modern or ancient, fit within this definition. Critics of the Flood model have posited that large reef buildups, modern and ancient, are impossible to explain within a young-earth model. Many creationists have attempted to answer this criticism by focusing on the definition of a reef (ancient reefs are nothing like modern ones), or suggesting that reefs may have grown faster in the past because of different conditions. The first response is problematic because ancient reefs have different organisms and therefore had different trophic and nutrient requirements. Therefore, they can't easily be compared to modern reefs. The second response is problematic because immediate post-Flood nutrient levels were probably high, creating unfavorable conditions for coral reef growth.

The fact that ancient reefs are unlike modern reefs is an important observation that has been well documented by creationists. We need to use this observation to explain the differences in Flood and post-Flood processes (table 1, figure 3). A consideration of these differences may help us understand the development of modern framework style reefs and their near absence in the ancient record deposited by the Flood. Many small ancient reefs may be unorganized piles of carbonate debris that accumulated during the Flood. However, some of these smaller structures may be true reefs that accumulated via microbial micrite production around a few in situ organisms.

The microbial formation of micrite has been underappreciated and may explain much about the rates of accumulation of small ancient mud-mound reefs. These processes may also help us understand the formation of larger ancient and modern carbonate buildups such as the Capitan Reef and the Eniwetok Atoll. Microbial production of micrite and geothermal endo-upwelling processes within guyots may help us understand how thick reefs may have built in turbid post-Flood conditions in the midst of high aqueous CO_2 concentrations.

This chapter is far from a complete answer to our critics. More work still needs to be completed, and therefore several suggestions of needed research and unresolved problems are included within this manuscript.

[Author's note: This manuscript was originally completed and submitted for review in March of 2006. After review, the final manuscript was submitted in February 2007. A few minor revisions were made to the manuscript in November of 2008. I thank the reviewers for their helpful suggestions in improving the manuscript.]

References

CRSQ: Creation Research Society Quarterly

Barnes, D.J., and B.E. Chalker. 1990. Calcification and photosynthesis in reef-building corals and algae. In Z. Dubinsky (editor). *Coral Reefs*. Amsterdam: Elsevier, p. 109–131.

Barton, H.A., J.R. Spear, and N.R. Pace. 2001. Microbial life in the underworld: Biogenicity in secondary mineral formations. *Geomicrobiology Journal* 18:359-368.

Bries, J.M., A.O. Debrot, and D.L. Meyer. 2004. Damage to the leeward reefs of Curacao and Bonaire, Netherlands Antilles from a rare storm event: Hurricane Lenny, November 1999. *Coral Reefs* 23:297–307.

Chavanich, S., A. Siripong, P. Sojisuporn, and P. Menasveta. 2005. Impact of tsunami on the seafloor and corals in Thailand. *Coral Reefs* 24:535.

Clark, H.W. 1968. *Fossils, Flood, and Fire*. Escondido, CA: Outdoor Pictures.

Cohen, A.S., M.R. Talbot, S.M. Awramik, D.L. Dettman, and P. Abell. 1997. Lake level and paleoenvironmental history of Lake Tanganyika, Africa, as inferred from late Holocene and modern stromatolites. *Geological Society of America Bulletin* 109(4):444–460.

Conaghan, P.J., E.W. Mountjoy, D.R. Edgecombe, J.A. Talent, and D.E. Owen. 1976. Nubrigyn algal reefs (Devonian), eastern Australia: Allochthonous blocks and megabreccias. *Geological Society of America Bulletin* 87(4):515–530.

Connell, J.H. 1997. Disturbance and recovery of coral assemblages. *Coral Reefs* 16 (supplement): S101-S113.

D'Armond, D.B. 1980. Thornton Quarry deposits: a fossil coral reef or a catastrophic Flood deposit? A preliminary study. *CRSQ* 17(2):88–105.

Darwin, C. 1897. *The Structure and Distribution of Coral Reefs*, third edition. New York: D. Appleton and Company.

Decho, A.W., P.T. Visscher, and R.P. Reid. 2005. Production and cycling of natural microbial exopolymers (EPS) within a marine stromatolite. *Palaeogeography, Palaeoclimatology, Palaeoecology* 219:71–86.

Duxbury, A.C., and A.B. Duxbury. 1997. *An Introduction to the World's Oceans*, fifth edition. Dubuque, IA: Wm. C. Brown Publishers.

Earle, S.A. 1976. Life springs from death in Truk Lagoon. *National Geographic* 149(5):578–603.

Fagerstrom, J.A., and O. Weidlich. 1999. Origin of the upper Capitan-Massive limestone (Permian), Guadalupe Mountains, New Mexico-Texas: Is it a reef? *GSA Bulletin* 111(2):159–176.

Faure, G. 1998. *Principles and Applications of Geochemistry*, second edition. Upper Saddle River, NJ: Prentice Hall.

Fox, H.E. 2005. Rapid coral growth on reef rehabilitation treatments in Komodo National Park, Indonesia. *Coral Reefs* 24:263.

Froede, C.R. Jr. 1999. The Florida Keys: Evidence in support of slow Floodwater retreat part 1: The Upper Keys. *CRSQ* 35(4):186–192.

———. 2000. The Key Largo Limestone: Correlating physical information models. *CRSQ* 37(1) 68–73.

Garrison, T. 2006. *Essentials of Oceanography*, fourth edition. Belmont, CA: Thomson Brooks/Cole.

Gattuso, J.P., and R.W. Buddemeir. 2000. Calcification and CO_2. *Nature* 407(6802):311, 313.

Gattuso, J.P., M. Frankignoulle, I. Bourge, S. Romaine, and R.W. Buddemeir. 1998. Effect of calcium carbonate saturation of seawater on coral calcification. *Global and Planetary Change* 18:37–46.

Guo, L., and R. Riding. 1992. Microbial micritic carbonates in uppermost Permian reefs, Sichuan Basin, southern China: Some similarities with recent travertines. *Sedimentology* 39:37–53.

Hodges, L.T. 1977. *Megafossil Orientation of Selected Silurian, Devonian, and Pleistocene Reefs of North America*. Dissertation. Loma Linda, CA: Loma Linda University.

———. 1987. Fossil binding in modern and ancient reefs. *Origins* 14(2):84–91.

Hodges, L.T., and A.A. Roth. 1986. Orientation of corals and stromatoporoids in some Pleistocene, Devonian, and Silurian Reef Facies. *Journal of Paleontology* 60(6):1147–1158.

Isdale, P. 1984. Fluorescent bands in massive corals record centuries of coastal rainfall. *Nature* 310(5978):578–579.

James, N.P. 1983. Reef Environment. In P.A. Scholle, D.G. Bebout, and C.H. Moore (editors). *Carbonate Depositional Environments*, Memoir 33. Tulsa, OK: American Association of Petroleum Geologists, p. 345–453.

James, N.P., and I.G. Macintyre. 1985. Reefs. *Colorado School of Mines Quarterly* 80(3):70.

Kawahata, H., I. Suzuki, and K. Goto. 1997. Coral reef ecosystems as a source of atmospheric CO_2: Evidence from PCO_2 measurements of surface waters. *Coral Reefs* 16:261–266.

Klevberg, P. 2001. More musings on the Key Largo Limestone. *CRSQ* 37(4):258–259.

Kleypas, J.A., R.W. Buddemeir, D. Archer, J.P. Gattuso, C. Langdon, and B.N. Opdyke. 1999. Geochemical consequences of increased atmospheric carbon dioxide on coral reefs. *Science* 284(5411):118–120.

Ladd, H.S. 1961. Reef building. *Science* 134(3481):703–715.

Ladd, H.S., and S.O. Schlanger. 1960. *Drilling Operations on Eniwetok Atoll*. U.S. Geological Survey Professional Paper 260-Y: 863–903.

Leclercq, N., J.P. Gattuso, and J. Jaubert. 2000. CO_2 partial pressure controls the calcification rate of a coral community. Global Change *Biology* 6:329–334.

Leggitt, V.L., and R.A. Cushman, Jr. 2001. Complex caddisfly-dominated bioherms from the Eocene Green River Formation. *Sedimentary Geology* 145:377–396.

Lirman, D. 2000. Fragmentation in the branching coral Acropora palmata (Lamarck): Growth, survivorship, and reproduction of colonies and fragments. *Journal of Experimental Marine Biology and Ecology* 251:41–57.

Logan, B.W. 1961. Cryptozoon and associate stromatolites from the Recent, Shark Bay, Western Australia. *Journal of Geology* 69(3):517–533.

Longman, M.W. 1981. A process approach to recognizing facies of reef complexes. In Toomey, D.F. (editor). *European Fossil Reef Models*, Special Publication No. 30. Tulsa, OK: Society of Economic Paleontologists and Mineralogists, p. 9–40.

Lough, J.M., and D.J. Barnes. 2000. Environmental controls on growth of the massive coral *Porites. Journal of Experimental Marine Biology and Ecology* 245:225–243.

McKenzie, J.A., and C. Vasconcelos. 2001. Micritic dolomite: a geobiological signature of anaerobic microbial activity? *Geological Society of America Abstracts with Programs* 33(6):400.

Murphy, R.C. 2002. *Coral Reefs: Cities Under the Sea*. Princeton, NJ: The Darwin Press, Inc.

Nevins, S.E. 1972. Is the Capitan Limestone a fossil reef? *CRSQ* 8(4):231–248.

———. 1974. Reply to Critique by Daniel Wonderly. *CRSQ* 10(4):241–244.

Oard, M.J. 1999a. A commentary on coral growth in south Florida after the Flood. *CRSQ* 36(2):101–102.

———. 1999b. The paradox of Pacific guyots and a possible solution for the thick "reefal" limestone on Eniwetok Island. *CENTJ* 13(1):1–2.

Peczkis, J. 1981. *Anastrophic Deposition in the Silurian Dolomites of the Chicago Area*. Master's Thesis. Chicago, IL: Northeastern Illinois University.

Polan, K.P., and C.W. Stearn. 1984. The allochthonous origin of the reefal facies of the Stuart Bay Formation (Early Devonian), Bathurst Island, Arctic Canada. *Canadian Journal of Earth Sciences* 21(6):657–668.

Read, P., and A. Snelling. 1985. How old is Australia's Great Barrier Reef? *Creation Ex Nihilo* 8(1):6–9.

Riding, R.E., and S.M. Awramik (editors). 2000. *Microbial Sediments*. Berlin: Springer-Verlag.

Riebesell, U., I. Zondervan, B. Rost, P.D. Tortell, R.E. Zeebe, and F.M.M. Morel. 2000. Reduced calcification of marine plankton in response to increased atmospheric CO_2. *Nature* 407(6802):364–367.

Riegl, B. 2003. Climate change and coral reefs: Different effects in two high-latitude areas (Arabian Gulf, South Africa). *Coral Reefs* 22:433–446.

Roehler, H.W. 1993. *Eocene Climates, Depositional Environments, and Geography, Greater Green River Basin, Wyoming, Utah, and Colorado*. U.S. Geological Survey Professional Paper 1506-F: 1–74.

Rosen, B.R. 1990. Reefs and carbonate build-ups. In D.E.G. Briggs and P.R. Crowther (editors). *Palaeobiology*. Oxford: Blackwell Scientific Publications, p. 341–346.

Roth, A.A. 1979. Coral reef growth. *Origins* 6:88–95.

———. 1995. Fossil reefs and time. *Origins* 22(2): 86–104.

———. 1998. *Origins Linking Science and Scripture*. Hagerstown, MD: Review and Herald Publishing Association.

Rougerie, F., and J.A. Fagerstrom. 1994. Cretaceous history of Pacific Basin guyot reefs: A reappraisal based on geothermal endo-upwelling. *Palaeogeography, Palaeoclimatology, Palaeoecology* 112:239–260.

Saller, A.H., P.M. Harris, B.L. Kirkland, and S.J. Mazzullo (editors). 1999. *Geologic Framework of the Capitan Reef*. Publication No. 65. Tulsa, OK: Society for Sedimentary Geology.

Saller, A.H., and R.B. Koepnick. 1990. Eocene to early Miocene growth of Eniwetok Atoll: Insight from strontium-isotope data. *Geological Society of America Bulletin* 102(3):381–390.

Sánchez-Román, M., Vasconcelos, C., Schmid, T., Dittrich, M., McKenzie, J.A, Zenobi, R., and M.A. Rivadeneyra. 2008. Aerobic microbial dolomite and the nanometer scale: Implications for the geologic record. *Geology* 36(11): 879–882.

Schlager, W. 1981. The paradox of drowned reefs and carbonate platforms. *Geological Society of America Bulletin* 92(4):197–211.

Senowbari-Daryan, B., and J.K. Rigby. 1996. Brachiopod mounds not sponge reefs, Permian Capitan-Tansill Formations, Guadalupe Mountains, New Mexico. *Journal of Paleontology* 70(4):697–701.

Shen, J.W., and H.L. Xu. 2005. Microbial carbonates as contributors to Upper Permian (Guadalupian-Lopingian) biostromes and reefs in carbonate platform margin setting, Ziyun County, South China. *Palaeogeography, Palaeoclimatology, Palaeoecology* 218:217–238.

Shinn, E.A. 1966. Coral growth-rate, an environmental indicator. *Journal of Paleontology* 40(2):233–240.

Smithers, S., and P. Larcombe. 2003. Late Holocene initiation and growth of a nearshore turbid-zone coral reef: Paluma Shoals, central Great Barrier Reef, Australia. *Coral Reefs* 22:499–505.

Sorokin, Y.I. 1990. Aspects of trophic relations, productivity and energy balance in coral-reef ecosystems. In Z. Dubinsky (editor). *Coral Reefs*. Amsterdam: Elsevier, p. 401–410.

Spalding, M.D., C. Ravilious, and E.P. Green. 2001. *World Atlas of Coral Reefs*. Berkeley, CA: University of California Press.

Sprachta, S., G. Camoin, S. Golubic, and T.L. Campion. 2001. Microbialites in a modern lagoonal environment: Nature and distribution, Tikehau Atoll (French Polynesia). *Palaeogeography, Palaeoclimatology, Palaeoecology* 175:103–124.

Stimson, J., S. Larned, and K. McDermid. 1996. Seasonal growth of the coral reef macroalga *Dictyosphaeria cavernosa* (Forskål) Børgesen and the effects of nutrient availability, temperature, and herbivory on growth rate. *Journal of Experimental Marine Biology and Ecology* 196:53–77.

Toomey, D.F. (editor). 1981. *European Fossil Reef Models*. Special Publication No. 30. Tulsa, OK: Society of Economic Paleontologists and Mineralogists.

Tsai, C.C., J.S. Chang, F. Sheu, Y.T. Shyu, A.Y.T. Yu, S.L. Wong, C.F. Dai, and T.M. Lee. 2005. Seasonal growth dynamics of *Laurencia papillosa* and *Gracilaria coronopifolia* from a highly eutrophic reef in southern Taiwan: Temperature limitation and nutrient availability. *Journal of Experimental Marine Biology and Ecology* 315:49–69.

Turner, E.C., and B. Jones. 2005. Microscopic calcite dendrites in cold-water tufa: Implications for nucleation of micrite and cement. *Sedimentology* 52:1043–1066.

van Lith, Y., R. Warthmann, C. Vasconcelos, and J.A. McKenzie. 2003. Sulphate-reducing bacteria induce low-temperature Ca-dolomite and high Mg-calcite formation. *Geobiology* 1:71–79.

Vasconcelos, C., S. Bernasconi, D. Grujic, J.A. McKenzie, and A.J. Tien. 1995. Microbial mediation as a possible mechanism for natural dolomite formation at low temperatures. *Nature* 377(6546):220–222.

Vasconcelos, C., A.M. Karpoff, J.A. McKenzie, R. Warthmann, and Y. van Lith. 2000. Microbial mediated dolomite precipitation; linking anaerobic culture experiments to natural environments in modern and ancient systems. *Geological Society of America Abstracts with Programs* 32(7):257.

Warnke, K. 1997. Microbial carbonate production in a starved basin: The *crenistria* Limestone of the upper Viséan German Kulm facies. Palaeogeography, Palaeoclimatology, Palaeoecology 130:209–225.

Warren, L.A., P.A. Maurice, N. Parmar, and F.G. Ferris. 2001. Microbially mediated calcium carbonate precipitation: Implications for interpreting calcite precipitation and for solid-phase capture of inorganic contaminants. *Geomicrobiology Journal* 18:93–115.

Weber, C.G. 1980. The fatal flaws of Flood geology. *Creation/Evolution* 1(1):24–37.

Whitcomb, J.C., and H.M. Morris. 1961. *The Genesis Flood*. Phillipsburg, NJ: The Presbyterian and Reformed Publishing Co.

Whitmore, J.H., and P. Garner. 2008. Using suites of criteria to recognize pre-Flood, Flood, and post-Flood strata in the rock record with application to Wyoming (USA). In A.A. Snelling (editor). *Proceedings of the Sixth International Conference on Creationism*. Pittsburgh, PA: Creation Science Fellowship and Dallas, TX: Institute for Creation Research, p. 425–448.

Wilson, P.A., H.C. Jenkyns, H. Elderfield, and R.L. Larson. 1998. The paradox of drowned carbonate platforms and the origin of Cretaceous Pacific guyots. *Nature* 392(6679):889–894.

Wise, K.P. 2003. The hydrothermal biome: A pre-Flood environment. In R.L. Ivey (editor). *Proceedings of the Fifth International Conference on Creationism*. Pittsburgh, PA: Creation Science Fellowship, p. 359–370.

Wise, K.P., and A.A. Snelling. 2005. A note on the pre-Flood/Flood boundary in the Grand Canyon. *Origins* 58:7–29.

Wonderly, D.E. 1974. Critique of "Is the Capitan Limestone a fossil reef?" *CRSQ* 10(4):237–241.

———. 1977. *God's Time-Records in Ancient Sediments*. 1999 reprint with minor corrections. Hatfield, PA: Interdisciplinary Biblical Research Institute.

Wood, R. 1993. Nutrients, predation and the history of reef-building. *Palaios* 8:526–543.

———. 1995. The changing biology of reef-building. *Palaios* 10:517–529.

Wood, R., J.A.D. Dickson, and B. Kirkland-George. 1994. Turning the Capitan Reef upside-down: A new appraisal of the ecology of the Permian Capitan Reef, Guadalupe Mountains, Texas, and New Mexico. *Palaios* 9:422–427.

———. 1996. New observations on the ecology of the Permian Capitan Reef, Texas and New Mexico. *Palaeontology* 39(3):733–762.

Woodmorappe, J. 1980. An anthology of matters significant to creationism and diluviology: Report 1. *CRSQ* 16(4):209–219.

———. 1982. An anthology of matters significant to creationism and diluviology: Report 2. *CRSQ* 18(4): 201–223.

Woodmorappe, J., and J.H. Whitmore. 2004. Field study of purported hardgrounds of the Cincinnatian. *TJ* 18(3):82–92.

Yap, H.T., R.M. Alvarez, H.M. Custodio III, and R.M. Dizon. 1998. Physiological and ecological aspects of coral transplantation. *Journal of Experimental Marine Biology and Ecology* 229:69–84.

Young, D.A. 1982. *Christianity and the Age of the Earth*. Grand Rapids, MI: Zondervan Publishing House.

Young, D.A., and R.F. Stearley. 2008. *The Bible, Rocks and Time*. Downers Grove, IL: InterVarsity Press.

Chapter 10

Do Mud Cracks Indicate Multiple Droughts During the Flood?

John H. Whitmore • PhD — Geology

Abstract

Mud cracks (or desiccation cracks) form when clay-rich sediment dehydrates, shrinks, and cracks. Critics of creationism contend that mud cracks are found throughout the geological record and are thus "proof" against a global Flood. A short catastrophic Flood could not have caused the bulk of the sedimentary rock record, they say, because of the multiple droughts indicated by the mud cracks. This chapter will review the literature of mud cracks and several similar features: clastic dikes, sand intrusions, diastasis cracks, synaeresis cracks, and molar tooth structures. Many of these can be mistaken for mud cracks, so criteria are presented to help properly identify and differentiate them. Also (surprisingly), rapid desiccation mud crack development has been documented during humid, rainy conditions and on modern shorelines during very brief intertidal exposure. Even though they are probably rarer in the rock record than Flood critics admit, it also appears that true mud cracks could have formed during the Flood.

Introduction

Features commonly referred to as "mud cracks" or "mudcracks" form when clay-rich sediment dehydrates, causing it to shrink and crack (figure 1). They are more properly referred to as "desiccation cracks" or "desiccation mud cracks" but sometimes are called "sun cracks." We see them form today when standing water underlain by mud

Figure 1. Mud-cracked surface, Anza Borrego Desert, California. Note how the edges of most polygons curl upward as the mud dries. This is due to a sand layer below the thin mud veneer.

Large playa cracks and small mud cracks, Lucerne Dry Lake

1 km

Figure 2. Giant playa mud cracks, Lucerne Dry Lake, California. Large playa polygons can have diameters of hundreds of meters in diameter. The cracks can act as waterways on the playa surface. Cracks often fill chaotically from material sloughing into the cracks from the crack walls. Smaller cracks can be found superimposed all over the playa surface.

examples of supposed desiccation cracks that have been proved to be otherwise.

Previous Creationist Work

Creationists have discussed mud cracks, but seldom in depth. Brief comments were by Austin (1984), Morton (1982, 1983), and Wood-morappe (1986) regarding mud cracks and synaeresis cracks. Longer comments have been made by Froede (1994) and Oard (1994). Most suggest the possibility that features previously interpreted as mud cracks may have formed by other mechanisms such as subaqueous synaeresis[1] or substratal diastasis cracking.[2] In a longer article and several abstracts, I have suggested that large, deep cracks in the Hermit Formation of the Grand Canyon are not mud cracks, but clastic dikes (2004, 2005; Whitmore and Peters 1999; Whitmore and Strom 2005). Clastic dikes have also been discussed by Austin and Morris (1986) and Froede (1998). I have also argued that some cracks found in the Hartford Basin of Connecticut may have formed by synaeresis instead of desiccation (1988). I argued (along with Paul Garner) that true desiccation cracks would primarily be preserved in rocks that represented post-Flood deposits (2008). This was one of many criteria that we suggested might be used to identify pre-Flood, Flood, and post-Flood sediments.

evaporates. Mud cracks typically form polygonal patterns with triple junctions and cracks that extend downward in a V shape. Polygon diameters can vary from a few centimeters in small, shallow mud puddles, to hundreds of meters on playa lake floors (figure 2). Sometimes open cracks can be filled and covered with sand, thus they have the potential to be preserved in the geological record. It is unlikely that true desiccation cracks would have formed at the height of Noah's Flood because of the time needed to expose, desiccate, and crack the sediments. It is even more difficult to imagine forming multiple layers of desiccation cracks during the Flood.

But there are many features similar to mud cracks that can form in other ways. These include synaeresis cracks, clastic dikes, sand intrusions, diastasis cracks, and molar tooth structures. These structures and their fillings involve processes other than desiccation by the sun, although in cross section, they resemble mud cracks. In this chapter, I will define the various types of cracks, list criteria that can be used to distinguish between them, and show some

---

1. Synaeresis cracks are formed underwater or even within buried sediments. The process is not well understood, but sometimes it has been related to changes in salinity.
2. Substratal diastasis cracks form and fill within buried sediments as loading and shear stresses interact with alternating layers of different kinds of sediment.

The Challenge: Multiple Droughts during the Global Flood?

One of the reasons that Morton (1982, 1983, 2003) believes that most sedimentary rocks were not deposited during the Flood is because many strata show supposed mud cracks. In his web article (2003), he gave specific examples of mud cracks (assumed to represent droughts) from every geological age, and then reasoned:

> One of the things that is [sic] very difficult for the global flood advocates to explain is why, during a global, wet water catastrophe, there are so many places in the world which experienced drought. These areas dried up and left mud cracks as evidence of the drying throughout the geologic column. Everyone is familiar with mud cracks and the fact that they take several days to several weeks of drought to dry out the sediments sufficiently to form. When we find such things in the fossil record, young-earth creationists often claim that they are synaeresis cracks, which are dewatering structures. This is a false claim as synaeresis cracks are easily distinguishable from genuine desiccation cracks. . . . The young-earth creationist,   Steve Austin, implies that all desiccation cracks are synaeresis cracks. He writes: "Thick sedimentary rock sequences containing shrinkage cracks are frequently claimed to have required repeated wetting and drying of the sediment surface, thereby requiring a lot of time in what would normally appear to be a rapidly deposited sedimentary sequence. Plummer and Gostin urge caution when interpreting 'mudcracks' in rocks as evidence of drying."

There are many problems with this statement. Many "mud cracks" have been identified without careful study or consideration of other processes that could have formed them.[3] Morton quickly dismisses synaeresis cracks and does not even consider other known mechanisms that can create "mud cracks." Furthermore, he is unfair to Austin (1984),

---

3. Recently I was on a GSA field trip with professional geologists in Pennsylvania. Several participants found some polygonal sand-filled cracks in the shales we were examining. Most participants quickly arrived at the conclusion that these were mud cracks without looking at the features for more than a few seconds! After carefully looking at the cracks and pointing out some irregularities, I was able to convince some of the participants that the mud crack interpretation they had so quickly arrived at was problematic. Caution is warranted when examining these features!

who merely suggested heeding Plummer and Gostin's (1981) caution in interpreting any crack as a mud crack, because some may be synaeresis cracks. Nowhere in Austin's short comment (1984) does he imply "all desiccation cracks are synaeresis cracks." Rather it is Morton who misquotes Plummer and Gostin (Woodmorappe 1986). They did urge caution in interpreting various kinds of cracks, because they *are* easily confused. Additionally, Morton wrongly assumes that true mud cracks only form during conditions of drought. Krynine (1935, p. 97), based on observations made in Connecticut during the spring of 1934, reported that "desiccation features can form, survive, and be incorporated into the fossil record under the climatic conditions of a rather wet New England spring." Dionne (1974) reported desiccation mud cracks forming in the lowest parts of tidal flats, exposed for only a short time during low tide.

Identifying "mud cracks" in the rock record is not simple. To avoid misinterpreting mud cracks in the Green River Formation, Smoot (1983) carefully outlined criteria for mud cracks and synaeresis cracks. He stated (p. 816, emphasis added):

> The interpretation of the bulk of the Wilkins Peak facies as subaerial deposits relies heavily on the assessment of the mudcracks as desiccation features. *Reaching this conclusion is not trivial, however,* since several other crack-forming mechanisms are known.

Cracks are difficult to interpret because very similar features can form by different mechanisms and in different environments. Hesse and Reading (1978) found it difficult to interpret between mud cracks and clastic dikes in the same sequence of rocks because the features were so similar. For example, clastic dikes often have polygonal patterns, too.

In an attempt to resolve these difficulties with regard to the Flood, criteria have been developed (Whitmore 2005), and are here expanded, so that *all* types of cracks can be properly identified. I believe that only a few examples of true mud cracks will be found in the parts of the geologic record deposited by the Flood. True mud cracks may occur in pre-Flood sediments and definitely are present in post-Flood sediments.

Various Crack Types

In order to determine the origin of different kinds of cracks, they must be carefully studied. What appears to be

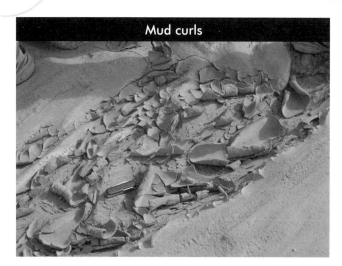

Mud curls

Figure 3. Mud cracks and mud curls, Anza Borrego Desert, California. Dried mud can curl up into tubes if it is underlain by a coarse sand layer. Pocket knife is about 9 centimeters in length.

Curls preserved in the rock record

Figure 4. Fossil mud curls near Sandstone Canyon, Anza Borrego Desert, California. U.S. penny is 19 millimeters in diameter.

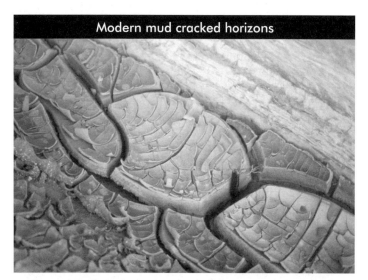

Modern mud cracked horizons

Figure 5. Multiple generations of polygonal mud cracks. Anza Borrego Desert, California. The vertical pocket knife handle is about 9 centimeters high.

a "mud crack" may actually be a synaeresis crack, clastic dike, sand intrusion, diastasis crack, or molar tooth structure. Many cracks share similarities and in some instances may be difficult to distinguish from one another without good three-dimensional exposure (rare) at multiple outcrops. Various crack types are described below and summarized in tables 1-5, which include references.

Mud cracks are features that form when clay-bearing sediment or soil becomes exposed to the air. The mud dries, shrinks, and cracks. It is a common misconception that mud needs to completely dry before it begins to crack. Experimental results show that contraction polygons can form while the mud is still damp (Baria 1977; Fellows 1951). Modern examples range in size from less than a centimeter to hundreds of meters in diameter. In experiments, principal (first-order) polygonal patterns can develop within an hour, though complete drying may take several weeks (Fellows 1951). Most mud cracks are polygonal with triple junctions, but slight variations have been reported (Neal et al. 1968; Reineck and Singh 1980; Shrock 1948). Most observed mud cracks occur in shallow basins, but can form on inclined surfaces as steep as 38° (MacCarthy 1922). It is significant that most variations which occur in "mud cracks" are in cracks that have been *interpreted* to be mud cracks.

Mud cracks do exhibit some variety. If the cracking mud layer is thin and underlain by sand, the mud curls upward, and can even roll up into a tube (Longwell 1928). These curls are common in the Anza Borrego Desert of southern California (figure 3) and have been preserved in the rock record (figure 4). However, some mud cracks have "downward" curls (Minter 1970). Modern mud cracked horizons may contain several generations (or orders) of cracks (figure 5). Usually cracks of the same generation have approximately the same depth, but smaller polygons can have the same depth, too, especially if underlain by a layer of sand, as in figure 6. Polygon size can often vary greatly even on the same horizon (figure 6). Modern mud cracked surfaces often contain raindrop imprints (figure 7) and animal tracks (figure 8).

Figure 6. Mud crack polygon size can vary greatly, even on the same cracked surface. Note the many smaller polygons in the upper right of the photo. Pocket knife is about 9 centimeters in length. Anza Borrego Desert, California.

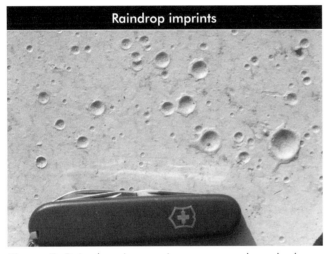

Figure 7. Rain drop impressions on a mud cracked surface, Anza Borrego Desert, California. Pocket knife is about 9 centimeters in length.

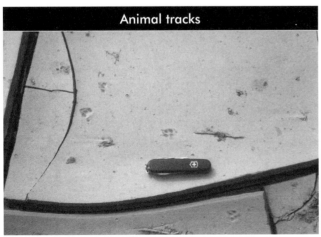

Figure 8. Animal tracks preserved on a mud cracked surface, Anza Borrego Desert, California. Pocket knife is about 9 centimeters in length.

These features can form before or after cracking, but must form while the mud is still relatively wet. Multiple layers of mud crack horizons can form during the same desiccation event (see Konrad and Ayad 1997). Figure 9 shows two layers of mud cracks of different sizes that may have formed during the same desiccation event.

The actual cracks are generally V-shaped. However, if shallow, as in figures 1 and 9, they may be U-shaped. Mud cracks often penetrate into uncompacted clays, whose lithification can cause deformation of the crack's shape (Bradley 1930; Smoot 1983). Based on field studies of modern playas, Smoot (1981) found that mud cracks are generally V-shaped but can be sinuous with lobate margins, have varying widths within a single crack and can sometimes propagate obliquely and horizontally. However, there appear to be theoretical constraints on the horizontal propagation of cracks and curls (Allen 1986). The amount and depth of cracking are mostly related to soil moisture and clay content (Neal et al. 1968; Olsen and Haugen 1998; Yassoglou et al. 1994), but factors such as the type of clay (Olsen and Haugen 1998) salinity (Dow 1964; Kindle 1917) and thickness of clay (Allen 1986; Fellows 1951) are important, too.

Mud cracks are filled by sediment from above (Plummer and Gostin 1981; Shrock 1948; Smoot 1981) that theoretically should be horizontally stratified (Davis 1889; Diller 1889; Plaziat et al. 1990; Shrock 1948). However, a great range of fill material, often chaotically arranged, can be present (Plaziat et al. 1990; Shrock 1948; Smoot 1981; Wilden and Mabey 1961). I have personally

Figure 9. An upper mud cracked surface has been peeled away to reveal a lower mud cracked surface. Note the upper polygons are much smaller than the lower polygons. The field book is about 20 centimeters in length. Anza Borrego Desert, California.

Table 1. Major characteristics reported for desiccation mud cracks.

Characteristics of Desiccation Mud Cracks	References
V or U cross sectional shape, can be parallel sided	Plummer and Gostin 1981; Shrock 1948
Cracks range in size from less than a cm to 100s of m in diameter	Baria 1977; Fellows 1951; Fife 1977; Goetz 1980; Lang 1943; Longwell 1928; Neal et al. 1968; Shrock 1948; Wilden and Mabey 1961
Derivation of infill from above	Neal et al. 1968; Plummer and Gostin 1981; Shrock 1948; Smoot 1981
Horizontal stratification of crack	Davis 1889; Diller 1889; Neal et al. 1968; Plaziat et al. 1990; Shrock 1948
Great range of crack fill material, often chaotic from sloughed sides of crack wall	Neal et al. 1968; Plaziat et al. 1990; Shrock 1948; Smoot 1981; Wilden and Mabey 1961
Often multiple generations (orders) of cracking	Konrad and Ayad 1997; Plummer and Gostin 1981; Reineck and Singh 1980; Shrock 1948
Often associated with other surficial features (tracks, rain drop impressions, etc.)	Krynine 1935; Plummer and Gostin 1981
Often the polygons form complete (connected) polygonal patterns but can be incomplete	Kidder 1990; Kindle 1917; Reineck and Singh 1980; Shrock 1948
Crack penetration is usually straight, but can be curved	Reineck and Singh 1980; Shrock 1948; Smoot 1981
Cracks of the same generation have similar depths (not widely reported in the literature, but often assumed)	Sipes and Peters 2000
Can branch and change in width	Smoot 1981
Horizontal cracking can develop at depth (perpendicular to the vertical cracks), but the extent of their protuberance is only about one-third the size of the polygon.	Konrad and Ayad 1997
Can be associated with "mud curls"	Allen 1986; Longwell 1928; Shrock 1948
Sediments with large amounts of clay are most susceptible to shrinkage.	Olsen and Haugen 1998
Can have "radial" and "striped" patterns	Shrock 1948; Snyman 1950; Neal et al. 1968
Can form during only brief times of exposure on the lowest parts of tidal flats	Dionne 1974
Can form in humid climates during periods of extended rainfall	Krynine 1935

observed giant desiccation cracks on Lucerne Dry Lake, California, acting as drainage paths for the playa (figure 2). Although the sediment within the cracks was not trenched, its bedding would probably mirror that of small streams. In many places the crack walls had sloughed in, likely producing a chaotic crack fill. The same phenomenon was observed by Wilden and Mabey (1961). Crack fills could also be from wind-blown material. Sand dunes were observed along the edge of Lucerne Dry Lake.

Table 1 summarizes various characteristics of mud cracks that may help in their identification. Many have found the interpretation of mud cracks to be difficult because they can often be confused with other types of cracks (Astin and Rogers 1991; Barclay et al.

1993; Donovan and Foster 1972; Plummer and Gostin 1981; Smoot 1983; Whitmore 2005). Synaeresis cracks can originate at the sediment-water interface (i.e., the seafloor), *or more commonly, substratally.* There are many reports of modern occurrences of cracks forming at the sediment-water interface (Burst 1965; Flower and Ives 1946; Moore 1914; Twenhofel 1923; Willard 1925). Synaeresis cracks can result from the contraction of mineral lattices in swelling clays in response to salinity changes (Burst 1965), shrinkage of argillaceous sediments during dewatering induced by earthquakes (Pratt 1998b), and loading and subsequent dewatering of mudstones overlain by sandstones and siltstones (Plummer and Gostin 1981). Synaeresis cracks can have a variety

Table 2. Major characteristics reported for synaeresis cracks.

Characteristics of Synaeresis Cracks	References
V or U cross sectional shape	Burst 1965; Kidder 1990; Plummer and Gostin 1981
Derivation of fill from above or below	Plummer and Gostin 1981; Pratt 1998b
Generally only one generation of cracks	Plummer and Gostin, 1981
Can develop from changes in salinity, compaction-induced loading, and shrinkage of mineral lattices	Burst 1965; Donovan and Foster 1972; Kidder 1990; Plummer and Gostin 1981; White 1961
Described cracks < 1 m in length	Burst 1965; Plummer and Gostin 1981; Pratt 1998b; Wheeler and Quinlan 1951; White 1961
Often a slight bending or branching occurs near the base of the crack.	Kidder 1990
Can form polygonal shapes, but are often incomplete and less regular than mud cracks	Donovan and Foster 1972; Kidder 1990; Moore 1914; Smoot 1983
Compaction of silt and mud often causes oblique orientation of the cracks to bedding planes	Donovan and Foster 1972
Cracks have been observed to form due to tectonic forces (shaking).	Flower and Ives 1946; Pratt 1998a, b
They can have preferred orientation.	Donovan and Foster 1972
If formed by a compaction mechanism, synaeresis cracks can be bulbous or have bulbous elements.	Donovan and Foster 1972
Curling of polygons can occur.	Burst 1965
High sinuosity	Plummer and Gostin 1981; Smoot 1983
Muddy infilling	Smoot 1983
They can form radiating (star-like) patterns.	Snyman 1950

of different morphologies that can overlap with those of mud cracks. Most typically, synaeresis cracks have been described as a single generation of sinuous, incomplete polygonal cracks, with irregular and/or U-shaped cross sections (Plummer and Gostin 1981; Raza et al. 1981; Smoot 1983; White 1961). However, they can also have V-shaped cross sections and polygonal patterns (Plummer and Gostin 1981), criteria that are usually assigned to desiccation cracks. Unlike mud cracks, synaeresis cracks can penetrate upward (Plummer and Gostin 1981; Pratt 1998b). This occurs when the synaeresis crack forms within buried strata and fluidized sediment is injected into a crack and fills the resulting void. To date, geologists have not clearly distinguished synaeresis cracks from clastic dikes.[4] Generally, synaeresis cracks have been described as smaller (<1 m) injected structures with mud crack-like characteristics that are filled with sand from a directly adjacent sedimentary layer. Clastic dikes are

larger structures that are often filled with sand derived from a more distant sedimentary layer. Table 2 summarizes the reported characteristics of synaeresis cracks.

Molar tooth structures, as reported by Pratt (1998a, p. 1,028), "appear as intricately crumpled, subvertical, microsparry calcite-filled veins, creating a pattern of bedding planes that resembles the upper surface of elephant molars." They are small (millimeters to a few centimeters), and have only been reported in Proterozoic *carbonate* strata. Some interpret them as forming by desiccation (Knoll 1984; Winston 1990), but Pratt (1998a, p. 1,028) interpreted them as "originating through syndepositional earthquake-induced dewatering and shrinkage of clay-lime mud sediment, filling of the resulting fissures by liquidized lime mud, and their rapid calcite cementation." The cracks are filled by downward-injected sediment slurries, and can be straight or highly folded (by differential compaction). They are similar in appearance to synaeresis cracks, but instead form in clay and lime-rich mudstones instead of clay and silt-rich units. Pratt made several distinctions between synaeresis cracks and molar tooth

---

4. Large tabular sand intrusions that penetrate more or less vertically (upward or downward) through preexisting rocks and sediments.

structures. The former can be open for a time and then later filled, generally with coarse sediment, while molar tooth structures are filled immediately with microsparry calcite and are restricted to carbonate rocks. A summary of their characteristics is found in table 3.

The term "diastasis cracks" was introduced into the literature by Cowan and James (1992) as an alternative to both desiccation and synaeresis cracks. They thought that diastasis cracks formed by "differential mechanical behavior under stress of stiff mud interlayered with loose ooid/peloid sand (p. 1,101)." The cracks are usually small (1–10 cm) and resemble desiccation and synaeresis cracks in cross section. The cracks they describe are filled with sediment and carbonate cement. On bedding planes, the orthogonal larger cracks resemble mud cracks, but smaller cracks are usually not connected and form incomplete polygons. Most of the cracks they described vary in width from top to bottom. In cross section, most are straight with V- or U-shaped cross sections, but some are jagged and bifurcate (up and down), and some have multiple branches. Some cracks penetrate through many successive layers, even when the layers consist of coarser material. Crack fills are not stratified. Cowan and James (1992) defined the cracks as being able to form at the sediment/water interface, or substratally. In a later abstract, Cowan et al. (2001) showed that diastasis cracks could be formed experimentally (2001) by shaking and differential loading of a water-saturated, unset plaster and sand mixture. Table 4 summarizes the characteristics of diastasis cracks.

Clastic dikes, sand intrusions, and sand sheets (or sills) are well documented. Clastic dikes often penetrate upward (Diller 1889; Harms 1965; Newsom 1903; Peterson 1968), but sometimes they can penetrate downward, too (Jenkins 1925a). Sometimes they transition to sand sheets or sills (Hiscott 1979; Truswell 1972). Width can vary from a few millimeters to many meters. Sand intrusions are usually large and pipe-like and can result in the formation of sand volcanoes. These types of structures can form during large earthquakes. Tectonic shaking and various types of loading can cause sand grains in water-saturated sands to temporarily gain buoyancy, becoming suspended in the surrounding fluid. A pressurized water-sand mixture can flow toward areas of low pressure (usually toward the surface), resulting in the formation of a clastic dike.

Clastic dikes can have polygonal patterns of large diameter but are often parallel to each other. They are often massive in appearance, but on closer inspection can demonstrate oriented sedimentary grains, flow structures, and grading. Some exhibit flute structures on their walls and others show slickenside-like features. Table 5 summarizes the characteristics of clastic dikes.

As noted above, many of the cracks share similarities. All types can have polygonal patterns, V-shaped cross sections, and sand fillings within clay-rich host rocks. These are features commonly attributed only to desiccation mud cracks. But true mud cracks should be distinguished by unique features such as mud curls, chaotic crack fill, varied crack fills, and horizontally bedded fills. Table 6 compares features of the various crack types and can be used as a guide to distinguish among them.

Reinterpreting Mud Cracks

Many supposed desiccation mud cracks have been misidentified. They have often been interpreted based on preconceived ideas of depositional environments, polygonal shapes, and V-shaped cross sections, while other criteria are overlooked. When some are examined critically, features have been found contrary to a desiccation origin. Here are a few examples.

Donovan and Foster (1972) argued compellingly that some cracks in the Caithness Flagstone of Scotland were formed by synaeresis. Astin and Rogers (1991) in turn argued that all of these cracks were formed by desiccation

Table 3. Major characteristics reported for molar tooth structures

Characteristics of Molar Tooth Structure	References
In plan view, resembles the upper surface of elephant molars	Pratt 1998a
Occur only in argillaceous lime mudstones	Pratt 1998a
Formed due to seismically induced compaction	Pratt 1998a
Complex, subparallel to reticulate pattern of folded, subvertical veins and sheets	Pratt 1998a
Cracks are filled with calcite	Pratt 1998a
Relatively small (usually 1–10 cm)	Pratt 1998a
Downward and upward injection of crack fill	Pratt 1998a
Polygonal patterns in plan view	Winston 1990

Table 4. Major characteristics reported for diastasis cracks

Characteristics of Diastasis Cracks	References
When viewed on bedding planes, they can have orthogonal intersections	Cowan and James 1992
Vary from complete to incomplete polygons	Cowan and James 1992
Most cracks are jagged and irregular	Cowan and James 1992
Many cracks bifurcate (downward) and can have multiple branches (up or down)	Cowan and James 1992
Cracks can be uniformly open (top to bottom), tapered (up or down), or dilated along part of their path	Cowan and James 1992
Cracks can bulge, pinch, and swell.	Cowan and James 1992; Kriz and Stepanek 1979
When effects of compaction are removed from distorted cracks, they can have differing lengths. The differing lengths show they were not initially straight, as are most mud and synaeresis cracks.	Cowan and James 1992
They have been experimentally produced with layers of hardening plaster and sand subjected to shearing forces.	Cowan et al. 2001

and that there was little evidence in the geologic record for any cracks forming via subaqueous shrinkage. Barclay et al. (1993) replied, arguing that Donovan's and Foster's conclusions could not be discounted completely. This "debate" demonstrates that cracks can often be difficult to interpret.

I have examined multiple layers of supposed mud cracks in the Hartford Basin in central Connecticut (1988) near the town of Rocky Hill. Many of them have second order patterns (figure 10). Adjacent layers contain dinosaur footprints, which is an indication of subaerial exposure. These might be good candidates for true desiccation cracks that formed during brief exposure during the Flood. However, in cross section (figure 11), some of the cracks occur immediately beneath channel deposits of cross-bedded sand. If they were true desiccation cracks, any current powerful enough to transport and deposit the sand would have ripped up any of the thin mud cracks. These processes typically produce flat-pebble conglomerates, not well-preserved mud cracks. Imagine what would be produced if the mud crack polygons of figures 1 or 3 were

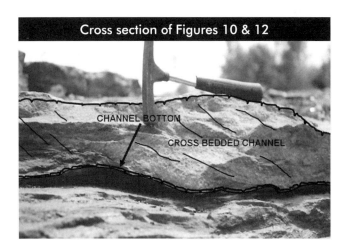

Figure 11. A cross section from the slab shown in figure 10. Cracks are found on the upper and lower surfaces of this slab, although they do not show up well in cross section. The slab contains cross-bedded sandstone and is interpreted as a small channel. The bottom surface of this slab is shown in figure 12. The shrinkage crack depths have been exaggerated for clarity. East Berlin Formation, Rocky Hill, Connecticut (from Whitmore 1988, p. 68).

Figure 10. Shrinkage cracks in the East Berlin Formation, Rocky Hill, Connecticut. This surface is the upper surface of the slab shown in the cross section of figure 11. Note there are several orders of cracks (from Whitmore 1988, p. 67).

Table 5. Major characteristics reported for clastic dikes and sand intrusions

Characteristics of Clastic Dikes and Sand Intrusions	References
Can develop as a result of tectonic activity	Austin 1984; Diller 1889; Dott 1966; Jolly and Lonergan 2002; Obermeier et al. 2002; Reimnitz and Marshall 1965; Stewart et al. 2002
Can develop as a result of sudden loading (from sediment or water)	Dott 1966; Feldl et al. 2002; Nichols et al. 1994; Pogue 1998; Seed and Lee 1966; Stewart 2003
Can develop as a result of the sudden failure of high-pressure fluids	Jolly and Lonergan 2002
Most are massive and have no internal structures, but some can have vertical flow structures and tabular grains showing flow directions.	Diller 1889; Dott 1966; Haff 1944; Harms 1965; Hiscott 1979; Jenkins 1925a, b; Laird 1970; Peterson 1968; Waterston 1950
Dikes can have occasional flute and groove marks on their sides.	Peterson 1968
Grading of sedimentary grains may occur parallel to walls of dike.	Peterson 1968
Most clastic dikes consist of coarse-grained silt or fine- to medium-grained sand.	Diller 1889; Dott 1966; Harms 1965; Lowe 1975, 1976; Newsom 1903; Peterson 1968; Shrock 1948
Well-sorted, spherical, fine-grained sand is most susceptible to liquefaction.	Jolly and Lonergan 2002
Dikes can vary greatly in thickness, spacing, and size (few millimeters to many meters).	Diller 1889; Harms 1965; Jolly et al. 1998; Newsom 1903
Dikes can branch, and then the branches can coalesce with one another. Dikes can intersect with each other.	Boehm and Moore 2002; Dott 1966; Harms 1965; Newsom 1903; Shoulders and Cartwright 2004; Truswell 1972; Waterston 1950
Dikes can have large polygonal shapes when viewed from above.	Reimnitz and Marshall 1965; Silver and Pogue 2002
Incomplete and complete polygonal patterns can exist.	Froede 1998; Raza et al. 1981; Silver and Pogue 2002
Dikes can show preferred orientation depending on tectonic factors.	Anderson 1951; Boehm and Moore 2002; Diller 1889; Harms 1965; Jolly et al. 1998; Jolly and Lonergan 2002; Silver and Pogue 2002
Slickensides or evidence of shearing can occur on the sides of dikes or possibly within the dikes.	Harms 1965; Petit and Laville 1987; Waterston 1950
Sand intrusions can be intimately associated with faulting and sometimes occur along fault planes.	Boehm and Moore 2002; Harms 1965; Jolly et al. 1998; Jolly and Lonergan 2002
Dikes can be injected downward.	Feldl et al. 2002; Newsom 1903; Pogue 1998; Silver and Pogue 2002; Stewart 2003
In order for a sand intrusion to form, there must be a trigger mechanism and there must be a sustained pressure differential between the fluid in the propagating fracture (the intrusion) and the fluid in the pores of the rock being fractured. The fracturing rock must have some tensile strength.	Jolly and Lonergan 2002; Lowe 1976; Nichols et al. 1994; Seed and Lee 1966; Walton and O'Sullivan 1950
The dike material is usually intruded during a liquefaction event, and the resulting grain fabric following liquefaction is more tightly packed than in the original host material.	Lowe 1976; Owen 1987; Seed and Lee 1966

Table 6. A comparison of selected observed characteristics of various crack types

Characteristic	desiccation mud cracks	synaeresis cracks	molar tooth structures	diastasis cracks	clastic dikes and sand intrusions
sand-filled cracks in clay-rich host rocks	x	x	x	x	x
complete polygonal shapes	x	x	x	x	x
incomplete polygonal shapes	x	x	x	x	x
multiple generations of cracking	x	x			
typically small (< 1 m) in size	x	x	x	x	
large sizes observed (> 1 m)	x				x
can bulge, pinch, and swell	x	x	x	x	x
horizontal stratification of crack fill	x				
massive or vertical stratification of crack fill		x	x	x	x
great range of crack fill material	x				
mud curls	x	x			
sediment infill from above	x	x	x	x	x
sediment infill from below		x	x	x	x
cracks intersect with one another (in cross section)			x	x	x
V-shaped cross sections	x	x	x	x	x
slickensides occur within some cracks					x
often associated with rain drop impressions and animal tracks	x				
usually all cracks have the same depth	x	x			
cracks can propagate and fill horizontally		x	x	x	x

ripped up. Instead, the channel sand was deposited directly on top of a thin silt-covered surface. Furthermore, some of the cracks extend up through the silt and into the next sand layer (figure 12). Although more study needs to be done at this site, it appears to be difficult to explain these features as desiccation mud cracks. Synaeresis or diastasis may be a better explanation for these cracks.

Another example is the supposed large playa mud cracks at the base of the Coconino Sandstone that extend down into

Bottom side of Figure 11

Figure 12. The bottom surface of the slab shown in figures 10 and 11. Note that several orders of cracks are present. East Berlin Formation, Rocky Hill, Connecticut (from Whitmore 1988, p. 69).

Clastic dikes

Figure 13. Large sandstone cracks (shown by arrows) penetrate into the top of the Hermit Formation, Grand Canyon, Arizona. This location is near the South Kaibab Trail. Cracks are up to 15 meters long near the Bright Angel Trail. These have been interpreted as mud cracks since they were first described in the 1920s.

Vertical flow structures

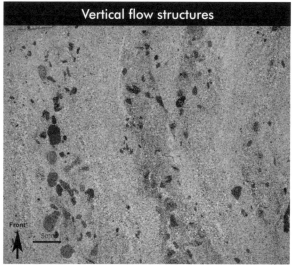

Front

5mm

Figure 14 (above). Sand-filled cracks at the base of the Coconino Sandstone in the Grand Canyon (like the ones shown in the previous figure) contain vertical flow structures. This is a section from a crack along the Hance Trail. Scale bar is 5 millimeters long. The section was made by slicing horizontally through the crack. Photo courtesy of Ray Strom, Calgary Rock and Materials Services, Alberta, Canada.

U-shaped cracks

the Hermit Formation in the Grand Canyon. They have been identified as mud cracks for decades without any serious study (Abbott and Cook 2004; Blakey 1990; McKee 1934; Noble 1922; White 1929). The Hermit Formation has been interpreted as having been deposited on broad, flat floodplains (Blakey 1990), which dried up and cracked. The Coconino has long been thought to have been a desert deposit that covered the Hermit, filling the deep cracks of the Hermit with sand (McKee 1934, 1979). Some of the cracks extend to a depth of at least 15 meters into the Hermit Formation. Others are shallower (figure 13). During the past several years, I have examined these cracks and found that they are not mud cracks (Whitmore 2004, 2005; Whitmore and Strom 2005). They are better interpreted as clastic dikes formed by seismic activity along the Bright Angel Fault. Among other things, they contain clear vertical flow structures (figure 14) and horizontal connections (figure 15), and the longest cracks are associated with the Bright Angel Fault.

Diastasis cracks were first described by Cowan and James (1992) because they found desiccation and synaeresis mechanisms incapable of explaining cracks found in Cambrian carbonates. They argued that those cracks could not be mud cracks because when crumpled cracks from the same layer were "decompacted" or "uncrumpled," lengths varied between cracks by as much as 30 percent. Therefore the cracks could not have been straight initially, and most of the "crumpling" was due to the crack forming process, not compaction of the mud. The explanation usually given for the "crumpling" of most so-called mud cracks is that the mud was compacted more than sand-filled cracks during lithification, resulting in highly folded and contorted "mud cracks."

Molar-tooth structures have been variously interpreted, including desiccation and synaeresis origins (Pratt 1998a). Pratt argued that these unique cracks are earthquake-induced deformation structures. He cited 12 different reasons why he believes they formed under water, including finding no unequivocal desiccation cracks and multiple evidences of underwater origin. Many of the photos of cross sections that appear in his paper are very similar to "mud cracks."

Figure 15. Some of the sand-filled cracks at the base of the Coconino Sandstone are horizontally connected with each other, making their mud crack origin highly improbable. Dripping Springs, Grand Canyon.

Could Desiccation Mud Cracks Develop in the Flood?

Although I personally believe they are probably rare, true desiccation mud cracks may have formed during the Flood. Experiments (Baria 1977; Fellows 1951; Konrad and Ayad 1997) and observations (Krynine 1935) have shown that desiccation mud cracks can develop within hours, even under humid, damp conditions. Perhaps there were brief times during the Flood when fresh sediments were temporarily exposed due to tectonic uplift. Creationists have cited the brief exposure of land above the Flood water as an explanation for the formation of dinosaur tracks and "nests" in Mesozoic rocks (Oard 1995). Occasional desiccation cracks could have developed at the same time. After all, well-developed desiccation mud cracks forming rapidly during brief exposure at low tide have been reported (Dionne 1974). He noted that these cracks remained open during high tides and therefore had preservation potential. This may be a possible explanation for multiple layers of true desiccation cracks that may occasionally occur in the record.

Many of the cracks described in the literature of this chapter occur in clay-rich rocks (mudstones and shales) and are filled with sand-rich sediment from an adjacent layer. When clay-rich rocks are compacted and dewatered, the clay mineral lattices realign themselves and take up less space (Kidder 1990; Plummer and Gostin 1981; White 1961). Tension in the sediment is created and cracking ensues. Shrinkage can take place in many ways, including desiccation, chemical changes, sedimentary loading, and seismic activity (Lowe 1975; Pratt 1998b). Some clays are "thixotropic," meaning that they change from a loose, flocculated structure to an aligned structure during shaking (Owen 1987). This process can also open void spaces in water-rich or unconsolidated sediments. Depending on the mechanism of compaction and/or dewatering, different types of cracks will result (mud cracks, synaeresis cracks, diastasis cracks, etc.). The reason that so many of these cracks have similar characteristics is that the primary mechanism of shrinkage, the rearrangement of the clay mineral lattice, is similar in all cases! All types of shrinkage tend to produce polygonal-shaped cracks in plan view and V-shaped cracks in cross section. If adjacent sandy sediment is susceptible to fluidization, liquefied sand may force its way into cracks as they open. This may occur on a small scale (synaeresis and diastasis) or on a large scale (clastic dikes). In some cases, it is thought that pressurized, liquefied sand can propagate its own cracks (Boehm and Moore 2002; Jolly and Lonergan 2002).

Conclusion

True desiccation mud cracks may have formed in limited areas during the Flood. Observation has proven that mud cracks can form quickly, even during times of brief exposure and with damp sediments. However, there are several other mechanisms that can lead to clay shrinkage and subsequent sand-filling of cracks that can closely resemble mud cracks. "Mud cracked" horizons need to be studied carefully to see if there is actually any true evidence of desiccation. Polygonal-shaped and V-shaped sand-filled cracks are insufficient criteria to identify periods of desiccation. Instead, such things as crack fill material, fill orientation, mud curls, and surficial features should be used as conclusive criteria to identify mud cracks (table 6).

[Author's note: This manuscript was originally completed and submitted for review in January of 2006. After review, the final manuscript was submitted in May 2007. A few minor revisions were made to the manuscript in November of 2008. I thank the reviewers for their helpful suggestions in improving the manuscript.]

References

CRSQ: Creation Research Society Quarterly

Abbott, L., and T. Cook. 2004. *Hiking the Grand Canyon's Geology*. Seattle, WA: Mountaineers Books.

Allen, J.R.L. 1986. On the curl of desiccation polygons. *Sedimentary Geology* 46:23–31.

Anderson, E.M. 1951. *The Dynamics of Faulting and Dyke Formation with Applications to Britain*. London: Oliver and Boyd.

Astin, T.R., and D.A. Rogers. 1991. "Subaqueous shrinkage cracks" in the Devonian of Scotland reinterpreted. *Journal of Sedimentary Petrology* 61(5):850–859.

Austin, S.A. 1984. *Catastrophes in Earth History*. Technical Monograph 13. El Cajon, CA: Institute for Creation Research.

Austin, S.A., and J.D. Morris. 1986. Tight folds and clastic dikes as evidence for rapid deposition and deformation of two very thick stratigraphic sequences. In R.E. Walsh, C.L. Brooks, and R.S. Crowell (editors). *Proceedings of the First International Conference on Creationism*, volume II, (technical symposium sessions and additional topics). Pittsburgh, PA: Creation Science Fellowship, p. 3–15.

Barclay, W.J., B.W. Glover, and J.R. Mendum. 1993. "Subaqueous shrinkage cracks" in the Devonian of Scotland reinterpreted — discussion. *Journal of Sedimentary Petrology* 63:564–565.

Baria, L.R. 1977. Desiccation features and the reconstruction of paleosalinities. *Journal of Sedimentary Petrology* 47(2):908–914.

Blakey, R.C. 1990. Supai Group and Hermit Formation. In S.S. Beus and M. Morales (editors). *Grand Canyon Geology*. New York: Oxford University Press, p. 147–182.

Boehm, A., and J.C. Moore. 2002. Fluidized sandstone intrusions as an indicator of paleostress orientation, Santa Cruz, California. *Geofluids* 2:147–161.

Bradley, W.H. 1930. The behavior of certain mud crack casts during compaction. *American Journal of Science* 220:136–144.

Burst, J.F. 1965. Subaqueously formed shrinkage cracks in clay. *Journal of Sedimentary Petrology* 35(2):348–353.

Cowan, C.A., J.W. Bishop, and N.P. James. 2001. Experimental and field examples of subaqueous synsedimentary cracks in sediments. *Geological Society of America Abstracts with Programs* 33(6):443.

Cowan, C.A., and N.P. James. 1992. Diastasis cracks: mechanically generated synaeresis-like cracks in Upper Cambrian shallow water oolite and ribbon carbonates. *Sedimentology* 39:1101–1118.

Davis, W.M. 1889. Discussion. *Bulletin of the Geological Society of America* 1:442.

Diller, J.S. 1889. Sandstone dikes. *Bulletin of the Geological Society of America* 1:411–442.

Dionne, J.C. 1974. Mud cracks and polygons on ice push ridges, in tidal flats of the St. Lawrence Estuary. *Canadian Journal of Earth Sciences* 11:489–494.

Donovan, R.N., and R.J. Foster. 1972. Subaqueous shrinkage cracks for the Caithness Flagstone Series (Middle Devonian) of northeast Scotland. *Journal of Sedimentary Petrology* 42(2):309–317.

Dott, R.H. 1966. Cohesion and flow phenomena in clastic intrusions. *American Association of Petroleum Geologists Bulletin* 50:610–611.

Dow, W.G. 1964. The effect of salinity on the formation of mudcracks. *Compass of the Sigma Gamma Epsilon* 41(2):162–166.

Feldl, N., T.J. Bralower, and K.G. Stewart. 2002. K/T impact-related features at Moscow Landing, Alabama. *Geological Society of America Abstracts with Programs* 34(6):137.

Fellows, R.H., Jr. 1951. *Experiments in the Formation of Desiccation Cracks in Sediments*. Master's Thesis, Dallas, TX: Southern Methodist University.

Fife, D.L. 1977. Engineering geologic significance of giant desiccation polygons, Lucerne Valley Playa, San Bernardino County, California. *Geological Society of America Abstracts with Programs* 9(4):419.

Flower, R.H., and W.G. Ives. 1946. Subaqueous mud cracks formed by settling. *Science* 103:85–86.

Froede, C.R. Jr. 1994. Comments on "underwater mudcracks." *CRSQ* 31(2):71–72.

———. 1998. *Field Studies in Catastrophic Geology*. Chino Valley, AZ: Creation Research Society Books.

Goetz, L.K. 1980. Giant desiccation polygons in Wildhorse Flat, west Texas. In P.W. Dickerson and J.M. Hoffer (editors). *Trans-Pecos Region*, New Mexico Geological Society Guidebook, 31st Field Conference, p. 285–287.

Haff, J.C. 1944. Petrology of two clastic dikes from the Placerville District, Colorado. *American Journal of Science* 242:204–217.

Harms, J.C. 1965. Sandstone dikes in relation to Laramide faults and stress distribution in the southern Front Range, Colorado. *Geological Society of America Bulletin* 76:981–1002.

Hesse, R., and H.G. Reading. 1978. Subaqueous clastic fissure eruptions and other examples of sedimentary transportation in the lacustrine Horton Bluff Formation (Mississippian), Nova Scotia, Canada. In A. Matter and M.E. Tucker (editors). *Modern and Ancient Lake Sediments*. Special Publication No. 2 of the International Association of Sedimentologists. Oxford: Blackwell Scientific Publications, p. 241–257.

Hiscott, R.N. 1979. Clastic sills and dikes associated with deep-water sandstones, Tourelle Formation, Ordovician, Quebec. *Journal of Sedimentary Petrology* 49:1–10.

Jenkins, O.P. 1925a. Clastic dikes of eastern Washington and their geological significance. *American Journal of Science*, fifth series 10:234–246.

———. 1925b. Mechanics of clastic dike intrusion. *Engineering and Mining Journal-Press* 120(1):12.

Jolly, R.J.H., J.W. Cosgrove, and D.N. Dewhurst. 1998. Thickness and spatial distributions of clastic dykes, northwest Sacramento Valley, California. *Journal of Structural Geology* 20:1663–1672.

Jolly, R.J.H., and L. Lonergan. 2002. Mechanisms and controls on the formation of sand intrusions. *Journal of the Geological Society*, London 159:605–617.

Kidder, D.L. 1990. Facies-controlled shrinkage-crack assemblages in Middle Proterozoic mudstones from Montana, USA. *Sedimentology* 37:943–951.

Kindle, E.M. 1917. Some factors affecting the development of mud cracks. *Journal of Geology* 25:135–144.

Knoll, A.H. 1984. Microbiotas of the Late Precambrian Hunnberg Formation, Nordaustlandet, Svallbard. *Journal Paleontology* 58:131–162.

Konrad, J.M., and R. Ayad. 1997. Desiccation of a sensitive clay: Field experimental observations. *Canadian Geotechnical Journal* 34:929–942.

Kriz, J., and P. Stepanek. 1979. False mud cracks in the Lower Silurian of Bohemia. *Bulletin of the Geological Survey*, Prague 54(2):115–117.

Krynine, P.D. 1935. Formation and preservation of desiccation features in a humid climate. *American Journal of Science*, 5th Series 30(176):96–97.

Laird, M.G. 1970. Vertical sheet structures — a new indicator of sedimentary fabric. *Journal of Sedimentary Petrology* 40:428–434.

Lang, W.B. 1943. Gigantic drying cracks in Animas Valley, New Mexico. *Science* 98:583–584.

Longwell, C.R. 1928. Three common types of desert mudcracks. *American Journal of Science* 215:136–145.

Lowe, D.R. 1975. Water escape structures in coarse-grained sediments. *Sedimentology* 22:157–204.

———. 1976. Subaqueous liquefied and fluidized sediment flows and their deposits. *Sedimentology* 23:285–308.

MacCarthy, G.R. 1922. Mud cracks on steeply inclined surfaces. *Journal of Geology* 30:702.

McKee, E.D. 1934. The Coconino Sandstone — its history and origin. *Papers Concerning the Palaeontology of California, Arizona, and Idaho*. Publication No. 440. Washington, DC: Carnegie Institution, p. 77–115.

———. 1979. Ancient sandstones considered to be eolian. In E.D. McKee (editor). *A Study of Global Sand Seas*. U.S. Geological Survey Professional Paper 1052. Washington, DC: United States Government Printing Office, p. 187–238.

Minter, W.E.L. 1970. Origin of mud polygons that are concave downward. *Journal of Sedimentary Petrology* 40(2):755–756.

Moore, E.S. 1914. Mud cracks open under water. *American Journal of Science* 188:101–102.

Morton, G.R. 1982. Fossil succession. *CRSQ* 19(2):103–111, 90.

———. 1983. Reply to Woodmorappe. *CRSQ* 20(1):56–59.

———. 2003. *The multiple droughts during the global Flood* (web article), http://home.entouch.net/dmd/droughts.htm.

Neal, J.T., A.M. Langer, and P.F. Kerr. 1968. Giant desiccation polygons of Great Basin playas. *Geological Society of America Bulletin* 79:69–90.

Newsom, J.F. 1903. Clastic dikes. *Geological Society of America Bulletin* 14:227–268.

Nichols, R.J., R.S.J. Sparks, and C.J.N. Wilson. 1994. Experimental studies of the fluidization of layered sediments and the formation of fluid escape structures. *Sedimentology* 41:233–253.

Noble, L.F. 1922. *A Section of the Paleozoic Formations of the Grand Canyon at Bass Trail*. U.S. Geological Survey Professional Paper 131-B:23–73, Washington, DC.

Oard, M.J. 1994. Underwater "mudcracks." *CRSQ* 30(4):213–214.

———. 1995. Polar dinosaurs and the Genesis Flood. *CRSQ* 32(1):47–56.

Obermeier, S.F., E.C. Pond, S.M. Olson, and R.A. Green. 2002. Paleoliquefaction studies in continental settings. In F.R. Ettensohn, N. Rast, and C.E. Brett (editors). *Ancient Seismites*. Special Paper 359. Boulder, CO: Geological Society of America, p. 13–27.

Olsen, P.A., and L.E. Haugen. 1998. A new model of shrinkage characteristic applied to some Norwegian soils. *Geoderma* 83:67–81.

Owen, G. 1987. Deformation processes in unconsolidated sands. In M.E. Jones and R.M.F. Preston (editors). *Deformation of Sediments and Sedimentary Rocks*. Geological Society Special Publication 29. Oxford: Blackwell Scientific Publications, p. 11–24.

Peterson, G.L. 1968. Flow structures in sandstone dikes. *Sedimentary Geology* 2:177–190.

Petit, J.P., and E. Laville. 1987. Morphology and microstructures of hydroplastic slickensides in sandstone. In M.E. Jones and R.M.F. Preston (editors). *Deformation of Sediments and Sedimentary Rocks*. Geological Society Special Publication No. 29. Oxford: Blackwell Scientific Publications, p. 107–121.

Plaziat, J.C., B.H. Purser, and E. Philobbos. 1990. Seismic deformation structures (seismites) in the syn-rift sediments of the NW Red Sea (Egypt). *Bulletin de la Societe Geologique de France* 6(3):419–434.

Plummer, P.S., and V.A. Gostin. 1981. Shrinkage cracks: desiccation or synaeresis? *Journal of Sedimentary Petrology* 51(4):1147–1156.

Pogue, K.R. 1998. Earthquake-generated(?) structures in Missoula flood slackwater sediments (Touchet Beds) of southeastern Washington. *Geological Society of America Abstracts with Programs* 30(7):398–399.

Pratt, B.R. 1998a. Molar-tooth structure in Proterozoic carbonate rocks: origin from synsedimentary earthquakes, and implications for the nature and evolution of basins and marine sediment. *Geological Society of America Bulletin* 110(8):1028–1045.

———. 1998b. Synaeresis cracks: Subaqueous shrinkage in argillaceous sediments caused by earthquake-induced dewatering. *Sedimentary Geology* 117:1–10.

Raza, M., S. Rais, and R.A. Akhunji. 1981. Occurrence of pseudo-mudcracks in Talchir sediments, near Ambikapur, Madhya Pradesh. *Current Science* 50(19):858–859.

Reimnitz, E., and N.F. Marshall. 1965. Effects of the Alaska earthquake and tsunami on recent deltaic sediments. *Journal of Geophysical Research* 70:2363–2376.

Reineck, H.E., and I.B. Singh. 1980. *Depositional Sedimentary Environments*. New York: Springer-Verlag.

Seed, H.B., and K.L. Lee. 1966. Liquefaction of saturated sands during cyclic loading. *Proceedings of the American Society of Civil Engineers, Soil Mechanics and Foundations Division* 92(SM 6):105–134.

Shoulders, S.J. and J. Cartwright. 2004. Constraining the depth and timing of large-scale conical sandstone intrusions. *Geology* 32:661–664.

Shrock, R.R. 1948. *Sequence in Layered Rocks*. New York: McGraw-Hill.

Silver, M.H., and K.R. Pogue. 2002. Analysis of plan-view geometry of clastic dike networks in Missoula flood slackwater sediments (Touchet Beds), southeastern Washington. *Geological Society of America Abstracts with Programs* 34(5):24.

Sipes, C.R., and R.A. Peters. 2000. Giant desiccation polygons in the surface of the Hermit Formation, Grand Canyon, Arizona. *Geological Society of America Abstracts with Programs* 32(7):310–311.

Smoot, J.P. 1981. Subaerial exposure criteria in modern playa mud cracks. *American Association of Petroleum Geologists Bulletin* 65(5):994–995.

———. 1983. Depositional subenvironments in an arid closed basin: the Wilkins Peak Member of the Green River Formation (Eocene), Wyoming, USA. *Sedimentology* 30:801–827.

Snyman, A.A. 1950. Note on unusual mudcracks in a pan on the Farm Oxford, Odendaalsrus, O.F.S. *Geological Society of South Africa* 52:203–204.

Stewart, K.G. 2003. Forcefully injected clastic dikes and sills associated with the K/T impact tsunami. *Geological Society of America Abstracts with Programs* 35(6):602.

Stewart, K.G., J.M. Dennison, and M.J. Bartholomew. 2002. Late Mississippian paleoseismites from southeastern West Virginia and southwestern Virginia. In F.R. Ettensohn, N. Rast, and C.E. Brett (editors). *Ancient Seismites*. Special Paper 359. Boulder, CO: Geological Society of America, p. 127–144.

Truswell, J.F. 1972. Sandstone sheets and related intrusions from Coffee Bay, Transkei, South Africa. *Journal of Sedimentary Petrology* 42:578–583.

Twenhofel, W.H. 1923. Development of shrinkage cracks in sediments without exposure to the atmosphere. *Geological Society of America Bulletin* 34(1):64.

Walton, M.S., and R.B. O'Sullivan. 1950. The intrusive mechanics of a clastic dike. *American Journal of Science* 248:1–21.

Waterston, C.D. 1950. Note on the sandstone injections of Eathie Haven, Cromarty. *Geological Magazine* 87:133–139.

Wheeler, H.E., and J.J. Quinlan. 1951. Precambrian sinuous mud cracks from Idaho and Montana. *Journal of Sedimentary Petrology* 21(3):141–146.

White, D. 1929. *Flora of the Hermit Shale, Grand Canyon, Arizona*. Publication 405, Washington, DC: Carnegie Institution of Washington.

White, W.A. 1961. Colloid phenomena in sedimentation of argillaceous rocks. *Journal of Sedimentary Petrology* 31(4):560–570.

Whitmore, J.H. 1988. *The Hartford Basin of Central Connecticut: An Evaluation of Uniformitarian and Catastrophic Models*. Master's Thesis. Santee, CA: Institute for Creation Research.

———. 2004. An alternative to the mud crack origin for sand-filled cracks at the base of the Coconino Sandstone, Grand Canyon, Arizona. *Geological Society of America Abstracts with Programs* 36(5):55.

———. 2005. Origin and significance of sand-filled cracks and other features near the base of the Coconino Sandstone, Grand Canyon, Arizona, USA. *CRSQ* 42(3):163–180.

Whitmore, J.H., and P. Garner. 2008. Using suites of criteria to recognize pre-Flood, Flood, and post-Flood strata in the rock record with application to Wyoming (USA). In A.A. Snelling (editor). *Proceedings of the Sixth International Conference on Creationism*. Pittsburgh, PA: Creation Science Fellowship and Dallas, TX: Institute for Creation Research, p. 425–448.

Whitmore, J.H., and R.A. Peters. 1999. Reconnaissance study of the contact between the Hermit Formation and the Coconino Sandstone, Grand Canyon, Arizona. *Geological Society of America Abstracts with Programs* 31(7):A235.

Whitmore, J.H., and R. Strom. 2005. Sandstone clast breccias, homogenized sand, and sand intrusions: evidence of substratal liquefaction in the basal Coconino Sandstone (Permian), Grand Canyon, Arizona. *Geological Society of America Abstracts with Programs* 37(7):440.

Wilden, R., and D.R. Mabey. 1961. Giant desiccation fissures on the Black Rock and Smoke Creek Deserts, Nevada. *Science* 133:1359–1360.

Willard, B. 1925. Mud cracks forming over water. *Journal of Geology* 33:286–287.

Winston, D. 1990. Evidence for intracratonic, fluvial, and lacustrine settings of Middle to Late Proterozoic basins of western U.S.A. In C. Gower, T. Rivers, and B. Ryan (editors). *Mid-Proterozoic Laurentia-Baltica*. Special Paper 38. St. John's, Newfoundland: Geological Association of Canada, p. 535–564.

Woodmorappe, J. 1986. Some additional comments concerning several matters: part II. *CRSQ* 23(2):79–83.

Yassoglou, N., C.S. Kosmas, N. Mousakas, E. Tzianis, and N.G. Danalatos. 1994. Cracking in recent alluvial soils as related to easily determined soil properties. *Geoderma* 63:289–298.

Chapter 11

Radiometric Dating: Challenging an Icon of Evolutionary Geology

Andrew A. Snelling • PhD — Geology

Abstract

Routinely used to calculate ages of millions and billions of years for rock strata and the earth itself, radiometric dating methods rely on radioactive parent atoms of several elements decaying at constant known rates to daughter atoms of other elements. Three crucial assumptions — initial conditions known, no contamination, constant decay rates — are necessary in calculating ages for a rock. Model ages are calculated for single rock samples, whereas isochron ages are derived from four or more samples from the same rock unit. However, persistent problems have been encountered with the four primary parent-daughter pairs used. Potassium-argon dating is plagued by problems with the inheritance or loss of argon gas. Excess argon in rocks and minerals yields excessively old, unreliable "ages." Inheritance, contamination, and open-system behavior also affect the rubidium-strontium system, so that it has lost credibility as a reliable dating method. Even the samarium-neodymium system, once thought to be immune from being perturbed, has been shown to be unreliable, due to Sm and Nd mobility at moderate to high temperatures, and transport by hot water migrating through rocks. Loss of uranium and/or lead from rocks and minerals has always made uranium-thorium-lead dating highly suspect. Yet the U-Th-Pb dating of zircon grains is now the most used method, in spite of documented Pb diffusion, compositional zoning, and inhomogeneities that yield spectrums of "ages," and the regular inheritance of zircons from older rocks. Now it has been shown that using all four of these methods on the same samples from the same rocks produces "ages" different by hundreds of millions of years. Interestingly, such "ages" vary in a systematic manner according to the type of radioactive decay, and the half-lives and atomic weights of the parent radioisotopes. Evidence indicates that radioactive decay rates were highly accelerated during some event(s) in the past. Thus, because all three crucial assumptions fail, radiometric dating is fatally flawed and cannot yield valid "ages."

Introduction

Without doubt, the most important and serious objection to Flood geology is the issue of time. Critics of Flood geology claim that the earth and its various rock strata are millions to billions of years old, immensely older than the straightforward reading of biblical history that explains most of earth's geologic features as the result of a recent creation and the Flood.

There have been many different ways geologists have attempted to measure the absolute age of the earth and its various rock layers and features. In each case, some physical or chemical process is involved whose present rate can be measured. The total accumulation of the products of the process is also measured. It is then a simple matter to calculate how long the process must have proceeded. However, most of these processes have proven inadequate in providing consistent and suitable ages because of the many unknown and immeasurable factors. That is why over the last century radiometric dating has become the most important geologic chronometer, yielding the now-accepted age of the earth at 4.55±0.07 billion years (Ga).[1]

What Is Radiometric Dating?

Radiometric dating is based on the radioactive decay of various isotopes found in many minerals. The present decay rates of these elements are known, so if both the parent and daughter elements are found in measurable quantities, then a relatively simple calculation yields the isotopic "age." This is then declared to be the age of the rock. The most important and routinely used of these methods measure the disintegration of the following:

1. uranium (U) and thorium (Th) into helium (He) and lead (Pb)

2. rubidium (Rb) into strontium (Sr)

3. potassium (K) into argon (Ar)

4. samarium (Sm) into neodymium (Nd)

More specialized methods involve the disintegration of lutetium (Lu) into hafnium (Hf), and rhenium (Re) into osmium (Os). All these parent elements decay very slowly, so the methods automatically "measure" millions to billions of years. For younger suspected ages (i.e., archeological relics), the short-age radiocarbon method is used. It is based on the formation of radioactive carbon (^{14}C) in the atmosphere by cosmic radiation, and its subsequent decay to stable nitrogen. Because carbon is the element on which organic materials are built, the radiocarbon method can only be used for "dating" organic-based materials, and because ^{14}C decays rapidly, the method only yields "ages" measured in thousands of years.

There is no question that these methods, apart from radiocarbon, give estimates for the age of earth and its rock layers immensely greater than any possible estimate based on biblical chronology. Furthermore, because they yield such precise numbers, the general public is easily convinced of their accuracy, too. However, all the scientific *measurements* of parent and daughter isotopes rest squarely on the assumptions made when *interpreting* them. If the assumptions are faulty, then the interpreted "ages" will also be faulty.

---

1. This date is based on the U-Th-Pb dating of meteorites, based on current (unprovable) theories about how the solar system formed.

Technical details of the analyses of rocks and minerals and the calculation of radiometric "ages" are provided in specialist textbooks. I recommend Dickin (2005) and Faure and Mensing (2005), as well as the good, simplified summaries of Austin (1994) and DeYoung (2000).

The Assumptions of Radiometric Dating

Measuring time by radioactive decay is often compared to the measurement of time by sand grains falling through an hourglass (figure 1). The sand in the upper chamber of an hourglass represents a radioactive parent element, while the sand in the lower chamber is analogous to the respective daughter element. The sand grains falling from the upper chamber at a constant rate are like radioactive decay. If all the sand grains started in the upper chamber, knowing the numbers of sand grains in the two chambers and the rate at which the sand grains fall enables a calculation of how much time has passed. For radioactive "clocks," this starting time is when the rock and its minerals form.

Thus the calculation of the "age" of a rock or mineral requires three crucial assumptions:

1. The initial number of atoms of the daughter element in the rock or mineral when it crystallized. In the potassium-argon (K-Ar) method, geologists usually assume no original daughter Ar, so that all the daughter Ar in the rock or mineral is from radioactive decay of potassium.

2. The numbers of atoms of the parent and daughter elements have not been altered except by radioactive decay since the rock or mineral crystallized.

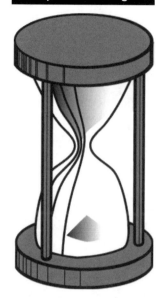

Metaphor of hourglass

Figure 1. An hourglass illustrates radioactive decay in a rock sample. The radioactive parent atoms and their daughter atoms are represented by the sand grains in the upper and lower chambers respectively. The rate of radioactive decay is controlled by the relevant half-life, just as the rate of falling sand grains is controlled by the width of the neck of the hourglass.

In other words, the rock or mineral has remained closed to loss or gain of either parent or daughter.

3. The rate of decay of the parent element is known and has not changed since the rock or mineral crystallized.

These assumptions impose certain restraints on the interpretation of radiometric "ages." They simply cannot be proven, because no human observers were present to determine the numbers of atoms of daughter elements originally present when most rocks or minerals crystallized. Nor were human observers present to determine that the rocks and minerals have remained closed to loss or gain of parent and/or daughter isotopes and that the decay rates have not changed. Thus it logically follows that these assumptions cannot be proven.

Scientists have been reticent to face this fact. They often claim that they know when assumption (2) fails, because "anomalous" results are obtained. But no one knows what results are "anomalous" unless they already know the true age. Thus, what they mean by "anomalous" is that a result does not agree with the age they expect. They fail to see that there is no way to know whether the expected "age" is correct. Admitting that the closed system assumption has failed in one case means that it might not be true in any other case — even when so-called acceptable results are obtained. Although the first two assumptions are shaky, scientists assume that the third is solid. But this means that radiometric dating is an extreme form of uniformitarianism. Decay rates have proven constant for (at the most) 100 years. But they must have been constant for millions and billions of years if the dating methods are valid — an extrapolation of up to seven orders of magnitude!

A radioactive date determined for an individual rock or mineral is called a *model age*. Calculating the model age can succeed only if the original amount of daughter element is known. For K-Ar dating, geologists assume that there was no daughter argon in the rock or mineral when it formed. Argon is an inert gas not expected to be chemically retained in the crystal structure of the mineral constituents of a given rock. But that is not always the case. Geologists expect daughter strontium to be present in rocks when they form, along with other isotopes of strontium not derived by radioactive decay. Because they cannot know the original ratio of parent/daughter strontium, geologists have devised a technique to circumvent that problem.

This technique is the *isochron age* method from the Greek, *isos* (equal) and *chronis* (time). For this method to

work, at least four rock samples from the same geologic unit, or at least three mineral samples from the same rock, must be obtained (since the whole-rock parent-daughter values can also be used for the isochron). The goal is to obtain samples that would have formed at about the same time. However, the geologic processes that formed the samples may not have evenly distributed parent rubidium and daughter strontium atoms. If the sample set is different minerals from the same rock, there will undoubtedly be different amounts of parent and daughter atoms because different minerals have different abilities to bind different elements in their crystal structures. Nevertheless, it is assumed that the sample has a uniform ratio of daughter strontium to other strontium isotopes. Of course, over time that ratio will be altered as radioactive decay transforms rubidium into more strontium. In any case, for the isochron dating method to work, all rock samples have to be from the same rock unit and possess a uniform ratio of daughter strontium to other strontium. These two conditions replace the first assumption — that the number of original daughter atoms must be known, which is used to obtain model ages.

The isochron dating method works by plotting measurements of parent and daughter isotopes from (in this case) six samples from a rock unit (figure 2). All samples are believed to have formed at the same time. A line with a positive slope can be plotted through five of the six samples (figure 2c). The sixth measurement lies off the line, and would thus be interpreted to have been altered by some geologic process. As an "outlier," it would usually be ignored in subsequent calculations. The interpretation in figure 2a assumes that the line provides the age for the five "good" samples. Figure 2b shows how the age is interpreted. When the samples (and the rock unit) formed, they all had the same abundance of the daughter element (zero time equals zero slope of the line). As time passed, the parent decreased and the daughter increased in a uniform manner according to the different abundances of the parent element in the rock samples. Since the ratio is the same, any point on the line will represent the same age (defined by the slope of the line). In figure 2b, it is evident that the slope of the line increases as time passes. The age is thus calculated from the slope of the isochron that best fits the analyses of the samples (figure 2c).

The isochron technique is the most widely used radiometric dating method for two reasons. First, no assumption about the initial conditions is thought necessary, because the isochron line itself can be used to determine the initial daughter element abundance (figure 2). Second, if contamination, weathering, or other geologic processes have perturbed the parent and/or daughter concentrations, then those samples will not plot on the isochron line (or so it is assumed). This technique is primarily used for the Rb-Sr, Sm-Nd, and U-Th-Pb methods, but can also be used for specialized applications of the Lu-Hf and Re-Os methods.

Anomalies that Defy and Disprove the Assumptions

One has only to research the uniformitarian literature to find numerous examples of problems with all of the radiometric systems that violate one or more of the crucial three assumptions. That being the case, these "absolute" dating methods all rest on a very shaky foundation and appear to be used more to reinforce uniformitarian bias toward deep time in reconstructing the earth's fascinating past.

An extensive survey of the many documented problems with each of four major radiometric dating systems is provided in an appendix. Many of these anomalies that defy and disprove the assumptions crucial to the radiometric methods are openly recognized in the conventional geology community, being documented in the main geochronology textbooks (Dickin 2005; Faure and Mensing 2005). These include much evidence that daughter isotopes not necessarily derived by radioactive decay are routinely inherited by magmas and lavas from their mantle and crustal sources, and that both parent and daughter isotopes easily migrate out of and/or into rocks and their constituent minerals. Heat can perturb the radiometric systems, as can both ground and hot volcanic waters migrating through rocks and minerals. Thus contamination and open-system behavior are rife. Mineral grains can also

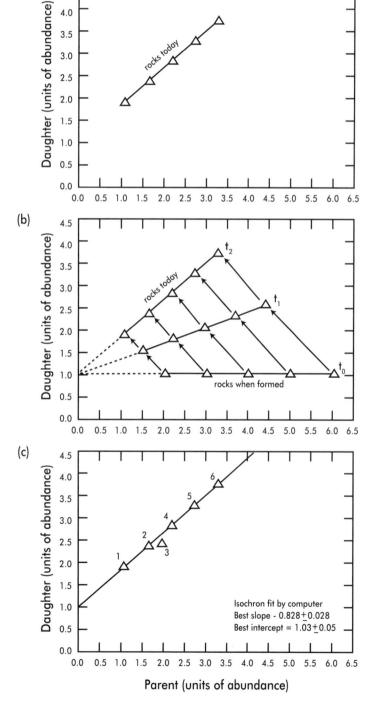

Examples of isochron dating methods

Figure 2. The assumptions and methods of isochron dating are illustrated by diagrams plotting the parent-daughter analyses of samples from a hypothetical rock unit. (a) Analyses of five samples from the rock unit indicate that their parent-versus-daughter compositions plot today as a linear array having a positive slope. (b) The isochron model suggests that the five samples, when the rock unit formed, all had the same abundance of daughter (1.0 unit of abundance in this case), but different abundances of parent. The compositions of the samples today are assumed to have been derived by significant radioactive decay of the parent and accumulation of the daughter. (c) Parent-daughter analyses of six samples from the rock unit are plotted with error bars. A computer program determines the "best-fit" line through the data points. The slope of the line can be used to estimate the "age" of this rock unit. The greater the slope, the greater the "age."

be compositionally zoned or contain inhomogeneities, both of which result in spectrums of vastly different "ages." So even if the constructed maze of these methods looks internally consistent, it is a house of cards, with foundations riddled with systematic errors and with questionable dates at every turn.

Systematic Differences

Despite these numerous problems with each method, geologists claim that results must be valid because large amounts of radioactive decay representing millions of years have occurred. They offer evidence that must be addressed by young-earth proponents, including the following:

1. the presence of decay products such as lead and helium occurring with parent uranium in proportions that indicate radioactive decay

2. radiohalos, which are physical scars left by radioactive decay (Snelling 2000b, 2005a)

3. fission tracks, which are physical scars left by the nuclear decay of uranium atoms as they split (Snelling 2005b)

Additionally, creationists must deal with the supposed agreement between different dating methods. Textbooks give the impression that the ages derived by different methods applied to the same rocks are generally always in agreement. Sometimes this is specifically stated:

> The achievement of concordant K-Ar, Rb-Sr, and U-Pb ages on rocks (where chemical systems have remained closed) supports the invariance of decay constants with time, since different radionuclides would be expected to respond differently if decay constants had changed (Dickin 1995, p. 14).

However, Dickin (2005), in the second edition of his 1995 textbook, does not repeat the above statement! Furthermore, detailed investigation of the relevant geologic literature indicates that rarely, if ever, have all the major radiometric methods been used to date the same sample. This seems to be because different methods are more suitable for different rock units and/or because the different decay rates of some parent isotopes are not suited to the expected ages of the rocks. Nevertheless, when two or more dating methods are applied to the same rock, different ages are often obtained. These "anomalies" are usually explained by the hypothetical action of some geochemical process or geologic event (e.g., circulating hydrothermal fluids) that

has selectively perturbed one or more of the radiometric systems.

For example, the Stuart dyke swarm of south-central Australia yielded a Sm-Nd mineral isochron age of 1,076±33 million years (m.y.) and a Rb-Sr mineral isochron age of 897±9 m.y. (Zhao and McCulloch 1993). Similarly, the Uruguayan dike swarm in South America yielded a Rb-Sr whole-rock isochron age of 1,766±124 m.y. and a Rb-Sr mineral isochron age of 1,366±18 m.y. (Teixeira et al. 1999). In neither case is a satisfactory and feasible explanation given for these differences. In contrast, an "explanation" was offered for the different radiometric ages yielded by the Great Dyke of Zimbabwe, southeast Africa. A Rb-Sr whole-rock isochron age of 2,477±90 m.y. (Davies et al. 1970) was subsequently confirmed independently in separate studies by Rb-Sr whole-rock and mineral isochron ages of 2,455±16 m.y. (Hamilton 1977) and 2,467±85 m.y. (Mukasa et al. 1998). Yet the latter study also reported a Sm-Nd whole-rock isochron age of 2,586±16 m.y., a Pb-Pb mineral and whole-rock isochron age of 2,596±14 m.y., and a U-Pb age using the mineral rutile of 2,587±8 m.y. Furthermore, another study reported identical U-Pb ages using the mineral zircon (Oberthür et al. 2002). Thus, even though three independent studies had all yielded an identical Rb-Sr age for this intrusion, it was rejected in favor of the approximately 120 m.y. older, identical radiometric age obtained by the Sm-Nd, Pb-Pb, and U-Pb methods. The reason given for rejecting the younger Rb-Sr age was that hydrothermal alteration must have reset the Rb-Sr system, in spite of the fact that there is no observational evidence, or any other geochemical indicators, of such hydrothermal alteration!

To investigate the extent of agreement between different methods, recent studies dated four rock units in the Grand Canyon using the four major methods on the same rock and mineral samples. This was done for rocks and minerals from the Bass Rapids diabase sill, the Cardenas Basalt flows, the Brahma amphibolites, and the Elves Chasm Granodiorite (figure 3).

The Bass Rapids diabase sill is ideal for radiometric dating because it formed as molten magma that was homogenized when injected between the host sedimentary strata. It yielded a K-Ar isochron age of 841.5±164 m.y., a Rb-Sr isochron age of 1,055±46 m.y., and a Pb-Pb isochron age of 1,250±130 m.y. (Austin 2005; Snelling et al. 2003) (figure 4). Additionally, minerals separated from one diabase sample yielded a Rb-Sr mineral isochron age of 1,060±24 m.y. and a Sm-Nd mineral isochron age of 1,379±140 m.y. Even though there are small overlaps

Dating rocks with different methods

Figure 3. Generalized geologic block diagram showing most of the strata sequence and topographic form below the north rim of Grand Canyon (from Austin 1994). The stratigraphic positions and relationships are shown for the Middle Proterozoic Cardenas Basalt and the likely related diabase sills, including the Bass Rapids sill, for the Brahma amphibolites and the Elves Chasm Granodiorite, and for the Quaternary Uinkaret Plateau basalts and the resultant lava dams.

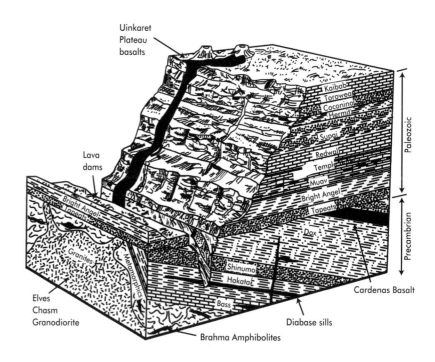

between the error margins of some of these dates, they are still quite different for each radiometric system. The Cardenas Basalt flows, believed to be related to the Bass Rapids and other nearby diabase sills, yielded a K-Ar isochron age of only 516±30 m.y., less than half the Rb-Sr isochron age of 1,111±81 m.y., while the Sm-Nd isochron age of 1,588±170 m.y. is more than three times the K-Ar isochron age (Austin and Snelling 1998; Snelling 2005c) (figure 5). The Brahma amphibolites, metamorphosed basalt lava flows, yielded K-Ar model "ages" ranging from 405.1±10 to 2,574.2±73 m.y. (Snelling 2005c). Furthermore, two samples collected only 0.84 millimeters (2.75 ft.) apart from the same outcrop yielded K-Ar model "ages" of 1,205.3±31 and 2,574.2±73 m.y.! Otherwise, these metamorphosed basalts yielded a Rb-Sr isochron age of 1,240±84 m.y., a Sm-Nd isochron age of 1,655±40 m.y., and a Pb-Pb isochron age of 1,883±53 m.y. (figure 6). And finally, the Elves Chasm Granodiorite, regarded as the oldest rock unit in Grand Canyon, yielded a Rb-Sr isochron age of 1,512±140 m.y., a Sm-Nd isochron age of 1,664±200 m.y., and a Pb-Pb isochron age of 1,993±220 m.y. (Snelling 2005c) (figure 7).

The major radiometric techniques yielded consistently different ages for the same samples from these four rock units. This totally destroys the popular idea (regrettably

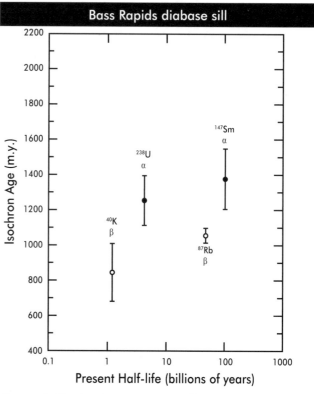

Figure 4. The isochron "ages" yielded by the four radioisotope systems for the Bass Rapids diabase sill, Grand Canyon, plotted against the present half-lives of those parent radioisotopes according to their mode of decay.

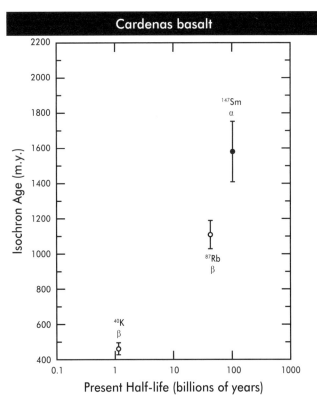

Figure 5. The isochron "ages" yielded by three radioisotope systems for the Cardenas Basalt, Grand Canyon, plotted against the present half-lives of the parent radioisotopes according to their mode of decay.

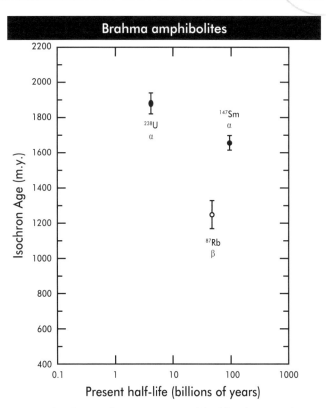

Figure 6. The isochron "ages" yielded by three radio-isotope systems for the Brahma amphibolites, Grand Canyon, plotted against the present half-lives of the parent radioisotopes according to their mode of decay.

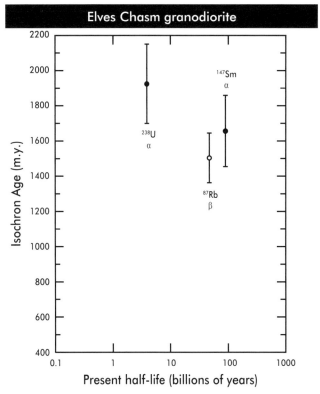

Figure 7. The isochron "ages" yielded by three radioisotope systems for the Elves Chasm Granodiorite, Grand Canyon, plotted against the present half-lives of the parent radioisotopes according to their mode of decay.

reinforced by textbooks) that these methods all agree. But creationists were not content to simply demonstrate that failure. Additional work was done to evaluate the positive meaning of these results. The different ages are not random but consistently follow several systematic patterns. For all four rock units, and also for the Great Dyke of Zimbabwe, the α-decaying parents (uranium and samarium) always yield older ages than the β-decaying parents (potassium and rubidium) (see figures 4–7). Furthermore, among the β decayers, the parent with the longer half-life (rubidium) always gives the older ages. In contrast, the α decayers (uranium and samarium) do not always follow this half-life versus age trend. But there appears to be another systematic relationship between isochron age and the atomic weight of the radioactive parents (figure 8). For many of these Grand Canyon rock units, the isochron ages increase in the same order as the increasing atomic weights of potassium, rubidium, samarium, and uranium, respectively. Further testing is obviously required to confirm one or more of these trends, but already there is sufficient evidence that there are systematic differences in the ages derived from the same rocks by the different radiometric methods. This hints at some underlying process or processes that act in tandem with radioactive decay to produce these ages. If there is another unknown factor(s), then the radiometric "clocks," as currently applied, cannot produce reliable valid ages for rocks.

Accelerated Decay

Although it is clear that arguments about mutually supporting methods are not valid, what about the evidence of million of years of decay presented at the beginning of the previous section? Both those and the systematic differences in radiometric ages from different methods can be explained by the same factor — the accelerated decay of isotopes in the past. This was conceded as a possibility by Dickin (1995), as quoted above, and explored more fully by the recent RATE project.[2] Researchers proposed that radioactive decay was accelerated by different amounts for different radioactive parents according to their atomic weights and half-lives (Vardiman et al. 2005). Thus, the U-Pb and Sm-Nd (α-decaying) "clocks" had their decay rates accelerated more than the K-Ar and Rb-Sr (β-decaying) "clocks" so that the former appear to have "ticked" longer, yielding older ages.

Potential accelerated decay during some event or events in the past is supported by other evidence:

1. A young (6,000 years) age based on helium diffusion for zircons that yield U-Pb dates of 1,500 m.y. (Humphreys 2005).

2. The concurrent formation of ubiquitous uranium and polonium radiohalos in biotite mica flakes in many granites (Snelling 2005a).

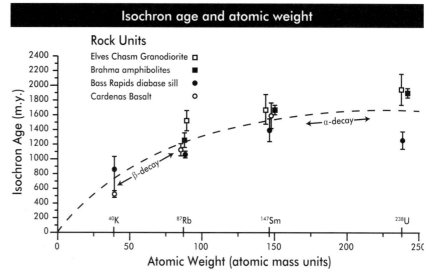

Figure 8. Composite plot of isochron "age" versus atomic weight for four radioisotope pairs and four Precambrian formations in the Grand Canyon from Austin (2005) and Snelling (2005c).

3. Resetting of the U-Pb system only within zircon grains by the intense heat due to the accelerated decay, while the volcanic ash beds containing those zircon grains were otherwise relatively unheated (Snelling 2005b).

4. The presence of measurable radiocarbon yielding young ages in coal and diamonds that are supposed to be millions and billions of years old, respectively, based on other radiometric methods (Baumgardner 2005).

These lines of evidence pointing toward accelerated radioactive decay during some event or events in the past are difficult to refute. This, of course, raises the question of a mechanism for accelerated decay. Several theoretical mechanisms have been suggested and discussed (Chaffin 2000a, 2000b, 2003, 2005; Humphreys 2000). The technical details are too complex to discuss here, but suffice it to say, they involve changes in the forces within the nuclei that control radioactive decay. More information is available in the references cited.

Responses to Critics

Because creationists have critiqued the reliability of radiometric dating for some time, there are a number of common criticisms from old-earth opponents, including those directed at the suggestion of accelerated radioactive decay to explain millions of years within a young-earth time frame. It is thus appropriate to respond to those in turn.

2. The eight-year RATE (**R**adioisotopes and the **A**ge of **T**he **E**arth) project was begun in 1997 by the Institute for Creation Research when it invited seven scientists (geologists, geophysicists, and physicists), with the support of the Creation Research Society, to research the radiometric dating methods, and to investigate their reliability and how the "ages" of supposed millions and billions of years they provide can be reconciled with the clear biblical teaching of a young earth.

Creationist Researchers Are Not Appropriately Qualified

Young-earth creationists have had formal university training in geochronology, up to and including the PhD level. Indeed, my own PhD focused on an Australian uranium deposit and involved geochemical and radiometric studies (Snelling 1982). Furthermore, analytical work in creationist studies has been done by PhD geologists through recognized, well-established university and commercial laboratories in consultation with PhD geochronologists in those laboratories. The calculation of all radiometric ages from the analytical results used software developed and used by the geochronology community (Ludwig 2001). Nevertheless, although these qualifications are important, the primary response to such criticism must be that ad hominem arguments are not answers to substantive problems raised by creationists. The validity of the *results* depends on the work done, not the individual doing it.

Poor Selection and Sampling of Rock Units

The rock units chosen for study, such as those discussed earlier from the Grand Canyon, are all rock units that old-earth geologists have already dated, so the suitability of those rock units for radiometric analyses is hardly in question! In most cases, radiometric dating by young-earth creationists simply duplicated and confirmed previous dating done by conventional geochronologists using the same radiometric methods. Our studies have simply increased the radiometric database on these rock units. As for the accusation of poor sampling of the rock units studied, it is blatantly false and slanderous. The PhD geologists who did the sampling were all trained to select the best samples from the outcrops for geochemical and geochronological analyses, and followed the best possible practices in sample selection. Since critics have not specified these "poor practices," it appears that this is another ad hominem attack. If that is their best response to the results, it only adds weight to our conclusions.

Selective Quoting and Citing of Problems by Creationists

Another ad hominem accusation (also lacking specifics) is that creationists misquote the relevant literature. Again, if these are their strongest criticisms, then their case is pretty weak. The examples of problems with the radiometric dating methods used by young-earth creationists are usually those cited by the conventional geology community in their own literature, and even in the standard geochronology textbooks (Dickin 1995, 2005; Faure 1986; Faure and Mensing 2005). Even the same selection of quotes has been made from those papers and textbooks. Thus, if young-earth creationists are selective of examples and quoting, then the conventional geology community is as equally selective!

All Radiometric Methods Still Yield "Ages" of Millions of Years Anyway!

Logically, demonstrated uncertainties in the radiometric methods place the burden of proof on those who assert the validity of the methods. The assumption that atomic concentrations and ratios have time significance has not been demonstrated conclusively, so their claim that these methods show a general, though not precise, old age is inherently fallacious. Indeed, one further example from the Grand Canyon should surely suffice to illustrate the complete absurdity of their claim. Across the Uinkaret Plateau on the north rim of the western Grand Canyon are up to 160 volcanic cones from which basalt lavas flowed southward into the inner gorge of Grand Canyon (Hamblin 1989, 1990, 1994, 2003) (see figure 3). These lavas are recent, erupting after the Grand Canyon had been eroded and cascading down the north wall. There they formed dams that temporarily filled the inner gorge, blocking the flow of the Colorado River. Geologists support their young age with K-Ar model ages of around 0.5–1.0 m.y. (Dalrymple and Hamblin 1998). However, the same basalts yield a Rb-Sr isochron age of 1,143±220 m.y. (Austin 1994; Snelling 2005c), which is almost identical to the Rb-Sr isochron age of 1,111±81 m.y. for the Cardenas Basalt! So the "youngest" basalts in the Grand Canyon are the same age as the "oldest"! The only explanation offered for this discrepancy is that the "young" Uinkaret Plateau basalts must have inherited their Rb-Sr isochron age from their mantle source, deep beneath the Grand Canyon region (Leeman 1982; Snelling 2005c). But if so, then why did not the Cardenas Basalt lavas also inherit their Rb-Sr age from the same mantle source? Another explanation would be that the millions of years are meaningless. Furthermore, the claim that we should place confidence in such shaky results to yield valid ages is even more absurd in the face of evidence for decay accelerated by up to five or more orders of magnitude (Humphreys 2005). After all, the 6,000 years measured by helium diffusion was "dated" to be 1,500 m.y. by U-Pb zircon ages. Any pretense that the radiometric methods yield ages of millions of years is simply arm waving!

The Heat and Radiation Produced by the Burst of Grossly Accelerated Radioactive Decay Would Be Destructive

These apparent problems have been acknowledged and discussed by creationists (Vardiman et al. 2005). A possible solution has been tentatively suggested by Humphreys (2000, 2005). Since radiohalos and fission tracks are obliterated at relatively low temperatures, if there had been a heat problem due to accelerated radioactive and nuclear decay, then we should not find radiohalos and fission tracks in the rocks today — but we do (Snelling 2005a, 2005b).

Sadly, many of the critics who make some of these claims against young-earth creationists and their research are not qualified to do geochronology research and/or they have not carefully read and comprehended all the appropriate technical details provided by the young-earth creationist researchers in their reports and papers.

Conclusions

There are many problems with each of the radiometric dating methods. These are admitted by the conventional geologic community in their own papers and textbooks, yet they fail to draw the common sense inference that these methods are highly questionable at best. In spite of these known problems, the millions of years demanded by the geologic time scale and evolution are accepted and research continues with these flawed methods because they are consistent with the evolutionary model of earth history. Though reluctantly admitted, the problems are usually ignored because radiometric methods are thought to be at least generally correct, in spite of the fact that these anomalies defy and disprove the very assumptions foundational to the methods. Furthermore, where more than one of these radiometric methods has been used on the same rocks and different ages have been obtained, geologists offer tenuous explanations for which physical evidence is often lacking. Recent careful research by young-earth creationists using common methods on the same samples has revealed systematic differences in the ages they yield. These can be explained by rapid radioactive decay in the past (i.e., during creation and/or the Flood). This possibility is strongly supported by several lines of impeccable evidence.

All these considerations taken together emphatically show that the radiometric dating methods are fatally flawed and cannot yield the valid absolute ages claimed by those who require the millions of years to prop up their belief in long, evolutionary ages of earth history.

Appendix

Potassium-Argon

Potassium-argon (K-Ar) dating is bedeviled by the mobility of argon, violating the assumptions of known initial daughter concentration and of a closed system. Many lava flows of known ages have yielded grossly incorrect K-Ar dates because they contain excess argon already in the rocks when they formed (Dalrymple 1969; Dalrymple and Moore 1968; Esser et al. 1997; Krummenacher 1970; Snelling 2000a). This argon must have been inherited from its parent magma, a fact confirmed by the presence of argon in gases released by volcanic eruptions.

Two examples illustrate this problem. On October 26, 1980, a new lava dome began to develop in the crater of Mount St. Helens. A sample of its lava that cooled in 1986 was analyzed ten years later (Austin 1996). It yielded a K-Ar age of 350,000 years for the whole rock, and up to 2.8 m.y. for the constituent minerals. Similarly, the June 30, 1954, lava flow on Mt. Ngauruhoe, central North Island, New Zealand, yielded K-Ar ages up to 3.5 m.y. (Snelling 1998). In both cases, excess argon had been preferentially trapped as minerals crystallized. That is not uncommon; a K-Ar date of olivine crystals in a recent basalt exceeded 110 m.y. (Damon et al. 1967).

If excess argon is not from atmospheric contamination or from radioactive decay of potassium, it must come from deep inside the earth. This was shown by samples from the 1800–1801 Hualalai flow in Hawaii. Excess argon in fluid and gaseous inclusions in olivine, plagioclase, and pyroxene grains in fragments of the mantle brought up in the basalt yielded K-Ar ages of 2.6 m.y. to 2,960 m.y. (Funkhauser and Naughton 1968). This is significant because analyses of gas bubbles in mid-ocean ridge basalt samples from the North Atlantic have suggested that excess argon in the upper mantle may be two to ten times previous estimates (Burnard et al. 1997; Moreira et al. 1998). Confirmation comes from diamonds, which form deep in the mantle. A K-Ar isochron age of 6 billion years (b.y.) obtained from ten Zaire diamonds convinced geologists; otherwise the diamonds would be older than the earth (Zashu et al. 1986)!

This mantle argon is probably primordial. Since it is not derived from radioactive decay of potassium, it can have no age significance, and since it emanates into the crust, all crustal rocks are susceptible to "contamination." Indeed, the composition of excess argon in carbon-dioxide-rich natural gas wells confirms its mantle origin, and its concentrations in some wells exceed those in mantle-derived, mid-ocean ridge basalts (Ballentine 1997; Staudacher 1987). Thus, any K-Ar date of a crustal rock is highly questionable.

But the problems do not end with argon inheritance. Since argon is mobile, it can also escape. When rocks are heated or melted deep in the crust, some or all of their argon may escape, resetting the K-Ar "clock" (Dalrymple 1991). That free argon is then incorporated in other minerals and rocks, resetting their "clocks," too (Laughlin 1969). Argon mobility can distort dates even within the same rock unit. Ten profiles across biotite grains in high-grade metamorphic rocks yielded 128 apparent argon-argon[3] (Ar-Ar) ages within individual grains ranging from 161 m.y. to 514 m.y. (Pickles et al. 1997) (figure 9). This naturally causes problems in regional dating studies. For example, rocks in the Precambrian Musgrave Ranges of northern South Australia showed a wide scattering of K-Ar mineral ages, ranging from 343 m.y. to 4,493 m.y. Of course,

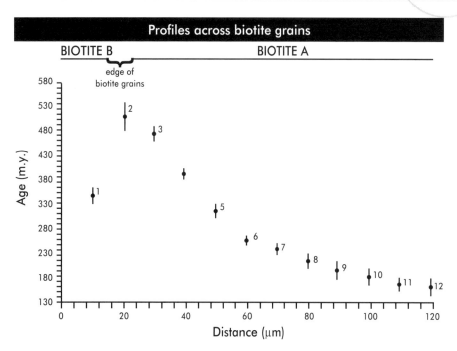

Figure 9. Apparent age versus distance profile across adjacent biotite grains in an amphibolite-granulite facies metamorphic rock from the Italian Alps (from Pickles et al., 1997 — their profile 8 across sample 85370). The high spatial resolution profile is along a "trench" produced by the beam from an ultraviolet laser ablation microprobe which is parallel to the biotite cleavage and perpendicular to the grain boundary. Apparent ages range from 515±27 m.y. at the edge of biotite A to 161±19 m.y. 100 m (microns) in from the edge of the biotite A. The high apparent ages at the grain boundary cannot be attributed to alteration because scanning electron microscope (SEM) photographs discount it.

no meaningful age interpretations could be drawn from those rocks (Webb 1985). Similarly, an Ar-Ar dating study of Precambrian high-grade metamorphic rocks in the Broken Hill region of New South Wales, Australia, documented widely distributed excess Ar, with the minerals plagioclase and hornblende most affected, yielding ages up to 9,588 m.y. (Harrison and McDougall 1981). Thus, when crustal rocks are dated by the K-Ar method, one can never be sure whether the argon in the rocks is from decay of potassium, from the mantle, or from other crustal rocks and minerals. So we have no way of knowing if any of the Ar measured in crustal rocks has any age significance at all!

Another explanation offered to resolve anomalous K-Ar ages is that argon gas can be lost from minerals (Faure and Mensing 2005). Argon loss was demonstrated at a contact metamorphic zone associated with the Eldora granite in the Front Range of Colorado. Biotite, hornblende,

and potassium feldspar apparently lost varying amounts of argon proportional to their distance from the granite intrusion (Hart 1964) (figure 10). K-Ar mineral ages were anomalously reduced even though the contact metamorphic effects were minor. This effect could be traced for more than two kilometers from the granite.

Finally, if recent lava flows contain excess argon, it is likely that ancient lava flows would, too. But whenever a K-Ar date of an ancient lava flow is not what is expected (according to the uniformitarian time scale), the perceived discrepancy is usually attributed to argon loss! This is the conventional explanation for the failure of K-Ar dates for the Precambrian Cardenas Basalt lavas of the eastern Grand Canyon (see figure 3) to match the "acceptable" Rb-Sr isochron age (Austin and Snelling 1998; Larson et al. 1994; McKee and Noble 1976). Yet the K-Ar isochron age of 516 m.y. (less than half the accepted uniformitarian age of 1,100 m.y.), when plotted, actually indicates some initial excess argon. Though there is a buildup of excess argon from the mantle in crustal rocks, argon loss can still be a

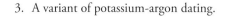

3. A variant of potassium-argon dating.

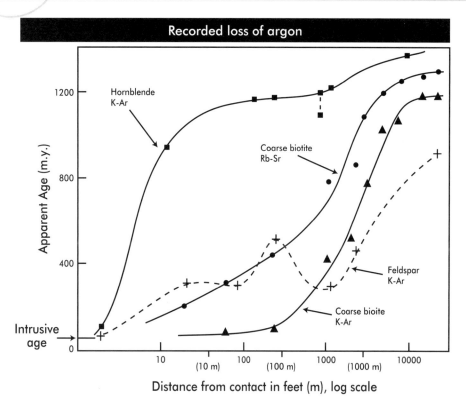

Figure 10. Plot of apparent mineral "ages" against outward distance from the contact of the Eldora stock, Colorado (from Hart 1964).

recent basalts on ocean islands, when plotted together, yielded an isochron with an "age" of approximately 2 b.y. (Sun and Hansen 1975). Even the basalts on individual islands produced isochrons showing vast ages due to strontium inheritance from the mantle (Brooks et al. 1976a). Similar problems have been found in both volcanic and intrusive continental rocks (Brooks et al. 1976b). For example, very young lava flows from two east African volcanoes, 160 kilometers (100 mi) apart, yielded an apparent isochron age of 773 m.y. (Bell and Powell 1969).

Crustal contamination can also perturb strontium in volcanic rocks (Faure and Powell 1972). Oceanic and continental rock units that apparently formed at the same time had significant strontium variations from crustal contamination and/or inheritance of strontium from the upper mantle and lower crust.

problem locally. With no method to categorically determine whether there has been argon loss or argon gain, K-Ar dates cannot logically provide an absolute time scale.

Rubidium-Strontium

Rb-Sr is one of the most widely used methods for rock and mineral dating, but it suffers from some of the same problems as K-Ar dating. It is claimed that strontium does not leave its host minerals like argon, but that claim has not been experimentally verified. It is not uncommon to find minerals that have lost both argon *and strontium* due to a thermal event (Hansen and Gast 1967). Both rubidium and strontium are relatively mobile elements that may be readily disturbed by either migrating fluids or heating (Rollison 1993). In the final analysis, Rb-Sr isochron ages — like dates from other radiometric methods — are evaluated by one crucial criterion: their consistency with the uniformitarian time scale.

Increasingly, Rb/Sr analyses yield anomalous isochrons that have no clear geological meaning, even when there is an excellent fit of the analytical data to the isochrons (Zheng 1989). Geologists admit that basalt lavas will invariably contain inherited strontium from mantle sources (Dickin 2005). Rb-Sr data from 14 different

Indeed, variations were found in initial strontium in groups of young lavas from a single volcano (Cortini and Hermes 1981) and in the rock units within an igneous complex derived from the same magma (McCarthy and Cawthorn 1980). This implies that the assumption of a single, well-defined value of daughter strontium in related rock units that formed at the same time (crucial for successful Rb-Sr isochron dating) is invalid.

Thus, geochemical factors may produce variations in initial strontium contrary to the assumptions of the isochron method (Allègre 1987; Hedge and Walthall 1963). Furthermore, if rubidium and strontium values are not independent of each other, the resultant isochron may not yield a valid age (Zheng 1989).

Magma contamination causes mineralogical and geochemical variations in granitic rocks and can lead to overestimating their Rb-Sr ages (Hall 1996). Furthermore, groups of samples with differing ages and different values of initial strontium can still be fitted to Rb-Sr isochrons (Haack et al. 1982; Köhler and Müller-Sohnius 1980). When geologists thought that pre-eruption processes had distorted the Rb-Sr system in some German volcanic rocks, they fixed the problem by rotating the isochron to derive a suitable age (Schleicher et al. 1983).

Because granitic rocks form from mixed mantle and crustal sources, their Rb-Sr isochrons may be inherited (Compston and Chappell 1978). Granites in southeastern Australia, regarded as 420 m.y. old, show Rb-Sr isochron "ages" of 1,100 m.y., and are believed to be the age of their source rocks because it agrees with U-Pb ages of zircons in the granites, supposedly from those source rocks (Chen and Williams 1990; Williams 1992). Since the presumed Precambrian source rocks have not been observed, either set of dates is arbitrary. And since strontium and neodymium values from some of the granites show that they formed from a mix of crustal and mantle components (Keay et al. 1997; McCulloch and Chappell 1982) (figure 11), Rb-Sr dates are also suspect (Zheng 1989). This is true of any rock derived from mixed mantle and crust sources. Even though an isochron can be drawn from measured Rb-Sr values, it would be a "mixed" isochron, and invalid. And within the uniformitarian paradigm, the problem would not be recognized unless the isochron age was at odds with the expected age.

Sr tends to migrate out of Rb-rich minerals, such as micas and potassium feldspar, if subjected to a thermal pulse (Dickin 2005) and into the nearest suitable mineral such as plagioclase. Thus, individual minerals will be open systems during metamorphism. A classic example of this is the varying mineral ages away from the contact of the Eldora granite in the Front Range of Colorado (Hart 1964) (see figure 10). Only six meters from the contact, coarse biotite in the surrounding Precambrian metamorphic rocks has apparently lost 88 percent of its daughter strontium. Indeed, similar Rb-Sr and K-Ar ages for the micas (Hansen and Gast 1967) indicate that the heat from the intrusion caused a redistribution of both strontium and argon. Patel et al. (1999) found that strontium can be redistributed

during regional metamorphism on a scale of at least tens of meters. Indeed, mounting evidence of whole-rock Rb-Sr open-system behavior has meant this widely used radiometric method has lost credibility (Dickin 2005). Even when Rb-Sr isochrons in metamorphic rocks look good, they yield meaningless ages. In some cases, the gain or loss of rubidium and strontium from rocks is so regular that isochrons are produced that look correct, but yield spurious ages (Zheng 1989). These problems have been confirmed by experiment; a mildly acidic solution will leach large amounts of rubidium from fresh samples of granites in less than a day (Irber et al. 1996). No wonder Zheng (1989, p. 1) concluded:

> As it is impossible to distinguish a valid isochron from an apparent isochron in the light of Rb-Sr isotopic data alone, caution must be taken in explaining the Rb-Sr isochron age of any geological system.

Samarium-Neodymium

Geologists claim that because samarium and neodymium are much less mobile than rubidium, strontium, uranium, and lead during regional metamorphism, hydrothermal alteration, and chemical weathering, the samarium-neodymium (Sm-Nd) method will "see through" younger events in rocks that distort Rb-Sr and U-Pb ages (Rollinson, 1993). Thus, it has frequently been used to date "original" igneous rocks that have undergone high-grade metamorphism where other "clocks" have been reset (Hamilton et

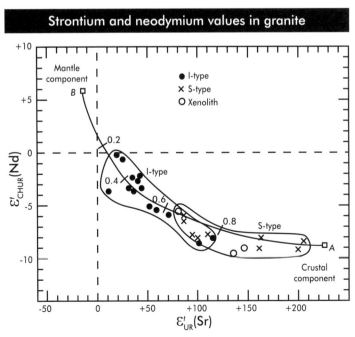

Figure 11. Epsilon values of Nd and Sr, corrected for decay, of granitic rocks and xenoliths from the Berridale and Kosciusko Batholiths (granites) of southeastern Australia (from McCulloch and Chappel 1982). Both I-type (igneous) and S-type (sedimentary) granitic rocks fit the same mixing line, indicating that both are mixtures of two components derived from "depleted" mantle and from the continental crust. The curve was fitted using the following end-member compositions: Crustal component (A): (Nd) = -9.0, Nd = 28.0 ppm, (Sr) = 227.2, Sr = 140 ppm; Mantle component (B); (Nd) = +6.0, Nd = 14.0 ppm, (Sr) = -14.20, Sr = 470 ppm.

al. 1979). However, a group of granitic and basaltic metamorphosed rocks in northwest Scotland showed that the Sm-Nd system in the non-basaltic rocks seemed to have been reset to the same age as the U-Pb (zircon) and other whole-rock systems, while the basaltic rocks retained an older Sm-Nd isochron age (Whitehouse 1988). So the Sm-Nd system only stayed closed in the basaltic rocks during metamorphism while in the *other* metamorphic rocks it was disturbed.

Under certain hydrothermal conditions, the mobility of rare earth elements can perturb the Sm-Nd system (Poitrasson et al. 1995), and, of course, the Flood offers a significant potential for hydrothermal action (chapter 4). Rare earth elements, including Sm and Nd, are not only leached by hydrothermal fluids, but are transported over distances exceeding hundreds of meters. Thus Sm and Nd are not immobile, nor does this method escape potential distortion, which raises doubts about its reliability, too.

There is another major limitation of the Sm-Nd technique. There are only small variations in samarium and neodymium values in rocks that form at the same time from the same source. Some investigators combine analyses from a wide range of rock types in order to obtain a spread of values to improve the statistics of the isochron (Rollinson 1993). However, rocks from different sources and with very different histories will produce a spurious isochron. Furthermore, variations in the initial Nd values have been found in groups of young lavas from a single volcano. This suggests that the assumption of a well-defined initial neodymium value for *different* rocks is difficult to defend (Chen and Frey 1983). These are critical problems for Sm-Nd whole-rock dating. A relatively small range of neodymium values in most groups of rocks means that any differences in the initial neodymium values larger than a laboratory's analytical uncertainty could affect the calculated age. For example, granitic rocks from Southern California, which are supposed to be about 100 m.y. old, plot on a Sm-Nd isochron of 1.7 billion years (DePaolo 1981a)! Even early Precambrian rocks yield an excellent whole-rock isochron with a grossly erroneous Sm-Nd age (Chauvel et al. 1985).

In spite of these problems, the Sm-Nd mineral isochron method has been widely used to date high-grade metamorphic rocks, because their minerals often have moderately large variations in samarium and neodymium values. Garnet is the mineral most often used. However, since any mineral's chemistry can be disrupted by metamorphism, there is still a problem. Geologists debate the temperature threshold for samarium and neodymium mobility in garnets (Ganguly et

al. 1998), but the point remains that they can be mobile, and their "clock" reset (Hensen and Zhou 1995). Thus geologists use U-Pb dating of mineral inclusions in the garnets as a check, but because such inclusions are invariably older than the garnets, the "check" is a problem, too (DeWolf et al. 1996; Vance et al. 1998).

Obviously, Sm-Nd mineral isochron dating still depends on calibration by other dating methods (each with its own inherent problems) and (more to the point) with the uniformitarian time scale (Mezger et al. 1993). As noted earlier, hydrothermal fluids are capable of carrying samarium and neodymium at least one kilometer through granites and their host rocks (Poitrasson et al. 1998). Even though the minerals in these granites produce statistically acceptable Sm-Nd isochrons, their ages are meaningless. Clearly, the Sm-Nd dating method in both whole rocks and minerals is not foolproof since it is subject to being reset by diffusion and fluid migration.

Nevertheless, Sm-Nd model ages are commonly calculated for individual rocks. These are thought to measure the length of time the rock unit has been separated from its original mantle source (Rollinson 1993). Of course, this assumes knowledge of the Sm and Nd in mantle sources, no separation of these elements from one another when the magmas leave their sources, and their subsequent immobility — all problematical. As if this were not enough, there are two popular models for samarium/neodymium values in the mantle (DePaolo 1976, 1981b; DePaolo and Wasserburg 1976), and the model choice makes a huge difference in the resulting Sm-Nd ages. For example, in metamorphic rocks in central Australia, the two models created age differences of up to 1.3 billion years (Windrim and McCulloch 1986). Consequently, credible Sm-Nd model ages require "precise" geochronological information, typically by U-Pb dating of zircons (DePaolo et al. 1991). So the Sm-Nd method depends on interpretive models and other "dating" methods. At best, it is only as good as these other methods.

Uranium-Thorium-Lead

Historically, uranium-thorium-lead (U-Th-Pb) dating was the first method used on minerals. Early studies showed it to be of little value because of the mobility of lead, thorium, and especially uranium (Dickin 2005). It has since been shown that open-system behavior is nearly universal in surface outcrops and down to depths of several hundred meters in granites because of circulating groundwater (Stuckless 1986). Thus, the emphasis has shifted back to dating minerals, particularly zircon, titanite or sphene, and monazite. But problems remain. Lead derived from radioactive decay can be inherited by minerals during crystallization. Furthermore, lead can be lost by diffusion because its atoms are not bonded in crystal lattices (Faure and Mensing 2005). Various models have been suggested for what appears to be a systemic loss of lead by diffusion, such as leakage of the intermediate radon by gaseous diffusion through microfissures in the minerals (Giletti and Kulp 1955). Wetherill (1956a) also suggested that episodic lead loss occurred in thermal events after minerals formed. These phenomena were used to explain incorrect "dates" that failed the crucial assumptions about initial conditions and a closed system (Wetherill 1956b). In any case, it has been experimentally confirmed that lead diffuses from zircons and uranium-bearing minerals even at low temperatures (Tilton 1960). Furthermore, lead diffusion is facilitated by radiation damage to host mineral lattices (Goldich and Mudrey 1972; Meldrum et al. 1998; Wasserburg 1963).

Higher temperatures increase the rate of diffusion (Lee et al. 1997), as was dramatically illustrated by the contact metamorphic effects on zircon crystals in regionally metamorphosed sediments and volcanics around a granite intrusion (Davis et al. 1968) (figure 12). Within 49 feet (15 m) of the contact, the U-Pb age decreased from 1,405 m.y. to 220 m.y. Furthermore, lead loss in zircons varies as a function of both grain size and uranium content (Silver and Duetsch 1963). Also, zircons are zoned because of their progressive growth during crystallization. Both zoned and unzoned zircons may be found in the same rock. Unzoned crystals are the result of recrystallization of zoned crystals, which causes the loss of uranium, thorium, and lead, producing erroneous U-Pb ages (Pidgeon 1992). Zircon recrystallization by regional metamorphism can reduce U-Pb dates by hundreds of millions of years, even within single samples (Kröner et al. 1994). Furthermore, even when a spectrum of apparently acceptable zircon U-Pb ages is obtained, they may be meaningless due to high-temperature lead loss during

metamorphism by volume and/or fracture-assisted diffusion (Ashwal et al. 1999).

So zircons — the most popular mineral for U-Pb dating — can show ages that are "too high" or "too low." When they are too high in metamorphic rocks, geologists interpret them as having been inherited from the original sediments without their "clocks" being reset by metamorphism (Froude et al. 1983; Kröner et al. 1994). When too high in granites, "older" zircons are likewise said to be inherited from the source rocks that melted to produce the granite magma (Williams et al. 1983; Chen and Williams 1990). But these explanations push the bounds of reason; some "inherited" zircons are five to ten times older than the age of the rock — up to 1,753 m.y. in a Himalayan granite supposed to be 21 m.y. old (Parrish and Tirrul 1989), up to 3,500 m.y. in a southeastern Australian granite supposed to be 426 m.y. old (Williams 1992), and up to 638 m.y. in a New Zealand granite supposed to be 370 m.y. old (Muir et al. 1996). Of course, if the true age of a rock is unknown, it follows that it cannot be verified by U-Pb dating — the point creationists have been trying to make for years.

Migrating lead creates many problems. For example, some feldspar grains in Precambrian rocks, which have never contained uranium, nevertheless contain daughter

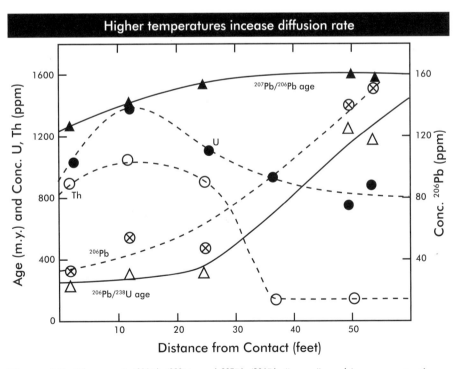

Figure 12. Change in $^{206}Pb/^{238}U$ and $^{207}Pb/^{206}Pb$ "ages" and in concentration of U, Th and ^{206}Pb in zircons in Precambrian metasediments and metavolcanics as a function of distance from the contact with the Eldora Tertiary granite stock, Colorado (from Davis et al. 1968).

lead (Ludwig and Silver 1977). In other cases, zircons contain excess daughter lead, giving them anomalously high ages (Williams et al. 1984) — up to hundreds of millions of years more than expected! Geologists are forced to explain it as mixing during the magma phase and/or subsequent migration caused by fluids, temperature, and pressure (Zhang and Schärer 1996; Copeland et al. 1998). This of course begs a question: should anomalously old zircons be interpreted as inheritance of the zircon crystals themselves or as the result of inheritance into the crystals of excess lead derived by radioactive decay? But it also begs a much larger question — why should we believe U-Pb dates at all?

These "clocks" are so temperamental that even technology can disturb their function. Recently developed, sophisticated analytical technology allows in situ analysis of 2-micron-wide spots within crystals, so that even different growth zones can be dated. Daughter lead has been found to vary on a 20-micron scale, with some spots being characterized by up to 30 times the expected values (Compston 1997). Pronounced age differences have also been demonstrated among four different faces of a large baddeleyite crystal, interpreted as a function of crystal growth (Wingate and Compston 2000). Even the angle of the analytical beam can affect the "age." Ages measured on the same crystal faces of 47 baddeleyite crystals at different beam orientations revealed a striking variation in U-Pb ages — hundreds of millions of years (figure 13). The same problems were found in monazite crystals that contained random submicroscopic, blotchy patches that varied up to 700 m.y. in age from one another (Cocherie et al. 1998). Monazite grains can even yield negative ages, such as -97 m.y. in a supposedly 20 m.y. old Himalayan granite that just happens to contains zircon grains yielding ages up to 1,483 m.y. (Parrish 1990), a disagreement of nearly 7,500 percent!

Clearly, the results of U-Th-Pb mineral dating, currently the most popular method, are highly interpretive. Since daughter lead easily migrates between crystals, and since the process is accelerated by heat, water, radiation damage, and weathering, any dating method that depends on its relative immobility faces major problems. Uranium presents a similar problem; it is readily leached by groundwater to considerable depths. Thus, without a geologic context and an expected age to guide the investigator, this method cannot determine the date of the formation of the rocks. Most published dates were derived without even the knowledge of these analytical challenges. After all, if ages vary significantly within crystals at submicroscopic scales, on different crystal faces, and at different crystal orientations, at what scale can geologists find valid results? These problems appear insurmountable, and the U-Th-Pb dating of rocks, whole mineral grains, or zones within them remains highly questionable.

Even though the U-Pb isochron method for dating whole rocks has been discredited, the lead-lead (Pb-Pb) method continues to be used. It was first used to date meteorites, yielding a Pb-Pb isochron age of 4.55±0.07 b.y., which was interpreted as the age of the earth (Patterson 1956). But this golden spike has been tarnished by analyses of daughter lead in recent basalt lava flows on ocean islands and at the mid-ocean ridges. These rocks yielded Pb-Pb isochron ages of between 1 and 1.5 b.y. (Gast et al. 1964; Sun 1980; Tatsumoto 1966)! This is a worldwide phenomenon that geologists have attempted to explain in three principal ways: (1) discrete magma-forming events in the mantle,

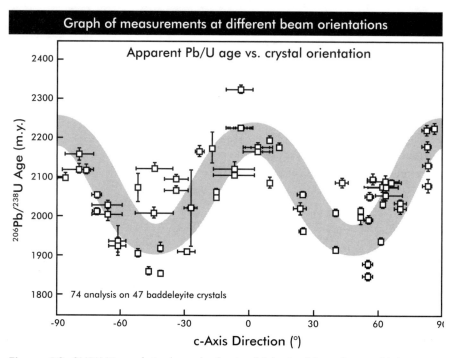

Figure 13. SHRIMP analytical results for baddeleyite (zirconium oxide), illustrating observed orientation effects (from Wingate and Compton 2000). Variation of apparent ^{206}Pb/^{238}U "age" with orientation for the same crystal (100) surfaces of 47 oriented baddeleyite crystals.

(2) two-component mixing processes, or (3) the continuous development of reservoirs (portions of rock materials) in the mantle and crust with changing U-Pb ratios (Dickin 2005; Doe and Zartman 1979; Taylor et al. 1984; Zindler and Hart 1986). Geologists have identified five of these reservoirs in the mantle and three in the continental crust. Multiple mixing scenarios supposedly explain the anomalously old Pb-Pb dates. Continental volcanic rocks also yield Pb-Pb results interpreted as mixtures derived from the crust and mantle. For example, volcanic and intrusive rocks on the Isle of Skye of northwest Scotland yield an apparent Pb-Pb isochron age of approximately 3 b.y. (Moorbath and Welke 1969; Thompson 1982). But if the whole-rock Pb-Pb dating of young volcanic rocks yields anomalously old ages because they inherit "old" lead from their magma chambers, then how can the same Pb-Pb dating of *ancient* volcanic rocks be trusted to yield valid ages? Even soil samples collected near a uranium deposit and surrounding areas up to 17 kilometers away yield an apparent Pb-Pb isochron age of 1,445 m.y. (Dickson et al. 1985, 1987).

Thus, U-Th-Pb dating involves many pitfalls that can only be surmounted by untestable assumptions and uncertain cross-checks. The mobility of both uranium and lead undermines whole-rock dating, and lead migration within and between individual mineral grains is so prevalent that interpreting the resultant analytical data is largely dependent on what date the investigator expects. Modern basalt lavas reveal inconsistent heterogeneities in lead caused by mixing in their mantle sources, even from successive volcanic flows on the same ocean island, which yield vastly erroneous old ages. Inheritance, migration, and mixing in the U-Th-Pb system are chronic problems at all observational scales. Even if the constructed maze of methods looks internally consistent, it is a house of cards, with foundations riddled with systematic errors and with questionable dates at every turn.

References

CRSQ: Creation Research Society Quarterly
CENTJ: Creation Ex Nihilo Technical Journal (now Journal of Creation)

Allègre, C.J. 1987. Isotope geodynamics. *Earth and Planetary Science Letters* 86:175–203.

Ashwal, L.D., R.D. Tucker, and E.K. Zinner. 1999. Slow cooling of deep crustal granulites and Pb-loss in zircon. *Geochimica et Cosmochimica Acta* 63:2839–2851.

Austin, S.A. (editor). 1994. *Grand Canyon: Monument to Catastrophe.* Santee, CA: Institute for Creation Research.

————. 1996. Excess argon within mineral concentrates from the new dacite lava dome at Mount St. Helens volcano. *CENTJ* 10:335–343.

————. 2005. Do radioisotope clocks need repair? Testing the assumptions of isochron dating using K-Ar, Rb-Sr, Sm-Nd, and Pb-Pb isotopes. In L. Vardiman, A.A. Snelling, and E.F. Chaffin (editors). *Radioisotopes and the Age of the Earth: Results of a Young-Earth Creationist Research Initiative.* El Cajon, CA: Institute for Creation Research and Chino Valley, AZ: Creation Research Society, p. 325–392.

Austin, S.A., and A.A. Snelling. 1998. Discordant potassium-argon model and isochron "ages" for Cardenas Basalt (Middle Proterozoic) and associated diabase of eastern Grand Canyon, Arizona. In R.E. Walsh (editor). *Proceedings of the Fourth International Conference on Creationism.* Pittsburgh, PA: Creation Science Fellowship, p. 35–51.

Ballentine, C.J. 1997. Resolving the mantle He/Ne and crustal ^{21}Ne/^{22}Ne in well gases. *Earth and Planetary Science Letters* 152:233–249.

Baumgardner, J.R. 2005. ^{14}C evidence for a recent global Flood and young earth. In L. Vardiman, A.A. Snelling, and E.F. Chaffin (editors). *Radioisotopes and the Age of the Earth: Results of a Young-Earth Creationist Research Initiative.* El Cajon, CA: Institute for Creation Research and Chino Valley, AZ: Creation Research Society, p. 587–630.

Bell, K., and J.L. Powell. 1969. Strontium isotopic studies of alkalic rocks: The potassium-rich lavas of the Birunga and Toro-Ankole regions, east and central equatorial Africa. *Journal of Petrology* 10:536–572.

Brooks, C., S.R. Hart, A. Hofmann, and D.E. James. 1976a. Rb-Sr mantle isochrons from oceanic regions. *Earth and Planetary Science Letters* 32:51–61.

Brooks, C., D.E. James, and S.R. Hart. 1976b. Ancient lithosphere: Its role in young continental volcanism. *Science* 193:1086–1094.

Burnard, P., D. Graham, and G. Turner. 1997. Vesicle-specific noble gas analyses of "popping rock": Implication for primordial noble gases in earth. *Science* 276:568–571.

Chaffin, E.F. 2000a. Mechanisms for accelerated radioactive decay. *CRSQ* 37:3–9.

————. 2000b. Theoretical mechanisms of accelerated radioactive decay. In L. Vardiman, A.A. Snelling, and E.F. Chaffin (editors). *Radioisotopes and the Age of the Earth: Results of a Young-Earth Creationist Research Initiative.* El Cajon, CA: Institute for Creation Research and Chino Valley, AZ: Creation Research Society, p. 305–331.

————. 2003. Accelerated decay: Theoretical models. In R.L. Ivey Jr. (editor). *Proceedings of the Fifth International Conference on Creationism*. Pittsburgh, PA: Creation Science Fellowship, p. 3–15.

————. 2005. Accelerated decay: Theoretical considerations. In L. Vardiman, A.A. Snelling, and E.F. Chaffin (editors). *Radioisotopes and the Age of the Earth: Results of a Young-Earth Creationist Research Initiative*. El Cajon, CA: Institute for Creation Research and Chino Valley, AZ: Creation Research Society, p. 525–585.

Chauvel, C., B. Dupre, and G.A. Jenner. 1985. The Sm-Nd age of Kambalda volcanics is 500 Ma too old! *Earth and Planetary Science Letters* 74:315–324.

Chen, C.Y., and F.A. Frey. 1983. Origin of Hawaiian tholeiite and alkalic basalt. *Nature* 302:785–789.

Chen, Y.D., and I.S. Williams. 1990. The zircon inheritance in mafic inclusions from Bega Batholith granites, south-eastern Australia: An ion microprobe study. *Journal of Geophysical Research* 95:17787–17796.

Cocherie, A., O. Legendre, J.J. Peucat, and A.N. Kouamelan. 1998. Geochronology of polygenetic monazites constrained by in situ electron microprobe Th-U-total lead determination: Implications for lead behavior in monazite. *Geochimica et Cosmochimica Acta* 62:2475–2497.

Compston, W. 1997. Variations in radiogenic Pb/U within the SL13 standard. *Research School of Earth Sciences Annual Report 1996*. Canberra, Australia: Australian National University, p. 118–121.

Compston, W., and B.W. Chappell. 1978. Estimation of source Rb/Sr for individual igneous-derived granitoids and the inferred age of the lower crust in southeast Australia. *U.S. Geological Survey Open File Report* 78-701:79–81.

Copeland, P., R.R. Parrish, and T.M. Harrison. 1998. Identification of inherited radiogenic Pb in monazite and its implications for U-Pb systematics. *Nature* 333:760–763.

Cortini, M., and O.D. Hermes. 1981. Sr isotopic evidence for a multi-source origin of the potassic magmas in the Neapolitan area (S. Italy). *Contributions to Mineralogy and Petrology* 77:47–55.

Dalrymple, G.B. 1969. $^{40}Ar/^{36}Ar$ analyses of historic lava flows. *Earth and Planetary Science Letters* 6:47–55.

————. 1991. *The Age of the Earth*. Stanford, CA: Stanford University Press.

Dalrymple, G.B., and J.G. Moore. 1968. Argon 40: excess in submarine pillow basalts from Kilauea Volcano, Hawaii. *Science* 161:1132–1135.

Dalrymple, G.B., and W.K. Hamblin. 1998. K-Ar ages of Pleistocene lava dams in the Grand Canyon, Arizona. *Proceedings of the National Academy of Sciences USA* 95:9744–9749.

Damon, P.E., A.W. Laughlin, and J.K. Precious. 1967. Problems of excess argon-40 in volcanic rocks. In *Radioactive Dating Methods and Low-Level Counting*. Vienna: International Atomic Energy Agency, p. 463–481.

Davies, R.D., H.L. Allsopp, A. Erlank, and J.W.I. Manton. 1970. Sr isotopic studies on various layered mafic intrusions in southern Africa. *Symposium on the Bushveld Igneous Complex and Other Layered Intrusions*. Geological Society of South Africa, Special Publication 1, p. 576–593.

Davis, G.L., S.R. Hart, and G.R. Tilton. 1968. Some effects of contact metamorphism on zircon ages. *Earth and Planetary Science Letters* 5:27–34.

DePaolo, D.J. 1976. Inferences about magma sources and mantle structure from variations of $^{143}Nd/^{144}Nd$. *Geophysical Research Letters* 3:743–746.

————. 1981a. A neodymium and strontium isotopic study of the Mesozoic calc-alkaline granitic batholiths of the Sierra Nevada and Peninsular Ranges, California. *Journal of Geophysical Research* 86:10470–10488.

————. 1981b. Neodymium isotopes in the Colorado Front Range and crust-mantle evolution in the Proterozoic. *Nature* 291:193–196.

DePaolo, D.J., and G.J. Wasserburg. 1976. Nd isotopic variations and petrogenetic models. *Geophysical Research Letters* 3:249–252.

DePaolo, D.J., A.M. Linn, and G. Schubert. 1991. The continental crustal age distribution: method of determining mantle separation ages from Sm-Nd isotopic data and application to the south-western United States. *Journal of Geophysical Research* 96:2071–2088.

DeWolf, C.P., C.J. Zeissler, A.N. Halliday, K. Mezger, and E.J. Essene. 1996. The role of inclusions in U-Pb and Sm-Nd garnet geochronology: Stepwise dissolution experiments and trace uranium mapping by fission track analysis. *Geochimica et Cosmochimica Acta* 60:121–134.

DeYoung, D.B. 2000. Radioisotope dating review. In L. Vardiman, A.A. Snelling, and E.F. Chaffin (editors). *Radioisotopes and the Age of the Earth: Results of a Young-Earth Creationist Research Initiative*. El Cajon, CA: Institute for Creation Research and Chino Valley, AZ: Creation Research Society, p. 27–47.

Dickin, A.P. 1995. *Radiogenic Isotope Geology*. Cambridge, England: Cambridge University Press.

————. 2005. *Radiogenic Isotope Geology*, second edition. New York: Cambridge University Press.

Dickson, B.L., B.L. Gulson, and A.A. Snelling. 1985. Evaluation of lead isotopic methods for uranium exploration, Koongarra area, Northern Territory, Australia. *Journal of Geochemical Exploration* 24:81–102.

———. 1987. Further assessment of stable lead isotopic measurements for uranium exploration, Pine Creek Geosyncline, Northern Territory, Australia. *Journal of Geochemical Exploration* 27:63–75.

Doe, B.R., and R.E. Zartman. 1979. Plumbotectonics. In H.L. Barnes (editor). *Geochemistry of Hydrothermal Ore Deposits*, second edition. New York: John Wiley and Sons, p. 22–70.

Esser, R.P., W.C. McIntosh, M.T. Heizler, and P.R. Kyle. 1997. Excess argon in melt inclusions in zero-age anorthoclase feldspar from Mt. Erebus, Antarctica, as revealed by the $^{40}Ar/^{39}Ar$ method. *Geochimica et Cosmochimica Acta* 61:3789–3801.

Faure, G. 1986. *Principles of Isotope Geology*, second edition. New York: John Wiley and Sons.

Faure, G., and J.L. Powell. 1972. *Strontium Isotope Geology*. Berlin: Springer-Verlag.

Faure, G., and T.S. Mensing. 2005. *Isotopes: Principles and Applications*, third edition. Hoboken, NJ: John Wiley and Sons.

Froude, D.O., T.R. Ireland, P.O. Kinny, I.S. Williams, and W. Compston. 1983. Ion microprobe identification of 4100-4200 Ma-old terrestrial zircons. *Nature* 304:616–618.

Funkhauser, J.G., and J.J. Naughton. 1968. Radiogenic helium and argon in ultramafic inclusions from Hawaii. *Journal of Geophysical Research* 73:4601–4607.

Ganguly, J., M. Tirone, and R.L. Hervig. 1998. Diffusion kinetics of samarium and neodymium in garnet, and a method for determining cooling rates of rocks. *Science* 281:805–807.

Gast, P.W., G.R. Tilton, and C. Hedge. 1964. Isotopic composition of lead and strontium from Ascension and Gough Islands. *Science* 145:1181–1185.

Giletti, B.J., and J.L. Kulp. 1955. Radon leakage from radioactive minerals. *American Mineralogist* 40:481–496.

Goldich, S.S., and M.J. Mudrey, Jr. 1972. Dilatancy model for discordant U-Pb zircon ages. In A.I. Tugrainov (editor). *Contributions to Recent Geochemistry and Analytical Chemistry*. Moscow: Nouka Publishing Office, p. 415–418.

Haack, U., J. Hoefs, and E. Gohn. 1982. Constraints on the origin of Damaran granites by Rb/Sr and $\delta^{18}O$ data. *Contributions to Mineralogy and Petrology* 79:279–289.

Hall, A. 1996. *Igneous Petrology*, second edition. Harlow, Essex, England: Addison Wesley Longman.

Hamblin, W.K. 1989. Pleistocene volcanic rocks of the western Grand Canyon, Arizona. In D.P. Elston, E.H. Billingsley, and R.A. Young (editors). *Geology of Grand Canyon, Northern Arizona (with Colorado River Guides)*. Washington, DC: American Geophysical Union, p. 190–204.

———. 1990. Late Cenozoic lava dams in the western Grand Canyon. In S.S. Beus and M. Morales (editors). *Grand Canyon Geology*, first edition. New York: Oxford University Press and Flagstaff, AZ: Museum of Northern Arizona Press, p. 385–433.

———. 1994. *Late Cenozoic Lava Dams in the Western Grand Canyon*. Geological Society of America, Memoir 183.

———. 2003. Late Cenozoic lava dams in the western Grand Canyon. In S.S. Beus and M. Morales (editors). *Grand Canyon Geology*, second edition. New York: Oxford University Press, p. 313–345.

Hamilton, J. 1977. Sr isotope and trace element studies of the Great Dyke and Bushveld mafic phase and their relation to early Proterozoic magma genesis in southern Africa. *Journal of Petrology* 18:24–52.

Hamilton, P.J., R.K. O'Nions, N.M. Evensen, and J. Tarney. 1979. Sm-Nd systematics of Lewisian gneisses: Implications for the origin of granulites. *Nature* 277:25–28.

Hansen, G.N., and P.W. Gast. 1967. Kinetic studies in contact metamorphic zones. *Geochimica et Cosmochimica Acta* 31:1119–1153.

Harrison, T.M., and I. McDougall. 1981. Excess ^{40}Ar in metamorphic rocks from Broken Hill, New South Wales: Implications for $^{40}Ar/^{39}Ar$ age spectra and the thermal history of the region. *Earth and Planetary Science Letters* 55:123–149.

Hart, S.R. 1964. The petrology and isotopic-mineral age relations of a contact zone in the Front Range, Colorado. *Journal of Geology* 72:493–525.

Hedge, C.E., and F.G. Walthall. 1963. Radiogenic strontium-87 as an index of geological processes. *Science* 140:1214–1217.

Hensen, B.J., and B. Zhou. 1995. Retention of isotopic memory in garnets partially broken down during an overprinting granulite-facies metamorphism: Implications for the Sm-Nd closure temperature. *Geology* 23:225 228.

Humphreys, D.R. 2000. Accelerated nuclear decay: A viable hypothesis? In L. Vardiman, A.A. Snelling, and E.F. Chaffin (editors). *Radioisotopes and the Age of the Earth: Results of a Young-Earth Creationist Research Initiative*. El Cajon, CA: Institute for Creation Research and Chino Valley, AZ: Creation Research Society, p. 333–379.

———. 2005. Young helium diffusion age of zircons supports accelerated nuclear decay. In L. Vardiman, A.A. Snelling, and

E.F. Chaffin (editors). *Radioisotopes and the Age of the Earth: Results of a Young-Earth Creationist Research Initiative.* El Cajon, CA: Institute for Creation Research and Chino Valley, AZ: Creation Research Society, p. 25–100.

Irber, W., W. Siebel, P. Möller, and S. Teufel. 1996. Leaching of Rb-Sr (^{87}Sr/^{86}Sr) of Hercynian peraluminous granites with application to age determination. *V.M. Goldschmidt Conference, Journal of Conference Abstracts* 1:281.

Keay, S., W.J. Collins, and M.T. McCulloch. 1997. A three-component Sr-Nd isotopic mixing model for granitoid genesis, Lachlan Fold Belt, eastern Australia. *Geology* 25:307–310.

Köhler, H., and D. Müeller-Sohnius. 1980. Rb-Sr systematics in paragneiss series from the Bavarian Moldanubium, Germany. *Contributions to Mineralogy and Petrology* 71:387–392.

Kröner, A., P.J. Jaeckel, and I.S. Williams. 1994. Pb-loss patterns in zircons from a high-grade metamorphic terrain as revealed by different dating methods, U-Pb and Pb-Pb ages for igneous and metamorphic zircons from northern Sri Lanka. *Precambrian Research* 66:151–181.

Krummenacher, D. 1970. Isotopic composition of argon in modern surface volcanic rocks. *Earth and Planetary Science Letters* 8:109–117.

Larson, E.E., P.E. Patterson, and F.E. Mutschler. 1994. Lithology, chemistry, age, and origin of the Proterozoic Cardenas Basalt, Grand Canyon, Arizona. *Precambrian Research* 65:255–276.

Laughlin, A.W. 1969. Excess radiogenic argon in pegmatite minerals. *Journal of Geophysical Research* 74:6684–6690.

Lee, J.K.W., I.S. Williams, and D.J. Ellis. 1997. Determination of Pb, U, and Th diffusion rates in zircon. *Research School of Earth Sciences Annual Report 1996.* Canberra, Australia: Australian National University, p. 121–122.

Leeman, W.P. 1982. Tectonic and magmatic significance of strontium isotopic variations in Cenozoic volcanic rocks from the western United States. *Geological Society of America Bulletin* 93:487–503.

Ludwig, K.R. 2001. *Isoplot/Ex (Version 2.49): The Geochronological Toolkit for Microsoft Excel.* University of California Berkeley, Berkeley Geochronology Center, Special Publication No. 1a.

Ludwig, K.R., and L.T. Silver. 1977. Lead isotope inhomogeneities in igneous K-feldspars. *Geochimica et Cosmochimica Acta* 41:1457–1471.

McCarthy, T.S., and R.G. Cawthorn. 1980. Changes in initial ^{87}Sr/^{86}Sr ratio during protracted fractionation in igneous complexes. *Journal of Petrology* 21:245–264.

McCulloch, M.T., and B.W. Chappell. 1982. Nd isotopic characteristics of S- and I-type granites. *Earth and Planetary Science Letters* 58:51–64.

McKee, E.H., and D.C. Noble. 1976. Age of the Cardenas lavas, Grand Canyon, Arizona. *Geological Society of America Bulletin* 87:1188–1190.

Meldrum, A., L.H. Boatner, W.J. Weber, and R.C. Ewing. 1998. Radiation damage in zircon and monazite. *Geochimica et Cosmochimica Acta* 62:2509–2520.

Mezger, K., E.J. Essene, and A.N. Halliday. 1993. Closure temperatures on the Sm-Nd system in metamorphic garnets. *Earth and Planetary Science Letters* 113:397–409.

Moorbath, S., and H. Welke. 1969. Lead isotope studies on igneous rocks from Isle of Skye, northwest Scotland. *Earth and Planetary Science Letters* 5:217–230.

Moreira, M., J. Kunz, and C.J. Allègre. 1998. Rare gas systematics in popping rock: isotopic and elemental compositions in the upper mantle. *Science* 279:1178–1181.

Muir, R.J., T.R. Ireland, S.D. Weaver, and J.D. Bradshaw. 1996. Ion microprobe dating of Paleozoic granitoids: Devonian magmatism in New Zealand and correlations with Australia and Antarctica. *Chemical Geology* 127:191–210.

Mukasa, S.B., A.H. Wilson, and R.W. Carlson. 1998. A multi-element geochronologic study of the Great Dyke, Zimbabwe: significance of the robust and reset ages. *Earth and Planetary Science Letters* 164:353–369.

Oberthür, T., D.W. Davis, T.J. Blenkinsop, and A. Höhndorf. 2002. Precise U-Pb mineral ages, Rb-Sr and Sm-Nd systematics for the Great Dyke, Zimbabwe — constraints on late Archean events in Zimbabwe cratons and Limpopo belt. *Precambrian Research* 113:293–305.

Parrish, R.R. 1990. U-Pb dating of monazite and its applications to geological problems. *Canadian Journal of Earth Sciences* 27:1431–1450.

Parrish, R.R., and R. Tirrul. 1989. U-Pb age of the Baltoro Granite, northwest Himalaya, and implications for monazite U-Pb systematics. *Geology* 17:1076–1079.

Patel, S.C., C.D. Frost, and P.R. Frost. 1999. Contrasting responses of Rb-Sr systematics to regional and contact metamorphism, Laramie Mountains, Wyoming, USA. *Journal of Metamorphic Geology* 17:259–269.

Patterson, C.C. 1956. Age of meteorites and the earth. *Geochimica et Cosmochimica Acta* 10:230–237.

Pickles, D.S., S.P. Kelley, S.M. Reddy, and J. Wheeler. 1997. Determination of high spatial resolution argon isotope variations in metamorphic biotites. *Geochimica et Cosmochimica Acta* 61:3809–3833.

Pidgeon, R.T. 1992. Recrystallization of oscillatory zoned zircon: some geochronological and petrological implications. *Contributions to Mineralogy and Petrology* 110:463–472.

Poitrasson, F., C. Pin, and J.L. Duthou. 1995. Hydrothermal remobilization of rare earth elements and its effects on Nd isotopes in rhyolite and granite. *Earth and Planetary Science Letters* 130:1–11.

Poitrasson, F., J.L. Paquette, J.M. Montel, C. Pin, and J.L. Duthou. 1998. Importance of late-magmatic and hydrothermal fluids on the Sm-Nd isotope mineral systematics of hypersolvus granites. *Chemical Geology* 146:187–203.

Rollison, H. 1993. *Using Geochemical Data: Evaluation, Presentation, Interpretation.* Harlow, Essex, England: Longman.

Silver, L.T.. and S. Deutsch. 1963. Uranium-lead isotopic variations in zircons: a case study. *Journal of Geology* 71:721–758.

Snelling, A.A. 1982. *A Mineralogical and Geochemical Study of the Koongarra Uranium Deposit, Northern Territory, Australia.* Unpublished PhD thesis, University of Sydney, Australia.

———. 1998. The cause of anomalous potassium-argon "ages" for recent andesite flows at Mt. Ngauruhoe, New Zealand, and the implications for potassium-argon "dating." In Walsh, R.E. (editor). *Proceedings of the Fourth International Conference on Creationism.* Pittsburgh, PA: Creation Science Fellowship, p. 503–525.

———. 2000a. Geochemical processes in the mantle and crust. In L. Vardiman, A.A. Snelling, and E.F. Chaffin (editors). *Radioisotopes and the Age of the Earth: Results of a Young-Earth Creationist Research Initiative.* El Cajon, CA: Institute for Creation Research and Chino Valley, AZ: Creation Research Society, p. 123–304.

———. 2000b. Radiohalos. In L. Vardiman, A.A. Snelling, and E.F. Chaffin (editors). *Radioisotopes and the Age of the Earth: Results of a Young-Earth Creationist Research Initiative.* El Cajon, CA: Institute for Creation Research and Chino Valley, AZ: Creation Research Society, p. 381–468.

———. 2005a. Radiohalos in granites: Evidence for accelerated nuclear decay. In L. Vardiman, A.A. Snelling, and E.F. Chaffin (editors). *Radioisotopes and the Age of the Earth: Results of a Young-Earth Creationist Research Initiative.* El Cajon, CA: Institute for Creation Research and Chino Valley, AZ: Creation Research Society, p. 101–207.

———. 2005b. Fission tracks in zircons: Evidence for abundant nuclear decay. In L. Vardiman, A.A. Snelling, and E.F. Chaffin (editors). *Radioisotopes and the Age of the Earth: Results of a Young-Earth Creationist Research Initiative.* El Cajon, CA:

Institute for Creation Research and Chino Valley, AZ: Creation Research Society, p. 209–324.

———. 2005c. Isochron discordances and the role of inheritance and mixing of radioisotopes in the mantle and crust. In L. Vardiman, A.A. Snelling, and E.F. Chaffin (editors). *Radioisotopes and the Age of the Earth: Results of a Young-Earth Creationist Research Initiative.* El Cajon, CA: Institute for Creation Research and Chino Valley, AZ: Creation Research Society, p. 393–524.

Snelling, A.A., S.A. Austin, and W.A. Hoesch. 2003. Radioisotopes in the diabase sill (Upper Precambrian) at Bass Rapids, Grand Canyon, Arizona: An application and test of the isochron dating method. In R.L. Ivey Jr. (editor). *Proceedings of the Fifth International Conference on Creationism.* Pittsburgh, PA: Creation Science Fellowship, p. 269–284.

Staudacher, T. 1987. Upper mantle origin of Harding County well gases. *Nature* 325:605–607.

Stuckless, J.S. 1986. Applications of U-Th-Pb isotope systematics to the problems of radioactive waste disposal. *Chemical Geology* 55:215–225.

Sun, S.S. 1980. Lead isotopic study of young volcanic rocks from mid-ocean ridges, ocean islands and island arcs. *Philosophical Transactions of the Royal Society of London* A297:409–445.

Sun, S.S., and G.N. Hansen. 1975. Evolution of the mantle: geochemical evidence from alkali basalt. *Geology* 3:297–302.

Tatsumoto, M. 1966. Genetic relations of oceanic basalts as indicated by lead isotopes. *Science* 153:1094–1101.

Taylor, P.N., N.W. Jones, and S. Moorbath. 1984. Isotopic assessment of relative contributions from crust and mantle sources to magma genesis of Precambrian granitoid rocks. *Philosophical Transactions of the Royal Society of London* A310:605–625.

Thompson, R.N. 1982. Magmatism of the British Tertiary Volcanic Province. *Scottish Journal of Geology* 18:49–107.

Teixeira, W., P.R. Renne, G. Bossi, N. Campal, and M.S. D'Agrella Filho. 1999. [40]Ar-[39]Ar and Rb-Sr geochronology of the Uruguayan dike swarm, Rio de la Plata craton and implications for Proterozoic intraplate activity in western Gondwana. *Precambrian Research* 93:153–180.

Tilton, J.R. 1960. Volume diffusion as a mechanism for discordant lead ages. *Journal of Geophysical Research* 65:2933–2945.

Vance, D., M. Meier, and F. Oberli. 1998. The influence of high U-Th inclusions on the U-Th-Pb systematics of almandine-pyrope garnet: Results of a combined bulk dissolution stepwise-leaching, and SEM study. *Geochimica et Cosmochimica Acta* 62:3527–3540.

Vardiman, L., S.A. Austin, J.R. Baumgardner, S.W. Boyd, E.F. Chaffin, D.B. DeYoung, D.R. Humphreys, and A.A. Snelling.

2005. Summary of evidence for a young Earth from the RATE project. In L. Vardiman, A.A. Snelling, and E.F. Chaffin (editors). *Radioisotopes and the Age of the Earth: Results of a Young-Earth Creationist Research Initiative*. El Cajon, CA: Institute for Creation Research and Chino Valley, AZ: Creation Research Society, p. 735–772.

Wasserburg, G.J. 1963. Diffusion processes in lead-uranium systems. *Journal of Geophysical Research* 68:4823–4846.

Webb, A.W. 1985. Geochronology of the Musgrave Block. *Mineral Resources Review, South Australia* 155:23–27.

Wetherill, G.W. 1956a. An interpretation of the Rhodesia and Witwatersrand age patterns. *Geochimica et Cosmochimica Acta* 9:290–292.

————. 1956b. Discordant uranium-lead ages, I. *Transactions of the American Geophysical Union* 37:320–326.

Whitehouse, M.J. 1988. Granulite facies Nd-isotopic homogenisation in the Lewisian Complex of northwest Scotland. *Nature* 331:705–707.

Williams, I.S. 1992. Some observations on the use of the zircon U-Pb geochronology in the study of granitic rocks. *Transactions of the Royal Society of Edinburgh* 83:447–458.

Williams, I.S., W. Compston, and B.W. Chappell. 1983. Zircon and monazite U-Pb systems and histories of I-type magmas, Berridale Batholith, Australia. *Journal of Petrology* 24:76–97.

Williams, I.S., W. Compston, L.P. Black, T.R. Ireland, and J.J. Foster. 1984. Unsupported radiogenic Pb in zircon: A cause of anomalously high Pb-Pb, U-Pb and Th-Pb ages. *Contributions to Mineralogy and Petrology* 88:322–327.

Windrim, D.P., and M.T. McCulloch. 1986. Nd and Sr isotopic systematics of central Australian granulites: Chronology of crustal development and constraints on the evolution of the lower continental crust. *Contributions to Mineralogy and Petrology* 94:289–303.

Wingate, M.T.D., and W. Compston. 2000. Crystal orientation effects during ion microprobe U-Pb analysis of baddeleyite. *Chemical Geology* 168:75–97.

Zashu, S., M. Ozima, and O. Nitoh. 1986. K-Ar isochron dating of Zaire cubic diamonds. *Nature* 323:710–712.

Zhang, L.S., and U. Schärer. 1996. Inherited Pb components in magmatic titanite and their consequence for the interpretation of U-Pb ages. *Earth and Planetary Science Letters* 138:57–65.

Zhao, J., and M.T. McCulloch. 1993. Sm-Nd mineral isochron ages of late Proterozoic dyke swarms in Australia: Evidence for two distinctive events of magma magmatism and crustal extension. *Chemical Geology* 109:341–354.

Zheng, Y.F. 1989. Influences of the nature of the initial Rb-Sr system on isochron validity. *Chemical Geology* 80:1–16.

Zindler, A., and S.R. Hart. 1986. Chemical geodynamics. *Annual Review of Earth and Planetary Sciences* 14:493–571.

Chapter 12

Fossil Distribution in the Flood

John K. Reed • PhD — Geology

Abstract

The argument that all extant species should be found randomly distributed throughout the rock record is examined and found to be misdirected in the main. Those aspects of the argument that are valid cast light on the significant uncertainty attached to any interpretation of the fossil record, by either uniformitarians or diluvialists.

Introduction

Morton (2003) asked, "Where were the plants and animals at the start of the flood?" Right away we see that he has satisfied his reputation as a clever polemicist — the question is unanswerable. Presumably it was asked to attempt to show that creationists cannot answer his "arguments." But turn it around. "Where are the plants and animals today?" Once we get past gross generalities and sparse specifics (e.g., Fido is on the sofa), we see that at any level of meaningful detail the question is a red herring — it cannot be answered accurately and precisely today, and both detail and our level of confidence of the answer degrades quite sharply with time. Where were the plants and animals when Darwin published in 1859, when Hannibal crossed the Alps, or when Moses came down from the mountain? Once we move far enough back in time, any answer must devolve from recorded observations to the fossil record, introducing an entirely new set of uncertainties.

However, there is an interesting issue behind Morton's obfuscation — the distribution of the fossil record — that can be addressed by diluvial geologists in a manner that not only overcomes Morton's point, but also opens new doors to productive research.

Much of Morton's challenge is similarly befogged by polemic, although he eventually gets to the more substantive argument that the distribution of fossils within the geologic column invalidates the young-earth creation model in favor of its old-earth evolutionist competitor. He reasons as follows: (1) there would have been extant creatures and plants present at the Flood's onset; (2) thus we should find all these creatures and plants fossilized in the lowest Flood strata and throughout the column. The created biodiversity present since creation should have provided for a thorough mixing of both extant and extinct categories throughout the geologic record. Since such a distribution is not reflected in the arrangement of the uniformitarian geologic column, the Genesis Flood could not have occurred as described. The known distributions, he argues, are better explained by evolutionary change across time, captured in snapshots by the fossil contents of various sedimentary strata.

This chapter will offer a specific response to Morton, illustrate the logical failures often employed by debunkers of Flood geology, and provide a general response to the underlying issue that the known order of fossil succession in the geologic column negates diluvial geology and creationism. More detailed statements of that argument can be found in Strahler (1999, parts VI and VII), and of course there exists a bloated corpus of literature arguing the evolutionary succession of fossils stretching back through shelves full of dusty scientific journals.

Certainty and Uncertainty

There are three types of errors. Although most people focus on *errors of fact* — those used in the "trivial pursuit" style of debate — *errors of reasoning* and *incorrect assumptions* are far deadlier to any argument. Morton's (2003) article is riddled with these. He consistently:

1. begs the question by assuming the validity and applicability of the points under debate (i.e., the uniformitarian geologic column and evolution);

2. does not address empirical or interpretive uncertainties;

3. selectively ignores weaknesses of his own model;

4. misrepresents the opposing view;

5. jumps between contrary sets of assumptions.

Morton's argument does touch on substantive geologic questions of interest to both diluvialists and uniformitarians. The most important challenge facing paleontology today is the need to describe the three-dimensional distribution of flora and fauna in the rock record. Gaps in our knowledge of fossil distributions require a corresponding caution in explanatory models — one sadly lacking in Morton as well as most other evolutionary paleontologists. It seems a universal human failing to attempt to explain what we know without pausing to consider what we do not.

Furthermore, Morton and many of his secular peers fail to realize that the type and level of uncertainty is not identical in both models. Naturalism relies wholly on empirical data for historical truth, while Christianity depends ultimately on recorded revelation. The latter is superior to empirical data in its truth value, and thus should guide its interpretation (Reed 2001). Therefore, naturalists must not only deal with descriptive and interpretive uncertainties, but must also recognize that their model lacks the counterbalance of a non-empirical truth source that biblical accounts give to Christianity. These also set boundaries for empirical investigation. However, Morton ignores *all* uncertainty, abandoning empirical paleontology for dogmatism. But he is not alone; paleontology as practiced today is *not* a descriptive branch of science. It is instead the forensic justification for speculation about an evolutionary natural history.

Though it is unlikely that the complete distribution of fossils in the crust will ever be ascertained, it is always worth considering just what percentage is known. For example, paleontologists interested in a particular formation may have carefully studied many cubic meters of outcrop and hundreds of meters of core from wells, identifying numerous flora and fauna. All too commonly, they then speak as if their investigation of a vanishingly small percentage of the fossil content of that formation (which may occupy thousands of km³) is known. In some cases, knowledge is greater and extrapolation less; in others, extrapolation is greater.

Descriptive uncertainties are exacerbated by interpretive bias, introduced by model-driven assumptions such as the assumption of the validity of the uniformitarian geologic column and evolution. Locked into those assumptions, adherents automatically pigeonhole rock units into time units based primarily on a few index fossils (see Mortenson 2006 for weaknesses in this method). Ignoring both their presuppositions and their sampling bias (Woodmorappe 1983), they trumpet their interpretations as empirical proof of their position.

Therefore, any broad interpretation of the presently known fossil record must include the recognition of these empirical and presuppositional caveats. It cannot be said that either model is false, based on the available empirical evidence, because that assertion would take the form of a universal negative — just as the hypothetical assertion "there is no gold on Pluto" cannot be demonstrated empirically. Specific predictions can be falsified, but recent history has demonstrated that predictive failures are often explained away without questioning the underlying model.

Distorting Creationism

Interpretation always adds further uncertainty, often in proportion to the relative balance between assumptions and data. Since data are incomplete, any objective evaluation of different interpretive models requires that their strengths and weaknesses be examined and compared. Biased analysis degrades rapidly to polemic, as Morton demonstrates, because (1) he does not address weaknesses in his model, and (2) he does not fairly evaluate the creationist alternative on its own terms.

Because evolution and uniformitarianism have been the ruling paradigms of natural history for many years, paleontology and stratigraphy have come to be considered virtually synonymous with those concepts. However, as Kuhn (1970) noted, nagging inaccuracies that appear minor to the advocates of a dominant paradigm appear much more significant to its opponents and probably will do so retrospectively to everyone following a paradigm shift. Evolution and uniformitarianism have both accumulated many such problems over the years, and Morton fails to acknowledge any of them.

It is well documented that the fossil record has not confirmed fundamental evolutionary predictions. These most definitely did *not* include (1) the abrupt appearance of all major taxa, (2) the absence of indisputable transitional forms, and (3) the surprising discovery of "living fossils" — all observed properties of the known record. Darwinian evolution proposes that all life forms have progressively developed, first from inorganic matter, then proceeding irreversibly from simple to complex forms over time by the natural selection of genetic mutations. Combined with the uniformitarian prediction of sedimentary preservation over time, evolutionists expect fossils to demonstrate an historical progression from the early life to man.

One of the more spectacular failures of this prediction is the sudden appearance of advanced life forms and their body plans in the fossil record. The most famous is the "Cambrian Explosion" where practically all 26 animal phyla and their corresponding body plans appear (Meyer et al. 2004; Weiland 1994). A corollary to abrupt appearance is the absence of transitional forms. In one sense, if evolution had occurred, all life forms would be expected to be "transitional" and classification quite difficult. The fossil record should contain innumerable examples showing the progressive development of body plans and specific parts (e.g., wings, eyes). Morton's silence on these topics is deafening.

Though evolutionists protest and cite examples of a few ambiguous transitional forms, their claims illustrate at least two failures. First, creationists have shown that commonly cited examples are ambiguous and not substantive (Sarfati 2002a). Not only do the most commonly cited examples such as archaeopteryx, the horse series[1] (Hastie 1995), and whales fail in their own right (Sarfati 2002b), but focusing on them masks evolution's most serious failure. Evolution does not predict a smattering of ambiguous examples — it predicts innumerable ones. Finding one "transition" when millions are expected is not a very good predictive percentage for a model claiming certitude.

A paradigm that asserts the seamless, age-old progression of life through time is hard pressed to explain the persistence of form and function without change. An additional challenge is presented when organisms are absent in multiple eras of geologic time but then reappear in the present. An example is *Platasterias* — the echinoderm that is found from the Ordovician to Devonian in fossil form, and then in the present, unchanged (Woodmorappe 1982). Numerous others have been documented (Morris 2000). When confronted with these examples, evolutionists resort to circular reasoning. Those that remain unchanged have reached some optimal form, while those that change have not. However, the only way to determine this optimal status is to appeal to the "progression" found in the geologic column, even though that progression is invalidated by such examples.

In addition to ignoring weaknesses in his own model, Morton (2003) consistently presents a caricature of creationism, misrepresenting its predictions about fossil distribution, sedimentary processes, and preservation. His use of equivocation and his tendency to argue to a "straw man" of his own imagination do not allow his readers to fairly compare the two models. For example, Morton (2003) stated:

> The young-earth paradigm holds that God created the world about 6,000 years ago along with all the animals we find both in the fossil record and alive today. . . . The YEC view has all groups, species, etc., created at the same time.

However, this argument fails to recognize that Linnaean taxonomy is not identical to the created taxa of Genesis. Genesis describes reproductive boundaries of unspecified "kinds," and creationists recognize a potential for genetic diversification within those boundaries, even proposing a systematic method of classification (Frair 2000). This point has been made so many times that Morton's continued attribution of the hoary "fixed species" concept to creationism verges on the dishonest (Sarfati 2000).

Since much of his argument depends on this equivocation, it is irrelevant. If diversification within genetic limits defined at creation occurred in the lower Linnaean levels after the Flood (in order to fill open habitats), then arguments about "species" are specious. Creationists would not predict that all extant species were present at the onset of the Genesis Flood — only that all extant "kinds" were. The true debate between the two models with respect to predicted speciation is whether or not changes at the lowest taxonomic levels add complexity — measurable

---

1. Cavanaugh et al. (2003) argue for a stratomorphic correlation of horse species within the context of baraminology. Even granting their argument, the correlation is not one of evolutionary development since it does not demonstrate an increase in genetic complexity over time.

in genetic information — or not. Evolution demands increasing information; creationism predicts the opposite. Observation presently supports the latter (i.e., Anderson 2005; Sanford 2005).

Another distortion of creationism lies in Morton's assumption that creationists accept the uniformitarian geologic column:

> So, what kind of fossil pattern should we expect to see in the geologic record? Partly it depends on where one places the global flood. . . .

He presupposes that the record of the Flood can be defined relative to some part of the uniformitarian column. That relationship is a matter of debate within creationism (Reed and Oard 2006), but few expect a one-to-one correlation. Nor do they accept the idea that fossils represent the in situ contents of ancient depositional environments — a crucial component of the uniformitarian version. So, when Morton states, "The earliest living fish genera appears in the Jurassic rocks not the Cambrian as would be expected by the young-earth paradigm," he presupposes that "Jurassic" and "Cambrian" have the same historical significance for creationists as they do for evolutionists.

Another misunderstanding is created when he says (2003): "Fossilization is incomplete and creationist claims that the record is essentially complete are false." He then proceeded to misquote creationists to support his point. Unfortunately, he misses the context completely. Creationist claims about the "completeness" of the fossil record apply to the failed prediction of Charles Darwin regarding the presence of innumerable evolutionary transitions between taxa through time. As noted above, although our empirical knowledge of the global three-dimensional fossil distribution is not complete, the record is *sufficiently* complete to falsify Darwin's prediction — a failure most commonly noted by creationists simply by citing evolutionary paleontologists . . . in context!

As an aside, Morton's error illustrates an unintended consequence illustrating how the two models differ with respect to certainty. Naturalism, which depends on empirical data for historical truth, cannot win either way. If the record is currently complete, then its failed predictions are magnified. If incomplete, then its conclusions possess uncertainty proportional to the degree of "incompleteness," unlike the creationist alternatives, in which assertions of historical truth depend ultimately on written records.

Morton (2003) also ignores the scale-dependent complexity of geologic processes within the Flood when he states: "A geologic column like that found in Oklahoma where 60,000 feet of sedimentary rocks are to be found requires that 164 feet of sediment be deposited each and every day. Surely some tired fish would get caught in such a cataclysm." This distortion of the rock record of Oklahoma carries with it a gross oversimplification of whatever processes deposited it. Any given spatial or temporal location on earth's surface could have experienced a variety of geologic processes during the Flood. Any realistic thought experiment, constrained by knowledge of hydraulics, geology, and the Bible, would anticipate such variety. In addition to the factual misrepresentation of sedimentary thickness (the average statewide thickness is only a few thousand feet, and the maximum observed thickness is ~40,000 ft), Morton's bias toward uniformitarianism shows in his attributing *uniform* deposition during the most catastrophic episode in history!

Morton (2003) also indulges in creating straw men:

> Most fish live less than 10 years, with a few, like the halibut, living 30 years. This means that in the preflood population there would be a significant fraction of old fish, ready to pass on to their reward. If there were 10 billion halibut, 330 million of them would be expected to die from old age during the flood.

In trying to make the point that sufficient halibut were available for fossilization in early Flood strata, he assumes: (1) a speculative initial halibut population, (2) its isotropic distribution, (3) death automatically leads to preservation, (4) the reality of the geologic column, and (5) a rigid uniformitarianism. Regular rates may be convenient for extrapolation but are devoid of any conceptual reality. Even granting this ridiculous scenario, it fails to acknowledge that the deposition of particular layers would occur not within the total *year* of the Flood, but often within days, hours, or even minutes, leading to a dramatic decrease in potential fossils by orders of magnitude!

Begging the Question

Confusing conclusions and assumptions, or "begging the question," is one of the classic fallacies of formal logic, and Morton repeatedly falls into that trap. Throughout his argument, uniformitarianism constantly surfaces, even (as shown above) in his discussions of the Flood — the antithesis of uniformitarianism. Varying rates, scales, depositional processes, and preservation are not even considered. His constant presumption of uniformitarianism makes many of his statements irrelevant to the real debate.

As already noted, Morton assumes the uniformitarian geologic column as an empirical fact rather than an interpretive construct. It is easy for laymen to confuse the rock record and the geologic column because uniformitarian geology uses the two terms synonymously in popular presentations. However, a scientist debating the paradigm itself should make that distinction clear. For the sake of clarity in this discussion, I will use the term *rock record* in a descriptive sense, and *geologic column* in a conceptual sense (Reed and Froede 2003).

Either paradigm can be distinguished vis-à-vis the rock record and the column. Both presume that forensic information can be derived from earth's crust. In other words, the crust is the product of events or processes occurring in history. Both models also assume that many of those processes or events have occurred in conformity to established scientific principles, properly applied. Thus, natural history is theoretically possible within both models, though the methodology differs. Beyond this, the two paradigms diverge, even in their definition of natural history. Uniformitarians view natural history as those events that happened prior to man's appearance, while the biblical paradigm presents it as a branch of history limited not by man's absence on earth, but by temporal and spatial gaps within recorded human history. Morton nowhere acknowledges this crucial distinction.

Further differences include uniformitarianism versus catastrophism, and the in situ preservation of assemblages in their paleoenvironments versus the sorting, transport, and deposition of fossils in the Flood. In other words, do fossil assemblages show a "snapshot" of history like the relics of Pompeii, or are they indicators of a particular hydraulic environment (e.g., Austin 2003)? Another difference is evolution: Morton sees it as the predicted variable that enables rock units to be calibrated into time periods. Creationists reject that approach. Finally, Flood models predict regional and megaregional signatures in the rocks, and attribute parts of the crust to a supernatural creation event not open to forensic investigation. The extent to which different assumptions lead to different stratigraphic constructs is discussed in Reed and Oard (2006).

Thus, when Morton equates Flood strata with particular uniformitarian eras, he is comparing apples and oranges. Even the *relative* time comparisons between the geologic eras may not be globally appropriate for creationists, given regional diachronous sedimentation occurring within days or weeks. When Morton asserts that the column shows a particular sequence of fossil forms, all he is saying is that the premises and conclusions of his model at that point are consistent. Contrary to his claims, he is not speaking to the validity of creationist models at all. This error is repeated throughout his presentation.

Selective Theology

In the past, presenting the argument over origins and earth history as one of "science versus religion" was used as a polemic device to avoid debate.

> The reason that we didn't know the truth concerning these matters is that the claim of an inevitable and bitter warfare between religion and science has, for more than three centuries, been the primary polemical device used in the atheist attack on faith. From Thomas Hobbes through Carl Sagan and Richard Dawkins, false claims about religion and science have been used as weapons in the battle to "free" the human mind from the "fetters" of faith (Stark 2003, p. 123).

Increasing numbers of people are realizing that creationists and evolutionists represent two opposing views of reality — worldviews — those of Christianity and naturalism. While it is true that one can advocate "theistic" evolution or "catastrophic" uniformitarianism, clearly such views are derivative hybrids, and the primary positions are those represented by creationists and atheistic views. Arguments between those worldviews range across a spectrum of theological, philosophical, and historical assertions and counter-assertions, because the two worldviews hold quite contrary views of everything from the nature of ultimate reality to the origin of the Grand Canyon.

Morton, however, cannot make up his mind. He cycles from one worldview to the other, choosing a position to suit whatever argument he is making at the time. For example, he states (2003): "Since Creation, especially since the Fall, creatures have only gone extinct." Does he believe in creation or in original sin? Does he believe in an historical Adam and Eve? If so, the only source of truth regarding these people and events is the Bible. But if the Bible is to be accepted when it speaks of "creation" and "the Fall," why not when it testifies to the Flood? Again he states (2003):

> Could God have created the new life after the flood? Yes, of course God could have. Of course this would be adding to the Scripture which is warned against in Galatians and Revelations. In other words, there is no evidence from Scripture that God engaged in a massive creation event after the flood.

Morton appears to be endorsing God, the Scripture, its specific moral imperatives, and its authority and unity. One does not even need to point out that the same passage in the Book of Revelation similarly warns against taking away from the Bible's words — which would, of course, include taking away such passages as Genesis 6–9 and 2 Peter 3 — to understand that there is a fundamental intellectual dishonesty in not arguing consistently within one particular worldview.

A point-by-point critique of Morton's polemic would be an exhausting slog through a bog of poor reasoning and self-serving assumptions, populated by more straw men than a casting call for *The Wizard of Oz*! Instead, it is more profitable to restate his argument, leaving aside those errors, and then proceed to points of genuine debate.

Would the Real Question Please Stand Up?

Beneath the numerous errors in Morton's article is the kernel of an argument that has been pressed against creationists for decades — the supposed order of the fossil record. Its longevity is because of its dual utility; it is useful (1) as an argument for biological evolution (fossils show evolution through time) and (2) for geological uniformitarianism (fossil order demonstrates deep time). While many have answered both sides of this argument in detail, it is worth reviewing a few important aspects of the debate.

First, the assertion that fossil order demonstrates evolution relies on a very selective examination of one aspect of the larger phenomena of fossils at the expense of others that paint a different picture. Just as some can cite individual Bible verses to prove any point (e.g., Judas went out and hanged himself. . . . Go thou and do likewise), evolutionists have long been guilty of selecting bits and pieces of the fossil record to bolster their case, while ignoring many facets that do not. Their focus has narrowed over the years as knowledge has increased, moving from Darwin's sweeping claims in 1859 to present-day focus on a few species.

But evolutionary selectivity must not define the debate. When creationists argue only questions defined by their opponents, they lose sight of the forest by zooming in on a few leaves, and they need to step back. For example, any explanation of fossils must account for the vast quantity of marine fossils found in sedimentary rocks on the continents at all elevations. Countless creatures were buried and preserved on a global scale — the primary prediction of the Genesis Flood. Increasing research demonstrates that much of the fossil record formed rapidly by catastrophic processes acting over large areas (Austin 1994; Reed 2002) — another prediction of the Flood. Furthermore, fossilization itself is relatively rare in the present (see chapter 14), reinforcing the creationist assertion that unique processes operated in the past that are not seen today. Examination of strata indicates that many fossils were transported (sometimes long distances) and then buried — contrary to the uniformitarian prediction of in situ burial in preserved ancient environments.

In addition to ignoring these broad characteristics, the uniformitarian/evolutionary position falls apart under its own weight. First, it is forced to ignore the large bulk of fossils in order to trumpet a few "index fossils," those supposedly showing a restricted stratigraphic range and widespread geographic distribution. Second, the succession of fossils — once confidently thought to illustrate the steps of evolution in minute detail — has fallen apart because all the links are missing. Third, the use of index fossils as time markers, telling geologists which era or period a particular rock unit should be, becomes increasingly problematic as continued research keeps shifting the temporal range of these fossils (Oard 2000), since index fossils require a restricted stratigraphic range. As they are found in "younger" and "older" formations, their stratigraphic utility decreases. More embarrassing, living fossils spectacularly invalidate both evolution and stratigraphic assignments.

Morton and his secular colleagues are caught on the horns of a dilemma. They claim to be open-minded empiricists, eagerly searching for new data, while decrying the dogmatism of their opponents. However, their actions say something quite different. They consistently refuse to place their pronouncements within the context of a poorly known three-dimensional distribution of the fossil record. In doing so, they demonstrate that they are guilty of the very "crime" of which they are so quick to accuse creationists! This selective presentation of evidence is a crucial logical error, and data gaps are commonly filled with the "conventional wisdom," which breaks down to nothing more than model-driven assumptions. These include the following:

- The geologic column (or geologic time scale) is an interpretive template — an accurate representation of the crust everywhere. This must be true a priori in order to expand the interpreted fossil succession at any particular location. Its use is rationalized by claiming that it is an empirical compilation, but data are not defined and organized absent assumptions — in this case evolution, uniformitarianism, and deep time.

- In order to assume the geologic column, stratigraphers must assume that rock units are ordered into globally synchronous, correlative time periods. In other words, a particular rock unit is "Cambrian" because it was deposited only between 542 and 488 Ma, regardless of lithology or depositional environment. This also means that "Cambrian" rocks can be unequivocally recognized and correlated all over the world simply on the basis of their supposed age. Clearly, creationists cannot accept this scheme unless inherent properties of rock units can be shown to be unique time indicators. Thus, when Morton (2003) expands on the relative abundance of fish in the "Devonian" and the "Cambrian," his argument is running in some parallel universe, with no relevance to biblical history.

- Evolution. The basis for ordering the fossil succession (often by correlating disparate strata physically separated by long distances) is the assumption that order and complexity increase steadily through time. The extent to which this assumption drives interpretation is seen in the absence of modification to the overall concept in spite of the numerous empirical "surprises" that have greeted paleontologists over many decades.

- Fossil assemblages and successions must represent in situ conditions to have interpretive meaning within the evolutionary paradigm. In other words, a limestone with corals, gastropods, and other shallow-water marine invertebrates *must* represent a reef that was buried and preserved as it existed hundreds of millions of years ago. Any evidence that fossils were transported into their burial position undercuts this fundamental assumption.

In summary, the confidence with which evolutionists and uniformitarians assert the truth of their position and the falsity of their opponents is shockingly at odds with their empirical approach to knowledge. If they were consistent, they would admit the gaps in the data, welcome competing hypotheses, and treat those that differ from them with greater respect.

Toward an Allocthonous Assessment of Fossils

Diluvial geologists expect fossil assemblages to be the artifact of sedimentary transport, deposition, burial, diagenesis, and differential preservation. Uniformitarians do, too, but on a much smaller scale. However, the more we examine the rock record, the more we see that these factors should be considered on a much larger scale. The roadblock to doing so is the set of expectations generated by assumptions about the geologic column, evolution, and deep time that comprise the reigning paradigm.

Thus the approach of the diluvialist is more "empirical," while the evolutionist remains fixated on speculative paleoenvironments, such as the mythological "coal swamp." If diluvialists are correct, then the rock record should show numerous instances of fossils being buried and preserved in ways analogous to clastic sedimentary particles transported and deposited in their present position. Whitcomb and Morris (1961) emphasized the creationist claim that the distribution of fossils will show the effects of hydraulic sorting (among other things), but this argument conflicts with the in situ paleoenvironment approach. In effect, that assumption has limited a fruitful area of research.

Thus, it is up to diluvialists to correct this oversight and open the door to this mode of investigation. Although it has been extensively used as an apologetic argument, it has seldom been studied in detail. I would strongly recommend that creationists rectify that oversight over the broad range of their investigations into the rock record. This can be done by examining the same steps applied to the analysis of clastic sediments in instances where the fossil contents of a rock unit show evidence of transport. This would include evaluating the density, shape, size, etc., of fossils, just as is done for other constituents that undergo transport and deposition.

First, to the extent possible, fossils should be traced toward their source. To facilitate this, the geometry of the rock unit in question must be determined. Then the direction and strength of the paleocurrents should be estimated. These can constrain the direction and distance that fossils were transported (e.g., Austin 2003). It may be possible to use varying hydraulic properties of different types of fossils, as well as their durability, to show a lateral sorting of fauna; similar to the way that conglomerate, sandstone, siltstone, and shale can show a lateral association based on the more rapid deposition of the heavier grains across a lateral area. If such a sorting can be shown, then the vertical time-dependent template commonly used to order the fossils would be invalidated.

Numerous sedimentary studies, both laboratory and field, have demonstrated that hydraulic parameters can often be derived from clastic sediments (Austin 1994; Berthault 1994, 2002a, 2002b, 2004; Lalomov 2003). Likewise, the hydraulic properties of fossils should be investigated to determine the flow conditions under which they would initiate motion, be transported, and then be deposited again. Often their association with sediments can facilitate this type of investigation, providing minimum current velocities, lateral extent, reach, and depth. Those fossils that might not be amenable to direct transport in aqueous currents might be subject to movement in sedimentary mass flows (Austin 2003).

Like rocks, most fossils are composed of minerals that can be subject to chemical and physical changes that occur after deposition. These run the gamut from simple compaction to complete dissolution of the organism. Sometimes even this extreme can be determined by the deposition of replacement minerals in the same form as the fossil, but it is certainly reasonable to infer that it might not be detected in examination of the current rock. Thus, the diagenetic history of any particular deposit should be considered when cataloging the fossil assemblages.

Like sedimentary rocks, the final step in evaluating the history of a particular unit must be an assessment of the preservation potential of the rock. In other words, how much of the unit was eroded? How does that erosion affect the way we see the present-day fossil distribution? For example, if particular fossils were sorted into the upper beds of a formation, and then those beds were eroded, our conclusion of the "complete" fossil assemblage for the formation would be in error. As with any forensic investigation of the past, it always pays to remember the uncertainties.

As continued investigation continues to reveal the true distribution of fossil forms in the rock record, as creationists refine their understanding of the rock record itself in terms of the mechanisms of the Flood, and as they explain the differences between extant and extinct species in terms of the Genesis "kinds" or *baramin*, then a clearer interpretation of the fossil record in its many particulars will follow. To the extent that evolutionists belittle such efforts and remain entrenched in their dogmatism, progress will be slowed . . . but not stopped.

Conclusions

Flood geology has nothing to fear from empirical efforts to understand the three-dimensional distribution of the fossil record in earth's crust. Those who believe otherwise, like Morton, are blinded by the mass of assumptions that supply most of the horsepower to their speculative models. Furthermore, that blindness hinders them from realizing that many of their "arguments" against creationism are in fact nothing more than the restatement of their own assumptions about evolution, uniformitarianism, and deep time and are therefore largely irrelevant to the real debate. Creationists should not be afraid to answer any question, but it is worth knowing that such a question is more than a disguised restatement of an extrascientific opinion.

References

CRSQ: Creation Research Society Quarterly

Anderson, K.A. 2005. Is bacterial resistance to antibiotics an appropriate example of evolutionary change? *CRSQ* 42(1):1–17.

Austin, S.A. 1994. *Grand Canyon: Monument to Catastrophe.* Santee, CA: Institute for Creation Research.

———. 2003. Nautiloid mass kill and burial event, Redwall Limestone (Lower Mississippian), Grand Canyon region, Arizona and Nevada. In R.L. Ivey (editor). *Proceedings of the Fifth International Conference on Creationism* (technical symposium sessions). Pittsburgh, PA: Creation Science Fellowship), p. 55–100.

Berthault, G. 1994. Experiments in stratification. In R.E. Walsh (editor). *Proceedings of the Third International Conference on Creationism* (technical symposium sessions). Pittsburgh, PA: Creation Science Fellowship, p. 103–110.

———. 2002a. Geological dating principles questioned, paleohydraulics: a new approach. *Journal of Geodesy and Geodynamics* 22:19–26.

———. 2002b. Analysis of main principles of stratigraphy on the basis of experimental data. *Lithology and Mineral Resources* 37:442–446.

———. 2004. Sedimentological interpretation of the Tonto Group stratigraphy (Grand Canyon Colorado River). *Lithology and Mineral Resources* 39:480–484.

Cavanaugh, D.P., T.C. Wood, and K.P. Wise. 2003. Fossil equidae: a monobaraminic stratomorphic series. In R.L. Ivey (editor). *Proceedings of the Fifth International Conference on Creationism* (technical symposium sessions). Pittsburgh, PA: Creation Science Fellowship, p. 143–153.

Friar, W. 2000. Baraminology — classification of created organisms. *CRSQ* 37(2):82–91.

Hastie, P. 1995. What's happened to the horse? *Creation* 17(4):14–16.

Kuhn, T.S. 1970. *The Structure of Scientific Revolutions*, second edition. Chicago, IL: University of Chicago Press.

Lalomov, A.V. 2003. Paleohydrology of Jurassic conglomerate of the Crimean Peninsula. In R.L. Ivey (editor). *Proceedings of the Fifth International Conference on Creationism* (technical symposium sessions). Pittsburgh, PA: Creation Science Fellowship, p. 197–208.

Meyer, S.C., M. Ross, P. Nelson, and P. Chien. 2004. The Cambrian explosion: biology's big bang. In J.A. Campbell and S.C. Meyer (editors). *Darwinism, Design, and Education*. East Lansing, MI: Michigan State University Press.

Morris, H.M. 2000. The profusion of living fossils. Back to Genesis #143, Acts & Facts 29(11), online at http://www.icr.org/newsletters/btg/btgnov00.html (April 2005).

Mortenson, T. 2006. The historical development of the old-earth geological time-scale. In J.K. Reed and M.J. Oard (editors). *The Geologic Column: Perspectives Within Diluvial Geology*. Chino Valley, AZ: Creation Research Society Books.

Morton, G. 2003. Where were the plants and animals at the start of the flood? http://home.entouch.net/dmd/whereanimals.htm (March 15, 2005).

Oard, M.J. 2000. How well do paleontologists know fossil distributions? *TJ* 14(1):7–8.

Reed, J.K. 2001. *Natural History in the Christian Worldview*. Chino Valley, AZ: CRS Books.

———. 2002. Reinventing stratigraphy at the Palo Duro Basin. *CRSQ* 39(1):25–39.

Reed, J.K., and C.R. Froede, Jr. 2003. The uniformitarian stratigraphic column — shortcut or pitfall for creation geology. *CRSQ* 40:21–29.

Reed, J.K., and M.J. Oard. 2006. *The Geologic Column: Perspectives Within Diluvial Geology*. Chino Valley, AZ: CRS Books.

Sanford, J.C. 2005. *Genetic Entropy and the Mystery of the Genome*. Dallas, TX: Ivan Press.

Sarfati, J. 2000. *Refuting Evolution*. Green Forest, AR: Master Books.

———. 2002a. 15 ways to refute materialist bigotry: a point by point response to Scientific American at http://www.answersingenesis.org/news/scientific_american.asp, answer to J. Rennie (editor). 2002. 15 Answers to Creationist Nonsense. *Scientific American* 287(1):78–85).

———. 2002b. *Refuting Evolution 2*. Green Forest, AR: Master Books.

Stark, R. 2003. *For the Glory of God*. Princeton, NJ: Princeton University Press.

Strahler, A.N. 1999. *Science and Earth History: The Evolution/Creation Controversy*. New York: Prometheus Books.

Weiland, C. 1994. Exploding evolution. *Creation* 16(2):38–39.

Whitcomb, J.C., and H.M. Morris. *The Genesis Flood*. Philadelphia, PA: Presbyterian and Reformed Publishing.

Woodmorappe, J. 1982. An anthology of matters significant to creationism and diluviology: report 2. *CRSQ* 18(4):201–223.

———. 1983. A diluviological treatise on the stratigraphic separation of fossils. *CRSQ* 20(3):133–185.

Chapter 13

The Joggins Polystrate Fossils

Ian Juby

Abstract

Polystrate plant fossils in the cliffs at Joggins, Nova Scotia, Canada, have long been seen as evidence of long, slow geological processes. These fossils are claimed to be evidence of in situ burial of ancient environments happening over and over again for long periods of time. However, there are numerous lines of evidence showing that the fossils were transported and catastrophically buried — a testament to the Flood rather than uniformitarianism. In this chapter we will examine evidence found in research by both uniformitarians and catastrophists, answer the uniformitarian and actualist skeptics, and discuss the strong indicators of the rapid deposition of the entire formation.

The Joggins Fossil Cliffs

The Joggins fossil cliffs (figure 1) are a fantastic, world-class formation on the east coast of Canada in Nova Scotia. Joggins is located about 20 minutes from Amherst, on the Bay of Fundy, site of the highest tides in the world (rising and falling as much as 49 feet [15 m] twice daily). These tides constantly erode the 82 foot (25 m) high cliffs, continually creating new exposures.

The cliffs have a combined thickness of some 16,400 feet (5,000 m), three times the depth of exposed strata in the Grand Canyon. They are generally tilted to the south, typically around 20°. The cliffs include conglomerate, coal, shale, sandstone, and small amounts of limestone. There is a wide variety of small-scale geological features, such as fossil ripple marks, supposed raindrop imprints, channels, and slickensides.

Figure 1. The fossil cliffs of Joggins, Nova Scotia, Canada. Located on the shores of the Bay of Fundy, these cliffs are eroded twice daily by the highest tides in the world.

217

Abundant body fossils found there include clams, lizards, occasional damselflies, horseshoe crabs, coelacanth body parts and scales, and a scorpion. Multiple layers of carbonized shale contain myriads of shells and fish scales. Trace fossils are also numerous and are mostly seen as tracks and trails from a variety of marine and terrestrial creatures. An interesting paleontological feature of Joggins is the presence of the lizard-like *Hylonomous* inside some hollow lycopod stumps.

The Joggins cliffs are now a fossil heritage site and no one may remove fossils or rocks from the cliffs without a heritage research permit (Falcon-Lang and Calder 2004).

The Polystrate Fossils

The cliffs are best known for their abundant fossil plants, which are commonly coalified or petrified. Throughout large portions of the cliffs, many of these plants are "polystrate," because they are buried vertically, cutting through many sedimentary layers (Coffin 1975; Morris 1999). The polystrate "trees" are not trees in the normal sense, but are giant, hollow reeds. Better known as lycopods and calamites, they are similar to modern club mosses and equisetum (horsetail), respectively.

The fossils are considerably larger than the modern forms. Modern horsetail seldom exceeds one meter in height and one centimeter in diameter. I have initially misidentified fossil horsetails as lycopods because of their size, about 4 inches (10 cm) in diameter. Calamites probably reach 66 feet (20 m) in height in the fossil record. The longest calamite log I have seen at Joggins was less than 13 feet (4 m). Figure 2 shows a typical fossil calamite beside its modern counterpart.

Modern club moss reaches a maximum of 1.6 feet (50 cm) in height, but their fossil counterpart, the lycopods, had trunks that were many meters tall and reached diameters of up to one meter! Figure 3 shows a polystrate lycopod from the Joggins Formation. It has a trunk diameter of roughly 2.5 feet (75 cm) and was at least 24.6 feet (7.5 m) tall.

In addition to the polystrate calamites and lycopods, there are actual fossil trees at Joggins called cordaitales, a type of pine. These are almost never polystrate but lie generally parallel to bedding.

The Challenge of "In Situ" Trees and Multiple Forests

The Joggins polystrate trees are considered a showcase for uniformitarian geology. Charles Lyell thought them a powerful evidence for uniformitarianism:

Figure 2. Fossil calamites (right) are common at Joggins and is one of the two predominant plants that are polystrate. It's modern counterpart is the horsetail reed (left). An excellent example of giantism in the fossil record.

Figure 3. A polystrate lycopod cutting vertically through over 7.5 meters of sediments. Ruler markings are 10 centimeters, I am pointing at the cavity left behind by the top of the plant which has fallen out of the cliff.

Hailed in 1842 by Charles Lyell (1881, p. 64–65) as "the most wonderful phenomenon perhaps that I have ever seen," Joggins is mentioned in his *Principles of Geology* (Lyell 1872) and Darwin's (1859) *On the Origin of Species*. This remarkable section, proposed as a UNESCO World Heritage Site (Falcon-Lang and Calder 2004), profoundly influenced the young science of geology by serving as a proving ground for the principles of uniformitarianism, in situ botanical origin of coal, and incompleteness of the fossil record (Waldron and Rygel 2005, p. 337).

The polystrate plants at Joggins are interpreted within the uniformitarian paradigm as trees that were buried in situ. In other words, they grew slowly in place for tens to hundreds of years before being buried and preserved. Thus they would be considered to exist in their growth position. Early researchers such as Dawson and Lyell observed that lycopods tended to be grouped together in specific sedimentary layers. At least 76 coal seams ranging in thickness from 0.16 to 5 feet (0.05 to 1.5 m) and 63 "forested" horizons with vertical lycopsid trees are known (Waldron and Rygel 2005). Most of the "forested" horizons are associated with thin, organic-rich horizons or mineral zones. So uniformitarians conclude that Joggins represents at least 63 forests that grew over hundreds of thousands, if not millions, of years. That opinion was first expressed by Charles Lyell and William Dawson when they visited the site in 1851, and has been assumed by uniformitarians ever since.

For instance, on the TalkOrigins website, Andrew MacRae (1997) refers to Dawson's (apparently an old-earth creationist) original work to support the uniformitarian position. He specifically uses Dawson's drawings from the late 1800s to build a case for in situ emplacement of polystrates at Joggins (figure 4).

Greg Neyman (2003), the author of the www.AnswersInCreation.org website, wrote a rebuttal to John Morris's (1999) article on the Joggins cliffs. Neyman disputed much of what Morris wrote and attempted to defend the idea that the Joggins formation was produced by several floods over the eons of time.

Berg (2002) did a literature search and concluded that the polystrate fossils were transported and deposited in a vertical position with few attached roots, which would not be expected in an in situ origin. Birkeland (2004) tried to discredit Berg's use of one of Dawson's original drawings, claiming that Dawson simply did not draw the roots:

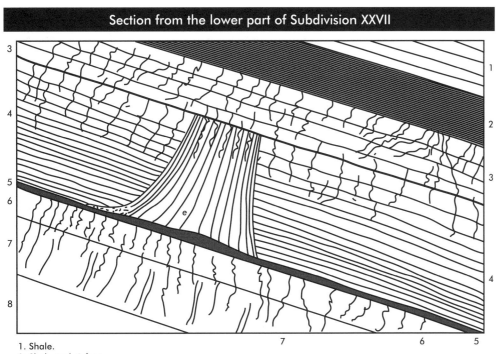

Section from the lower part of Subdivision XXVII

1. Shale.
2. Shaly coal, 1 foot.
3. Underclay with rootlets, 1 foot 2 inches.
4. Gray sandstone passing downwards into shale, 3 feet. Erect tree with Stigmaria roots (e) on the coal.
5. Coal, 1 inch.
6. Underclay with roots, 10 inches.
7. Gray sandstone, 1 foot, 5 inches. Stigmaria rootlets continue from the bed above; erect Calamites.
8. Gray shale, with pyrites. Flattened plants.

Figure 4. William Dawson's drawing of a polystrate lycopod at Joggins. Drawings still have their place today as photographing fossils has inherent problems. The fossils are usually the same color as their surrounding rock, and details visible to the human eye often do not show up on film. Nothing beats the human eye. (From Dawson 1855; other editions 1868, 1878, 1891). The Geology of Nova Scotia, New Brunswick and Prince Edward Island or Acadian Geology, Oliver and Boyd, Edinburgh. Public domain.)

Mr. Berg is taking a 140–160-year-old schematic figure, drawn by a fallible human, far too seriously. Unlike God, geologists are fallible beings, who make mistakes and oversimplify their drawing to the point of leaving out important details. Part of the problem is that some of [sic] roots weren't filled with sand or other sediment when the tree was buried. Thus, they are now preserved as carbonized compressions. These can be easily missed, if either the person looking for them doesn't know what they are looking for or if the outcrop is dirty and too dangerous to clean off. What Mr. Berg ignores is that later geologists have demonstrated, as an absolute fact, that the polystrate trees of Joggins do have roots. This later research completely renders Dawson's figures and text moot and meaningless as proof of anything, except that he over simplified [sic] his drawings to the point of leaving out important details and it is a serious mistake to regard his research as infallible.

Axel Heiberg Island, located in the northern Queen Elizabeth Islands, also has a section of polystrate trees with coal seams, similar to the Joggins site (Oard 1995a, 1995b). Birkeland (2004) claims that creationists have missed the roots in the Axel Heiberg "fossil forests," as well as at Joggins:

> Conventional geologists would consider this a remarkably ill-informed statement because [sic] both popular and scientific publications, it is obvious anyone [sic], except the vision impaired, can find pictures of the large tree stumps that have been found at Axel Heiberg Island. For example, in both Basinger (1987) and Lemonick (1986), there is an undeniable picture of one of the scientists studying the Axel Heiberg Island forests [sic] standing on the very tree roots that Young Earth creationists claim don't exist. . . . The inability of Young Earth creationists to observe rooted trees that quite clearly exist at the Axel Heiberg Island and in the Joggins, Nova Scotia, sea cliffs is a remarkable example of how people are so blinded by their preconceptions that they are totally deaf, dumb, and blind to reality. It is one of many reasons why conventional geologists regards [sic] much of incredibly bad science that Young Earth creationists publish as alleged "research" with disdain and much humor.

Rebuttal

I will address uniformitarian claims about the Joggins fossils. Although there are numerous advocates of that position, there is little need to deal with them individually, since most of what is written is simply a rehash of what is posted at the TalkOrigins website. Primarily, I will address the claim of "in situ" trees being preserved at Joggins.

It is convenient to divide the Joggins fossil cliffs into three parts, each of which is roughly 5,000 feet (1,500 m) thick. The Lower Cove section is the northernmost section and runs south from Boss Point to Lower Cove. This is known as the Boss Point Formation and is stratigraphically the lowest portion of the cliffs. The second part is the "classic" Joggins section, which contains the most polystrate fossils and runs south from Lower Cove to MacCarron's creek. The Ragged Reef section, the third part, runs from Mac-Carron's creek to Ragged Reef and includes the Springhill Mines and the Ragged Reef formations.

Despite claims of long ages, the evidence at Joggins points to rapid burial and preservation of the polystrate fossils. These plants show no signs of rot and were still soft and uncoalified when the formation underwent tectonic tilting. Consequently, the sediments must have also been soft and unlithified during this upheaval.

Because there are trees being deposited in the upright position in the bottom of Spirit Lake at Mount St. Helens, some creationists have mistakenly thought it a good modern analogue for Joggins. Although Spirit Lake does show that trees can be catastrophically deposited in an upright "growth" position (Morris and Austin 2003), the Joggins polystrate plants were not deposited in that fashion. Although the Joggins hollow reeds are polystrate, the fossil pine trees are always parallel to bedding.

Previous Creationist Investigations

Previous investigations of the Joggins cliffs have been performed by creationists (Coffin 1975; Berg 2002). Coffin documented ten pieces of evidence of allochthonous emplacement of the fossil plants at Joggins, refuting autochthonous burial theories. Berg's work was based strictly on literature research (mostly German), but is an excellent summary. He reached many of the same conclusions as Coffin, while pointing out nine pieces of evidence that suggest allochthonous emplacement of the Joggins deposits.

Since these men have already made an excellent case for the rapid deposition of the Joggins cliffs, I will not rehash their arguments. Rather, this article will complement the growing evidence that the Joggins Fossil cliffs are a testament to the global Flood of Noah.

Evidence the Polystrate Reeds Are Not In Situ

I have studied these cliffs for more than four years. I began after examining claims and counterclaims on the Internet about the significance of these exposures to the origins debate. I wanted to examine the evidence myself.

One of the strongest evidences that the trees did not grow in place is the *lack* of roots, which many evolutionists claim exist. Dawson (1855) claimed and MacRae (1997) repeated that the rootlets penetrating the clays had to have done so by growing through thick, dense clays. Dawson makes this claim in spite of the evidence he clearly saw, as seen in his drawing. Note (figure 4) that the very prominent stump (level 4) is clearly missing its roots. Point *e* in figure 4 shows a stigmaria, the root of the stump that has been sheared off at the coal seam on which the stump rests.

Figure 5 shows a specimen of the stigmarian roots in question. They are immediately identifiable by the pockmarks on them. The pockmarks on the mold of the root on the right show places where rootlets once radiated outward. Dawson clearly drew a stigmarian root at the base of the stump (point *e*, figure 4). His drawing shows numerous rootlets, even though they seldom exceed a centimeter in diameter. Yet none of them are attached to a main root! The only root drawn in the picture (attached to the stump) has clearly been stripped of its rootlets. Therefore, Dawson was careful to show the empirical detail contrary to his own hypothesis. Disarticulated rootlets are not an argument for in situ growth, but for catastrophic transport and deposition, although Dawson and MacRae attempt otherwise.

Birkeland (2004) thought that Dawson did see the roots attached to the stumps, but that is not supported by the meticulous drawing. While it is true that there are stumps with roots attached, sometimes the roots are crushed and difficult to see. Even when the roots are crushed (another evidence for rapid burial), they are easily seen, being at least several centimeters thick.

Although mud is constantly washing down and hardening on the cliff faces and often obscuring detail, Dawson's eye for detail is indicated by the centimeter-scale rootlets

Figure 5. A fossil stigmaria. Also very common at Joggins, this is the root of one of the giant lycopods. Looking carefully, one can see the cast of the root on the inside of the rock on the right. The black lines going into that rock are carbonized (coalified) rootlets. The roots had rootlets radiating out in all directions from the pock-marks visible in the root. These collected water and transmitted it to the root.

that he *did* draw. The stump in his drawing appears to have been at or near beach level. At that level, he could easily have cleaned the cliff face as he drew. If detail was obscured, *how could he see the small rootlets, yet miss the larger roots?* He shows rootlets below the coal seam but not above it. If the stigmaria were in the coal seam, but simply invisible, there should have been stigmarian rootlets radiating upward, too.

Figure 6 shows a stigmarian root with rootlets radiating in all directions. These rootlets are visible even though they are six meters off the ground. If there were large roots that had fallen out of the cliffs to which these rootlets had

Figure 6. Another stigmarian root, this time in-situ (in place). When rootlets are present and not stripped off, they radiate out in all directions. The discoloration in the surrounding rock could be interpreted as soil that was transported with the root when it was brought from its original location to where it sits now.

been attached, leaving behind the rootlets, the molds of the large roots should be visible. Since Dawson supported the in situ hypothesis, he would have known that the presence of roots would have been evidence for his belief and *certainly* would have drawn them — if present.

Coffin (1975) noted that the roots that are present show negative geotropism (figure 7). This means that the roots were not oriented down into the dirt as expected from in situ growth, but instead are bent *upward*, extending above what would have been ground level.

This implies that the stumps were uprooted and transported to their present position. Also, Coffin (1983, p. 123), Mackay (personal communication), and Juby (2006) have all reported *inverted* polystrate stumps. Figure 8 shows a portion of figure 7 with a cavity from an inverted stump highlighted. The longest roots I have encountered at Joggins extend to roughly 13 feet (4 m), and these are roots oriented in non-growth positions (figures 7 and 8). Figure 9 shows a closer view. The stigmarian root on the right may have come from the lycopod stump above; however, the one on the left could only have come from the inverted stump. Even the root oriented "correctly" does not help the uniformitarian argument; the roots of the two stumps are intertwined, with the upper one resting in an upright position on the lower, inverted stump. Furthermore, the roots from both stumps were on the same bedding plane as the roots of other stumps. Thus, intact roots (even on the same bedding plane as the roots from other stumps) are clearly not proof of burial in the growth position.

Roots that are found at Joggins are typically truncated, either by bedding or the ends of the roots having been broken off. This is consistent with other polystrate stumps found around the world, such as Specimen Ridge at Yellowstone Park, the Axel Heiberg Island "fossil forests," Alaska, and the lycopod trees of England (Oard and Giesecke 2007), and is evidence consistent with allochthonous emplacement, as was noted in Spirit Lake.

Calamites are just as common as lycopods at Joggins. At any given time, dozens of calamites are visible in the cliffs. Of all the calamites I have seen over four years of fieldwork, I have yet to see one with attached roots. Dawson documented one with partial roots and another with what looks like fairly intact roots (figure 10), while showing others in the same drawing as having none. In 2004 I observed some six or seven root balls exposed in the group of calamites located at the base of the entrance stairs to the beach. But not one of them had observable, intact roots.

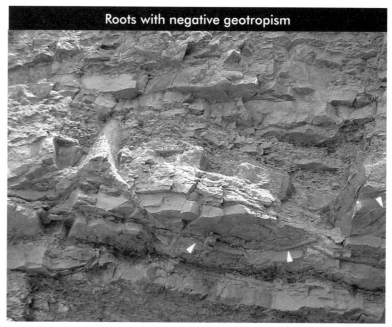

Figure 7. A giant lycopod. The arrows mark out its stigmarian root. This root shows "negative geotropism." The root is going up, not down. Roots normally grow down and out, so this implies that the roots were floating in the mud, not buried "in situ" (where they grew).

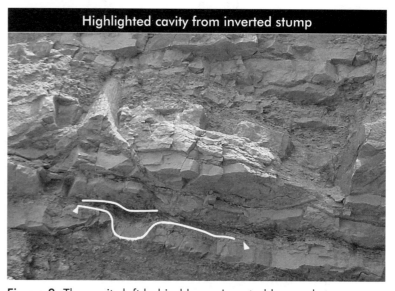

Figure 8. The cavity left behind by an inverted lycopod stump. The arrows mark the stigmarian roots which are still in place. Following the still-visible cavities left behind by the roots, the roots on the right were on the same level and apparently intertwined with the roots of the lycopod above.

These observations combine with common sense to lead to the conclusion that polystrate plants like those at Joggins are better interpreted within a catastrophic paradigm. While the 63 levels have been simply interpreted as growth horizons by uniformitarian scientists, other evidence suggests that the plants were transported and buried in their present positions in a very short time.

The Challenge of Polystrate Trees to the Uniformitarian Paradigm

Without their "buried forest" model, uniformitarians would be faced with yet another example of rapid geologic processes that would invalidate both their time scale and their paleoenvironmental assumptions about the past. But clearly, rapid burial is required to preserve the vertically oriented plant remains. The top of the "tree" would quickly decay if not buried within a short time frame.

When taken at the scale of the entire formation, this common sense conclusion puts a limit on the time available for the rocks to form. The conventional uniformitarian interpretation claims that the Joggins Formation took five to ten million years to accumulate. But the fossils refute this claim. Because the plants are vertical, sections of the formation must have formed quickly. Furthermore, because the vertical plants are found throughout much of the stratigraphic thickness of the formation, and the layers that are not cut across by polystrate fossils are identical to the layers that are, it is quite safe to conclude that the entire formation formed quickly. The only alternatives are that the plants stayed intact for thousands of years, without rotting or being petrified (or coalified), or that bursts of sedimentation occurred followed by hundreds of thousands of years of no geologic activity — or dead time. Both are difficult to imagine. To believe that plants would remain partially buried in a temperate environment without rotting requires much more faith than believing a catastrophist interpretation. For bursts of rapid sedimentation followed by long quiet periods, there should be abundant signs of erosion at the interface between bursts, but there are few signs of erosion.

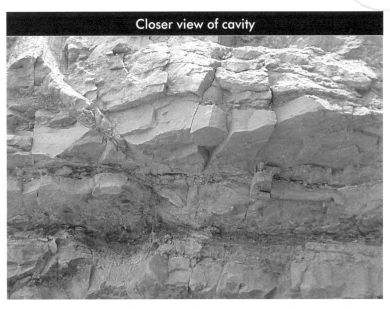

Figure 9. Close up of the inverted stump cavity in figure 8. The root at the far left of the picture is associated with the stump cavity; because some of the rock had fallen out of the cliff, it could not be determined whether the root still in place on the right was associated with the stump on top or the inverted stump.

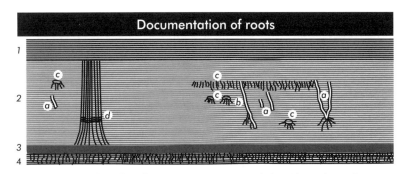

1. Underclay, with rootlets of Stigmaria, resting on gray shale, with two thin coaly seams.
2. Gray sandstone, with erect trees, *Calamites*, and other stems: 9 feet.
3. Coal, with erect tree on its surface: 6 inches.
4. Underclay, with Stigmaria rootlets.
(a) *Calamites*.
(b) Stems of plant undetermined.
(c) Stigmaria roots
(d) Erect trunk, 9 feet high.

Figure 10. Another drawing from Dawson, showing some calamites plants with reasonably intact roots (marked "a" in the drawing). Some of the calamites are obviously fragmented, no roots, yet still polystrate. Clearly, the roots are not an indicator for in situ growth and burial. (From Dawson 1855; other editions 1868, 1878, 1891.) The Geology of Nova Scotia, New Brunswick and Prince Edward Island, or Acadian Geology, Oliver and Boyd, Edinburgh. Public domain.

The Problem of the Reeds and the Trees

As noted before, the Joggins polystrate fossils are giant, hollow reeds; fossil pine trees, though present, are usually not polystrate (figure 11). To date, I have found only one

Figure 11. A petrified and coalified cordaitales tree trunk. Notice that the outside bark has been coalified while the inner core has alternating fossilization and coalification. Notice also it has been crushed flat — evidence of enormous pressures on top of the log. How much pressure does it take to crush a log to half its original thickness?

Figure 12. A segment of lycopod trunk and calamites trunk. These were giant, hollow reeds. Notice they are both split up the side, a pressure fracture. Outside pressures crushed the plants, fracturing them and forcing mud into them. It is highly unlikely that it was a horizontal pressure — so how did this happen?

All the other cordaitales trees that I have examined are parallel to bedding. The combination of horizontal solid trees and vertical hollow reeds presents a profound problem for the uniformitarian hypothesis: how could weak, hollow reeds remain upright during burial while stronger, solid pine trees did not?

At the base of Coal Mine Point, a deep undercut has exposed two different layers of cordaitales tree trunks. Both have the trunks oriented in a north-south direction, lying superimposed but separated vertically by about 2.5 feet (75 cm). Polystrate calamites connect these two layers and continue up into strata above the upper cordaitales! If the calamites were buried by a small flood (a common explanation) and remained upright during burial, how was the same flood able to transport solid tree trunks more than 2.5 feet (75 cm) in diameter?

While the reasons for plants being buried upright at Joggins is a mystery both to catastrophists and uniformitarians, a better explanation would be that all the plants were transported and buried *together* during rapid deposition.

Lizards in the Stumps

One of the more interesting features of the Joggins polystrate fossils is the presence of fossilized bones of small lizards that are found inside some of the broken stumps. Uniformitarians have proposed that the plants were partially buried, died, and then broken, leaving a deep hole into which the lizards fell. But the bones are commonly disarticulated, which is assumed to be evidence of predation. However, there are no fossil remains of predators. Another possibility is that the skeletons were broken up by mechanical forces. The uniformitarian scenario is also suspect in the instance of one trunk that was found containing 13 skeletons. Some stumps also contain plant debris and marine organisms (Mackay, personal communication, and personal observation).

Another problem for the uniformitarian hypothesis is that the stumps were subject to compression along their vertical axes (figure 12), which resulted in their sides being split open in places. It is thus possible that both the bones and sediment could have entered via

exception — a single cordaitales stump found in 2005 beside the Forty-Brine Coalmine drain tunnel. It was only 14.5 inches (37 cm) tall, was broken, and no roots were visible.

the fractures, rather than through an opening in the top. In a Flood scenario, the lizards might have been carried along with a mass of floating vegetation, or they might have been washed into the stumps between the time the stumps were deposited and the time they were covered by sediment.

Lastly, the fossil lizards have been flattened by lithostatic pressure. This obviously happened before the animals turned to rock, and before the sediments surrounding them hardened into rock, but such flattening requires enormous amounts of overburden.

The Local Flood Hypothesis

Both Birkeland (2004) and Neyman (2003) proposed small-scale, local floods as an alternate uniformitarian explanation (actually an "actualistic" explanation) for the polystrate reeds. However, their proposal must address the following observations:

1. With the exception of one small, polystrate stump, all of the tree trunks are parallel to bedding.

2. With the exception of one level, all of the lycopods are bent and/or leaning to the north, relative to the bedding planes. How would local floods have caused this orientation (opposite of the current direction) consistently for millions of years?

3. The Joggins cliffs are marked by parallel and continuous bedding throughout their 16,400 foot (5,000 m) thickness. Local fluvial flooding should have produced discontinuous bedding. Furthermore, to generate extensive parallel beds, thousands of meters of subsidence would have needed to occur over the entire area without tilting or tipping the land even a small amount.

4. Local flash floods would have eroded the well-preserved layers within the formation.

5. Arguing that some strata were quickly deposited (to cover the polystrate plants) and that identical sedimentary beds were deposited very slowly seems beyond the bounds of credibility.

6. Both the young-earth creationist and uniformitarian literature agree that there are no mature paleosols (ancient soils) at Joggins (Coffin 1975; Davies and Gibling 2003). Soil horizons can develop in relatively short periods (Klevberg et al.

Image of a stigmaria

Figure 13. A crushed stigmarian root. The roots at Joggins are flattened, and/or fractured from the surrounding pressures. This obviously happened before the plants had coalified, or the sediments had hardened inside or out. See text for details.

2003). If the formation is supposed to encompass some five to ten million years in an environment conducive to soil formation, there should be mature paleosols in abundance. Their absence makes it even more difficult to claim in situ burial of the calamites and lycopods.

Thus, the uniformitarian explanation is faced with numerous large problems and internal inconsistencies too great to overcome. The simplest and best explanation for the Joggins Formation is rapid deposition occurring over a large area — exactly what would be predicted by a Flood scenario.

The Story in the Crushed Roots

Figure 13 shows another stigmaria. Originally a hollow tube, it has been crushed and fractured under great pressure. The root has been changed into coal and the surrounding sediments lithified, creating a cast. The fossils are pristine, and the finest details are recorded in both the coalified root and the cast. They show no rot and are in pristine condition. We can safely draw several conclusions from these stigmaria: (1) the roots were crushed before they had a chance to rot, (2) the roots were crushed before they had turned to coal, and (3) the roots were crushed before any of the sediments had lithified.

As mentioned above, the plant fossils have been subjected to significant amounts of pressure prior to lithification. It would have taken significant overburden to crush

Sediment diagram

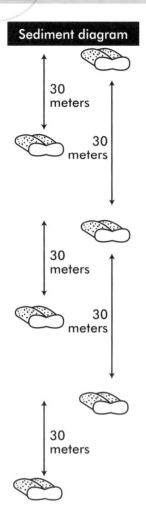

30 meters

30 meters

30 meters

30 meters

30 meters

Figure 14 (left). Schematic diagram of crushed stigmarian roots. These roots populate the entire classic Joggins section, which represents some 4,600 feet (1,400 m) of vertical sediments. See text for details and explanation.

Figure 15 (right). A polystrate lycopod that has been broken in half (vertically) with the top half shifted to the right of the bottom half. Note the break point on both halves are bent toward the other half. Clearly the plant was still soft when the break happened, which was most likely at the time of tectonic activity which tilted the Joggins Formation.

Image of lycopods

the roots — essentially hollow wooden tubes. In preliminary tests, I have been unable to crush similar wooden tubes under pressures in excess of 80 psi (575 kPa). To generate a pressure higher than that would require overburden well in excess of 100 feet (30 m) in thickness.

Figure 14 is an interpretive diagram. More than 100 feet of sediment must have been rapidly deposited to crush the roots prior to rotting or coalification, and prior to lithification of the surrounding sediments. The existence of crushed roots throughout the formation indicates *ongoing* rapid burial and thus the rapid deposition of the entire formation, just as predicted by the presence of polystrate fossils throughout the formation.

In addition to crushed roots, there are also crushed plants throughout the cliffs. I have documented numerous cordaitales trunks, especially in the lower two-thirds of the formation. These are also partially coalified and petrified, and were deformed prior to those diagenetic changes. The pressures required would have been much greater than those involved in crushing a hollow tube. Figure 11 shows that these logs are often distorted at a ratio of two to one. The overburden required to do this would be enormous, and would have to be present *before* the logs rotted, petrified, or coalified, and before the sediments hardened.

Offset and Bent Polystrate Reeds

Some lycopods are also distorted. Some are sheared in half, with the two pieces offset (figure 15). This must have occurred when the plant was still soft, since the fractured edges are bent. It would have broken cleanly had it been

Examples of polystrate plants (figures 16–18)

Figure 16

Figure 17

Figure 18

Figures 16, 17, 18. Polystrate lycopods exhibiting the very consistent bend or tilt to the north, relative to the bedding plane (the layers of rock). It is most likely that this happened at the time of the tectonic upheaval which tilted the Joggins formation on its side.

coalified. Also, if the sediments had already been lithified, there should have been no deformation of the plant at the point of shearing.

The overwhelming majority of polystrate plants are bent and/or tilted to the north — opposite the formation's tilting to the south (figures 16 through 18). Note that the plants were bent before they had a chance to rot or turn to coal, and before the sediments lithified.

Pair of polystrate calamites

Figure 19. Close-up of two calamites which are bent in unison. They are spriraling upward and clockwise. At the layer marked by the bottom of the ruler (12-inch scale), the calamites bend away from the camera, up and to the north, circling back toward the southeast while ascending roughly 8 inches. They then take on a more vertical ascension, coming toward the camera in a southwest direction, ascending approximately 5 inches before the rock containing the fossil is missing.

For example, figure 19 shows a pair of polystrate calamites found in 2002, near the middle of the Joggins formation. They were in pristine shape, with tremendous detail preserved in the casts and no visible rotting or cracking. The plants had obviously been bent while still soft. This was part of a group of calamites of which I verified that at least six of the ten were bent in this way (figure 20).

Experiments show that a reed cannot be bent in a radius smaller than ten times its diameter without their failure by kinking. Both modern horsetail and cattail reeds of varying diameters demonstrate this feature, and an estimate of ten times is generous. Because the Joggins fossil reeds are split vertically, I sliced some of the modern ones in the same way, but it made no difference in the point at which the plants failed under stress and kinked. A bend radius of ten diameters is the maximum I was able to achieve without kinking of the plant.

Surprisingly, the fossil calamites of the Joggins Formation are not only bent well beyond that failure point without kinking, but are also twisted in ascending clockwise spirals. This suggests that they were both surrounded and infilled by sediments, and then were deformed in an unusual stress field. Since the only stress exhibited by the sedimentary layers is tilting, then that episode must also have been responsible for the deformation of the plants.

It is difficult to reconcile the obviously rapid sedimentation, obviously rapid deformation of the plants and surrounding sediments, and then the coalification and lithification of the formation with any uniformitarian scenario stretched over millions of years. All evidence indicates that the

Figure 20. Group of polystrate calamites, all bent in unison. The two calamites from figure 19 are the farthest two on the right. I was able to confirm that at least six of the ten found were bent in the same spiral shape as the first two. Calamites are marked with arrows, and the ones that were exposed enough to determine their bend were (from left to right) numbers 2, 4, 5, 6, 7 and 8.

Figure 21. A second scour. This one was just north of Lower Cove and had fossil wave ripples exposed inside the channel, marked by the arrow. The line shows the approximate contour of the scour and sedimentary layers.

Figure 22. Close up of the fossil wave ripples showing a southerly current direction, not east or west. This is definitive: the current was going across the channel, not down it.

plants within the formation were soft, fresh, and buried in relatively unlithified sediments at the time of the tectonic shifting.

Scour Marks Do Not Indicate Much Time

There are a number of scour surfaces throughout the formation that are claimed to be eroded river channels (Ferguson 1988) (figure 21). But in a well-watered terrestrial environment, we would expect well-developed fluvial valleys and significant evidence of geomorphic erosion, especially over ten million years. Instead, all that are seen are scour marks — as would be expected during rapid sedimentation of the Flood with a few brief hiatus and minor scouring by rapid currents. The lack or rarity of erosion in and between sedimentary layers of the Joggins (and many other formations) is powerful evidence for generally continuous rapid sedimentation.

In 2005 I found a scour north of Lower Cove that had several exposed layers of ripple marks oriented at *right angles* to a "channel" (figure 22). The scours were likely formed by hydraulics as the current flow was *across* the "channel," not down it. These ripple marks were present throughout the layers that transgressed the scour.

Rebuttal to Axel Heiberg "Fossil Forests"

Uniformitarians compare the Joggins fossil plants to those found at Axel Heiberg Island, which also exhibits polystrate plants. Like Joggins, they interpret those plants as representing multiple layers of forests buried over long ages. There were a lot of strong and completely inaccurate claims made by Birkeland (2004) about these plants. His comments were originally made on the online "EVC forum" (Birkeland 2004) and contained so many flagrant errors it is difficult to know where to begin. Though quite dogmatic, his arguments were devoid of facts. His most compelling claims had to do with the supposed paleosols at Joggins — a claim that has recycled around the Internet.

Anyone who has read Christie and McMillan's (1991) exhaustively documented research bulletin on the Axel Heiberg "forests" would know that stumps with reasonably intact roots are the *exception*, not the rule. They show (p. 32) six photos, five of which are of stumps. Of those stumps, only one has roots — extending to a whole 1.5 m from the stump! In fact, in their entire book, that stump is the only one shown with reasonably intact roots, and even they are broken off short. So the Birkeland (2004) claim is off the mark for two reasons: (1) most of the stumps observed do not have roots, and (2) the presence of roots is not conclusive evidence of in situ growth. Oard (1995a,

1995b) provided evidence that the Axel Heiberg fossil forests indicate deposition in the Flood.

Conclusion

Contrary to the claims of skeptics, polystrate fossils are an impressive argument against the uniformitarian theory of multiple forests. The Joggins Formation illustrates their shortcomings. Not only are polystrate fossils found throughout the formation (indicating rapid, ongoing sedimentation), but the plants are giant hollow reeds which were undoubtedly more fragile than the fossil *prostrate* trees found also in the formation. Clearly, the hoary hypothesis of Lyell and Dawson cannot explain the Joggins fossils.

The evidence argues against any long period of deposition, diagenesis, and later deformation. Missing roots or rootlets, inverted stumps, and the orientation of roots that are present all point toward a rapid transport and burial scenario. The distortion of fossil plants indicates rapid deposition of the entire formation followed by tectonic deformation before the plants had a chance to rot or alter to coal.

Joggins is a powerful argument for Flood geology, and many of its secrets remain to be harvested by field research.

References

CRSQ: Creation Research Society Quarterly

Berg, R. 2002. http://earthage.org.

Birkeland, B. 2004. "Soracilla defends the flood" on the Evolution vs. Creation forum (EVCforum) http://www.evcforum.net/cgi_bin/dm.cgi?action=msg&f=7&t=116&m=1.

Christie, R.L., and N.J. McMillan (editors). 1991. *Tertiary Fossil Forests of the Geodetic Hills, Axel Heiberg Island, Arctic Archipelago.* Bulletin 403. Ottawa: Geological Survey of Canada.

Coffin, H. 1975. Research on the classic Joggins petrified trees. In G.F. Howe (editor). *Speak to the Earth: Creation Studies in Geoscience.* Chino Valley, AZ: Creation Research Society Books, p. 60–85.

———. 1983. *Origin by Design.* Hagerstown, MD: Review and Harold Publishing.

Davies, S.J., and M.R. Gibling. 2003. Architecture of coastland alluvial deposits in an extensional basin: the carboniferous Joggins Formation of eastern Canada. *Sedimentology* 50(3):415–439.

Dawson, J.W. 1855. *Acadian Geology*. London: Macmillan & Co.

Falcon-Lang, H.J., and J.H. Calder. 2004. UNESCO World Heritage and the Joggins cliffs of Nova Scotia. *Geology Today* 20(4):139–143.

Ferguson, L. 1988. *The Fossil Cliffs of Joggins*. Halifax, N.S.: Nova Scotia Museum.

Juby, I. 2006. The fossil cliffs of Joggins, Nova Scotia, photographic essay. *CRSQ* 43(1):48–53.

Klevberg, P., M. Oard, and R. Bandy. 2003. Are paleosols really ancient soils? *CRSQ* 40(3):134–149.

MacRae, A. 1997. www.talkorigins.org/faqs/polystrate/trees.html.

Morris, J.D. 1999. The polystrate trees and coal seams of Joggins fossil cliffs. *Acts and Facts Impact #316.* El Cajon, CA: Institute for Creation Research, p. i–iv.

Morris, J.D., and S.A. Austin. 2003. *Footprints in the Ash: The Explosive Story of Mount St. Helens*. Green Forest, AR: Master Books.

Neyman, G. 2003. *Creation science exposed — Joggins Fossil Cliffs*. http://www.answersincreation.org/joggins.htm.

Oard, M.J. 1995a. Mid and high latitude flora deposited in the Genesis Flood — part I: uniformitarian paradox. *CRSQ* 32(2):107–115.

———. 1995b. Mid and high latitude flora deposited in the Genesis Flood — part II: creationist hypotheses. *CRSQ* 32(3):138–141.

Oard, M.J., and H. Giesecke. 2007. Polystrate fossils require rapid deposition. *CRSQ* 43(4):232–240.

Waldron, J.W.F., and M.C. Rygel. 2005. Role of evaporite withdrawal in the preservation of a unique coal-bearing succession: Pennsylvanian Joggins Formation, Nova Scotia. *Geology* 33:337–440.

Chapter 14

Fossil Preservation

John H. Whitmore • *PhD — Geology*

Abstract

It is said by some that fossilization is a common process and can occur via non-catastrophic means, making it possible to explain much of the fossil record via slow, uniformitarian processes. This paper documents that decay of soft tissue and even hard skeletal material occurs quickly, making fossilization an unlikely event, absent special conditions. Numerous details about the fossil record suggest it formed quickly. These include Lagerstätten deposits, preserved soft-tissue, and unbiased preservation of thin versus thick shelly material in the fossil record.

Introduction

Fossils are the preserved remains or shapes of once-living organisms. Most fossil remains are found in sedimentary rock. *Taphonomy* is the science of fossil preservation. It includes the study of everything that happens between the death and eventual preservation of an organism. It is a growing and important discipline within paleontology, shedding light on the formation and meaning of the fossil record. It is commonly accepted that in order for something to be well preserved within the fossil record, it was likely buried rapidly, escaping the decay process. Numerous studies of multiple types of marine and terrestrial organisms have demonstrated over and over again that decay happens quickly after death. A common misconception is that oxygen-free (anoxic) environments inhibit decay. This is false; in some cases decay is just as fast, if

not faster in these environments (Allison 1988b; Kidwell and Baumiller 1990; Plotnick 1986; Whitmore 2003). In fact, most decay probably is anoxic and happens in many carcasses from the inside out.

Decay is a crucial part of nutrient recycling in both terrestrial and marine environments. Decomposers (bacteria, fungi), various invertebrate detritivores (mites, earthworms, millipedes, etc.), and scavengers feed on dead organic matter and convert it into inorganic nutrients such as carbon dioxide, nitrates, phosphates, and sulfates. Decomposers play a vital role in ecology because the decomposition process makes these nutrients available again to other organisms, like primary producers.

Is Fossilization Common under Non-Catastrophic and Modern Conditions?

In a web article, Morton (2003) accused young-earth creationists of believing the falsehood that fossilization must always occur quickly and is not occurring today. He writes:

> Young-earth creationists perpetuate the canard that fossilization only occurs in catastrophic conditions like the flood. People like Randy Wysong have written what many creationists erroneously state: *"After the Pre-Cambrian void we see a vast fossil record in the sedimentary rocks (water deposited) showing huge arrays of life. Finally, today, and for the past few thousand years, no fossilization*

to speak of is taking place" (Wysong 1976, p. 364). This is false. Anyone who reads the literature can find numerous articles on modern fossilization. Those like Wysong, who believe the young earth creationist canard have not done their research or is [sic] hiding from the data.

Morton argued that since fossilization occurs in various non-catastrophic settings today, young-earth creationists err in claiming that the fossil record strongly supports the Flood. He also argues that non-catastrophic fossilization can occur in fish and plants via microbial mats, that soft tissue preservation can occur via bacterial mineralization, that bones can last thousands of years without decaying, and that tree trunks and other wood objects can be preserved by water saturation. In summary he states:

> Thus we see that the claims of the young-earth creationists are false. They, as a group, ignore the vast literature on fossilization which shows that fossilization is occurring today without the need for a global flood.

However, Morton is the one ignoring the literature. He fails to mention, even once, the vast amount of literature describing the most commonly accepted reason for fossilization, namely rapid burial. Morton misleads the reader, making fossilization appear to be a common, everyday process. This is simply not the case. In this chapter, I will document that although fossilization can occur today (perhaps more often than Wysong implied), decay is far more likely. Actualistic experiments show that postmortem processes destroy a huge portion of all types of biomass — both soft tissue and hard skeletal material (Kidwell and Flessa 1995; Parsons and Brett 1991). The worldwide abundance of Lagerstätten type deposits, often produced by rapid burial, is consistent with the Flood account. Fossil deposits formed by rapid burial are far more common than the few specialized processes of fossilization Morton cited in his web article.

Previous Creationist Work

The creationist literature is full of references of fossils attributed to rapid burial and fossilization. Some examples include fossil fish (Calais 1989; Calais and Williams 1989; Wieland 1997a, 1997b), trees and wood (Sarfati 1999; Williams 1993; Williams and Howe 1993), marine reptiles (anonymous, 1997; Calais 1994), marine mammals (Oard 2004), various bone beds (Hoesch and Austin 2004; Holroyd 1992; Woodmorappe 2000), arthropods (Walker

2003), and soft-bodied invertebrates (anonymous 1981), not to mention hats (Mackay 1986) and bags of flour (Walker 2000)! Many of the articles simply cite exquisite preservation and fossil abundance as evidence of rapid burial. However, there are very few creationist publications that report actual experimental results on the decay and fossilization process. Woolley (2001) studied the disintegration of fish coprolites in order to better interpret the coprolites of the Green River Formation. I have studied modern fish decay to better understand the fish fossils of the Green River Formation (2003). It is reported in the creationist literature as part of a forum on the Green River Formation (Oard and Whitmore 2006; Whitmore 2006b), an article in *Answers* magazine (Whitmore 2006a), and the ICC Proceedings (Whitmore and Wise 2008).

Decay of Soft-Tissues Happens Quickly

Numerous experiments and observations have demonstrated that decay ordinarily happens quickly under many types of conditions. In an effort to understand how the fish fossils of the Green River Formation were formed, I performed over 400 decay experiments with modern fish (2003). Fish species, oxygen levels, salinity, temperature, and water depth were examined. Not surprisingly, it was found that obvious signs of decay (which could potentially be preserved in the fossil record) appear within days under all types of conditions. Fish have been noted to decay within days and weeks in natural settings, too. Table 1 is a summary of those observations.

Pristine fish preservation is more likely to occur if fish carcasses sink to the bottom in deep water.[1] In shallow water, a carcass must adhere to the bottom (perhaps by microbial mats) to prevent flotation by decay gases. Scavengers often consume part of the dead fish population (Ricker 1945; Schneider 1998), especially if the fish are in oxygenated bottom waters. Scavengers can venture into anoxic zones, but usually do not stay there long. However, anoxia and absence of scavengers in deep water are not enough to preserve fish. In my experiments and in natural settings, fish decayed just as quickly in anoxic conditions as in oxygenated ones. Even slight disturbances can quickly cause disarticulation following several days or weeks of decay. This is true even if water temperatures are cold (see table 1). After the soft tissue is gone, bones and scales can be lost, too. Vallentyne (1960) began his paper with the following statement: "Literally thousands of sediment cores have been collected from lakes and bogs, but only in one

---

1. Decay gases can eventually cause a carcass to float in water shallower than three meters.

Table 1. Summary of rapid decay rates of fish in natural settings. (Originally published as table 2.1 in Whitmore 2003.)

Author, location of observations	Summary of pertinent observations
Britton, 1988 California	Decay experiments with catfish showed they could decay rather quickly. Ten catfish disarticulated when slightly disturbed after three weeks when placed in a lake at 19.5°C, 7.5 mg/l O2, 8 m deep. In another experiment, two catfish disarticulated in a lake within four weeks at 15.0°C, 0.0 mg/l O_2, 18 m deep. Fish were protected from scavengers by placing them in five-gallon buckets with wire mesh lids.
Elliott, 1997 NW England	The experiment was performed with 20 boxes of 20 fish fry each, 10 of which were protected from vertebrate and invertebrate scavengers. The experiment used 20 boxes with 20 dead fry each in a streambed. It was discovered that invertebrate scavengers caused the fry to disappear at exponential rates with approximately 50 percent of the mass being consumed in just four days. Water temperatures averaged about 7.5°C.
Hankin and McCanne, 2000 N California	Thousands of fish died due to a chemical spill in the Upper Sacramento River. Small fingerling trout were in such an advanced state of decay after about one week that it was impossible to collect them. The water was well oxygenated and had a temperature of 11°C.
Krumholz, 1950 Indiana	Most of the marked green sunfish (90.8 percent) and largemouth bass (87.1 percent) floated to the surface over a ten-day period. Those surfacing late in the time period were in a very advanced state of decay and fell apart easily. The experiment was performed in an Indiana pond in June.
Minshall et al., 1991 Idaho	Experiments in the spring and summer were conducted when the average water temperatures were 4.2 and 8.6°C, respectively. Rainbow trout were allowed to decay in mesh bags and then observations were made at regular intervals. The fish were weighed to determine how fast decomposition was occurring. They found about half the fish mass was gone in 25 days during the summer and in 50 days during the spring when water temperatures were cooler.
Parmenter and Lamarra, 1991 SW Wyoming	Parmenter and Lamarra experimented with the decomposition of rainbow trout and pintail duck in a pond in southwestern Wyoming. The experiment was started in July and lasted until the following May. The fish bloated, although they would not float in the shallow water one meter deep and relatively warm 14–16°C. Most of the decomposition of the fish took place in the first 60 days of the experiment.
Schäfer, 1972 North Sea	He noted that fish carcasses are more vulnerable to decay than other vertebrates (p. 49) and suggested that only catastrophic events cause fish fossilization (p. 51). He studied the decay and disarticulation of eight different species of fish. Based on his experiments, he found that different species of fish decay in different ways, even with identical experimental conditions. Some fish tend to float during decay and others sink after death and never float. Higher temperatures, higher dissolved oxygen concentration, and lower salinities promoted bacterial decay and disarticulation in his experiments.
Schneider, 1998 Michigan	Schneider studied the fate of dead fish in a small Michigan pond by releasing dead marked fish during natural fish kills and then trying to recover them to find out how many fish may be sinking into deep water unnoticed. None of the fish he released in water deeper than 2.5 meters were recovered (0/50). Only 12/40 fish were recovered that were released in shallow water. He found that corpses that were not consumed by scavengers decayed rapidly, between 6 and 34 days. He estimated that only 22 percent of the dead fish in the lake were ever observed, the rest disappearing as a result of scavenging or sinking into deep water and decomposing.
Weigelt, 1989 SE Texas	Weigelt recorded the decomposition of a number of terrestrial and aquatic vertebrates in the mass kill around Smithers Lake because of a sudden drop in temperature (p. 69–70). Terrestrial vertebrate carcasses that were in water were reduced to skeletons within 3 months (p. 8–9). He extensively studied the gars that died in the lake (p. 137). The dead fish had a characteristic convex curvature toward the direction the current was coming from. The soft parts of the gar decay rather quickly, but the scales and skin are more resistant to decay and outlasted soft parts (p. 143–144). The lower jaw and opercular regions are especially susceptible to decay and scavenging (p.145, 147).
Zangerl and Richardson, 1963 Experiments in Idaho, Illinois, Massachusetts, and Louisiana	In a decay experiment in an Idaho lake (19°C) at three different depths it took only 14 days for all the fish to decay. The ones at deeper depths took longer. In a strip mine pond in Illinois (20–3.5°C) a fish took 45 days to decay. In a decay experiment in a Massachusetts tidal lagoon (23.3°C) fish took 7–10 days to completely decay. In experiments in Louisiana bayous (24.4–37.2°C), fish and shrimp only took 6½ to 11½ days to decay. They may have decayed sooner, but the cages were not checked in time.

Figure 1. Various boney fish remains from the Salton Sea, California. Any kind of fish remains are rare in modern lakes, but the Salton Sea has an abundance of them on its beaches and bottom. The pocket knife is about nine centimeters in length.

Figure 2. A well-preserved fish from the Green River Formation, Wyoming. Even though this fish is well-preserved, note that some subtle signs of decay are present. Note how the tail fin is "droopy." This condition has been observed in fish taphonomy experiments within a day or two after death. The specimen is about six centimeters in length and is from Whitmore's (2003) FBQ site.

Figure 3. Some fish in the Green River Formation show unequivocal signs of decay. This fish shows scales that are beginning to slough off and scatter, indicating this fish was dead and lying on the bottom for several days before it was completely buried and further decay was arrested. Specimen is from Whitmore's (2003) WSQ site.

instance have these been reported to contain fish remains." Britton (1988) searched for fish remains in seven lakes, only finding them in the Salton Sea of California.

Evidently, special conditions must be present to preserve fish remains of any kind. Rapid decay seems to be the rule, not the exception. The saline Salton Sea has abundant fish remains that occur on its bottom and on its beaches (figure 1). Massive fish kills often occur because of anoxic conditions that develop during the summer. Bones and scales are probably being preserved because of chemical conditions that are unfavorable for their dissolution. Conditions currently present in the Salton Sea may have been similar to the conditions responsible for the preservation of the fish in the Green River Formation (Whitmore 2003).[2] Even in this deposit, conditions must have been such that the fish were covered with a thin layer of calcite soon after death to prevent disarticulation (Whitmore 2003). Despite many well-preserved fish in the Green River Formation (figure 2), some show unequivocal signs of decay (figure 3). Morton discussed the spectacularly preserved fish from the Santa Ana Formation of Brazil. These fish are preserved in three dimensions (not in two, like the Green River fish) and are unusual in that some have soft tissue muscle structures preserved (Martill 1988, 1990, 1997). It is thought the fish were fossilized by calcium phosphate

within hours after death to preserve such detail. Experiments seem to have verified this process of fossilization (Briggs and Kear 1993b). However, this does not seem to be a very common mode of fossilization and cannot account for the bulk of fossil fish in the record. Experiments and observations of fish carcasses in modern settings overwhelmingly suggest they must be buried (or entombed in a mineral coffin) quickly; or decay of soft and hard tissues will result in complete disarticulation.

Of course, decay happens quickly in other groups of animals as well. Experimental and observational results in other groups of animals show similar results to those

_____

2. I believe that the deposits of the Green River Formation represent large post-Flood lakes, not deposits that were formed during the Flood.

for fish. Absent special conditions, soft tissue is typically gone within days or weeks. After soft tissue has decayed, the remaining hard skeletal elements quickly disarticulate. A cover of sediment or mineral entombment is necessary to preserve an articulated organism. Published examples of rapid decay and disarticulation include crabs (Plotnick et al. 1988), shrimp (Briggs and Kear 1994; Plotnick 1986), echinoids (Kidwell and Baumiller 1990), echinoderms (Allison 1990), polychaetes (Briggs and Kear 1993a), copepods (Harding 1973), diatoms (Ryves et al. 2001), chambered nautilus (Wani et al. 2005), plants (Gupta and Pancost 2004; Schoenhut 2005; Spicer 1981), birds (Behrensmeyer et al. 2003; Bickart 1984), cockroaches (Duncan et al. 2003), and various terrestrial vertebrates (Hill and Behrensmeyer 1984). This literature does cite a few special cases of prolonged decay and disarticulation (and even fossilization), but soft tissues of most animals disintegrate within short periods of time.

Disintegration of Hard Skeletal Material

Soft-bodied preservation is not normal in the fossil record, even when a carcass is rapidly buried. Bacteria can continue organic disintegration, probably even on deeply buried carcasses, since (surprisingly) microbes live at great depths (Balkwill and Wobber 1989; Gold 1999; Liu et al. 1997; Monastersky 1997; Sinclair et al. 1989). But what about hard skeletal material — what happens to it in modern marine and terrestrial settings? Obviously, if it is buried, it has good preservation potential. But what happens when it is left exposed?

Marine exoskeletal remains have been studied extensively. Many experiments and observations have been carried out using brachiopods, various mollusks, and other organisms with hard exoskeletons in modern marine settings (Best and Kidwell 2000; Carroll et al. 2003; Kidwell et al. 2005; Lazo 2004; Staff et al. 1986). Like soft-bodied organisms, the soft tissues in these organisms decay quickly, causing skeletal elements to disarticulate. Skeletal elements can be destroyed by any number of processes if they are not buried. These include dissolution, bioerosion, currents, and bioturbation or sediment reworking (Carroll et al. 2003; Cutler 1995; Kidwell et al. 2005; Kidwell and Bosence 1991; Wright et al. 2003). These experiments have been carried out, in part, to better understand the shelly fossil record. In uniformitarian models, sediments on the seafloor accumulate slowly, allowing more than enough time for shelly materials to be destroyed. The cited studies were done to understand how much of the shelly record has been preserved and how much may be missing within uniformitarian time constraints.

Experiments and observations in modern environments have repeatedly shown several trends.

1. A high percentage of living species with preservable hard parts are represented in death assemblages (Kidwell 2001; Staff et al. 1986).

2. Very few exotic organisms are transported into death assemblages (Kidwell and Flessa 1995).

3. Larger and adult individuals of all species are preferentially preserved compared to smaller and juvenile individuals (Staff et al. 1986).

4. The living ratio between various species nearly agrees with the ratio between species in death assemblages (Kidwell 2002).

5. Soft parts of organisms with hard skeletal material and organisms with no hard parts are rarely preserved (Staff et al. 1986).

6. Thin-shelled individuals are poorly represented compared to thick-shelled individuals (Behrensmeyer et al. 2005; Staff et al. 1986).

7. Post-mortem processes quickly destroy a huge portion of the hard skeletal material originally produced (Carroll et al. 2003; Kidwell and Flessa 1995; Olszewski 2004).

In modern studies, hard parts of marine organisms have been observed to be destroyed quickly. This creates a "paradox" for uniformitarian thinking. Olszewski (2004, p. 39) stated:

Actualistic studies show that taphonomic destruction of the remains of shelly marine organisms can be completed on the order of days to years. Yet, radiometric and amino-acid age dating show that shells in settings where taphonomic destruction is ongoing can be 10s, 100s, or even 1000s of years old. In order to resolve this seeming paradox, a number of authors have suggested that shells survive to great age by being sequestered temporarily from taphonomically destructive conditions and then reintroduced to the taphonomically active zone (that part of the sediment column in which a fossil can be modified or destroyed) by sedimentary mixing processes.

In order to resolve the paradox between "age" and the rate of taphonomic destruction, various authors have had to propose that individual organisms in modern settings are "sequestered" from taphonomic decay for many years before they are eventually destroyed. An additional, more serious problem has surfaced for uniformitarianism in a recent study (Behrensmeyer et al. 2005). Even though small, thin-shelled species disappear rapidly in modern settings, they were as likely to be present in the fossil record as large, thick-shelled species. The study used the Paleobiology Database (PBDB) and compared 150 of the most common genera of marine brachiopods, bivalves, and gastropods (450 total genera) to test the taphonomic expectation (from modern observations) that thick-shelled genera should be more commonly represented in the fossil record. They stated (p. 607):

> Contrary to taphonomic expectation, common genera in the PBDB are as likely to be small, thin-shelled, ribbed, folded, or spiny. In fact, only six of the 30 tests we performed showed a statistically significant relationship between durability and occurrence frequency, and these six tests were equally divided in supporting or contradicting the taphonomic expectation.

The authors appeared surprised by their results, and concluded that the fossil record (at least for these groups) is not biased toward more durable shelly material. One possibility that they did not consider was the catastrophic formation of much of the fossil record. It is important to note that their results suggest actualistic processes, and observations do not predict what is actually in the fossil record.

The taphonomic process of terrestrial bones has also been well studied. Bones can last almost indefinitely in cold settings (Sutcliffe 1990) and in deserts if protected from scavengers and ultraviolet light. Scavengers in many habitats will often chew and destroy bones to obtain nutrients from them; often only the largest and most durable bones from adults ever have a chance of preservation (Behrensmeyer et al. 1979). Even in arid and semiarid environments, bones will weather over periods of years if not buried. Behrensmeyer (1978) defined six stages (0 to 5) of bone weathering in East Africa. Bones reach the most advanced stages of weathering (4 or 5) within 6 to 15 years of exposure, even in that dry climate. Exposure to the sun and humidity may play a role in how fast bones weather (Cutler et al. 1999). It is not clear if bones in rain forests degrade as fast as bones on the African Savannah. Several reports have been published, but with conflicting results (Kerbis et al. 1993; Kidwell and Flessa 1995; Tappen 1994). Regardless, skeletons in rain forests and most other settings are susceptible to scavenging and dispersal. Complete disarticulation of medium to large carcasses has been noted to take place in time periods of weeks to years on the African Savannah (Hill and Behrensmeyer 1984; Hill 1980).

Because of its mineralized nature, hard skeletal material does not disintegrate as quickly as soft tissue. Soft tissues are usually gone within a time frame of days to weeks, but hard skeletal material usually lasts from years to tens of years. But it too disintegrates over time and its organic remains are recycled. Preservation almost always requires burial and protection from scavengers.

Fossilization of Soft Tissues

Soft tissues are preserved only under exceptional circumstances. Rapid burial (sometimes called obrution), stagnation, and bacterial coverings all can protect a carcass from taphonomic destruction (Allison 1988a). Burial must be deep enough for the organism to be protected from scavengers and burrowers in the sedimentary column. Rapid burial usually only preserves the morphology of an individual; it does not necessarily preserve the organic molecules themselves. Soft tissues (and in some cases, organic molecules) can also be preserved by amber, tar, pickling in salt or humic acids, freezing, and mineralization of soft tissues via microbes (Kidwell and Flessa 1995). These processes can seal organic molecules from normal decay. However, this usually only occurs on small scales and accounts for nearly all of the examples of nondecay cited by Morton.

When the literature speaks of "soft tissue" preservation in fossils, it normally does not mean preservation of actual cellular material still containing DNA, biomolecules, blood, etc. Usually it refers to simply the outline or morphology of soft tissues that were once present in the living organism. Mineralized soft tissue, including preservation of muscle fibers and cells, has been reported by Martill (1990). He describes the cellular structure of soft muscle tissues replaced by calcium phosphate, visible with scanning electron microscopy (SEM). Soft tissues (biomolecules) of most organisms decay rapidly and are not normally preserved unless they are frozen or mummified. Recently there have been several articles published that claim to have found soft tissue in dinosaur material (Schweitzer et al. 2005a; Schweitzer et al. 2005b; Stokstad 2005). In reading these articles carefully, the authors are cautious to explain that they do not know if they have found preservation of unaltered dinosaurian tissue or not. Schweitzer et al. stated (2005b, p. 1,955):

> Whether preservation is strictly morphological and the result of some kind of unknown geochemical replacement process or whether it extends to the subcellular and molecular levels is uncertain. However, we have identified protein fragments in extracted bone samples, some of which retain slight antigenicity. These data indicate that exceptional morphological preservation in some dinosaurian specimens may extend to the cellular level or beyond.

This discovery has excited many creationists who insist the discoveries represent unaltered dinosaur tissue (Allen 2006), and furthermore that these results support a young earth (Wieland and Menton 2005). The preservation of unaltered cellular material and structures since the time of the Flood (~4500 years ago) would be amazing in itself, let alone for 68 million years, which is the claimed age of these fossils. More recent analysis has confirmed the material contains proteins that are thought by the authors to be dinosaurian in origin (Asara et al. 2007; Schweitzer et al. 2007). However, this finding has been very controversial because relatively unaltered biomolecules, by the authors' own admission, are thought not to last more than a million years (Schweitzer et al. 2007, p. 277):

> It has long been assumed that the process of fossilization results in the destruction of virtually all original organic components of an organism, and it has been hypothesized that original molecules will be either lost or altered to the point of nonrecognition over relatively short time spans (well under a million years).

Some scientists remain skeptical of the discovery. Recently Kaye et al. (2008) claimed that no soft tissue at all had been found in the bones. Their study showed that the "soft tissue" was nothing more than bacterial biofilms that were relatively recent. They suggested the positive occurrence of collagen that was found by Schweitzer and her colleagues was in fact produced by the bacteria. In a 2009 paper, Schweitzer et al. effectively refuted that argument. Young earth creationists need to continue to monitor these reports and be cautious when reporting the positive occurrence of "dinosaur soft tissue." Personally, I have felt that creationist "announcements" of dinosaur "soft tissue" have been a bit premature. It is more likely from a

young earth perspective that these organic molecules and tissues exist, but it would still be incredible considering rates of biomolecular disintegration. For example, it is thought DNA can't typically last more than 10,000 years (Bada et al. 1999). Initially, I thought some dinosaur bone material that I collected in Alaska might be "unfossilized" (Davis et al. 1998), but I have since changed my mind based on our analysis (Whitmore 2005).

Recently, the importance of microbes in the fossilization of soft tissue has become better understood. Microbes, including bacteria, fungi, and diatoms, can colonize dead organic material as "mats" or "biofilms" and preserve delicate organic structures (Dunn et al. 1997; Harding and Chant 2000; O'Brien et al. 2002; Wilby et al. 1996). However, these same microbes are also apparently responsible for decay of organic matter. In the leaves they studied, Gupta and Pancost (2004) observed biofilms of bacteria and fungi with SEM. They suggested the biofilms observed after a 20-day period (p. 433) were the cause of rapid decay in the leaves. However, the biofilms could not degrade (or degraded more slowly) certain more resistant features like the cuticles of the leaves. They suggested that this was why most fossil leaves are represented only by their cuticles (p. 437). Bacteria probably induced calcium phosphate precipitation in experiments (Briggs and Kear 1993b; Briggs and Kear 1994) that showed some soft-tissue muscle preservation. This method may be responsible for the well-preserved fishes of the Santana Formation of Brazil (Briggs and Kear 1993b; Martill 1988, 1990, 1997). These fish have been found in both calcium phosphate and calcium carbonate concretions, and some show exquisite cellular preservation of muscle tissue.

A few misconceptions exist about soft-bodied preservation (Allison and Briggs 1991). It is often assumed that minimal transport has occurred when preservation is exquisite. But experiments have shown that soft-bodied organisms do not disarticulate until after several days of tumbling in a rotating drum (Allison 1986), implying that significant transport can occur in live or freshly dead organisms without significant loss of soft tissue. Anoxia has been assumed for all types of good preservation, but decay can occur rapidly in these environments (Allison 1988b; Kidwell and Baumiller 1990; Plotnick 1986; Whitmore 2003). The primary role that anoxia may play is inhibiting the presence of scavengers, most who prefer oxygenated bottom water.

According to Allison (1988a), several conditions must be met in order for soft tissue preservation to occur.

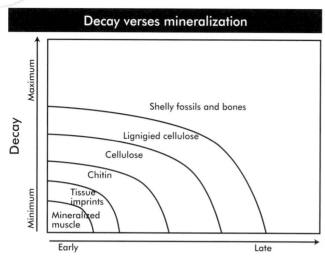

Figure 4. Decay and mineralization compete against one another in the fossilization process. In order for exceptional preservation to occur, mineralization must outpace the decay process. If mineralization does not occur quickly, decay will proceed more rapidly and only the most resistant tissues will be preserved. If permanent burial does not occur, even most shelly material is eventually destroyed in modern environments (see text). Tissues are arranged from the least resistant to decay (bottom left) to the most decay resistant (top right). This figure is redrawn and adapted from Allison (1988a).

Mineralization of the soft tissue must outpace the decay process. The most common types of mineralization are by pyrite, phosphate, and carbonate minerals. Various minerals cannot form unless certain chemical conditions are met after burial, making soft tissue preservation rather rare. *This is true even if the potential fossils have been buried rapidly.* Therefore, most fossil deposits do not consist of soft parts, but only hard skeletal remains. In most cases (even after burial), decay proceeds faster than mineralization, making soft parts difficult to preserve. Allison (1988a) illustrated this concept (figure 4).

Lagerstätten Deposits Are Common

Lagerstätten deposits contain fossils with exceptional preservation and are found worldwide. The term is used to describe exceptional skeletal or soft-bodied remains. Some of the most famous Lagerstätten include the Burgess Shale of Canada, the Solnhofen Limestone of Germany, and the Green River Formation of the United States. Table 2 lists some well-recognized Lagerstätten from around the world and throughout the geologic column, but it is by no means a comprehensive list.

Lagerstätten deposits have been classified into two different types. *Konservat* (conservation) Lagerstätten are characterized by mass mortalities and often display soft-bodied preservation. Most of the famous Lagerstätten deposits fall into this category. *Konzentrat* (concentration) Lagerstätten are characterized by concentrations of skeletal material and often exclude soft-part preservation. These include bone beds, shell concentrations, and collections of invertebrate skeletal material, such as crinoidal limestones. Because decay ensues quickly, Allison (1988a) stressed the importance of early diagenetic mineralization in the formation of Konservat-Lagerstätten deposits. Most authors cite the importance of rapid burial in the formation of any Lagerstätten deposit (Allison 1988a; Brett and Seilacher 1991; Briggs et al. 1994; Selden and Nudds 2004). From the data that show how fast soft parts and even hard skeletal material disappears in modern settings, it's obvious why most Lagerstätten are believed to have formed rapidly. Indeed, based on modern disintegration rates, most fossils in the geologic record need to be attributed to rapid burial.

Deposits with exceptional preservation can be found throughout the geologic record. Many young-earth

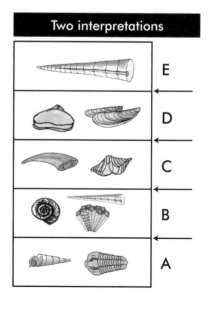

Figure 5. The same vertical section of rock may be interpreted two different ways. In a conventional interpretation, each rock layer containing fossils (A, B, C, D, E) is interpreted to form quickly because of good fossil preservation or other features that demand rapid accumulation. However, time must be placed within the column, so it is often placed between the layers (represented by arrows) as "hiatuses," or zones of non-deposition, often representing millions of years. In a Flood model, each layer may indeed be a separate event, but the events are separated by much less time. Hence, the biggest difference between the two models is the amount of time that passes between each event (A, B, C, D, E).

Table 2. Some well recognized Lagerstätten deposits from around the world. This list is only representative, not comprehensive.

Formation or Fauna	Location	Uniformitarian Age	Rock Type
Doushantuo	China	Precambrian	limestone, phosphates, shales
Ediacaran Fauna	worldwide	Precambrian	mostly sandstones
Burgess Shale	Canada	Cambrian	shale
Chengjiang Fauna	China	Cambrian	mudstone
Orsten	Sweden	Cambrian	shales
Sirius Passet	Greenland	Cambrian	mudstones
Soom Shale	South Africa	Ordovician	siltstone and mudstone
Ludford Lane Bonebed	England	Silurian	siltstones
Gilboa	New York	Devonian	shale
Gogo	Australia	Devonian	limestones
Hunsrück Slate	Germany	Devonian	mudstones
Rhynie Chert	Scotland	Devonian	chert, shales, sandstones
Mazon Creek	Illinois	Pennsylvanian	shales, mudstones
Buck Mountain	Nevada	Permian	carbonate concretions
Wellington Shale	Kansas	Permian	shale
Karoo Supergroup	South Africa	Permo-Triassic	various
Grès à Voltzia	France	Triassic	sandstone
Karatau	Kazakhstan	Jurassic	carbonates, shales
La Voulte-sur-Rhône	France	Jurassic	silty shales
Posidonia Oil-Shale	Germany	Jurassic	shale
Solnhofen Limestone	Germany	Jurassic	micritic limestone
Morrison	United States	Jurassic	various
Las Hoyas	Spain	Cretaceous	fine grained, carbonates
Liaoning	China	Cretaceous	fine grained, ash
Santana and Crato	Brazil	Cretaceous	shales and mudstones
Tlayúa	Mexico	Cretaceous	micritic limestones
Grube Messel	Germany	Eocene	mudstone
Monte Bolca	Italy	Eocene	carbonates and mudstones
Green River	Wyoming	Eocene	micritic carbonates
Florissant	Colorado	Eocene/Oligocene	mudstones, sandstones, tuff
Ashfall Fossil Beds	Nebraska	Miocene	ash
Riversleigh	Australia	Miocene to Present	limestone
Rancho La Brea	California	Quaternary	tar, sedimentary rocks

Most information in this table was obtained from Selden and Nudds (2004) and the following websites: http://palaeo.gly.bris.ac.uk/palaeofiles/lagerstatten/; http://peripatus.gen.nz/paleontology/defLagerstatten.html.

creationists believe much of the geologic column was deposited rapidly, and are thus not surprised to find Lagerstätten throughout the record. Uniformitarian geologists explain most of these deposits with unique events or circumstances that occur within their paradigm. Both groups agree that most fossils indicate rapid burial, but disagree about the amount of time represented by the physical rock record.

In a column of local bedrock, conventional geologists might believe that the fossil-bearing units were all deposited quickly, separated by large amounts of time (see figure 5). For example, the discoveries of the very rapid disintegration of thin, shelly material in modern environments, and yet the ubiquity of thin-shelled along with thick-shelled organisms throughout the fossil record (Behrensmeyer et al. 2005) is problematic for conventional paleontologists to explain using slow, uniform rates of accumulation. Therefore, much of deep time is placed between the fossil-bearing units (in the "cracks"), not within them. Occasionally, time is placed on top of hardground surfaces (if they can be found) or within concentrations of shell layers. Often there is little demonstrable evidence for the passage of great amounts of time (such as bioturbation). Derek Ager (1981), a conventional geologist vocally opposed to Flood geology, explained the stratigraphic record as follows (p. 106–107): "The history of any one part of the earth, like the life of a soldier, consists of long periods of boredom and short periods of terror." In other words, sedimentation happens quickly and is followed by long lulls, where the bulk of geologic time must be placed. An excellent series of articles has been written on these "time warps" from a creationist perspective (Reed 2002a, 2002b, 2004).

Concluding Remarks

Decay happens quickly — in both soft tissues and hard skeletal material. Decay, decomposition, and nutrient recycling are important parts of all ecosystems today. Therefore, fossilization is unlikely unless burial happens quickly and occurs to such a depth that decomposable tissues are protected from scavengers and any further disturbance. Even if an organism is buried quickly beyond the reach of scavengers, bacterial tissue decay and chemical dissolution will ensue unless specific conditions are met for special types of chemical preservation (like phosphate, pyrite, or carbonate).

Lagerstätten deposits are common and are predicted within a catastrophic Flood model. However, certain facts about the fossil record appear to be difficult to understand within a conventional paradigm. For example, it is well documented that thin shells rapidly deteriorate in modern marine environments. Yet they are ubiquitous throughout the fossil record. The presence of both shell types together in the fossil record, but not in modern environments, suggests the fossil record may have formed differently from processes that are occurring today. Contrary to the claims of anticreationists, modern fossilization is neither widespread nor common. Modern fossilization processes cited by Morton simply cannot explain the fossil record.

[Author's note: This manuscript was originally completed and submitted for review in February of 2006. After review, the final manuscript was submitted in February 2007. A few minor revisions were made to the manuscript in November of 2008 and September 2009. I thank the reviewers for their helpful suggestions in improving the manuscript.]

References

CRSQ: Creation Research Society Quarterly
PPP: Palaeogeography Palaeoclimatology Palaeoecology

Ager, D.V. 1981. *The Nature of the Stratigraphical Record.* London: Macmillan Press.

Allen, C. 2006. A fossil is a fossil is a fossil. Right? *Journal of Creation* 20(1):13–14.

Allison, P.A. 1986. Soft-bodied animals in the fossil record: the role of decay in fragmentation during transport. *Geology* 14:979–981.

———. 1988a. Konservat-Lagerstätten: cause and classification. *Paleobiology* 14(4):331–344.

———. 1988b. The role of anoxia in the decay and mineralization of proteinacious macro-fossils. *Paleobiology* 14(2):139–154.

———. 1990. Variation in rates of decay and disarticulation of echinodermata: implications for the application of actualistic data. *Palaios* 5:432–440.

Allison, P.A., and D.E.G. Briggs. 1991. The taphonomy of soft-bodied animals. In S.K. Donovan (editor). *The Process of Fossilization.* New York: Columbia University Press, p. 120–140.

Anonymous. 1981. Fossil jellyfish in Australia. *Creation* 4(2):31.

———. 1997. Buried birth. *Creation* 19(3):38–39.

Asara, J.M., Schweitzer, M.H., Freimark, L.M., Phillips, M., and L.C. Cantley. 2007. Protein sequences from mastodon and *Tyrannosaurus rex* revealed by mass spectrometry. *Science* 316(5822):280–285.

Bada, J.L., Wang, X.S. and H. Hamilton. 1999. Preservation of key biomolecules in the fossil record: Current knowledge and future challenges. *Philosophical Transactions of the Royal Society of London*, B 354:77–87.

Balkwill, D.L., and F.J. Wobber. 1989. Numbers, diversity, and morphological characteristics of aerobic, chemoheterotrophic bacteria in deep subsurface sediments from a site in South Carolina. *Geomicrobiology Journal* 7(1-2):33–52.

Behrensmeyer, A.K. 1978. Taphonomic and ecologic information from bone weathering. *Paleobiology* 4(2):150–132.

Behrensmeyer, A.K., F.T. Fursich, R.A. Gastaldo, S.M. Kidwell, M.A. Kosnik, M. Kowalewski, R.E. Plotnick, R.R. Rogers, and J. Alroy. 2005. Are the most durable shelly taxa also the most common in the marine fossil record? *Paleobiology* 31(4):607–623.

Behrensmeyer, A.K., C.T. Stayton, and R.E. Chapman. 2003. Taphonomy and ecology of modern avifaunal remains from Amboseli Park, Kenya. *Paleobiology* 29(1):52–70.

Behrensmeyer, A.K., D. Western, and D.E. Dechant Boaz. 1979. New perspectives in vertebrate paleoecology from a recent bone assemblage. *Paleobiology* 5(1):12–21.

Best, M.M.R., and S.M. Kidwell. 2000. Bivalve taphonomy in tropical mixed siliciclastic-carbonate settings. Environmental variation in shell condition. *Paleobiology* 26(1):80–102.

Bickart, K.J. 1984. A field experiment in avian taphonomy. *Journal of Vertebrate Paleontology* 4(4):525–535.

Brett, C.E., and A. Seilacher. 1991. Fossil Lagerstätten: a taphonomic consequence of event sedimentation. In G. Einsele, W. Ricken, and A. Seilacher (editors). *Cycles and Events in Stratigraphy*. Berlin: Springer-Verlag, p. 283–297.

Briggs, D.E.G., D.H. Erwin, and F.J. Collier. 1994. *The Fossils of the Burgess Shale*. Washington, DC: Smithsonian Institution Press.

Briggs, D.E.G., and A.J. Kear. 1993a. Decay and preservation of polychaetes: taphonomic thresholds in soft-bodied organisms. Paleobiology 19(1):107–135.

———. 1993b. Fossilization of soft tissue in the laboratory. *Science* 259(5100):1439–1442.

———. 1994. Decay and mineralization of shrimps. *Palaios* 9:431–456.

Britton, D.R. 1988. *The Occurrence of Fish Remains in Modern Lake Systems: A Test of the Stratified-Lake Model*. Master's Thesis. Loma Linda, CA: Loma Linda University.

Calais, R.C. 1989. Sudden burial and rapid fossilization. *CRSQ* 26(1):cover photograph.

———. 1994. Rapid fossils. *Creation* 16(3):50.

Calais, R.C., and E.L. Williams. 1989. Examples of rapid burial necessary for fossilization. *CRSQ* 25(4):181.

Carroll, M., M. Kowalewski, M.G. Simoes, and G.A. Goodfriend. 2003. Quantitative estimates of time-averaging in terebratulid brachiopod shell accumulations from a modern tropical shelf. *Paleobiology* 29(3):381–402.

Cutler, A.H. 1995. Taphonomic implications of shell surface textures in Bahia la Choya, northern Gulf of California. *PPP* 114:219–240.

Cutler, A.H., A.K. Behrensmeyer, and R.E. Chapman. 1999. Environmental information in a recent bone assemblage: roles of taphonomic processes and ecological change. *PPP* 149:359–372.

Davis, B., Liston, M., and J.H. Whitmore. 1998. *The Great Alaskan Dinosaur Adventure*. Green Forest, AR: Master Books.

Duncan, I.J., F. Titchener, and D.E.G. Briggs. 2003. Decay and disarticulation of the cockroach: Implications for preservation of the blattoids of Writhlington (Upper Carboniferous), UK. *Palaios* 18:256–265.

Dunn, K.A., R.J.C. McLean, G.R. Upchurch, Jr., and R.L. Folk. 1997. Enhancement of leaf fossilization potential by bacterial biofilms. *Geology* 25(12):1119–1122.

Elliott, J.M. 1997. An experimental study on the natural removal of dead trout fry in a Lake District stream. *Journal of Fish Biology* 50(4):870–877.

Gold, T. 1999. *The Deep Hot Biosphere*. New York: Springer-Verlag.

Gupta, N.S., and R.D. Pancost. 2004. Biomolecular and physical taphonomy of angiosperm leaf during early decay: Implications for fossilization. *Palaios* 19:428–440.

Hankin, D.G., and D. McCanne. 2000. Estimating the number of fish and crayfish killed and the proportions of wild and hatchery rainbow trout in the Cantara spill. *California Fish and Game* 86(1):4–20.

Harding, G.C.H. 1973. Decomposition of marine copepods. *Limnology and Oceanography* 18:670–673.

Harding, I.C., and L.S. Chant. 2000. Self-sedimented diatom mats as agents of exceptional fossil preservation in the Oligocene Florissant lake beds, Colorado, United States. *Geology* 28(3):195–198.

Hill, A., and A.K. Behrensmeyer. 1984. Disarticulation patterns of some modern East African mammals. *Paleobiology* 10(3):366–376.

Hill, A.P. 1980. Early postmortem damage to the remains of some contemporary East African Mammals. In A.K. Behrensmeyer and A.P. Hill (editors). *Fossils in the Making*. Chicago, IL: University of Chicago Press, p. 131–152.

Hoesch, W.A., and S.A. Austin. 2004. Dinosaur National Monument: Jurassic park or Jurassic jumble? *Acts and Facts Impact Article #370*. Santee, CA: Institute for Creation Research, p. i–viii.

Holroyd, E.W. 1992. Comments on the fossils of Dinosaur Ridge. *CRSQ* 29(1):6–13.

Kaye, T.G., Gaugler, G., and Z Sawlowicz. 2008. Dinosaurian soft tissues interpreted as bacterial biofilms. *PLoS ONE* 3(7):1–7.

Kerbis, J.C., R.W. Wrangham, M.L. Carter, and M.D. Hauser. 1993. A contribution to tropical rain forest taphonomy: retrieval and documentation of chimpanzee remains from Kibale Forest, Uganda. *Journal of Human Evolution* 25:485–514.

Kidwell, S.M. 2001. Preservation of species abundance in marine death assemblages. *Science* 294(5544):1091–1094.

———. 2002. Time-averaged molluscan death assemblages: palimpsests of richness, snapshots of abundance. *Geology* 30(9):803–806.

Kidwell, S.M., and T. Baumiller. 1990. Experimental disintegration of regular echinoids: roles of temperature, oxygen, and decay thresholds. *Paleobiology* 16:247–271.

Kidwell, S.M., M.M.R. Best, and D.S. Kaufman. 2005. Taphonomic trade-offs in tropical marine death assemblages: differential time averaging, shell loss, and probable bias in siliciclastic vs. carbonate facies. *Geology* 33(9):729–732.

Kidwell, S.M., and D.W.J. Bosence. 1991. Taphonomy and time-averaging of marine shelly Faunas. In P.A. Allison and D.E.G. Briggs (editors). *Taphonomy: Releasing the Data Locked in the Fossil Record*, volume 9, Topics in Geobiology. New York: Plenum Press, p. 115–209.

Kidwell, S.M., and K.W. Flessa. 1995. The quality of the fossil record: populations, species, and communities. *Annual Review of Ecology and Systematics* 26:269–299.

Krumholz, L.A. 1950. Some practical considerations in the use of rotenone in fisheries research. *Journal of Wildlife Management* 14(4):413–424.

Lazo, D.G. 2004. Bivalve taphonomy: Testing the effect of life habits on the shell condition of the littleneck clam *Protothaca (Protothaca) staminea* (Mollusca: Bivalvia). *Palaios* 19:451–459.

Liu, S.V., D.R. Cole, M. Gajdarziska-Josifovska, T.J. Phelps, C. Zhang, and J. Zhou. 1997. Thermophilic Fe(III)-reducing bacteria from the deep subsurface; the evolutionary implications. *Science* 277(5329):1106–1109.

Mackay, J. 1986. Fossil bolts and fossil hats. *Creation* 8(3):10–11.

Martill, D.M. 1988. Preservation of fish in the Cretaceous Santana Formation of Brazil. *Palaeontology* 31(Part 1):1–18.

———. 1990. Macromolecular resolution of fossilized muscle tissue from an elopomorph fish. *Nature* 346:171–172.

———. 1997. Fish oblique to bedding in early diagenetic concretions from the Cretaceous Santana Formation of Brazil — implications for substrate consistency. *Palaeontology* 40(4):1011–1026.

Minshall, G.W., E. Hitchcock, and J.R. Barnes. 1991. Decomposition of rainbow trout (*Oncorhynchus mykiss*) carcasses in a forest stream ecosystem inhabited only by nonanadromous fish populations. *Canadian Journal of Fisheries and Aquatic Sciences* 48:191–195.

Monastersky, R. 1997. Deep dwellers. *Science News* 151(13):192–193.

Morton, G.R. 2003. *Noncatastrophic and modern fossilization* (web article), http://home.entouch.net/dmd/fossilization.htm.

Oard, M.J. 2004. Dead whales: telling tales? *Creation* 26(4):10–14.

Oard, M.J., and J.H. Whitmore. 2006. The Green River Formation of the west-central United States: Flood or post-Flood? *Journal of Creation* 20(1):46–49.

O'Brien, N.R., H.W. Meyer, K. Reilly, A.M. Ross, and S. Maguire. 2002. Microbial taphonomic processes in the fossilization of insects and plants in the Late Eocene Florissant Formation, Colorado. *Rocky Mountain Geology* 37:1–11.

Olszewski, T.D. 2004. Modeling the influence of taphonomic destruction, reworking, and burial on time-averaging in fossil accumulations. *Palaios* 19:39–50.

Parmenter, R.R., and V.A. Lamarra. 1991. Nutrient cycling in a freshwater marsh: the decomposition of fish and waterfowl carrion. *Limnology and Oceanography* 36(5):976–987.

Parsons, K.M., and C.E. Brett. 1991. Taphonomic processes and biases in modern marine environments. In S.K. Donovan (editor). *The Process of Fossilization*. New York: Columbia University Press, p. 22–65.

Plotnick, R.E. 1986. Taphonomy of a modern shrimp: implications for the arthropod fossil record. *Palaios* 1:286–293.

Plotnick, R.E., T. Baumiller, and K.L. Wetmore. 1988. Fossilization potential of the mud crab, *Panopeus* (Brachyura: Xanthidae) and temporal variability in crustacean taphonomy. *PPP* 63:27–43.

Reed, J.K. 2002a. Time warp I: The Permian-Triassic boundary in the Texas Panhandle. *CRSQ* 39(2):116–119.

———. 2002b. Time warp II: Basalt flows at the Midcontinent Rift System. *CRSQ* 39(3):194–197.

———. 2004. Time warp III: The Proterozoic-Paleozoic hiatus in the northern mid-continent. *CRSQ* 41(1):75–78.

Ricker, W.E. 1945. Natural mortality among Indiana bluegill sunfish. *Ecology* 26(2):111–121.

Ryves, D.B., S. Juggins, S.C. Fritz, and R.W. Battarbee. 2001. Experimental diatom dissolution and the quantification of microfossil preservation in sediments. *PPP* 172:99–113.

Sarfati, J. 1999. The Yellowstone petrified forests. *Creation* 21(2):18–21.

Schäfer, W. 1972. *Ecology and Palaeoecology of Marine Environments*. Chicago, IL: University of Chicago Press.

Schneider, J.C. 1998. Fate of dead fish in a small lake. *The American Midland Naturalist* 140:192–196.

Schoenhut, K. 2005. Environmental implications of the preservation of chloroplast ultrastructure in Eocene *Metasequoia* leaves. *Paleobiology* 31(3):424–433.

Schweitzer, M.H., J.L. Wittmeyer, and J.R. Horner. 2005a. Gender-specific reproductive tissue in Ratites and *Tyrannosaurus rex*. *Science* 308(5727):1456–1460.

Schweitzer, M.H., J.L. Wittmeyer, J.R. Horner, and J.K. Toporski. 2005b. Soft-tissue vessels and cellular preservation in *Tyrannosaurus rex*. *Science* 307(5717):1952–1955.

Schweitzer, M.H., Suo, Z., Avci, R., Asara, J.M., Allen, M.A., Arce, F.T., and J.R. Horner. 2007. Analyses of soft tissue from *Tyrannosaurus rex* suggest the presence of protein. *Science* 316(5822):277–280.

Schweitzer, M.H., W. Zheng, C.L. Organ, R. Avci, Z. Suo, L.M. Freimark, V.S. Lebleu, M.B. Duncan, M.G. Vander Heiden, J.M. Neveu, W.S. Lane, J.S. Cottrell, J.R. Horner, L.C. Cantley, R. Kalluri, and J.M. Asara. 2009. Biomolecular Characterization and Protein Sequences of the Companion Hadrosaur B. canadensis. *Science* 324(5927):626–631.

Selden, P.A. and J.R. Nudds. 2004. *Evolution of Fossil Ecosystems*. London: Manson Publishing.

Sinclair, J.L., W.C. Ghiorse, and F.J. Wobber. 1989. Distribution of aerobic bacteria, protozoa, algae, and fungi in deep subsurface sediments. *Geomicrobiology Journal* 7(1-2):15–31.

Spicer, R.A. 1981. *The Sorting and Deposition of Allocthonous Plant Material in a Modern Environment at Silwood Lake, Silwood Park, Berkshire, England*. US Geological Survey Professional Paper 1143:1–77.

Staff, G.M., R.J. Stanton, Jr., E.N. Powell, and H. Cummins. 1986. Time-averaging, taphonomy, and their impact on paleocommunity reconstruction: death assemblages in Texas bays. *Geological Society of America Bulletin* 97:428–443.

Stokstad, E. 2005. *Tyrannosaurus rex* soft tissue raises tantalizing prospects. *Science* 307(5717):1852.

Sutcliffe, A.J. 1990. Rates of decay of mammalian remains in the permafrost environment of the Canadian high Arctic. In C.R. Harington (editor). *Canada's Missing Dimension*, Volume I. Ottawa, Canada: Canadian Museum of Nature, p. 161–186.

Tappen, T. 1994. Bone weathering in the tropical rain forest. *Journal of Archaeological Science* 21:667–673.

Vallentyne, J.R. 1960. On fish remains in lacustrine sediments. *American Journal of Science* 258-A:344–349.

Walker, T. 2000. Petrified flour. *Creation* 23(1):17.

———. 2003. Death March. *Creation* 25(2):54–55.

Wani, R., T. Kase, Y. Shigeta, and R.D. Ocampo. 2005. New look at ammonoid taphonomy, based on field experiments with modern chambered nautilus. *Geology* 33(11):849–852.

Weigelt, J. 1989. *Recent Vertebrate Carcasses and Their Paleobiological Implications*. Chicago, IL: University of Chicago Press.

Whitmore, J.H. 2003. *Experimental Fish Taphonomy with a Comparison to Fossil Fishes*. Ph.D. Dissertation. Loma Linda, CA: Loma Linda University.

———. 2005. "Unfossilized" Alaskan dinosaur bones? *TJ* 19(3):66.

———. 2006a. Exploding Fish. *Answers* 1(2):27–31.

———. 2006b. The Green River Formation: A large post-Flood lake system. *Journal of Creation* 20(1):55–63.

Whitmore, J.H., and K.P. Wise. 2008. Rapid and Early post-Flood mammalian diversification evidenced in the Green River Formation. In A.A. Snelling (editor). *Proceedings of the Sixth International Conference on Creationism*. Pittsburgh, PA: Creation Science Fellowship and Dallas, TX: Institute for Creation Research, p. 449–457.

Wieland, C. 1997a. Fast fossils. *Creation* 19(4):24–25.

———. 1997b. Frozen feeding. *Creation* 19(2):52.

Wieland, C., and D.N. Menton. 2005. Answering objections to creationist "dinosaur soft tissue" age arguments. *TJ* 19(3):54–59.

Wilby, P.R., D.E.G. Briggs, P. Bernier, and C. Gaillard. 1996. Role of microbial mats in the fossilization of soft tissues. *Geology* 24(9):787–790.

Williams, E.L. 1993. Fossil wood from Big Bend National Park, Brewster County, Texas: part II — mechanism of silicification of wood and other pertinent factors. *CRSQ* 30(2):106–111.

Williams, E.L., and G.F. Howe. 1993. Fossil wood of Big Bend National Park, Brewster County, Texas: part I — geologic setting. *CRSQ* 30(1):47–54.

Woodmorappe, J. 2000. The Karoo vertebrate non-problem: 800 billion fossils or not. *TJ* 14(2):47–49.

Woolley. 2001. Fish preservation, fish coprolites and the Green River Formation. *TJ* 15(1):105–111.

Wright, P., L. Cherns, and P. Hodges. 2003. Missing molluscs: field testing taphonomic loss in the Mesozoic through early large-scale aragonite dissolution. *Geology* 31(3):211–214.

Wysong, R.L. 1976. *The Creation-Evolution Controversy*. Midland, MI: Inquiry Press.

Zangerl, R., and E.S. Richardson, Jr. 1963. *The Paleoecological History of Two Pennsylvanian Black Shales*. Chicago, IL: Chicago Natural History Museum.

Chapter 15

Dinosaur Tracks, Eggs, and Bonebeds

Michael J. Oard • MS — Atmospheric Science

Abstract

Millions of dinosaur tracks, thousands of dinosaur eggs, and hundreds of dinosaur bonebeds have been observed and studied. The existence of these features has been used by secular scientists and some creationists to challenge the Flood. A hypothesis that accounts for both biblical and paleontological data is presented. Specific examples of tracks, eggs, and bonebeds are explained within the Flood model of earth history.

Introduction

During the past 20–30 years, dinosaur tracks (figure 1) have been found by the millions all over the earth, in at least 1,500 locations (Fastovsky and Weishampel 1996). The Paluxy River area (Texas) was one of the first locations where a large number of dinosaur tracks was discovered. The number keeps expanding; for instance, dinosaur tracks were recently discovered in northeast British Columbia (Silvestru 2004).

Dinosaur eggs from Mongolia have been known since the 1920s. However, little was known about dinosaur eggs until Marion Brandvold of Bynum, Montana, discovered not only eggs, but also embryos on "Egg Mountain" in the 1970s. John Horner has since discovered many more eggs and nests on Egg Mountain and elsewhere in Montana. Figure 2 references how dinosaur eggs have now been found worldwide at over 199 locations (Currie 1996).

The Creationist Challenge

Most creationists believe that dinosaurs not on the ark perished in the Flood (Oard 1997, 1998, 2004). According to the Bible, all terrestrial, air-breathing animals died by day 150 (Genesis 7:19–24). Since tracks and eggs are activities of live dinosaurs, they must have been made early in the Flood, the Inundatory Stage of the Flood according to Walker's (1994) model.

Anti-creationists have charged that dinosaurs could not possibly have produced these tracks and laid eggs in the midst of a catastrophe as devastating as the Flood. Furthermore, they claim that there was insufficient time for millions of tracks and thousands of eggs to be produced early in the Flood. Morton (2004, brackets added) exclaimed:

> Above the termite mounds were some dinosaur tracks. . . . In addition to the dinosaur tracks on top of them and below them, there are cicada burrows as well. . . . Features like these, termite nests, dinosaur tracks, cicada burrows and channels are not easily explained by the YECs [Young Earth Creationists]. They don't show their followers this type of data, and they have not explained it.

The claimed termite nests and cicada burrows are a matter of interpretation and need to be examined by creationists. Only the dinosaur tracks will be dealt with in this chapter.

Worldwide Distribution of Dinosaur Footprint Discoveries

Figure 1. About 1,500 locations have been known to yield dinosaur tracks.

Word. After that, we should examine such challenges as tracks and eggs within the classical Flood model (Whitcomb and Morris 1961) that has been generally accepted by most creationists.

First, an examination of the post-Flood explanation reveals many serious flaws. For example, how were the vast volumes of sediment (often marine) deposited on the continents after the Flood? And what about the massive tectonic shifts that accompanied that sedimentation? These and other challenges (Holt 1996; Oard 1996a, 1998) force the realization that features in the rock record should be explained by the Flood. Second, there is evidence of regional scale sheet erosion followed by channelized erosion, as one would expect during the Recessional Stage of the Flood (Walker 1994). For instance, in the western United States, hundreds of meters to possibly a kilometer or more of strata, much of it Mesozoic and Cenozoic, have been eroded (Oard 1996a; Oard and Klevberg 2005). One evidence for all this erosion is the existence of erosional remnants left behind, such as Devils Tower, Wyoming. This eroded material has been swept off the continent and deposited on continental shelves and in associated basins. How could all of this erosion and deposition have occurred *after* the Flood? However, these erosive processes involving the Mesozoic and Cenozoic strata would be expected in the latter stages of the Flood. Since it seems that the only biblically viable alternative is for the tracks and eggs to be emplaced early in the Flood, we need to examine how this might have occurred.

It is necessary to understand that the Flood was not a simple event. Anti-creationists (like Morton) distort the truth by oversimplification. They describe one particular aspect of the Flood at one particular place, and then imply that the same conditions existed everywhere all the time. The Flood was not just turbulent water rushing everywhere for 150 days. That is a straw man argument designed to invent unnecessary and unrealistic difficulties for the Flood model. Although particular areas at particular times would have been quite violent, the water would have been much less so at other places and

Several creationists apparently accept the arguments of their opponents and assert that dinosaur tracks, eggs, and bonebeds are post-Flood. Garton (1996, p. 82) wrote:

> If the Earth suffered a life-destroying catastrophe such as the Flood, and the event left a geological record of its destruction, that record should be devoid of fossil footprints.

Garner (1996, p. 101) expressed the same opinion in regard to dinosaur eggs that were laid on thousands of meters of Flood sediments:

> However, a study of the palaeontological literature reveals that in situ dinosaur nests occur at multiple levels throughout the Mesozoic. These nests stratigraphically overlie thousands of metres of Flood-deposited Palaeozoic sediments. Creationists [sic] arguments that attempt to accommodate multiple periods of nest building and nurture of juveniles within the limited time available during the Flood have not proven convincing. The nests are strong evidence that the Mesozoic host sediments are post-Flood.

An Early Flood Hypothesis

At first glance, the idea of dinosaur tracks and eggs produced early in the Flood seems impossible. However, we need to apply 1 Thessalonians 5:21: "But examine everything *carefully*; hold fast to that which is good" (NASB, emphasis added). We should hold to the Bible as God's at other times, especially deeper in the water column and within enclosed basins.

Rapid sedimentation would have occurred early in the Flood, especially in deeper, calmer areas. This would have rapidly infilled many rifts and basins, creating shallower areas subject to exposure with any change in relative sea level. At least five mechanisms could have caused exposure of freshly laid, flat-lying Flood sediments. These include (1) tides, (2) simple uplift of the area, (3) tectonically induced tilting (tilting a large area would result in significant elevation changes at each end), (4) tsunamis, and (5) the dynamics of Flood currents on shallow, large areas. These mechanisms, which are reasonable expectations in the Flood, would cause local sea level to oscillate, with effects occurring at a variety of scales. Tsunamis would be expected in association with rapid tectonic shifts, but if uplift were slow, a devastating tsunami would probably not develop.

In regard to the fifth mechanism, research performed by Barnette and Baumgardner (1994) showed that the Coriolis effect would produce very strong water currents of 90 to 180 mph (40 to 80 m/sec) over submerged areas greater than 1,560 miles (2,500 km) in diameter and shallower than about 5,000 feet (1,525 m). These currents would have caused drops in sea level of as much as 3,300 feet (1,000 m) in places, and that pattern would have remained more or less steady for weeks! This would have been a powerful force to create the temporary, yet extended, exposure of newly laid Flood sediments.

Given frequent relative sea level fluctuations, some areas on the edge of any exposed Flood sediments would be periodically inundated and then re-emerge, each time adding a thin layer of sediment. Flood water would have been violently erosive in some areas and less violent, even quiet, in others, depending on local conditions. Any surface exposed in this manner, especially those where fluctuating currents caused exposure, then burial, then exposure again, would have been excellent environments for the preservation of tracks and eggs, even at multiple levels.

Worldwide Distribution of Dinosaur Egg Discoveries

Figure 2. Worldwide distribution of the 199 sites where dinosaur eggs have been found. Major deposits are few. The fragile eggs were easily broken and then dissolved in groundwater. Most of those that were fossilized go unrecognized by the untrained eye.

Figure 3 shows an area that might have met these conditions. It is located in the western United States and contains millions of tracks, thousands of eggs, and dozens of bonebeds (Gillette and Lockley 1989; Lockley 1991; Oard 1995, 1997, 1998, 2002b). Extensive trackways, sometimes all orientated in a single direction, are found in central Texas, eastern Utah, northeastern New Mexico, Colorado, and most recently in Wyoming (Oard 2002a). These sites contain millions of tracks and are thus called megatrack sites. In some areas, tracks are found on more than one bedding plane (Gillette and Lockley 1989; Lockley 1991; Lockley and Hunt 1995). Other sites extend to Alberta, British Columbia, and northern Alaska.

Dinosaurs could have found their way into these areas in at least two ways. They could have survived limited immersion in Flood water, perhaps even on floating mats of vegetation, or they could have traveled from nearby higher areas down onto the newly deposited strata. Either way, once on these sediments, even a few individuals could have created millions of footprints. The stress of flight would have caused egg-bearing females to discharge any eggs. Scavengers would have fed on dead dinosaurs or even the eggs. That would account for modern observations of clutches with broken egg tops. As the Flood water washed back over the area, sediment would have buried tracks, eggs, and carcasses. Final submergence could have added great thicknesses of sediment over the sites. Later,

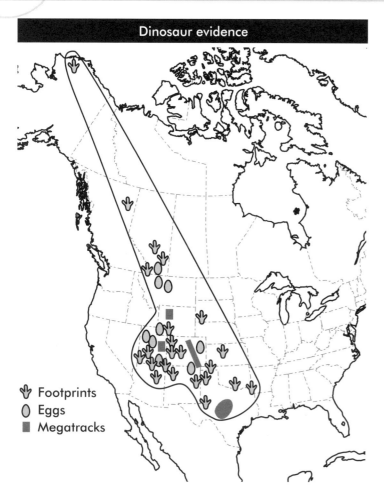

Dinosaur evidence

♧ Footprints
◯ Eggs
▮ Megatracks

Figure 3. Location of postulated strip of land or series of shoals in western United States generally parallel to the crest of the Rocky Mountains. There are four megatracksites in black, the newly discovered one in Wyoming contains two megatracksites on different beds (from Oard 2002a, p. 6).

Evidence for the Exposed Flood Sediment Hypothesis

There are many pieces of evidence that support this hypothesis, including unusual features of tracks, egg areas, and bonebeds that are difficult to explain in a uniformitarian setting. Although there are still many unknowns associated with the observed fossil data on dinosaurs, the available information is often incomplete and misinterpreted within the evolutionary/uniformitarian framework, and much of what is known so far is congruent with this hypothesis.

Evidence from Bonebeds

There are a number of observations of bonebeds that indicate catastrophic inundation. First, a sizeable number of dinosaur remains are entombed in marine strata (Oard 1997) that are identified as such by their containment of marine fossils (Paik et al. 2004). This would be expected in the Flood model. Of course, the lack of marine fossils does not automatically indicate a terrestrial environment.

Second, published descriptions of the bonebeds all suggest catastrophic inundations by water or mass flows of water and sediments (Oard 1997). Dinosaur remains are often found in large bonebeds or dinosaur graveyards. A few bonebeds contain thousands of dinosaurs. This requires at least a large "local" catastrophe. For instance, a single ceratopsian bonebed in Alberta contains probably

during the Recessional Stage, continental erosion would strip away much of that cover, leaving the buried tracks, eggs, and bonebeds on or near the surface.

This scenario would also explain dinosaur tracks found in coal (Froede 1996). Figure 4 shows a dinosaur footprint found in a coal mine near Price, Utah. If coal formed from the burial of mats of plant material (Austin 1987; Coffin 1983; Woodmorappe 1999), it is entirely possible that dinosaurs escaping mats that temporarily grounded on exposed sediments would leave footprints not only on the sediment, but also in the mat itself. Alternatively, the dinosaurs could have simply walked over the mat from the sediments. The tracks in the vegetation would be preserved by later sedimentation.

Dinosaur tracks found in coal

Figure 4. Dinosaur track in coal taken from a mine near Price, Utah (from the College of Eastern Utah Prehistoric Museum).

over 10,000 mostly *Centrosaurus* cerotopsian dinosaurs, believed to have died in a flood (Oard 2002b).

Another large bonebed is located in north-central Montana. Based on outcrop data, geologists estimate that over 10,000 duckbill dinosaurs are buried there. They are jumbled up in a thin, three-foot (1 m) layer extending 1.25 miles (2 km) east-west and 0.25 miles (0.5 km) north-south (Horner and Gorman 1988). The bones are disarticulated, disassociated, and are largely oriented east-west, indicating reworking by moving water. There are no young juveniles or babies in this deposit, and the bones are all from *one* species of dinosaur. Horner and Gorman (1988, p. 122–123, 131) described the catastrophic burial of this large bonebed:

> How could any mud slide [sic], no matter how catastrophic, have the force to take a two- or three-ton animal that had just died and smash it around so much that its femur — still embedded in the flesh of its thigh — split lengthwise? . . . This was no ordinary spring flood from the streams in the area, but a catastrophic inundation.

Other descriptions of dinosaur burial sound almost as violent. Colbert (1968, p. 173) described the stacked dinosaur bones at Howe Quarry, Wyoming, as being "piled in like logs in a jam." Bakker (1986, p. 39, brackets mine) cannot help but think of a cataclysm when viewing the dinosaur graveyard at Como Bluff, Wyoming:

> Anyone who cherishes notions that evolution is always slow and continuous will be shaken out of

his beliefs by Breakfast Bench [at Como Bluff] and the other geological markers of cataclysm.

There are so many bones from this graveyard that small houses have been built out of dinosaur bones (figure 5).

In addition to rapid burial, fossilization must have proceeded rapidly under special conditions with pressurized, mineral-rich hydrothermal fluids mineralizing the bones before they were destroyed (see chapter 14). Modern groundwater does not contain enough of the requisite chemicals, such as silicon dioxide (Pettijohn 1975), but this would certainly not have been true of the chemically rich connate waters during and after the Flood (see chapter 4).

Third, like those described above, many dinosaur graveyards contain only one or predominantly one type of dinosaur (Coombs 1991). Practically all the bones in the north-central Montana bonebed are disarticulated and broken. In modern catastrophes like mudslides, volcanic eruptions, or tsunamis, a multitude of different kinds of animals and plants are buried together. Ancient monospecific bonebeds imply herding behavior, thought to be a sign of stress, as observed in elk, especially during storms or cold weather.

Fourth, fossil bones of babies and young juveniles are not only missing from monospecific bonebeds, but are extremely rare as fossils anywhere:

> Except for nesting horizons, baby dinosaur remains are extremely rare in the fossil record, suggesting that most, if not all, baby dinosaur mortality occurred in the nesting area (Horner 1994, p. 121).

Since the "nesting areas" seem to be the only exception for finding embryos and babies (the interpretation of hatched babies is questionable), and these areas occur on thick Flood sediment, the nesting areas are from the Flood and not from the pre-Flood world. The fact that there are hardly any babies or young juveniles in the bonebeds is consistent with the Flood model. In the face of the coming catastrophe, dinosaurs abandoned their young and fled. Babies and young juveniles were unable to flee or keep up with the stronger adults. Those that were not destroyed would have been more easily disarticulated. Instead of reflecting normal herd

Figure 5. Como bluff bone house

Table 1. Unusual properties of dinosaur bonebeds that point to catastrophic burial.

1.	Many dinosaur remains in marine strata
2.	Practically always buried in catastrophic flood conditions
3.	Many bonebeds are monospecific
4.	Bones of babies and young juveniles rare

behavior, monospecific bonebeds suggest herding during catastrophic conditions.

Local catastrophes should preserve a high percentage of baby and juvenile remains, since animal populations today consist of a fair proportion of young. In referring to dinosaur fossils worldwide, Horner and Gorman (1988, p. 127, emphasis added) stated:

> As succeeding years yielded no other major finds of baby dinosaurs, the question grew in importance. If you think about it . . . more dinosaurs should have died young than died old; that's what happens with most animals. And the high infant mortality should have produced a lot of fossils over the course of 140 million years — a lot of fossils that had *never* been found.

Table 1 lists the unusual aspects of bonebeds. The pervasive lack of very young dinosaurs in bonebeds, the occasional monospecific bonebeds of broken and disassociated bones, burial by a watery catastrophe, and the marine nature of many dinosaur remains are most unusual within the uniformitarian paradigm. These occurrences are worldwide and are consistent with the Genesis Flood.

Evidence from Dinosaur Tracks

Details of dinosaur tracks reinforce the conclusions drawn from bonebeds. First, practically all the tracks are from adults and older juveniles, similar to bonebeds (Coombs 1991; Horner and Makela 1979; Lockley 1991). Coombs (1991, p. 42) wrote: "As with bones, footprints of juvenile dinosaurs are quite rare . . . but this apparent scarcity may be in part an artifact of taxonomic bias." This "taxonomic bias" is contrary to observations today. It has been observed in Amboseli National Park (Africa) that 50 percent of the tracks were made by juveniles (Lockley 1994). So one would expect a fair number of baby and young juvenile tracks along with the adult tracks, given "normal" conditions.

Second, trackways with more than one track from the same individual are practically always straight (Lockley 1991, 1994). Lockley and Hunt (1995, p. 165) stated: "First, the sauropod was changing direction, turning to the right, a phenomenon rarely recorded in trackways." Such straight trackways as observed in the rocks are unusual, since animals foraging for food or other daily activities commonly meander a lot. Frightened animals usually move in a straight line. Figure 6 shows three out of five straight tracks (two tracks heavily eroded) of a small three-toed dinosaur from northeast Wyoming in the Powder River Basin. Figure 7 displays a trackway from near the town of Shell in the northeast Bighorn Basin of north-central Wyoming. Could it be that the trackways represent dinosaurs fleeing encroaching Flood water?

Third, tracks of stegosaurs, ankylosaurs, and ceratopsians are rare (Lockley 1991). These likely were poor swimmers, based on their thick plates, bones, and spikes. It is not likely these dinosaurs would embark from swimming in the Flood water onto freshly exposed Flood sediments. They would drown before making it.

Fourth, a good number of dinosaur tracks in Utah and Colorado are from ancient "desert" sands, according to the standard geological interpretation. In reference to one set of tracks from carnivorous, three-toed theropods, Lockley (1991, p. 153) wrote:

Tracks in Wyoming

Figure 6. Straight trackway of a small three-toed dinosaur, northeast Wyoming.

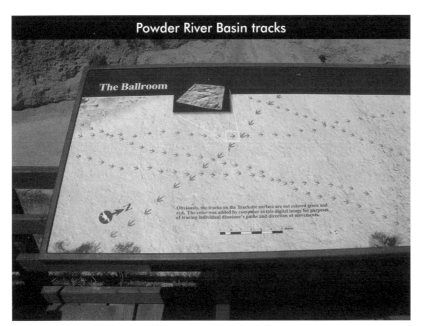

Figure 7. Plot of trackway from an exhibit of dinosaur tracks southwest of Shell, Wyoming.

The tracks occur at the top of the Middle Jurassic Entrada Formation. The main body of this formation represents an ancient sand sea of the type associated with the Sahara Desert today.

This brings up several problems with the uniformitarian paradigm. How would carnivorous dinosaurs survive in a desert? What would they eat? How would the tracks be preserved on loose sand? Perhaps the Entrada Formation is not a desert sand and the uniformitarian paradigm is wrong in its environmental interpretation of both the desert and the origin of the tracks.

Fifth, dinosaur tracks are practically always found on flat bedding planes, capping sedimentary units (Lockley 1991; Lockley and Hunt 1995). Finding a modern analogue is difficult: uniformitarian scientists attempt to explain this observation by stating that the dinosaurs were walking on a shoreline (Cohen et al. 1991). But many nearshore depositional environments would not produce flat beds. How would the tracks be preserved in such an environment? The uniformitarian interpretation seems far-fetched and could not possibly account for most dinosaur tracks. The Flood explanation of briefly exposed sediments is more logical; we would expect such exposed sediment to be generally flat with little or no relief and to undergo the rapid deposition needed to preserve the tracks.

Sixth, if the strata were deposited slowly over millions of years, we should see dinosaur tracks all through the strata and not on specific bedding planes. Although there can be multiple levels of dinosaur tracks in an area, the stratigraphic separation is usually large, and tracks should show no particular stratigraphic affinity.

Seventh, sometimes similar tracks are separated vertically in the same areas. The time span according to the evolutionary scenario can represent millions of years between track horizons, while the same interval in the Flood scenario might be minutes. Is it reasonable that the same type of dinosaur would make tracks on different strata separated by long periods of time? Once again, the Flood model of rapid sedimentation explains both the preservation and the stratigraphic separation of even very similar trackways.

One example of this is the "dinosaur freeway" or megatrack site found between northeast New Mexico and northwest Colorado (figure 3). The tracks are generally of two types and are found on multiple stratigraphic levels that span several million years according to the uniformitarian system. A second example, discussed further below, is that of trackways claimed to exist on 300 stratigraphic levels in South Korea that were made by one type of sauropod dinosaur (Lim et al. 1994; Lockley 1994; Paik et al. 2001). A third example is that of the two new megatrack sites near Shell, Wyoming. There, two trackway horizons are separated by three million years (Oard 2002a). The researchers estimated 380,000 tracks per mi^2 (146,680 tracks per km^2) on the upper track layer in the lower Sundance Formation. The tracks in the two layers were found in what was believed to be marine strata, but now the track sites have become "paleobeaches." Furthermore, the tracks from *both* horizons are all bipedal, tridactyl dinosaur tracks (Kvale et al. 2001).

Eighth, the mere existence of tracks in the rock record implies rapid burial. Cohen et al. (1991, p. 388) stated:

> A particular set of tracks within a limited area of track-bearing surface has a relatively brief (and in principal [sic], measurable) period of time in which to be both formed and buried; after that time, the tracks will be destroyed. These windows are measurable in terms of days (shoreline/Zones 1 or 2 equivalent) to months (Zone 3). . . .

Zones 1 and 2 are shoreline environments and Zone 3 is an underwater zone in which tracks are poorly defined. Lockley and Hunt (1995, p. 18) corroborated the

Table 2. Unusual properties of dinosaur tracks are consistent with the Flood paradigm but difficult to explain within the uniformitarian paradigm.

1.	Practically all tracks from adults and juveniles
2.	Trackways practically always straight
3.	Tracks of probable poor swimmers rare
4.	Dinosaurs supposedly living and/or traveling in "deserts"
5.	Tracks practically always on flat bedding planes
6.	Tracks should be all through strata between vertically separated track horizons
7.	Similar tracks in same area separated vertically by "millions of years" of strata
8.	Rapid burial required

requirement that tracks be buried within days to weeks for preservation to occur. Given the Flood scenario, they could have been buried within minutes or hours. All of these observations (table 2) are more consistent with the Flood model than with the uniformitarian paradigm.

Evidence from Eggs and Clutches

The Flood model would predict that egg-bearing females would lay eggs on newly exposed sediments. Actual finds of eggs show little evidence of normal nesting conditions expected by uniformitarians.

First, despite claims of abundant nests, there is physical evidence of only a few true nests out of the thousands of fossilized dinosaur eggs and egg clutches that have been discovered (Chiappe et al. 2004; Oard 2005). In the past, a nest was simply defined by the presence of eggs or eggshell fragments. But that definition begs the question of why most eggs are usually found in groups (called clutches) lying on bedding planes.

Second, the egg clutches sometimes form unique geometrical shapes, such as spirals (figure 8). One wonders how such features could form by dinosaurs having manipulated the eggs. Even the Maiasaur baby "nest" described below did not pass muster as a nest. It is indeed strange that mother dinosaurs simply laid eggs on bare sediment, since many reptiles build nests. A female laying eggs on bare unprepared ground correlates well with egg-bearing dinosaurs fleeing under stress from encroaching Flood water.

Third, most asymmetrical eggs are buried with the pointed end down, and intruded into the underlying soft sediment (Holt

1994). This is an unstable configuration, and eggs buried in this fashion would be knocked over by the hatching embryo or the mother — unless they were quickly buried.

Fourth, many fossil dinosaur eggs have extra-thick shells because of a pathological, second layer deposition, as revealed by scanning electron micrographs (Jackson and Varricchio 2003). This extra layer may indicate egg laying in a stressful environment, again, well in line with the diluvial model.

Fifth, only one dinosaur has been found with an egg preserved in its skeletal cavity (Sato et al. 2005). In the uniformitarian model, one would expect that to be more common. However, the rarity of this type of find may be due to unique factors of the Flood. These include: rapid decomposition before fossilization, the expulsion of eggs while the dinosaurs floated, or the female dinosaurs expelling eggs under stress.

Sixth, based on the three-dimensional orientation of many egg clutches, it appears sedimentation was occurring *while*

Figure 8. Underside of spiral-shaped clutch of Trodon eggs at Egg Mountain, west of Choteau, Montana.

the eggs were being laid (Barnhart 2004). Some clutches show eggs at different bedding levels, implying ongoing sedimentation while the eggs were being laid. This is consistent with rapid sedimentation during the Flood, but not with uniformitarian scenarios.

Table 3 summarizes the evidence from dinosaur eggs that is inconsistent with the uniformitarian paradigm.

Table 3. Summary of evidence from eggs and egg clutches of unusual circumstances contrary to the uniformitarian paradigm that would support a Flood paradigm.

1.	Physical evidence for only few nests
2.	Unique geometric shapes of some clutches
3.	Most asymmetric eggs have pointed ends down
4.	Some shells pathologically thick
5.	Eggs preserved in dinosaur skeletons very rare
6.	Some clutches show evidence of rapid sedimentation during egg laying

Possible Difficulties with the Hypothesis

Although much evidence seems to favor the Flood model, several features of the egg sites appear difficult to explain. For example, eggs and tracks at a few locations have been found at two or more levels, with little stratigraphic separation. One example is at "Egg Mountain" northwest of Great Falls, Montana, where three nesting horizons with multiple clutches and juvenile dinosaurs are found in a 10-foot (3 m) section (Horner 1982). About half a mile (1 km) north of Egg Mountain, 15 baby Maiasaur duckbilled dinosaurs up to three feet (90 cm) long appear to have hatched and been buried in and around a large nest. This evidence suggests that several months passed between hatching and burial. There are also isolated examples of babies actually hatching, primarily eggs with broken tops. Both of these are areas of further research to be done by creationists.

Three Examples of Mistaken Interpretation

Before discussing these problematic observations, the reader must be aware of the many unknowns associated with fossil evidence of this sort. Much detailed information collected in the field has not been published — but what might appear insignificant to a uniformitarian paleontologist might be quite important to his diluvial counterpart. Evidence that appears contradictory to the Flood paradigm may later be shown to fit after new data are revealed. Several examples are provided.

Paleontologists originally thought that the 15 Maiasaur babies north of Egg Mountain were feeding because some of their teeth were quite worn (Horner 1982). However, it was later concluded that this happened while the Maiasaur babies *were still in the egg,* based on worn teeth found in embryos (Horner and Currie 1994).

Apparently, there are only *one or two* claims of babies hatching and being reared in the nest by "good mothering lizards" (Horner 2000). One of these is near Egg Mountain. However, one "nest" with babies 45 centimeters long was later found to contain only embryos.

Maiasaur mothers supposedly reared the three-foot (90 cm) long babies in a second "nest" north of Egg Mountain. There is some doubt about this interpretation (Oard 1998). First, some researchers believe that the dinosaur remains are not in a nest, since true nests are actually very rare (Chiappe et al. 2004). The sediments in the area are contorted and the "nests" could simply be distortions in the strata. One paleontologist working the site believed the remains were deposited in an eddy. Some eggs and eggshells in the area likely were deposited in water (Kennedy 1997). Eggs and eggshells have also been discovered in water-transported mudstone and in cross-beds within a water-deposited, cross-bedded sandstone in Patagonia, Argentina (Kennedy and Spencer 1995). Second, some believe that the dinosaur remains could be precocial and did not need a "good mothering lizard," which means the whole idea of nesting dinosaurs would be wrong (Geist and Jones 1996). Precocial means that the baby did not need care from the mother after birth, while altricial means the baby needed care. Horner, who earlier assumed the babies were altricial, now concedes that these dinosaur remains were at least "semi-altricial" (Horner 2000). A few researchers have proposed that the few small dinosaurs that were found could be embryos (Horner 1999). Third, embryos of some hadrosaurs can be as long as three feet (1 m), such as the lambeosaurine hadrosaur *Hypacrosaurus stebingeri* (Horner 1999). When one considers how difficult it is to identify the type of dinosaur from embryos or babies (Horner 2000), and the absence of adult dinosaur remains with the group of Maiasaur "babies," then it is certainly possible that the remains are simply embryos.

Even if they were babies that had already hatched, their suggested life span of one to two months (Horner et al. 2000) would not be inconceivable within the Flood model. Fourth, there is little or no sign of vegetation in the "nest" (Horner 2000).

A second example of early misinterpretation is that of young juveniles found around the nesting horizons on Egg Mountain. These were originally assumed to have hatched from broken egg tops. Later it was confirmed that the egg clutches were from the small carnivorous dinosaur *Troödon formosus,* based on the identification of an embryo in one of the eggs. However, the larger juveniles were small, herbivorous hypsilophodonts, *Orodromeus makelai* (Horner and Weishampel 1996; Varricchio et al. 1997).

A third example of interpretations that need a second look is that of the abundant gastroliths — or gizzard stones — found in the widespread Morrison Formation in the central United States. These were once thought to indicate the passage of significant time; dinosaurs lived, died, and decayed, scattering their gastroliths widely about. In fact, this was one of three early challenges to my exposed Flood sediment hypothesis by those who believe that the dinosaurs are post-Flood (Garner et al. 1996, p. 234, brackets added):

> The problems are not limited to nest sites. Stokes (1987) has investigated gastroliths (stomach stones) from some Lower Cretaceous [actually the Late Jurassic Morrison Formation] dinosaurs. He found that many of these gastroliths were composed of lithified, fossil-bearing sedimentary rock which appeared to be derived from Palaeozoic and pre-Cretaceous Mesozoic sedimentary rocks. This is further evidence that these dinosaurs were living after the Flood. . . .

At the time, I did not have a ready answer to this challenge and had not read the Stokes (1987) reference, but pointed out that rocks probably lithified quite rapidly during the Flood and these rapidly cemented stones could potentially have been swallowed by dinosaurs (Oard 1996b). However, the Morrison Formation covers 1,800,000 km² from central Utah east to central Kansas, and from central New Mexico north to the Canadian border, if it is one continuous formation. It is generally less than 330 feet (100 m) thick and forms a flat-lying sheet. It provides evidence of rapid sheet deposition, not slow processes over millions of years (Oard 1997), which by itself nullifies the uniformitarian explanation of the gastroliths. According to Stokes (1987), there are

millions of the gastroliths. If so, their distribution would seem impossible in the time constraints offered by the Bible. The stones certainly are abundant; I found a polished stone a little over an inch in diameter and several less typical "gastroliths" during a cursory examination of an outcrop in Wyoming.

Once again, the Flood paradigm opens a new door of investigation. Are these stones really gastroliths (Oard 2006)? They are rarely found in Morrison Formation dinosaur graveyards (Stokes 1987), and dinosaur remains are rarely found with the "gastroliths" (Stokes 1987). It seems that the primary evidence for that theory is the polishing of the stones, but that evidence is equivocal (Darby and Ojakangas 1980). New information shows that the sediments containing these polished stones are probably *mass flow deposits* (Zaleha and Wiesemann 2005). The source of many of the stones, even those found with fossils, can be traced 125 to 250 miles (200 to 400 km) to the west. Many of the stones are quartzites that likely originated from southeastern Idaho. Evidence suggests a hyperconcentrated mass flow — one that contains much water. Zaleha and Wiesemann (2005) suggested that "gastroliths" from other formations are also stones from mass flow deposits. As anyone knows who has ever tumbled rocks, mechanical forces can also polish stones. It is also interesting that "gastroliths" were one of the diagnostic criteria used to identify outcrops as belonging to the Morrison Formation, but the new environmental interpretation has also allowed a stratigraphic reassignment of some of these rocks to the Lower Cretaceous Cloverly Formation (Zaleha and Wiesemann 2005). This "tale of the gastroliths" highlights the circular reasoning often found in uniformitarian stratigraphy, as well as demonstrating that things that appear to be problems for Flood geology are, in fact, opportunities for new and innovative interpretation of the rock record. As such, they should be met head on, and not with compromise.

Possible Solutions

With all of this information in mind, it becomes clear that dinosaur tracks, eggs, and bonebeds are not the challenge for Flood geologists that they once appeared. There are several hypothetical solutions within the Flood model. One is that closely spaced multiple levels of eggs and tracks represent rapid oscillations in sea level that would have periodically inundated and exposed Flood sediments. When sea level rose, the area would flood, dinosaurs would flee "inland," and sediment would cover existing tracks and eggs. When sea level fell, water would recede and dinosaurs would move back onto the newly exposed land to create more trackways.

Eggs with broken tops, actually rare in the fossil record, are assumed by uniformitarians to have been normally hatched. However, there are other mechanisms that might cause broken tops, including erosion as the next sediment layer was laid down, compaction, or scavengers (Barnhart 2004; Oard 1997). In the Egg Mountain area, where some eggs have broken tops, there is abundant evidence of scavengers, including small mammals, varanid lizards, pterosaurs, and other types of dinosaurs (Oard 1997). Teeth from three types of carnivorous dinosaurs are found in the egg area, including abundant *Troödon* teeth and those of *Albertosaurus*. Furthermore, shell fragments with the concave surface upward are often found within the intact lower shell (Barnhart 2004). But if the eggs had hatched normally, the shell fragments should be scattered outside the egg. A new egg find in South Korea provided clues to researchers that led them to conclude that some broken eggs were merely a result of collapse (Paik et al. 2004).

It has been claimed that there are 300 dinosaur footprint horizons in South Korea within a 360-foot (110 m) vertical section (Lim et al. 1994; Lockley 1994; Paik et al. 2001). However, there are a number of problems with the time implied by the find (Woodmorappe and Oard 2003). For instance, published stratigraphic sections indicate that lithological character, thickness, and stratigraphic intervals between dinosaur footprint horizons vary greatly over just a mile (a few kilometers). This makes it difficult to evaluate the true number of horizons. The number of real footprint horizons could be less, the result of fewer or simultaneous events over the study area. The fact that there are relatively few total footprints suggests a small time frame for each set. Moreover, the fact that there are usually only a few tens of centimeters of sediment between observed footprint horizons means that even small shifts in Flood water would have been sufficient to introduce new sediment to cover the tracks. If sedimentation had been fairly continuous, dinosaurs may have been stepping from one stratigraphic horizon to another in relatively short order. This scenario seems more reasonable than the uniformitarian scenario of repeated flash floods over hundreds of thousands of years, since all the tracks are of similar size and from only *one type* of sauropod. As with many of their ideas, the uniformitarian hypothesis requires the perfect synchronization of exactly the same kind of dinosaur walking in an area subject to flash floods, which also just happened to subside the requisite 360 feet (110 m) during that time. It makes little sense, especially since there is no evidence of

channels in the strata. The layers better support sheet flow and sheet deposition.

Summary

Dinosaur tracks have been found by the billions, eggs by the millions, and bonebeds by the hundreds at many locations. Both uniformitarians and those creationists who believe that dinosaur fossils are post-Flood phenomena look to modern processes acting over long periods of time to produce these features of the rock record. However, it is certainly not impossible to explain them within the context of the early Flood, and in many cases the rapid Flood model better explains the field data than do the uniformitarian speculations. The hypothesis advanced in this chapter was presented over a decade ago, and has since been able to explain new field evidence as it is discovered. There are at least five mechanisms to expose newly deposited sediments early in the Flood. It does not strain credulity to believe that dinosaurs crossed these exposed sediments, leaving tracks and even eggs before the exposed sediments were finally re-submerged. One of the biggest stumbling blocks for Flood geologists has been the stratigraphic assignment of the sediments containing the dinosaur remains. Since they are from the Mesozoic, Flood geologists who accept the relative dating scheme of the uniformitarian stratigraphic time scale see them necessarily as late to post-Flood. However, the flip side of the issue is the realization that these dinosaur traces are an argument for re-evaluating a rigid adherence to the geologic column in diluvial geology in the first place (Reed and Oard 2006).

Evidence for the exposed Flood sediment hypothesis, rather than slow processes over millions of years, comes from the tracks, eggs, and bonebeds. The bonebeds show (1) that a fair proportion of dinosaur remains are in marine strata as defined by fossils, (2) practically all descriptions of dinosaur graveyards include evidence of catastrophic flooding, (3) many dinosaur graveyards are monospecific, and (4) babies and young juveniles are rare.

The evidence from tracks includes (1) practically all tracks are from older juveniles and adults, (2) practically all trackways are straight, (3) tracks of probable poor swimmers are rare, (4) proposed uniformitarian environments (i.e., deserts) seem unsuited for dinosaurs, (5) tracks are practically always on flat bedding planes, instead of scattered randomly through the strata, (6) the same type of track can be found on track horizons separated vertically by "millions of years," and (7) tracks must be buried rapidly to be preserved.

The evidence from eggs includes (1) physical evidence for only a few nests, (2) unique geometric shapes of some clutches, (3) most asymmetrical eggs have their pointed end down in an unstable position, (4) some shells are pathologically thick, (5) eggs preserved within dinosaur skeletons are very rare, and (6) some clutches exhibit evidence for rapid sedimentation during egg laying.

Every hypothesis or theory has its challenges, and we must remember that those about historical events can never carry the weight and certainty of observational science. The ongoing reinterpretation of phenomena within uniformitarian circles illustrates this, even if its practitioners will not admit it. Flood geology has much to do, but it is evident that the way is clear ahead; even at this stage, its hypotheses are clearly a match for those of uniformitarians, and are often superior. Such is the case of dinosaur tracks, eggs, and bonebeds.

References

CRSQ: Creation Research Society Quarterly

Austin, S.A. 1987. Mount St. Helens and catastrophism. In R.E. Walsh (editor). *Proceedings of the First International Conference on Creationism*, volume I. Pittsburgh, PA: Creation Science Fellowship, p. 3–9.

Bakker, R.T. 1986. *The Dinosaur Heresies — New Theories Unlocking the Mystery of the Dinosaurs and Their Extinctions.* New York: Kensington Publishing Co.

Barnette, D.W., and J.R. Baumgardner. 1994. Patterns of ocean circulation over the continents during Noah's Flood. In R.E. Walsh (editor). *Proceedings of the Third International Conference on Creationism*. Pittsburgh, PA: Creation Science Fellowship, p. 77–86.

Barnhart, W.R. 2004. Dinosaur nests reinterpreted: evidence of eggs being laid directly into rising water under conditions of stress. *CRSQ* 41(2):89–102.

Chiappe, L.M., J.G. Schmitt, F.D. Jackson, A. Garrido, L. Dingus, and G. Grellet-Tinner. 2004. Nest structure for sauropods: sedimentary criteria for recognition of dinosaur nesting traces. *Palaios* 19:89–95.

Coffin, H.G. 1983. *Origin by Design.* Washington, DC: Review and Herald Publishing Association.

Cohen, A., M. Lockley, J. Halfpenny, and A.E. Michel. 1991. Modern vertebrate track taphonomy at Lake Manyara, Tanzania. *Palaios* 6:371–389.

Colbert, E.H. 1968. *Men and Dinosaurs.* New York: E.P. Dutton and Co.

Coombs, W.P. Jr. 1991. Behavior patterns of dinosaurs. In D.B. Weishampel, P. Dodson, and Osmólska (editors). *The Dinosaurian*. Berkeley, CA: University of California Press, p. 32–42.

Currie, P.J. 1996. The great dinosaur egg hunt. *National Geographic* 189(5):96–111.

Darby, D.G., and R.W. Ojakangas. 1980. Gastroliths from an Upper Cretaceous plesiosaur. *Journal of Paleontology* 54(3):548–556.

Fastovsky, D.E., and D.B. Weishampel. 1996. *The Evolution and Extinction of the Dinosaurs.* New York: Cambridge University Press.

Froede, C.R. Jr. 1996. Late Cretaceous epeiric sea or Floodwater? (A reply to Garner, Robinson, Garton, and Tyler). *CRSQ* 32(4):234–237.

Garner, P. 1996. Where is the Flood/post-Flood boundary? Implications of dinosaur nests in the Mesozoic. *TJ* 10(1):101–106.

Garner, P., S. Robinson, M. Garton, and D. Tyler. 1996. Comments on polar dinosaurs and the Genesis Flood. *CRSQ* 32 (4):232–234.

Garton, M. 1996. The pattern of fossil tracks in the geological record. *TJ* 10 (1):82–100.

Geist, N.R., and T.D. Jones. 1996. Juvenile skeletal structure and the reproductive habits of dinosaurs. *Science* 272:712–714.

Gillette, D.D., and M.G. Lockley (editors). 1989. *Dinosaur Tracks and Traces.* New York: Cambridge University Press.

Holt, R.D. 1994. *The Dinosaur Nest* (unpublished manuscript).

———. 1996. Evidence for a Late Cainozoic Flood/post-Flood boundary. *TJ* 10(1):128–167.

Horner, J.R. 1982. Evidence of colonial nesting and "site fidelity" among ornithischian dinosaurs. *Nature* 297:675–676.

———. 1994. Comparative taphonomy of some dinosaur and extant bird colonial nesting grounds. In K. Carpenter, K.F. Hirsch, and J.R. Horner (editors). *Dinosaur Eggs and Babies*. London: Cambridge University Press, p. 116–123.

———. 1999. Egg clutches and embryos of two hadrosaurian dinosaurs. *Journal of Vertebrate Paleontology* 19(4):607–611.

———. 2000. Dinosaur reproduction and parenting. *Annual Review of Earth and Planetary Science* 28:19–45.

Horner, J.R., and P.J. Currie. 1994. Embryonic and neonatal morphology and ontogeny of a new species of Hypacrosaurus (Ornithischia, Lambeosauridae) from Montana and Alberta. In K. Carpenter, K.F. Hirsch, and J.R. Horner (editors). *Dinosaur Eggs and Babies*. London: Cambridge University Press, p. 312–336.

Horner, J.R., A. De Ricqlès, and K. Padian. 2000. Long bone histology of the Hadrosaurid dinosaur Maiasaura Peeblesorum: growth dynamics and physiology based on an ontogenetic series of skeletal elements. *Journal of Vertebrate Paleontology* 20(1):115–129.

Horner, J.R., and J. Gorman. 1988. *Digging Dinosaurs*. New York: Workman Publishing.

Horner, J.R., and R. Makela. 1979. Nest of juveniles provides evidence of family structure among dinosaurs. *Nature* 282:296–298.

Horner, J.R., and D.B. Weishampel. 1996. A comparative embryological study of two ornithischian dinosaurs. *Nature* 383:103.

Jackson, F.D., and D.J. Varricchio. 2003. Abnormal multilayered eggshell in birds: implications for dinosaur reproductive anatomy. *Journal of Vertebrate Paleontology* 23(3):699–702.

Kennedy, E. 1997. Distribution of dinosaur eggshell fragments in an overbank deposit, Two Medicine Formation, Choteau, MT: a preliminary report. *Geological Society of America, Abstracts with Programs* 29(6):A-272.

Kennedy, E., and L. Spencer. 1995. An unusual occurrence of dinosaur eggshell fragments in a storm surge deposit, larargue Group, Patagonia, Argentina. *Geological Society of America, Abstracts with Programs* 27:A-318.

Kvale, E.P., G.D. Johnson, D.L. Mickelson, K. Keller, L.C. Furer, and A.W. Archer. 2001. Middle Jurassic (Bajocian and Bathonian) dinosaur metatracksites, Bighorn Basin, Wyoming, U.S.A. *Palaios* 16:233–254.

Lim, S.K., M.G. Lockley, S.Y. Yank, R.F. Fleming, and K. Houck. 1994. A preliminary report on sauropod tracksites from the Cretaceous of Korea. *Gaia* 10:109–117.

Lockley, M.G. 1991. *Tracking Dinosaurs — A New Look at an Ancient World*. New York: Cambridge University Press.

———. 1994. Dinosaur ontogeny and population structure: interpretations and speculations based on fossil footprints. In K. Carpenter, K.F. Hirsch, and J.R. Horner (editors). *Dinosaur Eggs and Babies*. London: Cambridge University Press, p. 347–365.

Lockley, M., and A.P. Hunt. 1995. *Dinosaur Tracks and Other Fossil Footprints of the Western United States*. New York: Columbia University Press.

Morton, G.R. 2004. While the Flood rages, termites dig, dinosaurs dance, and cicadas sing. http://home.entouch.net/dmd/termites.htm. Accessed September 1, 2006.

Oard, M.J. 1995. Polar dinosaurs and the Genesis Flood. *CRSQ* 32:47–56.

———. 1996a. Where is the Flood/post-Flood boundary in the rock record? *TJ* 10 (2):258–278.

———. 1996b. Polar dinosaurs: response to Garner, Robinson, Garton, and Tyler. *CRSQ* 32(4):237–239.

———. 1997. The extinction of the dinosaurs. *TJ* 11 (2):137–154.

———. 1998. Dinosaurs in the Flood: a response. *TJ* 12 (1):69–86.

———. 2002a. Newly discovered dinosaur megatracksites support Flood model. *TJ* 16(3):5–7.

———. 2002b. Watery catastrophe deduced from huge Ceratopsian dinosaur graveyard. *TJ* 16(2):3–4.

———. 2004. *The Missoula Flood Controversy and the Genesis Flood*. Monograph 13. Chino Valley, AZ: Creation Research Society.

———. 2005. Evidence of dinosaur nest construction is extremely rare. *TJ* 19(2):21–22.

———. 2006. "Gastroliths" deposited by mass flow. *Journal of Creation* 20(2):18–19.

Oard, M.J. and P. Klevberg. 2005. Deposits remaining from the Genesis Flood: rim gravels of Arizona. *CRSQ* 42:1–17.

Paik, I.S., M. Huh, and H.J. Kim. 2004. Dinosaur egg-bearing deposits (Upper Cretaceous) of Boseong, Korea: occurrence, palaeoenvironments, taphonomy, and preservation. *Palaeogeography, Palaeoclimatology, Palaeoecology* 205:155–158.

Paik, I.S., H.J. Kim, and Y. Lee. 2001. Dinosaur track-bearing deposits in the Cretaceous Jindong Formation, Korea: occurrence, paelaeoenvironments and preservation. *Cretaceous Research* 22:79–92.

Pettijohn, F.J. 1975. *Sedimentary Rocks*, third edition. New York: Harper and Row.

Reed, J.K., and M.J. Oard. 2006. *The Geological Column: Perspectives within Diluvial Geology*. Chino Valley, AZ: Creation Research Society.

Sato, T., Y. Cheng, X. Wu, D.K. Zelenitsky, and Y. Hsiao. 2005. A pair of shelled eggs inside a female dinosaur. *Science* 308:375.

Silvestru, E. 2004. Human and dinosaur fossil footprints in the Upper Cretaceous of North America? *TJ* 18(2):114–120.

Stokes, Wm. L., 1987. Dinosaur gastroliths revisited. *Journal of Paleontology* 61 (6):1,242–1,246.

Varricchio, D.J., F. Jackson, J.J. Borkowski, and J.R. Horner. 1997. Nest and egg clutches of the dinosaur *Troödon formosus* and the evolution of avian reproductive traits. *Nature* 385:247–250.

Walker, T. 1994. A biblical geological model. In Walsh, R.E. (editor). *Proceedings of the Third International Conference on Creationism*. Pittsburgh, PA: Creation Science Fellowship, p. 581–592.

Whitcomb, J.C. Jr., and H.M. Morris. 1961. *The Genesis Flood*. Grand Rapids, MI: Baker Book House.

Woodmorappe, J. 1999. *A Diluvian Interpretation of Ancient Cyclic Sedimentation. Studies in Flood Geology*, second edition. El Cajon, CA: Institute for Creation Research, p. 201–220.

Woodmorappe, J., and M.J. Oard. 2003. Reply to discussion of Woodmorappe's paper, "Dinosaur footprints, fish traces and the Flood." *TJ* 17(1):57–59.

Zaleha, J.J., and S.A. Wiesemann. 2005. Hyperconcentrated flows and gastroliths: sedimentology of diamictites and wackes of the Upper Cloverly Formation, Lower Cretaceous, Wyoming, U.S.A. *Journal of Sedimentary Research* 75:43–54.

Chapter 16

Conclusion

John K. Reed • PhD — Geology
Michael J. Oard • MS — Atmospheric Science

In this brief foray into the debate between modern secular geology and Flood geology, it is important to note the transition occurring on the secular side between the entrenched uniformitarianism of the past two centuries and a re-emerging secular catastrophism. If that trend continues, then the parameters of the debate must shift because many of the traditional arguments against Flood geology are derived from a uniformitarian understanding of earth's past.

At any rate, since the arguments presented often rely on the uniformitarian view, either explicitly or implicitly, then that is how the secular arguments have been examined. At a minimum, it is clear that there is more to the discussion than is commonly assumed. Belief in the historicity of the Flood and the subsequent development of geological models based on that belief are here to stay. Contrary to the wishes of the devotees of naturalism, it is not some form of extreme religious mania or a fringe pseudoscience. Rather, it is a growing conviction by many that current views of earth history are not adequate to explain the evidence — from an objective analysis of biblical accounts to field analysis of strata. And considering the progress of the small, unfunded creationist minority over recent decades, the promise of that viewpoint as a profitable research paradigm is well on its way to being established. Furthermore, the demise of the old "religion versus science" argument has stripped naturalism of its most potent weapon. Now that its thoroughly religious foundation in atheistic materialism has been revealed, the boundaries between science, history, philosophy, and theology can be more accurately assigned.

As the contents of this book have made clear, the "science" of secular earth history is often much less scientific than it first appears, while that of the so-called religious position is often surprisingly well-grounded in empirical observation and logical inference. Some of the arguments against the Flood are frivolous (e.g., chapter 2), illustrating the religious and philosophical prejudices of those making them. Some seem solid; it has taken years of concerted effort by creationists to begin to demonstrate the weaknesses of some arguments, like radiometric dating (e.g., chapter 11). But in every one of the arguments discussed in this book, one point comes across quite clearly — there is no aspect of Flood geology that an objective observer would dismiss as "pseudoscience" or "religious rant."

That being the case, it is worth asking why that characterization has been so often applied. Could it be that secularists are sufficiently insecure in their own position that they must denigrate their opponents to prevent a close examination of the real arguments? If so, that strategy, when it does fail, will fail spectacularly. That wall appears brittle, but thin; once breached, there is nothing behind it. Because arguments against the Flood are usually couched in pejorative terms, ignore the limits of forensic history, and ignore the solid arguments of diluvialists, the case for Flood geology can only become more convincing the more widely it is known. Scientists put up with many things, but deception by denigration has never been a winning strategy.

It is worth differentiating between the two groups of people that have demonstrated antipathy toward geological interpretations made within the framework of the Genesis Flood — the secular academic establishment and those Christians who disbelieve the historical account of Genesis. Both are influenced by the worldview of naturalism — the academics as its enthusiastic advocates and the compromising Christians as its intimidated victims.

Although there may be vast differences of beliefs in other areas, both of these groups make similar errors in their approach to natural history, and these fundamental mistakes lead to many others. Both believe the following:

1. The Bible is not reliable or authoritative in matters of history, especially the domain claimed by modern archeology and geology.
2. Science, as defined in the worldview of naturalism, is the final arbiter of truth in those domains.
3. Natural history is a subset of science; thus "scientific" (i.e., naturalistic) interpretations of the past are superior by default.

Advocates of naturalism add the assumption of atheism and attempt to define truth in such a way as to eliminate theistic explanation. The philosophers Kant and Hume were influential proponents of this strategy. Even today, diluvialists face these outmoded arguments. For example, more than one opponent of Flood geology has sought to define "actualism" to exclude theism a priori (see chapter 7). But Christians are not easily intimidated by epistemological parlor tricks, and will continue to point out that apart from a theistic basis, concepts such as "truth" and "science" cannot possibly be justified, as has been amply demonstrated by the postmodern philosophers on one hand, as it has been on the other by Christians too numerous to cite.

As the previous chapters demonstrate, Flood geology can certainly hold its ground, even on its opponents' home field. A more interesting question, and one that the "new atheism" is perhaps pushing us toward, is how the worldview of naturalism will fare on the theological and philosophical home ground of Christianity. Given the 20th-century descent into existentialism, and then into postmodern relativism, that question seems to already have a clear answer.

As Christians have often argued, the argument between the two worldviews needs to be resolved, and then the implications of that conclusion consistently applied throughout the relevant realms of knowledge. We firmly believe that in the realm of earth history a complete overhaul is needed; even secular geologists recognize this in their abrupt dismissal of uniformitarianism with its many inherent weaknesses, in favor of secular catastrophism.

But neocatastrophism stands on weaker ground vis à vis Flood geology than does uniformitarianism. If nothing else, the issue of finding certainty in the rock record to support the geological time scale is diminished, since every admission of catastrophic deposition within that record leads to the diminution of empirical evidence for deep time. We already knew the record was full of gaps; with the admission of the abrupt formation of another feature of the rock record, another increment of time once believed to be supported by field evidence becomes another gap. Such is the crisis that the International Commission on Stratigraphy has resorted to establishing stage boundaries with glorified highway markers.

The task of re-evaluating geology need not be a laborious slog through a morass of faulty geology. Rather, it is an exciting challenge. There is nothing wrong with the accumulated mass of geological data that exists today. It only requires a new interpretation from a different perspective. It is our belief that this new perspective of diluvialism offers incredible opportunities to unearth truths that have remained hidden within the data for some time, simply because the education and training of those evaluating it forced them into predefined pathways of interpretation. For example, the role of hydrothermal fluid migration in the formation of karst systems offers to solve many longstanding difficulties of that specialty (see chapter 4). The ability to see rhythmites as products of rapid deposition may open many doors to sedimentologic puzzles (see chapter 8).

For years, the uniformitarian establishment pursued a "bridge too far" by attempting to scare scientists away from any taint of catastrophism with arguments that such ideas are irretrievably linked to some dreaded "religious" leprosy called Flood geology. In doing so, they created a fault line within their own paradigm, closing off empirical indicators simply from religious bias — the very thing that they falsely accused their diluvial opponents of doing. Now that neocatastrophism has given the lie to that argument, how many other shibboleths of secular geology will be revealed as similarly without merit?

Uniformitarianism is a dying paradigm. Secular scientists seek to hold onto their philosophical position by pretending that the tectonic leap from Lyell back to Cuvier has no implications for the arguments for diluvialism. We have seen many revolutions in our lifetime, but the geological revolution of the past few decades holds the record for stealth. If the foundations of a discipline can be so easily overthrown, then what does that say about the integrity of the discipline?

Though no one has explored the question, it is certainly curious that the decline and fall of Lyellian uniformitarianism tracks nearly exactly with the rise of modern creationism, from the publication of *The Genesis Flood*[1] in 1961. The power of secular geology today lies in its monolithic dominance in academia, government, and the media. But one thing that history has proven is that control of institutions means little in the long run when the underdog possesses the truth. That is why we are confident that secular geology, whether displayed in a rigid uniformitarianism or a fringe catastrophism, will ultimately find that its view of the past will dissipate through their fingers, like the fog of a summer morning beneath the power of the rising sun.

Time will tell.

---

1. John C. Whitcomb and Henry M. Morris, *The Genesis Flood* (Philadelphia, PA: Presbyterian and Reformed Pub. Co., 1961).

GLOSSARY

acroperox — oxisol soils that are well drained with a perudic moisture regime that have a oxic or kandic horizon within 150 cm of the soil surface. They have low cation exchange capacity (CEC) with pH of 5.0 or more.

acrorthox — soils that have a short dry season or none at all and have an oxic horizon that becomes redder with depth. They have lost virtually all ability to retain bases in their mineral fraction. These soils have low productivity. Acrorthox is an older synonym for acroperox.

actualism — the modification of the principle of uniformitarianism that accepts the rates of some processes might have been higher at times in the past, or that environmental conditions may have been different. Although these processes are not observed today, they still must be "plausible natural process."

albic horizon — said of an eluvial soil horizon containing at least 85 percent material exhibiting a color determined largely by the primary sand and silt particles rather than particle coatings, implying that clay and free iron oxides have been removed from the materials or that the oxides have been segregated to such an extent that the colors largely reflect the natural mineral color of the sand and silt particles. Albic horizons usually occur beneath A horizons.

allochthonous — refers to material transported to a location prior to deposition or emplacement. Antonym of autochthonous.

andisol — a soil order composed of soils formed principally in volcanic ash

anisotropy — the physical state of a physical measurement varying along axes of different measurement

anoxic — without oxygen. When referring to groundwater, it means water with no free oxygen.

anthropogenic — refers to effects of human activities

antigenicity — the ability to induce an immune response.

aquiclude — a layer of low permeability that forms an upper or lower seal for an aquifer

Archaeopteryx — an ancient bird thought to represent a transitional form between reptiles and "modern" birds

argillic — said of a soil horizon characterized by accumulation of clays through illuviation

autochthonous — formed in situ

baraminology — a creationist approach to classification of biological organisms, loosely similar to cladistics

batholith — a large granitic rock that has more than 40 mi^2 (100 km^2) of surface exposure and no known floor

"begging the question" — a common name for the logical fallacy of assuming the consequent. It refers to the practice of implicitly assuming the conclusion of a logical progression at the outset.

benthic — pertaining to the ocean bottom or organisms living on or in the substrate

bioturbation — rearrangement of soil particles within and between horizons as a result of the actions of organisms

BP — before the present and used as a reference for dates

breccia — a rock composed of angular clasts up to boulder size embedded in a fine-grained matrix

caddis fly — a small, mothlike fly, the larvae of which live in fresh water in cocoons covered with sand, gravel, etc.

calcareous — containing calcium minerals, usually calcium carbonate

caliche — a soil cemented by calcium carbonate

cambic horizon — said of a mineral soil horizon that has a texture of loamy, very fine sand or finer, contains some weatherable minerals, and is characterized by the alteration or removal of mineral material. The cambic horizon lacks cementation or induration and has too few evidences of illuviation to meet the requirements of the argillic or spodic horizon (Brady and Weil 1999).

capillarity — the property of soil, a function of pore size, that draws water above the water table and against gravity until equilibrium is reached between the adhesive forces acting on the soil water and the increase in potential energy. Fine-grained soils have greater capillarity than coarse-grained soils.

cinnabar — a heavy, red mercury sulfide mineral that is the primary ore for mercury

circular reasoning — the fallacy of assuming part or all of the conclusion in a logical deductive scheme

clastic — refers to a sedimentary particle or rock formed by weathering, erosion, and transport

clay film — a thin coating of clay

coalification — the process of transforming organic plant material into coal

coprolite — fossil fecal matter

cutans — the surfaces of peds

cyclothem — a series of beds in which coal is one of the beds

diachronous — refers to a rock unit or contact that crosses time lines

diagenesis — all the changes undergone by a sediment after its initial deposition, not including weathering and metamorphism

diamict — a heterogeneous, unconsolidated, unsorted sediment, typically consisting of coarse material such as gravel in a fine-grained matrix

dike — a sheetlike igneous body that cuts across layering or contacts of pre-existing rocks

diluvialist — a person who accepts the historical reality of the Genesis Flood as a presupposition to earth science studies

dinoflagellate — a member of a group of primarily single-celled organisms that during some part of their life cycle have a free-swimming stage with two dissimilar flagella

disarticulate — to break apart

edaphalogy — the study of the relationships between soils and living things, particularly plants, including human use of land for agriculture

eluviation — removal of particles (particularly clays) from a soil horizon into a lower part of that horizon or into subjacent horizons

evulsion — escape of fluid from sediment during compaction

empirical — refers to the sensory apprehension of phenomena

empiricism — the belief that reality is apprehended through sensory perception rather than by rational deduction

endosymbionts — an organism that lives within the tissues of a host organism (either within the cell or outside of the cell) and provides some benefit to its host (i.e., has a symbiotic relationship with its host)

endo-upwelling — a process by which water circulates upward through a reef. Water enters conduits deep in the ocean, circulates upward, and exits near the top of the reef at sea level.

epigenesis — formation of new minerals from previous minerals through surficial processes, typically chemical weathering (e.g., formation of physils from feldspars). The new minerals are more stable in the surficial environment.

epimorphism — change in the outward form of mineral crystals and aggregates in response to weathering processes

epipedon — horizon that forms at or near the surface and in which most of the rock structure has been destroyed. It is darkened by organic matter or shows evidence of eluviation, or both.

epistemological — the discipline within philosophy that deals with the nature of knowledge and truth

evaporite — category of sedimentary rock, e.g., salt, characterized by chemical precipitation, thought to result from periodic drying cycles

facies — zones of rock units differentiated by their physical characteristics or presumed environment of deposition

fabric — preferred orientation of mineral grains in earth materials

flatirons — informal name for the geomorphic expression of the Rocky Mountain front. Flatirons are triangular features in sedimentary exposing bedding planes with a pointed apex and broad base resembling a flatiron for ironing clothes.

flocculation — the physical aggregation of small clay particles into larger sedimentary clasts, usually caused by changes in the chemistry of the surrounding medium

foraminifera — a small plankton marine animal that secretes a series of calcium carbonate chambered tests or round shells

glaciolacustrine — pertaining to a lake environment adjacent to a glacier or ice sheet

glaciomarine — pertaining to a marine water environment adjacent to a glacier or ice sheet

glaebule — a particle within the soil matrix that is distinct from it due to composition, fabric, or some recognizable boundary that encloses it. It does not appear to have resulted from the soil-forming processes that produced the soil in which it is found.

guyots — flat-topped seamounts

histosol — a soil order composed of soils characterized by a high percentage of organic matter

hydrothermal alteration — alteration of rock bodies by hot water, often associated with regions of active volcanism, such of Yellowstone National Park

hypogene — referring to the formation of mineral deposits by ascending fluids within the crust

illuviation — accumulation of clays in a soil horizon as the result of translocation

index fossil — a fossil of wide geographic range and limited stratigraphic range that can be used for correlation based on its presumed stage of evolution

induration — the process of becoming firm or hard. In rocks, it is a synonym for lithification.

in situ — refers to something forming in place, without transport from one place to another

isostasy — the condition of equilibrium, comparable to floating, of the earth's crust and upper mantle

karren — small-scale shaping of limestone or other soluble rock surfaces by rain or groundwater solution

lacustrine — the environments of deposition associated with lakes

lignite — a low-grade coal

lithify, lithification — the process that turns an unconsolidated material into stone

lithology — the physical aspects of a rock that describe mineralogy, whether igneous, metamorphic, or sedimentary

loess — a blanket deposit of mostly silt that is deposited by the wind

massif — a large mountain mass or a group of mountains forming a coherent whole within a range

maturity — a term often used in the past to indicate the extent of soil development; however, this term is associated with discredited concepts and is not presently favored. The term "steady state" is preferred and refers to dynamic equilibrium of soil-forming processes with environmental factors (Klevberg and Bandy 2003a; Lavkulich 1969).

mer operon — a group of genes that protect some bacteria from mercury by converting the metal to a less toxic form

mesic — the mean annual soil temperature is 8°C or higher but lower than 15°C, and the difference between mean summer and mean winter soil temperatures is more than 6°C either at a depth of 50 cm from the soil surface or at a densic, lithic, or paralithic contact, whichever is shallower

metaphysics — the branch of philosophy that deals with being or existence in the abstract

methylation — a chemical reaction that adds a methyl ($-CH_3$) to a substance

methyl mercury — simply, all organic mercury compounds

micrite — a limestone consisting of more than 90 percent very small particles

mogote — a steep-sided hill of limestone, generally surrounded by nearly flat alleviated plains

mollisol — a soil with strong surface horizon development

naturalism — the doctrine or philosophy that matter/energy is the only reality, and that everything in the universe, including thoughts, the will, and feelings, can be explained only in those terms without recourse to the supernatural. A synonym for materialism.

ooid — an ovate carbonate clast. Ooids form today on carbonate banks by the rolling of small clasts combined with the accretion of calcium carbonate.

orogeny — the process of formation of mountains

oxic — refers to an oxygenated state of a soil or groundwater

oxisol — a soil order composed of soils characterized by hydrated oxides and showing a high degree of leaching. They are typically reddish, tropical soils and include what were formerly referred to as "laterites."

paleontology — the study of fossils

paleopedology — the study of paleosols, a soil formed on a landscape of the past and usually buried

paraconformity — a term used for an obscure or uncertain contact or unconformity in which the strata are parallel with no signs of erosion between them

paradigm — a way of looking at a particular phenomenon; more encompassing than a theory or model, although sometimes used synonymously with those terms

pedogenesis — the formation of a soil from mineral and organic matter

pedology — the study of soils, including their formation, properties, and interrelationships

pedon — the smallest volume for which one should describe and sample the soil to represent the nature and arrangement of its horizons and variability in the properties that are preserved in samples. It has three dimensions. Its lower limit is the somewhat vague limit between the soil and "nonsoil" below. Its lateral dimensions are large enough to represent the nature of any horizons and variability that may be present.

peds — soil aggregates

pelagic — pertaining to the open ocean, rather than the bottom or shore areas

peloid — a small, rounded aggregate of calcium carbonate

per ascensum — the vertical rise of a gas or fluid

per descensum — the vertical descent of a gas or fluid

perudic — a perudic moisture regime is one that generally receives more moisture in all months than is used by evapotranspiration processes.

phototropic — an organism that is able to produce food from sunlight (i.e., photosynthesis)

phyla — in the classification system of animals, the next category down from the kingdom

physil — any of various hydrous, aluminosilicate minerals classified as phyllosilicates and often referred to as "clay minerals." The term "clay" is applied to particles smaller than about two microns, while physil particles (clay minerals) may be larger than this and some non-clay mineral particles may be smaller. Most clay particles are physils.

playa — a term used for a dry, vegetation-free, flat area at the lowest part of a desert basin, the deposits of which likely originated from a lake (playa lake)

polemic — a written statement of a position that includes attacks on opposing positions

polystrate — a fossil that passes through two or more strata or sedimentary layers.

positivist — one who believes that science provides a superior path to truth. Extreme positivists believe that science provides the only path to truth.

pneumatolytic — one of the later stages in the solidification of magma

positivism — a post-Enlightenment school of philosophy that elevates scientific investigation above other forms of knowledge. In its extreme form, it can assert that only scientific investigation can arrive at truth.

positivist — a practitioner of positivism

predation — the act of being a predator

protoplast — a cell without its protective cell wall

pseudogley — a term describing dense, silt-rich soils exposed to alternating saturation and drying.

QED — shorthand for the Latin phrase *quod erat demonstrandum*, meaning "which was to be demonstrated." It is a dramatic introduction of the conclusion of a logical progression.

red herring — informal name for an argument that leads away from the point being pursued

reduction — in chemistry, the opposite of oxidation

reinforcement syndrome — a psychological phenomenon or form of circular reasoning observed in scientific research wherein an hypothesis is repeatedly "verified" or reinforced by further data

salina — a salt marsh

seamount — an elevation of the sea floor, 3,300 feet (1,000 m) or higher, either flat-topped (a guyot) or peaked

sesquioxide — a highly oxidized molecule consisting of a cationic center (often metallic or organic) surrounded by hydroxyl ligands. Sesquioxides are typical of soil horizons subjected to significant chemical weathering and leaching, often under forest cover.

sigmoidal rate function — a curve that increases upward more in the middle of the graph and slower at the upper and lower ends

siliciclastics — pertaining to clastic noncarbonate rocks that are almost exclusively silocon-bearing, either as forms of quartz or as silicates

sill — a sheetlike formation of igneous rock intruded parallel to layering or contacts

sinkhole — the surface expression of karst. Sinkholes usually form in carbonates and are created by the subsurface collapse of caves.

slickenside — generally any polished or grooved fault surface, commonly with fibrous minerals, formed by frictional wear during sliding

solum — refers to the upper horizons of the soil where pedogenic processes occur; it overlies the C and R horizons (parent material)

spar (microsparry) — a term loosely applied to any transparent or translucent light-colored crystalline mineral, usually readily cleavable and somewhat lustrous

speleothem — secondary mineral deposits formed in caves by the actions of fluids, such as stalactites or stalagmites

s properties — independent variables defining the state of a soil (after Jenny)

spodic — said of a soil horizon characterized by accumulation of iron and aluminum sesquioxides, organic complexes, and organic matter, and frequently found beneath an E horizon in forested terrain

stratigraphy — the science of ordering, correlating, and interpreting the various sedimentary horizons of the crust

stratomorphic — an adjective applied to a presumed transitional fossil that is both morphologically intermediate and at the right evolutionary time between two other fossil forms

straw man — a logical fallacy that presents a distortion of an opposing view in order to more easily argue against it

subsidence — the downward settling of earth materials, often caused by dewatering

syndepositional — emplaced at the same time as the sediment

syngenetic — forming at the same time

taphonomy — the branch of paleoecology concerned with all processes occurring after the death of an organism until its discovery

taxa — the plural of taxon, a group of organisms of any rank, such as a particular species, family, or class

taxonomy — the theory of practice of classifying plants and animals

tectonics — the branch of geology dealing with the broad architecture of the outer part of the earth, that is the regional assembling of structures or deformation features

terra rossa — a reddish-brown residual soil found in a mantle over limestone berock

terrigenous — of the land, usually referring to the source of sediments

texture — the distribution of grain sizes in a soil, including both the most common size (clay, silt, sand, gravel) and range of sizes (well sorted/poorly graded, etc.)

truncate — to cut short

unconformity — a disruption between two layers of rock materials, caused by either nondeposition or erosion.

uniformitarianism — the fundamental doctrine of modern geology that believes that the rock record can be interpreted by reference to observed modern processes. In its earlier forms, advocates insisted on a strict uniformity of rates as well as processes.

vadose zone — the portion of the soil profile that is typically aerated, not saturated by water; it lies above the water table and superjacent to the capillary fringe

volcanism — the processes by which molten rock from earth's interior is extruded onto the surface

xeric — a moisture regime found in areas with a Mediterranean climate and characterized by moist, cool winters and warm, dry summers. The moisture, which falls during the winter when potential evapotranspiration is at a minimum, is particularly effective for leaching. In normal years, the soil moisture control section is dry in all parts for 45 or more consecutive days in the four months following the summer solstice and moist in all parts for 45 or more consecutive days in the four months following the winter solstice.

Subject Index